THE NATIONAL WELFARE RIGHTS MOVEMENT

THE NATIONAL WELFARE RIGHTS MOVEMENT

The Social Protest of Poor Women

Guida West

PRAEGER SPECIAL STUDIES • PRAEGER SCIENTIFIC

Library of Congress Cataloging in Publication Data

West, Guida.
 The national welfare rights movement.

 Bibliography: p.
 1. National Welfare Rights Organization. 2. Welfare
rights movement--United States. I. Title.
HV97.N34W47 362.5'82'06073 80-39554
ISBN 0-03-052166-1

Published in 1981 by Praeger Publishers
CBS Educational and Professional Publishing
A Division of CBS, Inc.
521 Fifth Avenue, New York, New York 10175 U.S.A.

© 1981 by Guida West

123456789 145 987654321

Printed in the United States of America

When we get our rights, we shall not have to come to you
for money, for then we shall have money enough in our
own pockets.

> Sojourner Truth
> Convention of the American Equal
> Rights Association, 1867

FOREWORD
Richard A. Cloward, Frances Fox Piven

The political movements that from time to time well up from
the bottom of our society are important. They are important because
they can transform the lives of the people who join them and because
they can transform the society that gives rise to them. In other words,
movements from below help to make history. But these movements
have usually not been paid much heed by students of politics. Instead,
politics is recognized as politics only when it is the normal activity
of electoral-representative processes, or when it is the exercise of
influence by those at the top of the society. Protest from the bottom,
if acknowledged at all, is defined as a temporary interruption of political life—and often as an irrational, misguided, and impotent interruption at that. These biases pervade the academic treatment of
popular protest through history and across nations. But nowhere are
these distortions more marked than in the academic dismissal of contemporary social movements in the United States.

Just because of these biases, this volume is valuable. It consti-
tutes a rich record of one episode of the exercise of power by the
poor, and it forces us to see how that power marked itself on our society. That one episode was the emergence of the National Welfare
Rights Organization in the 1960s, important both for itself and because
it was an expression of a large protest movement among black people
in the United States. The black movement is the most recent of a
series of protest movements among working-class and poor people
that has punctuated the history of the twentieth century United States,
a struggle that ebbs and flows partly in response to the changing economic fortunes of those at the bottom and partly in response to their
changing capabilities for political action.

These are struggles that transformed our society. Some ways
are obvious: the rights of capital were curbed by the winning of the
right to bargain collectively, and the caste system in the South was
toppled by the winning of a broad range of civil rights. Changes of
this order attest to the politics of the poor. But a transformation of
another kind, and on perhaps a greater scale, was also generated by
the social movements of the twentieth century.

In the Great Depression, an insecure New Deal administration
was forced to respond to an insurgent working class (huge numbers of
whose members were unemployed) with the skeletal social welfare
programs legislated under the Social Security Act. Then, some 30
years later, an insurgent black movement forced the expansion and
elaboration of these programs to the point that the United States has
now become a welfare state. The programs won are important, in
part because they provide some protection for the unemployed or unemployable who are the victims of the marketplace. But recent devel-

vii

opments suggest these programs have had an even more far-reaching significance for the organization of the U.S. political economy.

The centrality of the social programs is suggested by the new intensity of the conservative/corporate drive to cut them. And the arguments made are revealing. The U.S. economy is said to be in crisis, and the enlarging welfare state budget is given as a major reason. One variant of the argument simply asserts that U.S. capital cannot be competitive in a world economy unless the social programs are cut so as to stimulate investment. Another variant has it that the ready availability of social protections are weakening work incentives and contributing to inflation. Either way or both, it is clear that capital has launched a counterattack, and that the welfare state is the target. The conflict promises to be bitter, pervasive, and enduring. It will be bitter, pervasive, and enduring because it is major economic shares, and the institutional arrangements that determine economic shares, that are at stake.

The large numbers of people in the United States who depend upon the welfare state are likely to join that conflict and shape its outcome. They are likely to join the conflict because people have always mobilized as readily to protect past gains as to secure new ones. And if they join the conflict, the form their politics will take will be the mass movement, the only effective politics from the bottom. Should new movements emerge, then it is important that we have at hand studies such as this one, for there are lessons to be learned from the past.

Not least, the history of the National Welfare Rights Organization teaches—as do other movements—that much of the political capability of the poor is often dissipated by movement leadership. The reasons are human enough. Movements often lift some people from the lowliest origins to heights of recognition and deference that would otherwise have been thought inconceivable. Little wonder that with those heights reached, all effort turns to securing one's hold: even at the cost of expanding movement participation, or of militancy, or of strategies effective for the base but potentially risky to leadership. No movement can control its external environment; it can only exploit external vulnerabilities and absorb countervailing blows. But all movements can strive for greater control of internal processes, especially of leadership; otherwise, it is a virtual certainty that most of the leadership stratum will eventually succumb to co-optation. The forms of co-optation are numerous, and some are all the more insidious for not being recognized as what they are. When leaders take jobs or accept honors proffered by established institutions, the matter is clear enough. But when leaders try to turn movements into electoral organizations, arguing that electoral activity represents a more advanced stage in the struggle, the co-optational process is less obvious for being ideological rather than material. The conversion of mass protest to electoral organization obscures the nature of the essential political capability of the poor, for that capability inheres in the vulnerability of societal institutions to disruption, and not in the susceptability of these institutions to transformation through the votes of the poor. This sort of ideological conversion thus leads to the muting and, in the end, to the dissipation of the political power of the poor. It is about these perils confronting protest movements that the wealth of historical material in this book instructs us so pointedly.

COMMENTARY
Johnnie Tillmon, First Chair of the
National Welfare Rights Organization

Over 17 years ago on August 8, 1963, as a mother dependent
on welfare, I organized the Aid to Needy Children (ANC) Mothers in
Watts to try to find a way to help change and lift up the living standards, educational standards, and political standards of the poor—
mostly women and their children—in this area. This was the beginning of the welfare rights movement in California and, in many ways,
also the beginning of the National Welfare Rights Organization (NWRO).

Today (1980) I hear people saying that the welfare rights movement is dead. It is not dead. It has changed since those early days of
agitating and protesting in the streets. The movement is different
but still alive in many parts of the country. For example, in the
South there are welfare rights groups expanding in Louisiana under
the leadership of Annie Smart; in the East the Welfare Rights Organizations are involved in fighting for the rights of poor women and their
children. Frankie Jeter, a long-time leader in the national movement,
continues to lead the groups in Pittsburgh. In Nevada Ruby Duncan
has been extremely successful in developing and expanding job development programs for the poor, which has helped hundreds of poor
people, especially women. Here in the West the NAC Mothers continues to grow. We have a large staff and job-training and adolescent
pregnancy-prevention programs (under the Comprehensive Education
and Training Act), which are helping many every day. These and
many more activities—social services and political ones, too—are helping change the lives of poor women not only here but also in many
parts of the country.

As the originator and leader of welfare rights my goal has always been to lift people's living standards and educational standards
by getting them involved in political and social activities. Welfare
rights groups are still doing that today. Maybe the papers do not
write about us anymore and the country is not concerned about what
is happening to poor people, especially poor women and their children,
but we are still organized and fighting for our rights. So I say once
again: the movement has changed; the times have changed. The big
difference today is that we do not have the money to go places and get
together nationally as we once did. We still work in our separate
communities in various ways, and we keep in touch with each other
and help each other in any way we can. This is the welfare rights
movement today: different but still alive.

Guida West's story of the National Welfare Rights movement
tells it like it was and how it came to be. It is an excellent book
about the history of NWRO. It is important because it is the history
of poor women—especially poor black women, poor white women, and
poor Hispanic women—in the United States. This is a history that is

not often, if ever, written about. It is important because it shows who tried to help the welfare rights mothers, even if it was just for a short time. And it is important also because in order to keep going and learning, it is always good to look back and remember. I think much can be learned from this history of NWRO. Anyone who cares to understand about being poor in this country will learn much about our struggle in these pages.

PREFACE

In the mid-1960s I joined the National Welfare Rights movement as a Friend of Welfare Rights in support of this social protest for a guaranteed adequate income for the poor. In the earlier part of the decade—as an active, white, middle-class suburbanite anchored in the social action arm of the liberal Protestant denominations—I helped organize and participated in a local integrated effort to change some of the virulent racist practices in our community. At another level, I became a member of the United Presbyterian church's state-level Commission on Racial Justice. In the process, I learned a great deal about my own paternalistic behavior and attitudes as well as the institutional racism prevalent throughout our society. As I emerged from the quiescence of the 1950s into the political action of the 1960s, I also learned of innumerable obstacles one encounters when trying to promote social change. As an agent for change, I learned by doing. Later, the unanswered questions that had been raised by my activism in civil rights provided part of the impetus for me to return to graduate school in 1970 in order to study and analyze the strengths and pitfalls of social protest. As a sociologist, I had observed patterns and contradictions that intrigued me. As part of my doctoral research, I sought some explanations for these anomalies, even as I continued to be a participant in the spin-off from the civil rights movement— the welfare rights movement.

As a Friend of Welfare Rights, I was a supporter of this social protest and its goals, actively participating from 1967 through 1975, when the national movement collapsed. Initially as a participant, and later as both a participant and researcher, I became fascinated with the numerous paradoxes in the movement. First, its name: welfare rights. I had been taught that <u>welfare</u> was charity, not a right. I quickly learned the facts about welfare and poverty and the distortions promoted by the dominant myths of "lazy loafers" and "pink Cadillacs." Second, as I became part of the Friends group in Newark and witnessed the expanding national protest, I was curious about how poor women on Aid to Families with Dependent Children had been able to mobilize the resources necessary to become a political force in the country, albeit for only a short while. Where did they get support? Who had initiated this social movement and why? It was then that I read Richard A. Cloward and Frances Fox Piven's "A Strategy to End Poverty" in the <u>Nation</u> (May 1966) and numerous social-action articles on welfare-reform published by the main-line Protestant denominations. These articles began to answer some of my queries but, at the same time, raised others.

New strategies within this spin-off movement also interested me. In my civil rights days, the organizations within the movement in which I had participated had been racially integrated. Blacks and their white supporters were an integral part of the same groups. In the welfare rights movement, I found that supporters were supposed to remain outside the core group and function in an auxiliary fashion, rather than in an equal or leadership role. This twin-track strategy was intriguing to me and enhanced my interest in learning more about its origins, processes, and consequences. It was clearly a different cooperative model from the one that I had experienced and observed in the civil rights movement during the earlier part of the decade. I was curious to find out if this parallel model was prevalent within the movement and what its consequences were for the Welfare Rights Organizations (WROs). Did the Friends really help or hinder or both? At the local level, it was clear to me that, while the coalition was striving to achieve common goals, it was beset by numerous conflicts.

As I participated, studied, and talked to WRO women and leaders and their supporters throughout the country over the years, I uncovered more anomalies that whetted my appetite for further exploration. I became aware that, while the National Welfare Rights Organization (NWRO) was officially labeled by all as a poor people's movement, it was in fact a movement of poor women, mostly black. As I participated in their struggles as a supporter, my consciousness of women's issues and welfare as a women's issue rekindled the feminist leanings that had emerged during my civil rights activism. As a result of participating in the social protest of blacks, of poor women on welfare, I also became an active feminist.

Other paradoxes within this social protest fueled my research and ideological interests. I found that NWRO was a movement of the poor led and supported by educated, middle-class liberals in the universities, churches, foundations, and social welfare agencies, that it was a movement that proclaimed its support for the principle of racial integration at a time when others were calling for separatism. While NWRO subscribed publicly to racial inclusiveness, in practice it turned out to be overwhelmingly black and black controlled. While it endorsed the doctrine of maximum feasible participation of the poor in its organizations, in reality it was largely dominated by the nonpoor. These gender, race, and class contradictions in its structure and ideology further enhanced my interest in pursuing this research.

Over the years, as a participant observer and active supporter of NWRO at the local, state, and national levels, it became increasingly evident to me that welfare rights could not be defined as merely an extension of the civil rights movement. It was unique in its structure, strategies, and goals. Welfare rights, I realized, was not just a black protest movement, nor just a welfare movement of poor people. It was clearly a social protest of women who were poor, and

xiii

more particularly, of mothers with dependent children, most of whom were black. As a woman and a budding feminist, these new insights further instigated this research.

As a Friend of Welfare Rights I began to collect data at the local, state, and national levels through participant observation. I attended all the national conferences and conventions, as well as the eastern regional meetings during 1970-77. I taped many of the sessions and workshops and talked informally to leaders, members, and supporters. As a member of the national Friends of Welfare Rights group headed by the United Church of Christ (the Welfare Priority Team) and as a member and one of the organizers of the Friends of Welfare Rights in New Jersey, I gained access to additional information. I conducted over 50 in-depth personal interviews with leaders, members, and supporters at all levels of the movement. Available resources on NWRO, primarily the works of Richard A. Cloward and Frances Fox Piven, as well as four dissertations and other monographs on NWRO further supplemented my data. Articles from various newspapers, magazines, government documents, and publications from various organizations involved directly or indirectly in the movement were also analyzed. Public opinion polls were used to determine changing attitudes in the United States.

What had finally led to the initiation of a serious research project—and then molded my interest and observations into a dissertation and now a book—was the encouragement and continuous support of my adviser, Irving Louis Horowitz. His vast knowledge of social protest and public policy provided me with numerous theoretical insights into the problem I was researching. Without his enthusiasm, interest, and guidance, this book could never have been written.

Many others helped to make it possible. First, I owe an immeasurable debt to the national leaders and members of NWRO who taught me much of what follows in these pages. Johnnie Tillmon, , Beulah Sanders, Frankie Jeter, Marion Kidd, and Faith Evans are a few of the national leaders who gave of their time and shared with me their thoughts and experiences, as well as some of their dreams for a better world. At the local level, other welfare rights women helped me to grow and to eradicate the myths that continue to divide us by race, gender, and class. Among them were Catherine Hamer, Maud Davis, Margaret Rose, and Ruby Grace.

I owe much to the members of the United Church of Christ Welfare Priority Team, who accepted me as a Friend and as a team member and aided me in innumerable ways during three years. Hobart Burch, Helen Webber, Joe Merchant, and Paul Sherry gave generously of their time and support. Others who assisted me along the way and to whom I am very grateful were Hulbert James, Timothy Sampson, and Bert DeLeeuw. Most important, George Wiley, NWRO's executive director and the principal founder of NWRO, was an inspiration to all those who had the privilege of working with him before his tragic death in 1973.

I also wish to acknowledge with thanks the support given to me by the Research Council at Rutgers University, which subsidized in part the typing of this manuscript.

Finally, and most important, I acknowledge the love and support of my family and close friends—especially John West, Laura West, Paul West, Landa Wesely, and Mitzi Lau—who provided me with a continuous haven, which enabled me to complete this work.

A special—very special—vote of thanks goes to Lynda Sharp, my editor and friend, whose brilliant skills helped to remold this manuscript and whose patience and good humor kept frustration and despair to a minimum.

The NWRO is no longer in existence. The movement lives on only in scattered groups of WROs throughout the country. It is a movement becalmed. In the following pages I have attempted to recount the story of its origins and its decline, as viewed from the perspective of a middle-class, white supporter. A few others have tried to do the same. It is to be hoped that some day the story of NWRO will be retold by the women who helped create this unique social protest. In the meantime, the welfare struggle continues—with indelible marks left by NWRO.

CONTENTS

PART IV

THE CHANGING SOCIOPOLITICAL CLIMATE

LIST OF TABLES AND FIGURES

LIST OF ACRONYMS

ACORN	Arkansas Community Organizations for Reform Now
ADC	Aid to Dependent Children
AFDC	Aid to Families with Dependent Children
AFDC-UP	Aid to Families with Dependent Children with Unemployed Parent
AFSCME	American Federation of State, County, and Municipal Employees
ANC Mothers	Aid to Needy Children Mothers
BEDC	Black Economic Development Council
BJIP	Better Jobs and Income Plan
BLS	Bureau of Labor Statistics
BWRO	Brooklyn Welfare Rights Organization
CAP	Community Action Program
CETA	Comprehensive Education and Training Act
CLUW	Coalition of Labor Union Women
CORE	Congress for Racial Equality
DWAC	Downtown Welfare Advocate Center
EITC	Earned Income Tax Credit
EPSDT	Early and Periodic Screening, Diagnosis and Treatment (Program)
ERA	Equal Rights Amendment
ERJPT	Economic and Racial Justice Priority Team
FAP	Family Assistance Plan
FWRO	Friends of Welfare Rights
HEW	Department of Health, Education and Welfare
IFCO	Interreligious Foundation for Community Organization
MEJ	Movement for Economic Justice
MFY	Mobilization for Youth
MWRO	Massachusetts Welfare Rights Organization
NAACP	National Association for the Advancement of Colored People
NCAP	Newark Community Action Plan
NCC	National Coordinating Committee (NWRO)
NCHE	National Committee on Household Employment
NCLC	National Caucus of Labor Committees
NJFWRO	New Jersey Friends of Welfare Rights
NJWRO	New Jersey Welfare Rights Organization
NOW	National Organization of Women
NTO	National Tenants Organization
NU-NWRO	countermovement organization formed by the Labor Caucus Committee
NWPC	National Women's Political Caucus
NWRO	National Welfare Rights Organization

OEO	Office of Economic Opportunity
OIC	Opportunities Industrialization Center
PAC	Public Assistance Coalition
P/RAC	Poverty/Rights Action Center
PUSH	People United to Save Humanity
ROWEL	Reform of Welfare
SANE	originally National Committee for a Sane Nuclear Policy, now shortened to SANE (NJSANE—New Jersey State chapter)
SCAN	Social Concerns Action Network
SCLC	Southern Christian Leadership Conference
SDS	Students for a Democratic Society
SEDFRE	Scholarship, Educational, and Defense Fund for Racial Equality
SNCC	Student National Coordinating Council
SSI	Supplemental Security Income
UCC	United Church of Christ
VISTA	Volunteers in Service to America
WEAL	Women's Equity Action League
WIC	Women, Infants and Children (Program)
WIN	Work Incentive (Program)
WIP	Work Incentive Program—NWRO label for WIN
WPT	Welfare Priority Team (of UCC)
WRISC	Welfare Rights Information and Support Community
WRO	Welfare Rights Organization
YWCA	Young Women's Christian Association

THE NATIONAL
WELFARE RIGHTS
MOVEMENT

1

INTRODUCTION

In the mid-1960s the National Welfare Rights Organization
(NWRO) emerged as a social protest of poor women who demanded
increased benefits and more humane treatment for the poor in the
United States. Its rise was rooted in several factors. In general,
the sociopolitical and economic conditions converged to provide the
necessary climate and resources for the eruption of this protest.
More specifically, the Great Society programs of the Johnson Democratic administration created a national political environment that
supported and legitimated the grievances of the blacks and the poor.
As a result, various federal resources channeled into the inner cities
to wage war against poverty helped to catalyze the rise of this national movement. In addition, the decline of the civil rights movement by the mid-1960s contributed to the birth of MWRO by shifting
attention to the plight of the poor blacks in the inner cities and by
making available black and white leaders, organizers, and liberal
networks still committed to the ongoing struggle for racial justice.
Churches and foundations, which had been a major source of support
in the civil rights protest, began to shift their resources to community organization in the urban ghettos and to focus on the economic
sources of black oppression in U.S. society. Finally, economic conditions also enhanced the availability of monies for protest by subordinate groups. The decade of the 1960s was a decade of affluence, as
reflected in the low unemployment and inflation rates. (See Figure
1.1.) With the economy booming, poverty amid plenty was seen by
many as a contradiction that should and could be readily resolved by
concerted action. Given this widespread consensus among political
authorities, white liberals, and some black civil rights groups, the
political mobilization of the poor began to gain support.

Originally intended to address the needs of poor people in general, in practice, this collective effort came to focus more specifically on the grievances of poor women on welfare. As organizers
moved into the urban ghettos to mobilize the poor, they rapidly found

FIGURE 1.1

Unemployment Rate, 1959 to June 1980

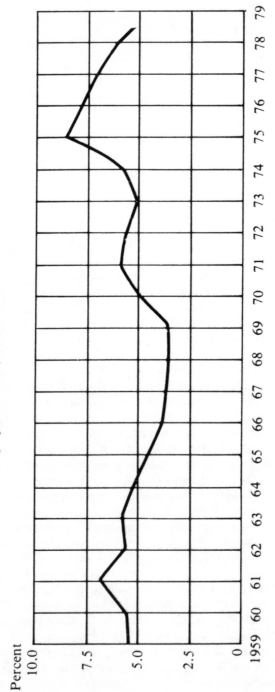

Source: Philip Shabecoff, "Jobless Rate Soars, Stirring Forecasts of a Deep Recession," New York Times, June 7, 1980.

that the heart of the problem rested in the inadequacy of income for households headed by women with dependent children. Since the structure of poverty in these areas was overwhelmingly female and primarily black, NWRO emerged not only as a movement of poor people but more specifically as a protest of poor, mostly black women on welfare. Although never defined as such by its organizers and architects in the early years, the structural reality of welfare as a women's issue became increasingly salient to all involved in the struggle. While repeated efforts were made to try and broaden its political base to make it a more inclusive movement of poor people, various factors inhibited the successful outcome of these strategies.

Few chose to join or become aligned with the protest of poor women. In part, this stemmed from the social stigmatization of welfare recipients; in part, from the racism and sexism within the dominant society. Poor whites remained largely uninvolved, perceiving NWRO as a militant black movement. Poor men, in general, rejected identification with a movement dominated by women. Others on welfare, the aged, blind, and disabled—or the "deserving" poor—appear to have seen few gains from such an association with these "undeserving" women. The stigmatization of class, race, and gender thus functioned to limit the potential numbers and groups in the struggle for economic justice. Not only the organizers' strategies, which emphasized the mobilization of poor women in the urban ghettos, but also the women leaders' reluctance to risk loss of power and prestige in an expanded movement resulted in an almost exclusive movement of poor women. Thus, external and internal conditions were interactive in bringing about this outcome.

The movement lasted for nearly ten years, from 1966 to 1975. In the process of this struggle, despite innumerable obstacles, NWRO was able to mobilize thousands of poor women and their liberal allies and, together, to confront the power structures on several levels in order to try to reform the welfare system. Gradually, counteroffensives by the political authorities and a deteriorating economy, together with rising tensions within the movement itself, eroded this national collective effort of poor women. Initial cooperation within the movement eventually gave way to rising conflicts between the poor and their allies. Questions of who should lead and who should follow and how coalitions should be structured and other issues split the movement into factions and weakened its solidarity. Although originally helping to mobilize the poor and their supporters, confrontations with the political authorities came to result in counteroffensives by those authorities that exhausted NWRO's resources. As protest gave way to bargaining and negotiations, further schisms emerged within the movement. Thus, NWRO lost most of its mobilized resources as the political climate became increasingly hostile to the demands of poor

women and as the "economy of affluence" in the 1960s became the
"economy of scarcity" in the 1970s. Faced with the realization of a
long, drawn-out struggle for welfare reform, many organizers, leaders, and supporters searched for new alternatives for bringing about
economic change. This resulted in further fragmentation and spin-
off organizations that competed for scarce liberal resources and further undermined NWRO. By 1975 the social protest of poor women had
become scattered and becalmed.

While interest in social movements in general and social protest in particular peaked after the turmoil of the 1960s in the United
States, NWRO and its protest for the rights of the poor gained relatively little public attention or support, especially when contrasted
with the civil rights movement from which it emerged. One obvious
explanation for this is that NWRO's membership base was composed
of welfare recipients, mostly black women, who were stigmatized
and devalued in the dominant society. It also failed to attract a large
following because "welfare as a right" conflicted with the sacred U.S.
values of work, achievement, and rugged individualism. While interest in the plight of the poor flared and spread in the 1960s, it dissipated rapidly in the 1970s, as the poor and their allies organized to
contest the status quo.

For a couple of years, however, NWRO's protest made the
headlines and, during its nine-year struggle, had an impact on the
welfare system that lasted long after its demise. NWRO was a unique
social movement in many respects. It was the first social protest of
women on welfare. NWRO was also unique in that it was characterized by numerous contradictions. It was a movement of women led
by men, a movement of the welfare poor financed by middle-class
liberals, a movement of blacks supported primarily by whites. Although NWRO's base constituency was composed overwhelmingly of
unemployed black women—mothers with dependent children—few
unions or black or women's organizations responded to its appeal for
allies.

That poor women, excluded from the labor force or at best relegated to isolated and menial jobs, should become political activists
appears anomalous. Women in general have long been socialized to
assume passive and apolitical roles in society. Historically, however, women as paid workers in certain sectors, unlike isolated
homemakers and domestic workers, have played a prominent role in
organizing and protesting in the United States. At certain times in
history, as Richard A. Cloward and Frances Fox Piven point out,
poor women, as wage earners and homemakers, black and white,
poor and middle-class, have united to fight for their economic rights
in order to provide for their families.[1] In the United States, despite
almost insuperable barriers, poor women with dependent children

succeeded in organizing themselves and defying the dominant norms in order to demand their rights for more income, food, and shelter for their families in the 1960s and 1970s. In a relatively short-lived, but momentous, effort, a small number confronted the welfare authorities, jamming welfare departments throughout the country to demand special grants for clothing and furniture, higher benefits, and the right to be treated with dignity and justice. Dispelling the myths and the prevalent stereotypes about the "laziness" of those on welfare, these women also fought for decent jobs and child care to enable them to gain some degree of economic independence. They lashed out against the system's attempt to limit their choices and to force them out of the home into menial jobs at slave labor wages. It was a gallant, but little recorded, fight by a small group of women, representing those on the bottom rungs of society.

To some, this social protest by poor women on welfare seemed doomed from the start. Given NWRO's powerless constituency and the ubiquitous public hostility toward welfare recipients in general, there were those who deemed such mobilization efforts a losing battle, especially in view of the differential in power between the protestors and their targets. From this perspective, the welfare mothers' struggle against the welfare authorities was pictured as a quixotic fight against intractable windmills. Some, on the other hand, saw the potential of organizing the welfare poor in order to create a crisis within the system and bring about some change in income distribution within the United States. A few contended that the poor were not powerless and that they could in fact be mobilized to help change their own economic conditions, and, more specifically, the welfare system that governed their lives.

Many of those who envisioned mobilizing welfare recipients as a political force were outsiders, that is, they were the nonpoor within the dominant sector, who saw a need for economic justice and new ways to achieve this goal.* They identified the rising turmoil in the

---

*Two sociological perspectives on "outsiders" are relevant here: Howard Becker's concept of "moral entrepreneurs" and Robert Merton's structural differentiation between "insiders" and "outsiders." The author uses the term outsiders to define those who were involved in the welfare rights movement as supporters, but who were structurally different from the welfare poor and consequently excluded from membership as an "insider" in NWRO, as mandated by its constitution. Generally speaking, "outsiders" in the movement were the nonpoor (mostly, but not exclusively, whites), who participated formally or informally as Friends of WRO and worked in some way in support of NWRO (Howard S. Becker, Outsiders: Studies in the

ghettos as evidence of deep-seated grievances among the poor that could become the basis for collective action. They uncovered contradictions within the welfare system that they felt could be exploited to increase the monies and benefits for the poor. Focusing originally in the urban areas, where poverty was starkly visible among the large black population, these outsiders sought to provide support and new strategies for changing the existing laws and regulations. The convergence of both spontaneous and planned actions by the poor and their allies against the welfare authorities in the mid-1960s thus gave rise to NWRO.

Setting its major goal as an adequate income program for all those in need, NWRO protested in the streets, lobbied in Washington and in the state capitals, and fought in the courts from 1966 to 1975. If the success of a protest movement is measured in terms of achievement of goals, then NWRO did not succeed. By 1980 the United States had not yet adopted a specific guaranteed minimum income program for the poor as part of its national social policy. If, however, success is measured in terms of other benefits that accrued to the poor, then NWRO's was a highly successful effort. NWRO played a major role in reshaping the food stamp program, in expanding other nutritional and health programs for poor children and mothers, and in securing other policies that added to the basic resources of poor families. For millions, poverty and hunger were, at minimum, attenuated as a result of NWRO's efforts. The organization also succeeded in politicizing poor women and adding their voices and perspectives to the ongoing debate about welfare reform. Speaking for themselves, they confronted the authorities in an unprecedented manner in order to "tell it like it is." For the first time, thousands of women, previously isolated, stigmatized, and intimidated by the power of the welfare authorities, came together and collectively exerted their influence on public policy to increase the income and benefits for their families. For the first time in the history of the federal welfare program, poor women became "challengers," rather than passive recipients within the political arena. Thus, NWRO left indelible marks not only on many of its participants but also on the federal and state public assistance systems.

The story of the National Welfare Rights movement is one about the protest and conflict between the poor and the existing power structures. It is an account of rising consciousness and anger as poor

---

Sociology of Deviance [New York: Free Press, 1963], pp. 147-63; also Robert K. Merton, "Insiders and Outsiders: A Chapter in the Sociology of Knowledge," American Journal of Sociology 78 [July 1972]: 9-47.)

women gained new awareness of the common sources of their economic grievances. It is also, however, a record of cooperation, primarily between the poor and their supporters in NWRO. At the same time, it is a documentation of how conflict can easily lead to cooperation and, conversely, of how cooperation almost inevitably results in conflict. It is, thus, a dynamic analysis of changing configurations of coalitions and power within a conflict setting and their consequences for this social protest of poor women.

For a short period of time, coalitions between the poor and nonpoor flourished and contributed to the successful creation of a national crisis around welfare reform. Powerful forces, however, quickly emerged to undermine NWRO and its collective efforts. Counteroffensives by the political authorities to quell the turmoil in the streets resulted in changes in the welfare laws and regulations and tightened social controls over the poor. These interactions led to the decline of open conflict, as NWRO shifted from street protest to negotiations with its opponents. Like many others dependent on the state for survival, increased social controls left members of NWRO little alternative but to accommodate the existing system and curtail political agitation. Internal cooperative efforts disintegrated as external pressures increased. Within a few years, turmoil subsided. Few welfare rights organizations (WROs) survived, as members and supporters dropped out.

Although welfare reform and a guaranteed annual income for the poor remained "live" issues in Washington at the close of the 1970s, the challengers within the political arena had changed. There was no longer an active national organization of poor women and their supporters ready to confront the authorities. Without resources, NWRO had folded in the mid-1970s. By 1980 welfare rights, as a political issue, had been subsumed under the rubric of "economic justice" by its supporters and organizers, partly reflecting an accommodation to more hostile conditions. At the state and national levels, administrators, legislators, and the courts continued to debate and to "tinker" with the system. Without agitation and a protest movement, the needs of the poor, although exacerbated by rising inflation and unemployment, remained a low priority on the agendas of political leaders in the country.

In studying the nature and morphology of social movements in general and social protest in particular, consensus exists among social scientists that such collective efforts indicate a desire for change in the status quo. Differences emerge, however, as to why some social movements succeed and others fail. Some theorists tend to emphasize the effects of internal conflicts. Others focus on the external pressures faced by fledgling movements as they concurrently mobilize members and supporters and confront their opponents. Still others suggest that both internal and external conditions interact to bring about the downfall of most social protest movements.

Another point in dispute in the analysis of social movements is whether this type of collective behavior is rational or irrational and whether or not it can legitimately be classified as political behavior. Historically, theorists can be found along this entire continuum. More recently, the trend among U.S. social-movement analysts has been to underscore the political and rational nature of social protest. Emphasis has shifted over the years from reporting such collective behavior as idiosyncratic actions on the part of a few individuals to analyzing it as planned collective efforts by subordinate groups and their allies to change the system. Economic rationality and resource mobilization theories have gained wide acceptance, especially since the turmoil of the 1960s and the proliferation of data confirming the validity of these perspectives.[2] In this study of the rise and fall of the NWRO, an analysis of resource mobilization within a triadic political context, rooted in Georg Simmel's[3] and Theodore Caplow's[4] works on triads, forms the basic theoretical framework. Simmel and Caplow both discuss the different roles available to third parties in conflict situations and explore the possible outcomes within different power triads. This analysis will define social protest as a triadic conflict: the protestors and their allies united against the political authorities. It will explore the interaction—both cooperation and conflict—that developed within the triad by examining the formation and dissolution of coalitions. The thrust is to identify the sources and consequences of resources mobilized or lost by NWRO over the years.

Both the structure of the core group of NWRO and that of its allies varied greatly over the nearly ten years of its existence. Membership and partnership in NWRO fluctuated widely, according to the real and perceived risks and rewards for those involved in the conflict. Participation in the movement both by the poor and Friends of Welfare Rights rose and fell in response to changing conditions within the movement and especially within the broader society. WRO women and their allies joined when the rewards were high and withdrew or abstained as the costs increased. Costs and rewards varied not only between different groups of participants but also over time. For example, at first the challenge of organizing welfare mothers was viewed as an opportunity by many activists. As conflicts emerged, this task came to be seen as less and less rewarding, especially as other alternatives emerged. As a result, many withdrew. Similarly, churches and foundations, which became major supporters of NWRO, at first defined visibility with welfare rights as an asset in promoting their common goals. Over the years, as conditions changed inside and outside the movement, identification with NWRO came to be seen as too costly. The consequence was the dissolution of many past partnerships. Given this fusion and fission within the movement, the mobilized resources of NWRO rose and fell. At any given period, the configuration of coalitions within the welfare rights movement varied considerably. While a few allies remained continuously aligned with NWRO, most provided only episodic support. Many also remained on the periphery of the struggle, participating independently, if at all. The decisions to participate or not participate in the protest of poor women and in what manner all affected NWRO's resources and, therefore, its rise and fall.

It is suggested that analysis of changing coalitions within a social protest movement thus provides a logical framework for determining the processes of mobilization and demobilization of resources. By examining the nature of different coalitions within the conflict setting, not only between the core group and its supporters but also with its opponents, social protest, as Caplow has indicated, can be defined as a triadic conflict of "two against one." The first step is to examine the changing internal dyad of the organized poor women and their different allies over time. The next step is to explore how they interacted with the "targets" of the protest jointly or independently, and what ties emerged in such relationships. The focus here is on the collective efforts of the protestors and their supporters against the welfare authorities. Finally, the analysis also must encompass the changing sociopolitical and economic settings within which the overt conflict evolves.

The book first investigates the processes of cooperation between groups that led to the birth of NWRO and then examines the internal conflicts that eroded these alliances. It then explores the consequences of the external struggles by NWRO and its various allies against the welfare target structures and the counteroffensives that ensued. The central question raised is, What factors, both internal and external, led to the decline of NWRO's mobilized resources? More specifically, it asks, Who were the major actors in this triadic conflict, what led to the development of cooperation between different partners, what conflicts arose, and how did they affect NWRO's resources over the years? In addition, the book seeks to discover the external conditions that had an impact on the rise and fall of this social protest. More succinctly, we will be investigating how shifting configurations of power within this triadic conflict affected the mobilized resources of the welfare rights protest and the decline of NWRO.

The book is divided into four parts. Part I covers the mobilization of poor women in the National Welfare Rights movement and the establishment of NWRO. Part II encompasses the mobilization of NWRO's supporters and the consequences of coalitions with different groups. It also includes a discussion of potential supporters who chose to remain as witnesses, rather than participants, in the social protest for welfare rights. Part III describes the confrontations of the poor and their allies with the welfare authorities and their effects on NWRO. Part IV provides an overview of the changing sociopolitical climate and its impact on the resources available for the welfare rights movement. Finally, there is a brief summary and conclusion.

In Part I the mobilization of the welfare rights movement is traced from its birth in 1966 to its becalmed state in 1980. Chapter 2 describes how cooperation between various groups resulted in the mobilization of thousands of members, millions of dollars, and numerous other organizational resources needed to activate and maintain this protest. Structural changes within the movement organization are analyzed to show the shift in the power within NWRO over time. Chapter 3 then focuses on the early cooperation that provided the impetus for the birth of the movement and the conflicts that emerged between blacks and whites, poor and nonpoor, and women and men within the core organization. It describes the consequences and conflict in terms of resources mobilized and lost over the years.

Part II analyzes the supporters of NWRO and, more specifically, their cooperation and conflicts with the organization. Chapter 4 describes the origins and consequences of the nonpeer coalitions between WROs and the middle-class Friends of Welfare Rights (FWROs) both at the national and local levels. In Chapter 5 we explore the coalitions between NWRO and black and women's organizations, its peer allies (given its predominantly black and female structure), and examine the ties that emerged or failed to emerge between these potential partners for welfare rights.

In Part III we move to the more salient struggle of NWRO and its allies against the welfare authorities. This section analyzes the overt triadic conflict of NWRO and its partners with welfare administrators, legislators, and adjudicators, the consequences of this conflict for the movement itself, and NWRO's goal to achieve a guaranteed income system for the poor in the United States.

Finally, in Part IV we examine the changing sociopolitical climate and its effects on NWRO. More specifically, the changes in social attitudes and actions of the policymakers, supporters, and the public in general toward welfare, a guaranteed income, and guaranteed jobs are explored. The decline in collectivism and the shift toward greater emphasis on individualism as a means of solving social problems is traced from the 1960s through the 1970s.

The final chapter summarizes the findings and conclusions related to the impact of the internal and external conflicts on NWRO's mobilized resources, as well as the legacy of NWRO in the continuing struggle for welfare reform. It suggests that a systematic and dynamic analysis of the resource mobilization and interactions of the protestors, their allies, and opponents within a changing society may help to explain the rise and fall of social protest movements of the poor.

NOTES

All taped interviews are coded to ensure confidentiality. The coding system does not reflect the actual numbers of interviews conducted. It is merely used to obscure the identity of the respondents but at the same time to provide a system facilitating easy identification by the author.

1. Richard A. Cloward and Frances Fox Piven, "Hidden Protest: The Channeling of Female Innovation and Resistance," Signs 4 (Summer 1979): 657.

2. Irving Louis Horowitz, Foundations of Political Sociology (New York: Harper & Row, 1972); Mancur Olson, Jr., The Logic of Collective Action (Cambridge, Mass.: Harvard University Press, 1965); William A. Gamson, The Strategy of Social Protest (Homewood, Ill.: Dorsey Press, 1975); Anthony Oberschall, Social Conflict and Social Movements (Englewood Cliffs, N.J.: Prentice-Hall, 1973); Michael Lipsky, "Protest as a Political Resource," American Political Science Review 62 (1968): 1144-58; Michael Useem, Protest Movements in America (Indianapolis, Ind.: Bobbs-Merrill, 1975); Mayer Zald and Roberta Ash, "Social Movements Organizations: Growth, Decay, and Change," Social Forces 44 (March 1966); John D. McCarthy and Mayer N. Zald, The Trend of Social Movements in America: Professionalization and Resource Mobilization (Morristown, N.J.: General Learning Press, 1973).

3. Georg Simmel, The Sociology of Georg Simmel, ed. and trans. Kurt H. Wolff (New York: Free Press, 1950).

4. Theodore Caplow, Two against One: Coalitions in Triad (Englewood Cliffs, N.J.: Prentice-Hall, 1968).

PART I
MOBILIZATION OF POOR WOMEN

2

THE MOBILIZATION OF POOR WOMEN

The National Welfare Rights Organization (NWRO) emerged in 1966 as the first national protest of poor women. Its goals were the reformation of the U.S. welfare system and the establishment of a guaranteed income based on need. In the first few years, it mobilized resources and became a recognized political representative of the poor and a challenger of the welfare system. Cooperation between the poor and nonpoor, between blacks and whites, and between women and men played a significant role in the rise and mobilization of this protest. These structural contrasts, and the reversal of traditional roles within the movement, however, also became the source of increasing tensions and conflict that eventually contributed to its decline.

NWRO was a movement characterized by contradictions. It was a movement of women led by men, a movement of the welfare poor financed by middle-class liberals, a movement of blacks supported mostly by whites. Although NWRO's base constituency was composed overwhelmingly of unemployed black women—mothers with dependent children—few unions or organizations of blacks or women responded to its appeal for allies.

While NWRO endorsed racial integration as one of its basic principles, in practice, its membership and leadership were overwhelmingly black. While it espoused "maximum feasible participation" and "power for poor people," the movement organization was dominated by its middle-class organizers and supporters, both at the national and local levels. Although it was a movement designed to empower poor women, it never openly addressed itself to the issue of women's liberation or the rights of women in U.S. society.

Moreover, not only the general term welfare but the specific name of the movement—welfare rights—epitomized the structural and ideological contradictions in U.S. society. Welfare, as defined in the dictionary, has two meanings that symbolize conflicting values: the "state of being healthy, properly fed, and comfortable" and the state of "receiving public financial aid because of hardship and need," a

status of poverty and dependence despised by all in a society that rewards independence, individualism, and achievement.[1] Similarly,
welfare rights was for many a contradiction of terms. Welfare, as
perceived by the public at large, was charity, not a right under the
law. These anomalies in the protest of poor women in the decade of
the 1960s had significant impact on the rise and decline of the movement.

While protest movements among the poor in the United States
have been relatively infrequent, as Piven and Cloward have pointed
out, at certain times in history, the sociopolitical conditions have
converged to give rise to mobilization and protest by the subordinate
elements of society.[2] The National Welfare Rights movement, composed primarily of poor, mostly black women, was an example of this
rare phenomenon in U.S. history. Its uniqueness was further rooted
in its structure. Although the intent of its organizers and architects
was to create a mass movement of "poor people," in reality, NWRO
turned out to be a protest of "poor women." How this came about—
the political conflict and cooperation that gave rise to such a collective
effort—is the substance of this chapter.

THE RISE OF THE WELFARE SYSTEM

With the onset of the Great Depression in the 1930s, public subsidies for the poor were institutionalized by the federal government
in the Social Security Act of 1935. Charity provided by private agencies at the local and state levels had failed to meet the rising needs
of millions, as jobs disappeared and people were left destitute. Despite resistance to government intervention into the economy and the
fear of undermining the "work ethic" in a free enterprise system, the
dimensions of this economic catastrophe combined to usher in new
economic security programs for some of the poor.

The public assistance legislation implemented in the 1930s was
categorical in nature, rather than universal. It emphasized the temporary aspects of relief and the ultimate solution as that of work.
Men temporarily dislocated from the labor force were perceived as
being most in need of federal aid. The goals of political leaders were
to abolish public dependency as quickly as possible and limit it to the
"deserving" poor, that is, "aged persons, blind persons, [and] dependent and crippled children."[3] From the time of President Franklin Delano Roosevelt, who instituted the federal programs for economic recovery, to President Richard Nixon, 35 years later, political leaders focused on finding ways and means of reducing the dole.
The espoused solution of the political establishment was to replace
welfare with "workfare" for the majority of this dependent population.[4]

As Piven and Cloward point out, however, governmental efforts to move people off welfare and onto the work rolls varied according to the intensity of civil disorder.[5] When outbreaks of protest caused by mass unemployment occurred, social controls were loosened and relief expanded. As soon as political stability was regained, provision of public assistance was tightened. Hence, the number of poor on welfare or in the labor force was regulated by the political leaders over the years.

The public assistance programs were categorical, and certain groups were excluded. Able-bodied individuals, childless couples, and families in which the father was present, regardless of need, were not eligible for the federal/state programs. The assumption was that they should be able to provide for themselves and their families through paid public or private work. The program for dependent children—Aid to Dependent Children (ADC)—covered families in which the father had died, deserted the family, or never been present. In the majority of the cases, the mother was the caretaker. Although written into the 1935 Social Security Act, ADC was, however, "almost an oversight and was not included in an original draft for the program."[6] Lucy Komisar notes that the purpose of ADC "was to promote family life and enable mothers to stay home and care for their children rather than work."[7] She adds, however, that, in a period of high unemployment, political leaders "welcomed the opportunity to keep women at home and give men the jobs." But this contradicted the "work ethic that was such a basic part of American poor-law tradition" and that "would cause constant dissatisfaction with the program." Komisar points out that "although Congress asserted in law that mothers without husbands should not work, the country in time rejected the spirit of the notion."

While the other "adult categories"—the aged, blind, and the disabled—were eventually shifted into a "guaranteed income program" in 1972 (the Supplemental Security Income [SSI]), Aid to Families with Dependent Children (AFDC) remained the source of the bulk of the welfare population and the welfare controversy in the 1960s and 1970s. Adopted by all the states, AFDC was available to mothers and their dependent children, despite later efforts to expand it to families with unemployed fathers.* "Welfare and poverty" thus became defined

------

*Gilbert Steiner states that "the Kennedy administration secured approval (in 1961) of federal financial assistance to states choosing to extend their aid to dependent children program to cover families whose heads are unemployed" (The State of Welfare [Washington, D.C.: Brookings Institution, 1971], p. 35). By 1980, however, only half of the states had adopted the unemployed parent option (AFDC-UP).

politically as a women's problem by those trying to modify the system.

As some have pointed out, it is not surprising that women comprised the bulk of the welfare poor. Komisar notes that "in a society where most women are dependent on their husbands, they become dependent on the state when their husbands leave them."[8] Lack of childcare facilities, low wages in traditional female occupations, and sex and race discrimination in the labor force combined to limit women's opportunities for economic independence. For many mothers with young children, welfare, or AFDC, was the only alternative for survival. Thus, in time, the problem of welfare became labeled more specifically as the problem of AFDC, or of women and children. AFDC was by far the largest program, the most costly, the most controversial, and the one providing the lowest benefits of any of the categorical welfare programs.[9] Condemnation of the program grew as its public image changed, and women, work, and welfare became central issues in the heated political debate to reform the system.

For several years, AFDC received little attention from policy makers.[10] At first, it had been accepted as a legitimate way of aiding helpless children and their widowed or deserted mothers. The typical AFDC recipient in the 1930s was described as "a West Virginia mother whose husband had died in a mine accident. Honest, hardworking, God-fearing white Protestant folk. Rural."[11] Over the years, the "widows and orphans were transferred to social insurance programs." As a result, the welfare rolls became "increasingly black, urban, and illegitimate" and thus the "whipping boy" for the public and policy makers.[12] For political leaders, the issue shifted from one of support for "deserving" women with dependent children to one of subsidizing women "to stay home, produce more children," and remain dependent on the state.[13] Little political support could thus be mobilized to increase benefits for these women and children, despite the fact that economic hardships continued to rise.

By the mid-1960s, it was becoming very clear that welfare was not going to "wither away" and that "a considerable fraction of the population was still outside the sweep of the country's prosperity," despite the availability of some federal/state programs of public assistance.[14] Unemployment was at its lowest in many years, but the AFDC rolls were burgeoning. * There were several reasons for this

---

*Gilbert Steiner notes that the unemployment rate was down to 3.4 percent in 1968 and that "during the 1960's the unemployment rate was halved, AFDC recipients increased by almost two-thirds, and AFDC money payments doubled. Whatever the relationship between

paradox of "poverty amid plenty." First, welfare benefit levels were
kept to a minimum, "lest some persons be better off with a combination of relief and part-time or casual employment than others . . .
with full-time employment alone."[15] Second, not only were the payments generally lower than the federally defined "poverty level" but
they also varied widely among the states. In 1951, for instance, the
average monthly benefit for a dependent child ranged from $5.25 in
Mississippi to $37.00 in California. A decade later, Mississippi was
paying $9.20 per month; Alabama, $10.20; and New Jersey, $65.00.[16]
Third, blacks were especially hard hit by unemployment after the
Korean War. Piven and Cloward note that "in the northern urban
ghettos, unemployment reached depression levels" in 1960.[17] Unemployment rates for women—especially black women—were even higher.[18]

Economic hardships among women with dependent children were
exacerbated because most had access only to menial jobs at the lowest wages, with little, if any, child care available. Furthermore,
the "rights" to welfare benefits were not publicized. In fact, information on relief was tightly controlled by the welfare authorities.
Rules and regulations were complex, fluid, and many times arbitrary.
The stigma of welfare, pervasive throughout U.S. society, further inhibited expansion of the rolls. Few among the poor applied. Of those
who did, "roughly one half were simply turned away."[19] Consequently,
the welfare rolls increased very slowly from 1950 to 1960 (only 17 percent) despite dire poverty, especially among women with dependent
children.

Economic hardships alone, however, were not enough to bring
about any change in the welfare system. Only with the rise of turmoil
in the inner cities and new actions and attitudes toward the urban
blacks and poor within the dominant society did the necessary conditions for the birth of the National Welfare Rights movement emerge.

THE ORIGINS OF THE NATIONAL
WELFARE RIGHTS MOVEMENT

Several factors converged in the mid-1960s to provide the political and economic conditions necessary for the rise of the welfare
rights protest in the United States. Among the most important were
the "favorable" attitudes and policies of the Kennedy and Johnson

---

workfare and welfare, it is not the simple one of reduced unemployment producing reduced dependency" (The State of Welfare [Washing-
ton, D.C.: Brookings Institution, 1971], pp. 32-33).

Democratic administrations, the rising agitation of the poor and black in the inner cities and the decline of the civil rights movement, and the development of "A Strategy to End Poverty" by the social scientists Cloward and Piven that helped to mobilize the needed resources (monies and people) to create NWRO.

The origins of the NWRO were rooted in two social movements of the 1960s, namely, the federal government's "War on Poverty," initiated by the Johnson administration shortly after President Kennedy's assassination, and the civil rights movement, which had climaxed in the early years of the decade. Daniel Patrick Moynihan argues that "NWRO was in large measure made possible by the antipoverty program."[20] Gilbert Steiner suggests that the movement "was an unanticipated consequence of the beginnings of the black power movement."[21] Both were right.

Out of these two political streams surfaced NWRO's resources —people and monies—as well as its principles, goals, and strategies. From the civil rights movement came its organizers, leaders, liberal supporters, their networks, and their monies. From the poverty movement emerged its theoreticians, other organizers, and federal funds. Its principles, strategies, and tactics developed from the synthesis of these two political currents. The interweaving of the civil rights conflicting doctrines of "racial integration" and "black nationalism" gave rise to NWRO's support of the pluralistic notion of "interracialism." The need for resources strengthened this belief, and the availability of civil rights allies led to the coalition of NWRO and white liberals in the struggle for a guaranteed income.

NWRO's goals and strategies reflected the endorsement of the principle of "maximum feasible participation of the poor," established by the Johnson administration's War on Poverty. NWRO's constitution specified that poor women on welfare were the voting members and elected leaders (the "insiders"). Technically, all others were classified as nonvoting supporters (the "outsiders").[22] From the civil rights movement, NWRO adopted the direct-action tactics of demonstrations and sit-ins against the welfare departments. Similarly, other civil rights strategies, such as lobbying in Washington, D.C., and waging legal battles in the Supreme Court, were incorporated by NWRO in its effort to change the welfare system.

Socioeconomic conditions in the 1960s also appear to have spurred the welfare rights protest. The generally favorable economic conditions in the country in the 1960s—low unemployment rates among the dominant white majority, single-digit inflation rates, and a rising gross national product—seem to have enhanced the willingness of various groups to support NWRO.[23] White liberals, many of whom had played a major role in the black civil rights struggle, provided not only their theories and ideas but also their monies, skills, staff, networks, and other organizational resources. As the economic scene changed and the country moved into the worst recession since the Great Depression, the resources available to NWRO in the 1970s dissipated rapidly.

The political conditions were also critical in the mobilization of resources and the rise of NWRO. The favorable political climate of the 1960s was a major factor in providing the impetus for the welfare rights protest. The actions of the nation's political leaders at that time reflected a rising concern for the problems of blacks and the poor. "Poverty" was reemerging as a social issue.[24]

With the publication of Michael Harrington's[25] The Other America in 1962, the paradox of "poverty amid plenty" surfaced as a political issue in the Kennedy administration. New solutions were sought. The Social Security amendments of 1962 called for the appointment of an Advisory Council on Public Welfare to investigate and recommend what should be done to improve the welfare system. The previous strategies of "rehabilitation" of the clients had not worked. In 1962 the new thrust was to increase social services to multiproblem families as a means of alleviating poverty and cutting down the welfare rolls. This "tinkering with the system" did not resolve the problem. President Johnson, in announcing to the nation his administration's decision to give priority to the elimination of poverty, said: "Today, for the first time in our history, we have the power to strike away the barriers to full participation in our society. Having the power, we have the duty."[26]

In 1966 the Advisory Council on Public Welfare, in its report to the president, recommended a new strategy to help eliminate poverty: a guaranteed income for the poor. The Advisory Council's report, Having the Power, We Have the Duty, called for drastic changes in the welfare system and concluded that "neither the War on Poverty nor achievement of long-range goals implicit in a Great Society concept can succeed so long as the basic guarantees of a practical minimum level of income and social protection are not assured to all."[27] The report, as Alfred Kahn points out, was "dedicated to the 'principle of welfare as a right.'"[28] President Johnson himself had announced, upon taking office in 1964, that his administration's policy would be "to eliminate the paradox of poverty amid plenty in the nation by opening to everyone . . . the opportunity to live in decency and dignity."[29]

The same year, Congress had passed the Economic Opportunity Act, providing not only the political but also the economic and ideological support for a new strategy to deal with the problem of poverty in the country. Part of the strategy rested on the principle of maximum feasible participation of the poor, required by this act. Peter Marris and Martin Rein point out that the Office of Economic Opportunity (OEO) "was determined that the poor themselves should share control of the new resources at least equally with government and professional agents of social services."[30] As Moynihan notes, this was a "period of great concern about poverty, especially black poverty."[31] Consequently, in the early 1960s, resources—people and monies—began to flow into the inner cities from the public sector.

Such propitious political and economic conditions on the national scene legitimated the fight against poverty and channeled resources into needy communities. As a result, this federal strategy of intervention helped to spark protests among the poor in major urban areas. One of the major sources of grass-roots grievances was the lack of income and, more specifically, the "inadequacy and inhumanity" of the welfare system. Three years before the birth of NWRO, local welfare rights groups were already beginning to emerge in various parts of the country around these issues. Stimulated by the civil rights agitation and protest of that decade, blacks in some urban areas had begun to organize around basic needs, such as welfare, housing, and food. Out of this politicization of the black urban poor, welfare rights groups emerged spontaneously in some parts of the country and through planned efforts in others. Federally funded Community Action Programs (CAPs), Volunteers in Service to America (VISTA), and social-welfare agencies, together with church agencies and social-action groups, provided organizers, volunteers, and other resources. Others came from the Students for a Democratic Society (SDS) and other radical groups involved in social protest during that period.[32]

Indigenous leadership and organizers also emerged within black communities. In California, for example, the ANC Mothers Anonymous was organized in 1963 by Johnnie Tillmon, a black welfare mother in Watts. Unemployed, ill, and with five children to support, she applied for welfare. The shift from self-support to the degradation of public assistance and the barriers she encountered propelled her into organizing the welfare women in her area. In less than four years, she had started her local WRO (one of the first in the country), helped to mobilize and coordinate other state groups, and become the first chair of the NWRO.[33]

At the same time, another group in California—the Alameda County Welfare Rights Organization—emerged through the efforts of outside organizers. Trying to find a way to get monies for poor women and their children, Timothy Sampson, a white organizer, was instrumental in the formation of this local welfare rights group. From there, he went on to play a major role in the organization of the NWRO.

Not only in California but elsewhere in the country, welfare rights organizing gained momentum as economic conditions for the urban poor deteriorated and outside resources helped spark confrontations against the welfare authorities. In Ohio, the worsening welfare crisis in late 1965, brought about by legislative cuts in benefits, precipitated the formation of a coalition of the poor and nonpoor to change the existing welfare system in the state. Agitation by the women on welfare, supported by private church and social-welfare agencies, gave rise to the Ohio Steering Committee for Adequate Welfare, which was to provide the focus and the site for the first national welfare rights confrontation in the country one year later.[34]

In the East, welfare rights organizing was spurred in New York City by the Mobilization for Youth (MFY), the precursor to the War on Poverty model. Lawyers and organizers had readily identified lack of income and welfare as the most critical issues affecting the poor in Harlem.[35] At the same time, they had become aware that one of the major sources of available, but generally untapped, income for poor people was the welfare department. Public assistance for women with dependent children, they found, existed as a statutory right under the program of AFDC. This program provided not only regular cash benefits on a monthly basis but also special grants for emergencies and other basic needs not covered by the regular allotment. Community organizers and lawyers soon discovered that relatively few women in desperate need of financial assistance knew anything about the availability of these special grants. Those who knew were afraid to apply because of the stigma attached to welfare as well as the fear of dealing with the welfare bureaucracy. Historically, these social controls had functioned effectively to limit participation by the poor. Only about half of those eligible for the benefits were receiving any in the 1960s.[36] Furthermore, those that were enrolled received minimal allotments, given the fairly arbitrary nature of the rules and regulations and the discretionary power of caseworkers and supervisors, the "gatekeepers" of the system.

It soon became apparent to those involved in MFY that this discrepancy between the actual disbursements to the poor and those available as a right under the law provided not only a means for increasing the income of poor families but also a way of organizing the community. Working with poor women who headed families, they taught them their "welfare rights," prepared lay manuals that could help to decipher the complex welfare regulations, bargained with the welfare administrations, and rapidly succeeded in increasing the income of some of the poor in Harlem. Success attracted others in need, and by 1967 the welfare rolls had burgeoned.[37] According to Larry Jackson and William Johnson[38] and Marris and Rein,[39] the MFY played a critical role in the rise of community organizing and, more specifically, the welfare rights protest.

Two social scientists in MFY were instrumental in the organization of the national movement for welfare rights. Radicalized by their involvement in the welfare crisis in Harlem, Cloward and Piven drafted "A Strategy to End Poverty" and circulated it widely within the liberal community in the spring of 1966. [40] These two white academicians from Columbia University had become convinced that, if eligible people were informed of their legal rights to welfare and were supported in making demands for these benefits, the existing welfare system would collapse. In its place, it was hoped, a more adequate and humane system—a guaranteed income system—would be adopted by the political leaders.

Cloward, describing the plan in 1966, stated that the intent of this "strategy of crises" was to increase the power of blacks in the cities by organizing "people to claim their full benefits and recruiting large numbers of eligible people to the (welfare) rolls."[41] Both Cloward and Piven also felt that this would enable blacks "to create a major political crisis in the cities." They contended that the welfare crisis "would exacerbate strains among Negro and white working class and middle-class elements in the urban Democratic coalition," which would lead to major economic and political reforms and redistribution of income on a more "equitable and less tyrannical basis." Cloward argued that, while those detached from the labor force lacked the economic leverage of the employed, they did have "a form of power in government itself, in making it adhere to its own laws." Recognizing that "it will not amount to the same continuing power that labor has," Cloward contended that it would be "sufficient power to create a crisis, a crisis that could lead to some kind of reform of traditional means of distributing income in the country."[42]

The favorable political and economic climate in the country, the rising agitation and organization of welfare rights groups, and growing liberal support for the Cloward and Piven theory converged with other events to bring about the birth of the National Welfare Rights movement. One such event was the emergence of a national black leader dedicated to the plight of the poor. George Wiley, a black professor of chemistry at Syracuse University, had become active in the civil rights movement, organizing and heading a chapter of the Congress for Racial Equality (CORE) in Syracuse, New York. In time, Wiley's interest in racial justice began to focus increasingly on the needs of the poor blacks who had not shared equally from the successes of the civil rights movement. [43] Deeply committed to this cause, Wiley relinquished his prestigious post at the university at a time when his career and scientific contributions were gaining national recognition. He moved his family to New York and worked full time for CORE as its associate director under James Farmer. During these years in the civil rights movement, he met Cloward and Piven and learned of their proposed strategy of mobilizing the welfare poor. This focus on the economic needs of the black poor immediately appealed to him. Together, these three intellectuals were to provide the major leadership in the rise of the national welfare rights protest.

As it happened, Wiley's stay in CORE turned out to be very brief. Internal political conflicts within this organization set the stage for him to organize and lead the National Welfare Rights movement. When James Farmer announced his resignation as director of CORE late in 1965, Wiley became one of the two contenders for this top position. In a bitter contest, Wiley lost to Floyd McKissick in January 1966 and, shortly thereafter, resigned from the organization.

The major underlying issue in the election campaign for the top post in CORE was racial integration, the extent of continued white participation in the black movement. It was a time when racial integration versus separation of white within the civil rights movement was being hotly debated. It was also a time when middle-class dominance in poor people's movements was beginning to create conflicts between the poor and nonpoor. White liberals, as well as many black leaders, were becoming polarized, as August Meier and Elliott Rudwick point out in their seminal study of CORE. [44] Accusations of racism and classism within the "integrated" civil rights movement were beginning to split former allies. In CORE, this conflict led ultimately to Wiley's defeat and resignation. There were basic ideological and strategic differences between Wiley and McKissick in terms of how to cooperate with whites and how to organize the black and poor.

Wiley was an "integrationist who believed that whites could play an important role in the movement."[45] Throughout the years, Wiley's belief in racial inclusiveness in the struggle for racial and economic justice never waivered. Support for interracialism remained one of his basic principles throughout his life. When he set out to organize the NWRO, this commitment to cooperation with whites was incorporated into the new movement, even though he was criticized by black leaders who were moving in the opposite direction. As a result of this internal conflict, Wiley left CORE and organized NWRO. As one of his close colleagues remarked, "If George [Wiley] had not lost [to McKissick], NWRO would not have been founded."[46]

Upon leaving CORE in January 1966, Wiley attended a meeting in Syracuse that was to change the course of his life. At the "Poor People's War Council on Poverty," he met Cloward, who pointed out to him the paradox that, while the meeting was for poor people, "there was not a single workshop on welfare."[47] Cloward then described the strategy that he and Piven "had been developing, that they felt gave significant promise as a source of political power for welfare recipients and other poor people."[48] Their "Strategy to End Poverty" combined immediate benefits for the poor together with long-range reforms in public policy that might well usher in a guaranteed income system.[49]

While other black leaders had rejected the Cloward and Piven strategy of mobilizing around the welfare issue, Wiley was immediately attracted to its central focus on an economic issue. He set about mobilizing support for it. He first took a job as the national action coordinator of the Citizen's Crusade against Poverty, "a private liberal establishment group which sought to ensure that the government's War on Poverty programs lived up to their promises."[50] Convinced that "the most basic problem of Black people was the economic problem," Wiley proposed to them the strategy of organizing poor people across racial lines.[51] Despite his untiring efforts, he was unable to convince the Citizen's Crusade to endorse his plan. According to Wiley, the feat was that, once organized, the poor would turn around and make demands on the Citizen's Crusade.[52] Given this conflict of interests, Wiley resigned in the spring of 1966.

Interest in the welfare issue and welfare rights organizing was emerging among former civil rights activists and organizers throughout the country. The question was how to coordinate the isolated efforts across the nation and when to start. On May 21, 1966, at a conference on guaranteed income at the University of Chicago, Wiley and Cloward found the opportune moment. Meeting with some 40 welfare mothers and other activists who were present, the two leaders set up a special meeting to discuss their welfare rights strategy. At that meeting, one of the welfare mothers, Edith Doering, announced that the newly formed Ohio Steering Committee for Adequate Welfare was planning "a 150-mile protest march from Cleveland to Columbus on June 30 to dramatize cutbacks in the Ohio budget" and invited others to join.[53] As a result of this report, the decision was made to have "a national thing on June 30 [1966]," which was to coincide with the Ohio demonstration. Wiley offered to coordinate the effort. Two days later, on May 23, 1966, he officially opened the Poverty Rights Action Center (P/RAC) in Washington, D.C.,[54] which was to function as the national coordinating agency. Together, the poor and their allies "laid the groundwork for a national effort in welfare, culminating eventually in the formation of NWRO."[55]

P/RAC's first actions were to send out its two staff members across the country to identify existing welfare recipients and to help others to mobilize for the June demonstrations. The plan was to have as many groups as possible involved in protest around the issue of welfare at the time of the "Walk for Decent Welfare" in Ohio. On June 30, 1966, approximately 5,000 recipients and supporters participated in some part of the long march from Cleveland to Columbus to protest the cutbacks and the inadequacy of the benefit levels and to demand increased grants and more humane treatment by the welfare authorities. Concurrently, throughout the country, as a result of P/RAC's efforts, welfare demonstrations were held in "24 to 27 cities" to demand changes in the welfare system.[56] This first major confrontation of the poor and their allies with the welfare establishment marked the birth of the National Welfare Rights movement.

Originally, Wiley had not envisioned P/RAC as a means for creating a national movement of poor people. His objective was more modest. His hope was that he would be able to establish a national network of poor people. P/RAC was "simply going to be a communications center to link together the poor people in the many grassroots organizations that already existed, and to help stimulate their development."[57] Wiley felt that "although community organizations were being developed, the efforts were isolated, one from another, and they were not getting maximum clout or maximum use of their political potential. They were unable to act in concert on national issues." At the beginning, the principal aim of the core organization was "to try to provide a communication link that could help [poor] people make a move on the national level."[58] This collective effort would, he felt, provide a unique opportunity for "a new configuration of forces to promote social change in the United States."[59]

Despite serious misgivings by some of his colleagues, Wiley had become convinced that the Cloward and Piven strategy to create a "financial crisis in welfare" would eventually "force Washington to institute a guaranteed income." He felt that it was a viable way of empowering the poor on welfare and argued that sufficient resources could be mobilized among potential allies to bring about change.[60] Critics of the plan questioned the payoffs of such a strategy for the recipients, voicing concern that the poor could easily be victimized when welfare authorities reduced rather than expanded benefits.[61] Opponents in the liberal camp argued that organizing the poor to demand welfare, rather than jobs, would alienate the political leaders and the public, given the deep-seated values of work and achievement in U.S. society.[62] Cloward and Piven countered by asserting that "most of the people whom we now call very poor are not going to participate in occupational roles, at least not in this generation."[63] Furthermore, they and Wiley contended that welfare was a unique issue for organizing, since it "was a basic economic issue affecting a lot of poor people." The welfare system was also unique in that it was "operated jointly by the Federal, state, and local governments." Once the poor were mobilized at the local levels, "eventually they would see the crucial importance of change at the national level. Their involvement would likely be a continuing process of education."[64] Confrontation at the local and state levels would lead to political action to change the federal welfare system.

In order to mobilize the poor and transform his vision into reality, Wiley knew that he had to mobilize resources—people and monies—to establish P/RAC and link together the widely scattered groups of poor people throughout the country. Consequently, in the spring of 1966, he set about to seek support for a national "communications center" for poor people. In the process, this changed into the building of a national movement organization of poor women on welfare.

MOBILIZING MONEY

With a limited number of individual donations, Wiley's own savings, and one small foundation grant, P/RAC began functioning with not more than $10,000 in May 1966. [65] "Within two or three months," Cloward stated, "Wiley was $20,000 in debt; by August 1966 [three months later] he was not only bankrupt, but he was twenty to thirty thousand dollars behind." By the end of the year, Wiley had raised $50,000 and was hiring organizers as quickly as they could be found. As a result, welfare rights burgeoned. [66]

Raising money for welfare rights was no easy task. White liberals, who earlier in the decade had supported the black struggle, were reluctant to support this "unpopular" cause. As Piven noted, "Civil Rights was a popular cause among liberals; Welfare Rights was not." [67] Piven, Cloward, and Wiley's efforts to raise money for the movement in New York City were only partially successful. Few funds were mobilized among "rich liberals in Westchester and Eastside New York," but some "grants from small foundations" were finally forthcoming by 1967. [68]

While monies were scarce in the first few months, organizational needs were relatively limited, since "the movement was just a network." [69] Most of the action was at the local level, and groups functioned by "bootlegging" staff and organizers, mimeograph machines, and other needed equipment and supplies from federally funded poverty-action programs and friendly churches. As the national movement expanded, its needs also increased.

By August 1967 NWRO had become institutionalized as a formal movement organization with a constitution, bylaws, elected leaders, offices in Washington, D.C., and a paid staff. As a result, its budget and expenditures skyrocketed. Its yearly operation costs exceeded $200,000 in 1968. [70] By the end of 1969, this had increased to almost half a million dollars. (See Table 2.1.) By 1970 NWRO's proposed budget was $900,000. (See Table 2.2.) Throughout its history, the national organization developed budgets for its programs but seldom succeeded in meeting their financial goals. NWRO was continually in debt.

To keep the national operation going, fund raising became Wiley's almost full-time job as NWRO's executive director. Despite his "juggling acts" and untiring efforts, there were never enough monies to

TABLE 2.1

NWRO Financial Statement: October 1, 1968–September 30, 1969

	Dollars
Income	
Individual contributors	50,821.65
Foundations	32,345.73
Church denominations	74,242.50
Inter-Religious Foundation for Community Organization (IFCO)	90,000.00
National Association of Social Workers	36,500.00
Other organizations	26,270.07
Membership and dues	23,733.74
Literature, jewelry, and miscellaneous sales	17,329.20
Government grants and contracts	105,859.21
Total income	457,102.10
Expenses	
National headquarters	
Salaries	204,588.69
Rent and utilities	10,044.75
Office expenses	7,801.63
Postage and shipping	6,074.13
Telephone	29,981.39
Travel	18,353.16
Conferences	21,675.47
Summer student stipends	36,000.00
Consultants and auditors' fees	2,471.06
Total	336,990.28
Field operations	
Salaries	133,922.47
Office space and expenses	15,310.72
Travel	10,485.62
Total	159,718.81
NWRO officers and national meetings	12,323.54
Total expenses	509,032.63

Source: National Welfare Rights Organization, Prospectus, March 1970, p. 7.

TABLE 2.2

NWRO 1970 Proposed Operating Budget

	Dollars
National headquarters	250,000
National meetings and leadership development	140,000
Field organizing	300,000[a]
Backing for citywide and statewide WRO's	50,000[b]
Organizing new constituencies, for example, aged, working poor	50,000
Southern organizing drive	200,000[c]
Welfare rights information and education program	100,000
Lobbying and developing middle-class support	60,000
Bail and emergency fund	50,000
Total	900,000

[a]This budget does not include funds for special programs or projects, for example, summer student project, WIN and PHS contracts. The welfare rights information and education program is for work supplementary to these contracts and to pick up vital parts of these programs in the event of nonrenewal.

[b]This does not include funds for citywide and statewide WRO operations raised with national assistance estimated at $1 million.

[c]The minimum needed to develop ten key areas.

Source: National Welfare Rights Organization, Prospectus, March 1970, p. 1.

cover the outstanding bills. It was a major feat to keep the national organization alive and the creditors appeased while carrying out strategies of confrontation against the welfare authorities. For a few years, however, Wiley succeeded in mobilizing some funds through pledges from NWRO's major supporters in the liberal camp.

During the first three years (1966-69), the "major source of financial support for NWRO came from the organized church, private foundations, the United States Government and contributions from individuals."[71] The Protestant churches were by far the "largest private source of welfare rights money" and, in fact, contributed 47 per-

cent of the NWRO budget in 1968 ($106,893). This sum did not include
the contributions of the Interreligious Foundation for Community Organization (IFCO), an arm of the National Council of Churches.
IFCO's support alone totaled $500,000 over four years. (See Chapter
4.) The white Protestant churches, especially the main-line denominations, turned out to be NWRO's major financial support.

According to Wiley, the United Church of Christ was NWRO's
"top contributor." Other denominations, such as the Methodists,
Presbyterians, and Episcopalians, provided some support. The
Methodists' highest cash donation to NWRO reached $35,000 one year
and then dropped the following year to $30,000. Periodically, addi-
tional monies were transferred to NWRO through the purchase of advertisements in its programs books. The Presbyterians contributed
$25,000 in the early years, followed by an additional $15,000 for the
"Children's March for Survival" in 1972, which was described by
NWRO officials as "the peak of their giving." The Episcopalians donated about $3,000 to the national office and provided in-kind resources
and some cash contributions to local groups, especially in New York
City.[72] While white Protestant commitment to welfare reform remained as part of its social-action agenda long after NWRO had folded,
church contributions to the protest movement declined significantly
after 1972.[73] By the end of 1973, all Protestant financial support for
NWRO had vanished.

Support from black churches for NWRO and the welfare rights
protest failed to materialize, despite concerted efforts by staff members and Wiley himself.[74] In contrast to their role in the civil rights
movement, the black churches and black church leaders ignored
NWRO's appeals for assistance, according to Wiley.[75] While Wiley
contended that black churches had very limited resources in relation
to the white mainline denominations and, therefore, could not be
faulted for their lack of contributions to the movement, he acknowledged
that the antiwelfare ethic had inhibited middle-class blacks from giving
to NWRO. Wiley admitted that several efforts "to pull the black
churches in . . . had not been successful."[76] (See Chapter 5.)

Financial support by the Catholic church varied at the national
and local levels of the movement. The U.S. Catholic Conference opposed NWRO's position on welfare reform and consequently refused
to contribute to the national movement.[77] In 1968 another group, the
National Catholic Conference for Interracial Justice, provided some
funds to NWRO and symbolically supported it by taking an advertise-
ment in the movement's publication, NWRO in Action, "pledging its
full cooperation in working to secure the rights of America's poor."[78]
The U.S. Catholic Conference's Campaign for Human Development, a
national program designed to financially assist organized groups of
poor people, funded three local WROs for one year.[79] Its major sup-

port, however, went to the United Farmworkers movement, the Southern Christian Leadership Conference (SCLC), and organizations of American Indians, according to NWRO officials. [80]

At the state and local levels, financial support for the welfare rights movement by Catholics was more salient, especially in some areas of high concentration of Catholics. The state WRO in Rhode Island, for instance, was funded almost exclusively by the Catholic church. [81] Its membership, according to its state chair, was white and overwhelmingly Catholic. In this area, activist priests were described as the catalysts in mobilizing church support for the Rhode Island WRO and underwriting its entire budget. Some Catholic church support was also reported in New Jersey. In Patterson, local Catholic monies replaced the funds provided to the local WRO when the poverty funds from CAP disappeared. [82] In Camden, the Catholic church supported a Hispanic WRO group. However, another local WRO group, mostly black and Protestant, gained its funds from Protestant churches and the federally funded poverty agencies. According to Nicholas and Mary Kotz, the Catholic church provided "major support" in "several urban dioceses. "[83] The exact nature of such support is not known. It is clear, however, that support by the Catholic church varied considerably at the national and local levels and that, in comparison to Protestant contributions, its financial assistance to the welfare rights protest was negligible.

Jewish support, according to Wiley, came principally from "individuals and foundations and not through synagogues." Wiley added that this "was the pattern [of giving] in Jewish communities. "[84] He emphasized that these donations were generally "large" and that the support from 1966 through 1972 had been "continuous. "[85]

Within the secular world, foundations played a major role in the contribution of monies to the welfare rights protest—about seven or eight transferred thousands of dollars to NWRO during its first six years. After Wiley resigned from the movement in 1972, this pattern of giving changed dramatically. The last major foundation grant to NWRO was shortly before Wiley left the NWRO. [86] In the early years, Wiley, as NWRO's principal fund raiser, obtained several grants from the "Stern Family and the Aaron E. Normal [foundations]," as well as from "the Field, Hess, Ottinger, New York, Whitney, Voluntary Service and Loeb Foundations. "[87] Through 1968 these foundations contributed approximately 30 percent of the monies for NWRO's yearly budget.

Labor unions, which had played a central role in the liberal coalition in the 1960s civil rights struggle, remained as witnesses in the welfare rights struggle. [88] The goals of these two movements were "at obvious cross-purposes. "[89] Although both sought "adequate levels of income for their members," Hulbert James of NWRO pointed out that, while its protest focused on the "rights for poor people on welfare . . . to stay home and get some money," the labor movement "believes in people working for their money."[90] As a result of these divergent views and objectives, only a few local unions contributed any funds to NWRO.[91]

Paradoxically, allies for NWRO were found not only among liberals in the private sector but also within the federal government —the major target of the welfare rights movement. In the final weeks of the Johnson administration, the U.S. Department of Labor signed a contract with NWRO. This federal contract was slated to provide NWRO the amount of $434,930 over a one-year period for training of Work Incentive Program (WIN) participants.[92] As we shall see in the next chapter, there were critical differences of opinion within NWRO about this financial "windfall" that created tensions and polarized some factions within the movement. The federal contract, however, did add to NWRO's financial resources, even though it never received the entire allotted funds. In practice, because the grant had been given to NWRO by a lame-duck administration, only $105,859.21 were actually transferred to the movement organization by the Department of Labor by the end of September 1969.[93]

By 1969 the sociopolitical conditions had changed dramatically. The Johnson Democratic administration had been replaced by the Nixon Republican administration, with its stated policy of dismantling the Great Society programs of the previous decade. (See Chapter 6.) Economic conditions were also changing. The country was heading toward the worst recession since the depression of the 1930s. Unemployment and inflation were on the rise. The general social conditions were less conducive to "sharing" with and "giving" to the poor. Such trends boded ill for NWRO's financial state.

In seeking to maximize its sources of income, NWRO tapped individuals as well as groups. It raised monies by collecting dues from its members and its supporters, the Friends of Welfare Rights. An elaborate dues-collecting structure was developed by the P/RAC to differentiate between the poor and the nonpoor in the movement. Members (the poor) paid $1 per year to join the national organization through a local WRO chapter. Friends of Welfare Rights were assessed $10 per year, half of which was supposed to go to the national office and half to the local unit.

In fact, these fund-raising strategies among individuals added little to NWRO's coffers. Membership dues brought in only $24,000 (or less than 5 percent of its yearly budget) in its peak year (1968/69).[94] With a base constituency of female-headed families on welfare, and a small contingent of Friends of Welfare Rights, economic support from individual participants was one of the least productive fund-raising strategies for NWRO. Over the years, as organizational support from churches and foundations declined, NWRO leaders made several unsuccessful attempts to bolster fund-raising among members and Friends, but these, too, failed. (See Chapter 4.) Its Friends contributed only a small amount to NWRO's budget. At the height of their activism, Friends' dues and donations amounted to about $50,000, or about 10 percent of NWRO's budget. (See Table 2.1.) Additional "emergency donations" by a few wealthy Friends also added to NWRO's resources, but data are not available on these amounts. [95]

It is clear that, given its membership base, NWRO remained an economically dependent organization, relying almost exclusively on outsiders for funds to run its offices and programs. This economic dependency, in the long run, became its Achilles' heel and in many ways hastened its decline. (See Chapters 3 and 4.) Wiley, aware of this danger of dependency on liberal contributions, sought ways to make NWRO self-supporting. He wanted a "self-sufficient, dues-supported organization" that would not have to depend on "churches, unions, or the poverty program." [96] At the same time, the demand by NWRO's members and leaders for a national movement organization required a budget that far exceeded the resources available among its own membership. With a poverty constituency, a self-supporting and independent organization remained an unfulfilled goal.

Over the years NWRO's organization and programs expanded and its budgetary needs grew. [97] Despite George Wiley's continuous efforts to raise funds among liberal groups, changing political and economic conditions had an impact on the financial support available to NWRO. Following the urban riots in the 1960s and the assassination of Martin Luther King, Jr. in 1968, it had been relatively easy to get money for black causes. [98] Since NWRO was perceived as a black movement by many, these political conditions stimulated liberal contributions. By 1971, however, political agitation by the black and poor had died down. The themes of "law and order" and "benign neglect" under the new Republican administration and the public backlash against welfare recipients and rising welfare costs dampened political support for NWRO.

By the end of 1972, almost seven years after its birth, the leaders of NWRO acknowledged that the movement was "in serious financial trouble." [99] Describing NWRO's plight in September 1972, Wiley stated that the national office was in the midst of the "most serious financial crisis" in its history. [100] He announced that NWRO was burdened with a $150,000 debt. While the mobilization of funds had been a continuous problem for NWRO throughout its life span, by 1973 it was evident to all those involved that the sources of funds were rapidly drying up and the national organization's staffing and expenditures had to be drastically curtailed. Wiley, however, in his report on the state of NWRO at the end of 1972, predicted optimistically that "with a crash fundraising effort NWRO . . . should be out of debt" within a few months. [101] He cited the fact that NWRO had already raised $125,000 in pledges and "another similar amount in renewable grants and contributions." Elimination of the debt was based on the expectation that "a reasonable program and fundraising effort" would be continued.

This, however, did not come to pass. By the end of January 1973, Wiley had resigned as the executive director of NWRO in order to organize a new movement called the Movement for Economic Justice (MEJ). Wiley's resignation dealt a fatal blow to NWRO. His role as its major fund raiser and his easy access to liberal support left a void within the movement that could not be easily filled. At least 80 percent of its donations and pledges "went out the door when George Wiley went to the Movement for Economic Justice." [102] Hence, as NWRO struggled to continue as a national protest organization in 1973, it remained burdened with a $100,000 debt, from which it never recovered. [103]

Following Wiley's resignation, NWRO's financial situation deteriorated rapidly. Its 1973 budget for $200,000 was never funded. [104] Additional efforts by NWRO leaders to raise monies failed. A fundraising dinner in tribute to Wiley in April 1973 raised only a few thousand dollars. An appeal for donations after Wiley's untimely and tragic death a few months later was also unsuccessful. Finally, Tillmon's call for support from NWRO members and Friends in 1974 also went unheeded. [105]

From 1973 to March 1975—from Wiley's resignation to the day NWRO closed its national headquarters—two additional strategies to save the protest movement failed. The Welfare Rights Information and Support Community (WRISC), the church Friends' strategy to mobilize liberal supporters, brought in only $500 in a direct appeal to over 10,000 individuals in 1974. (See Chapter 4.) Another fundraising strategy developed by Tillmon in 1974 also failed. The "Half-A-Chance Campaign" was Tillmon's plan to make the welfare rights movement self-supporting by appealing to "the estimated 12 million poor people in this country to give 50 cents each to the National Welfare Rights Organization." [106] Tillmon was well aware that economic dependency had always been a major weakness of the national movement organization. However unrealistic her strategy, she was determined not to go "begging from outsiders anymore." [107] She pointed out that NWRO had "always had to depend on money from foundations and Churches, but now the whole economy is hurting . . . and NWRO has been put on the low priority list." [108] By asking the 12 million poor people to donate 50 cents each, she hoped to meet a "6-year goal of six million dollars."

The "Half-A-Chance Campaign," formally inaugurated in October 1974, failed. Only a few thousand dollars were collected. [109] By then, there were few incentives for poor people to contribute to a cause that seemed to offer little in return. By December 1973 NWRO's major financial and political supporters had vanished. Protestant monies and foundation support were gone. NWRO's attempts to raise funds among the middle-class Friends and among poor people were unsuccessful. A major barrier to financial solvency was the $100,000 debt that remained after Wiley's resignation. Continuing efforts by Faith Evans, Tillmon, and a few others did succeed in reducing the deficit to $20,000 by 1975. Without a continuing base of support, however, in March 1975 NWRO was forced to declare bankruptcy and close down its headquarters in Washington, D.C.

NWRO's other mobilized resources—its members, leaders, and staff—followed the same pattern of rise and fall during these years. Expanding rapidly in the early days during the turmoil of the 1960s, their numbers plummeted as external political conditions and internal conflicts eroded NWRO's base constituency and supporters. Not only loss of monies but also of people reflected the decline in the power of the protest movement of poor women.

MOBILIZING MEMBERS

Another basic resource of the NWRO was its organized grass-roots constituency, which expanded rapidly in the late 1960s and then dropped precipitously. How to mobilize the poor to effect change was debated continuously in the early days by its architects and organizers. Although there was consensus among the planners of the national protest that special strategies had to be developed to create power for poor people, there were differences as to how this should be accomplished. Some argued for a formal organization; others, for loosely structured cadres. Wiley, for example, contended that the poor had to be organized in order to wield any kind of influence within the system. He believed that, in order to overcome economic deprivation and redistribute power within the system, it was imperative to create a "tough political organization" of poor people.[110] Economic problems, he asserted, were "generally very nitty-gritty kinds of problems that have to be worked on over a long period of time." Solving these problems required a "sustained effort," and, therefore, an organization was needed.[111]

Many of the organizers that joined NWRO tended to support this view that "the only way to effect this transfer of power was to build poor people's organizations," in order to confront the power structures that ruled their lives.[112] James, for example, emphasized that "only power can bring about change so people in this society will have enough money and a decent life for themselves and their families."[113] Wiley asserted that the white middle class of the United States would not willingly "move over and share their wealth and resources with the people who have none."[114] At the same time, he believed that "if the poor people who have problems can organize, can exert their political muscle they can have a chance to have their voices and their weight felt in the political process of this country."[115] Wiley felt that a movement organization had to be built in order to have any influence on the dominant welfare system. He also believed that in order to have their needs addressed, the poor had to control their own organization. In Wiley's view, therefore, it was imperative that there be a national organization and that it "be a grassroots organization run democratically by and for recipients."[116]

Piven and Cloward, the other architects of the welfare rights protest, disagreed with Wiley's emphasis on organization, contending that it used up scarce resources and created the problem of providing ongoing incentives to attract participants. They also emphasized that poor people in the country were now a numerical minority and could wield little political influence through the electoral process. Protest, not organization, they stated, presented the best means for mobilizing resources for poor people. Piven and Cloward argued "that political influence by the poor is mobilized, not organized."[117] They added that "a disruptive strategy does not require that people affiliate with an organization and participate regularly. Rather, it requires that masses of people be mobilized to engage in disruptive action."[118] They suggested that, if families could "be encouraged to demand relief," these acts of defiance "could contribute to a fiscal and political crisis."[119] If, however, the poor were asked to join a formal organization, pay dues, and contribute time and energy to maintain local and national organizations, organizers would be hard pressed to find ongoing incentives to sustain participation by poor people.

Piven and Cloward suggested an alternative strategy: the development of "a national network of cadre organizations rather than a national federation of welfare recipient groups." Rather than just people on welfare, the national network would include both the poor and nonpoor. It would be an "organization of organizers—composed of students, churchmen, civil rights activists, antipoverty workers and militant AFDC recipients" that "would in turn seek to energize a broad, loosely coordinated movement of variegated groups to arouse hundreds of thousands of poor people to demand aid."[120] The purpose of this strategy, from Cloward and Piven's perspectives, was "to build the welfare rolls," rather than "organizational membership rolls."

Wiley and his organizers disagreed. As Piven and Cloward point out, the strategy they were proposing "struck organizers as exceedingly manipulative."[121] Wiley and his staff felt that the role of outsiders in the movement of poor people should be a subordinate one —an enabling, rather than a controlling, one. Poor people, they said, should be helped to build and run their own political organizations, with organizers eventually fading or withering away. Within the movement of poor people, the political power was to be reversed. The poor would govern; the nonpoor would advise and support.

While at the beginning these differences in strategies were clear to all, they were not seen as paramount, since there were enough areas of agreement. As a result, mobilization of the new movement proceeded, "animated by a belief that agitation among the poor around welfare issues had great potential for success." Piven and Cloward add that "the differences in strategy seemed less important then the imperative of action itself. In a word, the omens were good; every one was eager to begin."[122]

From the outset, the decision was made to focus on the largest welfare group—those receiving AFDC. AFDC was by far "the largest public assistance program," and those on its rolls were clearly suffering from extreme economic hardships.[123] In 1965 there were about 1 million adults (mostly women) and over 3 million children in the AFDC program.[124] Yet this number represented only a fraction of those in need and those legally eligible for assistance.[125] Piven and Cloward's research in the early 1960s had documented "that for every family on the AFDC rolls, at least one other was eligible but unaided."[126] These findings indicated that "a huge pool of families with incomes below prevailing welfare grant schedules had built up in the cities as a result of migration and unemployment" and that many of those eligible for AFDC were not receiving any aid. The strategy, then, of NWRO's architects was to close the gap between the law and its practice by getting as many of the eligible poor as possible onto the welfare rolls. Millions of dollars would thus be transferred to the poor. The resulting fiscal and political crises would, according to its theorists and organizers, help to change the welfare system and usher in a guaranteed income for all in need.

Despite Cloward and Piven's serious reservations about building a "superstructure," Wiley and his staff set out in 1966 not only to organize at the grass-roots level but also to establish "a national organization of welfare rights groups."[127] Following the birth of the movement in June, a meeting was called by P/RAC that summer, bringing together social scientists, organizers, and women welfare leaders from various parts of the country to discuss the "history and future of the welfare rights movement." The poor women present enthusiastically supported Wiley's proposal for a national organization of recipient leaders.[128] Consequently, a temporary National Coordinating Committee of Welfare Rights Groups (NCC) was established to develop overall plans for a national organization.[129] At

Wiley's suggestion, the P/RAC in Washington, D.C., became the national headquarters for the new movement. The initial meeting in Chicago was quickly followed by others in which the constitution, by-laws, and goals of the NWRO were developed and adopted.

By August 1967 NWRO had held its first national convention; Tillmon, a welfare mother, had been elected chair of the national movement organization; and its ruling bodies—the National Coordinating Council and the Executive Committee—had been established. In setting its national goals, NWRO emphasized both "decent jobs with adequate pay for those who can work, and adequate income for those who cannot."* Central among NWRO's principles was that welfare was a basic right of poor people, given its mandate in the federal and state laws. To reinforce this belief, NWRO developed its "Welfare Bill of Rights."[130] This was a 13-point statement covering abstract ("the right to fair and equal treatment") as well as very specific ("the right to be a member of a welfare rights organization") rights. Thus, within one year, Wiley and his staff of organizers had developed a formal organization, linking together isolated groups throughout the country into the first national movement of the welfare poor, that is, the poor women on AFDC.

Within a politically "receptive" climate in 1967, NWRO's grass-roots organizing "took off."[131] The numbers of dues-paying members soared, and the groups of WROs expanded rapidly, as organizers used the monies of special benefits available from the welfare department in the AFDC program to mobilize the poor. From 1966 through 1969, the major thrust of NWRO organizers was to create as many WROs as possible in order to establish a mass movement with a dues-paying membership. Organizers fanned out across the country, while a growing staff in Washington tried to run the national organization and link

---

*NWRO's blueprint for a better welfare system included, in its words, four basic principles:

1. Adequate Income: A system which guarantees enough money for all Americans to live dignified lives above the level of poverty;
2. Dignity: A system which guarantees recipients the same full freedoms, rights, and respect as all American citizens;
3. Justice: A fair and open system which guarantees recipients the full protection of the Constitution; and
4. Democracy: A system which guarantees recipients direct participation in the decision under which they must live.

See "About the National Welfare Rights Organization," NOW! (Washington, D.C.: Poverty Rights Action Center, February 9, 1968).

the atomized groups into an integrated national movement for welfare rights. Success, according to NWRO criteria at that time, was measured in terms of the numbers of paid-up members and affiliated WRO groups. Victories were also counted in terms of added benefits received by the AFDC women and children, as a result of their protests at the local welfare departments. As the political climate changed and became increasingly hostile by the late 1960s, NWRO was forced to shift its strategies in response to the counteroffensives launched by the welfare authorities. (See Chapter 6.) Internal conflicts emerged, as NWRO was buffeted by numerous political forces, hastening the movement's disintegration. As Piven and Cloward had predicted, success in terms of organized numbers was very difficult to maintain.[132] For a few years, however, the movement organization thrived, as thousands of poor women eligible for AFDC joined the ranks of NWRO.

NWRO's two major strategies for mobilizing AFDC women involved "solving individual grievances of existing recipients" and taking "actions on collective grievances."[133] Piven and Cloward note that solving individual grievances "usually worked to build groups, for grievances were legion."[134] For example, "families were often capriciously denied access to benefits, or failed to receive checks, or received less than they were entitled to, or were arbitrarily terminated, or were abused and demeaned by welfare workers." When organizers promised some redress through membership in NWRO, many of the poor women joined the movement.

When the "individual grievance" approach did not prove to be effective in building and maintaining a mass membership, the other strategy used was that of "collective grievances" for "special grants." Special grants for clothing and household furnishings and other items were available to AFDC clients, but "few people knew about these provisions, even fewer applied for them, and still fewer received them."[135] By acting collectively, instead of individually, on similar grievances, added benefits could be gained in confrontations with the welfare authorities, while the movement's membership could be expanded.

As these protests escalated in the late 1960s, benefits flowed from the welfare departments' treasuries to poor women and their families. Millions of dollars were transferred to the poor.[136] Monies attracted members. NWRO organizers in most areas kept information on special grants restricted to women who paid their dues and joined a welfare rights group. This created the unique, but temporary, incentive needed for building local organizations. Only members were provided with forms and assistance to obtain the special grants from the welfare department. As long as this information and assistance remained an exclusive payoff for members only—a "private good"—

the NWRO membership and number of affiliated WRO groups multiplied. [137] When these monetary incentives disappeared, or became widely available, the membership dropped almost as fast as it had risen. Once their grievances were settled, many members ceased to participate for there were few other incentives "to contribute to the group." [138] Thousands joined in the early days; a few remained with the movement over the years.

Criteria for membership in NWRO was specified by its constitution. People on welfare, of any race or ethnic background, were eligible to become full-fledged members of a local WRO and affiliated with the national organization once they had paid their dues. In theory, the only restriction to membership was "welfare" status, later modified to "low-income" status. In practice, however, other factors helped to determine who became a member. Structural cleavages and organizing strategies restricted the numbers, race, and gender of NWRO's grass-roots membership.

Membership was limited to poor people, in what William Whitaker called "welfare separatism." [139] In the first years, only a few nonpoor were allowed to become members with voting rights. The first constitution made it clear that "the majority . . . has to be current welfare recipients, and the rest immediate past recipients, or low income persons, with no more than 10% 'other' persons." After 1970 these rules were revised and tightened. Outsiders were eliminated as voting members. Voting rights were granted only to those who were welfare or Social Security recipients, having a net income below the NWRO income level for a particular family size. [140] In practice, however, there was little control by the national leaders over the local groups and their membership. Local WROs were, in fact, autonomous units. [141]

This eligibility formula had been "carefully designed" to prevent the recurrence of what had happened in the civil rights movement, namely, the poor being dominated by the nonpoor. Integrating the poor and nonpoor into the same organization with the same rights, according to NWRO organizers and ex-civil rights activists, had not worked. Middle-class whites tended to take over and dominate. The organizers' objective was to ensure that WRO remained a truly "indigenous group of poor people." [142] Edwin Day, an early NWRO organizer, adds that "we didn't want these groups to be taken over by church people or social work people or other dogooders. The civil rights cadre organizations disappeared because the middle class members just walked away and did something else." [143]

Since only the poor could become members, NWRO had to define a specific criteria for poverty. It chose to use the figures of the U.S. Bureau of Labor Statistics (BLS), rather than the official federal poverty level established by the U.S. Department of Agriculture.[144] The latter was consistently much lower than the BLS figure. In 1964 the first poverty level was set at $3,220 per year for a family of four, thereby designating about 34 million U.S. residents as living in poverty.[145] Since the median annual income for a four-person family that year was $7,490, NWRO rejected this index as totally inadequate. It chose, rather, to define the poor using the BLS lower living standard or the lower standard budget, which, like the poverty index, was adjusted annually to reflect the cost-of-living increase. Welfare standards, in contrast to these indexes, were not automatically adjusted to reflect the changes in economic conditions within U.S. society. The BLS figure specified "the minimum amount of money a family needs to live in dignity, meeting all its basic needs."[146]

NWRO called "on the Federal Government to guarantee every American this minimum income."[147] This guaranteed income level was readjusted periodically to reflect the changes in the BLS figures. (See Table 2.3.) In 1968 NWRO called for $4,000 as a minimum annual income for a four-person family. In 1970 this was raised to $5,500, then to $6,500 in 1971. By 1974 it was revised to $7,500. Two years later some WRO leaders were calling for $10,000.

Based on these figures, those people whose family income matched or fell below the BLS figure were considered poor and were eligible to join as voting members once they had paid their dues and joined a local WRO group. Using this criterion, Wiley asserted that there were at least 50 million poor people in the country who potentially could be mobilized to fight for a guaranteed income and guaranteed jobs, NWRO's major goals. Others who were not poor but who subscribed to the movement's goals, were allowed to join as Friends of Welfare Rights, with limited membership privileges. (See Chapter 4.)

Not only were all the poor urged to join the movement but all racial and ethnic groups within the poverty population were welcomed, according to NWRO's stated principle of racial inclusiveness incorporated in its constitution, publications, and the speeches of its leaders. Poverty, as Wiley repeatedly pointed out, was not confined to blacks. While he was convinced that poverty was the basic problem for blacks and had to be attacked, Wiley was just as firmly convinced that other groups, including whites, were victims of similar economic injustices. He asserted that while "it is absolutely critical for Black people to solve this basic economic problem . . . at the same time it is the same problem that exists for literally millions of whites, Chicanos, Puerto Ricans, and Indians."[148] He noted also that the majority of poor people were white. The paradox, he said, is that "the majority of Black people are poor, but the majority of poor are white!"[149] He thus saw that this economic issue was "really an important link between blacks and whites."[150]

TABLE 2.3

Poverty Levels
(in dollars)

Year	U.S. Poverty Level	Bureau of Labor Statistics "Lower Budget" (Metropolitan Area)	NWRO Poverty Level (based on BLS "lower budget")
1966	3,317	n.a.[b]	n.a.[a]
1967	3,410	5,994	n.a.[a]
1968	3,553	n.a.[b]	4,000
1969	3,743	n.a.[b]	4,000
1970	3,968	7,061	5,500
1971	4,137	n.a.[b]	6,500
1972	4,275	n.a.[b]	6,500
1973	4,540	8,305	7,500
1974	5,038	9,323	7,500
1975	5,500	9,720	n.a.[b]
1976	5,815	10,189	7,800
1977	6,191	10,481	10,000

[a]No NWRO poverty level set on this year.
[b]Data not available

Notes: The three poverty levels are calculated for the annual income of a non-farm family of four. The U.S. poverty level was "originally developed by the Social Security Administration in the 1960's, [and] calculates the poverty threshold by first estimating the market cost of a basic but minimal diet, and then multiplying that cost according to the proportion of their budget the poor spend on food. Among several problems with that procedure, the key one has been that the food standards underlying the poverty thresholds are too low, since they are based on an emergency diet plan suitable only for short-term use, not on a set of nutritional standards adequate to maintain a healthful diet over the long run."

"This not only underestimates the amount of food the poor need to eat minimally, but, by extention, artifically lowers the estimate of their overall income needs. This often-noted bias helps explain why the SSA poverty threshold for a nonfarm family of four, in 1977, was only 59 percent of the 'lower living standard' estimated for the same family by the Bureau of Labor Statistics (BLS) of the U.S. Department of Labor" (National Advisory Council on Economic Opportunity, Twelfth Report, Critical Choices for the 80's [Washington, D.C.: U.S. Government Printing Office, 1980], pp. 22-23).

Sources: Compiled by the author based on U.S., Bureau of the Census, Statistical Abstract of the United States: 1979, 100th ed. (Washington, D.C.: Government Printing Office, 1979), pp. 462 and 487; and NWRO documents.

NWRO leaders proudly underscored interracialism as one of their organizing principles and a central characteristic of their movement. It was not a black movement; it was a poor people's movement made up of all racial groups. As Lawrence Bailis points out, "The welfare rights movement explicitly rejected any emphasis on 'black power' in favor of an emphasis on 'poor people's power' and gave prominence to its poor white, Spanish-speaking and Indian members."[151] Wiley repeatedly pointed out the fact that different racial and ethnic groups were part of the welfare rights movement. His thrust was "to unite the efforts of people of all races and ethnic backgrounds into cooperative action against poverty and injustice."[152]

Over the years, Wiley's emphasis shifted from integration to interracialism, reflecting the political tenor of the times. For him, pluralism was the key to strengthening and expanding the movement's base. He insisted that it was "possible to develop a pluralistic movement, if not an integrated one."[153] This almost imperceptible shift mirrored the temper of the times—the increasing focus on black nationalism and the rise of ethnic pride among various groups—as well as the internal political tensions based on race within NWRO. (See Chapter 3.) Wiley, however, never compromised on the principle of racial inclusiveness for NWRO.

Other leaders also upheld this doctrine of interracialism. Tillmon, the first chair of NWRO, openly supported this interracial principle and strategy for organizing poor people around their common economic grievances. She repeatedly pointed out the uniqueness of NWRO, noting that its integrated structure was a "fairly unusual thing" for poor people and disconcerting to "the power structure."[154] She emphasized "that NWRO is not a black organization, not a white organization . . . [but] a poor people's organization." She noted that "in some instances the poor whites have stopped fighting the poor blacks," and this new solidarity among the poor "kind of shakes people" in the power structure. She pointed out that "white women in Kentucky" were uniting with "black women, talking about working for a common goal." Tillmon emphasized that this was an event that had never happened before.[155] She insisted that NWRO had to remain inclusive and that, if it ever became "all Black or all Brown," she would "get out."[156] Since its birth in 1966, its leaders and supporters had repeatedly underscored what Dick Gregory had said on its founding day: NWRO was not a "civil rights movement" but rather a "human rights movement."[157]

Despite this solid support for racial integration and the determination of its architects and organizers to make NWRO a movement of poor people, in practice its grass-roots membership turned out to be overwhelmingly black. Although the AFDC population was about

50 percent white nationally,* organizers of NWRO focused their efforts in the urban areas, where there was a high concentration of black women on welfare. This seems to be the major explanation for the discrepancy between NWRO's rhetoric or racial inclusiveness and its overwhelmingly black composition. Another reason for this gap between theory and practice was that racial antagonisms in many areas led poor whites to reject the movement as being "black-oriented and inhospitable to whites."[158] Organizers made some efforts to organize other ethnic groups in Massachusetts, New York, Rhode Island, and some midwestern states.[159] In some areas they succeeded. For example, the Rhode Island WRO had an all-white membership and leadership, according to its state chair, Bertha Cavanaugh.[160] Some groups in New York State and Massachusetts had large white memberships but black leaders.[161] While there are little data on the exact racial distribution of its members, George Martin suggests that "85 percent of the memberships was black, 10 percent white, and 5 percent Latin."[162] Piven and Cloward state that "all observers agree that NWRO's membership was almost entirely black."[163]

Over the years, some Hispanics and American Indians formed welfare rights groups.[164] Spanish-speaking WRO groups were most prevalent in the Southwest, where they established a separate movement organization, stating that, while they had common goals with NWRO, they wanted to direct and control their own organization, given their different cultural needs.[165] NWRO attempted to attract and integrate Hispanics into the movement by providing a leadership position for a Hispanic woman on the Executive Committee, publishing its newsletter in Spanish as well as in English, and urging organizers to seek out different ethnic groups. In 1970 Wiley announced that "some Spanish-speaking people . . . are active in the organization and are working well together."[166] Their numbers, however, were never large.

In terms of gender, NWRO's membership base was composed almost exclusively of women, with only a few male recipient members

---

*According to Gilbert Steiner, the number of white women on AFDC in 1967 was slightly higher than that of nonwhite women (51.3 percent white and 48.7 percent nonwhite) with no more than 3 percent change since 1961 (The State of Welfare [Washington, D.C.: Brookings Institution, 1971], p. 41). A HEW publication in 1971 reported that 49 percent of those on AFDC were white, 46 percent black, and the remaining 5 percent American Indians, Orientals, and other racial minorities (U.S., Department of Health, Education and Welfare, Welfare Myths vs. Facts [Washington, D.C.: Government Printing Office, 1971]).

and WRO groups. Piven and Cloward, contrasting the protest of the
unemployed in the 1930s and the welfare poor in the 1960s, stated that
"the [Worker's] Alliance was composed mostly of unemployed white
men, whereas NWRO is composed mostly of black women who are,
practically speaking, unemployable in today's market."[167] They
also noted that a few groups in the movement were predominantly
male, such as the Welfare Union of the Westside Organization in Detroit ("composed of unemployed black men") and the East Kentucky's
Committee to Save Unemployed Fathers ("consisting of unemployed
white miners").[168] Whitaker, writing in 1969, observed that there
appeared to be a "growing involvement of Appalachian white men."[169]

This trend of male participation—white or black—failed to materialize. Few males joined NWRO. One possible explanation is that
men had alternative sources of economic support. Because of greater
and more continuous ties to the labor force and participation in military service, many were eligible for unemployment compensation,
Social Security insurance, and veterans benefits. Most low-income
women, on the other hand, given their primary role in the home and
their limited training, generally had tenuous and intermittent ties to
the labor market, making them ineligible for unemployment compensation or Social Security benefits. For poor women, welfare was often
the only alternative when left with children to support and no way to
earn a living.

Men on welfare were also limited by the laws and regulations.
The AFDC-UP program, which allowed unemployed fathers to receive
benefits, was, as we have previously noted, adopted by only half of
the states, after its enactment in 1961.[170] Even then, the rules governing eligibility were very restrictive, partly reflecting the society's
rejection of males in dependent roles. In other welfare programs,
such as those in the "adult categories" of the aged, blind, and disabled, there were more men, but NWRO made little effort to organize
these groups. Its primary focus was on the AFDC program and thus
on mobilizing poor women.

Paradoxically, this aspect of the AFDC population or of the
NWRO membership was seldom highlighted. While the poverty (or
"class") status of the AFDC population and NWRO's constituency was
underscored, racial and gender characteristics were obscured. Welfare authorities, policy makers, social scientists, and journalists,
as well as NWRO's own organizers, leaders, members, and supporters, tended to use gender-free terms when referring to the AFDC
population or NWRO's membership, for example, welfare recipients,
welfare clients, welfare poor, single parents, and poor people.[171]
Within the movement, members were called at times "welfare mothers"
or "welfare women," and their collective efforts were termed "motherpower."[172] Organizers also liked to address the women as "the

ladies." In general, however, the common usage of gender-neutral language, when referring to the welfare or welfare rights population, functioned effectively to obscure the high incidence of poverty among women, especially female heads of families. It also tended to blur the reality that NWRO was a women's movement, structurally, if not ideologically.

With few exceptions, welfare was never identified explicitly by NWRO's organizers as a "women's problem." NWRO women leaders, however, increasingly pointed out that "every woman is one man away from welfare," as Tillmon emphasized in her speech before the National Organization of Women (NOW) in the late 1960s. At that time, few heard it and few believed it. Only in the mid-1970s did her statement gain increasing recognition within the women's movement as being a fact and not a myth. (See Chapter 5.)

Tillmon and some of the other national women leaders acknowledged that NWRO was a movement of welfare mothers who had "banded together to survive."[173] She emphasized, however, that this had not been the original intent of the movement organization. She pointed out that at the first organizing meeting in Chicago in 1966, the suggestion that the national movement be exclusively for welfare mothers had been rejected. The consensus was that it would be a movement open to all poor people and not just poor women on welfare. In practice, as she and others noted, NWRO had become an organization of AFDC women with dependent children.[174]

Not only was the movement made up primarily of women but most, as we have seen, were poor black women. White women, despite their large numbers in the AFDC program, remained in the minority within NWRO. The concentration of NWRO's organizers on the inner cities and the high percentage of black families dependent on public assistance accounted for this racial imbalance. Some suggested that another reason for this predominance of blacks was that white women seemed to be more apolitical than black women, who had become politicized in their historical struggle against racial and sex discrimination. Carol Glassman, a WRO organizer in Newark who tried to mobilize white women, suggests that "white welfare women, as compared to their black sisters, are much more in retreat from the world due to the absence of the male. . . . They view welfare as a disgrace and their own lives as failures and thus seek self expression through their children." She adds that "many live in welfare for years without telling their friends or families" because of their fear or actual experience of "abuse, ridicule, or exploitation." This fear of stigmatization makes them "retreat further into their shells" and keeps them isolated and atomized. She concludes that, "unlike many black women, they are usually unwilling to fight for their rights and are more easily cowed."[175]

This pattern of nonparticipation by poor white women seemed to be changing as agitation by feminists for woman's rights brought many "out of the closet" to demand more income, education, jobs, and child care in the 1970s. Demographic changes, especially the explosion of the divorce rate and the consequent rise of female-headed families, seemed to be changing attitudes and the political behavior of some poor white women.[176] Rising consciousness of their common plight as women seemed to have spurred greater numbers to join NWRO despite the presence of racial antagonisms. (See Chapter 5.) By the mid-1970s, more white women appeared to be joining the welfare rights movement, even as NWRO was rapidly declining. At NWRO conventions in 1974 and 1977, their attendance was higher than it had ever been.[177]

Independent of the original movement, new welfare rights groups were surfacing by the end of the decade. In New York City, the Downtown Welfare Advocate Center (DWAC), organized by white feminist/ socialists, emerged in 1974. By 1980 they were gaining support and visibility and were the most active welfare rights group in the city (and perhaps the state).[178] Unlike other welfare rights groups in New York, the major impetus for DWAC had come from the feminist and socialist movements, rather than the civil rights turmoil and the efforts of welfare rights organizers. For these women, poverty was rooted in sexism and classism. They emphasized that welfare was a women's issue, since there were few jobs available at decent pay and no day care they could afford.[179]

In New Jersey, there were also signs in the late 1970s that white women in poverty were beginning to join others in demanding economic justice. At the state's celebration of the International Women's Year in 1976, workshops on welfare (entitled "Wives of the State: Women on Welfare") were attended only by white women.[180] About 15 identified themselves as being AFDC mothers, some of whom had organized groups to fight for their welfare rights. Their major goal was to get more education and better jobs to move off welfare. They emphasized that they wanted the federal government to pay for them to attend college so that their employment options could be expanded. Ruby Grace, the black chair of the state WRO and a panelist, pointed out the differences between the black women in the WRO and these new groups of white women. She explained that, for most black women, the struggle had always been for income and the basic needs to survive. Poverty, racism, and sexism had aborted the educational and employment dreams of many black poor women.[181] For them, the fight was income, not college, to enable them and their children to survive. Hence, while there appeared to be increasing politicization of poor white women on welfare, many were emerging within the context of the expanding, white feminist movement, rather than the declining, black-dominated welfare rights movement.

Across the country in California, other groups of white women were also organizing around welfare rights in the mid-1970s. Young feminists demanding their rights to more income, education, and child care attended the NWRO conference called by Tillmon and other WRO leaders in 1977. [182] They identified themselves as being part of the feminist movement and also part of the welfare rights movement. By the end of the 1970s, the economic issue of poverty was gaining momentum as a common cause for women in both protest groups.

Over the years, NWRO women leaders came increasingly to define welfare as a women's issue and to see their movement as a poor women's movement. At one point, the Executive Committee considered a proposal to change its name to the National Women's Rights Organization. It failed to gain enough support among the women. Class and race, rather than gender, continued to be considered the basic sources of economic injustices.

Although the racial and gender characteristics of the NWRO membership remained relatively stable, the numbers of poor women in the organization changed significantly over the years. It has been mentioned previously that, as long as there were immediate economic payoffs for participating in the movement organization, the membership expanded. When these disappeared and the costs of participation increased, the numbers dropped. As many social scientists have pointed out, the poor are economically rational, generally participating and investing their limited resources in a movement only when there are immediate payoffs, whether economic, social, or political. [183]

Membership rewards for the women included not only monies received through the added special grants provided by the welfare departments but also the social rewards of participation in the movement itself. While there were risks involved (fear of being cut off the rolls, of being arrested, of having to spend time away from their families), other incentives attracted some members. Participation in a WRO and in the national movement decreased their isolation, provided opportunities for sociability, and increased their self-esteem. [184] Members learned to blame the system, rather than themselves, for their economic plight. For the few who became leaders, there were the added benefits of new political status and recognition within the movement and within their communities. Many were invited to assume positions on advisory boards and on mayors' and governors' committees and to attend international meetings sponsored and paid for by their "peace" allies. [185] Incentives decreased over time, as welfare authorities tightened social controls and internal conflicts within the movement emerged, eroding NWRO's grass-roots base.

For a short while, however, in the mid- and late 1960s, NWRO's membership expanded, following the turmoil in the welfare centers.

At the same time, the national AFDC rolls exploded. Of the 2 million adult AFDC recipients in 1969, the NWRO succeeded in enrolling "between 1 and 2 percent of the total."[186] Although a relatively small number, Steiner points out that it was "some client participation where before there was none."[187]

NWRO's rise and fall was also reflected in the expansion and contraction of its membership, groups, and attendance at its yearly conferences and conventions. These indexes of its organized strength showed a rise for the first three years, peaking in 1969. According to various sources, its members ranged from 30,000 to 100,000, * with most concentrated in the "nine major industrial states."[188] While rewards for participation lasted, the numbers expanded. As the economic, social, and political payoffs declined, so did its members, affiliated groups, and attendance at the national meetings. In 1967 there were 5,000 paid members. In 1968 this figure had doubled to 10,000. By 1969 NWRO had a paid membership of 22,500 to 24,500.[189] By 1971 the decline was in evidence. Leaders reported privately that NWRO's paid membership had dropped to 11,500. The figures released to the press, however, remained unchanged. For public consumption, its number was 100,000. Within the movement, nonetheless, it was generally acknowledged that NWRO's base constituency had been dropping rapidly since 1970. In 1974, when asked for membership figures by one of its major supporters, Executive Committee members admitted that the organization no longer had an accurate count of its members.[190] NWRO leaders noted that welfare rights groups were still in operation at the local level, but few continued to pay their dues or affiliate with the national organization. †

---

*Lawrence Bailis explains this wide range by stating that movement leaders who note that "each dues-paying member is the head of a family that probably averages three or four members and thus about 25,000 families could be calculated to contain at least 75,000 individuals." He adds that "the states with the largest membership were, in descending order, New York, California, Pennsylvania, Michigan, Virginia, Massachusetts, Ohio, New Jersey, and Illinois." New York City had by far the largest membership. Boston had the second largest group (Bread or Justice: Grassroots Organizing in the Welfare Rights Movement [Lexington, Mass.: D. C. Heath, 1974], pp. 11 and 207).

† In contrast to the declining NWRO numbers, the national AFDC rolls, which had less than 5 million women and children (about 1 million adults and 4 million children) in 1966, had, by 1979, grown to include almost 11 million (about 3 million adults, mostly women heading single-parent families, and 8 million children). In 13 years, the num-

An example of the dramatic decline in membership was reflected in New York City, as documented by Piven and Cloward. [191] In 1967 half of the national movement's members were located in New York City (2,550 out of 5,000). By 1968 membership in the city had climbed to 5,870 (out of 10,000) and then declined to 4,030 (out of a total of 22,500) in 1969. From 51 percent in the mid-1960s, New York City's share had dropped to less than 18 percent of the movement's total membership by the close of the decade. Four years later, NWRO leaders reported that there were only 48 paid members left in the city. [192]

In 1973, after George Wiley's resignation, a final attempt was made by the women leaders to revitalize grass-roots organizing and to rebuild NWRO's base constituency, which had declined so dramatically since 1968. Its leaders voted "to redevelop field operation, so that [it could] provide continuing build up and support to local organizing groups. "[193] By then, however, it was too late. The national political climate, once receptive to the demands of the poor and black in the urban areas, had changed. Wiley, NWRO's principal fund raiser, was gone. Liberal support had vanished. All that remained of the movement was an empty shell, an entrenched national leadership without a base constituency. Without tangible benefits to offer as incentives for participation, most members dropped out and the WRO groups folded. Only a few survived. Without a grass-roots base, it could no longer attract liberal supporters by claiming to be the legitimate representative of the organized poor. Without funds, it could not maintain its national headquarters, coordinate the movement, or hire field organizers to implement its programs. Without protest or the necessary resources to maintain a national movement organization, NWRO lost its political clout and visibility as a challenger within the political arena.

As might be expected, the number of local WRO groups, another indicator of NWRO's strength, also followed the same pattern as its membership rolls during these years. * In December 1966 there were 130 groups in 23 states. By 1971 NWRO claimed 800 groups in 50

---

ber of children receiving AFDC assistance had doubled; the number of women, tripled (Gilbert Y. Steiner, The State of Welfare [Washington, D.C.: Brookings Institution, 1971], p. 32; and Guide to Welfare Reform [Washington, D.C.: Food Research and Action Center, 1979], p. 2).

*Affiliated groups were those that recruited at least 25 paid members and sent to the national headquarters $1 dues per member along with a membership card. A formally affiliated group could send one delegate to the national convention ("How NWRO Works, " NOW!, February 14, 1969).

TABLE 2.4

Estimated Participation at NWRO Annual Meetings

Year	City	Estimated Number of Participants (members and supporters)
1966	Chicago	80–90
1967	Washington, D.C.	350–375
1968	Chicago	a
1969	Detroit	3,000–5,000
1970[b]	Pittsburgh	1,500–2,500
1971[b]	Providence	1,200–1,500
1972[b]	Miami Beach	800–900
1973[b]	Washington, D.C.	800
1974[b]	St. Louis	500–750
1975	San Francisco	200
1976[b]	Pittsburgh	30–40
1977[b]	Little Rock	100

[a]Estimate not possible.
[b]Personal participation by the author.

Source: Compiled by the author.

states. In New Jersey, for example, there were 24 WRO groups in 1968. By 1971 there were only four affiliated with the national movement.[194] By 1974 no one would venture a guess as to how many groups still existed. Some survived as independent organizations long after the national movement had folded. Attempts to reestablish a national NWRO network in 1979 did not succeed.[195] To survive, new strategies had been developed by local groups. Several had learned the art of grantsmanship and were operating as service, job training, and advocacy centers with small grants from the federal government (many using the funds from the Comprehensive Education and Training Act [CETA] programs), local agencies, and churches.[196]

Linkages between the national offices and local groups also deteriorated over the years. Participation in NWRO conferences and conventions mirrored the declining strength of its grass-roots base and support. Attendance rose sharply and peaked in 1969 and then declined steadily through 1974. The meetings held after March 1975, following the closing of NWRO's headquarters, indicated minimal local welfare rights activity. They were sparsely attended. (See Table 2.4.) At the first official NWRO convention in August 1967, about 350 to 375 poor people and their supporters were present. This rose rapidly in the next two years. Estimates of participation at the Detroit convention in 1969 ranged from 3,000 to 5,000. Just as quickly participation began to drop. By 1972, the year of the Democratic Convention in Miami Beach, NWRO's conference in that city attracted only 800 to 900 people. Three years later, at the San Francisco convention called by Tillmon, the attendance was down to 200. Another final attempt in 1977 to revitalize the national movement organization at a meeting in Little Rock, Arkansas, brought out about 100 participants. However, Tillmon, its organizer, refused to concede that the movement was dead.[197] She acknowledged that the movement was greatly weakened but still alive.[198] Unlike the 1960s, there was little hope among the remaining members that the becalmed and fragmented movement could be revived in the 1980s.

MOBILIZING LEADERS

The Formal Leaders

NWRO's resources also included its national and local leaders. Its national leaders were elected at the first official convention in August 1967. At that meeting, NWRO's constitution was adopted by those present, establishing its ruling bodies and lines of authority. The constitution, drafted primarily by the P/RAC staff, incorporated the principles of maximum feasible participation of the poor and racial inclusiveness. The formal decision-making power was vested in the poor—the representatives of the WROs from all over the country. Since AFDC women comprised the bulk of the organization's members, they became the elected leaders at the national, state, and local levels of the movement. Most were black, reflecting the composition of its grass-roots base. The racial and gender structure of its formal leadership, like that of its membership, changed little over time. While the national offices remained in operation between 1967 and 1975, black females dominated the elected leadership positions and the two national ruling bodies of the movement organization, the NCC and the Exeuctive Committee

The NCC, NWRO's policy-making body between national conventions, was composed of elected delegates from each state having affiliated WROs. It met four times a year. The nine national officers, elected at the national conventions, formed the Executive Committee, which was supposed to carry out the policy of the member-

FIGURE 2.1

Organizational Structure of NWRO

160 Members Local WRO	25 Members Local WRO	125 Members Local WRO	25 Members Local WRO	25 Members Local WRO	95 Members Local WRO

Citywide Coordinating Committee   Countywide Coordinating Committee

50

Statewide Organizations

National Coordinating Committee

National Executive Committee

Eastern Regional Representative	Southern Regional Representative	Sergeant-at-Arms	Chairman	1st Vice Chairman	2nd Vice Chairman	3rd Vice Chairman	Central Regional Representative	Western Regional Representative
Eastern Alternate	Southern Alternate	Sergeant-at-Arms	Treasurer	Financial Secretary	Corresponding Secretary	Recording Secretary	Central Alternate	Western Alternate

Executive Director

National Staff

Source: Distributed by NWRO in 1970, publication date unknown.

ship in the intervening periods between national conventions. It met at least eight times a year. According to the constitution and bylaws, the "general program and goals" were decided by the delegates at a yearly national meeting. At other times, the NCC and the Executive Committee were granted the formal policy-making power. (See Figure 2.1.) Theoretically, this political structure ensured maximum feasible participation of the poor women in their national movement organization.

In accordance with its principle of racial inclusiveness, NWRO's ruling bodies included blacks, Hispanics, and whites. Black women, however, dominated the conventions, the NCC, and the Executive Committee. Throughout the years, the top positions remained not only in the hands of blacks but also with the original group of elected leaders. In six years (1967-73) NWRO elected only two national chairs, Tillmon and Beulah Sanders, both of whom had been in the vanguard of welfare rights organizing and came from the states with the highest membership. In 1974 (a nonelection year) a coup d'etat within NWRO resulted in the ouster of Sanders and her replacement by another black woman, Frankie Jeter, the head of the Pittsburgh WRO.

Although the highest elected positions in NWRO remained exclusively in the hands of black women, the Executive Committee was carefully integrated. While Tillmon underscored the fact that they did not "talk about color," it was clear that the structure of the Executive Committee had been carefully designed to include not only black women (who were in the majority) but also whites and Hispanics. "The third Vice-President," Tillmon reported, "had to be from a Spanish-speaking group." At least one white was added because, according to Tillmon, "people thought she was qualified."[199] The remaining officers were black women. Thus, of the nine women on the Executive Committee, six were black, two white, and one Hispanic. NWRO leaders conscientiously adhered to their stated principle of racial inclusiveness, albeit with token representation of other groups. Blacks, who were in the majority within NWRO's membership, maintained leadership control. A similar pattern of power existed within the NCC and at the national conventions.

The gender profile of the ruling bodies remained fairly stable over the years. Tillmon proudly pointed out that NWRO's membership was composed of "98%. . . women and [that] the leadership has always been women."[200] There were two black male representatives on the NCC, and eventually both were elected to the Executive Committee. Faith Evans, one of them, played an increasingly important role within the leadership of the movement.[201]

Over the years, the numerical, racial, and gender composition of the members of the Executive Committee changed. By constitutional amendment, the number of committee members rose from 9 to

TABLE 2.5

Race and Sex of NWRO Executive Committee

	1967-69		1969-71		1971-73		1973-75	
	Number	Percent	Number	Percent	Number	Percent	Number	Percent
Black females	6	67	7	78	10	72	13	76
Hispanic females	1	11	1	11	1	7	1	6
White females	2	22	1	11	1	7	1	6
Black males	0	0	0	0	2	14	2	12
Hispanic males	0	0	0	0	0	0	0	0
White males	0	0	0	0	0	0	0	0
Total	9	100	9	100	14	100	17	100

Note: In terms of class, all board members were "poor."

Sources: 1967-69—Taped interview with Johnnie Tillmon, July 1974; The National Welfare Rights in Action, NWRO, 1968-69; Welfare Fighter, November 1969. 1969-71—Taped interview with Johnnie Tillmon, 1974; letterhead of NWRO stationery, March 1970; Welfare Fighter, August 1971. 1971-73—Welfare Fighter, April 1972; field notes, November 19, 1973. 1973-75—Field notes, July 11, 1974 and August 15, 1975.

17, almost a 50 percent increase. This altered the percentage of blacks, Hispanics, whites, and males. Black female representation increased 9 percent (from 67 to 76 percent), and black male representation rose by 12 percent (from 0 to 12 percent). In contrast to this increase in the number of blacks on the Executive Committee, the one position for a Hispanic woman on the committee remained constant. Thus, the percentage of representatives of Hispanics in fact declined from 11 percent to 6 percent. White women also held token positions on this board, and their participation also decreased from 22 percent to 6 percent from 1967 to 1971, as the absolute number of board members increased. (See Table 2.5.)

While the numbers involved in this analysis are relatively small, the percentages indicate significant shifts in NWRO's structure, namely, a relative decline of white and Hispanic women and an increase in black male participation and black representation in the top leadership and policy-making positions. Racial inclusiveness was still technically maintained, but the proportion of whites and Hispanics changed. Racial integration decreased as gender integration increased at the national leadership level. Class composition remained constant, given NWRO's constitutional guidelines, which limited elected leadership posts to those who were poor. As we shall see in the following chapter, these structural shifts within the Executive Committee reflected rising tensions within the movement. Internal power struggles between blacks and whites, the poor and nonpoor, and women and men eventually erupted and changed the leadership of NWRO.

The Informal Leaders

NWRO's staff represented still another of its mobilized resources. Its structure also changed over the years, mirroring and modeling NWRO's power within the political arena. In general, the terms staff and organizers were used interchangeably, especially at the grass-roots level.202 Theoretically, their role was a supportive, rather than a policy-making one. In reality, many of them turned out to be the informal leaders at the national and local levels.

At the local level, the staff were the field workers who mobilized AFDC women and organized them into welfare rights groups throughout the country. At the national level, they were the individuals who ran the daily operations at the NWRO headquarters in Washington, D.C., and helped to design and implement strategies and programs for local groups. From the perspective of the welfare rights women, organizers were considered to be outsiders. They were not members, since the overwhelming majority of them were not poor. Most had never experienced being on welfare. Furthermore, unlike the insiders who participated in the movement as <u>volunteers</u>, the staff, for the most part, were <u>paid</u> employees (or supposed to be) of NWRO, CAP, or VISTA programs.[203] Some were volunteers. Most, however, received income from a supportive agency and considered themselves to be professional organizers. On the other hand, from the perspective of NWRO's targets (the welfare authorities and political leaders), they were also part of the movement and viewed as insiders, given their allegiance and participation in the movement at the local and national levels. Nonetheless, as we shall see, for the most part they tended to be drawn from the dominant groups in society and, as such, contrasted sharply with the formal leaders, who were subordinate in status based on class, gender, and race. Over the years, the formal leaders of NWRO—the elected officers—increasingly criticized the taking of power by the informal leaders—the staff and organizers.

At the state level, the Massachusetts Welfare Rights Organization (MWRO), the largest grass-roots organization within the movement, was probably representative of WROs organized by "outside professionals." On the whole, however, most local WRO groups had little, if any, contact with organizers on a continuing basis. New Jersey, for example, had one or two during the first two years (1966-69). Thereafter, the WRO groups in the state functioned on their own. Only a few states, such as Massachusetts, New York, Michigan, Illinois, and Ohio, had large numbers of organizers financed by various private and public agencies. Thus, NWRO was able to increase its mobilized resources by attracting VISTA and CAP personnel, social workers, and university students as field organizers, expanding its outreach among the poor throughout the country. Some states were more successful than others in recruiting organizers for welfare rights.

Structurally, the office and field staff differed significantly from the membership and leaders of the local WROs and the national organization. Organizers were generally "white, middle-class and recent college graduates" at the local level.[204] Most were male, with the possible exception of members of the staff of the MWRO. Here Bailis reports a fairly even distribution between men and women in the field.[205]

Black organizers were the exception, rather than the rule. While Bailis points out that, in Massachusetts, MWRO leaders "would have preferred to have more black organizers," they found it "difficult to recruit them," given the rising tide of black nationalism.[206] NWRO, as an integrated movement organization, did not appeal to this faction among blacks. This was the common pattern at the local level throughout the country, according to several observers.[207] There were exceptions. Robert Curvin, in Newark, was one of the principal organizers of welfare rights in 1966-67.

Women were also rarely found as organizers or staff in NWRO. While some did work at the local level, they were few in number, either white or black. [208] Whitaker indicates that "the paucity of female organizers reflects the status of women and stems both from 'male chauvinism' . . . and the preference of the 'unliberated' female recipients for male staff leadership. "[209] He also notes, however, that many women were engaged "in the movement for female liberation," which left them "little time for welfare rights activity." At the local level, one of the most prominent white female organizers was Rhoda Linton, who, in Brooklyn, helped organize the largest WRO group in the country. Linton, together with Bill Pastreich, the leading organizer in Massachusetts, also developed the "Boston model" for organizing recipients, which was adopted as the major mobilizing strategy in various parts of the country. (See Chapter 3.) She was later promoted from the local staff to the national headquarters.

Black female organizers and staff were even more rare in NWRO. Bailis notes that, in Massachusetts, (as probably elsewhere) there were only "a few." In New Jersey there was one. [210] Shirley Lacy, an organizer for CORE, played a central role in establishing the welfare rights movement in Newark from 1966 to 1968. In New York, Andrea Kydd was another black woman who took Linton's place in Brooklyn when she went to the national office. [211]

At the national level, the composition of the staff was similar to that at the local level. It was mostly middle-class, male, and overwhelmingly white. In Washington, however, the top staff position, that of executive director, was held by Wiley, a well-educated, middle-class black. He had been hired by the women leaders on the Executive Committee, given his initial role in the organization and his proved commitment to the cause. Responsible for hiring and firing the staff at the national level, he added them as fast as the monies became available. By 1969 the original staff of four had grown to 50 or more. [212] At the height of NWRO's grass-roots organizing activity, the number reached 200, according to one report. [213] The numbers fluctuated, however, depending on the rewards and cost of participation.

At first, NWRO's emphasis on grass-roots organizing attracted many young people, many of them ex-civil rights activists. When the decision was made by NWRO leaders to shift its resources from local organizing to national lobbying after 1969, there was attrition in the field staff. As NWRO's financial resources rose and fell, its staff expanded and contracted. By March 1975, just before the closing of its headquarters, NWRO had only two staff members left in Washington, and these had gone unpaid for weeks.

The job of office and field staff was very demanding and the material rewards very limited. Salaries were low and payments irregular. Hours were long. While the work was seen as challenging by the young activists, and described as "fun" by some, it was also arduous, frustrating, and at times very isolated. Many organizers "burned out" in a short period of time, according to Wiley.[214] He underscored this by pointing out that after four years, in 1970, he was "the only one who is still doing it," of the "people who originally started welfare rights."[215] When funds were unavailable but commitment remained high, many of the staff continued to work as volunteers, surviving on unemployment benefits or on the resources of family and friends.[216] Despite the generally high commitment on the part of the national staff, deterioration of NWRO's financial resources, the intensity of the organizing pace, increasing tensions within NWRO, and emerging alternatives (such as the antiwar movement) gradually eroded the numbers who stayed in NWRO. For a few years in the mid- and late 1960s, the challenge of organizing the poor and black in the inner cities had attracted many young people interested in "changing the system." As the turbulent 1960s gave way to the subdued and narcissistic 1970s, and as the costs of participation in NWRO increased, many dropped out.

NWRO's national staff, as were those in the professionally organized WROs, was racially integrated. From the very beginning, as we have previously noted, Wiley's deep-seated commitment to racial integration led him to hire both blacks and whites in setting up the P/RAC. The first hired was Bruce Thomas, a black resident of Syracuse, who had been attracted first to CORE and then to NWRO by Wiley's charismatic leadership. The second was Edwin Day, a white colleague in the Syracuse CORE, who agreed to work with Wiley in Washington.

As NWRO's staff expanded in the first few years, it remained racially integrated, but the balance tipped in favor of whites.[217] Wiley appointed Sampson, the white welfare rights organizer from California, as his associate director in charge of the Washington office. Other high positions within the national staff were also awarded to whites. John Lewis, a black civil rights leader and one of the founders of the Student National Coordinating Council (SNCC), became the publications director, one of the few top posts assigned to a black male. Kotz and Kotz note that "Wiley was perfectly comfortable to have white aides but the appearance of whites in key jobs, he insisted, was principally a matter of economics."[218] Wiley explained that few blacks could afford to live on "subsistence pay" or as volunteers. Furthermore, he added, many did not want to work in a "multi-racial organization," given the rising black nationalism. Finally, few wanted to be involved in a movement "dominated by black women."[219]

In contrast, then, to NWRO's base constituency and its formal leaders, the national staff and field organizers emerged as predomi-

TABLE 2.6

Race, Sex, and Class of NWRO Top Staff Positions

	1967	1968	1969	1970	1971	1972	1973	1974
Executive director								
Race								
(black/white)	B	B	B	B	B	B	B	B
Sex								
(female/male)	M	M	M	M	M	M	M	F
Class								
(poor/nonpoor)	NP	NP	NP	NP	NP	NP	P	P
Associate director								
Race								
(black/white)	W	W	W	B	B	B	B	B
Sex								
(female/male)	M	M	M	M	F	F	M	M
Class								
(poor/nonpoor)								
Liaison to the UCC-WPT								
Race								
(black/white)	—*	—	—	W	B	B	B	—
Sex								
(female/male)	—	—	—	M	M	M	F/M	—
Class								
(poor/nonpoor)	—	—	—	NP	NP	NP	P	—

*There was no liaison to the UCC-WPT in this year.

Sources: Compiled from personal taped interviews with NWRO leaders and organizers in 1974, news items in Welfare Fighter, the letterhead of NWRO stationery, and participant observation at meetings and as a member of the UCC-WPT.

nantly white, middle-class, and male. However, while the staff remained predominantly white for the first few years, it gradually "got
blacker as time went on."[220] Eventually, it also came to be dominated by women, the poor women who previously had served only as
volunteers in elected positions. Ironically, when the women finally
demanded and began to assume some of the paid staff jobs, the national organization was near bankruptcy, and there were few funds
left to hire anyone.

These structural changes in terms of race, class, and gender
occurred from 1967 through 1974 within the national staff in Washington, reflecting shifts in power and the loss of office and field workers.
(See Table 2.6.) In Washington, people in key positions, such as
executive director, and staff liaison to the United Church (a major
supporter of NWRO), were replaced over the years. Wiley remained
NWRO's executive director from 1967 through the end of 1972, when
he resigned to form the MEJ. The post was then taken over by Tillmon, a black welfare mother and the first elected chair of NWRO,
thus reversing gender and class. For one year, while Tillmon was
on a leave of absence, this top position reverted to Evans. Evans,
unlike Wiley, came from a poverty background and had experienced
being poor and living on welfare. Like Wiley, he was also a black
male deeply committed to the plight of poor people, especially black
women with dependent children. In 1974 when Tillmon resumed her
position as executive director of NWRO, the top leadership closely
resembled the core membership of the movement.

The position of associate director, the second-highest staff position, directly under George Wiley, shifted from a white nonrecipient,
Sampson, to a black male, Hulbert James, in 1969. In 1971 this position was taken over by Tillmon, the first woman and welfare mother
to assume a high staff position in NWRO. * This, as we shall see, reflected as well as created internal tensions and struggles for power
between the national women leaders and the paid staff.

Another important staff position was the NWRO staff liaison with
the United Church of Christ Welfare Priority Team, NWRO's principal
ally from 1970 through 1973. The responsibilities of this job included
attending regular monthly meetings of the Welfare Priority Team in
New York City, reporting on the latest developments and strategies
of NWRO, and cooperating with the church supporters in establishing
linkages of WROs and middle-class church constituencies. The first
NWRO liaison was Sampson, the man who conceived of the coalition
between the NWRO and the United Church of Christ. He was the as-

---

*Earlier, recipient leaders Joyce Burson and Jackie Pope from
Brooklyn had been given minor positions on the staff in Washington.

sociate director at the time and temporarily assumed the position of liaison on the Welfare Priority Team. Almost immediately, he was replaced by Mel Turner, a black staff member in Washington. In September 1972 Sanders, the second elected chair of NWRO (and a black welfare mother), and her staff assistant, Audrey Colom (also a black woman), took over this assignment. When Wiley resigned from NWRO shortly afterward, Colom did, too. She was replaced by Evans, who was then the associate director under Tillmon. Sanders and Evans were black and from poverty backgrounds, closely resembling the membership they represented in terms of race and class. They held these positions on the team until the alliance between NWRO and the Welfare Priority Team dissolved at the end of 1973. From 1970 through 1973, the position shifted from a white, middle-class male to a black female and male, both of whom had lived on welfare.

During the eight years that NWRO maintained its national headquarters in Washington, D. C., the structural gap between its membership base and its paid staff was gradually closed. By 1974 race, class, and gender characteristics of the paid employees on the national staff closely resembled those of its grass-roots membership. These shifts evolved as solutions to the structural contradictions within the movement, which reflected similar cleavages and antagonisms within U.S. society. The changes in NWRO's structure also traced and mirrored its declining power.

NWRO thus became the first national protest of welfare mothers in the history of the United States. Various resources were mobilized in order to organize the poor women and confront the welfare authorities. Cloward and Piven, as theoreticians and practitioners, contributed both their plan of action ("The Strategy to End Poverty"), which released untapped monies within the welfare departments, and their own time, money, and efforts. Wiley adopted their strategy and modified it, creating a mass-movement organization of welfare recipients that could function as a political force in order to exert influence on state and national legislators and administrators. As its national "informal" leader, Wiley attracted and mobilized the poor as members and leaders and the young, middle-class activists as organizers and supporters, from a wide spectrum of public and private agencies. Their collective efforts contributed to the development of local WROs throughout the country, which Wiley and his staff linked together into a highly structured and complex national movement organization. Wiley, as NWRO's principal fund raiser, mobilized monies from churches, foundations, wealthy individuals, and even the federal government. He and his staff also developed alliances with various supporters, which provided NWRO with other needed resources to sustain its national headquarters.

Having mobilized funds, members, leaders, organizers, and supporters, the welfare rights movement took off in 1966 and for a short period of time became a viable challenger of the welfare system. As NWRO fought to change the economic conditions of the poor, internal conflicts, rooted in its structural contradictions, erupted. These clashes hastened the downfall of NWRO, already buffeted by the changing political tide. In the process, its principal resources—people and monies—were lost, as we discuss in the next chapter.

NOTES

1. The Random House Dictionary (New York: Ballantine Books, 1978), p. 1006.
2. Frances Fox Piven and Richard A. Cloward, Poor People's Movements: Why They Succeed, How They Fail (New York: Pantheon Books, 1977). See especially chap. 1.
3. Social Security Act of 1935, 42 U.S.C., Section 301 et. seq. (1970).
4. Gilbert Y. Steiner, The State of Welfare (Washington, D.C.: Brookings Institution, 1971), p. 1. Also see, Frances Fox Piven and Richard A. Cloward, Regulating the Poor: The Functions of Public Welfare (New York: Pantheon Books, 1971); Joe R. Feagin, Subordinating the Poor: Welfare and American Beliefs (Englewood Cliffs, N.J.: Prentice-Hall, 1975); Walter I. Traetner, From Poor to Welfare State (New York: Free Press, 1974); Lucy Komisar, Down and Out in the U.S.A.: A History of Social Welfare (New York: New Viewpoints, 1974).
5. Piven and Cloward, Regulating the Poor, p. xiii.
6. Komisar, Down and Out, pp. 63-64.
7. Ibid.
8. Ibid., p. 137.
9. Steiner, State of Welfare, pp. 26-27; Larry R. Jackson and William A. Johnson, Protest by the Poor: The Welfare Rights Movement in New York City (New York: Rand Corporation, 1973), p. 3; William Howard Whitaker, "The Determinants of Social Movement Success: A Study of the National Welfare Rights Organization" (Ph.D. diss., Brandeis University, 1970), p. 104.
10. Whitaker, "Social Movement Success," p. 106; Steiner, State of Welfare, p. 35.
11. Whitaker, "Social Movement Success," p. 106; quoting Moynihan.
12. Ibid., p. 107.
13. Steiner, State of Welfare, p. 53.
14. Ibid., pp. 31-32.
15. Ibid., p. 27.
16. Ibid., p. 78.

17. Piven and Cloward, Poor People's Movements, p. 267.

18. U.S., Department of Labor, Bureau of Labor Statistics, U.S. Working Women: A Databook (Washington, D.C.: Government Printing Office, 1977), p. 3.

19. Piven and Cloward, Poor People's Movements, p. 268.

20. Daniel Patrick Moynihan, The Politics of a Guaranteed Income: The Nixon Administration and the Family Assistance Plan (New York: Random House, 1973), p. 331.

21. Steiner, State of Welfare, pp. 283-84. See also Jackson and Johnson, Protest by the Poor, pp. 26-29.

22. Jo Freeman, The Politics of Women's Liberation (New York: David McKay, 1975), p. 67. Freeman defines "networks" as an important resource.

23. John D. McCarthy and Mayer N. Zald, The Trend of Social Movements in America: Professionalization and Resource Mobilization (Morristown, N.J.: General Learning Press, 1973), p. 27.

24. Alvin L. Schorr, Explorations in Social Policy (New York: Basic Books, 1968), pp. 10-11.

25. Michael Harrington, The Other America: Poverty in the United States (Baltimore: Penguin, 1962). This book is credited by some observers as having revived the interest of the political establishment in the problem of poverty.

26. U.S., Department of Health, Education and Welfare, Having the Power, We Have the Duty (Washington, D.C.: Government Printing Office, 1966), p. 3.

27. Ibid., p. xii.

28. Alfred Kahn, Studies in Social Policy and Planning (New York: Russell Sage Foundation, 1969), p. 118.

29. U.S., Congress, House, Poverty: Message from the President of the United States and Draft of a Bill, 88th Cong., 2nd sess., 1964, H. Doc. 243, pp. 2-6 (as quoted in Whitaker, "Social Movement Success," p. 134).

30. Peter Marris and Martin Rein, Dilemmas of Social Reform: Poverty and Community Action in the United States, 2d ed. (Chicago: Aldine, 1973), p. 210.

31. Moynihan, Guaranteed Income, p. 36.

32. Lawrence Neil Bailis, Bread or Justice: Grassroots Organizing in the Welfare Rights Movement (Lexington, Mass.: D.C. Heath, 1974), p. 11.

33. Taped interview with Johnnie Tillmon, Washington, D.C., July 1974.

34. Taped interview with Bert DeLeeuw. Also, Whitaker, "Social Movement Success," p. 163, n. 1.

35. Metropolitan Applied Research Center, A Relevant War Against Poverty: A Study of Community Action Programs and Observable Social Change (New York, 1968).

36. Richard A. Cloward and Frances Fox Piven, "The Weight of the Poor: A Strategy to End Poverty," The Nation, May 2, 1966, p. 510, reprint. They state that "nearly 8 million persons (half of them white) now subsist on welfare, but it is generally known that for every person on the rolls at least one more probably meets existing criteria of eligibility but is not obtaining assistance." In June 1967, they stated that the 8 million on welfare "are less than a quarter of the poor." See "Improving Social Welfare," Current, October 1967, p. 21.

37. Sar A. Levitan and Robert Taggart, The Promise of Greatness (Cambridge, Mass.: Harvard University Press, 1976), p. 14.

38. Jackson and Johnson, Protest by the Poor, p. 161.

39. Marris and Rein, Social Reform, pp. 177, 289, and 293.

40. Cloward and Piven, "Strategy to End Poverty."

41. "Strategy of Crisis: A Dialogue," American Child 48 (Summer 1966): 21.

42. Ibid., p. 29.

43. Nicholas and Mary Lynn Kotz, A Passion for Equality: George Wiley and the Movement (New York: W. W. Norton, 1977). This book is a biography of George Wiley by two journalists who became his close friends in the National Welfare Rights movement. See chapter 21, pp. 181-93.

44. August Meier and Elliott Rudwick, CORE: A Study in the Civil Rights Movement, 1942-1968 (New York: Oxford University Press, 1973), p. 315.

45. Ibid., pp. 406-7.

46. Field notes, speech by Carl Rachlin, legal counsel of CORE and later of NWRO, at the "Service in Commemoration and Celebration of the Life and Work of Dr. George A. Wiley and the Welfare Rights Movement" at the Mariner's Temple in New York, September 12, 1973.

47. Kotz and Kotz, Passion for Equality, p. 182.

48. Ibid.

49. Ibid., p. 183.

50. Ibid.

51. Taped interview 201. Bayard Rustin, another civil rights leader, analyzed the problem of blacks in similar economic terms. He felt that the blacks would never have equal opportunity without basic changes in socioeconomic conditions. He also believed in a strategy of coalition formation across race and class lines. See Bayard Rustin, "From Protest to Politics: The Future of the Civil Rights Movement," Commentary 39 (February 1965): 25-31.

52. Hobart A. Burch, "Conversations with George Wiley," Journal of Social Issues, November/December 1970, p. 6, reprint.

53. Kotz and Kotz, Passion for Equality, p. 187.

54. Whitaker, "Social Movement Success," pp. 158-59.

55. Jackson and Johnson, Protest by the Poor, p. 126.

56. Whitaker, "Social Movement Success," p. 159; Piven and Cloward, Poor People's Movements, pp. 290-91.

57. Burch, "Conversations with George Wiley," p. 6.

58. Ibid.

59. Jackson and Johnson, Protest by the Poor, pp. 55-59.

60. "Strategy of Crisis," p. 27.

61. Ibid., p. 28.

62. Ibid., p. 24.

63. Ibid.

64. Burch, "Conversations with George Wiley," p. 6.

65. Richard Cloward, taped radio show, "Always on Sunday," New York City, August 11, 1973; taped interview with Frances Fox Piven, New York City, September 1974.

66. Ibid.

67. Taped interview with Frances Fox Piven, 1974.

68. Ibid.

69. Ibid.

70. Whitaker, "Social Movement Success," p. 222. He states that 47 percent of the budget was equal to $106,893. Therefore, 100 percent would be over $200,000.

71. Field notes, report by George Wiley to WPT, September 29, 1972.

72. Ibid.

73. Ibid.

74. Ibid.

75. Ibid.

76. Ibid.

77. Moynihan, Guaranteed Income, pp. 298-99. NWRO opposed Nixon's FAP. The U.S. Catholic Conference endorsed it, according to Moynihan.

78. NWRO in Action (Washington, D.C.: NWRO, n.d. [1969?]). This is a compilation of newspaper clippings telling some of NWRO's story from 1966 to 1968 and apparently funded, in part, by paid advertisements from supporters, listed in its last pages.

79. Taped interview 151.

80. Ibid.

81. Interview with Bertha Cavanaugh, the chair of the Rhode Island WRO, August 1972.

82. Guida West, "Twin-Track Coalitions" (Paper, Rutgers University, 1971).

83. Kotz and Kotz, Passion for Equality, p. 245.

84. Field notes, September 29, 1972.

85. Ibid.

86. Taped interview 151.

87. Ibid.

88. Frances Fox Piven and Richard A. Cloward, "Social Movements and Societal Conditions: A Response to Roach and Roach," Social Problems 26 (December 1978): 172-78. On p. 174, Piven and Cloward state:

> Obviously the black struggle against caste and discrimination, and the struggle of the welfare poor for the means to survive, did not erupt from the ranks of organized labor. . . . Indeed, dominant elements within labor have been an important source of opposition to most of these movements.

See also Richard A. Cloward and Frances Fox Piven, "Workers and Welfare: The Poor against Themselves," Nation, November 25, 1968, reprint. They state:

> Union leaders have traditionally resisted encouraging their members to apply for welfare wage supplements, believing this an admission of their failure to obtain higher wages through collective bargaining. . . . Many workers do not know that these payments are available or how to calculate their eligibility. Some workers who do know shy away because of their traditional contempt for the dole and for those who subsist on it.

89. Whitaker, "Social Movement Success," p. 216. Also, see Piven and Cloward debate with Jack Roach and Janet K. Roach, "Mobilizing the Poor: Road to a Dead End," Social Problems 26 (December 1978): 172-77 and 160-71, respectively.

90. Whitaker, "Social Movement Success," p. 215.

91. NWRO in Action. In the final pages of this compilation of reprints of newspaper stories on the movement, a section begins "Publication of NWRO in Action has been made possible by the contributions of the following individuals and organizations." The labor unions and labor union members listed were as follows: John Coleman, president, Hospital Local 420; Joseph Rogoff, president, Department of Social Services Local 371; Harry Gray, vice-president, School Lunch and School Aides Local 372; Victor Gotbaum, executive director, District Council 37; American Federation of State, County, and Municipal Employees, ALF-CIO; also U.A.W. Western Region 6, Los Angeles, Paul Schrade, director; also National Federation of Social Service Employees, New York City; Social Workers Local 535, Los Angeles; Local 1199 Drug and Hospital Employees Union, RWDSU, AFL-CIO, New York City, Leon J. Davis, president. Also taped in-

terview with Frances Fox Piven, September 1974. One local union, according to Piven, contributed $100 per month for one year to the New York Citywide WRO.

92. Steiner, State of Welfare, p. 293.

93. "NWRO Financial Statement for Twelve Months," October 1, 1969 to September 30, 1969.

94. NWRO Prospectus, March 1970.

95. Taped interview 215.

96. Steiner, State of Welfare, p. 288.

97. Kotz and Kotz, Passion for Equality, p. 238. They report the following budgets for NWRO:

1967 – $ 63,000	1970 – $535,000
1968 – 232,000	1971 – 650,000
1969 – 457,000	1972 – 400,000

98. Field notes, Eastern Regional WRO Conference, Baltimore, November 11, 1972.

99. Field notes, Beulah Sanders's speech at Eastern Regional Conference, November 11, 1972.

100. Field notes, September 29, 1972.

101. George Wiley, "Memo to Members and Friends and Supporters," December 15, 1972, pp. 1-4 (mimeographed).

102. Taped interview 151.

103. Field notes, Beulah Sanders's report, Washington, D.C., January 30, 1973.

104. Field notes, January 12, 1973.

105. Memorandum from Johnnie Tillmon and Faith Evans, "To All WROs and Friends," August 16, 1973.

106. "Giving the Poor Half-A-Chance to Contribute to Independence," For Our Welfare (October 1974): 8 (published by WRISC, Washington, D.C.). See also taped interview with Johnnie Tillmon, Washington, D.C., 1974. The correlation between philanthropic giving to social movements and economic conditions has been posited by John D. McCarthy and Mayer N. Zald. They conclude that "where the classical model of social movements predict less activity in prosperous times, our analysis predicts just the reverse" see John D. McCarthy and Mayer N. Zald, The Trend of Social Movements in America, p. 17.

107. Taped interview with Johnnie Tillmon, Washington, D.C., 1974.

108. Ibid.

109. Field notes, October 1974.

110. Burch, "Conversations with George Wiley," p. 5.

111. Ibid.

112. Bailis, Bread or Justice, p. 94.

113. Memorandum from NWRO associate director to all WROs, September 24, 1969. See Steiner, State of Welfare, p. 287, on Wiley's thrust for organizing.

114. Kotz and Kotz, Passion for Equality, p. 231.

115. Ibid.

116. Ibid., p. 234.

117. Piven and Cloward, Poor People's Movements, p. 284.

118. Ibid.

119. Ibid.

120. Ibid.

121. Ibid.

122. Ibid., p. 288.

123. The HEW identified the AFDC program as "the largest public assistance program." In fact, in one of their publications, they state, "The term 'welfare' in this leaflet refers to Aid to Families with Dependent Children (AFDC), the largest public assistance program." See U.S., Department of Health, Education and Welfare, Social Rehabilitation Service, Welfare Myths vs. Facts (Washington, D.C.: Government Printing Office, 1971).

124. U.S., Department of Health, Education and Welfare, Having the Power, We Have the Duty (Washington, D.C.: Government Printing Office, 1966), p. 9.

125. Report of the Steering Committee of the Arden House Conference on Public Welfare, held on November 2-3, 1967, in Harrison, New York, p. 15.

126. Piven and Cloward, Poor People's Movements, pp. 275-76.

127. Ibid., p. 291.

128. Piven and Cloward, Poor People's Movements, p. 292.

129. Whitaker, "Social Movement Success," p. 161; Piven and Cloward, Poor People's Movements, pp. 291-92.

130. Jackson and Johnson, Protest by the Poor, p. 64.

The Welfare Bill of Rights included the following points:

1. The right to be a member of a welfare rights organization.

2. The right to fair and equal treatment, free from discrimination based on race and color.

3. The right to apply for any welfare program and to have that application in writing.

4. The right to have the welfare department make a decision promptly after application for aid.

5. The right to be told in writing the specific reason for denial of aid.

6. The right to appeal a decision thought to be wrong, including denials and reductions of assistance, and to be given a fair hearing before an impartial referee.

7. The right to get welfare payments without being forced to spend the money as the welfare department wants.

8. The right to be treated with respect.

9. The right to be treated in a way that does not invade your privacy.

10. The right to receive welfare aid without having the welfare department ask you questions about who your social friends are, such as who you are going with.

11. The right to have the same constitutional protections all other citizens have.

12. The right to be told and informed by the welfare department of all of your rights, including the ways you can best make sure that you can get your welfare money.

13. The right to have, to get, and to give advice during all contacts with the welfare department, including when applying, when being investigated, and during fair hearings.

See Welfare Bill of Rights (Washington, D.C.: National Welfare Rights Organization, n.d.).

131. Jackson and Johnson, Protest by the Poor, p. 89.

132. Piven and Cloward, Poor People's Movements, pp. 307-8.

133. Ibid., p. 297.

134. Ibid.

135. Ibid., p. 301.

136. Jackson and Johnson, Protest by the Poor, p. 283. See also taped interview with Hulbert James, September 1974.

137. Mancur Olson, The Logic of Collective Action: Public Goods and the Theory of Groups (Cambridge, Mass.: Harvard University Press, 1965). See also Jackson and Johnson, Protest by the Poor, pp. 19-20; Bailis, Bread or Justice, pp. 121-23.

138. Bailis, Bread or Justice, p. 65.

139. Whitaker, "Social Movement Success," p. 157.

140. NWRO Constitution, 1970.

141. Bailis, Bread or Justice, p. 17. "The only major power that NWRO holds over its local groups is the power to recognize them as affiliates."

142. Kotz and Kotz, Passion for Equality, p. 214.

143. Ibid.

144. Ben B. Seligman, Permanent Poverty: An American Syndrome (Chicago: Quadrangle Books, 1970), pp. 28-31. The Social Security Administration "poverty index" theoretically "specified the minimum money income required to support an average family of a

given size at the lowest level consistent with a decent standard of living." Basically, "total income requirements" were estimated "at three times the food bill" that would buy an adequate diet based on Department of Agriculture criteria. In 1963 this came to about $3,220 per year for a family of four living on an "economy diet." By 1979 the "poverty level," reflecting the cost of living increases, was up to $6,490.

145. Ibid., p. 38.

146. Guide to Welfare Reform (Washington, D.C.: Food Research and Action Center, 1979), p. 13.

147. "NWRO's Guaranteed Adequate Income Plan," NOW!, n.d. See also, Burch, "Conversations with George Wiley," p. 11.

148. Burch, "Conversations with George Wiley," p. 5.

149. Ibid.

150. Ibid.

151. Bailis, Bread or Justice, pp. 79-80.

152. Kotz and Kotz, Passion for Equality, p. 160.

153. George Wiley, taped radio show, "Always on Sunday," interview with Paul Sherry of UCC, New York City, April 15, 1973.

154. "Insights of a Welfare Mother," Journal of Social Issues, (January/February 1971), p. 21, reprint.

155. Ibid.

156. "Arizona," Welfare Fighter, March 1970.

157. "Birth of a Movement," Welfare Fighter, November 1971.

158. Whitaker, "Social Movement Success," p. 202.

159. Kotz and Kotz, Passion for Equality, p. 228; Bailis, Bread or Justice, p. 103.

160. Personal interview with Bertha Cavanaugh, chair of Rhode Island WRO, August 1972; Kentucky, see Whitaker, "Social Movement Success," p. 202; Massachusetts, see Bailis, Bread or Justice, p. 103; Michigan, field notes, NWRO Convention, July 1974, St. Louis, Missouri; West Virginia, Kotz and Kotz, Passion for Equality, p. 222; New Jersey data collected through participant observation from 1967 through 1979.

161. Bailis, Bread or Justice, p. 104. He mentions that a white WRO chose a black woman as its leader because blacks were more militant. In New York, Evans reported a white group that was led by blacks.

162. Piven and Cloward, Poor People's Movements, p. 317, n. 32; David Street, George T. Martin, Jr., and Laura Kramer Gordon, The Welfare Industry: Functionaries and Recipients of Public Aid (Beverly Hills, Calif.: Sage, 1979), p. 124.

163. Piven and Cloward, Poor People's Movements, p. 317, n. 32.

164. Field notes, NWRO Convention, Rhode Island, July 1971.

165. Field notes, Washington, D.C., January 30, 1973.

166. Burch, "Conversations with George Wiley," p. 5.

167. Piven and Cloward, Regulating the Poor, p. 321.

168. Ibid., p. 322.

169. Whitaker, "Social Movement Success," p. 202.

170. Steiner, State of Welfare, p. 44 and chap. 3, n. 143. Only in 1978 was "the unemployed mother" in a two-parent family considered by the courts for eligibility for welfare benefits. See "Current Supreme Court Cases Relating to Welfare," prepared by the Center on Social Welfare Policy and Law, New York and Washington, D.C., March 21, 1979, especially the Califano v. Westcott and Sharp v. Westcott cases.

171. Lynne B. Igletzin, "A Case Study in Patriarchal Politics," American Behavioral Scientist 17 (March/April 1974): 487-505. Igletzin has also made this same observation about the gender-free terminology used in referring to AFDC women, and its consequences in obscuring poverty among women.

172. "NWRO Mothers Launch Campaign," NOW!, June 6, 1978.

173. Johnnie Tillmon, "Profile of a Welfare Fighter," Welfare Fighter, August 1971; Richard Rogin, "Now It's Welfare Lib," New York Times Magazine, September 27, 1970, p. 75.

174. Taped interview with Johnnie Tillmon, Washington, D.C., 1974.

175. Carol Glassman, "Women in the Welfare System," in Sisterhood is Powerful, ed. Robin Morgan (New York: Vintage, 1970), pp. 102-14.

176. See Heather L. Ross and Isabel V. Sawhill, Time of Transition: The Growth of Families Headed by Women (Washington, D.C.: Urban Institute, 1975), especially chap. 3.

177. Field notes, NWRO Conventions 1974 and 1977. July 1974 in St. Louis, Missouri, and August 1977 in Little Rock, Arkansas.

178. Correspondence with DWAC, New York City, April 8, 1975, and July 22, 1975. Also see Sheila Rule, "Relief Recipients Rally in Albany," New York Times, March 15, 1979; Enid Nemy, "'As You Go Up the Ladder, Pull Other Women Along,'" New York Times, March 19, 1979; Children on Welfare . . . Families in Need: The Case for a Welfare Grant Increase (New York: DWAC, 1979); "Welfare Protest Draws 2000 in NY," Just Economics 7 (April/May 1979): 2-3. In 1979 Richard Cloward, Bert DeLeeuw, and Hulbert James, all formerly with NWRO, were on DWAC's board of directors.

179. Correspondence with DWAC, April 8, 1975; DWAC letter, July 11, 1975; field notes, International Women's Year celebration, Princeton, New Jersey, June 18, 1977. Poor women within the socialist-feminist movement were apparently having a difficult time getting welfare recognized as an important women's issue. At the

Socialist-Feminist Convention in Ohio in July 1975, the issue of women in poverty was "neglected again," according to a DWAC leader. Poor women at this convention urged the socialist-feminists to speak out on changing the welfare system but apparently were not successful.

180. Field notes, New Jersey, International Women's Year celebration, Princeton, N.J., June 18, 1977.

181. Ibid.

182. Field notes, WRO Conference, St. Louis, Missouri, July 1977.

183. Bailis, Bread or Justice, pp. 65 and 122; Jackson and Johnson, Protest by the Poor, pp. 283-85.

184. Field notes, Montclair WRO, 1968-71. Also see Piven and Cloward, Poor People's Movements, p. 293.

185. Ibid., p. 323.

186. Steiner, State of Welfare, p. 310.

187. Ibid.

188. Bailis, Bread or Justice, p. 207.

189. Piven and Cloward, Poor People's Movements, p. 296. The figures for 1969 (22,500 and 24,500) are Piven and Cloward's and my data from NWRO documents, respectively.

190. Taped interview 151.

191. Piven and Cloward, Poor People's Movements, p. 296.

192. Taped interview 151.

193. "Local Community Organizing" (Report from NWRO to 1973 Convention, August 1, 1973).

194. Whitaker, "Social Movement Success," p. 161; field notes, July 30, 1971; conversation with Marian Kidd, NJWRO chair, November 9, 1971.

195. Guide to Welfare Reform; conversation with Ruby Grace, Newark WRO coordinator, May 1979.

196. Field notes, Pittsburgh, Pa., August 15, 1975; field notes, Little Rock, Ark., August 6, 1977; Welfare Righter (published by the WRO of Allegheny County, Pittsburgh, Pa.), 1975-77 issues; "They Said It Couldn't Be Done," Welfare Righter 10 (April 1977); field notes, May 1979.

197. Welfare Fighter (published by the WRO of Los Angeles), n.d. (but received July 1977).

198. Field notes, Little Rock, Ark., August 6, 1977.

199. Taped interview with Johnnie Tillmon, July 30, 1974.

200. NWRO Press Release, "Mrs. Johnnie Tillmon Succeeds George Wiley as Head of NWRO," January 12, 1973.

201. Kotz and Kotz, Passion for Equality, p. 218. They state that Evans was "the only male member on the National Coordinating Committee." Analysis of the Welfare Fighter and other NWRO comcunications indicates that there may have been two. In either case, male representation as elected leaders was limited, but significant.

202. Bailis, Bread or Justice, p. 2.

203. Ibid., p. 78.

204. Ibid., p. 79.

205. Ibid.

206. Ibid., p. 80.

207. Whitaker, "Social Movement Success," p. 203; Bailis, Bread or Justice, p. 80; Wiley report, September 29, 1972; taped interview with Bert DeLeeuw, July 1974.

208. Bailis, Bread or Justice, p. 19, n. a; Kotz and Kotz, Passion for Equality, p. 234; taped interview with Bert DeLeeuw, July 30, 1974; Madeline Adamson, "Women Organizers Spell Out Concerns," Just Economics 6 (October 1978): 10-13. Adamson and others discussed the problems faced by women organizers.

209. Whitaker, "Social Movement Success," p. 203. One recent article on the lack of black and female organizers, in which recent black and Chicano organizers were interviewed, suggested that most blacks still did not "believe that the primary reason for discrimination is economic, or class; they believe it is racial" and that black organizers "want to organize something that deals specifically with racial issues as sort of the focal point for the organization." Gary Delgado points out that "there's a primary contradiction in terms of our attempting to hire people from within our constituency. Basically, organizing skills are middle-class skills." In terms of attitudes toward women organizers, more specifically, of black men's attitudes toward black female organizers, Don Leaming-Elmer, director of WISH in Washington, D.C., states that "the feeling was that they could not organize, period" see "Organizing Needs Affirmative Action," Just Economics 7 (April/May 1979): 12-15.

210. Bailis, Bread or Justice, p. 82.

211. Kotz and Kotz, Passion for Equality, p. 235.

212. Taped interview 203; Piven and Cloward, Poor People's Movements, p. 351. They indicate that the paid staff reached 30 to 50.

213. Bailis, Bread or Justice, p. 78.

214. Burch, "Conversations with George Wiley," p. 12.

215. Ibid.

216. Taped interview 203.

217. Ibid.

218. Kotz and Kotz, Passion for Equality, p. 283.

219. Ibid.

220. Taped interview with Frances Fox Piven, New York City, September 1974.

3

CONFLICTS WITHIN NWRO

Almost as rapidly as the NWRO was able to mobilize its resources, internal conflicts erupted that undermined its power as a national protest organization of the poor. Organizers withdrew, membership dropped, leaders resigned, and supporters and their monies disappeared. The major sources of these internal conflicts were rooted in the movement's structural and ideological contradictions, reflecting those in the larger society. Attempts to find new strategies of cooperation to change the existing welfare system called for models of equal partnership within a world of unequals. The traditional hierarchy of race, class, and gender within the dominant social order set parameters in alliances between the poor and nonpoor that were difficult, if not impossible, to change. While ideology was minimized and action emphasized to achieve the movement's goals, the practice of reversing power roles, or at minimum, sharing them equally between the poor and nonpoor, blacks and whites, and women and men proved to be a continuous source of tension for the fledgling movement. The concurrent strategies of mobilizing the poor and their supporters and confronting the welfare power establishment competed for and exhausted NWRO's limited resources. It was a period of turbulence and experimentation, of trial and error, of debating and testing new and old strategies of organizing. Differences on how best to bring about changes in the welfare system grew over the years, deepening schisms within the NWRO and undermining its limited resources.

In the beginning, both the poor and nonpoor, blacks and whites, and women and men felt that "unequal" power partners not only should but could find ways of developing cooperative strategies as equals to achieve common goals and, more specifically, to increase the power of poor people in U.S. society. Working together, combining resources, and mobilizing and organizing as many of the poor as possible seemed not only feasible but also the most effective way of creating political power and of transferring economic power to those at the bottom rung of the social ladder.

This chapter explores the cooperation and conflicts that emerged as the NWRO evolved into a national protest movement. It focuses on the common principles underlying the movement and the conflicts that surfaced over the years, as organizing practices collided with basic beliefs and goals, undermining NWRO's mobilized resources. More specifically, the chapter attempts to describe how structural contradictions within NWRO gave rise to conflicts at every level of the movement, with the central issue of who rules surfacing more and more openly. Dominance by the nonpoor, in a movement that called for the empowerment of the poor, thus became one of the weakest links in the coalitions and cooperative efforts between different groups within NWRO.

As previously noted, NWRO was a federation of welfare rights groups, whose members and leaders were overwhelmingly poor, black women and whose organizers and staff were primarily white, middle-class men—with the notable exception of George Wiley and a few others. While these structural anomalies were recognized, they were also minimized, given the commonality of goals. Over time, however, these differences became increasingly accentuated, as goals and strategies proposed by the poor women and those designed by the organizers diverged. It then became a question of who would make policy decisions—the poor women or the middle-class supporters and organizers. This issue festered over the years and created schisms along class, race, and gender lines that its architects, leaders, and members had sought originally to obscure. The poor struggled increasingly to gain more authority in determining their agendas and priorities. Blacks called for more control, and the welfare rights women eventually demanded the right to be the "real" policy makers, after years of being led and directed by men.

As a result of such conflicts, NWRO's structure changed. In practice, as in theory, NWRO became a movement of poor women, for poor women, and run by poor women—mostly black. For a brief period of time, they gained increased control over their organizations. In the process of taking power, however, they lost the economic and social support of outsiders. Organizers, leaders, supporters, and their monies disappeared. Many of these resources, once mobilized to empower the welfare poor, were shifted to new movement organizations run by some of NWRO's exorganizers. These became NWRO's competitors for people and funds. With these changes in resources within the movement, along with an increasingly hostile political climate and a deteriorating economy in the 1970s, NWRO collapsed.

Before proceeding with this analysis of cooperation and conflict within NWRO, and the consequences for its mobilized resources, three points of clarification should be made. First, although this discussion focuses on internal conflicts, the assumption is that the external political and economic conditions impinged on and aggravated the tensions within NWRO. Internal and external antagonisms are thus considered to be interactive in the process of bringing about the decline of the national protest of poor women. It is difficult, it not impossible, to disentangle cause and effect. The rise of black nationalism in U.S. society in the mid-1960s, for instance, exacerbated the racial conflict within NWRO's integrated structure. It also provided alternatives for black organizers, as is evidenced by the small numbers who chose to become involved in welfare rights organizing, and created a pool of white ex-civil-rights activists who were no longer as welcome to lead and participate in black or "integrated" organizations.

Another example of the interactive effects of internal and external tensions on NWRO is the role played by the women's liberation movement in the 1960s and 1970s. The women's liberation movement, emerging (as did the welfare rights movement) in 1966, heightened the consciousness of poor women about male dominance in U.S. society and, at the same time, created the opportunity for them to be the catalysts in defining welfare as a women's issue. (See Chapter 5.) The antiwar movement and student rebellion in the 1960s also provided alternatives for white, middle-class organizers, especially as the incentives for participating in the welfare rights movement decreased and the costs of organizing the poor increased. The deteriorating economy in the early 1970s also affected NWRO's funding and support. Changes in the political administrations in Washington forced NWRO to shift strategies and reallocate resources, adding to the conflicts within the movement. Both internal and external factors, therefore, gave rise to conflicts and their resolutions within NWRO, altering its structure and its resources.

Clearly, internal conflicts within NWRO were inevitable, given the sharp cleavages and antagonisms within the movement and U.S. society. Paradoxically, however, these differences also proved to be sources of bonding and cooperation. Alliances between nonpeers supplied NWRO with needed resources and its supporters, in turn, with opportunity for participation in the protest. At the same time, nonetheless, these alliances exacerbated the internal clashes.

Another point of clarification addresses the decision to analytically categorize conflicts as being primarily rooted in racial, class, and/or gender contradiction, with little attempt to identify their separate effects. In many cases, the data were not available. In most, the complexity of their interactions would make it impossible, if not misguided, to attempt such a task. In most of the conflicts discussed, the assumption is made that these structural factors were interactive, with some clearly more salient than others in different episodes. For example, the clashes between blacks and whites within the Washington office were obviously rooted in racial contradictions, highlighted by participants and by other observers. The issue of class differences may well have been a factor also, although the data are not as evident. In another episode, the visible controversies emerged between black males and females, reinforcing the "gender" roots of this conflict. Again, however, the class sources of tension were present as well. In the clashes between the welfare women leaders and the white, middle-class organizers, we find class, race, and gender contradictions exacerbating the tensions within their cooperative efforts.

Finally, some assumptions are made about power distribution within U.S. society in the 1960s and 1970s as well as within NWRO, namely, that whites have greater access to wealth, status, and power than blacks; that the poor rank lower than the nonpoor on these criteria; and that women are less powerful than men, both socioeconomically and politically. Consequently, we begin with a stage set in which the Welfare Rights Organization (WRO) women and their allies (as well as their opponents) contrast sharply in power within the society and within the movement. Not only is it suggested that this structural heterogeneity aggravated internal conflicts but also that the specific script—that of reversed roles—selected by NWRO's organizers added to the internal tensions.

Defying the traditional dominant/subordinate mode of cooperation, architects of NWRO set up a new, nonpaternalistic model that abolished the stereotypes of poor people as subordinates in alliances with the nonpoor. NWRO attempted, thus, to mesh its belief in equal rights and power for poor people by practicing what it preached. It was a pioneering effort, and, as the data show, ultimately, many of these attempts failed. Traditional roles rapidly reemerged for the poor as followers and the nonpoor as leaders. Middle-class, white males (the dominant group in U.S. society) ended up dominating the movement of poor black women. Alliances proved to be short-lived and unstable when "reversed roles" were attempted. For middle-class organizers, this pattern of interaction became too costly in practice. After some initial rewards of participating in the unique, exciting, and semiexclusive movement of poor people, the glamour wore off. Many males, socialized to lead, found it difficult, if not impossible, to assume subordinate roles within the local and national organizations. Poor women on welfare, on the other hand, socialized to be subordinate and passive, found the risks of aggressive political protest and the costs of leadership too high.

Gradually, however, some chose to break the stereotypes and take power, changing their attitudes and behavior. Politicization and leadership brought its rewards. For the few who assumed positions of power as elected officers, political action brought them into the public limelight and provided them with new status and recognition. Few were readily willing to give up such benefits for the sake of the greater cause. For poor women, as for any group with limited opportunities for social mobility and achievement, the rise in power within their own organizations provided rare and unique occasions to develop talents and gain new perquisites.

However, while some poor women gained rewards as leaders and fought to hold on to them, many of the rank-and-file members found few incentives for continuous participation in the movement. Conflicts between elected women leaders and the outsiders as organizers and staff intensified over the years and centered on the question of how to build power for the poor and, more specifically, on who should decide. Definitions as to what was best for the movement and for the poor women themselves increasingly diverged over the years. As a result of all these cleavages and conflicts, NWRO lost organizers, leaders, and members.

Three conflict episodes are analyzed in this chapter. The first examines the interaction between the black, poor, female leaders and the white, middle-class, male organizers (race, class, and gender conflicts); the second, the disputes between black and white staff organizers (race and class conflicts); and the third, the rising clashes between Wiley and the women leaders of NWRO (class and gender conflicts). Changes in goals and strategies are traced over time, to highlight the shift in power from middle-class males to the poor women, which had major consequences for the movement. We begin by examining some of the principles that provided a common ground for cooperation in the early years.

Discussions of ideology and principles within NWRO were relatively limited. Time and energies of planners and organizers, as well as members and leaders, were spent on strategies for action. The immediate objective was to attain visible and tangible results, or "victories," that could in turn be used to mobilize additional recruits to the movement. Once Wiley and his colleagues had endorsed the general concept developed by Cloward and Piven in their "Strategy to End Poverty," the motto of NWRO, as Sampson liked to put it, was "Do it!" (implying "don't talk about it"). Wiley, as Kotz and Kotz point out, was a pragmatist who felt that ideology "was not important in NWRO."[1] His goal was "simply to organize the poor, black and white" and to focus on specific benefits that the organization could provide recipients.

Wiley and his principal organizers subscribed to the Saul Alinsky philosophy and strategy of organizing. Alinsky believed that "the only thing the poor have as far as power is their bodies"[2] and that, in fact, the only power that can be mobilized among the have nots rests in their numbers.[3] The more people organized, the more power available to the poor. To achieve change, power is a prerequisite. According to Alinsky, power, or "organized energy," could be "a man-killing explosive or a life-saving drug."[4] He also contended that "to know power and not fear it is essential to its constructive use and control." He added that "life without power is death."[5]

NWRO's organizers subscribed to this theory of organizing and fully endorsed "the goal of 'building the power of the poor'" as their "highest priority."[6] Following in Alinsky's footsteps, most organizers "felt the only way to effect this transfer of power [from the nonpoor to the poor] was to build poor people's organizations."[7] Their major interest focused on creating power, rather than discussing abstract goals. Ideology was minimized. The closest they came to exploring their beliefs was over the dilemma of endorsing and practicing the principle of "participatory democracy." The issue of "using the poor" was a constant source of concern among many.[8] Most seemed aware of this inevitable contradiction of creed (participation of the poor) and deed (control by the organizers). In general, they came to terms by accepting the need for some compromise in "democracy" within NWRO in order to achieve the desired results, namely, a protest movement of poor people strong enough to effect change in the welfare system. The consensus was that, in the trade-off between ideals and pragmatism, sacrifices had to be made to ensure the outcome.[9] Success was measured in terms of numbers of welfare rights groups organized, and in most areas, this proceeded "almost on a production line basis."[10]

Despite the limited attention given to the discussion of ideology, two major underlying principles of organizing were generally accepted as givens within the movement. These were assumed to form the framework for the strategies to mobilize welfare recipients and were incorporated into NWRO's constitution and bylaws. A third principle was rarely mentioned at first but gradually gained recognition, as the women leaders assumed more control within the national movement.

The first major principle addressed the issue of race. NWRO strongly endorsed racial inclusiveness within the movement. Among the poor and nonpoor, there was general consensus that NWRO should be integrated at all levels. Every opportunity was seized to stress this theme. It was emphasized that both its membership and staff included all racial groups and that "poverty was colorblind." Consequently, NWRO's base constituency, as well as its staff, was designed to be racially integrated. For Wiley, racial inclusiveness within NWRO was a central principle that was not to be compromised.

A second major principle dealt with the issue of class. Maximum feasible participation of the poor in its own organization was part of NWRO's espoused doctrine. This concept had been introduced and supported by President Johnson's War on Poverty and coincided with the Alinsky view that the poor had to control their own organizations.[11] The nonpoor in the movement were to assume supportive roles.

A third principle evolved out of the first two. Although NWRO's membership was to be open to all races and to be controlled by its members or representatives, in practice, as we have seen, the overwhelming majority consisted of black women in the Aid to Families with Dependent Children (AFDC) program. Consequently, women were, in theory, the policy makers within the movement. The principle of the poor women's right to rule was thus formally, but never explicitly, incorporated into NWRO's Bill of Rights.* Poverty was not defined as a women's issue.

Over the years, the differences in goals and strategies between members and staff became more salient. Participatory democracy and "power to the poor" meant rule by black women who comprised NWRO's majority base. As long as the poor women were willing to accept the symbolic and "formal" power positions, and to allow the men to be the "informal" leaders, cooperation was maximized and conflicts muted. As the women became more vociferous in their demands for power and control, conflicts escalated. As power shifted, the incentives for middle-class organizers diminished, and many withdrew. Groups, created on the basis of "dependence" on outsiders, generally collapsed. A few WROs, established independently by poor women, survived by accommodating their goals and strategies to changed conditions. However, as they became de facto leaders within their own movement, and the gap closed between NWRO's principles and practices, the poor women found themselves bereft of resources. Few in society in the 1970s were willing to support a movement of poor women run by poor women.

RACE, CLASS, AND GENDER CONFLICTS

As early as 1966, signs of underlying conflict between the poor women and the middle-class organizers were already beginning to emerge, even before the formal organization of the national movement. The anomalous structure of black women as leaders and white males as supporters, further differentiated on the basis of class, was

---

*NWRO's Bill of Rights called for "fair and equal treatment, free from discrimination based on race and color," with sex not included. See Chapter 2.

a constant source of tension that erupted repeatedly and increasingly over the years in different parts of the country. The major issue raised was, Who was going to run the organization, establish goal priorities, and choose the strategies for expanding NWRO's power base? Succinctly, the question in every case came down to, Who decides?

Locally, an incident involving Tillmon and Sampson in California illustrates the underlying power struggle that would continue to beset the national organization as long as the whites and nonrecipient males remained in control. Tillmon was a dynamic individual struggling to support her six children. An indigenous welfare rights leader in Watts, she had worked since 1963 to organize the AFDC women in her area. Her personal experience, after being forced to accept welfare, led her to try to mobilize other women to fight for their welfare rights. [12] She also tried to develop programs of jobs, education, and child care to enable the mothers to move off the welfare rolls. Being on welfare had been a dehumanizing experience for her, since she had worked and supported her family for many years. Poor people needed services, she felt, but they also needed opportunities to move out of poverty. [13] To help accomplish these objectives, she organized the Aid to Needy Children (ANC) Mothers in Watts with a small-core group of loyal adherents.

At the same time, Sampson, a white, Alinsky-trained organizer and social worker, had been active in the northern part of the state, trying to bring poor people together around welfare problems to form their own local organizations in order to build power. Structurally, he was an outsider, since he was middle-class, white, and male among a predominantly black, female, AFDC population. He believed in the Alinsky strategy of organizing the poor and had been committed to the struggle of blacks in the civil rights movement and the poor in the farmworker's movement. Now, welfare and lack of income were emerging throughout the country as the central problems for poor people. Welfare, as a basic need in various communities, thus provided Sampson with a new handle for continuing his longtime commitment to organizing and empowering poor people.

While Tillmon and Sampson basically agreed on the nature of the problem facing the poor in California, the differences in strategies and tactics became quickly apparent. There were divergent views as to how poor people should be organized and who should organize them. Sampson, a professional organizer, noting the rising numbers of welfare rights groups in the state in 1966, saw the need to coordinate their efforts. He proposed a statewide welfare rights group for California. Tillmon reacted immediately, contesting the right of white nonrecipients to assume leadership within the fledgling movement of welfare mothers. Believing that Sampson and his colleagues were "or-

ganizing . . . so they could have the control," Tillmon decided to
challenge their authority within the new movement. [14]

On the night that Sampson had set for the organizational meeting,
Tillmon and her group, the ANC Mothers, decided to challenge his
leadership role and to take control. She recalled that "Tim Sampson
and other folks" had written a constitution and had invited her and her
members to discuss it at the first statewide meeting. Tillmon suggested to her group that they "go up and look at this thing and if we
don't like it, we'll dispose of it."[15] When they walked in, they found
Sampson and another white organizer leading a group that "was mixed,
but heavily black populated." Tillmon "read the Constitution they had
written" and then asked, "Who wrote the Constitution?" When Sampson replied that he had, she said, "Well, this is what I think of it,"
and she tore it up. "Ladies," she added, addressing the women in
the audience, "write your own Constitution!" Tillmon stated that
she "wanted to show to Sampson's men that you just don't come into
somebody's neighborhood and run it." You come in and "inspire
them." What she was looking for was "support . . . in doing our own
thing." Support, not control, was what she felt was needed.

As a result of this incident, Sampson, who had been chosen to
represent the newly formed California WRO at the national level, resigned, fully aware that this new movement of welfare mothers intended to keep control in the hands of poor people. Ironically, he was
almost immediately hired as NWRO's associate director by Wiley and,
in this national administrative post, turned out to wield more power
and influence than many of the formally elected women leaders.

Another consequence of this episode was that NWRO adopted the
principle of "recipient hegemony," as some called it, and incorporated
it in its organizing model. [16] Unlike the dominant pattern in society,
where the poor are seldom given any power to control their own lives
and organizations, within NWRO, the roles were reversed. According to its constitution and bylaws adopted in 1967, the women ruled
and the men supported. As the dominant majority within the movement, blacks governed and whites assisted. The poor set the agenda,
and the nonpoor helped to carry it out. It was a "new" model in which
the powerless were expected to take power and gain prestige by becoming the decision makers and setting the goals and strategies within
the movement.

In theory, then, the formal power rested with the black, female
recipients, the elected representatives of NWRO's dominant majority.
As Bailis points out, this was the plan adopted throughout most of the
country. [17] The paid staff was to serve "at the pleasure of a board of
elected lay leaders who retain final responsibility for determination
of basic policy."[18] The power to hire and fire organizers and staff
ultimately rested with the women leaders, according to the stated

policy. Bailis adds that "this formal description does not accurately portray the actual distribution of influence" because the staff in practice "exercised far more influence than might be assumed on the basis of this description alone."[19]

For a few years, signs of discontent were muted. The contradiction between theory and practice in terms of who was really running the national organization was not salient and, when questioned, was accepted by both the women and the organizers as a necessary and temporary arrangement to achieve the desired goals. Gradually, however, the conflict between these two groups began to surface, and the women expressed their anger more openly over organizer/staff dominance. Internal tensions between the "welfare mothers who are in command and the staff which advises them" was even reported in the press.[20]

At the local level, conflicts between the female leadership and the organizers erupted episodically over the issue of the latter's tendency to dominate and control. Wiley and his staff were well aware of the need to involve the poor women at every stage of planning in order to maintain credibility and minimize frictions. The nature of organizing a protest movement and responding to daily crises, however, demanded that decisions be made immediately and by a few. Wiley and his staff assumed this role at the national level, as did the organizers in the field. This resulted in added tensions between the women and the men.

To enhance the distinction between the roles of "leaders" and "supporters"—the AFDC women and the organizers, respectively— Bailis states that

> NWRO staff members were always careful to see that the recipients received all public credit for what was accomplished; lay leaders were encouraged to run all NWRO meetings, to lead demonstrations and marches, and to engage in negotiations themselves while their organizers remained in the background. NWRO never made statements to the press; only lay leaders and members were permitted to do so.[21]

This was designed to make the recipients "less inclined to perceive white organizers as personal threats; instead they saw them as assistants to help maintain their own positions of public prominence."[22]

Despite these strategies to emphasize control by the poor of their organization, other actions by the staff and organizers at the national and local levels increasingly made clear who was really in charge. This led to clashes between the leaders and organizers, or the "insiders" and "outsiders." In February 1967, conflict erupted over the setting of NWRO's priorities. Discussion of long-range objectives had seldom been given much time by the organizers, as was consistent with their strategy for maximizing action rather than talk. When, however, the issue of NWRO's goals was raised and priorities specified, the differences between the two groups surfaced.

Theoretically, a guaranteed income for poor people was the major goal of NWRO. Even though NWRO had originated at a national meeting in May 1966 that specifically addressed "the guaranteed annual income," such a goal was not discussed at the first organizing meeting and was never officially adopted by the national organization until the end of August 1968. One explanation was that the organizers felt that the women on welfare "were not ready to cope with so sophisticated an idea."[23] The women, however, knew what they wanted.

At one of the early meetings, some of the poor women rejected the prepared list of goals proposed by the Poverty/Rights Action Center (P/RAC) staff. The white organizers had recommended that NWRO "support . . . AFDC-UP [the public assistance program for families with unemployed fathers, that is, two-parent rather than single-parent families], work incentive payments, and food stamps." The women objected. Their top priority was getting government support for families headed by women, both through adequate welfare benefits and through jobs at decent wages. Some reacted strongly to this staff domination and withdrew from the National Coordinating Committee (NCC), accusing the organizers in P/RAC once again of trying to control the movement of poor people.[24]

Similarly, when NWRO became involved in formulating its platform for the Poor People's Campaign in 1968, the staff once again took the initiative in determining NWRO's goals. Their choice was to demand increased welfare benefits for the AFDC women and poor families and more jobs for men as breadwinners. The platform called for "a minimum guaranteed income of $4000 for every American family," along with "three million jobs for men."[25] Reflecting the dominant and traditional views of the family, they rationalized that "there is a desperate need for jobs in the ghettoes for men to permit them to assume normal roles as breadwinners and heads of families."[26]

The male-dominated staff gave top priority to goals that reinforced the "intact" and traditional family (where both father and mother are present), ignoring the fact that the majority of NWRO's members represented female-headed households. Forced to combine two major roles, child rearing and breadwinning, AFDC women listed their major needs as higher welfare benefits for women, more jobs and training, and child care, rather than jobs for men and more funds for "intact" families.

The goals of "welfare for women" and "jobs for men," although at first not a source of controversy within the movement, eventually surfaced as a major area of conflict. Data on poor women's work motivations, compiled by social scientists and public opinion polls, repeatedly confirmed their desire to get off the welfare rolls. Data also underscored, however, that poor women want the freedom of choice to determine whether to work in the home caring for their children or to work in the labor market or to do both. For affluent women, theoretically, there had always been a choice (as Tillmon pointed out), although socialization and social pressures emphasized their primary role in the home. Research findings confirmed that lack of job opportunities and social support for female-headed families, rather than lack of motivation, were major factors in women's dependence on welfare.* Sexism and racism compounded the obstacles to women's employment at all levels of the social hierarchy.

---

*Leonard Goodwin found that recipients have "essentially the same work ethic as middle-class people." Both blacks and whites "identify their self-respect with work." The only major difference he found was that blacks were "much less confident of their ability to succeed at work" than whites. Women in the mandated work incentive programs had "high life aspirations and work ethic," and those who gave up did so because they had failed repeatedly at work and thus "find welfare an acceptable alternative" (Do the Poor Want to Work? [Washington, D.C.: Brookings Institution, 1972], pp. 3, 4). Berry Bluestone and Anna Hardman also underscored the structural barriers faced by poor women within the labor market, pointing out that the employment problems they confronted were

> by far the most complex and involve a myriad of psychological, cultural, social, and economic barriers. The average welfare mother has all of the following going against her when she attempts to enter the labor force: her sex, her race, her skill level, her education, the structure of the labor market, and the cultural conflict between the roles of mother and financial head of household. Together these factors pose a nearly insurmountable barrier to self-supporting employment.

They underlined the fact that "women who head households are caught in the cross fire between two competing models of their roles"—the maternal ethic and the work ethic. The maternal ethic states that "the mother's place is in the home." The work ethic states that she must earn the money to support her family (Women, Welfare, and Work, Social Welfare Regional Research Institute Region I, SWRRI Publication No. 9 [Institute of Human Sciences, Boston College, July 1972].

Originally, when the Social Security Act of 1935 had been enacted, such a choice had been incorporated in the public assistance legislation for the AFDC program. By the 1960s, however, this choice—to work or not to work outside the home—was rapidly losing its support among legislators and the public, with work requirements for poor mothers added on to the Social Security amendments. Alvin Schorr notes that in the early years, "if a mother desired to work and could find employment, she did. If she preferred to stay home, her right to do so was affirmed in accepting her for ADC."[27] The Handbook of Public Assistance in those days stated "that ADC should 'make it possible for a mother to choose between staying home to care for her children and taking a job away from home.'" The role of the agency, Schorr adds, was "to help the mother arrive at a decision that will best meet her own needs and those of her children. The emphasis was on "choice and particularly on free choice to stay home."[28]

As times changed and women's influx into the labor force in the 1960s and especially the 1970s soared, creating the largest "silent revolution" since the industrial revolution, economic dependency of mothers on public assistance came to be viewed by many political leaders and others as less and less acceptable. The choices for poor women "ended from opposing directions." The choice to stay home was "ruled out by fiat and the choice to work made meaningless by the budget process."[29] Some policy makers continued, however, to call for such options. Moynihan, writing about "the problem of dependency" among poor women in the early 1970s, endorsed as a partial solution the redefining of women's work in the home "as productive work to be included in the national economic accounts."[30] Among legislators, this issue was also gaining prominence in congressional debates, as policy makers confronted the contradiction of the accelerating influx of women into the labor force and the soaring AFDC rolls. Robert Lampman points out that by the late 1960s, "Congress was changing its expectation about work by women who head families" and trying to resolve their economic problem by creating "working incentives" within the welfare structure.[31] At the same time, little attention was given to the glaring realities of restricted employment and training opportunities, which forced women with few skills into low-paying and dead-end jobs and disregarded their need for child care.

NWRO's organizers and architects strongly supported the view that it was the economic system that was flawed, not the women dependent on welfare. While they agreed that these women should have a choice to work in the home or in the labor market, they underscored the fact that jobs were not available.[32] Wiley, for example, pointed out that, contrary to the rhetoric of policy makers (who contended that people had to be forced to work), the Work Incentive (WIN) programs designed to put AFDC women to work had "always been over-subscribed with people wanting to get into them."[33] He underscored the fact that over 150,000 welfare recipients had been trained, but only 27,000 had gotten jobs. Like Cloward and Piven, Wiley believed that employment as a solution to poverty among the unskilled, especially the welfare mothers, was totally unrealistic. AFDC women, they felt, "will not become economically mobile," regardless of their strong work motivations and desire for economic independence. "Economically immobile" groups, they said, included "the aged, the disabled, [and] female-headed families." While they asserted that some might "like to work," they also pointed out that "many would just like to be mothers." The problem, in their view, was not a simple matter of welfare or work. The central question was "how to provide a minimum condition of sustenance for them without governmental coercion, intimidation and degradation."[34] The solution, according to Wiley, was to have the federal government guarantee the basic "right to life" for every human being by providing an adequate income for all in need. [35]

NWRO's women leaders supported the goal of a guaranteed income, but they also emphasized that they wanted choices, as did nonpoor women, in terms of more training opportunities, jobs, and child care. Sanders, the second chair of NWRO, repeatedly asserted that poor women were willing to work and get off welfare, when there were jobs with adequate wages and decent child care. [36] If these were not available, then a guaranteed income through the welfare system might be a better alternative. "If you're going to slave for nine hours a day and get nothing but the same welfare check . . . you can sit home and take care of your family, instead of paying someone else to take care of them and get them the same nothing."[37]

Tillmon also stressed the idea that there had to be choices. She emphasized that women were already working, and what they wanted were choices as to when and where to employ their time and talents in the best interests of their children. For Tillmon and Sanders, and probably the majority of the women in the welfare rights movement, issues affecting their children received top priority on their agendas. [38] In Tillmon's view, women worked when they reared their children and maintained a home for their families. The political and economic solution to the problem of welfare was payment for this work that had never been classified as productive. The vast majority of AFDC women had been producers, as well as consumers, within the economy. Most of them, however, had been relegated to intermittent and dead-end jobs, with the additional responsibility of full-time child rearing.

Tillmon had "hoed and picked cotton," worked as a maid for $2 a day, worked as a laundry worker, and held other menial jobs that barely enabled her family to survive. [39] Sexism and racism had converged to restrict her options. Only as a last resort, when her health had failed, did she reluctantly apply for welfare and become dependent on public charity. After years of ironing shirts ten hours a day to support her family, personal health and family problems forced her to become another "statistic" in what many in the United States labeled the "welfare problem."[40] While she continued "working in the home, raising her [six] children," within the dominant society she was no longer classified as productive.* As such, she was stigmatized, labeled a charity case, because she had to rely on state aid rather than on her own or on her husband's income to support her children.

Tillmon commented bitterly on the difference in choices available to poor and nonpoor women.

> If you're a society lady from Scarsdale and you spend all your time sitting on your prosperity paring your nails, well, that's okay. Women aren't supposed to work. They're supposed to be married.
>   But if you don't have a man to pay for everything, particularly if you have kids, then everything changes. You've "failed" as a woman, because you've failed to attract and keep a man. There's something wrong with you.[41]

Tillmon increasingly underscored that poverty and welfare were women's issues, highlighting the plight of AFDC mothers.

Like others, Tillmon emphasized that most of the poor women on welfare were working "but at such pitifully low wages" that they could barely survive. She pointed out that a woman "earning the full minimum wage of $1.60 an hour" (in 1970) and raising three children was "still stuck in poverty." Poor women, she added, wanted to be "able to support [their] kids through honest labor," but there were few opportunities to do so. Given the alternative of low-paying, menial jobs or welfare, women should have the right to choose what was best for their families.[42] The solution to the welfare problem, she suggested, lay partly in the redefinition of what dominant society remunerated as "work." Long before Moynihan or government researchers made similar recommendations,† Tillmon had already advanced this proposal:

---

*Johnnie Tillmon pointed out that she has six children, not five, as quoted in this article. (Personal conversation with Tillmon, November 3, 1980.)

†The 1973 Department of Health, Education and Welfare came out with the following recommendations:

If I were President, I would solve this so-called welfare
crisis in a minute and go a long way toward liberating
every woman. I'd just issue a proclamation that women's
work is _real_ work. In other words, I'd start paying women
a living wage for doing the work we are already doing—
child raising and housekeeping. And the welfare crisis
would be over. Just like that. Housewives would be getting wages, too—a legally determined percentage of their
husband's salary—instead of having to ask for an account
for money they already earned. [43]

According to Tillmon and other women welfare rights leaders,
NWRO's goals and priorities had to emphasize these issues of central
concern to women in poverty. Increased welfare benefits through a
national guaranteed income, meaningful job training, and child care
for women had to be part of NWRO's blueprint for a better society.
"Instant" benefits, through protest and organization, were necessary,
but not enough.

From the earliest days of organizing in the Watts area, Tillmon
had tried to mesh her beliefs with practice. One of her goals was to
organize welfare mothers to get jobs and become self-sufficient. She
explained:

Our theme on the local level is to try to do things through
self-motivation, so when our mothers are motivated through-

In the discussion of welfare, our analysis indicates that our
welfare problems are predominantly definitional and fami-
lial. . . . With regard to the definitional problem, it is time
to give full recognition to the fact that keeping house and
raising children is work, and it is as difficult to do well
(and is as useful to the larger society) as paid jobs producing goods and services. Counting housewives in the labor
force would be a useful step in redefining a portion of our
welfare problems and constructing judicious alternatives.
[Work in America: A Report of a Special Task Force to
the Secretary of Health, Education and Welfare (Cambridge,
Mass.: MIT Press, 1973), p. xix)

The Comprehensive Employment and Training Act (CETA) of 1979 also
incorporated recognition and support for the "displaced homemaker."
Its definition of a displaced homemaker included, among other women,
those "receiving public assistance on account of dependent children in
the home."

out the organization, they are able to go into training and
come out and be able to go into jobs and be self-sustaining.
This is what the [welfare rights] organization is all about. [44]

Tillmon's group, the ANC Mothers, emphasized not only services but
also jobs and training for women.

In 1963, three years before the national mobilization of welfare
rights, Tillmon had surveyed the needs of poor women in her Watts
housing project to determine what they wanted: work or welfare.
Her findings revealed that all but one of the 600 women who responded
wanted jobs and training rather than welfare. [45] One wanted to be a
mortician. The group figured out that it would cost only $1,000 and
take two years of training: one year of schooling and one year of apprenticeship. Tillmon added that "we could see her in two or three
years being completely off the welfare rolls." They arranged with a
local mortician for the training and a guaranteed job at the end of the
period. All they lacked was $1,000 to retrain this woman. But, as
Tillmon reported, they "could not get that out of the welfare department." They would not go along with this job program initiated by
the welfare mothers. [46]

Ironically, ten years later, CETA, enacted by the U.S. Congress, provided a similar model for apprenticeship training to that
which Tillmon had envisioned and tried unsuccessfully to implement
in Watts before the riots of 1964. [47] Her findings confirmed that women
wanted to work outside the home to earn more income for their families, but there were no public revenues to get their job program off
the ground in 1963.

Tillmon and her group in California did not give up. A few
years later, they confronted the welfare authorities in their county
and told them they were tired of being on welfare and wanted jobs.
They had "1000 applications already filled out for jobs." They "didn't
care where the jobs came from; but if they couldn't come up with jobs,
then they should leave them alone and put some money in the
checks. "[48]

They also sought child care. "One of the first priorities" of the
organized welfare mothers in Tillmon's county in 1963 was to try to
get a child-care center in the Watts area. In 1974, after 11 years of
concerted efforts, the ANC Mothers opened the child-care center
named in her honor: the Johnnie Tillmon Child Care Development
Center. [49] To Tillmon and many other women welfare rights leaders,
the issue was not simply a question of welfare or work. In their
opinion, solutions to the problem of dependency included expanding
choices for poor women within the home and the labor market, redefining work, fighting for adequate wages and child care, and emphasizing the needs of children. [50]

In other parts of the country, other WRO leaders also called for similar goals: "free day nurseries, job training programs," and more day care centers so mothers can go out and work."[51] Over the years, these themes were increasingly emphasized by the NWRO women. Welfare rights women wanted job opportunities, not "workfare," as national social policy. For instance, Louise Brookins, a WRO leader in Pennsylvania, stated in 1974 that NWRO's focus should be "on fighting for a guaranteed income . . . jobs and job training, but not WIN" (the federal government program labeled "workfare" by the poor women). Another WRO leader in South Carolina added that "the guaranteed income is important" but that jobs were also needed.[52] One of the most successful groups in establishing jobs and training for poor women was the WRO in Nevada, founded and headed by Ruby Duncan. Operation Life, as it was called, was still in operation in 1980, partially funded and supported by CETA grants.[53] Clearly, adequate benefits and adequate jobs were both high on the poor women's agenda.

While elected leaders in WROs were cognizant of the obstacles faced by poor women in trying to find decent jobs and raise their children, they were unwilling to limit their choices and NWRO's goals to welfare for women and jobs for men. While supporting the need to reform the welfare system in order to guarantee an adequate income for those who chose to work in the home, many felt the NWRO should also fight for jobs, better educational opportunities, and child care for poor mothers. These feelings surfaced repeatedly in workshops and conferences, as the women clashed with organizers who gave priority to jobs for unemployed males in the AFDC-UP program, rather than for mothers in the AFDC category, and who tended to ignore the child-care issue. This clash became salient when welfare rights women began to demand paid jobs within their own movement. Volunteer positions for poor women as elected leaders and delegates in NWRO and paid staff positions for men became less and less acceptable.

For NWRO's organizers, employment did not seem to be a realistic solution for increasing the income of poor, female-headed families, who comprised the movement's base constituency. Wiley and others, as we have noted, categorized AFDC women, along with the aged and the disabled, as "economically immobile." Furthermore, many, including Wiley, supported the traditional roles for women in the home as child rearers and fathers in the labor force as breadwinners.[54] They endorsed the strategy of expanding NWRO's base constituency to include "low paid male workers" and strategies that called for wage supplements under the local home relief and general assistance programs.[55] While wage supplements for men in two-parent families were accepted as a legitimate goal of poor people, the women did not consider this a priority for them.

By 1971 NWRO was becoming increasingly identified by its elected leaders as a movement of poor women, even though in public speeches and written communications they still continued to describe it as an inclusive poor people's movement. By then the entrenched female leadership was questioning the direction chosen by the predominantly male staff and demanding that NWRO's scarce resources be devoted to their priorities. Coalitions with other groups of poor people were resisted, since the women felt that such inclusiveness would dilute the emphasis on women's and children's needs, as well as undermine their own hard-won power and influence within the national organization.

Over the years, changing political conditions inside and outside the movement gave rise to new demands by the women leaders. While in the early days the goals of jobs, child care, and training had rarely created a stir, gradually these issues emerged as new sources of tensions between the women and the organizers. This was evidenced in the new demands of poor women for paid jobs within NWRO, especially within the Washington, D. C., headquarters. Elected officers, who had served for years in a voluntary capacity, now questioned why they were not being offered paid administrative positions within their own movement. In the process of politization, the expectations of poor women had been raised for "new careers" as experts on welfare rights. Some saw employment within the movement organization (despite the limited number of jobs available) as a means of moving off welfare. In addition, staff jobs for them also meant more control by the poor women within the local and national organizations.

Organizers and staff members at first resisted such a structural shift, contending that NWRO had very limited resources to pay salaries, that many staff members in fact went unpaid for weeks when funds were unavailable, and that most field organizers were federally funded, hired through VISTA programs or "donated" by friendly social agencies and churches. NWRO's budget paid for only a few. Underlying these realities was also the general, but unstated, feeling that the poor women on welfare did not possess the educational level, skills, or sophistication needed to lead a national protest movement. [56] Some organizers seemed to feel that placing poor women in administrative positions within NWRO might well undermine, if not reverse, the desired results of the movement.

Pressures from NWRO's national convention and the NCC (the two large ruling bodies), however, led to the hiring of a few token women in 1969 for minor staff positions in the Washington headquarters. [57] Added demands in 1971 resulted in Tillmon being hired as Wiley's associate director, the only welfare mother to hold this top, paid staff position within the national organization. NWRO was now recognized as an almost exclusive movement of poor women, and the constituency's demands increasingly conflicted with that of the broader goals of middle-class organizers and staff, who still believed in and continued to implement the original plan for a "real" poor people's movement. As this conflict grew and NWRO women resisted the proposed strategy of expansion and inclusiveness, many organizers, including Wiley, quit.

Another source of tension emerged over the strategy of how to achieve NWRO's goal of a guaranteed income. One faction supported the strategy of lobbying in Washington, D. C. Another proposed continuing the protests at the local level and in the welfare departments, as originally proposed by Cloward and Piven. These strategy differences further polarized NWRO. The women in the national leadership favored lobbying as a top priority, with continuing attention to grass-roots organizing. The field organizers, on the other hand, saw the need to continue mobilizing at the local level in order to create and maintain a power base for the poor. In 1971 George Wiley attempted to revitalize grass-roots activity by organizing the unemployed and underemployed. He met with little success. Declining support from all sectors for welfare rights and the strong opposition by women leaders finally led to the abandonment of this strategy.

Whether to focus NWRO's limited resources on the "streets" or in the congressional "suites" became a new source of conflict. The basic question revolved around who was to decide. While recipient hegemony was the espoused principle within the movement, organizer control was deemed necessary by the staff to achieve the desired results. In the long run, the organizers argued, the poor would benefit. This was a necessary compromise between principle and practice. Consequently, for the first five years, from 1966 to 1971, the office and field staff wielded significant influence in determining when and how to focus on a "guaranteed income."

Some observers criticized the staff for being deliberately vague as to its long-range goals and for its choices of strategies that seemed to be directed at enhancing the organization rather than furthering the cause of income redistribution. [58] Generally, organizers designed strategies that provided "instant" benefits for poor people. First, they concentrated on special grants from the welfare departments. Then, as these were eliminated by the state authorities, they shifted to credit rights, consumer rights, utility rights, and rental "strikes." According to Whitaker, the broader issues of work definitions, minimum wages, and regressive taxes were "virtually left untouched."[59]

By 1971 some of the women welfare rights leaders at the local and national levels began to criticize such strategies and priorities. In a report from the Virginia WRO to the NCC, disagreement with the national staff's lack of a specific plan for bringing about "a guaranteed income" was expressed. [60] NWRO was accused of reacting, rather than acting, as a vanguard in proposing new ways to change the welfare system. Organizers and staff were criticized for developing "media-staging" tactics that brought about only temporary and "instant" bene-fits to a few, instead of forging long-range guidelines for social policy in order to guarantee economic security for poor people. Counter-offensives by the political establishment, in response to welfare rights agitation, had increased the penalties imposed on the poor and exacer-bated public hostility toward AFDC women and their families. Some local and state leaders felt that, unless NWRO developed and pressed for some basic national policy changes in the welfare system, most of the poor would continue to suffer.

Earlier successes in the "streets" and in the courts (see Chapter 6) had raised the hopes and expectations of NWRO's members and leaders that their nationally recognized movement of poor people had the power to influence policy at the federal and state levels. Despite its meager resources (members, funds, and supporters), past actions and victories seemed to justify such optimism. Given this view in the early 1970s, the women in NWRO began to make more demands on the staff.

In part, this confusion and the mismatch of goals and strategies were rooted in NWRO's heterogeneous structure and its policy (but not practice) of "recipient hegemony."[61] As we have seen, for the AFDC mother, single parenting and survival of her children were paramount realities in everyday living. Not only more income but also child care, food, clothing, jobs, and training were among these moth-ers' major needs. For the predominantly white, middle-class, male organizers, on the other hand, these women's issues were defined simply as the common problems of poor people in general. They were not identified specifically as poor women's problems. As the women gained more control, they began to insist on their priorities and to de-velop different strategies for achieving them. At first muted, the tensions between the women leaders and the male organizers gradually became more visible. A "women's agenda" for child care, adequate jobs, training, and education, originally part of Tillmon's welfare rights program in 1963, gained attention only in the later years.

Much sharper than the differences in goals were those in the or-ganizing strategies developed by local welfare rights women and the outside organizers. Two basic contrasting models emerged, one de-signed by women on welfare within their own communities and the other by the field staff working with NWRO. The latter came to be known as the "Boston model"; the former, the "Johnnie Tillmon model." Both had similar objectives, namely, empowering the poor to gain greater benefits from the bureaucratic institutions that dominated their lives, especially the welfare departments. Both also emphasized the need to build organizational bases in order for poor people to achieve greater power and control over their own lives. Both believed that changes in the system were needed but varied in their approaches as to how these should be achieved. The two models developed strategies and incentives to attract members by trying to help the poor resolve some of their multiple grievances. They also, to different degrees, sought outside support. Most important, perhaps, both built WROs throughout the country that became linked to the national movement.

There were, however, some very basic differences in these two organizing models. The most salient ones were those in their structures and, more specifically, in their hierarchies of power and authority. The Boston model, the "dependent" model, was created, organized, and run by outsiders—middle-class organizers and staff (mostly white males). The Tillmon model was defined as an independent model, since it was developed by indigenous, local leaders with only minimal outside support from community individuals or agencies. It underscored the need for poor women's self-sufficiency and autonomy. Control, in theory and in practice, rested with its members and leaders, the poor women on welfare. Strategies for building the organizations of the two models also differed, as did the means for dealing with the systems they were trying to change. The Boston model, developed in the mid- to late 1960s, became the pattern adopted by most of NWRO's organizers. The Tillmon model, which had emerged as early as 1963, gained wider acceptance within the movement in the final years, as the women leaders gained greater control.

From the earliest days, tensions between the poor women and the outside organizers were evident but minimized by all. As the women became increasingly politicized, their demands for more power and control at the local and national levels became more open and vocal, leading to increasing conflicts between the two groups. By 1971 the Boston model had all but disappeared, since most of the organizers had withdrawn from NWRO. By the mid-1970s, the few surviving WRO groups appeared to be those patterned on the Tillmon model, reflecting a shift in political control within the movement, as well as the loss of organizers.

The Boston model, developed by Pastreich for the Massachusetts Welfare Rights Organization, was unofficially endorsed as the organizing plan for NWRO's field organizers throughout the country. [62] It was staffed by paid and volunteer organizers recruited and funded mostly through the Office of Economic Opportunity VISTA programs. NWRO, according to Bailis, paid the salaries of only a few of their national organizers. [63] The major objective was to create, as rapidly as possible, many WROs across the nation, with numbers of members and groups becoming the measure of the Boston model's success.

The basic strategy used for mobilizing welfare recipients was to identify the poor and their grievances in urban communities, invite them to meetings with the promise of helping them resolve their problems, and then enroll them as members of WRO, once they had paid their dues. Following a general strategy meeting on rights of welfare recipients, the assembled group was encouraged to confront collectively the welfare authorities to obtain their benefits under the law.

Organizing the poor, however, was no easy task. There were numerous obstacles to overcome in terms of not only attracting the women to the first meeting but also maintaining their membership and participation in the grass-roots organization. The ubiquitous stigmatization of welfare recipients by the dominant system was one barrier. Getting the women to identify themselves as recipients of public welfare was a major hurdle to overcome. The practice of labeling recipients as "deviants" and categorizing them as charity cases functioned effectively to keep the welfare poor hidden, isolated, and powerless. Few ventured out to seek public assistance, despite grave hardships. Few, when approached by the organizing teams, readily acknowledged their ties with the despised system of welfare. Not many willingly disclosed their dependent status to strangers and outsiders in a society that prized rugged individualism and achievement. The stigma of being on relief thus functioned as a major obstacle in the early mobilization attempts by NWRO's organizers.

Another barrier in organizing local groups was the fear of outsiders, as well as of authorities.[64] Women dependent on AFDC for survival of their families felt intimidated by the welfare caseworkers, supervisors, and administrators, given the power differential between the poor and the "gatekeepers" of the nonpoor. They feared the loss of their meager benefits and questioned the role of organizers, most of whom resembled the authorities in race and class. Many at first shunned proposed confrontations, afraid of the risk of such militant tactics.

To overcome these barriers, the organizers in NWRO developed the Boston model for mobilizing the poor.[65] This plan was designed to highlight the rewards of participation and reduce as much as possible the real and perceived risks involved. Three underlying principles formed the core of this strategy. First, there had to be immediate and tangible benefits for the participants. Second, there had to be "continuous personal contact" between the organizers and the women in order to overcome the fears and negative attitudes about being on welfare. Organizers made a point of teaching the welfare mothers "how the system really worked." They redefined the problem of poverty as being rooted in systemic, rather than individual, pathologies. It was the task of "WRO organizers and leaders, therefore . . . to convince the mothers through participation in WRO activities that the system was the 'enemy.'"[66] Third, minimum demands were made upon the membership. Bailis reports that "aside from paying the nominal NWRO dues of one dollar per year and any dues that the local group might have established, all the welfare rights organization asked of its membership was they demand benefits in an organized way."[67]

Members were mobilized by guaranteeing solutions to individual grievances and increased welfare benefits through collective action. Recipients attending the meetings were carefully instructed as to their rights and the procedures to be followed in order to obtain their legal benefits.

The meetings were planned and tightly controlled by the organizers to ensure the desired results. The rule was that all work together, using group pressure to resolve their common problems. As Piven and Cloward point out, this "heightened solidarity, helping to engender the feeling that the welfare of each depended upon the welfare of all."[68] The results of the collective, rather than individual, efforts were deemed effective because they minimized personal costs and risks and maximized rewards. Generally, everyone "won." Demands for special grants in the early years transferred millions of dollars to the poor.

At the meetings, the organizers reproduced and distributed the application forms for the special grants and provided technical assistance to all who became paid members of WRO. They assisted the mothers in filling out the bureaucratic forms, underscored their rights to such monies, and then moved them into collective confrontations with the welfare authorities. In general, the outcome was increased benefits for all members who participated. Consequently, in the beginning, the Boston model was assessed as successful by its architects, because it resulted in the rapid growth of WROs throughout the country.

While funds from the welfare departments lasted, mobilization of the welfare mothers continued. In the process, some of the women found additional incentives for continuing participation. Organizers underscored the special status and prestige of being a welfare rights member, part of a national movement, and the legitimacy of their cause. Leaders were identified, groomed, and supported. They moved from the obscurity and isolation of being welfare mothers into the political limelight, gaining visibility and new status as WRO officers.[69] Before their involvement in the welfare rights protest, most women had seen themselves as "deviants," reflecting the dominant values about welfare. Now, with rising politization and new consciousness, many began to identify themselves as nonconformists who visibly chose to protest the existing values and the welfare system. In their new roles, they enjoyed the perquisites of political leadership and the elimination of a stigmatized status.[70]

For organizers following the Boston model, the rewards were varied in the mid- and late 1960s. While the material incentives for individuals were small in terms of money, the organizing experience attracted many young, white, middle-class males and a few females. Some were searching for different careers, while also seeking ways to put into practice some of their ideals for a new society for the poor and black. There were new challenges, especially the opportunity to work in a predominantly black movement at a time when whites were being rejected by some civil rights groups. As Piven and Cloward point out, many activists in the mid-1960s were "in limbo" as separatism resulted in decreased participation by whites within the civil rights movement. [71] Thus, NWRO emerged as a challenging alternative, given its support for integration within its staff.

The payoffs for organizers were also measured in terms of members and WRO groups organized. In the early days, the Boston model for organizing the poor led to a rapid rise in NWRO's membership rolls and the number of WROs throughout the country. These successes helped to attract even more organizers into the movement. Maintaining the groups on an ongoing basis, however, proved to be a much more difficult task. What at first was defined as challenging and "fun" by the organizers eventually was seen by many as a tedious and almost impossible task.

Once grievances had been solved, few women found any incentives for continuing their affiliation or participation in the local WRO groups. Those that remained were generally the leaders, who received the unique rewards inherent in their special role. As has been pointed out, with rising recognition of their new status, the women leaders gradually came to demand more authority and greater attention to their personal needs and to insist that their organizations be supported, but not controlled, by the organizers. Bitter clashes were reported in some parts of the country. Eventually, such costs became too high for the organizers, and, by 1971, as conflicts grew, most withdrew from NWRO.

Several factors contributed to the loss of organizers. Not only conflicts within the movement but also changing external political conditions affected their withdrawal from NWRO. Some, as Wiley pointed out, just "burned out." [72] Others, such as Cloward and Piven —NWRO's staunchest allies since its birth—left because they opposed NWRO's emphasis on lobbying in Washington, D. C., rather than grass-roots organizing. Finally, many found new alternatives for activism in the anti-Vietnam War movement or in building other protest movement organizations. Wade Rathke, for example, left NWRO to organize the low-income and working-class group in Little Rock, Arkansas, at Wiley's suggestion. Arkansas Community Organizations for Reform Now, Rathke's new organization, expanded rapidly and by 1980 had become recognized by many as one of the most successful grass-roots movements of the working poor. [73]

With the decline in the number of organizers, NWRO's grass-roots membership also decreased. The erosion of its constituency base also indirectly affected the mobilization of middle-class, liberal support, as we shall discuss in Chapter 4.

NWRO was caught in the classic dilemma of having to choose where and how to allocate its limited resources. It had to build a following and at the same time confront its opponents.* The situation was further exacerbated by the fact that the protest was a national effort carried out at various levels. Competition for scarce resources between organizers and the women leaders heightened tensions both at the local and national levels.

The Johnnie Tillmon model contrasted sharply with the Boston model, underscoring some areas of conflict between the staff and the women leaders. First, unlike the organizers' model, which required dependence on outsiders, the Tillmon model emphasized independence and reliance on indigenous leadership among poor women. Its structure consisted exclusively of the welfare poor, mostly AFDC mothers. The nonpoor were relegated to supportive, but peripheral, roles. It was what Tillmon liked to describe as the "organizing of all women on welfare to try and do something for ourselves and by ourselves to the extent that we could."[74] Second, in the Tillmon model, the authority rested with the women members and leaders of the group. However small in number, they were the decision makers, generally with one woman as a dominant leader. Poor women in such groups held the power within their own organizations (even though many organizers pointed out the lack of democracy within them). Third, the major thrust was on services and not on political action. The local group attempted to attract members by responding to their multiple needs with whatever resources they could mobilize within their communities and among friends.[75] They also became advocates for each other when forced to confront the welfare bureaucracy.[76] Organizational maintenance, loyalty, and participation were emphasized. Those who were helped were expected to help others. Those who refused to cooperate in this informal exchange were dropped. Groups

---

*Joyce Gelb and Alice Sardell, in their analysis of NWRO, suggest that the movement organization failed in part because it tried to combine both "service" and "political" strategies. They posit that "urban groups must often choose to expend their energies on either providing services or engaging in political action. Welfare Rights . . . attempted to forge a link between the two" but was unsuccessful (Organizing the Poor: A Brief Analysis of the Politics of the Welfare Rights Movement," Policy Studies Journal 3 [Summer 1975]: 348).

were generally small, but the emphasis was not on numbers, but solidarity.

Developed in Watts in 1963 by Tillmon, the ANC Mothers Anonymous* symbolized such a model that was adopted and developed spontaneously in other parts of the country where there were few or no outside organizers.[77] Dependence on outsiders was minimized and, in fact, rejected, except under special conditions, as revealed in the first clash between Tillmon and Sampson. Service, rather than confrontations with the welfare department, comprised the large share of the groups' actions. The emphasis was on "women helping women" to meet immediate basic needs and to lessen the fear of the welfare authorities, who dominated the lives of the AFDC women. Welfare rights membership also provided them with a new status within a movement that highlighted the dignity of poor people.

In addition to the service strategy to help people cope with the daily crises in their lives, the Tillmon type of group attempted to develop ways to alter the dependent position of poor women. Tillmon's ANC Mothers, as we have seen, tried to find jobs and training for women, helped to establish a child-care center, and sought to develop internships with local professionals and agencies in the surrounding communities. Their efforts were directed toward making poor women with dependent children more self-sufficient through employment in new careers.

To achieve long-rance changes in the welfare system, the Tillmon model called for alliances with Legal Services. The major strategy of "two against one" was to file class-action suits. Confrontations with welfare authorities and street protests were minimized as the years went by. More traditional political and legal strategies were espoused, such as voter registration, running for elected office, and the use of established political processes and the courts.[78]

Over the years, welfare rights organizing shifted from the organizers' model to the poor women's model (the Boston and Tillmon models, respectively), reflecting the declining role of the outsiders in the movement and the growing control of the women. Fewer organizers and rising demands for autonomy by the women leaders, both at the local and national levels, reinforced this trend.[79] By 1974 Sampson, one of the earliest NWRO organizers, commented on this change, noting that "the women were now doing their own thing."[80]

---

*The original group was called ANC Mothers Anonymous because in the early days fear of the repercussions from the welfare authorities forced the women to work "underground." Later, the "anonymous" was dropped.

Tillmon, in evaluating the survival rates of WRO groups through-out the country in 1974, concluded that the organizers' model had not helped to expand the base of the movement. She contended that inde-pendent groups, organized by indigenous leaders and not by outsiders, had fared better in the long run. In her opinion, there were several reasons for this. The Tillmon model had built-in incentives and re-wards for its members, besides just money and increased benefits from the welfare department. People joined, she said, for more than just "to get a buck." The thrust of the indigenous and independent local groups was toward social service, rather than political protest. There were multiple rewards and fewer risks. For the groups depen-dent on outsiders and special grants provided by the welfare depart-ment, the rewards of participation in the movement organization van-ished once these grants were gone.[81] Tillmon also suggested that the Boston model of organizing reinforced women's dependency on men and eroded the outsiders loyalty to the larger movement. She was critical of the organizers' apparent lack of commitment to the poor, stating that "they weren't concerned about welfare recipients . . . [but] only . . . about themselves." She added:

> In Massachusetts when the organizers left, the action
> left. You see, them folk weren't organized like the John-
> nie Tillmon model. They didn't organize themselves.
> Somebody organized it for them. You see, the welfare
> mothers depended on the Bill Pastreichs, on the Tom
> Glynns, on the Wade Rathkes, and all of those folks.
> And those folks weren't into nothing because they weren't
> concerned about welfare recipients. Sixty percent of those
> folks were only concerned about themselves. And when
> they got through doing their thing, they went on about their
> business.[82]

A variant of the Boston model, in which the organizers were fe-male (both white and black), seems to have encountered fewer con-flicts, according to the data collected by Kotz and Kotz.[83] For in-stance, the Brooklyn Welfare Rights Organization, organized by Rhoda Linton, a white woman, took deliberate steps to minimize organizer control and develop leadership among the poor women. Working with her were two black women, Andrea Kydd, a social worker, and Joyce Burson, a welfare mother. For women organizers, perhaps, given their socialization pattern, the supportive role seemed less costly and less frustrating than for the male organizers traditionally raised to assume dominant roles in society. Linton insisted that the poor women be allowed to make their own decisions and defined her job as giving "technical help." She pointed out that the group was "an organization of women run by women," unlike others that were dominated by men. She noted also that "a lot of men organizers in NWRO were very much macho and talked down to the 'ladies.'"[84] This added to the internal tensions within local WRO groups.

According to Tillmon, Wiley eventually came to endorse the Tillmon model of organizing poor people in preference to the Boston model. She recalled that upon returning from a visit to Texas in 1972, Wiley told her that in his travels throughout the country he had found several WRO groups that appeared to be functioning very well without outsider organizers. More specifically, Wiley told her that

> we've got something going in Texas. I have decided to leave it alone. There is something there. They have a "Johnnie Tillmon model" organization. . . . They do things on a day-to-day basis. They don't do a lot of demonstrations and hollering in the streets. . . . People don't depend on organizers to come and do things for them. The people who are hurting do it themselves.[85]

As Kotz and Kotz note, "Wiley was always very uncomfortable with the dominance of outside organizers."[86] He felt that "the tactics of the Boston-style organizers defied a fundamental Wiley-principle—that NWRO should be a grassroots organization run democratically by and for its recipients." Therefore, the Tillmon model, which he identified in 1972, received his endorsement because it adhered more closely to his vision of poor people controlling their own organizations.

Wiley, however, was not oblivious to the weaknesses in both models. In the Tillmon model, entrenched leaders sometimes became overly concerned with organizational maintenance and their perquisites and lost sight of the original goals of the group. This led to narrowed perspectives and resistance to expanding the base of the movement.[87] On the other hand, in the Boston model, organizer dominance became a constant source of tension and conflict within the movement. This ultimately led to the loss of organizers and members, and solidarity among the members of the movement eroded. Wiley, reviewing the problems encountered in organizing the welfare rights movement, recalled that

> as the effort became more difficult the glamor wore off, and it was harder to recruit and keep good organizers. New organizers just didn't hang in. A lot of them got discouraged and went into other things. The poverty program people copped out as welfare rights became less voguish. The organization was not able to respond to those changes.

It responded some and developed some new techniques, relying more on the women members themselves but not
enough. [88]

Internal conflicts, rooted in structural contradictions within
NWRO, along with decreasing support from the public and private sectors around poverty issues after 1969, gradually led to the withdrawal
of most organizers and the abandonment of the Boston model for organizing poor women. Dependency on outsiders came to be resented
by many leaders, as politization of welfare rights women increased
their demand for power and control within their own organizations.
Mobilization of poor women on welfare, as a means of creating a poor
people's movement, had become a two-edged sword. It had politicized
a group of isolated and oppressed women but at the same time had
raised their expectations into a growing demand for control of their
own organizations. They demanded the right to define their problems
and issues and to develop strategies that addressed their specific
needs as poor women with dependent children, rather than as poor
people in general. As a result, the men left and the women took control in the groups that survived, reinforcing the shift of WROs to the
Tillmon model in the early 1970s.

The structural contradictions, leading to differing strategies
and tactics, gradually widened the schism between the poor women and
the organizers. Alliances between these two groups disintegrated as
both parties found the ties too costly to maintain. Organizers left,
WROs folded, and NWRO's membership base withered. For a few
short years, however, the unique cooperative efforts between the
poor and nonpoor succeeded in building the foundation of a new national
protest movement, before internal conflicts surfaced to erode the collective effort.

RACE AND CLASS CONFLICTS

Support for the basic principle of racial integration remained
firmly established within NWRO but was slowly redefined as support
of interracialism. As NWRO sought to increase its political power
by establishing coalitions with different groups, a pluralistic perspective emerged. However, as an organization, NWRO remained largely
a black movement, with limited integration of whites and Hispanics.
Its staff in the office and in the field, on the other hand, at first integrated and dominated by whites, eventually became "blacker," reflecting the rising racial conflicts within NWRO and the tide of black separatism within the country in the 1960s.

In 1966 Stokely Carmichael, the black civil rights leader, had
sounded the call for "black power," criticizing the low and uneven

progress for blacks through strategies that espoused racial integration and nonviolence. Within NWRO, as early as 1968, similar signs
of racial tension were beginning to surface. Whitaker observed that
as the movement became "more truly inter-racial," internal conflicts
escalated. [89] Clashes occurred within the national headquarters between black and white staff/organizers over who was dominating the
movement organization. The formation of a "Black Caucus" reflected
the polarization in 1968. Whites "who questioned the propriety of a
Black Caucus were severely chastised by other white and Black organizers who accepted the philosophy of separation."[90] The differences,
however, were minimized at first by the leadership, with the hope
that they could be resolved without fracturing the movement.

Wiley, for example, downplayed the racial tensions within
NWRO but acknowledged that they existed. He admitted that "a militant black nationalism in the country is impinging on the Welfare
Rights movement," making it "difficult to operate." He pointed out
"rampant white racism in the country" had been "carried over by
some individuals into the organization—in their attitudes and the way
they operate," which added to the internal difficulties. Conflict, however, from Wiley's point of view, was rooted "in the conditions in society that breed more tensions and problems around racial issues."[91]

In the summer of 1969, the tensions between blacks and whites
within the national headquarters reached a crisis, "nearly destroying
the organization in the process."[92] As Kotz and Kotz note, for Wiley,
this was

> a grim reminder . . . of a similar struggle in CORE five
> years earlier. No issue more bitterly split civil rights
> and social activist groups in the late 1960's than matters
> of race, and NWRO was not exempt, despite Wiley's ef-
> forts to turn the focus of the movement away from tradi-
> tional civil rights concerns towards a coalition of multi-
> racial economic interests. [93]

The basic source of tension was the growing concern among some
black staff members that whites were coming to dominate the movement, which was predominantly black. They accused Wiley of showing "favoritism to white staff" and tried to oust him from leadership. [94]
Blacks within NWRO, some said, were relegated to the menial, or
at least, lower-ranking positions and excluded from the elite inner
circle of policy makers within the staff.

As we have seen in Chapter 2, the staff in the national headquarters for the first few years was integrated, but, as Wiley hired
more organizers, the ratio of whites to blacks tipped in favor of
whites. [95] The top administrative positions were held by whites, with

the exception of Wiley himself, who was executive director. In 1966 Sampson, a white organizer, had "come aboard as the 'Number Two person' in the operation." Two years later, the office and field staff had become "very heavily white . . . all Massachusetts people."[96] All the field organizers, with the exception of Hulbert James in New York City, were white. Even in New York City, the WRO—"Citywide," as it was called—was staffed almost totally by whites. In Washington, everyone else on the staff was white, except for the clerical support staff, which was black and female. Consequently, as one white staff member reported, "Any time you'd have a gathering of significant people around the country, it was two to one white, and increasingly, as the national office developed in 1969 and 1970, whites came to dom-inate it."[97] Given this racial and class structure, with its inherent maldistribution of power, the racial crisis blew up in 1969 at the National Staff Conference.[98]

At that time Sampson, the white associate director of NWRO, directly under Wiley in terms of power and authority, was "running the operation with a number of lieutenants under him who were all white: Bert DeLeeuw, Rhoda Linton, John Kaufmann and Tom Glynn." These were the "key movers" in the national organization at that time. One staff member recalled that "when Wiley would have a strategy session, that would be the list, plus John Lewis, who was black and in charge of the newsletter [NOW!]."[99]

Lewis, the black former leader of the Student National Coordi-nating Committee, ran the "back shop" with an all-black staff. The decision makers were white. In addition to the policy makers, there was the "legal team," a group of lawyers, which was also white. The legal team, however, was not "on the inside" and was generally ex-cluded from strategy meetings. According to one report, "When George [Wiley] would have key policy meetings at midnight to three in the morning to decide what to do next, the people that would attend . . . were all white except Wiley and Lewis. It was clearly a heavily white thing . . . in terms of who had the control."[100]

In the summer of 1969, James, the black organizer in New York City, was asked to move into the national offices as the field director. At the same time, Sampson had persuaded a white organizer and editor of the United Farmworker's newsletter to take over the position of editor of NOW!, the NWRO newsletter. Under him was an all-black staff working in production roles. The setting, as one staff member described it, was one in which the whole black staff was now faced with "a white outsider running the newsletter." He added that "there was a lot of tension around that, to put it mildly."[101] One incident fed another, fueling the rising racial antagonisms among the blacks within the staff. The crisis worsened when the black printer was fired. A Black Caucus was immediately formed within the national staff, although the black women leaders outlawed it and threatened to fire anyone who joined. These actions, however, did not stem the rising conflict.

Just before the first National Organizers' Conference in August 1969, with over 80 people from all over the country present for a weekend of training, a verbal and physical fight erupted in the "back shop." The tension spilled over into the conference with charges being made by blacks that there was "a conspiracy by whites in the [national] office to exclude blacks from running it." Wiley tried to intervene and made a "moving plea for unity."[102] Wiley appealed for cooperation, stating that "racial prejudices should have no place here as they should have no place in other elements of our country's life." He acknowledged the reality of the "black revolution" in which many were deeply involved but begged everyone to set aside differences in order to attain the goals of the movement.[103]

That same summer at the NWRO convention in Detroit, Lewis and his group of dissidents repeated their accusations. Members of the Black Caucus "claimed they were being manipulated by white people" and that professionals were "consistently making policy decisions that recipients themselves should have made."[104] The black protestors contended "that the only way to achieve recipient control would be to replace the top non-recipient leaders, including Wiley, with recipient leaders."[105] They insisted that only then could "the problems caused by white professional manipulators" be eliminated.

The outcome of this conflict was a redistribution of power within the national office. Although the national women leaders condemned this polarization, they did not oppose the structural changes that took place. The top posts were shifted to black men (not the welfare women) by order of the Executive Committee and Wiley. James replaced Sampson as the associate director with "Wiley's authority" to decide on the staff. He immediately fired everyone and almost immediately rehired all those who would stay. Sampson stepped down and shortly afterward resigned from the staff.[106] Blacks were assigned to all the top, paid leadership positions. Two black welfare mothers, Joyce Burson and Jackie Pope, were given minor posts on the staff.[107] Very soon after the shift in power, "the whites began to leave."[108]

Some of them moved into Wiley's "shadow staff"—an unofficial policy-making group, parallel to, but separate from, the NWRO staff. Predominantly white, it functioned at Wiley's beck and call. It was totally separate and isolated from the national office and its staff, which now was almost entirely black.[109] As one member of the "shadow staff" observed, the cost of participation on the reorganized NWRO staff was just too high. According to this individual, "In 1970-71 a 'disease' set in."[110] While this "shadow staff" member continued to work "for George [Wiley] continuously during that period," he never worked in the national offices anymore. He felt that this was "the only way of protecting myself from the terrible staff situation," adding that it was impossible to get any work done there and that "the only reward for good work was being shit on."[111] The immediate conflict subsided, but the schisms and antagonisms remained, eroding the fragile racial alliances within the headquarters. Power now rested in the hands of blacks within the national staff.

By 1970 the formal ruling bodies of NWRO, the NCC and the Executive Committee, and the national staff were dominated and controlled by blacks. One woman leader on the Executive Committee underscored the general feeling among the blacks at that time: "The whites . . . tried to run the show, so we expelled all of them by 1970."[112]

Similarly, at the local level, racial tensions were also on the rise by 1968. White organizers in New York City, for instance, clashed with black militants in the fight for "poverty leadership," with resultant reorientation and reorganization of many groups. Those that survived were "dominated by non-whites from within the community."[113] In Massachusetts, Bailis reports that the issue of race did not become a problem as long as the white organizers were able to "deliver material benefits."[114] Racial conflicts erupted, however, when political struggles within the Massachusetts Welfare Rights Organization emerged between two factions. When the incumbents were defeated, they "refused to accept the results" and "joined with other community groups, including the Black Panthers and others to attack the new leaders as 'lackeys' of the white middle class organizing staff."[115] Bailis adds that "this was the first time that the race of the staff members had ever played a significant role in the NWRO affairs."

While NWRO leaders and staff members continued to emphasize interracial cooperation and a continuing role for whites, the strategies adopted after 1969 increasingly projected a black image for the organization. First, the name of NWRO's newsletter, selected by the white organizers, was changed. Instead of the name NOW!, which recalled the civil rights slogan of "Freedom Now!" and the racially integrated movement, the new black staff members chose the more militant name of Welfare Fighter. [116] Observers reported that the newsletter became more black oriented with the change in editors. [117] Second, Wiley, while continuing to support interracial cooperation within the movement, increasingly emphasized his own black background. He grew an Afro hairstyle and "frequently wore a dashiki,"[118] and these practices were picked up and reported in the press. [119]

Other strategies by NWRO's majority black leadership also revealed the changing emphasis from white to black dominant orientation. For instance, the "live on a welfare budget" strategy, designed

by white organizers to attract white liberal support for NWRO, originally took place around the national Thanksgiving celebrations in order to highlight the inadequacy of the welfare food budgets and contrast
them to the sumptuous repasts of the more affluent groups in U.S.
society. Two years later, in 1971, this same strategy was repeated
by the black women leaders to mobilize public support, but the activity was planned to "coincide with the date of the last week of the life
of Dr. Martin Luther King," who had been assassinated in 1968. [120]

Not only the women leaders but also Wiley emphasized the black
structure and support of NWRO. In reporting the results of NWRO's
"Children's March for Survival" in 1972, he described it not only as
"the most massive demonstration of poor people in recent history"
but also emphasized that it was "the largest protest gathering of predominantly Blacks in many years." [121] NWRO's newsletter also reported that it was "the largest predominantly Black march since the
1963 March on Washington." [122] At this national rally, the major
speakers were prominent black leaders from a variety of fields: Ralph
Abernathy of the Southern Christian Leadership Conference (SCLC);
the black film star, Richard Roundtree; Congressman Ronald Dellums;
Jesse Jackson of "Operation Breadbasket" and People United to Save
Humanity (PUSH); and Coretta King, widow of Martin Luther King, Jr.
The following year, the NWRO "Spring Offensive," another strategy designed to attract public support, was scheduled by the women leaders
to take place around the anniversary of the death of Martin Luther
King, Jr. [123]

Other evidence of the increased black focus within NWRO, mirroring its black structure, was found in the increasing presence of
black speakers at its annual conferences and conventions. Originally,
the speakers included an almost equal representation of blacks and
whites, mostly middle class. Year by year, there were more black
keynote speakers and prominent guests in the program; and, in time,
not only the race but the class of the participants changed. Representatives of organizations of the "poor," rather than those from more
"middle-class" civil rights organizations, were the ones attending and
addressing the meetings of the welfare rights women in the later years.
At first there were speakers from the Urban League and the National
Association for the Advancement of Colored People. Later, they came
from the organizations representing the poor blacks, such as the
SCLC, the Household Workers, and the National Tenants Organization
(NTO). While the Executive Committee members invited black leaders from all groups to participate as keynote speakers at the NWRO
annual meetings in 1973 and 1974, most did not accept. [124] Many
black organizations and leaders did not seem willing to align themselves visibly with the welfare rights protest, especially as the political establishment became increasingly hostile to their demands.
There were notable exceptions, as we shall discuss in Chapter 5.

In the early years, blacks and whites had shared the podium at NWRO's first few national meetings. Dick Gregory (the black comedian), Wiley, and three whites (Sampson, Cloward, and Robert Theobald) played major roles in the first organizational meeting in Chicago in 1966. In 1969 white "peace" leaders, including Benjamin Spock, held top billing along with Whitney Young, the black director of the National Association of Social Workers and the National Urban League. A year later, at the NWRO Pittsburgh conference in 1970, the principal political attractions were the white and black national legislators, Senator Eugene McCarthy (a Democrat from Minnesota) and Congresswoman Shirley Chisholm (a Democrat from New York), respectively. Other speakers included Howard Spragg, the white top executive of the United Church Board of Homeland Ministries, and Lucius Walker, the black director of the Interreligious Foundation for Community Organization (IFCO), an arm of the National Council of Churches. In 1971 NWRO's Rhode Island convention highlighted the theme of "coalitions" and attracted speakers from various minority-power groups, including Native Americans, Hispanics, and the elderly, among others. The principal speakers were blacks and whites: Congressman Dellums, a black Democrat from California; Congresswoman Bella Abzug, a white Democrat from New York; and Senator George McGovern, a white Democrat from South Dakota. Coretta King addressed the participants as the keynote speaker at the concluding dinner. By 1972, at the annual NWRO conference in Miami Beach, speakers representing black protest organizations were clearly in the majority. The striking number of blacks on the program led some white WRO members to protest to the NWRO leadership that the conference had become "a black thing and was not interracially slanted," as they had expected. [125]

NWRO's choice of coalition partners in the political struggle also underscored its black image. Its principal and visible coalition allies in 1972 were organizations representing the black poor. For instance, the Poor People's Platform, developed for the Democratic National Convention that year, was the result of the coalition of three groups that were predominantly black, namely, NWRO, SCLC, and NTO. This political partnership emphasized, intentionally or not, the public identity of NWRO as a black movement, even as it continued to promote (through its statements and literature) its support of all poor people, regardless of color.

By 1973 only a few individuals and organizations were willing to be identified publicly with NWRO. Various "big name" black performers were invited to participate in that annual convention, but all declined. [126] By then the movement had undergone considerable changes. Wiley had resigned. The membership base had withered. The major political fight to defeat President Nixon's welfare reform plan had ended. Public hostility toward welfare recipients and the poor in general was on the rise, as the U.S. economic situation worsened. Neither NWRO's structure nor the political climate provided the necessary conditions to attract allies. Few were willing to associate with the "deviant" protest movement for welfare rights led by poor black women.

Some black leaders did attend. The keynoters that year were Ralph Abernathy of SCLC, Jesse Jackson of PUSH, and George Wiley, now head of the new Movement for Economic Justice (MEJ). These three men represented protest organizations of the poor; the first two, of the poor and black.

At the last national NWRO conference held in 1974, Ralph Abernathy, NWRO's staunchest black supporter, was the major speaker. Most of the others participating as "prominent guests" were also black: Whiteman Mayo of NBC-TV's "Sanford and Son"; William Lucy, the black labor leader of the American Federation of State, County, and Municipal Employees; Edith Sloane of the National Committee for Household Employees; Brother Owusu Saduski of the African Liberation Support Committee; and Hulbert James of the National Council of Churches. There were also two white speakers: Bert DeLeeuw of MEJ and a representative of the Gray Panthers, the movement of the organized elderly. One white supporter at this conference observed paradoxically that "there were more white [WRO] groups there than ever before, but the rhetoric was 'black' from all the major speakers. It was not 'welfare' oriented; it was a 'black' conference." He added that in his opinion this was "very sad" because he felt that it was "a serious mistake on [NWRO's] part," since it appeared to be shrinking its potential base of support, instead of expanding it, as Wiley had been attempting to do in MEJ. [127]

While NWRO's black women leaders continued to maintain their support for the principle of racial inclusiveness within the welfare rights movement, they also revealed their deep commitment and allegiance to the black struggle. In their strategy choices at conferences and conventions and other activities, they projected a "black image" for NWRO, which Wiley in the early years had tried to underplay. For instance, in the final months of the movement, the "Half-a-Chance Campaign," designed to attract "seed money" from white liberals as well as contributions from the poor, was held at the Museum of African Art in Washington. Once again, the public image was that of a black organization, rather than a poor people's movement. This "black image" had serious consequences for NWRO in terms of mobilizing white liberal support, as we shall see in the following chapter.

In summary, over the years internal race and class conflicts appear to have led to the withdrawal of middle-class, white organizers and staff at the national and local levels of the movement. As power within its national headquarters shifted to blacks, NWRO strategies also became increasingly black oriented, although its rhetoric continued to support racial inclusiveness. With decreased numbers of organizers, its grass-roots membership also declined. Its black structure and salient black image seem to have been added factors inhibiting white recipient participation. The rising racial exclusiveness of NWRO and the attrition of its political base among the poor lessened the interest of its white liberal supporters and thus affected the alliances between the poor and nonpoor. Consequently, internal racial and class conflicts appear to have contributed directly and indirectly to the erosion of NWRO's mobilized resources.

CLASS AND GENDER CONFLICTS

While racial tensions eased at the national level with the withdrawal of most of the whites, conflict on the basis of class and gender worsened over the years. More specifically, the tension between Wiley, NWRO's middle-class, male executive director, and the poor black women on the Executive Committee increased as women demanded more control and proposed strategies clashed. For several years, men continued to hold most of the paid staff positions in the poor women's movement. These class and gender contradictions seem to have aggravated the cooperative relationship between the formal and informal leaders within the national office. By the early 1970s, there were signs of growing unrest in the Washington, D.C., headquarters over the lack of power of the women within their own organization. Wiley, at the same time, was growing restless with the slow pace of political change and increasingly concerned with the hostile climate toward the poor and the black in the country. Consequently, he was seeking new strategies to respond to the changing political times. He was also becoming worried about the rigidity of the entrenched female leadership, who, having attained symbolic (if not real) power and status within the movement, were now reluctant to adopt new strategies that might undermine their present positions. As a result of rising political consciousness and demands of the women, tensions increased between Wiley and the elected leaders when he began insisting that NWRO make some radical changes in its structure and strategies in order to survive.

Although Wiley and other organizers had repeatedly endorsed and supported leadership and control by the members of NWRO, it was a recognized fact that Wiley had always been the "captain of the ship." He developed and proposed strategies to the Executive Committee and the NCC. As a former college professor and a middle-class black man, he contrasted sharply with the poor women in NWRO. As a civil rights activist, however, he had proved his deep commitment to the plight of the poor and black. [128] Originally, his goal of a national organization of poor people fighting for a guaranteed adequate income had meshed with those of the welfare rights leaders. Together they had cooperated and succeeded in creating the first national protest of welfare mothers. Wiley's commitment to welfare rights and the women's need for higher welfare benefits for their families (as well as the desire for leadership and recognition in their struggle) had converged in 1966.

Unlike many other black civil rights leaders, Wiley, despite his middle-class background, empathized with and responded to the plight of poor women on welfare. Wiley was critical of black civil rights leaders who had abandoned "their own people." One of his colleagues stated that "George Wiley always thought that the black leaders rapidly left behind their own people." According to this report, Wiley felt "that if you wanted to know what's happened to blacks in America you had to look at the welfare rolls. He knew that anyone who's black runs away from those issues." He felt he had to join the struggle in which were found "the poorest of the poor—the very worst off of the blacks blacks."[129]

Wiley was respected by the women leaders not only for his visible commitment to the poor but also for his outstanding ability to mobilize funds for their cause. He was NWRO's principal fund raiser, and they depended almost entirely on him and his staff to provide the monies to carry out their programs. They were well aware of their dependence on Wiley and of the valuable resources he was able to contribute to the movement. In Wiley they had a committed and talented executive director who had access to white liberal support and entry into the dominant society, which were unavailable to the women in poverty. One member on NWRO's staff noted that "most of the money that got raised got raised for Wiley, not [for] NWRO."[130] He added that whatever issue Wiley might have decided to champion, he would have been able to mobilize liberal support.

Wiley was also respected by the women for his expertise in negotiating and bargaining with legislators in Congress and administrators in the Department of Health, Education and Welfare (HEW). He was also an attraction for the media, which in the early years gave him and the movement exposure and political visibility. These attributes made him a recognized leader by the women. As Kotz and Kotz report:

> At the beginning things worked smoothly. The women saw Wiley as their helpful teacher and guide. They treated him like a son, protecting him, buying him clothes and sending him home to his family when they thought he was neglecting that responsibility. [131]

As Tillmon described it, it was a mutually satisfying "partnership."[132] He worked with them, shared with them his organizing and speaking skills, and helped many of them to become "articulate and impassioned speakers for the movement."

Despite Wiley's recognized power within NWRO, he and others, including the women leaders, insisted on projecting the public image of a movement run and controlled by the poor members. Wiley, for instance, was "fond of saying that they [the poor women] are his boss in the struggle."[133] This meshed with the espoused principles of recipient hegemony and maximum feasible participation of the poor. The rhetoric of NWRO leaders emphasized the "reversed roles" within the movement and a structure in which the poor were dominant, thus shattering the prevailing stereotypes that the poor were unable to organize or to lead. In practice, however, the traditional power relations remained. George Wiley ruled NWRO. He not only organized the national movement, with outside support, but also mobilized the necessary funds to keep it in operation. He made the decisions on how the monies were to be spent.[134] Contrary to one report, the data indicate that recipient hegemony within NWRO was more a myth than a reality.[135]

Gradually, however, the women's acceptance of Wiley's informal power and authority began to change. They began challenging him and demanding more say in the decisions affecting the use of the available funds and other resources. As they acquired more skills, status, and some public recognition, the women became increasingly politicized. Their awareness of their limited and symbolic power within the organization expanded over the years, and with it came rising frustrations. From defining and supporting Wiley as a partner in the early years, they gradually came to view him as "a rival for power."[136] Kotz and Kotz note that "the women often came to meetings angry not only at the society but enraged at Wiley and the staff. They could curse him and scream at him, rake him over the coals."[137] This rising anger would soon peak and explode in a crisis with shattering consequences for the movement organization.

The rising tide of feminism in the 1960s and 1970s also fueled the fires of conflict between the women and men in NWRO. Although the ties between NWRO and the middle-class, white feminists had remained fragile at best (despite their similar origins in 1966), some linkages had begun to emerge in 1971. (See Chapter 5.) This rising feminist consciousness appears to have reinforced the demands by poor women for more power in running their own organization.

By the fall of 1972, the political fight in the U.S. Congress to eliminate the Family Assistance Plan (FAP)—the administration's proposed "welfare reform" plan—had been won. FAP was temporarily defeated. President Nixon, almost assured of a landslide victory in the November elections, vowed to rekindle the issue. From NWRO's perspective, this guaranteed four more years of "repressive" measures for poor people in the country. There was no alternative but to continue the struggle.

For Wiley, given these political realities, the only recourse was to build as quickly as possible a much broader and more inclusive movement. Other groups of poor people had to be mobilized, namely, the working poor, the unemployed, and the elderly. [138] More middle-class, liberal support had to be enlisted. Wiley's vision was that of creating a majoritarian coalition to increase the organized power of poor people. This had always been his dream from the earliest days. It was clear to him now that a movement of welfare mothers harnessed the power of only a small segment of the poverty population. It was burdened by the stigma of welfare, which inhibited the participation of other groups of poor people. Alone, NWRO lacked the political clout needed to bring about a guaranteed income or a comprehensive economic program of income redistribution. Consequently, NWRO had to be restructured and new strategies designed.

Wiley also felt that the labels of welfare and welfare rights were becoming too costly and had to be changed. In a hostile political climate, the visibility of this stigmatized group had to be lowered in order to attract other groups. The goals of jobs and full employment, which meshed with the sacred U.S. values of work and achievement, had to be emphasized. Welfare, which violated the norms of individualism and independence, had to be downplayed. In his view, these were the only politically feasible strategies in 1972, if NWRO's goals were to be achieved. Wiley sensed that the political mood of the country had changed and that welfare and welfare rights had now become losing issues. [139] He felt that, if NWRO revised its strategies and adapted to these realities, the movement would be strengthened and its power within the political arena (which had greatly dissipated) increased.

The women leaders, on the other hand, disagreed with Wiley. They found his proposal to radically restructure the movement organization too threatening. In their view, NWRO ran the risk of losing its political recognition as the representative of the poor if it expanded its membership to include various other groups. Individual leaders were also afraid that they would lose power and prestige in a broader and "integrated" coalition with others of higher status. Since welfare women were at the bottom of the status hierarchy, it was clear to them that any alliance with others might well place them in a subordinate and less powerful position. In addition, in such a broad coalition, many feared that attention to their unique problems as female heads of household would be diminished. Many were aware that an expanded movement among various other groups might well mean downward mobility for those in leadership positions.

NWRO had created for many of its leaders and members a new identity as citizens and political participants, thus increasing their feelings of solidarity and power. Welfare rights, as many repeatedly asserted, had lessened their sense of stigmatization, isolation, and powerlessness. These rewards of participation in NWRO would not easily be relinquished for the sake of a bigger cause. The movement organization, both at the local and national levels, had become a new and better way of life for many of the poor women. What had begun as the means to an end had now become an end in itself. For Wiley, on the other hand, the organization still remained a means, not an end.

By 1971 another area of conflict had emerged. Wiley began to reverse his prior position and suggested that NWRO use its limited resources to rebuild its grass-roots base, rather than maintain a large staff and headquarters in Washington. Many other organizers and supporters endorsed this renewed attention to the local level, including Cloward and Piven, who felt that was where the power could be mobilized to change the welfare system. The issue was one of changing the current priorities and reallocating more of NWRO's resources to grass-roots organizing, rather than to lobbying in Congress and HEW. NWRO's women leaders were not opposed in essence to the revitalization of the grass-roots base of the movement. In fact, they were aware of the need to rebuild their membership, which had been declining precipitously since 1969. Their concern, however, was that the national office and its budget would have to be cut drastically to support such a new strategy. That meant, in part, a reduction of staff jobs in Washington, D. C., and less money for meetings, conferences, and other organizational activities, which were among the perquisites of leadership.

Ironically, just about this time, several recipient leaders had begun questioning Wiley's existing policy of hiring outsiders to work on his staff and were beginning to pressure him for paid jobs for the poor women instead. (Three had been hired since 1969.) There was growing unrest and disaffection among these women, as they became aware that while the women remained dependent on welfare and won the "elected" positions, nonrecipients were getting the paid jobs and the policy-making control within NWRO. Many resented the fact that, in general, the men were put on the "Management Team" and the women in the "Operating Departments" within the Washington, D. C., headquarters.* Given these rising expectations for employment within NWRO, they rejected the idea of dismantling the national office.

---

*In the fall of 1972, Wiley issued new staff assignments. On the "Management Team" were George Wiley, fund raiser and executive director; Johnnie Tillmon, associate director; Jim Evans, executive

Finally, the issue of drastically revamping NWRO's budget and staff became another source of increasing tension between Wiley and the women. NWRO had always been plagued by lack of monies, despite Wiley's indefatigable efforts at fund raising. As fast as the money came in, it was spent, with deficits running into the thousands each year. By 1970 two major sources of support for NWRO had vanished, while expenditures continued to rise. The contract between NWRO and the Department of Labor had been terminated, and the IFCO/National Council of Churches' contributions had been halted.[140] In the light of this financial crisis, Wiley issued a call for a program of austerity within the national office and a freeze on hiring.[141]

For the national women officers, this strategy of retrenchment signified the demise of the National Welfare Rights movement and individual losses of power, status, and other perquisites of leadership. Therefore, they now refused to go along with Wiley's policy decisions. They were no longer willing to have Wiley set policy and run NWRO. In this conflict, they had some allies. One of them was Faith Evans.

Since the racial upheaval in August 1969, the issue of recipient control had remained simmering and unresolved within the national office. In 1971 Evans, a black man who had lived in poverty and on welfare as an AFDC father, joined the Executive Committee.[142] Since becoming an NWRO organizer in New York State, he had been a strong advocate of female recipient control.[143] Coming from a poverty background, he contrasted sharply with Wiley. Evans, left with four small children to raise after his wife had walked out on him, turned to welfare for support and training. Despite months of training in industry, no jobs were open to him as a machine tool operator. Consequently, he accepted a position as organizer in a Community Action Program agency, where he first learned about the welfare rights movement. Although he had never organized before, within a short period, he had formed over 50 new WRO groups. Eventually, this led to organizing demonstrations and his arrest for "interference with

director of Misseduc Foundation; and Jack Sorren, business manager. In other words, there were three males and one female recipient in the policy-making slots. In the "supportive Operating Departments," there were three females and one male: Audrey Colom, "special assistant in the areas of legislation, politics, coalitions"; Leslie Wolfe, research assistant; Joyce Burson, communications center; and Rudy Wilson, editor of the Welfare Fighter. The legal representative was John Kinney, who was technically on the staff but not involved in any policy or programs of the organization. (These data were provided by Wiley at a Welfare Priority Team meeting in New York City on September 29, 1972.)

the governmental administration and justice."[144] After spending six months in jail, he was released and immediately elected as a representative to the NCC.

Evans's personal experience in poverty and welfare, plus his organizing successes without any "professional" training, made him a firm believer in the latent potential abilities of the NWRO women. He was convinced that the women on welfare could and should run their own movement organization with some limited outside support. As a result of these convictions, he fought to make the women the de facto policy makers in NWRO. This led to a head-on collision with Wiley.

Although Wiley reportedly understood the women leaders' needs and was sympathetic to their aspirations, he disagreed with Evans on this issue. Wiley felt that the broader goal of economic justice for poor people had to supersede personal needs. In his opinion, a movement of women on welfare, run by women with few skills and training, could not achieve this goal without substantial support from outsiders. NWRO had been designed by its planners and supporters as a means to an end, not as an end in itself.

From the very beginning, the struggle had been to change the welfare system that dehumanized the poor and dominated their lives. One supporter and admirer asserted that Wiley's efforts within the movement had never been inconsistent. His "basic commitment was always to racial justice by way of economic justice." His move from civil rights to welfare rights was "entirely consistent." In 1966 welfare rights had "presented itself as a means toward this end." Wiley, he added, had a mission—economic justice. The welfare rights movement was simply "a specific limited application of his mission."[145] In 1972 Wiley felt that unless drastic changes were made, NWRO would become an obstacle, rather than a means, of achieving economic justice. He did not see how a limited movement of women on welfare could mobilize enough support to become an effective political force in the continuing struggle. For him, the principles remained the same, but the strategies had to be changed.

Given these contrasting needs, it was just a matter of time before the conflict between Wiley and the women leaders (supported by Evans) reached a crisis stage. Declining resources and a series of other events led to a final showdown in the fall of 1972.

In the spring of 1972, the women of the Executive Committee decided to organize a "Children's March for Survival" to help mobilize support to defeat Nixon's FAP, which they defined as "the greatest threat to the wellbeing of children in recent years."[146] According to Evans, it was the first time that the Executive Committee not only had come up with its own strategy but had also seen it implemented, despite resistance from the staff.[147] At the same time, Wiley and his "shadow staff" had designed a different strategy to mobilize support among the Democrats for NWRO's guaranteed income plan and the Poor People's Platform. NWRO had formed a coalition with SCLC and NTO and had outlined the platform, planning to get it adopted at the Democratic National Convention in Miami Beach in July 1972. Thousands of dollars were needed to implement both of these plans.[148] Both sides defended their strategies and set about implementing them. The result was that NWRO's budget deficit soared. By the end of the year, it had reached $150,000, and the payroll was behind four weeks.[149]

This economic crisis within the national headquarters finally brought the simmering conflict to a head. Wiley and Evans clashed openly. Frustrated and angered, Wiley confronted Evans and told him that if he did not change his tactics, they were going to end up having a fight because of their radically different view on who should run the organization. Evans recalled that Wiley said that he objected to his "telling the ladies that they should run this organization," adding that he, as executive director, ran NWRO.[150] According to Evans, Wiley emphasized that he did not want the women interfering with the "administration of this operation," contending that they "had their job to do" and he had his job to do.[151] Evans disagreed with Wiley and argued that the women "should know all the parts of the organization." He also stated that he opposed keeping the women uninformed about NWRO's finances and failing to provide the Executive Committee with any financial reports.[152] Evans asserted that "no one ever knew where the money came from and when George Wiley left, we were left in a vacuum."[153] Clashes continued not only over money matters but also regarding hiring practices, with the women criticizing Wiley's choice of nonrecipients for the staff.[154]

The final crisis erupted in late November 1972, shortly after the defeat of FAP in Congress in October and Nixon's landslide victory at the polls a few weeks later. The mood was one of tension and pessimism, according to one executive officer present.[155] At an Executive Committee meeting called to discuss the "future staff and operation of the national office," conflict surfaced over Wiley's unprecedented power within the movement.[156] According to Kotz and Kotz, "It started out as just another executive board meeting, with the members badgering Wiley with questions and criticisms, but the argument soon became an indictment: Wiley had usurped for himself the policy-making role of the board."[157] Arguments continued and "old disputes were rehashed."[158] Kotz and Kotz state that "the disputes played into a prearranged plan of a board faction which believed that the time had come for a woman and a former welfare recipient to lead NWRO."[159]

The conflict, according to a number of participants, was bitter and unreconcilable. The major issues narrowed down to who should be kept on the staff to run the organization and what direction the movement should take in the coming months. Wiley wanted to cut the staff to three: himself and two others. He also proposed moving in a new direction, which the women opposed. [160] Earlier, a motion to fire Wiley hit a deadlock when the chair refused to break the tie. [161] Wiley then confronted the women, emphasizing the fact that they were afraid to take over the leadership responsibility, regardless of how much they wanted the power. [162] Although "peace was temporarily restored . . . the unique partnership which had begun six years earlier and given birth to a new movement was fatally ruptured."[163] Wiley resigned. So did Evans. Tillmon assumed the post of executive director of NWRO.

Following this episode, Wiley submitted his formal resignation to the Executive Committee on December 15, 1972, and sent a letter to members and friends announcing his decision. [164] He was leaving, he wrote, to organize a broader-based movement that would include many more poor people. He emphasized that women on welfare represented a political minority (only about 3 million adults) that did not have the power to effect change in the system working by itself. The population of poor people, on the other hand, numbered at least 50 million, according to the NWRO level of poverty and the Bureau of Labor Statistics's figures for low-income people. This political reality made it imperative to seek new ways of mobilizing the poor. Welfare rights, which unintentionally had become almost exclusively a movement of AFDC women, no longer seemed to provide a politically feasible means of bringing about income redistribution in the United States. These facts, he felt, had to be faced and incorporated into any future plans. He added that strategic differences between him and the elected leaders had led him to resign, but he would continue to support and aid their cause.

Evans, in announcing his resignation to the membership and supporters, maintained that he had "been responsible for some of the conflict" because he had urged the women "to get rid of George Wiley and . . . run the organization themselves."[165] He stated that he believed that such a change would lead to "a much better recipient movement." He acknowledged that while he had succeeded in convincing the women to dismiss Wiley, he had "failed to get across a plan for the future of the Organization."[166] He remained adamant, however, in his belief that the women should and could run their own organization. He added:

> I feel we have many recipients that could be hired to run
> the national operations, even though they have never run
> this type of operation before. The reason they haven't
> is because no one is giving them a chance. Time and time

again we have had the opportunity to place recipients into
positions, but we haven't. . . . If recipients aren't given
the chance to try by their own organizations, then who will
give it to them? All one has to do is take a look at our
local organizations around the country and ask how many
times we've given our people a chance at organizer's jobs
when we've gotten monies. [167]

He concluded by stating that he believed that "we have a responsibility
to recipients both at the national and local levels and that we at the
national level should lead the way." He noted that it had been a struggle to get Tillmon hired for the post of associate director. He felt it
was imperative that NWRO "survive, if people are to have better
lives."

Before Wiley resigned, he approached Evans and asked him "to
take over the organization."[168] Evans refused, stating that the Executive Committee had chosen Tillmon as its new executive director
and that he felt it had to be the committee's decision, not Wiley's.
He decried the fact that Wiley, like many other black leaders, had so
little faith in poor women running their own organizations. In most
cases, he noted, they were only given the illusion of power, while
others "ran the show."[169]

The gender roots of this conflict were clearly highlighted in a
press release issued by the new women leaders in January 1973, after
Wiley's resignation. While acknowledging his invaluable contributions
to NWRO, they announced publicly for the first time that NWRO was
and had always been a women's movement and should be run by women.
The press release stated:

NWRO feels that it is time to utilize the capabilities of
women who have been associated with the welfare movement. Approximately 98% of the organization's membership is comprised of women. The leadership has always
been predominantly women. NWRO views the major welfare problems as women's issues and itself as strictly a
women's organization. They are willing to cooperate
fully with men in activities but will maintain responsibility
for NWRO policies and programs. [170]

Publicly, efforts were made to present a united front and an
image of amicable separation. In April 1973, the NWRO leaders held
a testimonial dinner for Wiley, partially as a public reconciliation and
partially as a new fund-raising effort. When Wiley resigned, NWRO
had a debt of $150,000, which he tried to reduce before leaving. He
was only partially successful. As of January 1973, the figure still

stood at $100,000. By then, without Wiley at its stern, foundations and churches were no longer interested in funding NWRO. Many told Evans that they would have "to wait and see." No one in NWRO had been trained to replace Wiley as a fund raiser, and in 1973 few organizations were willing to undertake the risk of investing in a movement led by poor black women with a label of welfare rights. Furthermore, as one supporter observed, people were "tired of welfare."[171] There seemed to be few incentives for investing in such a movement. Its grass-roots base had withered, its charismatic leader was gone, and its constituency represented the least powerful group in society, black women on welfare.

From January 1973 to March 1975, NWRO struggled to survive on its own. While it made several attempts to project a new image of strength and political autonomy as a movement run _for_ and _by_ poor women, it also revealed, paradoxically, its continuing dependence on men. Evans, as Tillmon's associate director, remained an important decision maker within NWRO, working tirelessly to try to keep the movement alive. He approached churches and foundations, trying to secure the necessary monies to eliminate NWRO's debts. In two years, he succeeded in reducing it to $28,000. But there were no funds for continuing the operation. The staff that remained went unpaid. The Welfare Fighter, NWRO's newsletter, was no longer published. Repeated efforts by the leadership to rebuild its national and local base failed. In March 1975, NWRO was forced to file bankruptcy papers and close its Washington, D.C., headquarters. Its debt was finally liquidated by some friends' contributions. On paper, as a legal organization, NWRO continued to function, periodically surfacing as a plaintiff in Legal Services lawsuits. As a national protest movement, it ceased to exist.

From 1966 through 1975, the national movement organization was buffeted by major internal conflicts rooted in racial, class, and gender contradictions. In the process, the power within the national (and some local) organizations shifted from whites to blacks, from nonrecipient organizers to the poor, and from the men to the women leaders. Political victory for the black women on the Executive Committee, however, resulted in economic disaster for the movement. Political power without an independent economic base proved to be an "empty" victory. Mere political independence, without economic resources, resulted in short-lived and symbolic power for the poor women. Without monies and supporters, the movement of poor women eventually collapsed.

NWRO AND THE MOVEMENT FOR
ECONOMIC JUSTICE

One major consequence of the internal conflicts within NWRO and Wiley's resignation as its executive director was the birth of the MEJ in 1973. Planned and organized by Wiley, this spin-off from the welfare rights movement in some ways appears to have hastened NWRO's downfall by further eroding its support base. Wiley's new organization was designed to eliminate some of the "costs" involved in participating in NWRO for the poor and their supporters, while at the same time working for the broader goal of economic justice within the system. Given its apparent greater appeal in terms of its structure, strategies, and goals, MEJ soon gained sufficient funding and recognition from the working poor and middle-class liberals to become a new movement of poor people. As such, therefore, it emerged as a competitor of NWRO.

Wiley's new strategy called for the mobilization of the poor with incomes below the NWRO poverty level in 1973—$6,500 for a family of four—rather than just the welfare poor. To him, this group represented a target population of about 50 million people that had the potential of becoming a political force to bring about economic change in the nation. With state governors and the Nixon administration taking increasingly "repressive" actions against the poor (and especially the welfare poor), Wiley felt that new allies were needed "to forge an effective poor people's movement."[172] He also believed that another group of low-income people in the $5,000 to $15,000 income range (approximately 70 million), who were generally "very hostile to welfare recipients and adamantly opposed to NWRO's plan" for a guaranteed income, might be mobilized around other economic issues.[173] Instead of welfare, the issues would be "tax reform, national health insurance [and] housing."[174] The projected image of the new movement was to be "an organization of taxpayers," with the emphasis on the needs of working people and other poor people, rather than on welfare benefits for poor women and their dependent children.[175] Eventually, Wiley hoped to link these newly organized groups around "a common economic agenda."[176]

Outsiders—the nonpoor—in the overall plan for MEJ were to be mobilized as supporters in a separate, but parallel, group. A Citizen's Lobby for Economic Justice was to include people "who might not benefit economically from a redistribution of income" but who perceived ideological and social rewards in living "in a more just society —one free from poverty and deprivation." The role of the middle-class allies was to include both supportive and active political actions. Like the Friends of NWRO, the Citizen's Lobby for Economic Justice was designed primarily to provide "financial support at the national and local levels for poor people's issues and organizations."[177] Wiley's new plan was expected to maximize the resources of the movement by including both the poor and nonpoor, while at the same time delimiting the role and potential dominance of the latter.

As a new movement organization of poor people, the MEJ appears to have had more political appeal within the liberal sector than had NWRO. Its emphasis on values, goals, and strategies that were consonant with the basic U.S. principle of income through work and achievement decreased the costs of participation for potential members and supporters at a time of increasing hostility toward the dependent poor. In 1973 social-welfare expenditures for the poor were being slashed, and work, not welfare, for poor women was being emphasized by the political establishment, as the unemployment rates escalated and the country edged closer to the worst recession since the Great Depression in the 1930s. In the 1970s welfare and poverty were no longer viable issues around which to mobilize support.

Thus, MEJ was in several ways a potentially more attractive political ally for prospective liberal allies because of its proposed structure and strategies. First, it was to be organized and directed by Wiley, a respected and recognized leader among white liberals. Second, it planned to mobilize a broader class of poor people, which would include the working poor. While its blueprint endorsed racial inclusiveness, its mobilizing strategies called for organizing groups from all races. This was to be accomplished in part by concentrating not only on blacks in the urban areas but also on whites and Hispanics in various areas of the country. Third, unlike NWRO, MEJ guaranteed equal status for all who joined. Although there was a separate category for those in the Citizen's Lobby for Economic Justice, MEJ eliminated the dichotomy between voting and nonvoting members, which had separated the poor from the nonpoor participants in the welfare rights movement. The rule now was, "Once you pay, you're all equal."[178] Finally, MEJ was a potentially attractive movement among liberals because it emphasized in its name and goals the less controversial issue of economic justice and obscured the visibility of welfare in organizing the poor. The political costs of alliances with MEJ thus seemed to have been lessened for potential members and supporters. Consequently, MEJ gained various resources, while NWRO lost support in terms of members, organizers, money, and political recognition within the social movement sector.[179]

Given NWRO's precarious financial state in January 1973, the loss of any funding sources became critical for its survival as an ongoing national movement organization. Wiley, upon resigning from NWRO, had stated that "welfare rights would be central to the movement [MEJ]"[180] and pledged that he would "remain committed to working to build an even stronger NWRO."[181] To minimize competition between the two movement organizations of poor people, Wiley allegedly reached an informal agreement with NWRO leaders on "dividing" the potential funding sources between the two. The unwritten rules were that "NWRO would take the churches and MEJ would take the foundations."[182] Despite these early efforts to ensure cooperation, the competitive relationship between the two organizations became evident, as contributors shifted their support from NWRO to MEJ.

According to Evans, "90 percent of the funds to run NWRO basically came from either national church groups or mainly foundations. . . . 80 percent of those funds went out the door when George Wiley went onto the Movement of Economic Justice."[183] The last foundation grant received by NWRO was $50,000 in 1972 from the Field Foundation.[184]

In contrast to NWRO's economic skid in 1973-74, MEJ's financial situation gained in strength. Foundations and churches were MEJ's principal supporters. According to DeLeeuw (who assumed MEJ's leadership after Wiley's accidental death in August 1973), by the middle of 1974 MEJ "had raised about $220,000."[185]* MEJ's annual report in 1974 listed donations from the National Council of Churches amounting to $38,396 during the past year. Funds received by MEJ through the Misseduc Foundation reached $101,366.[186] In addition, $37,500 came from the New World Foundation, $67,000 from the Field Foundation, and $5,242 from individual contributions. These donations, according to the same report, were "used for grants to the Poverty Rights Action Center," which originally had been the vehicle for organizing NWRO. Previously, these same foundations and churches had supported NWRO, but in 1974 their funds were no longer available for the welfare rights movement. MEJ also received a substantial contribution from the Campaign for Human Development of the Catholic Church, whose support NWRO had never succeeded in attracting. Protestant agencies were also shifting their funds to the new movement, as continuing participation in the welfare rights movement was assessed as being too costly.[187]

It seems clear that while NWRO was struggling to find funds during 1973-74, MEJ was able to mobilize substantial monies for its operation from sources that had withdrawn support from NWRO. As noted above, MEJ seems to have provided an alternative for churches and foundations that by the early 1970s was more attractive as an

----

*The sources were as follows: "$100,000 from the Catholics; 45,000 from the Field Foundation; 25,000 from the New World Foundation; 25,000 from some big contributors; plus 20,000 from members" (taped interview no. 213).

ally than NWRO. [188] As a coalition partner, MEJ's goals and strategies seemed less costly. The issue of economic justice was less threatening to liberals than the issue of welfare rights, given the political and economic climate. [189]

In its competition with MEJ, NWRO lost not only potential sources of funding but also political recognition as the representative of poor people. For example, in 1973, when a task force among mainline denominations had to make a choice, Wiley as the head of MEJ was selected over Tillmon in NWRO. Some questioned this decision, arguing that Tillmon, as head of the welfare rights movement, was still the representative of the movement of poor people. The decision, however, remained unchanged. [190] A few months later, when a coalition of liberal churches, civil rights groups, labor unions, and other minority groups organized a "Convocation of Conscience" in Washington, D.C., to protest the impoundment of funds and cutbacks in social welfare programs by the Nixon administration, NWRO was not invited to send a representative. [191] Speakers, representing other movement organizations of the poor, however, were asked to participate, including Wiley of MEJ. The explanation given was that welfare was not a major agenda item but was subsumed under the broader rubric of economic justice.

From the perspectives of the NWRO women leaders, MEJ had undermined NWRO. They criticized this "splintering" that they felt divided, rather than united, the groups within the same struggle. Beulah Sanders, early in 1973, commented on MEJ's lack of concern for welfare recipients and the welfare issue.

> George Wiley wants to reach workers with low income who don't want to identify with welfare. He wants to help them get a wage supplement. The Movement for Economic Justice is really like WRO, people who are working class, but who refuse to identify with welfare. . . . They won't come out publicly and admit it, but in fact they are on welfare and they can't be separated from welfare. Ninety percent are probably receiving some form of welfare: hospital workers, cartpushers in the garment districts, domestic workers. These are the people he's going to look for. I say to them, "Come and join NWRO." But they think it's a crime to be part of our group. We must change attitudes. [192]

From the very beginning, tensions between MEJ and NWRO were evident. Shortly after Wiley's death, MEJ leaders attempted to establish a formal relationship with NWRO, but no agreement could be reached. Ties were never established with the poor women's organization at the national level, [193] although DeLeeuw, Wiley's succes-

sor as MEJ's executive director, did address the 1974 NWRO conference in St. Louis, calling for greater cooperation between workers
and welfare recipients. [194] In the first few years of MEJ, its policy
makers deliberately avoided a welfare rights image. Welfare rights
organizing was rarely mentioned in its newsletter, Just Economics. [195]
In 1975, as NWRO struggled to survive, some of its leaders contacted
MEJ and asked permission to print its welfare rights news on one
page of MEJ's regular publication, since it had no more funds to issue the Welfare Fighter. The request was denied, with MEJ leaders
explaining that they "were reluctant to get into Welfare Rights" at
that time. [196] Welfare was seen as being too costly, since it might
inhibit the mobilizing of the working poor, the population that MEJ
had targeted for its base constituency.

While Wiley had asserted when he resigned that his new movement organization would continue to support and strengthen NWRO,
in practice, this did not materialize. The need to mobilize the working class, with its assumed social hostility toward welfare recipients,
resulted in limited ties between NWRO and MEJ and little support for
welfare rights by the latter. NWRO leaders criticized MEJ for not
being "grounded in welfare recipients," contending that "if George
Wiley had lived, [he] would have addressed himself to the issue of
welfare."[197] They added that, while Wiley "believed the issue and the
base had to be expanded to include people with incomes of $10,000 to
$15,000," they were "convinced that [he] felt that the heart of the
movement had to start with welfare recipients."[198]

Over the years, however, some cooperation between the two
organizations did emerge. Some local welfare rights groups, unable
to get help from the failing NWRO, turned to MEJ. MEJ responded
with assistance in leadership training and some organizing support,
which led some to link up with MEJ. [199] NWRO leaders and former
staff members, who had remained with the movement until its demise,
were highly critical of this development, asserting that the issues of
importance to poor women would not be given top priority in the expanded MEJ. [200]

In practice, DeLeeuw of MEJ became increasingly concerned
by 1977 "that the direction of massbased, majority strategy, citizen
action organizing [was] moving increasingly away from poor people
and their issues."[201] He noted that, while MEJ had been designed
"to bridge the gap between poor people and working and middle-income
people," since Wiley's death, no one had "replaced him as the chief
advocate of organizing poor people." There was, he added, "no poor
people's constituency organized to lobby its interests against the fiscal interests of the cities and states, the self-interests of municipal
unions, the we-know-betterisms of the liberals and all-out attacks of
conservatives." He urged that poor people be given a larger role in

the local grass-roots organizations and that greater attention be directed to organizing them. He concluded by stating that

> if our purpose in organizing is to rearrange the balance of power so that we can have an economic system that is more just, I think we must face up to the need to organize among those who suffer the most from inhumanity of that system. [202]

By 1977, as the "second round" of the welfare struggle (now under the Carter Democratic administration) gained momentum, MEJ began shifting its policy of limited involvement with welfare, urging its constituency and supporters to become involved in the continuing fight. MEJ then acted in support of these new goals by organizing conferences and mobilizing protests throughout the country against the proposed legislation. [203]

By the end of the 1970s, there were signs that "the veterans of George Wiley's National Welfare Rights Organization and the Movement for Economic Justice" were turning their attention "back toward the poor." Cloward and Piven, writing about this reversal, noted:

> In the years since [the 1960s], community organizers have remained with us, but the direction of their efforts has changed. In the early 1970s, they moved from focusing on organizing "the poor" to focusing on organizing a more stable, homeowning stratum of the working class. Now, in the late 1970s, the direction may be changing again. At least some organizers are beginning to turn back toward the poor —to the unemployed and underemployed, to people on the dole—with a new approach born of the political circumstances of the 1970s. [204]

A number of NWRO's former organizers, including DeLeeuw, Rathke, and Mark Splain, had "joined forces [in the] summer [of 1978] to begin the process of directly building a base of the unemployed, the underemployed and the unorganized service workers." [205] According to Cloward and Piven, there was "a growing secondary labor market" that included the long-term unemployed and the new or episodically unemployed, low-wage workers and CETA workers, and welfare recipients. [206] Most, they added, "were locked into a cycle of low-wage employment, unemployment, and welfare." For these groups in this secondary labor market, "there had been no end to the 1973-1974 recession," and, on the basis of actions of political leaders in the late 1970s, it seemed likely that "there never would be an end of the recession for them." [207]

In the spring of 1978, these former NWRO organizers, DeLeeuw, Rathke, and Splain, developed a new plan of action, called Jobs and

Justice, with the "aim to force major changes in national economic policy." They hoped to organize the "unorganized to engage in local direct action," and their target population included youth, CETA workers, AFDC recipients, and the unemployed. [208] Their goal was to get jobs for all groups through organization and protest throughout the country.

Thus, it seems that by 1980 concern for the welfare poor and the AFDC women had reemerged among a small core of former NWRO organizers and supporters. There was at least one basic difference now. In the 1960s, their emphasis had been directed to increasing welfare benefits for women. By the end of the 1970s, the new goal was "jobs for AFDC recipients through the WIN program," as well as jobs for several other economically subordinate groups. [209] Analysis had reconfirmed what many poor women had previously argued, namely, that AFDC women preferred decent jobs to welfare, given adequate opportunities and child care. Many in the home rearing children considered themselves "unemployed," given the reality of an economy that did not provide enough jobs or supports for those willing and wanting to work the labor market. [210]

In 1980 the struggle for adequate income continued, long after the collapse of NWRO as a national protest movement. The issues were similar, but the leadership, structure, and strategies had changed. The spin-off organizations had survived and appeared to be expanding, while the movement of poor women remained fragmented and, at best, becalmed. Former organizers of NWRO, who had coordinated the struggle for welfare rights in the 1960s and for economic justice in the 1970s, appeared to be narrowing their focus on jobs in the 1980s. Given the political tensions abroad, the landslide victory of Governor Ronald Reagan and other conservatives in November 1980 presidential elections, and a deteriorating economy, mobilization of the working and welfare poor remained a formidable task for middle-class organizers at the start of the new decade.

In summary, conflicts based on racial, class, and gender contradictions within the National Welfare Rights movement resulted in loss of organizers, members, leaders, and monies in the late 1960s and early 1970s, contributing to the demise of NWRO. Racial disputes between blacks and whites within the national staff led to the withdrawal of most of NWRO's white organizers. Conflicts between white, middle-class staff/organizers and the black women leaders at the local and national levels led to the revolt and the exodus of other NWRO organizers, as differences emerged over strategies of mobilization and confrontation. Finally, class and gender conflicts, reflected in the clash between Wiley and the national women leaders, hastened Wiley's resignation. The loss of this charismatic leader proved to be a fatal blow for NWRO, as liberal supporters withdrew their already diminishing contributions. Additionally, a new spin-off organization, developed by Wiley and some of his former staff and organizers from NWRO, emerged as a stronger competitor for scarce liberal funds and support. MEJ, in NWRO's final years, succeeded—where the poor women failed—in mobilizing the needed resources to build a national constituency in the 1970s. Consequently, MEJ appears to have further eroded both the support of the poor and nonpoor for the fragile and weakened movement of welfare rights. An increasingly hostile political climate, deteriorating economic conditions, along with the rise of other competing movements impinged on the welfare rights movement, exacerbating the internal conflicts and eroding its mobilized resources.

For a few years, however, NWRO succeeded in attracting and organizing liberal support among white main-line denominations at the national and local levels. These groups became known in NWRO as the Friends of Welfare Rights and played a role in the rise and fall of the movement, as we shall see in the following chapter.

NOTES

1. Nicholas Kotz and Mary Lynn Kotz, A Passion for Equality: George Wiley and the Movement (New York: W. W. Norton, 1977), p. 232.
2. Marion K. Sanders, The Professional Radical: Conversations with Saul Alinsky (New York: Harper & Row, 1970), p. 75.
3. Saul Alinsky, Rules for Radicals: A Pragmatic Primer for Realistic Radicals (New York: Vintage Books, 1971), p. 19.
4. Ibid., p. 51.
5. Ibid., pp. 52-53.
6. Lawrence Neil Bailis, Bread or Justice: Grassroots Organizing in the Welfare Rights Movement (Lexington, Mass.: D. C. Heath, 1974), p. 93.
7. Ibid., p. 94.
8. Ibid., p. 96.
9. Ibid., p. 98.
10. Kotz and Kotz, Passion for Equality, p. 232.
11. Alinsky, Rules for Radicals, p. 80.
12. Taped interview with Johnnie Tillmon, July 1974; Kotz and Kotz, Passion for Equality, p. 219.
13. Taped interview with Johnnie Tillmon, 1974.
14. Ibid.
15. Ibid.
16. William Howard Whitaker, "The Determinants of Social Movement Success: A Study of the National Welfare Rights Organization" (Ph.D. diss., Brandeis University, 1970), p. 208.

17. Bailis, Bread or Justice, p. 16.

18. Ibid.

19. Ibid.

20. Richard Rogin, "Now It's Welfare Lib," New York Times Magazine, September 27, 1970, p. 85.

21. Bailis, Bread or Justice, p. 80.

22. Ibid.

23. Whitaker, "Social Movement Success," p. 187.

24. Ibid., p. 162.

25. "NWRO Demands for the Poor People's Campaign," NOW!, August 21, 1968.

26. Ibid.

27. Alvin L. Schorr, Explorations in Social Policy (New York: Basic Books, 1968), pp. 27-31.

28. Ibid.

29. Ibid.

30. Daniel Patrick Moynihan, The Politics of a Guaranteed Income: The Nixon Administration and the Family Assistance Plan (New York: Random House, 1973), p. 17.

31. Robert J. Lampman, "Concepts of Equity in the Design of Schemes for Income Redistribution," in Equity, Income, and Policy: Comparative Studies in Three Worlds of Development, ed. Irving Louis Horowitz (New York: Praeger, 1977), p. 23.

32. Hobart A. Burch, "Conversations with George Wiley," Journal of Social Issues, November-December 1970, p. 10.

33. Ibid.

34. "Strategy of Crisis: A Dialogue," American Child 48 (Summer 1966): 22-23, 29.

35. Statement prepared for delivery at the Institute for Black Elected Officials, Washington, D. C., September 13, 1969.

36. "Beulah—from the Chair," Welfare Fighter, November 1971.

37. Vicki Morris, "The Woman from Welfare Rights," World Magazine, September 11, 1971, reprint.

38. Johnnie Tillmon, "Welfare Is a Women's Issue," in The First Ms. Reader, ed. Francine Klagsburn (New York: Warner Books, 1975), p. 58; Mary Quintana, "The Right to an Income?" (Speech by a WRO leader before the National Assembly for Social Policy and Development, Denver, Colorado, 1971), pp. 1-5.

39. Kotz and Kotz, Passion for Equality, p. 219.

40. Ibid.; taped interview with Johnnie Tillmon, July 1974.

41. Tillmon, "Welfare Is a Women's Issue," p. 54. See also U.S., Commission on Civil Rights, Women Still in Poverty (Washington, D.C.: Government Printing Office, 1979), p. 13.

42. Tillmon, "Welfare Is a Women's Issue," p. 58.

43. Ibid., p. 58. Nona Glazer, in a report to the Joint Economic Committee of the Congress of the United States, in September 1977, states:

> Doing housework, taking care of children, and carrying
> out assorted jobs for husbands are work just as much as
> leaving home each day for paid employment in an office
> or factory. To ignore this is to do a disservice to women
> in the labor force. These women, their children, and
> eventually all Americans suffer from the consequences:
> harried unhappy women; ill-cared for children; and angry,
> puzzled men. . . . We realize that it may sound strange
> to hear women's activities in the home called work. Since
> women who do housework and child care receive no salary
> or wages, homemaking is not considered "work." Econo-
> mists have finally helped us to recognize the importance
> of women's work in the family by estimating the monetary
> value of homemaking.

Glazer, however, cited several reasons for not accepting wages for housework as a solution for the problem of women's lack of income. Noting the isolation of the job, the reinforcement of occupational stereotyping, the lack of definition for "housework," and the possibility that the potential evaluators might be either husbands or federal agents, she emphasized that "wages for housework" overlooked the central fact that women work to increase the family income, and, where they are the only parent, their income is that of the breadwinner. She noted that "most women who head families are already in the labor force," most in the lowest-paying jobs. Nona Glazer et al., "The Homemaker, the Family, and Employment," American Women Workers in a Full Employment Economy (A compendium of papers submitted to the Subcommittee on Economic Growth and Stabilization of the Joint Economic Committee, 95th Cong., 1st sess., September 15, 1977), pp. 161-62.

44. "Insights of a Welfare Mother: A Conversation with Johnnie Tillmon," Journal of Social Issues, January-February 1971, p. 23.

45. Taped interview with Johnnie Tillmon, July 1974.

46. Ibid.

47. CETA was the first of the "special revenue-sharing programs" enacted by the Nixon administration in December 1973. There were job-training opportunities included, but discrimination against women kept female enrollees to a small percentage. See U.S., Commission on Civil Rights, Women in Poverty (Chicago: Allied Printing, 1974), pp. 30-33; and idem, Women Still in Poverty (Washington, D.C.: Government Printing Office, 1979).

48. "Insights of a Welfare Mother," p. 16.

49. Taped interview with Johnnie Tillmon, 1974.

50. Tillmon, "Welfare Is a Women's Issue," pp. 111-16.

51. "WROs see Governor," Morning News (Wilmington, Del.), March 6, 1968.

52. "Focus," Welfare Fighter, February 1974.

53. Field notes, June 24, 1979; and Guide to Welfare Reform (Washington, D.C.: Food Research and Action Center, 1979), p. 66.

54. Conversation with Wilma Scott Heide, April 8, 1978, re-counting Wiley's report to the NOW Executive Board on NWRO's "hidden agenda"—to reestablish the male as head of black families.

55. Richard A. Cloward and Frances Fox Piven, The Politics of Turmoil: Essays on Poverty, Race, and the Urban Crisis (New York: Pantheon, 1974), p. 72.

56. Kotz and Kotz, Passion for Equality, p. 282.

57. Ibid., p. 226.

58. Whitaker, "Social Movement Success," p. 261.

59. Ibid., p. 246.

60. Andrew Bowler, Debra Vaida, Tyrone Chapman, "A Strategy for a Guaranteed Income" (Paper presented to the National Coordinating Council by the Virginia WRO, Norfolk, February 4, 1971), pp. 1-10.

61. It should be noted here that some disagree with this analysis. See, for example, Whitaker, "Social Movement Success," p. 108.

62. Bailis, Bread or Justice, pp. 19-54. See also Frances Fox Piven and Richard A. Cloward, Poor People's Movements: Why They Succeed, How They Fail (New York: Pantheon Books, 1977), p. 308; and Kotz and Kotz, Passion for Equality, pp. 230-31.

63. Bailis, Bread or Justice, pp. 19-54.

64. Ibid., p. 20.

65. See Bailis, Bread or Justice, pp. 19-54; Piven and Cloward, Poor People's Movements, p. 308; and Kotz and Kotz, Passion for Equality, pp. 230-31.

66. Susan Hertz, "The Politics of the Welfare Mothers Movement: A Case Study," Signs 2 (Spring 1977): 605.

67. Bailis, Bread or Justice, p. 21.

68. Piven and Cloward, Poor People's Movements, p. 198.

69. See Hertz, "The Welfare Mothers Movement"; and Bailis, Bread or Justice.

70. See the excellent analysis and discussion of the differences between deviance and nonconformity and the role of visibility in Robert Merton's Social Theory and Social Structure (New York: Free Press, 1968), pp. 411-22.

71. Frances Fox Piven and Richard A. Cloward, Regulating the Poor: The Functions of Public Welfare (New York: Pantheon Books, 1971).

72. Burch, "Conversations with George Wiley," p. 25.

73. John Herbers, "Activist Groups Intensify Role in Presidential Race," New York Times, April 27, 1980. "A grass-roots political movement called ACORN is known by many people in Arkansas for its ability to inflict pain on public officials, utilities, banks and landlords in its efforts to help the poor. Since its founding here in the early 1970's, the racially mixed organization of low-income and moderate-income people has spread to 20 states, opened an office in Washington and become active in a number of large cities, including Philadelphia, Pittsburgh and Detroit."

74. Taped interview with Johnnie Tillmon, July 1974.

75. "Insights of a Welfare Mother," p. 15.

76. Field notes, July 14, 1974.

77. See also Hertz, "The Welfare Mothers Movement," for a discussion of different WRO organizing models in Minnesota.

78. Field notes, July 14, 1974.

79. Taped interview with Johnnie Tillmon, 1974.

80. Kotz and Kotz, Passion for Equality, p. 215. Several other writers on NWRO comment on the tensions between the poor women and the middle-class organizers: Bailis, Whitaker, Piven and Cloward, Hertz, and others.

81. Taped interview with Johnnie Tillmon, July 1974.

82. Ibid. See also Chapter 8 on the rise of local and regional spin-off, grass-roots organizations started by former NWRO organizers in other parts of the country, such as ACORN (Arkansas), Fair Share (Massachusetts), and CAL (California), among others. Nationally, the largest spin-off movement was MEJ, later changed to Jobs and Justice.

83. Kotz and Kotz, Passion for Equality, 234-35.

84. Ibid. Quotes by Burson and Kydd are also taken from this same source.

85. Taped interview with Johnnie Tillmon, July 1974.

86. Kotz and Kotz, Passion for Equality, p. 234.

87. Ibid,, p. 291.

88. Ibid.

89. Whitaker, "Social Movement Success," p. 202.

90. Ibid. See also Kotz and Kotz, Passion for Equality, pp. 282-83.

91. Burch, "Conversations with George Wiley," p. 5.

92. Kotz and Kotz, Passion for Equality, pp. 282-83.

93. Ibid.

94. Whitaker, "Social Movement Success," p. 202. See also Gilbert Y. Steiner, The State of Welfare (Washington, D.C.: Brookings Institution, 1971), pp. 291-93.

95. Taped interview no. 203.

96. Ibid.

97. Ibid.

98. Ibid. This same respondent emphasized, however, that within the Executive Board and the NCC, as well as within the national membership as a whole, there was an absence of racial tension. It is clear, however, that the absence of racial conflict within these ruling bodies of the NWRO was probably related to the fact that the blacks were overwhelmingly in control, as we have seen in Chapter 1.

99. Ibid.

100. Ibid.

101. Ibid.

102. Ibid.

103. Kotz and Kotz, Passion for Equality, p. 283.

104. Steiner, State of Welfare, pp. 291-92.

105. Ibid.

106. Sampson remained a loyal supporter of NWRO, contributing his organizational expertise for many years in a variety of ways. See WRISC in Chapter 5.

107. Kotz and Kotz, Passion for Equality, p. 283.

108. Taped interview no. 203.

109. Ibid.

110. Ibid.

111. Ibid.

112. Field notes, April 18, 1973.

113. Larry R. Jackson and William A. Johnson, Protest by the Poor: The Welfare Rights Movement in New York City (New York: Rand Corporation, 1973), p. 105.

114. Bailis, Bread or Justice, p. 81.

115. Ibid.., p. 15.

116. Steiner, State of Welfare, p. 286, notes that the NWRO newsletter NOW!—"a title with symbolic appeal both to those involved in the civil rights fight for 'freedom now' and those who had been supporting a guaranteed income now"—was "retitled The Welfare Fighter after an upheaval in the NWRO's publication section in 1969." NOW! was first published on October 31, 1966.

117. Taped interview no. 203; and analysis of most of the issues of Welfare Fighter, 1969-74.

118. Whitaker, "Social Movement Success," p. 201.

119. William Borders, "Welfare Militant on the Way Up, George Alvin Wiley," New York Times, May 27, 1969.

120. Letter to WRO leader and staff from Johnnie Tillmon, chairperson of NWRO, February 24, 1971.

121. Memo to WRO leaders, staff, and friends from George Wiley, executive director, about Children's March for Survival, April 12, 1972.

122. The March on Washington took place in August 1963 and was part of the civil rights movement. It attracted over 200,000 demonstrators to Washington, D.C.

123. Letter from Johnnie Tillmon, executive director of NWRO, to "Dear Friends," March 22, 1973 (mimeographed).

124. Field notes, May 15, 1973, and July 11, 1974.

125. Field notes, July 6, 1972.

126. Field notes, March 7, 1973.

127. Taped interview no. 203.

128. Kotz and Kotz, Passion for Equality.

129. Taped interview no. 203.

130. Ibid.

131. Kotz and Kotz, Passion for Equality, p. 281.

132. Ibid.

133. Borders, "Welfare Militant."

134. Personal taped interview no. 151, September 1974; field notes, June 6, 1972; field notes, November 2, 1972; interview with Bertha Cavanaugh, Rhode Island WRO chairperson and member of the Executive Committee, September 12, 1972; field notes, April 17, 1973; and letter from Faith Evans to the Executive Board and NCC, November 21, 1973.

135. Whitaker, "Social Movement Success," p. 203. Whitaker was a white, middle-class, male organizer who wrote about NWRO from 1966 through 1969. He states that "in keeping with the NWRO emphasis on recipient hegemony, auxiliary support personnel [the staff] have no formal avenue for their participation in movement policy-making" (emphasis added). He goes on to add that "within the framework of recipient [black female] hegemony the NWRO objective of democracy turns out to mean the limitation of participation in decision-making to those only whose immediate self-interests most narrowly defined are involved."

136. Kotz and Kotz, Passion for Equality, p. 281.

137. Ibid., p. 282.

138. Richard Cloward, taped radio show, "Always on Sunday," New York City, August 11, 1973.

139. Ronald Smothers, "Welfare Activist Plans New Group," New York Times, December 17, 1972.

140. Kotz and Kotz, Passion for Equality, p. 291.

141. Welfare Priority Team minutes, April 22, 1971.

142. Fathers in some states were eligible under AFDC-U. Mothers were not. In 1977 the Women's Bureau of the U.S. Department of Labor planned several conferences throughout the country on the employment and economic issues affecting low-income women. The objective was "to bring together low-income women and their advocates to discuss this problem . . . to make recommendations for

change at the national level." The "extension of AFDC-U to unemployed mothers" was suggested by Legal Services lawyers as a partial solution to the lack of income for women with children. Women, if defined as unemployed, rather than dependent welfare recipients, would hopefully eliminate some of the stigma attached to this income-transfer system. The source of these data is a "Memo from the Center on Social Welfare Policy and Law in New York City to Welfare Specialists" regarding the "upcoming conferences" sponsored by the Women's Bureau, January 4, 1977. On June 25, 1979, "poor women and their families were victorious . . . when the United States Supreme Court held that the federal AFDC-U program . . . unconstitutionally discriminates against unemployed women and their families and that the remedy for the unconstitutional discrimination is to provide benefits to two-parent families in which either the father or the mother meets the federal test of unemployment." Memorandum to Welfare Specialists: AFDC-U: U.S. Supreme Court Finds Unconstitutional Sex Discrimination (New York and Washington, D.C.: Center on Social Welfare Policy and Law, July 19, 1979).

143. Taped interview with Faith Evans, September 1974. This entire section on Evans is based on this source.

144. Ibid.

145. Taped interview no. 201.

146. "NWRO Executive Committee Sets Goals," Welfare Fighter, April 1972.

147. Taped interview with Faith Evans, 1974; and interview with Bert DeLeeuw.

148. Letter from George Wiley and Beulah Sanders to "Dear Friends," undated but distributed at the Eastern Regional Meeting, New York City, February 25, 1972. Wiley hired David Ifskin, the immediate past president of the National Student Association, to coordinate the political strategy at the Democratic National Convention.

149. Letter from George Wiley resigning from NWRO, December 15, 1972.

150. Taped interview with Faith Evans, 1974.

151. Ibid.

152. Ibid.

153. Ibid.

154. Taped interview with Johnnie Tillmon, July 1974; field notes, personal interview with Bertha Cavanaugh, Rhode Island WRO chairperson, Providence, September 12, 1972; and field notes, September 11, 1973.

155. Field notes, November 12, 1972.

156. Welfare Priority Team minutes, November 21, 1972; and Kotz and Kotz, Passion for Equality, p. 290.

157. Kotz and Kotz, Passion for Equality, p. 290.

158. Ibid.

159. Ibid.

160. Field notes, December 12, 1972.

161. Taped interview no. 203; and Kotz and Kotz, Passion for Equality, p. 290.

162. Taped interviews nos. 151 and 203.

163. Kotz and Kotz, Passion for Equality, p. 290.

164. Memorandum to welfare rights leaders, members, friends, and supporters from George Wiley, December 15, 1972.

165. Letter from Faith Evans to the Executive Board, dated November 21, 1972.

166. Ibid.

167. Ibid.

168. Taped interview with Faith Evans, 1974.

169. Ibid.

170. "Mrs. Johnnie Tillmon Succeeds George Wiley as Head of NWRO," press release from NWRO, Washington, D. C. , January 12, 1973.

171. Field notes, November 19, 1973.

172. Memorandum to welfare rights leaders, members, friends, and supporters from George Wiley, December 15, 1972.

173. Ibid.

174. Smothers, "Welfare Activist."

175. George Wiley, speech at the "Debut of MEJ," New York City, March 5, 1973.

176. Wiley memorandum, December 15, 1972.

177. Ibid.

178. Taped interview with Bert DeLeeuw, July 1974.

179. Social movement sector is the term coined by John D. McCarthy and Mayer N. Zald in their article "Resource Mobilization and Social Movements: A Partial Theory," American Journal of Sociology 82 (May 1977): 1220.

180. Letter from George Wiley to welfare rights leaders, members, friends, and supporters, December 15, 1972. See final section on MEJ.

181. Ibid.

182. Field notes, December 14, 1973.

183. Taped interview with Faith Evans, September 1974.

184. Ibid.

185. Taped interview with Bert DeLeeuw, 1974.

186. The report noted that "the Misseduc Foundation makes grants to the Poverty Rights Center for projects of research, training and public education relative to the support of the Movement of Economic Justice." "MEJ Annual Report," February 1974 (for the period January 1, 1973 through January 1, 1974).

187. Taped interview no. 214.

188. Taped interview no. 213.

189. Ibid.

190. Field notes, February 13, 1973.

191. Field notes, May 3 and 15, 1973.

192. Field notes, meeting in Washington, D. C. , January 30, 1973.

193. Field notes, November 10, 1973.

194. Field notes, July 13, 1974.

195. Analysis of 27 issues of Just Economics, MEJ's newsletter, and over 300 articles revealed the following: one article in the December 1973 issue, five articles during 1974, and one in June 1975 mentioned "welfare" or "welfare rights."

196. Field notes, February 24, 1975.

197. Field notes, August 15, 1975, Pittsburgh.

198. Ibid.

199. Taped interview with Bert DeLeeuw, 1974; and report by NWRO chairperson, Pittsburgh, August 15, 1975.

200. Field notes, August 15, 1975.

201. Bert DeLeeuw, "Some Thoughts on Organizing Poor People," Just Economics 5 (July-August 1977): 7-8.

202. Ibid.

203. Memorandum to grass-roots action organizations from Bert DeLeeuw and Tobi Lippin of MEJ, Washington, D. C. , May 29, 1978; and "Eighteen Cities Join May 11 Protest," Just Economics, May 1978, pp. 6-8. Included in these protests coordinated by MEJ were the following welfare rights groups: WRO in Columbus, Ohio; Kent County Welfare Rights in Grand Rapids, Mich. ; Houston WRO in Texas; Black Hills Client Council in Rapid City, S. Dak. ; Southside WRO in St. Louis, Mo. ; Alabama WRO in Montgomery; Dane County Welfare Rights Alliance in Madison, Wis. ; Downtown Welfare Advocate Center in New York City; Welfare Recipient League in San Jose, Calif. ; Coalition for Consumer Justice in Providence, R. I. ; ADA County Rights Organization in Boise, Idaho; Minnesota Coalition for Welfare Reform in St. Paul; Baton Rouge WRO in Louisiana; WRO in Jackson, Miss. ; WRO in Newark, N. J. ; Neighborhood WRO in New Orleans, La. ; and Carolina Action in Charlotte, N. C.

204. Richard Cloward and Frances Fox Piven, "Who Should Be Organized? 'Citizen Action' vs. 'Jobs and Justice,'" Working Papers, May-June 1979, p. 35, reprint.

205. Memorandum to "Friends, Allies and Supporters of Jobs and Justice," from Bert DeLeeuw, Wade Rathke, and Mark Splain; and Organizing Report #1 (Washington, D. C.: Jobs and Justice, May 24, 1978).

206. Cloward and Piven, "Who Should Be Organized?" p. 41.

207. Ibid.

208. Memorandum from Jobs and Justice, May 24, 1978. See also "Jobs and Justice: A Social Action Report," Social Policy, November-December 1978, p. 58.

209. Ibid.

210. Harry Brill, "The Official Unemployment Rate: Fact or Fiction," Organizing Report #6 (Washington, D.C.: Jobs and Justice, October 23, 1978). Brill, a sociologist at the University of Massachusetts, writes:

> In fact, substantial numbers of AFDC recipients who are not required to register with WIN have attempted to do so because they want jobs and training, both of which the WIN program has inadequately provided. There are also enormous numbers of poor women, and the not-so-poor as well, who need to work but are unable to because of inadequate childcare facilities. According to the Household Survey, which periodically inquires about those who want a job now but are not seeking work, more than 1,200,000 women explained they are constrained by home responsibilities. From the perspective of employers, these women are out of the labor force because, practically speaking, they are unavailable for work. But from the perspective of these out-of-work women, they are unemployed.

PART II
MOBILIZATION OF SUPPORTERS

4

NWRO AND FRIENDS OF WELFARE RIGHTS

In order to mobilize monies and other organizational resources, the National Welfare Rights Organization (NWRO) developed strategies to attract middle-class liberals to the movement. Individuals, as well as organizations, who contributed various kinds of support became known as "Friends of Welfare Rights or "Friends of NWRO." From the outset, Wiley and other architects of the movement viewed the network of liberals involved in the civil rights movement as an almost ready-made base of Friends of "auxiliary" for NWRO. There were those, however, who disagreed, contending that welfare was too stigmatized to function effectively as an organizing issue for the liberal sector in U.S. society. While racial justice, the theme of the civil rights movement, meshed closely with the society's sacred values, welfare rights did not. In 1966 some doubted whether these coalition partners in the civil rights struggle would continue as allies in the welfare rights movement. In reality, a few individuals and groups did become active supporters of NWRO, both at the national and local levels. Others, as some had predicted, remained as "witnesses" in the conflict, assuming a peripheral role in this social protest. The decisions of these potential groups to abstain, join, or (at times) withdraw from the welfare rights movement in the 1960s and the 1970s had an impact on NWRO's mobilized resources and, ultimately, on the outcome of the national protest of poor women.

Within the civil rights traditional coalition—blacks, churches, and labor—the only group that failed to establish ties with NWRO at the national level was labor. While at the local level there was episodic support by a few unions, the basic contradictions between NWRO's thrust for welfare rights and the unions' fight for job rights, in part reflecting their contrasting structures,* seem to have func-

---

*In general, unions were and, with a few exceptions, still are largely male-dominated. NWRO, as we have seen, was made up pre-

tioned to keep these two groups apart. Others in the traditional civil rights coalition, however, did join the National Welfare Rights movement at different times and in different ways. Various coalitions between NWRO and its Friends of Welfare Rights—"twin-track" coalitions—emerged at the national, state, and local levels. This chapter examines those that developed primarily as a result of white church support. The following chapter explores NWRO's linkages with black organizations and the women's groups and their consequences.

While labor chose to remain as a "witness" within the welfare rights struggle, white mainline denominations and their agencies joined at all levels as early as 1966 and continued their support through the 1970s. Most were Protestant. More specifically, at the national level, the National Council of Churches, through its agency the Interreligious Foundation for Community Organization (IFCO), and the United Church of Christ, through its Welfare Priority Team (WPT), became major contributors to NWRO in terms of financial, political, and social resources. They not only provided monies but mobilized other allies, confronted the power structures, and enhanced the legitimacy of NWRO's cause. At the local level, the mainline denominations provided the stimulus for mobilizing their middle-class constituencies and others into groups of FWROs.

Some white churches were much more involved than others. As we mentioned earlier, the Catholics were involved with welfare rights groups in scattered areas at the state and local levels but not at the national level. Similarly, many of the white Protestant denominations assumed peripheral and episodic roles, and still others remained as witnesses in this social protest. A few developed a continuous alliance for extended periods of time, providing considerable political and economic support for NWRO and maintaining a salient profile with their welfare rights ally. Others chose to participate sporadically and inconspicuously. Together, the white churches contributed thousands of dollars to establish and maintain the NWRO headquarters in Washington and to aid local WROs. The withdrawal of this support in the later years had a major impact on the movement's decline.

While most of the white Protestant involvement was restricted to episodic financial support of NWRO, there were singular exceptions. The coalitions of NWRO with the National Council of Churches and the United Church of Christ were both comprehensive and continuous in

---

dominantly of women on AFDC, supporting children in single-parent families. Furthermore, most of the traditional female occupations requiring few skills and training (domestic work, waitressing, clerical, and others) are not yet unionized.

nature. Each lasted over three years, and both provided substantial sums of monies, networks, and other needed resources to the fledgling social protest of poor women. This chapter begins by examining the coalitions at the national level between NWRO and IFCO and between NWRO and WPT. It ends by analyzing the alliances that emerged at the local level between organized WRO groups and FWROs. The general thrust here is to assess the impact of "outsiders," the Friends, on the movement of poor women.

In terms of composition, the white churches and their middle-class constituencies represented an antithesis to NWRO's black, poor, and female membership. Although white churches had a predominantly female population, they were usually dominated by males at the policy-making levels. Thus, NWRO and these allies reflected polar extremes in terms of power and privilege in U.S. society. While dissimilar in structure, they espoused common goals and ideologies and worked together for more than eight years to bring about a guaranteed income system for poor people. This chapter explores the changing configurations of coalitions within the welfare rights movement between the poor and nonpoor and their consequences for the movement itself, as well as for the goal of welfare reform. Implicit in this analysis is the question "Under what conditions did these outsiders strengthen or undermine the movement of poor women, and how was this accomplished?"

We start with a brief overview of the historical ties between the church and the poor and then analyze the mobilization strategies that developed in the mid-1960s and 1970s and the changes that shifted them from "service" to "social action" to "evangelism."

HISTORICAL LINKS BETWEEN THE CHURCH AND THE POOR

The rationale for the Protestant churches' involvement with the poor is grounded in their espoused theology. Biblical imperatives in both the Old and New Testaments emphasize the responsibility of the rich toward the poor. The "religious factor," as Gerhard Lenski suggests, undergirds this involvement between the church and the lower classes.[1] Putting into practice these religious beliefs, however, entailed both costs and rewards, as Georg Simmel has outlined so cogently in his essay on the poor.[2] This "inconvenient gospel," as Alinsky liked to describe it, was costly in worldly terms but had its transcendental rewards. Church activists were constantly reminded "that they should be protagonists for the poor."[3]

There were two major traditional Protestant themes that underlined this commitment to the poor: the belief in the "holiness of the poor" and the "principle of radical equality before God." Emphasis on the former led to a "service" strategy; emphasis on the latter thrust the church into the political arena as an ally of the poor and powerless. For a few years in the 1960s and 1970s, a shift from "service" to "social action" became increasingly visible in the inter-actions between the middle-class activists within Protestant churches and the organized poor. By 1980, however, this trend had become much less evident as conservative social forces gave rise to renewed emphasis on "evangelism" within the Protestant denominations. (See Chapter 7.) In the 1960s, however, the new direction was toward so-cial action.

The new currents emerging with the social gospel movement gradually underscored the "liberation of the oppressed," rather than just "feeding the needy."[4] Harvey Cox writes that "in the 1960's the mainstream of religious liberalism turned away from neo-orthodoxy to a more worldly, secular Christianity, which found its most radical expression in Death of God and Liberation Theology."[5] Cox points out "that the latter movement views God as working through history to free humanity from political oppression and sometimes identifies His will with specific historic movements of reform and revolution." This liberation theology emphasized "radical equality before God" and called for a new mode of cooperation between the poor and the nonpoor, namely, a relationship of equal partnership. The church, as a dominant institution in society, was not to lead, but to support, the efforts of liberation. It was to act "more as a supporter and strengthener of movements already under way than as a vanguard."[6] This began to supplant, but not replace, the traditional service-ori-ented strategies of the past. The historical, paternalistic orientation was becoming more openly rejected by increasing numbers of activist clergy and laity, because, as one church report explained, paternal-ism "destroys autonomy and self respect." Demands from many sec-tors for the elimination of paternalistic service programs—which some decried as a Band-Aid approach—were "growing louder and more vehement" in the 1960s. Noninvolvement in empowering the poor to gain political autonomy was described by some as "a serious delinquency."[7]

In order to eliminate paternalism, the church activists empha-sized that the poor had to participate in the decision-making processes that affected their lives. They "should have significant though not necessarily an absolutely determinative voice in deciding how their needs shall be met."[8] Specifically, on the issue of welfare, the principle of maximum feasible participation of the poor was to "be embraced in a positive and wholehearted manner." People on welfare, or with welfare needs, were to be given a major voice in "setting goals and shaping policies" around issues affecting their needs.[9]

Given these "new" interpretations of the social gospel, the white
Protestant churches in the 1960s provided a timely rationale for those
within their circles who wanted the religious sector to play an active
role in the rising struggles of the blacks and the poor. These principles reflected the changing social conditions as well as helped to mold
the growing involvement of white churches in alliances with the oppressed. In a time of rising social turmoil, it was now felt that "an
image of the church as a supporter of inequities in the status quo was
being sustained" and that it had to become "more aggressive in the
critical struggles for justice, equity, and human dignity" that were
presently under way. The means to be used to implement these principles was to be the channeling of church resources into community
organizing to "help the poor and excluded achieve self-determination
and full participation. "[10]

Along with these shifts in emphasis on theological teachings,
there were also structural changes taking place in white main-line denominations that reinforced the new direction toward social action and
legitimized the activism within the Protestant churches in the 1960s.
Cox suggests that the rise of militant, politically conscious church
activists at this time stemmed in part from the bureaucratization—
the "managerial revolution"—within the Protestant denominations.[11]
Lay control, according to Cox, seemed to lead to a greater "social
service mentality" and "opposition to social action." On the other
hand, "where the managerial revolution has freed ministers and
church executives from subservience to laymen, there is more of a
tendency toward social involvement."

These structural and ideological shifts within the leadership of
the Protestant denominations meshed with other emerging social
forces. The War on Poverty of the Johnson Democratic administration in 1964 had legitimated the strategy of maximum feasible participation of the poor. Rising turmoil in the inner cities, where the poor
were concentrated, was seen by the political establishment as a threat
to social order. The decline of the civil rights movement and the
dominant role of whites in the black struggle was coming under increasing scrutiny, if not attack, by some black leaders. Integration
as a goal and a strategy to empower blacks within the dominant white
society was being criticized by many who subscribed to separatism
and black power. Separation and autonomy were the emerging themes
for blacks, women, and other minorities in the 1960s. For activists
in the white churches who had been deeply involved in the civil rights
movement, the trend was viewed with mixed feelings.

Separation between the poor and the nonpoor was seen as costly
by theologians and church leaders who espoused universalistic concern for all people and whose theme in the 1960s (especially among
the Presbyterians) was "reconciliation." Racial separation and class

antagonisms contradicted the mandate for a united and "blessed" community. Consequently, these social currents within and outside the church structures were forcing some church leaders to search for new ways of reuniting the poor and nonpoor and blacks and whites in a joint struggle for great equality within society.

Coalition-building emerged as one possible solution. This strategy assured both separation and community control for the minority-power groups within their own organizations, while at the same time providing a participatory role for church supporters. There was mutual self-interest in such alliances. They furnished a strategy of "reconciliation" for the church and economic support with self-determination for the organized poor. This combination of needs thus set the stage for the rise of "twin-track" coalitions between white, middle-class church activists and the black poor in the cities in various parts of the country. Emerging first in the civil rights movement, they gained momentum in the National Welfare Rights protest.[12] Many such alliances between the poor women in NWRO and their supporters in the liberal sector emerged within the movement, functioning in various different ways and having different consequences for NWRO and its affiliates around the country. One of the national coalitions that emerged at this time was that between NWRO and IFCO, an agency of the National Council of Churches.

THE NWRO/IFCO COALITION

IFCO was organized in the early part of 1967, about the same time that NWRO was just getting started as a national movement. The "troika" of the liberal Protestant demoninations involved in urban work—the United Presbyterian church, the United Church of Christ, and the Episcopal church—conceived of a plan to support community organization of the poor and set about to implement it.[13] Later, other denominations—the Methodists and the Lutherans—joined the IFCO.[14]

IFCO was viewed as a pragmatic response to the question "In an age of racial separation and polarization, is it possible for persons of different ethnic groups to work together in a coalition?"[15] It was envisioned as a cooperative, racially integrated coalition of different groups of the poor that would establish and maintain communications with the liberal church leaders. It was to be an alliance of "whites and non-whites who are equally committed to the principle of equality and social justice in society and could come together and attempt to resolve their differences over strategies, tactics, and priorities for programs." It was also designed to transfer the decision-making power from the powerful to the powerless.[16]

One of IFCO's primary objectives was to become "a support structure for community organization and economic development efforts in minority communities." The foundation was to function as a fund raiser, as well as a coordinator of "member and cooperating agencies."[17] It was also listed in the <u>Directory of National Black Organizations</u> as a black agency whose goal was to fund and assist "community organizations committed to eliminating racial oppression and exploitation."[18] It was also a fund-raising arm of the National Black Coalition, which included the Black Economic Development Council (BEDC), the National Committee of Black Churchmen, the Southern Christian Leadership Conference (SCLC), and the NWRO.[19] IFCO's strategy was to promote training and self-development for local minority groups through the allocation of monies to different organizations throughout the country. Policy was made by the IFCO board and implemented by its staff. IFCO began its operation in September 1967, one month after the formal organization of NWRO.

In principle, IFCO was to address the needs of all poor people and to be an "integrated" organization with both blacks and whites and poor and nonpoor serving on its board. In practice, however, it began by being dominated by whites. This changed when Lucius Walker, a black leader and minister, assumed the post of executive director in 1967.[20] As a result of his efforts, the IFCO board gradually came to be dominated by blacks.[21]

Cooperation between NWRO and IFCO stemmed from their similar structures and goals. Both executive directors, Wiley and Walker, were black, middle-class, and well-educated men who became catalysts in bringing about the alliance between the two groups. Both appealed to the poor in the inner cities, although NWRO, in practice, turned out to have a limited constituency of poor women on welfare. Both were theoretically designed to empower poor people but were dependent on outsiders for funding. IFCO was an arm of the long-established National Council of Churches. NWRO was a fledgling movement organization, created largely through the efforts of middle-class organizers in cooperation with poor women on welfare. Both groups reflected similar responses to the rising turmoil in the inner cities in the 1960s. The two organizations espoused the principles of racial equality and maximum feasible participation of the poor. In reality, however, both were dominated by blacks and "informal leaders" who were mostly middle-class.

While both organizations were federations of local groups, NWRO was a national political movement with a formal membership. IFCO, on the other hand, was a foundation whose principal mission was allocating funds to community organizations. As such, it held a nonprofit, tax-exempt status and was restricted by law in terms of its "political activity." NWRO, in contrast, was a protest movement organization, whose major strategy was political action to change the system. Except for its Misseduc Foundation, NWRO's "educational" arm, Wiley's movement was not tax-exempt, given its political nature.

Both IFCO and NWRO were dependent on the religious sector for their funds. IFCO's power base was rooted in the white Protestant denominations. Approximately 96 percent of all its contributions came from Protestants. The remaining 4 percent came from Catholic and Jewish sources.[22] NWRO, as we have seen, received its major funding from IFCO and other religious groups and foundations. As political and economic conditions changed over the years, these funding sources disappeared. By 1980 neither organization was being supported by this sector. NWRO had long since folded as a national organization. IFCO, as a result of internal conflicts and changing priorities within the National Council of Churches, had separated from this body and become an independent organization in Harlem.[23] NWRO and IFCO were similarly buffeted and shaped by the shifting political tides of support within the social movement environment in general and the white Protestant sector in particular.

For almost four years, IFCO was the main vehicle through which white denominations channeled their monies to NWRO. This reduced the risks of donating directly to NWRO and yet contributed to the goal of community organizing that had been endorsed by the white churches. Between 1967 and 1971, IFCO transferred over $500,000 to NWRO, * plus "emergency grants when Wiley was in desperate need of money to pay long overdue bills."[24] According to both NWRO and IFCO officials, however, the decision to support NWRO was not easily made. Many church board members were not convinced that welfare rights organizing fell into the category of community organizing. They had to be convinced of "the legitimacy of WRO as a community organization."[25] Proponents of this alliance argued that there was mutual self-interest in the relationship. IFCO would serve as an advocate for NWRO among the churches, and Wiley, in turn, would bring welfare rights and its grass-roots groups and organizers to support the work of IFCO. Walker pointed out that "both of us knew it was a working partnership. The rules of the game were clearly spelled out. We had common commitments—mutual professional organizational self-interest."[26]

IFCO provided not only monies for the national movement of welfare rights but also organizational training, legitimation, and access to additional liberal funding within churches and foundations. Walker pointed out that NWRO needed to have the established credibility of IFCO within white churches rub onto Wiley so as to establish the necessary links.[27] Walker worked closely with Wiley and trained him to

---

*IFCO's contributions to NWRO from 1967 to 1971 were as follows: $99,212.00 in 1968, $159,521.16 in 1969, $216,444.93 in 1970, and $38,647.52 in 1971, for a total of $513,825.61.

tap the white churches for funds and other support. He praised Wiley
as the "best student" he had ever had, since he "used IFCO successfully to build relationships and get monies for his organization, funded
through IFCO, in addition to other direct grants."[28]

In exchange for what Walker called IFCO's "Good Housekeeping
seal of approval" for NWRO, Wiley contributed his time and energy
in helping Walker build IFCO as "a credible black organization."
Walker, critical of Alinsky's Industrial Areas Foundation, which was
white dominated, wanted IFCO to become a "black organizer's training center." Wiley, according to Walker, helped him to move IFCO
in this direction by bringing " 'the cream of the crop' of black organizers into IFCO."

IFCO used various strategies to help increase NWRO's financial
base and political visibility as a black movement. In 1969 IFCO became the catalyst for the development and publication of the Black
Manifesto, which demanded, among other things, $500 million in
reparations for past racial discrimination by whites against blacks.
It accused the "white Christian Churches and the Jewish synagogues
in the United States" of being "racist institutions" and called among
other things for the recognition of NWRO and for "ten million dollars
to assist in the organization of welfare recipients" as well as "welfare
workers" in order to bring about "better administration of the welfare
system in this country."[29]

The partnership of IFCO and NWRO, rooted in common racial
and class concerns, lasted for almost four years. The dissolution
of the alliance stemmed both from internal and external pressures.
According to Walker, the federal government, through the Internal
Revenue Service, "tried to harass the life of IFCO" because of its
close ties to the welfare rights movement. He asserted that their
"major beef was our support of NWRO."[30] Despite this harassment,
Walker insisted that this was not the major reason for terminating
support of its ally. Rather, he added, it "was its [NWRO's] poor administrative practices" that led to the severance of their ties. Walker
explained that, while Wiley was "a genius at organizing," there were
"serious problems" with NWRO's administration, specifically with
financial reports. He added:

> NWRO did not supply documentation needed for our ac-
> counting for use of grants. We were very careful and
> we had to be. We got it in the earlier years because at
> the beginning, IFCO could do the documentation itself.
> Later, as our own funding declined and with no staff,
> we could not do it.[31]

Wiley, on the other hand, contended that IFCO had withdrawn
because of the harassment by the political authorities "when the IRS

threatened to take away IFCO's tax-exempt status."[32] Other observers
suggested that perhaps the partnership ended because of both internal
and external pressures.[33] Declining support of IFCO by major denominations also contributed to the reduction of contributions to NWRO,
which was forced, in turn, to cut back on all its programs by the early
1970s.

Despite these eroding factors in the alliance, the NWRO/IFCO
coalition lasted close to four years and supplied NWRO with the major
portion of its budget during that period. Another payoff for NWRO was
the enlistment of the United Church of Christ as an ally, which played
a significant role within the movement of poor women.

NWRO AND THE UNITED CHURCH OF CHRIST'S
WELFARE PRIORITY TEAM

At the national level, the coalition between NWRO and the United
Church of Christ resulted in the mobilization of both economic resources and additional political allies. The United Church of Christ
(UCC),* a long-established institution within the dominant society,
provided NWRO with both material and other resources, namely,
money, staff, networks, media coverage, and legitimation of its cause
among the liberal sector. UCC also functioned as a catalyst in developing and stimulating the expansion of the network of Friends of WRO
throughout the country. This network became known informally as the
National Friends of WRO. The church, in turn, gained a visible role
in the movement as an ally and a Friend of NWRO. This coalition between the poor and nonpoor lasted for almost four years and mobilized
various resources for NWRO. Together, these allies confronted the
political establishment and struggled to defeat the proposed "welfare
reform" plan of the Nixon Republican administration. As the costs
of participation in the movement of the welfare poor increased and the
political outlook for achieving the goal of a guaranteed income declined,
UCC dissolved the alliance. As a result, NWRO lost one of its major
supporters. This section examines the origins and nature of this coalition between nonpeers and the consequences for NWRO, both politically and economically.

The coalition between NWRO and UCC emerged as a result of
mutual self-interest. In the early days, both partners viewed the relationship as a politically feasible and effective means of achieving the
common goal of greater economic security and a guaranteed income

---

*The specific branch involved was the United Church Board for
Homeland Ministries. For brevity's sake, it will be referred to as
the UCC.

for poor people in the United States. By 1970 NWRO had begun to seek additional allies, as the struggle against FAP escalated and its expenditures and other needs increased. At the same time, UCC was seeking new strategies to respond to the rising turmoil in the cities, the growing demands for "black power," and the decline of the civil rights movement. More specifically, many church leaders were searching for nonpaternalistic models for bringing about greater economic justice not only for blacks but for all the poor. Wiley was now increasingly concerned about the rising counteroffensives by the dominant authorities against the poor in general and NWRO in particular and decided that new ways had to be found that "move beyond the organization of just black and poor people to counteract Nixon's repression."[34] One of the strategies he proposed was to enlist the white Protestant denominations as allies. IFCO had been assisting him in these efforts, and in 1969, with the advent of FAP, he assigned this task to his associate director, Sampson.

Sampson sought out the UCC, suggesting that it consider establishing a formal alliance with NWRO. He recalls that, while other Protestant denominations had already contributed some monies to NWRO, UCC as yet had not.[35] It had, however, in its recent pronouncements, committed itself to a guaranteed income for the poor as well as to working to bring about welfare reform. Since these goals meshed with those of NWRO, it became a potential ally, whose resources were greatly needed by the fledgling and impoverished movement organization.

UCC, a predominantly white and middle-class church, had been among the Protestant denominations in the vanguard of "social action" for many years.[36] As early as 1967, the Sixth General Synod of the United Church (its national ruling body) had voted "support . . . of proposals for assuring an adequate income when employment possibilities and opportunities are not sufficient."[37] By 1969 it had specifically endorsed a platform on "welfare reform."[38] Although UCC supported this new concept of the right to unearned income (when jobs were not available), it was not until three years later, on April 29, 1970, that the Board of Directors of the United Church Board for Homeland Ministries came out specifically with a statement on policy and program "advocating a monetary criterion at this time of at least $5500 per year for a family of four as one prerequisite for a humane standard of living."[39] Just as significant was its vote supporting NWRO as a means through which to achieve the goal of an adequate income for all U.S. residents.

When Sampson of NWRO approached the UCC officers with the possibility of establishing an alliance between the two, the new social-action policy and strategy within the denomination was to create "priority teams" to study and act on specific social issues. In its first trial, UCC had selected three areas on which to focus its attention and resources: race, peace, and welfare. In 1970/71 it had voted to spend $1 million to implement this policy.[40] As a result, the conditions were present for the emergence of the Welfare Priority Team within the church and its linkage with NWRO.

The two partners represented widely contrasting organizations and constituencies. NWRO was a fledgling movement of the poor. UCC was a long-established, prestigious denomination. NWRO's membership was poor and mostly black and female, while UCC's was middle-class and white and primarily female. The formal leadership of both groups also differed, reflecting their different constituencies. On the other hand, the "informal" leaders of both organizations (the paid staff and directors) were more similar, since they were mostly white and male. The two allies contrasted sharply in terms of resources, including money, power, and prestige. White Protestant churches, representing the dominant class, ranked at the top of the social hierarchy; and black women on welfare, at its bottom. It was clearly a coalition of nonpeers in terms of power and status.

Although structurally different, the two organizations subscribed to similar principles, goals, and strategies. Both endorsed racial justice and equality, urged a more humane system for the redistribution of income within the country, called for maximum feasible participation of the poor, and sought a partnership as equals, rather than the traditional paternalistic relationship between the "haves" and "have-nots." The representatives of the organized poor, despite their lower status and power within the society, were regarded as codecision makers within the alliance. It was a new model that sought to shatter stereotypes about the poor and the relationship of the church to those in need.

Both sides saw potential rewards in such an alliance. NWRO sought material rewards, such as economic and political resources to maintain its organization and fight against the political authorities to change the welfare system. UCC, in turn, was manifestly interested in this long-range goal, as well as continuing its historical and theological commitment to the poor. Alliances with the poor also added to its constituency a group that was noticeably absent from its membership and whose absence contradicted its universalistic beliefs. Given the existence of common grounds for cooperation, the coalition emerged in 1970.

Negotiations between NWRO and UCC, which had been initiated the previous year, were finalized in the spring of 1970. Since the UCC Synod had adopted welfare reform as one of its priority issues, the UCC's Planning Council and NWRO, with Sampson as the primary resource person, developed a policy position on "welfare rights and adequate income in general." At the spring meeting of the corporate board, this position was presented, debated, and finally "passed virtually unchanged."[41]

The "action" adopted by the board of directors was very comprehensive, but also explicit, in outlining the parameters of the relationship, including its goals, strategies, and tactics. Specifically, the policy supported the right of "all persons . . . to a humane standard of living" and assigned the ultimate responsibility to "the Government . . . for providing the means to protect this right." It also endorsed the right of people "to organize non-violent efforts to secure their rights, one of which is a humane standard of living." More than a mere social pronouncement by a church body, it outlined an explicit program and process by which its goals were to be achieved and implemented.

UCC's strategies were basically twofold: support of NWRO and its affiliates and mobilization of its own middle-class constituency and others as a new political constituency in support of welfare reform and welfare rights. The UCC pledged numerous kinds of resources to NWRO but, at the same time, stated that it was equally committed "to building this general support within our membership" and others of "all races and income levels." It endorsed the concept of welfare rights as a means to enhance the dignity and economic status of welfare recipients. It also endorsed NWRO as one means of achieving that end. Ultimately, however, its stated objective, like NWRO's, was much broader than empowering the poor on welfare. The UCC policy statement called for "the achievement of equal economic and social opportunity for all persons." NWRO was seen as a viable movement organization that endorsed universalistic principles similar to those of the church. It was perceived by UCC "as an essential component of its efforts toward equality of Blacks, Indians, Puerto Ricans, Chicanos, Whites, and all others" in their struggles for "basic life needs" and "political freedom."

In the spring of 1970, the corporate board voted to "implement immediately aspects of the policy" and authorized "the establishment of a working relationship with the National Welfare Rights Organization and its affiliated units so that mutual goals and purposes can be fulfilled." The "rules of the game" were clearly delineated and the parameters of its contributions and ties to NWRO spelled out. It would aid NWRO "in increasing its visibility and interpreting its goals, purposes, and programs to the general public." In addition to monies, UCC promised to provide "staff services," to develop "literature and other materials" on welfare and welfare rights, and to facilitate "access of NWRO to the mass media."

To add to its personnel resources throughout the country for the national movement, it pledged to assign "substantial numbers of persons" in its Volunteer Service Program to work "under the guidance

and general supervision of NWRO or local welfare rights organizations." Students were also identified as another potential source of
volunteers for the movement. Those attending the "Urban Semester"
in UCC-related colleges would be recruited to work for NWRO. Finally, to expand the support base for NWRO at the grass-roots level,
UCC pledged to help establish or strengthen alliances between local
WROs and "local Friends of NWRO." A "clearinghouse" was planned
to put these various volunteers and potential Friends "in contact with
local welfare rights organizations which seek and need their help."

Concurrently, while it mobilized support for the social protest
of the poor, UCC pledged to mobilize its peers in the middle class as
a means of aiding NWRO and bringing about a change in the welfare
system. A variety of educational strategies were called for to involve
the UCC constituency "in the welfare rights effort; to help them understand and interpret welfare issues; to build organization bases which
support the welfare rights movement; and increase the expertise of
persons engaged in programs related to welfare concerns." In addition, UCC promised to try to mobilize support for NWRO among other
Protestant denominations. Thus, its resources for the issue of welfare were to be divided between two basic strategies: direct aid to
NWRO and indirect political and economic support through mobilization of its middle-class constituency and its peer denominational leaders.

To administer this program priority around welfare, the board
immediately appointed a WPT, composed of ten staff members from
various divisions, to implement its stated policy. Immediately,
$30,000 were allocated for this task, $15,000 of which was to be
"transmitted by the Team to the National Welfare Rights Organization
as an undesignated grant." In order for the WPT to be able to operate,
a budget line was guaranteed for its staff and organizational needs
within the total church budget.

While there were few strings attached to the donations by UCC
to NWRO, some controls were clearly spelled out in the initial policy
statement. To assess the consequences of the alliance with NWRO,
the work of the WPT was to be reviewed "regularly" by the Policy and
Planning Committee in order "to affirm or terminate the Team's mandate." If found wanting, the team could "be disbanded and its functions
terminated upon administrative action of the Executive Vice-President
or by failure of the Directors to extend the mandate to the Team beyond the calendar year 1971, or any year thereafter."

The NWRO/UCC coalition was by far NWRO's most comprehensive and formal alliance with a middle-class ally.* The exchange

---

*One church executive summarized the exchange as follows:

The way we saw the ties from the very beginning were very
programmatic in nature: that we were two organizations

was clear to both partners. The church pledged to provide a wide variety of needed organizational resources to NWRO, and NWRO promised to give the white, middle-class church a role in the movement of poor people. Both sought to bring about a guaranteed income for poor people in the United States by combining their different resources in the political struggle against the welfare authorities.

To minimize conflict within the partnership, the "rules of the game" had been developed jointly by NWRO and the church leaders. Both accepted them and were anxious to put them into practice. UCC emphasized that the alliance encompassed specific areas "where our concerns came together." As one church executive observed, "There were specific points of contact, for specific goals, a specific time span, and a specific evaluation." To him and to others on the church board, this was underscored as being very, very important in establishing any kind of coalition relationship."[42] At the outset, the unwritten, but projected, duration of the alliance was approximately three years, with a yearly evaluation review. If deemed "successful" by the UCC, the issues of guaranteed income and welfare reform would be integrated and institutionalized into the existing program and budget of the Health and Welfare Division of United Church Board for Homeland Ministries.[43] Historically, other struggles by the poor and powerless had eventually been incorporated into the ongoing programs and structure of the UCC, including the civil rights issues into its Commission for Racial Justice and its Racial Justice Priority Team and those of the farmworkers into the Ministry for the United Farmworkers. This left open the possibility that a welfare rights ministry might also evolve within UCC. The alliance with NWRO in 1970 was seen as a beginning and a testing ground.

Although the church board of directors had adopted the "Action" paper on welfare rights, this had not been an easy task for its proponents. Many on the board had serious reservations about the feasibility of such a coalition. The sociopolitical costs of such an alliance with the welfare poor, beyond the mere pledging of economic support, were perceived as very high. Some questioned the effect of such a

---

with similar concerns in this given area; and that being the case, we had several things we could bring for them. (1) We had a network of people, which we could alert and inform; (2) we had staff that were willing to work on given issues; (3) we had financial support to give; (4) we had given structures through which NWRO could move . . . to route foundation funds and in a lot of ways, we opened our publications and media to them. [Taped interview no. 213, emphasis added]

strategy of social action on UCC membership. Others disputed the NWRO goal of $5,500 per year for a family of four. There were board members "who came from primarily the Midwest rural areas [and] felt that they knew a lot of people who weren't on welfare who weren't getting that level of income." This concern over the specific amount for a guaranteed income extended to the issue of whether the NWRO/ UCC alliance was only supporting welfare people. These doubts were allayed when staff members explained that "we weren't talking about welfare people in the policy position . . . [but] a standard for all families of four in the nation below which no family should be allowed to fall."[44]

Other risks were identified by church officials. There was "the risk of alienating large segments of your constituency who don't understand what you're into and, if they do understand, disagree with it." Another risk was that "when you enter into any relationship as potentially explosive as this one, you are in danger of being overly identified with the group you're into and so their sins become your sins and their virtues become your virtues." Finally, there was the risk of people who are most closely involved in the relationship on an issue being always in danger of losing objectivity and becoming so involved personally that the issue and the goal become secondary to the relationship," that is, the risk that "methodology replaces ideology and that social activists become ideological methodologists."[45] In sum, the risks involved not only alienation of the church constituency but also possible goal displacement—with the means becoming an end in itself.

Despite these potential risks, the alliance with NWRO seemed to offer UCC some rewards. As one church official explained, UCC wanted to achieve the goal of an "adequate income for everybody in the country," and it felt that "the means most appropriate for dealing with the problems of the lowest income group . . . was through welfare rights and welfare reform." Since the church did not have "many poor people" among its members who could identify these needs, NWRO offered an attractive source of allies and experts on poverty.[46] NWRO members were considered an asset because of their firsthand knowledge of poverty and also because they were involved in the movement out of rational self-interest, not abstract values. As one church official explained: "We need NWRO [because] they have something else going for them that we haven't . . . that is self interest. . . . We searched out the organization to relate to on this and welfare recipients have the greatest self interest in welfare reform and an adequate guaranteed income." Because of this economic self-interest in the struggle, he felt that "they're likely to work harder on it and hang in longer through more frustration than anyone else." In addition, he added, "they also keep us honest in the sense that the liberal record is a bit faddish, almost dilettantish in social change."[47]

Support of NWRO also offered UCC an opportunity to unite its creed and deeds. There were theological rewards in such an alliance with the poor. One church official stated that "insofar as the church retains any relationship to the Gospel on which it is supposed to be based . . . the church can't help but be concerned that every person has a right to life and the wherewithal to live." He added that "like Luther, one can do no other."[48] The relationship with NWRO "could help us clearly by who they were and the strengths they represented and the constituency they represented to further the goal." The white, middle-class churches in the United States, he emphasized, had a need for "ongoing contact" with people who were representative of other segments of U.S. society, if "their perspectives" were to be "more accurate" than they had been in the past. To a great extent, he added: "We are who we run with. And we felt that if we could run more with the people from this segment of American society, we would become different personally and institutionally."[49]

For NWRO, the rewards were primarily material: monies, staff support, networks, and other organizational resources. Politically, the alliance had the potential of mobilizing additional liberal allies within the dominant sector that might help more monies trickle down to the movement organization, as well as strengthen the tide for welfare reform. From NWRO's point of view, it was hoped that the alliance would strengthen the movement organization at the national and local levels not only by adding to its material resources but also by mobilizing middle-class support for the goal of a guaranteed income for poor people.

Another attractive feature of the proposed alliance was that it was designed to be a relationship between equals, despite the real gap in power and status between the two allies in the broader society. The nonpaternalistic model of coalition was one espoused both by NWRO and UCC. Theoretically, each would have the right and the power to agree or disagree on policies and programs affecting both groups. Another added reward, from NWRO's point of view, was the legitimation of the welfare rights cause by its higher-status partner.[50] Finally, both groups felt that by establishing a formal alliance cooperation would be enhanced and competition between the two minimized. One observer noted that Wiley "was as eager" as the church for this coalition because he did not want "a strange unbranded calf riding out in left field and in one sense trying to do something that might not jibe with NWRO strategy and policy."[51] By working together, there was the potential of greater control over each other's activities.

NWRO was also aware of the costs and risks involved in an alliance with a long-established, middle-class organization. In general, there was the underlying fear of being dominated or used by the stronger ally, especially under conditions of economic dependency.

Domination by white liberals in the civil rights movement had been, in the opinion of many black and white activists, a ubiquitous problem, Domination by the nonpoor within the movement of poor people was seen to be just as threatening. Like UCC, NWRO saw the risk of becoming overidentified with its nonpeer allies. Too much interaction with middle-class church people might well alienate its base constituency and other potential peer allies among the organized poor and black. Both NWRO and UCC were well aware that such a twin-track coalition (in which the visibility of ties are high independent actions by one or the other would reflect on both) could bring praise or criticism from their peer constituencies or the public in general. Finally and more specifically, there were the bureaucratic costs for NWRO in having to file reports on funds donated by the church. Although there were no strings attached to the UCC contributions, it was agreed at the very beginning that NWRO would file reports on a regular basis, attend the monthly WPT board meetings, and cooperate throughout the country in helping the church to organize its middle-class constituency around welfare rights and welfare reform. Given the potential rewards in the alliance, these risks and costs for NWRO seemed, at best, negligible and, at worst, controllable.

As a result of the prenegotiations between NWRO and the UCC staff, the church board adopted the "Action" paper on welfare rights and established the WPT as the specific group linking the church and NWRO. This relationship began in April 1970 and continued for over three and a half years. During this period of time, the team provided NWRO with monies, staff, networks, media time, literature, and other materials. In the external conflict with the welfare authorities, it also joined NWRO in demonstrations and in lobbying in Washington against FAP and other social policy opposed by the poor. At the same time, it worked to expand the network of Friends of NWRO throughout the country. NWRO, in turn, donated its time and expertise to the church by providing a liaison and other consultants to the WPT, who participated in various leadership roles at regional and national meetings organized by the church as it attempted to mobilize its middle-class constituency around welfare reform.

The major resource sought by NWRO in this alliance was money. Money remained one of the movement's major problems, as it expanded its national headquarters and staff. Over the years of the coalition, WPT transferred to NWRO directly a total of $142,500 in cash contributions, or about 65 percent of its total operational budget during those years. (See Table 4.1.) This direct and regular cash transfer does not reflect, however, the total monetary contributions of the church. Part of the remaining WPT budget also found its way to NWRO through a variety of special arrangements, some spontaneous, others planned. First, NWRO's liaison representatives on the team

TABLE 4.1

Budget and Allocations of WPT to NWRO

Year	WPT Con- tributions to NWRO (dollars)	Percent of Total	WPT Con- stituency Develop- ment and Other Programs (dollars)	Percent of Total	Budget Total (dollars)
1970	15,000	50	15,000	50	30,000
1971	42,500	61	27,500	39	70,000
1972	42,500	67	20,500	33	63,000
1973	42,500	73	15,500	27	58,000
Total	142,500	65	78,500	35	221,000

Source: Compiled by the author.

were paid as consultants. Second, the purchase of advertisements in NWRO's annual convention program books transferred some additional monies to the movement organization. Finally, in emergencies, WPT contributed funds at the request of NWRO.

The remaining WPT budget was allocated, in general, to mobilization of its middle-class constituency around welfare rights and welfare reform. This was labeled "constituency development" by the church policy makers. This included designing and implementing various educational conferences on welfare and training in lobbying; the publication of numerous articles, policy analyses, and alerts; and publication of Sampson's book on welfare reform and welfare rights issues.[52] The church also used its magazines and other periodicals, as well as its radio programs, to interview NWRO leaders and to disseminate information on their goals and activities around welfare reform. As training and support, WPT paid its staff to attend all NWRO public meetings and traveled throughout the country to establish support groups for NWRO.

Staff time of the WPT was devoted to work directly with NWRO as well as with middle-class constituency groups. The chair of WPT, Hobart Burch, reported that about half of his time as head of the Division of Health and Welfare within the church was allocated to the programs and actions of the team. Two or three other people on his division staff were assigned full-time to the welfare rights project. The team also periodically lent staff to NWRO for special projects. These in-kind contributions, in terms of paid staff time and other organizational perquisites, added to NWRO's mobilized resources and enhanced its rewards within the coalition.

In addition to its own cash and in-kind contributions, WPT, from the start, sought to supplement its financial support to NWRO by developing outside sources of funding. By August 1970, three months after the formation of the coalition, the team was actively involved in negotiations with a number of foundations.[53] Over a two-year period, these efforts reportedly led to additional indirect contributions to NWRO amounting to over $250,000.[54] These monies from individuals and foundations were channeled to NWRO through UCC. It "passed through" almost $150,000 per year to NWRO—"an appropriation to NWRO based on the level of contributions received for the Board's [United Church Board for Homeland Ministries] work in the area of welfare . . . through special gifts."[55] One church official noted that NWRO "used our offices at times to route foundation funds simply because we had an administrative machinery which was not available to them."[56]

As the overall revenues of the church declined, its allocations to its three priority teams involved in social action (race, peace, and welfare) were reduced. From 1971 to 1973, all priority team budgets were cut. By 1972 the "across the board" cuts within UCC had reduced the original $1 million budgeted for the priority teams to $650,000. One church staff member suggested that "this church action reflects societal attitudes toward increasing conservatism in all of American life."[57] New priorities within the church were emerging and siphoning off monies "at the expense of social action."[58] WPT's existence and the continuation of the alliance with NWRO became increasingly precarious, as pressures mounted within the leadership of the UCC to dissolve the coalition with the welfare rights movement.

As social-action priorities were shifted away from welfare within UCC, reflecting the rising conflicts not only within the religious sector but also within society in general, WPT's budget was trimmed every year while the coalition lasted. Despite these continuous cuts in its total operational budget, the team voted repeatedly to maintain the same level of cash support for NWRO. In essence, then, it chose to reduce its own financial support for "constituency development," or the mobilization of middle-class supporters, in favor of strengthening the mobilization of the poor within NWRO. In its choice of strategies, therefore, the team indicated its preference for mobilizing the poor, rather than the middle class, in the struggle for welfare reform. As its annual budget was cut from a high of $70,000 in 1971 to a low of

$58,000 in 1972, the team maintained its total pledge to NWRO in the amount of $42,500 per year.

The commitment of most of the team members to NWRO was high, as is evidenced by their decision not to decrease their contribution to the movement despite their budget reduction. There was, however, growing opposition within the team to this emphasis on support for organizing the poor, rather than on expanding the indirect strategy of organizing the middle-class constituency for welfare reform. This became salient in 1973, when after Wiley's resignation NWRO, bereft of support, was struggling to survive. When it came time to decide on how to divide the WPT's budget, conflict developed between those in favor of mentioning the same level of support for NWRO and those in favor of reducing it. The issue thus revolved around how much money should be allocated for what strategy in order to be most effective in achieving the team's goal. The options were support of NWRO or mobilization of the church's middle-class constituency. The existence of similar conflicts at the local level underscores the competitive nature of the strategies within this twin-track coalition.

Certain questions were repeatedly raised in the alliances of the poor and nonpoor within the welfare rights movement. "How do we allocate our limited resources? Should they be used to enhance the base of the organized poor or that of the middle-class liberal supporters, or both?" For WPT, the strategy from the outset of the coalition had been to distribute a higher percentage of its funds to NWRO than to its own constituency development around the issues of welfare rights and welfare reform. Similarly, NWRO had to confront this issue of what part of its meager resources should be spent on mobilizing its supporters, such as FWROs. Ultimately, the basic question debated continuously at different levels of the movement was, Which of these strategies was the most effective in bringing about the desired change? From NWRO's point of view, the resources should be used to mobilize the poor. From UCC's perspective, middle-class support in the political struggle was also needed. NWRO leaders, for the most part, defined the role of Friends of WRO simply in terms of providing monies and other resources to enhance the movement's organization. No effort was made to coordinate the Friends of NWRO until 1970, when the coalition with UCC was formally established.

Some team members, favoring constituency development, argued for the indirect or trickle-down strategy, that is, the mobilization of middle-class supporters who would then provide monies to the welfare rights groups around the country and to the national office. The proponents of this strategy contended that if the middle-class grass-roots support within the church withered, the church revenues for welfare rights would ultimately be reduced. One team member expressed his views as follows:

> If we keep reducing our own educational budgetline . . .
> we will not be able to establish grassroots support within
> our own church, for that's where the support should come
> from. And gradually we won't have any money or support
> for NWRO or the whole welfare movement. We need money
> to publish booklets, mailings, and further develop and
> strengthen the non-poor constituency. In the long run we
> will be helping NWRO. We will be developing a grassroots
> middle class movement for NWRO. [59]

Another team member, supporting this same trickle-down approach,
added that "we have a responsibility to our churches to develop interest and conscience in this welfare area. Our staff should be working
with our people. Most of our resources should be spent on our constituency."[60]

The majority of the team members, however, refused to accept
this argument and voted to hold the line on their contribution to NWRO,
despite the budgetary reductions. The most important need, they felt,
was to keep NWRO alive as a "voice" and "forum" for the poor. The
decision in support of this strategy thus decreased political mobilization of its middle-class constituency and denominational development
in favor of support for the organization of the poor. In many ways, the
decision reflected the ongoing struggle between paternalistic and nonpaternalistic strategies within the church.

A much more serious crisis emerged in the early part of 1973,
when all the priority team budgets were cut. [61] NWRO was assured,
at first, that "even if the Welfare Priority Team ceased to exist in
1974, 'welfare' will still be a priority" for UCC. While the welfare
issue was to remain among the church's concerns, the continued support of NWRO appeared to be in jeopardy. Other vehicles for achieving economic reform were being considered. Continuation of the coalition strategy with the welfare poor seemed to be in doubt. Team members expressed the need "to prepare NWRO for the possibility of no
more funding at the end of the year [1973]."[62]

Six months later, the rumors were confirmed. The total budget
for the three priority teams had in fact been cut to $150,000 for the
following year. It was officially announced that WPT would "not exist
after December 1973."[63] The entire budget of the Health and Welfare
Division, which administered WPT, had also been reduced by 10 percent.

Sampson, the original architect of the NWRO/UCC coalition,
upon hearing this news, bluntly criticized the team in 1973 for having
"failed to generate new monies for [NWRO] to enable it to survive."[64]
He acknowledged that they had tried and that perhaps it had been "ab-
surd" of him and other organizers to expect "dramatic changes in the

welfare system in such a short time." The effort, he added, would take "continuous years of struggle."[65] Where the support was to come from for the long fight ahead remained unanswered.

The decision to dissolve the coalition with NWRO had been made at the highest policy-making level of the church. WPT members had argued in favor of continuing the alliance but had failed in their efforts. They tried to explain to NWRO representatives the reason for dissolving the alliance. The budget committee, it was reported, had decided in 1974 "to put its money where it can have what is realistically achievable. 'Welfare Rights' was no longer considered a fruitful effort, since it had not been successful in achieving its goal of a guaranteed income."[66] Goals and strategies had to be revised to adapt to the changing political and economic conditions. The movement for social change had to have a broader base that included all the poor, not just welfare recipients. Its goal had to be expanded to encompass a variety of economic security programs. The new theme was economic justice, not just welfare rights or welfare reform. As one church executive explained, the problem was not the goal but the means. In other words, welfare rights was no longer viewed as a politically feasible strategy in light of the changed political climate and the new structure and leadership of NWRO. Furthermore, as one team member suggested, although the church had limited resources, it had several different alternatives in achieving its mission with the poor.[67]

This differentiation between welfare rights and economic justice was criticized by Sampson and Evans, the NWRO liaison representatives to the team that year. Sampson questioned the new label, pointing out that welfare was in fact "an economic issue."[68] Evans also challenged the shift from welfare to economic justice. Why, he asked, was "working for adequate welfare for the poor" not the same as "working for 'economic justice?'" Why, he questioned, had this shift in policy occurred?[69] Some tried to suggest an answer.

Sampson felt that the move to "cut out welfare rights" and substitute economic justice simply meant that internal politics within the Board for Homeland Ministries had "reshuffled the priorities and monies." He surmised that the symbolic change in the priority team's name—from "Welfare" to "Economic and Racial Justice"—mirrored basic political and policy changes within the church regarding the groups of poor people they would support. There was some evidence that the church leadership was shifting its resources to help mobilize the working poor. Sanders, the national leader of NWRO that year, commented sadly that only groups with "economic development" goals, not "welfare" goals, were getting funded by the churches. Political alliances with NWRO were assessed by many policy makers within the Protestant denominations, including UCC, as being too costly. Some said that the middle-class constituencies were becoming alienated with the continuing demands for welfare rights and their churches' overidentification with this movement. Another factor undermining the church's support for NWRO was the emergence of attacks by the radical Labor Caucus Committee against the national leaders of the welfare rights movement. Whatever their motivations, the caucus succeeded in splintering the social protest of poor women, which was at its most vulnerable state, and in confusing NWRO's middle-class supporters by creating a parallel organization called the NU-NWRO (pronounced "new" NWRO). Its violent tactics in various parts of the country frightened many supporters and heightened UCC's concern with its highly visible ties with the welfare rights movement. In many ways, this attack from the radical left became the last straw. It solidified support within the church to dissolve the alliance with NWRO.

Responding to the political realities of increased hostility to the poor and black by the political establishment and the public, both white Protestant churches and NWRO had begun revamping their policies and strategies. In NWRO, women leaders made an attempt to emphasize the "rights of children" on AFDC, rather than the general welfare rights of the poor, most of whom were women.[70] Rising public resentment to welfare, inflammatory rhetoric about "lazy loafers on welfare" by national political leaders, and the internal conflicts within NWRO were forcing it to reevaluate its structure and direction. As a result, as we have seen, Wiley resigned from NWRO and established the Movement for Economic Justice (MEJ).

Within WPT and the white Protestant churches, strategies were also changing. Over the years, programs with greater appeal to the middle class, such as health, day care, and abortion (all issues of concern to NWRO women as well), were gaining in priority over welfare and a guaranteed income. This stemmed, in part, from the rising frustration of trying to achieve this long-range goal, which seemed increasingly unattainable. It also reflected the gathering momentum of the women's liberation movement in the 1970s. Within the mainline denominations, "the top priority issues" for social action had shifted from welfare in 1972 to health in 1973 to woman's rights in 1975.[71] Interest in welfare and welfare rights, never high, was on the wane by the mid-1970s. Health and job rights, much less controversial issues within U.S. society, were gaining new allies.

While the principles undergirding continuing support for the poor and the powerless remained constant, changing times called for different strategies. New coalition partners were being sought by the activists within UCC. In 1973 church leaders announced that the existing Welfare and Racial Justice Teams would be combined into one called the Economic and Racial Justice Priority Team (ERJPT). Economic justice thus formally replaced welfare rights as a major area of social action. Two other priority teams funded by the church that year focused on peace and evangelism. After three years, new goals and revised strategies had been adopted by the board of directors that had originally approved the coalition with NWRO. Its actions mirrored the rising conservatism within the society and reflected, in part, UCC's serious misgivings about NWRO as a political partner. NWRO's internal conflicts had weakened the movement and altered its structure. Wiley had resigned, its grass-roots base had practically disappeared, and control now rested with the women leaders. For UCC policy makers, these changes had decreased NWRO's attractiveness as an ally in the ongoing struggle. They no longer felt that the national organization represented the legitimate movement of poor people.

At the final coalition meeting of NWRO and WPT in December 1973, the structure and strategy for the new ERJPT were described. First, its major thrust would be around health and not welfare, even though the latter would be included as one of the team's continuing responsibilities. Second, its ties to movement organizations of poor people would be more limited. While representatives of various groups, including NWRO, would be invivted to present their program needs to the new team periodically, there would be no permanent seats for these representatives on the team. This was designed to minimize the risk of overidentification of the church with any one group, which, in the NWRO/WPT coalition, had become perceived as increasingly costly to the church supporters. Partnerships with organizations of the poor were still to be a central part of the mission of the church, but these alliances were to be much more restricted and specific in their interactions and exchange. The decision-making process was to be limited to the church team, with consultations with the organized poor as deemed necessary. No long-range commitment of funds was to be made to just one group. Support was to be more diffuse. Finally, NWRO leaders were assured that while health and racial justice would be the top priorities on the new team's agenda, "welfare reform" (not welfare rights) would remain a major concern. [72]

NWRO representatives argued against this new church policy and strategy, criticizing Wiley as well for having played a role in creating an artificial dichotomy between economic justice and welfare rights. [73] One of the team members tried to explain that the new strategy was designed to make the movement more inclusive and to unite the poor, not to divide them. The strategy of economic justice, he added, was "just an expansion of the idea of welfare rights" and a way of "expanding upwards to include other poor people," since NWRO, intentionally or not, had "excluded the working poor." The new strategy of economic and racial justice was designed to include both groups, those on welfare as well as the working poor. Its thrust would still be for "a guaranteed income but through jobs and welfare." The rationale for this new team, he explained, was that church leaders felt the "need [for] a broader coalition of the working poor and substrata groups to bring about legislative reform."[74]

NWRO leaders seriously questioned this strategy of creating another new organization within the movement of poor people. They felt that another structure would stimulate competition among the poor for the limited funds from the liberal sector. Choices would have to be made as to the allocation of badly needed resources, which were already scarce. Some would lose. It was seen as a situation of "triage" or "lifeboat ethics."* An NWRO representative added that the church policy makers "will have to pick and choose who [they] are going to support and my concern is about what is going to happen to the Welfare Rights struggle."[75] He pointed out that the lack of solidarity among the poor and the proliferation of protest organizations among them (many times supported by the liberal white churches) helped aggravate the competitive situation and ultimately weakened many of them. He urged the church to work to enhance cooperation, rather than competition, among the poor.

In a final attempt to lessen the impact of the break with NWRO, WPT, at its last meeting, adopted several resolutions in support of continuing ties with NWRO. First, the team voted unanimously to recommend "the continuation to the fullest extent of Welfare Rights in the

---

*During World War I the wounded were separated into three groups. The first group included "those likely to die no matter what was done for them"; the second, "those who would probably recover even if untreated"; and the third, "those who could survive only if cared for immediately." With scarce supplies, the strategy was to provide care only for the third group. "Such a practice was called triage—from the French verb trier, to sort." In warfare this was the system developed to make "the most efficient use of scarce medical resources" (Wade Greene, "Triage: Who Shall Be Fed? Who Shall Starve?" New York Times Magazine, January 5, 1975, p. 9).

Lifeboat ethics refers to the moral dilemma confronted by those in a lifeboat with others less fortunate than they swimming in the ocean around them, trying to get in or at least trying to cling to the sides to survive. If all are pulled into the lifeboat, the boat will probably sink and all will perish. If some are allowed to come aboard, while others are left in the ocean, the latter almost inevitably will die. Here again the dilemma is set in a context of scarcity, namely, space, which means survival (James W. Howe and John W. Sewell, "Let's Sink the Lifeboat Ethics," Worldview 18 [October 1975]: 13–18). The authors discuss both "lifeboat ethics" and "triage."

Economic and Racial Justice Team and that an NWRO representative be invited to sit on the new Team." Second, it voted to recommend that the relationship between the United Church Health and Welfare Division (of the Board for Homeland Ministries) and NWRO be continued in some way. Finally, it urged that special funds be sought to support NWRO in whatever way possible. [76]

Given the lame-duck nature of the team in December 1973, its actions were at best symbolic. There seemed little evidence that these recommendations would carry much weight in the new team, given the changed policies and strategies within the church. An NWRO representative, while applauding the team's "good intentions," pointed out that realistically, at this stage of the game, "some ties" with the church would not suffice to save NWRO. Without continuous support from UCC, "the chances were that NWRO would not survive." Since Wiley's resignation, it was reported, foundation support had also disappeared. [77] According to this NWRO spokesperson, the white liberal churches "had always been and would have to continue to be" the major contributors to welfare rights if the movement were to survive. Funding still was and had always been the most critical problem in the organizations of the poor. Without church support, NWRO would have no choice but close down its national offices. The dissolution of the alliance between WPT and NWRO, he predicted, would reverberate with negative consequences at the local level. [78]

Although the issue of NWRO's survival remained unresolved at that last meeting of the NWRO/WPT coalition, in reality there were no choices left for either partner to make. Decisions had been made at the highest policy-making levels of UCC that the coalition should not continue to exist, regardless of the consequences for NWRO. The configurations of power were shifting again within the movement, as alliances dissolved and new ones were established. Those with the power to decide established the frameworks for the new coalitions in the continuing struggle for welfare reform.

Through its WPT, UCC, in accordance with its 1970 "Action" statement, had made repeated attempts to mobilize a national organization of middle-class Friends of NWRO in order to lessen its own burden and risks in its alliance with NWRO and to develop another means of continuing liberal support for the movement of poor women. It failed in these efforts, despite the fact that it had succeeded over the years in expanding the network of Friends throughout the country. Numerous factors intervened to undermine this parallel strategy of mobilization of middle-class supporters. The national Friends network, in the final years, became known as the Welfare Rights Information and Support Community (WRISC). It was an idea that never gained enough support from either the poor or the nonpoor and thus failed to be implemented.

THE WELFARE RIGHTS INFORMATION
AND SUPPORT COMMUNITY

Although UCC's policy statement in April 1970 called for the development of its own and other denominational support for the welfare rights movement, as part of its multipronged strategy to expand NWRO's political and economic resources, in terms of its priorities, a national Friends network remained a "residual operation" for the team, according to its chair, Hobart Burch.[79] Efforts were made to bring together Friends at NWRO's conventions, and a regular communications system was established to disseminate information on the movement and the status of the legislative battle. Thus, throughout the active years of NWRO, the network consisted of a loosely structured group of liberals throughout the country (some of whom were organized at the local level) who supported the social protest primarily by participating in the grass-roots movement and by contributing some monies to the national organization. By 1973, as UCC began to withdraw from the movement, the Friends' network reportedly had around 3,000 on its list.[80] There had been little effort to coordinate or formalize the Friends into a national network until it became apparent to the members of WPT and to the new women leaders of NWRO that the end of the coalition was in sight. Concerned about leaving a potential vacuum of support, with its dire implications for NWRO, UCC sought to share the financial burden with others. The idea of ecunemical and coordinated, middle-class, grass-roots support, which had been simmering in the background for a number of years, finally began to gain adherents and greater endorsement by both allies.

The decision to create a middle-class support structure for NWRO in 1973 reflected a reversal of its strategies and a last effort by WPT to expand its alliance with the welfare rights movement to include other Protestant denominations. A few of these had more sporadic contributions to NWRO in the early years, but none had established the continuous ties with, or commitment to, the movement demonstrated by UCC. As it became clear that support for NWRO was eroding within UCC, other sources were sought to possibly strengthen this support by making it more ecumenical.

For NWRO the decision to endorse this concept of a national Friends support organization was also a reversal of strategies. In some ways, it symbolized the loss of NWRO's power over the years. In the early days of the movement, NWRO had repeatedly rejected the idea of organizing middle-class liberals for fear of being dominated by a more powerful ally. By 1970, as it entered into the alliance with UCC, NWRO, in accordance with the agreement made with its new partner, indicated that it would try to allocate some of its resources for coordinating FWROs throughout the country. In NWRO's view, however, the financial rewards of such a network were limited and the political risks high. As a first step, that year NWRO appointed the first national Friends coordinator to its staff, Joanne Williams, to "service the network."[81] From then on, Friends were regularly invited to attend all NWRO meetings and participate in various activities. However, their major function, in NWRO's perspective, was to contribute funds both locally and nationally. There was no need, its leaders felt, to organize a formal and potentially competitive movement organization for the Friends on the national level. When this was suggested at the 1970 NWRO conference in Pittsburgh, it was firmly rejected.

WPT, on the other hand, had entered into the partnership with NWRO with one of its objectives being the development of its church constituency and other Protestant denominations in support of NWRO. Three months after the coalition between NWRO and the church had been formalized, WPT began to gather names of Friends around the country, thus forming the basis of the informal national network of Friends of NWRO. For three consecutive years, WPT undertook the responsibility to maintain and service a network of communications with middle-class supporters of the movement. It organized church caucuses and workshops for FWROs at NWRO conferences and conventions and invited denominational leaders to join it in discussing the feasibility of a joint "Ministry of Welfare Rights."[82] From 1970 through 1976, the repeated efforts of the team were met by lukewarm support at best, and outright rejection at worst, from NWRO leaders and Protestant denominational leaders, both of whom were not receptive to this cooperative strategy.

By 1973 the attitudes of NWRO's leadership began to change, and WPT's efforts gained added momentum as its members foresaw the approaching dissolution of their alliance with the poor women and the need to find an alternative source of support. By then, NWRO's structure and financial state had changed considerably since its early years. Wiley had now resigned as its executive director, the funds he had succeeded in raising within the liberal sector had all but vanished, and control of NWRO rested with the black women leaders. The original organizers who had opposed the Friends strategy as a waste of time and resources were gone. The structure, power, and perspectives had changed, as economic imperatives mandated compromises. The original thrust for autonomy and separation was now giving way to greater integration with outsiders, despite the risks involved. Economic exigencies had forced NWRO leaders to reconsider their political policies within the movement. As a result, the organization began to cooperate with WPT in developing a formal national network of Friends to undergird its declining base of support.

Two consultants were called in by the team to help in implementing this task. James and Sampson, both former associate directors

of NWRO now working elsewhere, were selected to design and organize
the meeting to get the national network off the ground. James sent out
invitations to Friends across the country, asking them to attend the
1973 NWRO convention in Washington, D. C. , to form "another organization." Its major thrust would be to raise monies and to "aid
NWRO as it faces its next seven years." He suggested that, with a
national Friends network, it would be possible to create "a survival
fund of $100,000 by getting 4,000 members at $25 a member."[83]

The response was very limited. No more than 40 people attended. Few denominational executives were present, a disappointment
to WPT, who had hoped to gain ecumenical support for this endeavor.
At this meeting, UCC representatives reasserted that they would not
participate in a new national organization unless there was "hard evidence" of ecumenical financial support and commitment. The church
could not, they stated, continue to function as the only major supporter
of NWRO among the Protestant denominations.

The plan designed by Sampson for the national Friends' organization was endorsed and adopted with few changes by those present.
Sampson, who had originally conceived of the idea of the Friends as a
role and special status for middle-class supporters in the movement,
suggested that changing times demanded some alterations. Since
there was growing opposition to welfare rights within the society,
the new group should reduce the visibility of this label and call itself
the Welfare Rights Information and Support Community, or WRISC.
The use of an acronym might lessen the risks of participating in the
movement and attract more liberal supporters. Half in jest and half
seriously, Sampson pointed out that he had selected this name because
of the appropriateness of its acronym. WRISC symbolized the perceived and real risks involved in coalitions with the welfare poor.
Next, he outlined WRISC's objectives and strategies: "to provide information and connect in other welfare rights concerned people," to
"support NWRO" by giving it 80 percent of the dues collected, to "hook
up" and work with "both local WROs and Friends," and, finally, to
"distribute a newsletter called For Our Welfare."[84]

WRISC incorporated the new idea of equal, but different, roles
for the Friends and the welfare rights members within the movement.
Friends were no longer asked to provide just services and monies to
NWRO but to join as active, organized, political allies out of "enlightened self-interest." This was reflected in the title Sampson had
chosen for the newsletter. WRISC was to provide an active role for
the middle-class liberals, as well as support for the movement organization of NWRO. For the latter, the underlying risk was that this
new organization of middle-class supporters might come to dominate
the movement of poor women or "take off" on its own. By 1973 Sampson was convinced that the middle class had to be mobilized around

welfare reform in terms of its own self-interest, rather than the traditional liberal idea of service for others. Sampson emphasized that WRISC could not "exist only to support WRO." In his opinion,

> Those days of support by other people—that service model —are over. They're out and happily so. Everyone has to be active—if they want to be active—for their own self-interest. What we have to find answers to—besides support for NWRO—is "what's in it for the middle class?" That's the only way they will ever link up with Welfare Rights today. [85]

Sampson also pointed out that, after the turmoil of the 1960s, people were tired of fighting other peoples' battles. Given the deteriorating economic conditions in the society and the disillusionment with the Watergate scandal in the Nixon administration, the mood of the country was shifting from social involvement to self-concern. The decade of the 1970s was to become known as the "me" decade. (See Chapter 7.)

All these trends underscored the need for new strategies in bringing about social change. Incentives for participation by the middle class and the working class had to be built into the movement. In its 1974 appeal for membership, WRISC emphasized that

> Americans are beginning to understand that the welfare system is not just for the poor but is vital to all. The purpose of WRISC is to meld and encourage this healthy self-interest with continuing commitment to support the self-determined efforts of the poor. Fair welfare and adequate income for all is WRISC's aim. [86]

Despite the cooperative efforts of UCC and NWRO to get WRISC off the ground in 1974, the strategy failed. Although a small group at the NWRO conference in St. Louis that year adopted the WRISC proposal (the "Agreement of St. Louis," as Sampson called it), set up a steering committee, and gained the public blessings of Tillmon and Evans of NWRO, the fledgling organization collapsed within six months. A promotional appeal mailed to 10,000 people resulted in only 50 people paying their dues to join WRISC. Support for welfare rights among middle-class liberals had vanished by the mid-1970s. The number of such supporters—never large in the first place—had dropped. Despite Sampson's plans and predictions, there appeared to be little understanding or perception of how mobilizing around welfare might be in the self-interest of the nonpoor.

Only two other Protestant denominations joined UCC and the National Council of Churches in funding WRISC. Various efforts to mobilize ecumenical support had not succeeded. Ironically, one stumbling block was the confusion that resulted when two simultaneous appeals were presented to the liberal denominations for funding: the proposal for WRISC by WPT and the "Half-a-Chance Campaign" of NWRO. One denominational executive recalled that since they were introduced at the same meeting, the two "collided" and created a "tremendous amount of confusion.[87] Denominational leaders questioned the soundness of these two competing strategies for funds. For example, they asked, "If a group decides to support 'welfare rights,' in which plan should it invest its limited resources—in the NWRO "Half-a-Chance Campaign" or in the middle-class WRISC proposal?" In other words, should available resources be channeled directly to the movement organization of poor people or to one of middle-class supporters? Would the resources in fact trickle down to NWRO? Which one of the strategies would most efficiently mobilize sufficient political power to achieve the desired economic changes? Given the lack of interest in the welfare rights cause at this time, these unanswered questions caused the denominational leaders to decide not to participate in either plan.

In retrospect, it seems clear that WRISC—the strategy formulated by UCC, the National Council of Churches, and NWRO to mobilize a national Friends of Welfare Rights network—had emerged at the wrong time around the wrong issue. Whereas the Protestant churches had been successful in establishing constituency support for the causes of the blacks in the civil rights movement and for those of the farmworkers in the United Farmworkers movement, welfare rights, by 1973/74, carried little appeal for these potential liberal supporters. The mood of the country and the political establishment were no longer receptive to the needs of the poor, especially those on welfare. Moreover, the social trends pointed toward less collectivism and more individualism in finding solutions to problems and toward less centralization at the national level and more decentralization. Reflecting this political climate and the reality of declining membership and revenues, the main-line Protestant denominations were shifting strategies. The drift in the religious sector was away from social action and toward evangelism,[88] away from welfare rights and toward job rights, and away from welfare reform and toward economic justice. All these social forces added to the barriers in mobilizing resources for NWRO.

With the demise of WPT, NWRO eventually collapsed at the national level, as the NWRO leaders had predicted. On March 31, 1975, it closed its national offices, unable to find the funds to pay the rent or its remaining staff, much less to function as a national movement of poor people. While the alliance at the national level between the poor and nonpoor lasted, it succeeded in mobilizing monies and people, including middle-class supporters for NWRO. When UCC decided to withdraw from the coalition, NWRO did not have the power to continue. Middle-class support, therefore, emerged both as a source of power for the movement of poor women and the root of its major problems and conflicts. While this parallel coalition at the national level had attempted to create a model of equal partnership between unequals, in practice, the final decision to continue or terminate the coalition rested in the hands of the church policy makers. As their needs changed, they selected new alternative strategies to achieve their ongoing goals for economic justice. NWRO, with few, if any, alternatives, collapsed. Political power within this twin-track coalition thus remained with the partner who had control over economic resources.

Although WPT ceased to exist in December 1973, UCC, through its new team (ERJPT) and its Commission on Racial Justice, continued its commitment to welfare reform into the 1980s, as this social policy resurfaced for debate in Congress. (See Chapter 6.) Early in the spring of 1978, a coalition of religious groups joined together "to rebuild the base of church support for welfare reform."[89] Lack of support and the tabling of the welfare issue by Congress and the Carter Democratic administration undermined these renewed efforts. In New Jersey, a concurrent mobilization of the poor and nonpoor by the National Council of Churches' Health and Welfare Working Group (of which UCC was a member) attempted to bring together new and old supporters to fight for increases in welfare benefits and for a guaranteed income. The plans were discontinued after a few months, when it became apparent that there was little support within the religious community in New Jersey for social action, especially around the issue of welfare.[90] In the last years of the 1970s, the thrust by Protestant churches around the country was to mobilize members around evangelism. As one New York _Times_ reporter observed in 1977:

> America's mainstream Protestant churches, spurred by recent declines in membership, are showing a renewed interest in evangelism, which they have long neglected and even shunned. Among the bodies reflecting this ferment are the . . . churches not considered aggressively evangelical in the past.
>
> For the first time in two decades they are providing money and resources for evangelistic initiatives designed to strengthen the commitment of lapsed members and to convert outsiders to Christ. Though the trend is just in its beginning stages, it could mark the most dramatic shift in emphasis since these churches became embroiled in social activism in the 1960's.[91]

While NWRO and national Protestant leaders were involved in building alliances at the national level, groups of FWROs had surfaced, partially in response to church influence at the state and local levels. The following section examines the origins, structure, and consequences for NWRO of the coalitions between the poor and their middle-class supporters at the local level.

LOCAL COALITIONS OF WROs AND FRIENDS OF WRO

The Friends of Welfare Rights was an "auxiliary"[92] of the National Welfare Rights movement designed by its organizers to meet two organizational needs in the protest against the welfare system: the economic need for monies and services to support its local, state, and national headquarters and the political need to minimize middle-class control within the movement organizations of the poor. In theory, the plan was envisioned as enlisting individuals, rather than organized groups, as supporters who would contribute their time, money, and services to WROs in exchange for a participatory role in the quasi-exclusive movement of the poor. The economic contributions from the liberal sector would thus be maximized, while middle-class involvement in internal decision making would be minimized. A peripheral, but contributing, role for the nonpoor would ensure, it was felt, maximum control by the poor over their own organizations. In practice, however, some individuals, attracted by the potential of political action, organized into groups of Friends of Welfare Rights and linked up with WROs in different parts of the country. Some formed parallel or twin-track coalitions (WRO/FWRO). Others joined in integrated coalitions of the poor and nonpoor. Still others organized independent coalitions with the nonpoor that were concerned only with welfare reform. In general, the ties between the coalitions of women on welfare and their middle-class supporters were tenuous and episodic, beset by structural contradictions and competing needs and loyalties that gradually eroded cooperation around the common cause. In the process, however, FWROs appear to have had some impact on NWRO's mobilized resources and its goals at the local level.

The major architect of the model of Friends of Welfare Rights was Sampson, Wiley's associate director from 1966 to 1969. Out of his experience in the civil rights and farmworkers movements, he had become aware of both the risks and advantages involved in white liberals' participation in the protests of these groups. While some funds and other resources had been mobilized for the black protest, it seemed to him that white activists inevitably had come to dominate the integrated groups. Consequently, he felt a new strategy had to be developed for the movement organization of poor women on welfare.

Originally, Sampson's model called for a separate category of membership for the nonpoor within the movement, namely, the Friends of Welfare Rights. Individuals would be invited to join NWRO and pay their dues in exchange for membership in the movement. Their status and roles, however, were to be clearly differentiated from those of the regular members. This separation was designed not only to enhance the status of the welfare rights women but also to minimize the risk of domination by the stronger ally. Friends were not to be given voting rights or leadership roles. They were to service the needs of the WROs by providing whatever resources were needed. As Sampson explained it, Friends were "supposed to support the development of a strong WRO" and to "assist and not takeover."[93] Simply put, Sampson said, "Support means . . . that they lead, we follow."[94] In fact, then, this model called for reversed roles. Those from the dominant society were to take a subordinate role, rather than the traditional leadership role. The empirical question was whether this reversed-role model would succeed in practice, given the poor women's dependence on economic resources provided by these outsiders. As we shall see, these contradictory needs of economic dependence and political independence within WROs became sources of tensions and gave rise to conflict and restructuring within the protest movement.

Political forces within society reinforced the necessity for a new strategy in mobilizing supporters. Both the civil rights and the War on Poverty movements in the early 1960s had emphasized the principle that blacks and poor people should control their own organizations. Growing numbers of blacks (and some whites) were now calling for separatism to strengthen black power within the civil rights movement and within the dominant society. At the same time, the War on Poverty had adopted, as one of its basic doctrines, maximum feasible participation of the poor. Given the poor women's limited resources, however, dependence on outsiders for various resources was an acknowledged reality. Nevertheless, the counterforces of separatism and autonomy among blacks gave rise to increasing demands for constraints on unrestricted white participation in their organizations. This limitation of white involvement in the black protest thus created a pool of organizers and liberal supporters in search of new ways to continue their participation in the black struggle. The political conditions of 1966 thus helped to shape the structure of the welfare rights movement and, more specifically, the twin-track model of organizing supporters.[95]

Whitaker, an early organizer in NWRO, writes that this kind of separatism within the movement could be justified in three ways: the poor were the "experts" on poverty; there was a danger of domination by the middle class in an integrated structure; and the poor had to have their own organization to develop a "revolutionary consciousness" to protect them from the proverbial risk of "cooptation."[96]

For the first few years (from 1966 through 1968), NWRO felt little need of, and did little to develop, a formal membership category for its supporters. First, its major strategy at that time—the "street strategy" at the grass-roots level—required few resources, most of which could be begged or borrowed from CAP agencies, churches, and wealthy individuals. Second, both the organizers and the national leadership had serious misgivings about middle-class, liberal support, both in terms of its ability to provide the needed resources and its tendency to control. Wiley stated that "in a crunch you could not count on middle-class groups" to support the poor, and there was always the risk of "being dominated."[97] Several of the women leaders, including Tillmon, tended to agree.[98] Third, in the mid-1960s, the political climate was relatively friendly toward the black and poor. The political leaders' rhetoric and actions in designing and implementing the Great Society programs reflected their support. At the same time, the national economy was thriving and expanding. Resources, especially in terms of organizers and funding, were more readily available as a result of the decline of the civil rights movement and the rise of the War on Poverty. Monies for organizing the poor could be had from foundations, white Protestant churches, and the federal government. Although limited, these funds were sufficient to stimulate protest in the early days.[99] Given these favorable conditions in terms of available resources, the national leadership of NWRO and its staff found little reason to invest much time or energy in mobilizing middle-class individuals as supporters.

By 1968-69 the political and economic conditions had begun to change, providing some of the impetus for the development of FWROs within the movement. Interest was emerging both among white liberals and NWRO's organizers. With the rise of turmoil in the cities in 1967 and 1968 and the assassination of Martin Luther King, Jr., that spring, white liberals began to organize and join the protest of the black and poor in increasing numbers. James of NWRO noted that support groups "just sprung up" all around the country "calling themselves Friends of Welfare Rights."[100] As a result, NWRO staff attempted to link these independent groups to the national movement.

Whites, as James points out, found various incentives for joining the Friends' groups in those days. First, there was the opportunity for activists to participate in a period of heightened racial conflict. Second, the visibility of their alliance with the cause of the welfare poor was an added payoff for the "nonconformists" in the early days.[101] Finally, the separation of the poor from the nonpoor assured those whites who had "anxieties . . . about a relationship with predominantly black groups at that time." James emphasized that "despite what people like to say, NWRO has been a predominantly black group."[102]

With spontaneous support emerging in different parts of the country, NWRO decided to recognize and incorporate these activists and their resources into the national movement. In 1968 the Friends of Welfare Rights became an integral "link in the welfare rights chain."[103] Membership forms were developed and distributed widely, dues established, and a special Friend's pin and a subscription to NWRO's newsletter were sent to all who paid their dues.

The number of paid-up Friends was relatively small. From 1969 to 1970 the numbers, however, doubled, rising from about 700 to 1,500.[104] By 1973 NWRO's lists claimed a total of 3,000 nonpoor supporters, mostly white and middle-class. There are little data available to determine their actual contributions. In 1970 a NWRO report stated that the expected donations of Friends was $10,000 per year, or, at most, 4 percent of its annual budget. According to Sampson's design, half of the Friends' dues were to be returned to the local WROs. In practice, however, this complex system of collection and distribution of dues rarely worked. Local WRO leaders complained that they received few, if any, of these funds collected by NWRO. The economic rewards for NWRO were relatively insignificant, and, consequently, its staff and leadership showed little interest in expanding the base of these supporters throughout the years.

Contributing monies to NWRO was only one aspect of the Friends' role, albeit the major one from NWRO's perspective. Political support was another. At first, however, NWRO restricted the political involvement of Friends in the movement and made every effort to reinforce differentiation of statuses, rights, and responsibilities. DeLeeuw recalls that "in those early days there was a lot of tension and jealousy." The women leaders felt that "this is our organization and no one else can be part of it." Consequently, they rejected the idea of having the Friends involved in their meetings. Friends were allowed to attend conferences and conventions but could not be present in any of the NWRO sessions.[105] By 1970 this had begun to change.

As the numbers of Friends grew, so did their organized groups. This led to greater involvement in political actions at the local and national levels. By 1969 NWRO was also beginning to exhibit signs of rising interest in formalizing and institutionalizing this spontaneous rise of support for welfare rights. Some efforts were initiated to publicize the special membership for individuals who wanted to contribute to NWRO. Isolated Friends seemed to pose little threat of dominating the movement. Organized groups presented greater risks. Within NWRO, there appears to have been an underlying fear of the rise of a parallel movement of middle-class supporters, which might dominate the poor women's movement.

At the local level, groups of Friends began to emerge in 1968. By January 1971 NWRO reported that there were approximately 50 FWROs in 47 cities and in 22 states. (See Table 4.2.) In contrast,

TABLE 4.2

Friends Contact List

States and Cities

Arizona	Missouri	Virginia
Tempe	St. Louis	Norfolk
Arkansas	Nebraska	Washington
Little Rock	Lincoln	Seattle
California	New Jersey	Wisconsin
San Francisco	Montclair	Madison
Connecticut	Newark	Milwaukee
Bridgeport	Westfield	
New Haven	New York	Regions
Watertown	Albany	
Florida	Auburn	East
Tampa	Binghamton	Connecticut
Illinois	Buffalo	Maryland
Champaign	Elmira	Massachusetts
Chicago	Ithaca	New Jersey
Columbia Friend	Londonville	New York
of WRO*	New York	Pennsylvania
Madison County,	Rochester	Rhode Island
Edwardsville	Syracuse	Vermont
Indiana	Utica	West
Evansville	Ohio	Arizona
Green Castle	Cleveland	California
Indianapolis	Delaware	Washington
Iowa	Lima	Central
Des Moines	Pennsylvania	Illinois
Waterloo	Philadelphia	Indiana
Maryland	Pittsburgh	Iowa
Baltimore	Rhode Island	Michigan
Silver Spring	Providence	Mississippi
Massachusetts	Texas*	Nebraska
Stoughton	Houston	Ohio
Michigan	Vermont	South
Bloomfield Hills	Chester Depot	Florida
		Virginia

*NWRO mailing list, 1973.

Note: Totals 23 states, 49 cities, 50 groups.

Source: Material distributed by NWRO, undated, but received February 6, 1971.

however, WROs were estimated to number 800 groups in all 50 states. Relatively speaking, then, the support movement of the local Friends was limited, even at its peak. Despite their small numbers, NWRO staff and organizers repeatedly emphasized the need for Friends to adhere to the "rules of the game and to avoid taking control in the fledgling WRO groups."[106]

In time the tensions in this parallel coalition between the poor and nonpoor intensified, both at the national and local levels. In many cases, the passive, subordinate role for middle-class activists proved to be too costly. NWRO organizers reported that many of the Friends would not conform to the service role and organized independently to take political actions at the local and state levels. This aggravated the partnerships, since local WRO leaders expected the Friends to contribute monies and help them to respond to daily crises and emergencies. Many Friends, however, resented being placed in a "glorified social worker's role."[107] Wiley and his staff, on the other hand, at first saw this as the primary function of a support group. To them, FWROs were potential "auxiliaries." Friends, on the other hand, seemed to find greater rewards in social action around welfare reform than in social service for welfare families. DeLeeuw described the tensions as arising from these conflicting needs. WROs wanted "money and warm bodies," and the Friends wanted political action. In his view, "The Friends were way ahead of the movement organization. They were ready to move right into welfare reform . . . but in the early days of the movement, there wasn't any . . . real political lobbying action until the Family Assistance Plan was introduced in August 1969."[108]

As the political scene changed and NWRO shifted its resources from organizing at the grass-roots level to lobbying in Congress, its attitudes and actions toward middle-class supporters began to alter. By the end of 1968 counteroffensives by state welfare authorities had eliminated the special benefits in many states, removing the monies that had been NWRO's major organizing incentive. A few months later, the Nixon administration's plan for welfare reform was introduced, and NWRO geared up to defeat it. This required increased expenditures for the national headquarters. At the same time, major sources of income were being threatened. NWRO's $400,000 contract with the Department of Labor, approved in the final days of the Johnson administration, terminated at the end of fiscal year 1969. Continued financial support from IFCO was in question, as the Internal Revenue Service increased its pressures to rupture the alliance.

Confronted with such financial reversals and new political realities, NWRO began to view middle-class Friends as an increasingly attractive alternative source for needed resources. In its search for new allies, NWRO had established formal ties with UCC in 1970, as

discussed in an earlier section. One of the objectives of this partnership was to expand the middle-class, grass-roots base of support for
welfare rights. Changing economic and political conditions thus provided the stimuli for the endorsement of middle-class Friends, despite
continuing reservations by some of NWRO's leaders and organizers.
In part, NWRO's new interest also stemmed from the fact that groups
of Friends were emerging spontaneously throughout the country following the urban turmoil.

By 1970 NWRO had begun to encourage liberals to join in political actions to defeat Nixon's FAP. Friends attending the NWRO conference that year were urged to "Zap FAP." The following year,
NWRO's theme was openly one of "coalition politics."[109] Representatives of other oppressed groups were invited to participate and to
join NWRO in its struggle for welfare reform. Blacks, American Indians, farm workers, labor unions, students, the elderly, and feminists were sought as allies in the emerging political fight. Middle-
class churches were also enlisted as partners, given their established
resource base, their prestige, and their public commitment to social
justice. Thus, by 1970/71 the Friends were being asked to work not
only as passive service providers but also to join actively in the political struggle as allies.

This created tensions within NWRO, as disagreements emerged
over the expansion of the role of the middle-class Friends within the
movement of poor women. Some argued that by relegating activists
to a passive and subordinate role, Friends were becoming alienated,
withdrawing from the movement or organizing independently and thus
eroding NWRO's potential political support. Whitaker notes that "although many liberal sympathizers may for a time participate out of
guilt feelings, they tend toward non-involvement as they tire of their
subordinate, second-class status."[110] Some organizers were insisting that the costs of participation had to be reduced and the incentives
increased in order to attract more allies. The political conditions,
they contended, demanded additional Friends and a broader base to
achieve long-term change in the welfare system.

A few within NWRO's staff set about developing new ways to attract Friends and to engage them in political actions. In 1969 a special strategy was developed for the middle-class supporters. NWRO
appealed to the Friends to live on a welfare food budget for one week,
to report their experiences to the press, and to mobilize public opposition to the inadequacies of the Nixon-Moynihan FAP.[111] This strategy
was designed to make "the Friends a political part of the movement
[and] to get them really involved politically." Those on the staff who
opposed this strategy contended that it deflected attention from WROs
and consumed NWRO's scarce resources. Some criticized NWRO for
"moving too much toward middle-class people and . . . deserting 'the
ladies.'"[112]

Despite these internal conflicts over the role of Friends, James, as associate director in 1969, endorsed and promoted this strategy. Friends throughout the country were called on "to test the inadequate Nixon workfare plan by living on his proposed food budget for the week of November 16-23 [1969]."[113] That month, the Welfare Righter, in a rare article about the Friends' activities, also urged their participation in this political campaign against the Nixon plan.[114] In 1970 NWRO announced that it was actively seeking to expand the movement's base by mobilizing both the poor and nonpoor. It called for "the active support of 'middle Americans' for a new coalition with organized poor people to change the priorities of our nation."[115]

To emphasize its commitment to the mobilization of middle-class allies, NWRO assigned one of its few national staff members to coordinate the network of Friends. On the eve of establishing a formal alliance with UCC (a potential source of new middle-class Friends), Williams, a young black woman, was appointed as the Friends' coordinator in NWRO's headquarters in Washington, D.C. For the first time in its four-year history, NWRO was now actively encouraging greater involvement of middle-class liberals. New political strategies and an expanded national organization required additional money and allies.

Incentives for participation for Friends were increasingly highlighted in NWRO communications. In return for their time, money, and commitment, NWRO promised Friends that they would not only be put on NWRO's mailing list to receive various publications but also be given a greater opportunity for political involvement. As one observer noted, "the servicing of the Friends network" was to be improved.[116] In March 1970 Williams sent out what was to be the first in a series of communications "to establish a bond among all the groups" in the country. She added that she hoped that, in the coming months, "our family of Friends will greatly multiply."[117] Wiley, although still skeptical about organized, middle-class support, also spoke out in 1970 in favor of greater involvement by the Friends in the movement. While emphasizing their role as financial supporters, he now offered them an opportunity to participate in the NWRO conference in Pittsburgh and become active in defeating FAP.[118]

By August 1971 it was clear that NWRO's policy was shifting and that it no longer mandated a limited role for Friends. Opposision to the Friends strategy was not as noticeable. One black, male leader in NWRO, who had consistently opposed the formal organization of Friends, stated that he felt that it was time to change the relationship given the fact that "we're in a 'war' to eliminate inequality."[119] Thus, as NWRO's needs changed, reflecting the new political conditions, Friends became less threatening and more attractive as potential allies. While there was continuing reluctance on the part of some leaders to expand the middle-class role, political pragmatism won out over ideology. By May 1973, after Wiley's resignation, Tillmon announced that NWRO needed "local groups of Friends" and "anything they can will do with us."[120] For her, as for others, it was a reversal of strategies. Sanders, the second chair of NWRO, also urged the Protestant churches to help expand the groups of Friends throughout the country. Her hope was that this support at the grass-roots level would aid in revitalizing the movement of poor women. Although UCC, as we have seen, did undertake to develop a national Friends network, it did not succeed. [121]

By 1973 the tables had turned. In the early years, the Friends' participation had been restricted and, at best, tolerated by NWRO. From 1969 to 1972, NWRO somewhat reluctantly expanded the role of the Friends to encompass both financial and political involvement, as the external political attacks by welfare authorities at the national and state levels grew worse. With Wiley gone and heavily in debt, NWRO leaders reluctantly allocated some of their scarce resources to mobilize the Friends. A strategy that had at first been repudiated as too costly was later adopted by the women leaders as a means for trying to save the movement organization. All attempts failed, although the efforts continued into 1975. For the middle-class activists, the costs of alliances with the welfare rights women had increased, and the rewards had declined. Moreover, new alternatives for social activism had emerged. For NWRO, the opposite had happened. The payoffs of an organized, middle-class support structure seemed to be much greater than its risks, given the weakened state of the national movement organization.

While NWRO had specified the rules for alliances between local WROs and their organized FWROs, in practice the national office had little, if any, control over what actually occurred at the local level, with a few exceptions. Thus, different models emerged, some supporting NWRO's guidelines for cooperation, others opting for integration of the poor and nonpoor, and still others developing independent coalitions that excluded (by design or by accident) the welfare poor. In each, the potential rewards and risks for the partners varied. In the parallel, or twin-track, model, the WRO women were to be the leaders, the Friends their supporters. Both would be separate, yet interdependent. In the integrated model, rules called for the sharing of power among several groups, regardless of their status within the larger society. The independent model was structured to keep the control in the hands of the middle-class allies by directly or indirectly limiting the participation of WROs in the coalitions. This model was highly criticized by NWRO leaders and some supporters as being "paternalistic" and undermining, rather than strengthening, the national movement. In the following sections, we examine how these three models functioned in practice in different parts of the country and what their consequences were for the mobilized resources of NWRO.

Twin-Track Coalitions in New Jersey

Unlike some other FWROs, the Friends of WRO in New Jersey was not organized to play a limited auxiliary role, as proposed by NWRO. Its goals were consonant with those of NWRO's, but its strategies included both support of local WROs and the mobilization of peer groups in the middle class. Its newsletter stated that its aims were

> to help bring about needed changes in the welfare system and to redirect our nation's priorities, by supporting the Welfare Rights Organization through education and mobilization of ourselves and others. [122]

It was a twofold strategy that eventually led to increasing conflict within this coalition, as support of WROs' needs collided with the mobilization and expansion of the Friends movement. Structural changes caused the power and decision making to gradually shift to the middle-class supporters, thus leading to the final withdrawal of the New Jersey Welfare Rights Organization (NJWRO) from the coalition. In the end, the movement of poor women had gained few resources. The Friends, on the other hand, had found an opportunity to participate as social activists in the political arena in the struggle for welfare reform. The long-range goals had not been attained. At best, some proposed cuts in New Jersey's AFDC benefits were restored and a new commissioner for the Department of Human Services appointed partly as the result of lobbying efforts by the middle-class supporters.

The Friends movement in New Jersey emerged shortly after the 1967 urban riots. It gained momentum and middle-class, suburban support as a result of a series of educational conferences in 1968 and 1969. Through the sponsorship of the locally based Greater Newark Council of Churches, a "Churchman's Seminar on the Public Welfare Crisis" was organized in February 1968. It was a cooperative effort with the newly organized WRO in Newark, which played an active and visible role on the planning committee and in the conference. As the chair of the conference, the Reverend Kim Jefferson stated that the use of "WRO members as consultants in the workshops . . . was a tremendous success. . . . They played an extremely important role in making the issue come alive . . . to the participants."[123] More people commented on this aspect of the conference, he added, than

on any other. Out of this gathering, a network of "concerned church
people" began to organize around the welfare issue.

A few months later, white and black church leaders organized
the Urban Training Institute in response to the urban crisis arising
from the 1967 riots and the assassination of Martin Luther King, Jr.,
the following spring. One of the central issues in the institute was
welfare. Suburbanites were invited to attend a series of educational
sessions in the winter of 1968/69. Once again, the leaders of the
WRO cooperated in the planning and participated as consultants in the
workshops. Out of this mobilization of middle-class liberals emerged
the New Jersey Friends of Welfare Rights in 1969.

The rationale for such an organization, according to its chair,
the Reverend Glenn Hatfield, was that "belonging to a membership
organization will give us a greater group coherence than if we are
merely a loose group of concerned persons." He added that "it will
also keep us honest and relevant by keeping us in touch with the genuine
concerns of the grassroots folk in the Welfare Rights Movement."[124]

The two groups, the WRO and the FWRO, had separate organizations, held separate meetings, and recruited different constituencies.
WRO leaders and members were always present at the Friends' meetings and functioned in the role of consultants. Friends, in theory,
were supposed to listen to their needs and to respond to their agenda,
in addition to developing their own. In reality, the interactions between
the WROs and the FWRO were very limited, as was the participation
by the welfare rights leaders in the middle-class organization. When
they did make requests, it was generally to ask for financial support
to keep their organization alive, to attend NWRO meetings, or to respond to individuals' emergencies.

The raising of funds for the WRO was a constant source of tension within the group of Friends. Despite various strategies, their
efforts met with little success. The basic question repeatedly raised
was, For whom should the monies be raised—WRO or the Friends?
The majority of the supporters believed that social change could be
brought about more quickly and efficiently by mobilizing the middle
class, rather than by expending time and energy raising monies to
help the AFDC women's organization. Furthermore, it was clear that
some Friends were not overly anxious to support any groups that might
add to the turmoil in the inner cities. New Jersey had had its riots
in 1967 and 1968, and suburbanites were, for the most part, wary of
a strategy of protest. There were some important exceptions. For
example, the Friends' leader and other officers repeatedly joined
WRO members in demonstrations, and its chair, Hatfield, was arrested in Newark in 1969 along with several poor women.

Only limited amounts of funds were mobilized and transferred
to the WRO in the state. Although the Friends had adopted member-

ship dues that allotted $10 out of the $13 to NWRO and its state affiliate, little was actually collected. Another attempt to raise monies by getting middle-class supporters to live on a welfare food budget for one week and to donate the resulting savings to WRO was not successful. At most, 150 families participated, and about $1,000 was collected.[125]

Given the costs and frustrations of service and protest strategies, most of the Friends' resources were spent in planning and running educational programs to mobilize the middle-class liberals. Mobilization of their peer groups, rather than support of WRO's needs in terms of money or protest, provided more rewards and fewer risks. Through various conferences, the New Jersey Friends gradually identified supporters and established a statewide network. Loosely structured and run by a small core group of activists, it succeeded, at its peak, in mobilizing about 300 to 400 Friends for a period of one or two years.

Some political strategies were developed by the New Jersey Friends in cooperation with the WROs in the state. One of their first joint actions was to try to change the structure of the Essex County Welfare Board. Success was achieved when a black AFDC mother, Nannette Adams, was appointed to the board. It was the first time in the history of the welfare system in the state that a black woman recipient and resident of Newark had held a seat on the board. Tokenism, however, proved to have its problems, and little change was made in the system as a result of this political action. As a "conduit" to the welfare power structures, the expectation of WRO leaders and members was that Adams would be able to voice their needs and gain support for their agenda. As one minority woman in a board of eight (mostly white and male), with few skills and experience with bureaucracy, her views and votes carried little weight. She later described it as a "powerless" position.[126]

Another political action of the Friends and the NJWRO was the mobilization of suburbanites and public leaders to live on a welfare food budget in order to gain support to defeat the Nixon-Moynihan FAP. In 1971 the "Mobilization against Hunger" united the resources of the WRO, the FWRO, and the peace organization New Jersey SANE to fight against the revised FAP (now called H.R. 1) and to call for tax expenditures on domestic welfare programs, rather than on military items. H.R. 1 was eventually defeated in 1972. (See Chapter 6.) Another objective of the 1971 mobilization was to fight the proposed cuts in the New Jersey AFDC benefits and to endorse and support the appointment of Ann Klein, an informal Friend of welfare rights, to the New Jersey Department of Human Services. Some cuts were blocked or reduced, and Klein was appointed to the top state welfare post.

These cooperative efforts, however, were beset by conflicts between WRO leaders and the Friends. One major source of tension was funding. WRO was critical of the inadequacy and inconsistency of the Friends' financial support. The Friends, on the other hand, were frustrated by NJWRO's lack of planning and the constant appeals for monies as well as their own inability to secure foundation or church grants for their allies. A second source of tension was the high visibility of the Friends in the coalition. Some Friends wanted to minimize their salience in the relationship, while others felt that to remain "legitimate" partners of the welfare organization, high visibility with WRO had to be maintained. The conflict not only polarized the Friends but also intensified the tensions between the Friends and the WROs. Two episodes illustrate the contrasting needs within the Friends' group and within the WRO/FWRO coalition.

At the first organizational meeting of the statewide network of the Friends of Welfare Rights in 1970, "there was considerable struggle and debate over the name" for the new organization. The original group formed at the Urban Training Institute in 1969 had adopted the label New Jersey Friends of Welfare Rights (NJFWRO). Some felt that this "close identity with a controversial group would be a barrier in mobilizing support in the suburbs." Others felt that "they had to take a clear and public stand in support of the Welfare Rights Organization." One participant reported that "the first group wanted the name of the support group to be 'Concerned Citizens of Welfare Reform' to minimize its direct linkage to NWRO. When the decision was made to call ourselves 'Friends of Welfare Rights,' we lost a lot of those present."[127] For some middle-class liberals, high visibility with the movement was defined as too costly, from both a personal and a political point of view, given the stigmatization of welfare in U.S. society. For others, high visibility with the movement of poor women and the welfare rights issue was seen as a personal and political reward, inasmuch as it helped to publicize the existence of middle-class liberal support for changing the system and endorsement of the national and state WROs.

The issue of the degree of identification and visibility with the WRO resurfaced when plans were being made for an educational conference for the middle-class supporters. The conflict once again erupted over the name for the conference. Basically, the debate was whether to include or eliminate the word <u>welfare</u> from the title. The WRO leaders had selected the slogan "Welfare Not Warfare," the theme of the 1971 NWRO convention. Most of the middle-class Friends were in favor of a nonalienating name, such as the Mobilization against Hunger. This faction argued that since the main objective of the conference was to mobilize more middle-class supporters for the political struggle to defeat FAP, any tactic that inhibited this effort should be eschewed. The Friends' choice, Mobilization against Hunger, rather than the WRO title, was adopted.

In the earlier years, high visibility with welfare rights had been perceived as a payoff by the small cadre of middle-class activists. Nonconformity was part of the political struggle. Close identification with NWRO underscored their belief that the poor had "rights to welfare," in violation of the U.S. value that the needy on public assistance were dependent on society's charitable impulses. In the mid-1960s, with the political climate supporting the idea that the poor had some basic rights, participation in this social movement held political and ideological rewards for many social activists. As public hostility to welfare recipients increased, the AFDC rolls and costs soared, and the Nixon administration and congressional leaders berated the poor women on welfare, participation in NWRO by Friends became less attractive. By 1971 this conflict over identification with welfare rights reflected these trends in the larger society and the growing power struggle within the coalition of WRO and FWRO. It culminated in the major restructuring of the alliance by the NJFWRO, the adoption of a new name, and, eventually, the withdrawal of the NJWRO from active participation in the new coalition.

Following the Mobilization against Hunger, participants were invited to attend an organizational meeting for a new coalition for welfare reform in December 1971. Theoretically, it was to expand the movement within the state by creating a federation of groups of the poor and nonpoor. The "umbrella" coalition was to include not only WROs and FRWOs but also representatives of labor unions, churches, civil rights groups, women's organizations, and student groups.

Leaders within the welfare rights movement strongly objected to this proposed reorganization. Their demands, however, were largely ignored. The New Jersey Friends and other interested groups undertook to restructure the parallel coalition into an integrated and more inclusive alliance for welfare reform. It was clear to WRO leaders in New Jersey, whose movement organization was by now greatly weakened and fragmented, that within the new structure their power would be very limited. They would be one among many, most of whom represented middle-class organizations. With their power diluted in the new coalition, many of the WRO leaders withdrew and refused to let their organization participate.

Their withdrawal, however, failed to impede the restructuring. The new movement organization chose to minimize its visibility with the welfare issue, choosing as its name the Social Concerns Action Network (SCAN). Most of the leaders of SCAN were former officers in the NJFWRO. Although they were concerned about the defection of WROs, they argued that it was politically necessary at this time to expand the middle-class base if they were to stop the "cuts and repression in New Jersey." They also asserted that the NJWRO was no longer a viable movement organization and that it no longer had any legitimacy among the organized poor.[128] Consequently, political realities demanded new strategies and tactics.

SCAN was active for a few years but succeeded in mobilizing only limited numbers in the mid- and late 1970s. Among its members were representatives of Protestant, Catholic, and Jewish religions; social-welfare agencies; one labor union; two civil rights groups; one peace organization; and several of the major women and feminist organizations. According to its annual reports, its budget never exceeded $1,000, although its staff was at times donated by social agencies, churches, and CETA. While welfare reform remained a central goal for SCAN, it was subsumed under the broader and more abstract objective of "elimination of poverty and racism and injustice."[129] This spin-off from the twin-track coalition of WRO/FWRO had emerged out of the turmoil and protest of the black and poor in the cities. When turmoil subsided and the cost of partnership with WRO became too high for the middle-class supporters, a new movement organization emerged. SCAN became an alternative vehicle through which to continue the welfare struggle. The goals remained the same, but the strategy had changed and was now controlled by the nonpoor liberals in an "integrated" movement organization.

In assessing the results of the WRO/FWRO coalition in New Jersey, there were varying reports from participants and observers on both sides. WRO leaders in New Jersey were mostly critical of the role of the Friends in the welfare rights movement, stating that much had been promised and little accomplished as a result of the alliance. One WRO officer in the state asserted that most of the Friends had "copped out" and joined other movements, contending that "they can't work with us because we have a lot of dissension in our organization."[130] Hatfield, the chair of NJFWRO, also admitted that the coalition of the poor and nonpoor had had some successes and some failures. He asserted that the Friends and their middle-class allies "can take most of the credit for getting the passage of 'transitional payments' to alleviate some of the welfare cuts imposed by Governor Cahill's Administration." He noted that this "amounted to six million dollars in additional money for welfare recipients" and emphasized that "if the Friends hadn't raised these issues and kept them visibly before the public, it would never have been done. WRO was too disorganized at that point to mobilize a campaign independently without middle-class support from all liberal sectors."[131] On the other hand, he was quick to add that the coalition had failed because the Friends had "lulled them [NJWRO] into thinking that we are stronger and can deliver more than we can. We lulled them into a false sense of security." Hatfield felt that the WRO in Newark "tends to overestimate what we can do and thus we . . . added to the level of their frustrations' quotient." He agreed that "our Friends group certainly has not delivered any major support in money terms" and that "the only thing we have done is provided entry for them into the suburbs and provided forums where they can be heard."[132]

Other critics of the WRO/FWRO coalitions in the welfare rights movement stated that little change had occurred as a result of this alliance between the poor and nonpoor. Philip Nyden, an observer and social analyst, suggested that the "reliability of middle-class support appears to be quite dubious."[133] Ed Chambers, Saul Alinsky's successor in the Industrial Areas Foundation, was highly critical of the Friends' strategies in New Jersey.[134] He decried the fact that the middle-class Friends did not understand "what power was" nor how to organize it and maximize it. He criticized church people as amateurs "playing at organizing" and raising the expectations of welfare recipients, without ever developing any "power" among the client population itself. Chambers cited the "naivete of a strategy of expanding the Welfare Board as a means of gaining power." He pointed out that this was just tokenism, and "OEO had always seduced the poor and black that way." An effective strategy, he suggested, was to create a majority base and develop independent means of support. Referring to the civil rights struggle, he emphasized that, as had been shown repeatedly, economic dependence—"asking whites to help blacks with financial support"—just did not work. Other strategies, such as Living on a Welfare Budget, the Utility Rights Campaign, and other "gimmicks," were, in his opinion, a waste of time and effort. The only successful way of creating power was to build a majority coalition of board interests with a multiissue focus. Only this strategy, he insisted, would be "a move in the right direction."

Despite the unresolved tensions in the cooperative efforts of the poor and nonpoor in New Jersey, other WRO/FWRO satellite coalitions emerged in some suburban areas following the turmoil in the cities and major mobilization by the liberals in Newark.* In all cases observed, the memberships were small and the alliances fragile. Some lasted a few weeks. Others continued for over two years. Similar conflicts arose in all of them. Unmet expectations on both sides raised the tensions in such alliances and decreased the rewards of involvement. The major issue leading to conflict was the question of who rules. Despite the espoused subordinate role for the middle-class supporters, in most of the twin-track coalitions observed, the Friends tended to dominate. This type of coalition, however, was a new and

---

*Some data are available on WRO/FWRO satellite coalitions in the New Jersey towns of Morristown, Montclair, Westfield, Patterson, and Somerville.

unique experiment to try to empower the poor without taking control.
In many instances, it failed—both in terms of providing financial support and political autonomy for the fledgling movement organizations
of poor women at the local level. These attempts at new cooperative
models once again underscored the inevitable "prisoners' dilemma"
in bringing about social change.

In sum, from the furor of the urban disorders in 1967/68, the
New Jersey Friends and some satellites in the suburbs emerged to
coalesce with the state and local WROs. The goal of the alliance was
to bring about welfare reform at the state and national levels. Its
means was to be the support and empowerment of the WROs in the
state and the mobilization of a parallel, middle-class support structure. This coalitional strategy added little to the mobilized resources
of the movement in New Jersey. At best, it brought some public visibility to the issue of welfare reform and kept the debate in the political arena, as the NJWRO declined in power and was torn by internal
dissension. Perhaps its biggest success was in mobilizing some liberal, middle-class support for welfare reform in general and, to a
much lesser extent, for welfare rights in particular.

The most significant change in the alliance over the years was
the restructuring of NJFWRO into a broader umbrella coalition called
SCAN. NWRO's fear that the Friends might come to dominate the
movement organizations of the poor had in fact come to pass in New
Jersey. While the state WRO collapsed, SCAN survived, despite its
declining activities, into the 1980s.

Other parallel, or twin-track, coalitions between WROs and
the Friends of WRO emerged in various parts of the country, but little data are available. Some evidence indicates that many, like the
ones in New Jersey, were fragile, short-lived, and small in size.
Conflicts over unmet expectations on both sides and complaints about
middle-class dominance seem to have been ubiquitous and helped to
undermine these cooperative efforts. While they lasted, they represented, at minimum, symbolic, if not real, support for the welfare
rights movement.

Integrated Coalitions of the Poor and Nonpoor

Wisconsin

In Wisconsin the statewide Public Assistance Coalition (PAC)
emerged in response to the "drastic cuts in the welfare budget by the
State Legislature for [the] biannual budget in the Fall of 1969."[135]
Led by the State Council of Churches, a diverse group of organizations
concerned with poverty coalesced to develop a strategy to bring about
legislative reforms and restore the welfare cuts. Over the first year,

over 40 state and local organizations joined the coalition, which included not only the WRO but also the League of Women Voters, the AFL-CIO, the United Auto Workers, social workers, and others. Using the annual legislative seminar of the Council of Churches as a public forum from which to air the issue, PAC moved on to develop educational materials, publish a newsletter, hold meetings around the state, and mobilize widespread support among a diverse group of organizations. While the organized poor women were represented, middle-class liberals dominated in terms of numbers.

The paid director, Ken Scholen, according to one participant, "did a fantastic job of getting the PAC established as an effective political grassroots force and getting communications of pertinent information to the new Governor and key legislators."[136] Success came about in the fall of 1971, when all the welfare cuts of 1969 were restored. From actions at the local level, the coalition moved to mobilize in support of NWRO's agenda to defeat FAP at the national level. Statewide meetings, educational programs, and lobbying of key congressional representatives followed. As a result of these actions, it was felt that some impact had been provided by the Wisconsin coalition in helping defeat FAP in 1972.[137]

The major consequence of the coalition, according to Scholen, "has been the growing awareness among its members of the importance and potential of organized groups of welfare recipients." The coalition funded the WRO's efforts to write and publish a comprehensive handbook on AFDC rights and also provided monies to strengthen and sustain the "first two years of an embryonic Wisconsin Welfare Rights Coordinating Committee" for the state. It lobbied together with NWRO, as well as conducted research and provided technical assistance to the organization of the poor.

In 1973 the Wisconsin PAC was still functioning and cooperating with the state WRO. This integrated model appears to have been successful in achieving its goal at the state level and to have established a functioning relationship between the poor and nonpoor. No data were available, however, on the conflicts and their outcomes within the coalition. Neither is it known how the WRO leaders rated its effectiveness in terms of support and the degree of middle-class control. Based on this limited evidence, it seems clear, however, that these Friends of WRO also dominated the alliance, even though the WROs were included as equal partners "to ensure a realistic reading of the issue." In numbers, at least, the middle-class liberals appear to have been in control.

Rhode Island

Another integrated coalition of the poor and nonpoor emerged in Rhode Island in early 1971.[138] As in Wisconsin, a state budgetary

crisis gave rise to the mobilization of the Friends of WRO and the organized welfare recipients. In February 1971, the state legislature
attempted to reduce the state budget by cutting down on welfare expenditures. This provided the impetus for middle-class involvement in
the conflict between the WRO and the state legislature. The coalition
of Friends lasted for a short period of time; was broad-based; and
included churches, social-welfare agencies, labor unions, women's
groups, and some civil rights organizations. Black churches, however, apparently remained outside the conflict as witnesses. While
the coalition lasted, it was a loosely integrated alliance of the poor
and nonpoor.

The rationale for political action by church leaders and their
constituencies was that churches "have power and political clout" and
should use it to "convince people . . . to function as a lobby." One of
the major organizers of the coalition, a Catholic priest, noted that
the driving force for the mobilization against the actions of the state
in Rhode Island "sprung from moral outrage at the suspension of the
special grants, as well as from a motivation of self-interest." White
church and social-welfare leaders in the state, he added, realized
that the burden of supplying the special needs to the poor would fall
on them, once the state withdrew the public funds and revised its
welfare policy. These church and social-welfare representatives
feared that such a crisis might well create a demand on them by the
poor of "catastrophic proportions," which they were totally unpre-
pared to meet "financially or staffwise." The cost to the nonpoor
within the church and the social-welfare agencies in the private sector—whose stated mission was to serve the poor—was estimated as
potentially disastrous if the state proceeded with its proposed social
policy.

To avert this, a strategy was developed to mobilize public support to pressure the legislature. After research and compilation of
the "facts on welfare," the Friends and state and local WROs joined
together to present programs on television and radio and from church
pulpits and other forums to expound their economic and moral arguments against the proposed welfare cuts. In addition to these public
presentations, teams of three—a member of the clergy and two welfare rights representatives—visited homes in a door-to-door campaign.
It was an intense and all-encompassing effort, employing a variety of
sophisticated tactics and economic and political resources of the middle-class supporters together with the cooperation of welfare rights
groups. It was a barrage of information through the media, public
forums, and personal contacts with key leaders.

The organizers "highlighted the discrepancies that existed in
the system." For example, they pointed out that "a heating allowance
of $18.50 per month and the reality of heating bills reaching $55-60"

penalized the poor. They also "tried to make very clear . . . the negative impact that [the cuts] would have on the middle-class." The emphasis was that "the working poor" were also in need of assistance and that the coalition was interested in "establishing emergency funds" for them, too. One organizer summarized the overall strategy as an "educational strategy—unemotional, clear and concise—with hard facts on 'what is' and 'what might be' if this action were taken by the Legislators."

Although the outcome of the "first round" of the contest of the poor and their allies against the political establishment in Rhode Island was successful, the organizers asserted that they had won not only through political mobilization but also through legal and educational actions. Fighting concurrently in the courts, the coalition was able to get a temporary injunction on the proposed legislative welfare cuts. The outcome was also deemed a success because the "people were advocating for themselves." The "poor and their middle-class supporters had our self-interests at heart" in the joint struggle. The WRO's contributions and input were described as "invaluable" by their supporters, since "they knew what the problems were very specifically and could help us target in on them very directly." Finally, the coalition was assessed as a success by its chair because it had provided "a voice for the welfare recipients when no one would listen."

From the reports of the middle-class supporters, it is clear that this integrated coalition succeeded at least temporarily in achieving its short-run goals. Little data are available on the feelings and reactions of the welfare rights leaders. The existing evidence suggests that the WRO played an important role in defining the problem and cooperated in carrying out the strategy decisions of the coalition. However, it is clear that here, as in other coalitions of the poor and nonpoor, the latter probably were in control. Nevertheless, at least for a limited time, commonality of needs superseded differences and possibly attenuated the conflicts inherent in such coalitions. This cooperative experiment in itself was termed a success by participants and observers.

An Independent, Middle-Class
Coalition for Welfare Reform

Whereas the parallel coalition of the WRO and the FWRO in New Jersey eventually changed into an integrated alliance dominated by middle-class liberals, in Missouri a movement organization emerged within the context of the welfare rights struggle that eschewed cooperation with the welfare recipients. Reform of Welfare (ROWEL), an independent, middle-class coalition, deliberately decided to exclude the WRO and worked independently to increase the benefit level for the poor in Missouri.

Like the other coalitions examined, ROWEL emerged as a result of the stimulus of church action and study groups around the issue of welfare.* During the summer and fall of 1972, a coalition of Protestant church leaders and lay persons sponsored a couple of welfare legislative workshops for "persons interested in understanding the welfare system in Missouri and in becoming advocates for needed changes in the system."[139] As a result of the workshops, ROWEL was organized. Its membership was theoretically open to anyone, although one interviewer of ROWEL members reported that "black participation was never made clear." Black leaders in the community indicated that while some had been invited to participate, a decision seems to have been made by the white leadership not to saliently involve them "in the legislative fight." In the blacks' opinion, this underscored the conscious or unconscious racism present in the coalition and within society.[140]

ROWEL was gradually expanded to include Catholics and Jews and various religious and social-welfare agencies concerned with the problem of low AFDC benefits in Missouri. The WROs in the state, however, were deliberately excluded or, at best, not invited to participate in the coalition of middle-class church groups.

Repudiating NWRO's militant tactics, ROWEL bypassed the use of welfare recipients in the struggle for welfare reform in Missouri, calling only on its middle-class members and allies. This created anger within the local and national movement, but it did not stop the middle-class liberals from proceeding with their political plans.

According to one participant, the rationale for the exclusion of welfare rights was based on the fact that previous attempts to use "demonstrations, witnesses, and confrontations" in the state had failed to bring about any changes in the welfare system. Consequently, ROWEL had decided to try a new strategy. Their strategy, said one observer, was to be "collaborative not confrontative."[141] A collaborative strategy was defined as involving careful planning, development, and close nurturing of ties with various members and friends of the legislature. Technically, in the welfare rights struggle, these were the "targets" and the opponents. ROWEL, on the other hand, attempted to attract them to their side. ROWEL researched the laws,

---

*UCC's WPT, discussed in an earlier section, was active during this time in several regions in the country developing its own constituencies and that of other liberal groups in support of welfare reform and the welfare rights struggle.

established contact with key legislators, and cooperated in drafting a bill. It also enlisted the support of the mayor of St. Louis to introduce the bill and other key legislators to sponsor it. In contrast to the early militant demonstrations and sit-ins by the WRO, ROWEL's was a traditional "low-key and sophisticated" political strategy, according to one participant.

In terms of legislative reforms, the outcome of these independent lobbying actions was successful. After organizing in October 1972, ROWEL succeeded in getting a bill into the Missouri legislature in January 1973 and having it adopted that summer. While the amount they demanded was not met (they had asked for an $80 increase for the ADC* monthly payments), the legislature did grant an increase of $20 per recipient per month. ROWEL termed this a victory for Missouri, which had one of the lowest public assistance benefit levels in the country. Among all the states, Missouri ranked thirty-seventh in the AFDC program. According to ROWEL leaders, this "victory" resulted in the distribution of about $11 million to recipients in one year and moved Missouri up from thirty-seventh to thirty-fifth place in AFDC benefit levels in the country. To one middle-class observer, the "amazing thing" was that "it was accomplished without militancy" and by "working through the system."

Like the "parallel" and "integrated" state coalitions of Friends that mobilized around the welfare issue, ROWEL's actions resulted in some benefits for the poor in that state. It failed, however, to make any long-term impact on the welfare system and its inadequacies. Unlike the other alliances, moreover, ROWEL failed to empower the WRO, either by providing it with needed organizational resources or by helping it to join as a political partner in the struggle. Most important, unlike the others, ROWEL failed to recognize the WRO as a representative of the poor or to accord it a legitimacy to participate as an equal partner in the coalition.

One white church official asserted that "this model, while in some ways successful, conveyed continued paternalism: doing 'for' instead of 'with.'" In many ways, he added, "it undercut a basic Christian principle which demands that we eliminate paternalism." He criticized not only this "blatant paternalistic" strategy but also ROWEL's "racist" behavior, whether conscious or unconscious. In his opinion, these basic structural "weaknesses" undermined ROWEL's economic and political successes. The means, he felt, did not justify the end. Another church official, closely associated with ROWEL, sug-

---

*In Missouri, the program is called Aid to Dependent Children (ADC) rather than Aid to Families with Dependent Children (AFDC), as in many other states.

gested that lack of cooperation between the poor and nonpoor decreased the power of those involved in the welfare reform struggle. He emphasized that both kinds of strategies were needed—both "abrasive and collaborative." He explained:

> If we play a separate game, without consulting one another
> we may lose more than we win. The best strategy appears
> to be to keep outwardly divided and in disagreement on
> strategy, while inwardly we maintain close communication
> and continuous linkages. The facts are clear that we need
> both kinds of groups to achieve change: those with abrasive
> tactics and those employing collaborative ways. [142]

He added that the key was to adjust the "visible connections" depending on the political climate. "In the present hostile environment," he suggested, "visible connections should be minimized."

In sum, cooperation between organized groups of poor women in the National Welfare Rights movement and middle-class liberals emerged in various parts of the country as a result of the political turmoil in the cities in 1968 and 1969 and later as a result of active mobilization by NWRO and its church ally, UCC. Most coalitions examined appear to have been short-lived and episodic, rising and falling with crises. Although coalitions of the poor and nonpoor were observed at all levels of the movement, there were clear structural differences among them. Some were twin-track coalitions in which the two allies were separate but visibly linked around a common goal. Here, theoretically at least, the poor led and the nonpoor supported. In the integrated coalitions, various middle-class and WRO organizations joined together under one umbrella coalition to develop joint and independent strategies against the welfare power structures. All coalition members in such umbrella groups were, in theory, equal partners. In the independent, or separatist, model, middle-class activists within the welfare rights movement excluded the poor by design or by accident. In these, therefore, WROs gained no support either economically or politically.

The outcomes of these different cooperative experiments varied. While conflict appears to have been prevalent in all three to some extent, the major sources of tension in these coalitions among unequals seems to have been the question of who rules. In the parallel WRO/FWRO coalitions, the proposed "reversed roles" in practice exacerbated conflict, since supporters from the middle class generally refused to accept a passive service role. As they organized and took political initiatives, they tended to dominate the movement of the poor, despite NWRO's continuous admonitions against control by the nonpoor. Based on the evidence available in New Jersey, the parallel coalitions added only limited resources to the WROs in the state, although they appear to have enhanced the visibility and legitimacy of the welfare rights cause within the dominant sector. The coalition was more successful in expanding the middle-class base of support than that of the poor women. In terms of changing the state system, its efforts were limited and temporary. It seems to have helped attenuate some of the more repressive measures proposed by the state legislature but did not succeed in blocking major cuts, institutionalizing cost-of-living increases, or preventing the expansion of more repressive tactics by the state, such as of "fraud squads." Conflicts between WRO and its Friends, as well as the changing political and economic conditions, led to the demise and restructuring of the coalition into an "integrated" coalition known as SCAN. By then the NJWRO was suffering from internal factionalism and lack of resources. Its supporters chose to move on independently with the challenge, rather than to undergird the challenger.

The integrated coalitions observed achieved some success in inhibiting welfare cuts for the AFDC mothers in the campaigns in Wisconsin and Rhode Island. In these alliances, the WRO was recognized as a legitimate representative of the welfare poor and was considered an equal partner. Middle-class supporters appear to have been in control in terms of numbers, although there is evidence that WRO was accorded a leading role in defining the problems and issues. Here again, these coalitions appear to have enhanced the visibility of the welfare rights cause within the political arena but done less to empower the WROs by providing needed resources. The emphasis seems to have been on political actions to achieve changes in the welfare system rather than on service to strengthen the movement organizations of poor women.

Finally, the independent coalition of middle-class activists in Missouri, which excluded the WRO, succeeded temporarily in raising the benefit level for recipients by $20 per month. Its effect on the WRO was probably debilitating, since it siphoned off potential supporters and resources and failed to recognize the organization of the poor as a legitimate challenger in the political arena.

This chapter has tried to explore the sources of cooperation from the middle-class sector and their consequences for NWRO. We first examined the coalition between NWRO and the church agencies, IFCO and the United Church of Christ's WPT and found that these alliances, although limited in time, transferred substantial monies and political allies to NWRO. The local and state coalitions examined, on the other hand, appear to have been much shorter in duration and beset by lack of clear-cut rules of the game and disappointed expectations on both sides. While some temporary gains were made for welfare recipients in general in the parallel coalitions in New Jersey, the benefits for the WROs in all cases seem to have been minimal at best. Perhaps the "success" of the middle-class, liberal involvement in the welfare rights struggle was primarily in helping keep the issue in the political arena and providing legitimacy for the cause and the national movement organization. Only at the national level were substantial monies transferred from the Protestant churches to NWRO. When these were withdrawn, along with other support, NWRO, by then without alternatives, collapsed.

Both cooperation and conflict thus helped to shape and structure the alliances within the welfare rights movement at all levels. The process of mobilization of allies and their resources in the ongoing conflict with the welfare power structures was a continuous one for NWRO and its local affiliates. As supporters joined or withdrew—or even abstained from the struggle—NWRO's power rose and fell. The political and economic forces also continuously affected this fusion and fission within the protest movement. Both internal conflicts and changing conditions altered the costs and rewards of participation for those involved. As we shall see in the next chapter, alliances with black and women's organizations—NWRO's racial and sex peer groups —also were riddled with tensions that had an impact on NWRO's mobilized resources and, ultimately, its survival.

NOTES

1. Gerhard Lenski, The Religious Factor, rev. ed. (Garden City, N.Y.: Doubleday, 1963).

2. Georg Simmel, On Individuality and Social Forms, ed. Donald N. Levine (Chicago: University of Chicago Press, 1971), pp. 150-78. In a passage on the obligation of the giver, Simmel notes that "Christian alms . . . represent no more than a form of asceticism, of 'good works,' which improve the chances of salvation of the giver" (pp. 153-54).

3. "The Church and Welfare Rights," Grapevine, Joint Strategy Action Committee, New York, September 1972. See also Luke 4:18.

4. "The Church and Welfare Rights."

5. Francine du Plessix Gray, "To March or Not to March," New York Times, June 27, 1975, p. 6.

6. This discussion is based principally on Harvey Cox's article "The 'New Breed' in American Churches: Sources of Social Activism in American Religion," in Religion in America, ed. William McLoughlin and R. N. Bellah (Boston: Houghton Mifflin, 1968), pp. 368-82.

7. "Social Welfare Ministries in a Time of Radical Social Change—A Report to the Churches for the 1970's" (Prepared by Haskell M. Miller for the Committee on Social Welfare, National Council of Churches of Christ in the U.S.A., n.d., distributed 1970/71).

8. Ibid., p. 20.

9. Ibid., p. 23.

10. Ibid., pp. 50-52, 54.

11. Cox, "New Breed," pp. 374-75.

12. See Guida West, "Twin-Track Coalitions in the Black Power Movement," Interracial Bonds, ed. Rhoda Goldstein Blumberg and Wendell James Roye (New York: General Hall Press, 1979).

13. Taped interview no. 207, September 1974.

14. Ibid.

15. Report of IFCO, 1970, p. 5.

16. IFCO's annual report, April 1970, p. 23.

17. Ibid., p. 9.

18. Directory of National Black Organizations (New York: AFRAM, 1972).

19. Richard Fitzgerald, "IFCO: A Black-Controlled Philanthropy," Non-Profit Report 4 (June 1971), reprint. This is a national monthly magazine published for foundations and individuals interested in philanthropy.

20. Interview with Lucius Walker, first executive director of IFCO, New York, 1974; and taped interview with Ann Douglas, acting executive director of IFCO, New York, 1974.

21. "IFCO," Tempo (National Council of Churches, New York), June 1, 1971. See also Fitzgerald, "IFCO"; and H. H. Ward, "IFCO—What It Is, What It Does, What It Wants," Tempo (National Council of Churches, New York), June 1, 1969, p. 9.

22. Ward, "IFCO."

23. George Vecsey, "Church Council Body Moving to Harlem in Protest," New York Times, January 7, 1979.

24. Nicholas Kotz and Mary Lynn Kotz, A Passion for Equality: George Wiley and the Movement (New York: W. W. Norton, 1977), p. 245.

25. Interview with Lucius Walker, New York, 1974. The following section is based on this interview.

26. Ibid.

27. Ibid.

28. Ibid.

29. August Meier, Elliot Ludwick, and Francis Broderick, eds., Black Protest Thought in the Twentieth Century, 2d ed. (Indianapolis: Bobbs-Merrill, 1971), p. 543; and Kotz and Kotz, Passion for Equality, p. 245.

30. Interview with Lucius Walker, 1974.

31. Ibid.

32. Report of George Wiley to WPT, New York, September 19, 1972.

33. Field notes, November 19, 1973.

34. Hobart A. Burch, "Conversations with George Wiley," Journal of Social Issues, November-December 1970, p. 5, reprint.

35. Conversation with Timothy Sampson, 1972.

36. Paul Sherry, Hobart Burch, and Mel Turner, "UCC/NWRO," in Voluntarism in America's Future (Washington, D. C.: Center for a Voluntary Society, 1972), p. 37.

37. "Guaranteed Income—HOW?" Social Action, vol. 34 (November 1967).

38. Taped interview no. 213.

39. "Action Taken by the Board of Directors for Homeland Ministries—Welfare Rights," April 29, 1970 (mimeographed).

40. The decline in social action priorities over these years is reflected in the amount of allocations for the priority teams. According to this same source, the allocations went from a high of $1 million in 1971 to $650,000 in 1973 to a low of $150,000 in 1974. Field notes, October 24, 1973; and December 14, 1973.

41. Sherry, Burch, and Turner, "UCC/NWRO."

42. Taped interview no. 213.

43. Ibid.

44. Ibid.

45. Ibid.

46. Ibid., p. 39.

47. Ibid., pp. 41-42.

48. Ibid., p. 39.

49. Taped interview no. 213.

50. Sherry, Burch, and Turner, "UCC/NWRO," p. 41.

51. Taped interview no. 207.

52. Timothy J. Sampson, Welfare: A Handbook for Friend or Foe (Philadelphia: Pilgrim Press, 1972).

53. Field notes, July 6, 1972.

54. WPT memorandum, August 15, 1972.

55. Taped interview no. 213.

56. Ibid.

57. Field notes, October 24, 1972.

58. Ibid.

59. Field notes, September 29, 1972.

60. Ibid.

61. Field notes, January 11, 1973.

62. Ibid.

63. Field notes, June 8, 1973.

64. Ibid.

65. Ibid.

66. Ibid.

67. Ibid.

68. Field notes, June 8, 1973; and Timothy Sampson, "For Our Own Welfare," Just Economics, vol. 2 (April 1974).

69. Field notes, June 8, 1973.

70. It should be noted, however, that another factor influencing this shift in strategy was the interaction and political impact of the women's middle-class movement on NWRO women leaders. By 1972 they were demanding and apparently asserting greater power within the national headquarters. (See Chapter 3.)

71. Field notes, conversation with church executive, August 15, 1975.

72. Field notes, December 14, 1973.

73. Ibid.

74. Ibid.

75. Ibid.

76. Ibid.

77. The last grant was from the Field Foundation in 1972 in the amount of $50,000, according to this respondent. Taped interview no. 151 in 1974.

78. The facts in 1973 indicated, however, that the local base had already eroded considerably. This appears to have been one of the important reasons given by the elites in UCC for not continuing the alliance with NWRO. One team member described the movement at the end of 1973 as being an "empty shell."

79. Field notes, November 19, 1973.

80. Field notes, January 30, 1973.

81. NWRO, after the establishment of the coalition with UCC/WPT and before its end, made few references to the role of Friends in its newsletter, the Welfare Fighter. One occurred immediately after the coalition formation between the NWRO and the UCC/WPT in the May 1970 issue. After the termination of the coalition, the Welfare Fighter (the last issue published in May 1974) had a lengthy article strongly supporting the organization of a national Friends support group. The first article was limited to a few lines stating that periodically they hoped to publish "a regular Friends news column . . . to bring the Friends network closer together by publicizing the activities of local groups and the National office." "Friends to Start Column," Welfare Fighter, May 1970, p. 12. This never happened. It is clear that with limited resources in terms of money and staff servicing the Friends was never given priority, even though periodically staff members were assigned the responsibility of being the national Friends coordinator. There were many perceived and real costs and limited payoffs in such a strategy for NWRO.

82. Hobart A. Burch, "Conversations with Cesar Chavez," Journal of Social Issues, November-December, 1971; and field notes, July 18, 1972.

83. Memorandum from Hulbert James, director of economic concerns in the National Council of Churches, to Friends of Welfare Rights, New York, June 21, 1973.

84. Original notes of Timothy Sampson on WRISC at the July 1973 meeting and workshop of the 1973 NWRO convention in Washington, D. C.

85. Field notes, St. Louis, Mo., July 12, 1974.

86. "WRISC Membership Form," For Our Welfare 1 (October 1974): 7. This was the first and only issue of the WRISC newsletter.

87. Field notes, July 12, 1974.

88. Kenneth A. Briggs, "Protestant Churches Are Reviving Evangelism in Membership Drive," New York Times, April 10, 1977. The UCC "formed its first working group on evangelism, a subject in which its previous interest had been slight." See also taped interview no. 207.

89. Conversation with Ruby Grace, chair of Newark WRO, April 1978. See also "Program on Welfare Reform: 1978-1980," National Council of Churches; and field notes, April-September 1978.

90. "Churches Combine for 'Festival of Faith,'" Star Ledger (Newark, N. J.), April 1, 1979.

91. Briggs, "Protestant Churches."

92. The word friend, used commonly in the English language, implies support. It generally symbolizes an auxiliary structure to achieve the goal of another already-existing institution. The nature of such auxiliaries in the social protest movements (which this writer has labeled twin-track coalitions), in which powerless groups organize and then are linked up with other, existing, more powerful allies, differs from the traditional "auxiliaries" in at least one significant way. In the latter, both the internal and external power rests with the core group from the dominant sector, not with the subordinate supporting group. In the twin-track model—the parallel coalition— the internal political power rests with the subordinate core group. Outside the movement community, however, the political and economic power resides in the supporters from the dominant majority. In the twin-track model, the protestors are economically dependent on their dominant political allies. In the traditional model, the elite group is economically and politically independent and the "auxiliary" functions merely as an appendage. It is not dependent on its "friends" politically or economically. In many instances, the auxiliary provides a traditional voluntary service role for women in the support of professional male organizations and reinforces, in practice, the "supportive" rather than "leadership" positions into which women are social-

ized. The traditional model is generally found in "service" contexts; the twin-track model, in political protest situations.

The "friends" track in protest movements implies existence of a politically subordinate core group that provides the leadership for the coalition. The "ideal" twin-track coalition is an interdependent and a symbiotic coalition model. There are risks and incentives for both partners. The goal of twin-track is power redistribution. The goal of auxiliary is support of the status quo. In the former, the participants are challengers. In the latter, the members are supporters of the status quo.

93. Sampson, as the NWRO liaison to WPT in 1970, helped develop materials for distribution for the church's middle-class constituency. One of the letters was to the Friends of Welfare Rights, sent out by the United Church Board of Homeland Ministries, November 10, 1970, of which a section is quoted.

94. Sampson, Welfare, p. 200.

95. Conversation with Timothy Sampson, Deering, N.H., July 1972. Sampson provided this writer with the original notes he had made in planning the Friends structure: "Comments on the Nature of the Relationship." He also said that the Friends of SNCC in the civil rights movement had served as model in his thinking and developing of the FWRO.

96. William Howard Whitaker, "The Determinants of Social Movement Success: A Study of the National Welfare Rights Organization" (Ph.D. diss., Brandeis University, 1970), pp. 156-57, n. 1.

97. Taped interview no. 205. Also see Anne Carol Spencer, "A History of the National Welfare Rights Organizations" (Paper, University of Pennsylvania, School of Social Work, 1976), p. 23.

98. Taped interview with Johnnie Tillmon, July 1974.

99. John D. McCarthy and Mayer N. Zald, The Trend of Social Movements in America: Professionalization and Resource Mobilization (Morristown, N.J.: General Learning Press, 1973).

100. Taped interview with Hulbert James, New York, September 1974.

101. Robert K. Merton, Social Theory and Social Structure (New York: Free Press, 1968), pp. 411-22. Merton conceptually distinguishes nonconformity from other forms of deviant behavior. He states:

> Under certain conditions, public non-conformity can have the manifest and latent functions of changing standards of conduct and values which have become dysfunctional for the group. Other private forms have the manifest function of serving the interests of the deviant and . . . the latent function of re-activating sentiments of the group which have

grown so weak as no longer to be effective regulators of behavior. To lump together functionally (and not only morally) different forms of conduct in one concept of "deviant behavior" is to obscure their sociological import. [P. 420]

102. Taped interview with Hulbert James, New York, September 1974.

103. Memorandum from George Wiley to Friends, July 4, 1970.

104. "Friends," a report from WPT, n.d., probably June 1970.

105. Taped interview with Bert DeLeeuw, July 1974.

106. Whitaker, "Social Movement Success," pp. 208-9.

107. Taped interview with Bert DeLeeuw, July 1974.

108. Ibid.

109. Nicholas Kotz, "Welfare Rights Eyes Coalition," Washington Post, August 1971, reprint.

110. Whitaker, "Social Movement Success," p. 210, n. 1.

111. "Friends Exist on a Welfare Diet," Welfare Fighter, July 1969.

112. Taped interview no. 203.

113. Memorandum to all WROs from Hulbert James, NWRO associate director, September 24, 1969.

114. "Wife of Senator Calls for Fast," Welfare Fighter, November 1969.

115. Prospectus, NWRO, March 1970.

116. Field notes, November 1971.

117. Letter from Joanne L. Williams, NWRO Friends coordinator, to "Dear Friend," March 31, 1970.

118. Memorandum from George Wiley, executive director, to All Friends of Welfare Rights, July 4, 1970.

119. Field notes, February 3, 1972.

120. Field notes, Washington, D.C., meeting, May 1, 1973.

121. "National Friends Organization," Prospectus, NWRO, 1974.

122. Welfare Writer, FWRO Newsletter, February 1970.

123. Personal interview with Kim Jefferson, December 11, 1971.

124. Glenn Hatfield, Welfare Concerns Newsletter, vol. 1 (March 11, 1969).

125. Analysis of a questionnaire on participation in the New Jersey Live on a Welfare Budget.

126. Interview with Nannette Adams, Newark, N.J., December 1971.

127. Personal interview no. 259.

128. Taped interview no. 264.

129. Undated brochure, Social Action Concerns Network, Newark, N.J., printed and distributed in 1972.

130. Taped interview no. 108.

131. Personal interview with the Reverend Glenn Hatfield, chair of FWRO, December 1971.

132. Ibid.

133. Philip Nyden, "Welfare and Welfare Rights: An Analysis of Organizations in the Newark Metropolitan Area" (Paper, Drew University, Madison, N.J., 1972), pp. 42, 45.

134. Field notes, Deering, N.H., July 1973.

135. Personal correspondence from the Reverend George Munger, Wisconsin, to the Reverend Glenn Hatfield, New Jersey, April 14, 1972. This section on Wisconsin is based on data reported by Ken Scholen, coordinator of the Public Assistance Coalition, at a meeting in Washington, D.C., May 1, 1973, and in his article "Making a Difference: A Model," Colloquy, October 1973, pp. 32-33.

136. Munger correspondence.

137. Scholen, "Making a Difference."

138. This section is based on a report at a workshop at the July 1971 NWRO convention.

139. Field notes from a meeting on November 19, 1973; "Rowel," mimeographed (undated); taped interview with a white, male participant on July 13, 1974, St. Louis, Mo.; and Mary Jo Halderman Ross, "Letter to an Editor," Colloquy, October 1973, pp. 34-37.

140. Field notes, November 19, 1973. The rest of this section is based on these notes.

141. Ross quotes the theological rationale of ROWEL as follows:

> Involvement is at the very heart of the Christian's faith and life. To say that one is Christian is to say that he or she is dedicated to healing the hurt in the hearts of human beings, binding up the wounds of the world, becoming a part of the solution to human problems rather than an extension of the problems themselves. . . . We want to work for a Christian reforming of the welfare system—our faith calls us to do that.

The staff coordinator of ROWEL, a young woman, stated that her philosophy of living was "Out of the pew and do!"

142. Field notes, November 19, 1973.

5

NWRO AND ALLIANCES WITH
BLACK AND WOMEN'S ORGANIZATIONS

Other potential allies of NWRO, given its predominantly black and female structure, were black and women's organizations. Historically, these two groups had periodically united across class, race, and gender lines in their struggles for equality in the United States. This past pattern of cooperation between minority-power groups in a dominant white, male society suggested that such coalitions might once again emerge within the National Welfare Rights movement. Some did but were few in number and added little, in terms of political and economic resources, to the protest of poor women. In practice, racial and gender solidarity was relatively limited. Basic antagonisms based on class and gender undermined the bonding between the poor black women in NWRO and members of the middle-class civil rights organizations. Similarly, historical race and class contradictions between black and white women eroded the ties between the Aid to Families with Dependent Children (AFDC) women and the women's organizations. Finally, class anomalies weakened the bonds between NWRO women and black women's organizations.

Over the years, however, as the feminist movement gained momentum, there were signs of rising solidarity between women in poverty and those in more affluent circumstances. Even more salient was the mounting evidence of the integration of poor black women— and their welfare concerns—into the emerging black feminist movement in the mid- and late 1970s. These changing coalition patterns between NWRO and its allies among black and women's organizations, like those with the white church's Friends, both mirrored, as well as modeled, the changes in the political conditions within NWRO and within the broader society. To some extent, these alternating configurations of power within the political arena had an impact on NWRO's mobilized resources and the ongoing struggle for welfare reform in the 1960s and the 1970s, as well as implications for any future protest for economic justice in the 1980s.

We begin by analyzing the nature and the consequences of the alliances that developed—or failed to develop—between NWRO and the black, male-dominated organizations. The second section explores NWRO's ties with black women's and white women's organizations.*

NWRO AND BLACK ORGANIZATIONS

Class cleavages between middle- and lower-class blacks inhibited racial solidarity in the National Welfare Rights movement, in contrast to the black struggle in the South in the 1960s.[1] While Wiley was able to develop ties with some black groups, with others all his attempts failed. When cooperation did emerge, class and gender cleavages and ideological conflicts heightened the tension among potential racial allies. In some cases, major black organizations remained on the periphery of the welfare rights conflict as witnesses, rather than active supporters.

Internal conflicts within the civil rights movement, the traditional social antagonisms between the black poor and middle-class blacks and between women and men, further weakened racial bonding.[2] With a few exceptions, black organizations that linked up with the National Welfare Rights movement were only episodically involved. Many lacked a strong power base, and few had access to enough resources to share with their partners on welfare. In fact, many black organizations had to compete for the same liberal support. Competitiveness for scarce resources within the protest community further limited the development of strong alliances between NWRO and black organizations.[3] Consequently, during the life span of the welfare rights movement, peer alliances based on common racial structures failed to empower NWRO economically or politically. Both limited economic resources and lack of class solidarity inhibited the support for NWRO by black organizations.

Although NWRO was defined as a movement of poor people by its organizers and leaders, in reality, as we have seen, it attracted largely a black constituency. While this racial characteristic provided a common basis for alignment with other civil rights and black

---

*I have chosen to group black and white women in one section, since this entire analysis is based on the assumption that NWRO was a women's movement, although not organized or defined as such. New research on blacks and women is now considering, as it should, black women as a separate and distinct category. See U.S., Commission on Civil Rights, Social Indicators of Equality for Minorities and Women (Washington, D.C.: Government Printing Office, 1978).

power organizations, class differences, the ubiquitous stigmatization of the welfare poor, and the rejection by many of NWRO's militant tactics by poor women inhibited cooperation. NWRO's goals and strategies to reform the welfare system were seen by many—both black and white activists—as misguided and out of step with the political realities. NWRO's call for welfare, rather than for jobs, and the mobilization of black welfare mothers as leaders in a society in which whites and males ruled and blacks and women were subordinated violated dominant values and norms and increased the costs of participation for potential allies. Finally, NWRO antagonized black organizations on both extremes of the political spectrum. The more militant black groups "avoided NWRO because of its interracial character," while the "moderate Black organizations such as the NAACP were put off by NWRO's militant tactics and radical goals."[4] Symbolic of NWRO's "split personality," in terms of race, was the observation by one participant, Audrey Colom, who noted that "the Black community identified George [Wiley] with whites, and the white community identified him with Blacks."[5] For leaders in some of the civil rights and black power organizations, an alliance with NWRO thus seemed to offer few rewards and entail too many risks.

When such barriers were overcome, some cooperation emerged. Coalitions between black organizations and NWRO, however, varied greatly in the nature and extent of support provided to the movement of poor women. The younger, "poorer," and more militant black organizations—more congruent in structure and ideology with NWRO—linked up with NWRO as symbolic, if not real, political allies. Given their limited resource base, there were generally few material contributions they could make other than lending their presence, name, and "warm bodies" at meetings and demonstrations. On the other hand, the older and more established middle-class civil rights organizations, which had greater resources and legitimacy in the dominant white society, offered little visible support in the political arena and only a limited amount of monies. Their ties to the white funding sources appear to have functioned as a constraining factor in their participation in the welfare rights protest.[6] Competition for scarce resources within the liberal sector by various minority power groups seems to have undermined cooperation between the black movement organizations. Those whose goals were more congruent with dominant values appear to have attracted liberal support more easily than those who flagrantly violated them. Ultimately, therefore, both economic and political ties with NWRO were limited mostly because of its highly visible identification with welfare rights and its "deviant" membership, goals, and strategies.[7]

Over the eight-year period (1966-74), only a few black groups coalesced with NWRO. These alliances, or nonalliances, between the

black organizations and the protest movement of poor women on welfare had an impact on NWRO's political and economic resources and
possibly on the outcome of its goals. We begin by examining the alliances that emerged, focusing first on the ones that attempted to provide some continuous link with NWRO and then on other black groups
that were less involved in the movement. The major thrust is to
identify the areas of cooperation as well as those of conflict that
affected the peer partnerships.

NWRO/SCLC

The coalition between NWRO and the Southern Christian Leadership Conference (SCLC) emerged out of both internal and external
contradictions. Both groups were protestors of racial and economic
inequalities within the system. While NWRO focused on the issue of
welfare, SCLC centered its efforts on the needs of blacks and especially poor blacks. Thus, they sought to mobilize similar constituencies, even though NWRO espoused the organizing of poor people in
general.

Structurally, NWRO contrasted with SCLC in terms of the gender of its formal leadership and the economic status of its membership.
NWRO, as we have seen, was a movement of welfare mothers headed
by black women. SCLC, on the other hand, mobilized support and
members from various economic levels and was led by Martin Luther
King, Jr. and later, after his assassination in 1968, by another black
male, Ralph Abernathy. Given the fact that Wiley was NWRO's nationally recognized leader within black and white communities, NWRO and
SCLC were similar in this respect. While the overlapping social issues of race and poverty tended to unite the two organizations in a
common cause, other factors functioned to pull them apart. As Piven
notes, "There was an uneasy alliance (only 'uneasy' in terms that in
every alliance there is tension and competition) with SCLC."[8]

On the issues of "integration" and "interracialism," the two
groups held similar views. Like NWRO, SCLC supported racial cooperation between blacks and whites. As it broadened its strategy to
include poverty issues, SCLC's leader, Abernathy, publicly called
attention to the fact that this issue "has nothing to do with race, creed
or color. If you are poor, you are poor," he said. Ultimately, "we
are all black and white keys on the same keyboard."[9]

This common concern about the needs of poor people theoretically
provided grounds for cooperation. In reality, however, the similarity
of their constituencies and goals at first created tension and competition between the potential allies. SCLC had emerged in the civil rights
movement in the early 1960s to support the black protest in the South.

As the civil rights movement shifted its attention to the North and to economic issues affecting poor blacks, SCLC, under the leadership of King, announced the expansion of its goals to include "a guaranteed adequate income." At this point, conflict erupted between NWRO and SCLC. [10]

Basically, the clash arose because both movement organizations were seeking to mobilize around the same goal and attract similar constituencies. By the mid-1960s, SCLC, unlike NWRO, was a recognized black protest organization with a nationally respected leader and considerable white liberal support. NWRO, on the other hand, was a fledgling movement with little public recognition. Consequently, it was threatened by SCLC's independent decision to adopt the guaranteed income issue as part of its new campaign. Whitaker notes that "such a campaign by an established civil rights organization seemed likely to 'upstage' the fledgling welfare rights movement." [11] He adds that Wiley was "concerned with both the strategic differences and the fate of the welfare movement." Wiley sought repeatedly to contact King and wrote him "criticizing his failure to take into account 'the emerging local movements of welfare recipient groups in cities across the country' and 'the strategies they have decided upon at their first national meeting.'" Wiley insisted that King and his staff meet with the leaders of NWRO to discuss their common goals and needs. According to NWRO reports, SCLC ignored NWRO's communications and requests for cooperation. Response only came when SCLC began to plan its "Poor People's Campaign," at which time it decided to seek NWRO's support.

SCLC leaders contacted NWRO and requested a meeting. The meeting almost collapsed, however, when SCLC sent its "fourth lieutenants" to negotiate with NWRO leaders, rather than their top men, King and Abernathy. One NWRO staff member, who accompanied Tillmon and the other women officers, described it as "that infamous meeting in Chicago" because King did not feel that it was important enough for him to be present personally. [12] The women leaders were outraged and announced that "they would only meet with Dr. King." As a result of this clash, King, Abernathy, and his "top lieutenants" flew to Chicago and spent the whole day together "hammering out" the rules of the game. The outcome was a coalition between the two groups as equal partners in the emerging struggle for a guaranteed income.

Tensions had been high over SCLC's apparent lack of knowledge about the problems of special concern to the black women on welfare and the needs of their families. NWRO was in the throes of fighting Congress and the administration over the Work Incentive Program (WIN), and the women leaders were infuriated that the men in SCLC "didn't know what it was all about." [13] For Tillmon and the other women present, this signified a lack of concern or, at minimum, a lack of understanding of the plight of women on welfare.[14] She stated that "the ladies told Dr. King that it was a disgrace that SCLC had ignored the welfare issue and the [NWRO] movement for so long."[15] After angry confrontations between the black male leaders of SCLC and the black female leaders of NWRO, King admitted that he had been remiss in not dealing with this central question and promised NWRO that he and SCLC would cooperate to counter the repressive measures in the 1967 Social Security amendments. He also agreed, henceforth, to support publicly the organizing of welfare recipients and the welfare rights movement. In return, NWRO agreed to back the SCLC's "Poor People's Campaign" that spring of 1968.[16] Two months later, however, King was assassinated. The promise was not broken. His wife, Coretta King, and Abernathy, his successor as head of SCLC, continued the ties with NWRO through its final years.

The relationship, as might be expected, remained in many ways a competitive one. There was competition in the "Poor People's Campaign" for public recognition as "the representative of the poor." NWRO stipulated that the campaign demands to be presented to the political leaders include "the legislative enactment of its proposals as a 'living memorial' to the memory of Dr. King."[17] In "a continuation of the NWRO struggle for domination or at least co-leadership of the Poor People's Campaign," its leaders sent Abernathy telegrams demanding inclusion of a list of items of interest to NWRO, such as "repeal of the repressive portion of the 1967 Social Security legislation . . . a guaranteed income of $4000 for a family of four . . . and federal funds to create immediately at least three million jobs for men."[18]

To gain wider publicity for NWRO's role in the campaign, 31 welfare rights mothers staged a vigil for King on Capitol Hill the night before the launching of the campaign. All were arrested and jailed. Shortly afterward, representatives of the Poor People's Campaign's Steering Committee, which now included NWRO leaders, met with the welfare administration. While little resulted from this joint confrontation with the political establishment, the incident served, in NWRO's opinion, to make it a recognized and legitimate partner in the struggle for the black poor. It also taught NWRO that before any coalition formation, the "rules of the game" had to be carefully negotiated by the partners.[19]

The problem of funding also seems to have undermined the linkages between NWRO and SCLC. Between the two, there was a "silent," but continuous, struggle for liberal monies and, more specifically, for support from the white churches and other black and white movement organizations.[20] UCC, for example, provided SCLC not only with monies but also staff support. Moreover, SCLC's agenda was

institutionalized as part of UCC's ongoing ministry in the area of racial justice.[21] Abernathy, in describing the close ties between SCLC
and the white churches in general, stated that it was the "social action
arm or division of the church."[22] NWRO's alliance with the white
churches, in contrast, was episodic and short lived, as we have seen.
Part of the explanation for this difference in liberal support seems to
have been that SCLC's goals and principles, centering around the concept of racial justice, were congruent with the dominant values, while
NWRO's clashed with them in calling for welfare rights.

Overlapping goals, constituencies, and supporters added to the
tensions between the two organizations. Not only was SCLC more
successful in gaining white liberal resources, especially among the
churches, but it was also able to attract black support. Unlike NWRO,
SCLC was rooted in and had always had continuous support from black
churches. According to Abernathy, "The 'Black church' has really
been the backbone of the movement." He added that he did not "know
what we would have done without the 'Black church.'" Throughout
the black struggle, he had "never found the door of these churches
closed to us." NWRO, on the other hand, failed to attract any support
from the black churches.[23] One NWRO leader commented that "there
has always been a lot of money for Civil Rights but very little for Welfare Rights" within the black or white churches. Referring to the
competition for liberal monies, he added that the groups remained
"separate" when they should be "coming together," given their common problems and concerns. He acknowledged, however, that the
"money sources determine the issues and people do not want to invest
in . . . a movement for welfare rights."[24] Church leaders confirmed
this, with one stating that in U.S. society the churches "shy away
from defining a problem in 'class' terms. 'Race' is much more acceptable."[25]

Despite these underlying antagonisms between NWRO and SCLC,
the two worked together off and on throughout an eight-year period.
SCLC attended all NWRO annual conferences and conventions, providing speakers and other resources, such as moral and political support.
At the 1974 NWRO conference in St. Louis, when practically all other
allies had deserted NWRO, Abernathy, in an electrifying speech,
brought immediate applause from the black and white audience when
he promised continued support for NWRO, saying:

> SCLC is with you in your struggle. We're with you when
> you're down. We'll be with you when you're up. We'll
> march together. We'll confront them in the streets.
> We've got to go back to Washington, D.C., together:
> poor whites, Puerto Ricans, Chicanos, Blacks, and Amer-
> ican Indians. We must form a coalition. That's the only

way to deal with the problems in the country. Poor whites
have to be educated. They didn't come over on the same
ship, but I'll be damned if we're not sinking together.[26]

SCLC pledged to continue fighting along with NWRO to defeat any
"new" Family Assistance Plan (FAP) that the political leaders might
try to introduce. SCLC had good intentions; provided NWRO with symbolic, if not material, support; and incurred risks by identifying with
the protest of poor women on welfare, because of the public hostility
to NWRO in society and to its demands for welfare as a right. In
1974 Abernathy pointed out that "NWRO and SCLC are the only organizations in the country today fighting for the rights of poor people."
He noted that "many organizations today have bourgeois goals and
aims. They have forgotten the disinherited and the downtrodden."[27]
    SCLC remained a strong political ally of NWRO. When NWRO
was mobilizing supporters to defeat FAP, SCLC, whose stronghold
was in "eight Southern states which would have benefited significantly
from this Nixon plan," remained loyal to NWRO's goal to defeat it.[28]
    Thus, this peer alliance between NWRO and SCLC, although
episodically buffeted by internal conflicts and tensions, contributed
to NWRO's political recognition and support in the protest for poor
women's rights.

NWRO/CORE

    Another black civil rights group that temporarily aligned itself
with NWRO in some parts of the country was the Congress for Racial
Equality (CORE). Conflicts both at the national and local levels, however, inhibited any continuous cooperation between these two predominantly black organizations. Nationally, the support of CORE was eschewed by NWRO leaders because of its "capitalist orientation."[29]
Furthermore, ideological clashes over "integration" and "separatism," most vividly reflected in the bitter struggle between Wiley and
McKissick for leadership of CORE, resulted in a "breach [that] was
never healed and . . . created a lot of political problems down the
road."[30] However, at the local level, at least one NWRO/CORE alliance emerged and survived for about two years.
    In the early years of NWRO, the Scholarship, Educational, and
Defense Fund for Racial Equality (SEDFRE), an arm of CORE, sought
to help organize WROs in some parts of the country. Various kinds
of resources were mobilized in support of this cause, such as paid
organizers, technical assistance, black leadership, and funds to organize AFDC women in the urban areas. One of the major tactics
used was to work with the women to develop "lay welfare manuals" in
order to inform them of their statutory rights.

In Newark Robert Curvin and Shirley Lacy, black organizers from the national CORE staff, mobilized one of the first groups of welfare rights mothers by writing and distributing the publication known as Your Welfare Rights.[31] Lacy explained that the manual served as an important organizing tool for welfare rights because the information was highly guarded by the welfare department and inaccessible to the recipients. "Friendly" caseworkers supplied the welfare department manuals with the rules and regulations that were unavailable to the public in general. They then heiped the AFDC women to "rewrite" the sections in lay terms to eliminate another barrier for the poor, namely, the complexity of the bureaucratic rules and regulations. This tactic, used widely throughout the country, was felt to be a good organizing tool because it was a cooperative effort of the women and their supporters. Lacy added that "SEDFRE [CORE] provided the funds for publication of the booklet . . . and felt it was very important to have direct contact and involvement with the client groups . . . as part of a team." She emphasized that "the questions in the book came directly from their own personal questions [since she] felt very strongly that the welfare mothers had to do their own organizing and have their own organization." Ultimately, the intent was to use the "welfare booklet" as a "facilitative process to get members and to strengthen the organization."[32]

From 1966 to 1968, SEDFRE in Newark provided about $30,000 to organize the United Welfare Group of Essex County, which became an affiliate of NWRO. Its first leader, Marion Kidd, went on to become NWRO's national treasurer for several years. While funded by SEDFRE, it opened offices, printed a newsletter, trained organizers, and participated in various sit-ins and confrontations with the welfare department. The purpose of SEDFRE's support in this area was to "create a Welfare Rights Center in Newark, New Jersey, which [would] focus and coordinate the multilateral community efforts to pressure for rights and entitlements of the welfare recipients." Its long-range objective was "to bring about effective structural changes in the welfare system."[33] Before withdrawing from Newark, Lacy mobilized support for WRO from another black organization. She convinced the National Urban League's chapter in Essex County to take over SEDFRE's role as a partner and supporter of the WRO.

CORE's economic and political support appears to have been limited to the first two years of the welfare rights movement and also to have been restricted to organizing at the local level. No ties developed at the national level between NWRO and CORE, possibly because of the differences between Wiley and McKissick. As CORE's internal conflicts heightened and its resources declined, it withdrew from community organization of the welfare poor.[34] While the alliance lasted in New Jersey, it played an important role in helping expand the base of the movement in its beginning years. With CORE's withdrawal of financial and political support, along with the loss of other allies, the WRO in New Jersey eventually collapsed.

NWRO/Black Panthers

The Black Panthers, a protest movement of poor blacks, was also a visible ally of welfare rights in many urban areas but never established formal ties with the movement at the local and national levels. Their linkages with WROs and their contributions were episodic and scattered. One major explanation seems to be the continuous harassment of the Black Panthers by government agents in the late 1960s, which greatly weakened their base and activities around the country.[35]

In some areas, however, Black Panthers joined welfare rights groups in public demonstrations against the welfare authorities. For instance, in 1969 the Black Panthers and the WRO in Baltimore took over the welfare department for a short period and succeeded in getting some of their demands met.[36] They were also active during this time in street demonstrations in New York City and Newark.[37] Joint militant actions between the organized poor black women and men seem to have added to WRO's political power in such confrontations, but its leaders also suffered severe reprisals at the hands of the agents of social control. In Iowa, for example, when Charles Knox of the Des Moines Black Panther party came to the support of the WRO women, who were demonstrating for higher welfare grants, both leaders were maced and jailed.[38] Observers within the welfare rights movement tend to agree that where these two groups existed at the local level, strong bonds of solidarity emerged, especially in the confrontations with the authorities.[39] Some suggest that the Black Panthers functioned as "a buffer between NWRO and the forces of political repression." James of NWRO, for example, stated that "if there were not a Black Panther movement in the country right now [1969], it would be the National Welfare Rights Movement that would be hauled off to jail."[40]

Black Panthers, with a constituency of poor blacks, seem to have identified readily and spontaneously with the cause of the welfare rights mothers. Both were protests of poor people, and racial bonds clearly strengthened the ties between the black women and black men. Both groups were involved in protest strategies around basic needs and survival issues. While limited data are available on alliances throughout the country, cooperation between these two groups appears to have ended in 1969, when the Black Panthers were almost totally destroyed by the political authorities after having been designated by the FBI as the country's "Number 1 enemy."[41]

NWRO/PUSH

Another black organization with a constituency of poor people that linked up with NWRO in the early 1970s was People United to Save Humanity (PUSH). Headed by a black leader, Jesse Jackson, the ties between these two movement organizations were loose, informal, and episodic. In its early years, PUSH's major thrust was for jobs and employment. With limited resources, it struggled, like NWRO, to survive as a black protest group dependent largely upon white liberal support.

For one year, after Wiley's resignation in 1973, PUSH became a visible ally of NWRO. That year, Jackson of PUSH, Abernathy of SCLC, and Sanders of NWRO jointly planned a spring offensive around the anniversary of King's assassination "to secure as national policy a program for full employment—socially useful peacetime jobs—and a reform of the tax structure which will require the rich to pay their fair share and put an end to present tax injustices."[42] In July 1973, Jackson was a keynote speaker at NWRO's annual convention and was introduced symbolically by Abernathy as "the offspring" of the "marriage" of SCLC and NWRO.

This public cooperation was designed to promote political solidarity among the three movement organizations and a show of unity among blacks, especially poor blacks, in their struggle for economic justice. In reality, however, the three were also competitors for the same constituencies and a common liberal base of support. This helped to undermine the partnership. By 1974 PUSH had withdrawn from public alignment with NWRO. It rejected an invitation to participate in NWRO's annual meeting that year. Yet, when welfare rights women made a final appeal for help to keep the movement alive, PUSH was one of the few that responded, contributing $500 to the cause.[43]

In some areas in New Jersey, PUSH attempted to provide some support to local WROs after the Friends of Welfare Rights had withdrawn from the movement. Some of the WRO women leaders in the state joined PUSH, attended its national meetings, and reported that they had been invited to link their WRO groups as "satellites of PUSH."[44] From the evidence available, this does not seem to have come to pass.

PUSH's support of the welfare rights movement was at best symbolic, since it, like SCLC and other younger civil rights groups, had few resources to share and had to compete with NWRO for scarce liberal support. Thus, this alliance appears to have had little impact on NWRO's mobilized resources, although it did reinforce NWRO's image as a black protest movement. As we have seen, this in turn affected white church support, for these liberal allies asserted that they were interested in aiding an integrated movement of poor people, rather than an increasingly exclusive movement of poor black women. In 1980, while the welfare rights movement remained fragmented and becalmed, PUSH was gaining new recognition and support as it shifted its goals and strategies to the "education of youth."[45] Furthermore, unlike NWRO, PUSH was still headed by a black, male leader, Jackson, who was respected and accepted by the dominant society.

NWRO/NTO

The National Tenants Organization (NTO), another protest organization of poor people, temporarily aligned itself with the National Welfare Rights movement in the late 1960s and early 1970s. Headed by a black male, Jesse Gray, it was a direct spin-off from both the civil rights and the welfare rights movements and emerged in 1969.[46] While some cooperation emerged between these two movements of poor people, rising tensions and competition eroded political bonds.

Within two years, rising tensions between the two groups began to surface and were reported in the media.[47] At issue was the possible consolidation of the two movement organizations into one protest movement of poor people. Given their fairly similar goals and constituencies, Gray of NTO proposed in 1971 that the two merge and form "a real people's movement." Gray insisted that there was a greater potential politically in uniting than in working independently. By then NTO had "established affiliates in forty states" and was continuing to expand. NWRO, already five years old, claimed to be even larger and stronger, with a membership "estimated at 150,000." NWRO leaders saw few benefits in such a merger. When questioned, Wiley stated that there "had been some discussion" but that NWRO "felt it wasn't something to be rushed." He acknowledged also that both groups were "dealing with the same people," since "people on welfare are tenants, too," and indicated that perhaps there might be some "linking together" of the two organizations in the future. This, however, never materialized as the women leaders remained strongly opposed to any restructuring that would undermine their authority and political visibility.

The only major cooperation between NWRO and NTO occurred during the 1972 presidential elections. At that time, in the face of President Nixon's bid for reelection and his actions to cut back on the poverty programs, NWRO joined with NTO and SCLC to try to have some political impact on the Democratic platform. NTO was interested in "guarantee[ing] the election of a pro-tenant Governor in this country." NWRO wanted the election of political leaders receptive to the promotion of an adequate guaranteed income system. SCLC was

interested in improving the economic opportunities for poor black
workers, especially in the South. As a consequence of overlapping
goals, the three united to develop and present to the Democratic National Convention the Poor People's Platform. Their common grievances were stated in the preamble as follows:

> Poor people have been excluded from democratic processes.
> They have been victims of racism, discrimination and eco-
> nomic exploitation. As welfare recipients they have been
> slandered by vicious myths. As tenants they have been ex-
> ploited. As low paid workers they have been denied the
> benefits of Federal minimum wage protections and the
> right to organize. And all the while the gap between the
> rich and poor has broadened.

In view of the "major issues confronting poor people," they prepared a "joint platform" to be "presented to the Democratic Convention and the people of America" by the "three major poor people's
organizations—National Welfare Rights Organization, National Tenants
Organization, Southern Christian Leadership Conference."[48] The
Poor People's Platform called for representation of poor people in
the Democratic party in proportion to their numbers in the country,
an adequate income for all U.S. residents, the defeat of Nixon's FAP,
the end of the war in Vietnam, economic security for all U.S. residents, decent homes, special programs for children, and recognition
and support of organized groups of poor people as the legitimate way
of including the poor in the democratic processes.

At the Democratic National Convention in Miami Beach in July
1972, all the points of the Poor People's Platform were adopted, except for the guaranteed income provision. This was not interpreted
as a defeat, since Wiley and others within NWRO defined the "999 3/4
votes" for a guaranteed income at the convention "as having been a
victory." In their view, the needs of the poor people had been heard
and endorsed by a major political body. For the first time in the history of the country, a welfare mother had addressed the Democratic
National Convention and called for its support to help eliminate the
existing economic injustices.

After this one initial effort at building an alliance of poor people's organizations, the coalition dissolved. With President Nixon's
reelection and Wiley's resignation from NWRO, NTO dropped any
further plans for a merger.

The NWRO/NTO coalition between poor black groups thus appears to have failed to empower the welfare rights movement in any
way. Some argue that it in fact decreased NWRO's resources by
siphoning off some of its leaders and supporters and becoming a com-

peting organization within the political arena. Others disagree, stating that this differentiation of protest organizations should be seen "as a good thing and not a bad thing."[49] It is clear that in the increasingly hostile environment toward the poor and black of the early 1970s, the proliferation of poor people's organizations (and their resulting competition) did not increase agitation and protest in the streets, nor did it succeed in integrating their common cause into an effective political-electoral strategy. By 1980 neither NTO nor NWRO were viable national protest organizations, having lost their base constituencies and their sources of support. Only a few local chapters of each remained scattered throughout the country.[50]

While these organizations of poor black people were the most noticeable partners of NWRO, some of the long-established, middle-class civil rights organizations also joined the welfare rights struggle, providing some funds and political solidarity. Others, however, remained uninvolved.

NWRO/National Urban League

The National Urban League, although differing significantly from NWRO in terms of its class structure, organized resources, and major goals, also established some ties with NWRO at the national and local levels. Structurally, as Andrew Young has pointed out, "The Civil Rights movement up until 1968 . . . was really a middle-class movement. There were middle-class goals, middle-class aspirations, middle-class membership, and even though a lot of poor people went to jail . . . it was still essentially a middle-class operation." Young pointed out in contrast that "Cesar Chavez and George Wiley had poor people's movements."[51]

Founded in 1910, the Urban League was considered "the nation's wealthiest Civil Rights Organization," with its major goal being full employment and "a decent job and decent salary" for everybody in the country.[52] Unlike NWRO, the National Urban League's primary focus was on employment, not welfare, for blacks. Its strategy and tactics for social change were nonmilitant and utilized institutionalized political processes. According to its executive director, Vernon Jordan, these had proved to be the "most basic and effective weapons" in the long run.[53] NWRO, on the other hand, had combined various strategies but had gained national visibility in the mid-1960s from its direct actions and "street strategy" against the welfare authorities.

Structurally, both organizations were led by black, middle-class males, and, while both were recognized for having racially "integrated" memberships, in general they were acknowledged as black organizations. NWRO, unlike the Urban League, had been organized as a poor people's movement—more specifically, as a poor women's movement. Similarly, both depended primarily on white liberal support for their organizational resources. NWRO received most of its monies from churches and foundations, while the Urban League was funded by white liberals, industry, and foundations.[54]

At the national level, Wiley and Whitney Young, the Urban League's executive director until 1971, developed a close friendship. As a result, the latter provided some support for local community organizing, especially after the riots of 1967–68. Young, as president of the National Association of Social Workers, also participated in NWRO's 1969 convention as one of its keynote speakers. After Young's untimely death in January 1971, Jordan continued to maintain close personal ties with Wiley but had little connection with NWRO. In 1972, at the height of the political battle against FAP, Jordan, as the executive director of the Urban League, arranged for Wiley to meet with top editors of leading newspapers in the country to explain NWRO's opposition to the proposed FAP legislation. As a result, "the press never openly criticized NWRO's stand, even though they did not support it."[55] When NWRO and its supporters were battling the Nixon administration and its allies in Congress over FAP, the Urban League joined NWRO to help defeat it. While Jordan testified against FAP, the Urban League did not endorse the "NWRO plan" for a guaranteed income of $5,500 per year for a family of four.[56] After FAP was defeated, the National Urban League continued to speak out "in public debate on welfare reform."[57] Jordan insisted that the Urban League had "to take a position" and that this "advocacy . . . must be carried to Congress, the Statehouses, and the City Halls of the nation."[58]

Politically, then, the Urban League was willing to become involved with the issue of welfare reform but not with NWRO. NWRO was militant in its confrontations and demanded a high benefit level as an adequate income for the poor. The Urban League, as an interest group for middle-class blacks, opted for more traditional strategies for bringing about changes in the welfare system. Given the stigma of welfare in U.S. society, the linkages between the two were generally obscured to minimize reprisals from the Urban League's supporters, blacks and white liberals in the dominant sector.

For a period of time in the late 1960s, the National Urban League, according to some reports, was the strongest supporter of NWRO among the civil rights groups. One NWRO leader asserted that "the strongest support both politically and in terms of what they did for NWRO of all the Civil Rights groups came from the Urban League." He added that the Urban League had replaced its "traditional social service" for a new thrust of "organizing in the ghetto" after Wiley and his staff had urged it to become involved. After several meetings, NWRO "worked out an understanding with the Urban League that they would try to get someone into local Welfare Rights groups and let the local Welfare Rights groups organize recipients." According to this report, "A very close relationship [was] worked out with the Urban League and the local Welfare Rights groups."[59] The available data indicate that this appears to have materialized only in a limited number of places.

In Newark, for example, the Urban League announced publicly in 1969 that it was supporting the Newark WRO by giving it a grant of $21,900 to set up an office, train organizers, and educate the poor about their rights.[60] It also invited welfare rights representatives to sit on its local board.[61] The partnership was described as "the first of its kind in the country" and "the only program in the nation in which the Urban League has a working relationship with the Welfare Rights Organization."[62]

In a joint press release in July 1969 announcing the coalition, the two allies underscored that the two groups would cooperate but "retain separate identities." The purpose of the alliance was "to help low-income people make effective use of the welfare system." For some of NWRO's allies, the welfare rights partnership entailed the risk of becoming overly identified with the stigmatized issue of welfare. However, as a fledgling protest organization, NWRO's identity as an advocate of welfare rights was seen as politically necessary by its organizers and leaders. Consequently, a coalition strategy that guarded and separated the identity of both partners and did not undermine the visibility of either in the political arena meshed well with the needs of both allies at the beginning.

Although a very detailed contract was worked out between the two organizations in New Jersey, conflict soon erupted, as both contended that the other had violated the established "rules of the game."[63] Urban League leaders called the coalition "a big mistake," complaining that the welfare rights women in Newark wanted total control over expenditure of funds. The Urban Leagues in Essex County refused to go along with that. They asserted that the Newark WRO also wanted "to promote their own organization," rather than use the monies to educate poor people in the area about their welfare rights.[64] James Pawley, the head of the Urban League in Essex County, emphasized that it was not a disagreement over ideology but, rather, different perspectives on strategy and tactics that led to conflict and dissolution of the coalition. Both organizations, he added, were "pressing for rights rather than charity for black people in the country." The Newark WRO, however, wanted "to keep its office open" and "to gain publicity by participating in demonstrations." The Urban League "did not agree with their tactics."[65] While the Urban League stated that it had "nothing against demonstrations and confrontations," it contended that "confrontations are not the only way."

Despite the tensions and the short-lived partnership, the WRO women in Newark generally praised the alliance. Ultimately, for the ones who had been selected and trained as organizers with Urban League monies, new and rare opportunities opened up that led to work and economic independence. Of the 15 trained as organizers, 13 left the organization and returned to work or to college. Most of them developed new careers. Thus, the alliance was individually beneficial but organizationally devastating. It not only resulted in the loss of potential leaders but also created factions within the local organization between those selected for training and leadership and those who were not. Without ongoing programs for leadership maintenance and membership recruitment, once the organizers left, the Newark WRO began to decline. Temporarily, it gained some support as a result of its alliance with the Urban League. Ultimately, however, it lost several of its leaders, as new alternatives for social mobility opened up to them.

There were varying opinions on the costs and benefits of this alliance for the welfare rights movement in this area. Curvin, a black CORE leader and an early organizer of welfare rights in Newark, assessed the coalition between these two racial peers as having strengthened the WRO, although he acknowledged that the internal conflicts it had created within the organization had contributed to its dissolution. Curvin explained that part of the problem was that "the Urban League is oriented to a passive educational approach—a non-militant approach—while the women wanted to demonstrate."[66] He observed that "when the League withdrew its support at the end of the year, WRO started to go down."[67] Other observers also criticized the impact of this coalition on the WRO in Newark. The chair of the Friends of Welfare Rights felt that "the funding by the Urban League split the group apart because some of the mothers were getting paid to organize and others were not. It was very bad for the morale of the organization." The national leaders of the organization, he added, were also "against this kind of funding" because they "didn't want WRO to become dependent on the Urban League and take orders and directions from them."[68]

After one year, rising conflict led to the dissolution of the coalition between WRO and the local Urban League. This was the last grant that this local WRO received from private sources, and this loss of funding hastened its decline as an active challenger within the political arena. Continuing attempts to find outside monies for the Newark WRO largely failed. Some of the women leaders sought support from local churches or public funding under the "Model Cities" program to strengthen their own WRO groups. These individualistic and competitive efforts, rather than collective and cooperative actions, created cleavages within the local movement. Factionalism exacer-

bated personal antagonisms that never healed, despite repeated intervention and mediation by the national staff. [69] The competition for
scarce resources by individuals and local WRO groups undermined
the fragile movement that had been in operation for three years. As
Kidd, the first WRO leader in Newark, stated, "Money was always
the source of our problems—when we had it and didn't have it."[70]

At the national and local levels, there appear, therefore, to
have been minimal political and economic ties between NWRO and the
Urban League. The linkages that emerged were short-lived and
led to little transfer of economic resources to the welfare rights movement. One of the unintended consequences of the alliance was the
loss of the women trained for leadership. As new economic opportunities emerged for them, the need for personal social mobility
superseded organizational loyalty. A few gained as other alternatives
to welfare arose. The movement organization, however, suffered
from the loss of these resources, as well as from added factionalism.

In 1980 the National Urban League continued to function as an
advocate of black people's needs. It was still "organizationally sound
and financially strong," while its onetime ally, NWRO, had vanished
as a national protest organization. The Urban League, while still
fighting for "welfare reform," focused more of its efforts on "a full
employment program." In its view, "jobs with adequate pay and
fringe benefits" were defined as the critical issues. [71] Jordan suggested that part of the problem with NWRO and similar protest groups
was their militancy. Many such movement organizations had "difficulty putting together a program that would attract support because
the nature of the issues is different in the nineteen-seventies and you
cannot attract funding for movements of mass demonstrations."[72]
The issues were the same, but the times had changed. The implication was that those who adapted to the dominant values and norms survived and that those who did not vanished from the political arena.

NWRO/NAACP

Another long-established civil rights organization, and a potential ally of NWRO—the National Association for the Advancement of
Colored People (NAACP)—developed few ties with the welfare rights
movement, although both represented predominantly black constituencies. The two organizations differed in many ways, some of which
became the sources of tensions and conflicts that inhibited cooperation in the welfare rights struggle.

The NAACP, unlike NWRO, was the "oldest and largest civil
rights group in the United States" and "essentially middle class and
moderate."[73] While both endorsed the principle of racial integration

and similar goals of racial justice, the NAACP emphasized strategies of litigation, rather than militant tactics, for bringing about social change. Its strength and funding, over the years, had come primarily from its own membership, described as "a secure black middle class," and from some white liberal support. By the end of the 1970s, observers were questioning "whether the Black underclass" had "any representation" within the NAACP. Some suggested that "the gap between the upwardly mobile [blacks] and those stuck in the ghettoes is widening."[74]

According to NWRO leaders, welfare and welfare rights were not accepted as viable mobilizing issues by the NAACP.[75] Although the NWRO staff made some attempts to link up with the NAACP's Office of the Rights of Indigents, the existing antagonisms between the leaders of these two black movements and their differences in goals and strategies seem to have precluded cooperation.[76] Despite, therefore, their common racial bonds, ties between NWRO and NAACP failed to materialize at the national and local levels. There were only scattered reports of intermittent cooperation between local NAACP chapters and WROs in NWRO's publications.[77] The most prominent support apparently came from NAACP's militant wing, the Brown Berets.[78]

Relatively speaking, therefore, the NWRO/NAACP alliance was nonexistent. According to Wiley, acceptance of the dominant values and attitudes by middle-class blacks governing this black organization had inhibited support for the mobilization of women on welfare.[79] Thus, the NAACP remained, for the most part, as a "witness" in the welfare rights struggle, providing few, if any, resources for NWRO.

NWRO/Black Churches

In contrast to their decisive role in the civil rights movement, black churches also remained on the periphery of the welfare rights struggle.[80] Black churches and their national Protestant leaders, especially within the main-line denominations, were markedly absent from the list of NWRO's supporters. Individual black ministers in some local communities participated and protested alongside welfare rights women. In general, however, most black churches chose to stay outside the welfare rights struggle, despite their common racial bonds with NWRO's largely black constituency.

The sources of conflict between WRO and black churches seem to have been rooted in class antagonisms. While expressing concern about the needs of the poor, many black churches seemed to oppose the strategies and militancy of the welfare rights women. In New Jersey, WRO leaders attempted unsuccessfully to enlist some aid from local black churches, although a few joined the middle-class movement of Friends of Welfare Rights. Some observers explained this failure as stemming from NWRO's primary emphasis on welfare, rather than on jobs and income, which were principle items on the agenda of black churches. Ironically, jobs and income had always been the movement's stated goals, but this twofold objective was distorted by the visibility of the welfare rights issue and the organizers' apparent concern for "jobs for men" and "welfare for women." (See Chapter 3.) Others contended that the source of antagonism stemmed from NWRO's mobilization of women as heads of households.[81] This seems to have alienated many black church leaders, who worked hard to underscore the strengths of the black family and the need "to bring men back as head of the home."[82]

The lack of racial solidarity between NWRO and the black churches was repeatedly raised by other supporters, especially within the white main-line denominations. In 1972, for example, a white church executive expressed his feeling that black churches "had a responsibility to support NWRO" and questioned why they, "who are symbolically related to the Welfare Rights movement," did not contribute to NWRO. Wiley responded that "while an attempt had been made to develop that area of support through the Black Caucus—the National Council of Black Churchmen—and IFCO," the effort had not been successful. Wiley explained that, first, the black churches did not "have a lot to put into the National Council of Churches." Second, NWRO had never "put a lot of work into this area of fundraising" because it tried to "go where there's a lot of money—where the pool of resources is large."[83] Third, Wiley stated that an "anti-welfare ethic" was "afflicting the middle-class blacks," primarily because of "the continuous negative publicity in the media and by the nation's top leaders."

Blacks, Wiley acknowledged regretfully, were to a great extent being taken in by the white majority's "anti-welfare arguments" and "were supporting the conservative views on welfare." As one example, he pointed to Leon Sullivan's Opportunities Industrialization Center (OIC) in Philadelphia, which had received "close to twenty million dollars through federal programs" and which wanted NWRO to unite with it "in preventing welfare."[84] Wiley rejected this strategy, since NWRO's goal was to try to increase the adequacy of welfare benefits for all poor people through a guaranteed income system. Most of the welfare population, Wiley contended, could not find jobs that paid enough to support a family, nor could many work, given family responsibilities as heads of household and the ubiquitous problem of poor health. He was highly critical of black leaders who would not help organize the black and poor.[85]

Other blacks who supported or worked in NWRO also criticized this lack of racial solidarity in the welfare rights movement. One black woman leader in a Protestant denomination urged black church executives to stop their boycott of the National Welfare Rights movement and called on all blacks "to stop rejecting ourselves."[86] Another black NWRO leader explained this lack of support in terms of too many options. Given the number of protest organizations, there were many choices for black (and white) supporters, many of which were considered to be "better alternatives" to welfare rights. Investment in such groups as SCLC and PUSH, he added, was perceived as offering lower risks and potentially higher rewards. Organizing around racial issues was more acceptable to most black and white church leaders than organizing around welfare issues.

Other NWRO officers felt that black leaders within white-dominated denominations had been "co-opted" by whites. As part of the white church structure, they were accused of having ignored, rather than supported, the welfare rights cause. One black NWRO staff member suggested that perhaps they had "avoid[ed] the statistics you get afraid of looking at when you're black in America." "Large numbers of black leaders," he added, "do not want to recognize that welfare is one of the key systems in our country that we [as blacks] find ourselves having to deal with . . . [because] the major part of your people are on welfare rolls." Many black leaders, he noted, "do not want to speak of the issue of welfare as a black issue."[87]*

Not only the absence of black church support but the lack of black organizational support in general within the welfare rights movement was repeatedly raised at meetings, workshops, and conferences by its leaders, members, and supporters. For example, in 1970 one black WRO woman leader from the South jarred the audience at the NWRO Eastern Regional Conference when she publicly denounced the existing antagonisms among blacks. She stated:

> The power structure knows we're fighting. . . . They [our opponents] come in all colors. Some of us say the power structure is all white. It's a lie. It's not all white. There's the black power structure which looks down on us worse than the white power structure. . . . We say the white man is splitting us up. Wrong! We're splitting up ourselves. . . . The white man doesn't separate us. We separate ourselves.[88]

Others pointed out that the existing schisms between "integrationists" and "separatists" within the civil rights movement had

---

*By 1977 there were some signs that this was beginning to change (see Kenneth Briggs, "Some Black Church Leaders Plan Drive to Help Poor," (New York Times, August 5, 1977).

eroded black support for NWRO. This, they contended, was reflected in the antagonisms felt by some black leaders toward Wiley and NWRO's interracial strategies. One close associate of Wiley's suggested that it was Wiley's "lack of popularity" among "black leaders" that had inhibited black support for welfare rights. Wiley "really disliked them and they disliked him," because he "thought that black leaders very rapidly left their people behind." To Wiley, "if there was any symbolic constituency of blacks, it was welfare recipients," and, "if you wanted to know what was happening to blacks in America," you had "to look at the welfare rolls."[89] In addition, Wiley differed from some of the more militant black power leaders over the issue of integration and separation of blacks and whites in the ongoing struggle for racial justice. According to one NWRO officer, this "presented a lot of problems in relation to the black movement." He added that many did not consider Wiley to be a "black leader" because he was an integrationist.[90] Another source of conflict between Wiley and other black leaders was the organization of black women. Day asserts that "the Black power guys were also disdainful of George [Wiley] because he was organizing women." At that time, he explains, black men "were very intent on freeing themselves from the idea of a maternalistic, matriarchal Black society and here we are, out organizing Black women, and white ones, too." He summed up the controversy between Wiley and other black leaders by saying that "everybody was going one way and George was going another, all by himself."[91]

Others felt that the underlying conflicts between NWRO and black groups stemmed not so much from differences over integration or organizing women as from differences over the issue of mobilizing around welfare. Piven, for example, stated that "Civil Rights groups and Civil Rights leaders did not think 'welfare' was a good issue. They did not want a welfare constituency." She added that "they had values of white Westchester liberals."[92]

Evans of NWRO also supported this view that welfare had been the overriding factor in exacerbating the cleavages among blacks, specifically in terms of black support for NWRO. Jeter, the third chair of NWRO and an AFDC mother, also decried the lack of black support for the welfare rights movement. Appealing for allies in 1975, she noted that NWRO was "being overwhelmed by forces of repression," and she criticized the "so-called civil rights forces or 'Black leadership' for having become absorbed into the system with the 'Great Society,' promises of equality and the right to wear three-piece suits." She claimed that the poor had "been abandoned to the bowels of the welfare mess."[93]

As NWRO had gained power and recognition within the political arena in the late 1960s, black groups had begun to pay more attention to Wiley and his movement of black women. At that point, black leaders could no longer afford to ignore him, since membership was increasing and NWRO was gaining political visibility in most parts of the country. At the height of its mobilization success, some black organizations chose to cooperate with Wiley and NWRO. When the political tide began to turn, and NWRO was increasingly buffeted by internal conflicts and outside forces, the existing links between NWRO and its black allies disappeared, with the few exceptions discussed earlier.

In sum, as had been the case with the white church allies, the number of black groups who supported NWRO were limited. Moreover, black organizations' relationships with the organized poor women of NWRO varied at different levels and among different groups. At the national level, the younger, poorer, and more militant black movement organizations, such as SCLC, PUSH, and NTO, were the most visible and continuous allies of NWRO. SCLC remained visibly aligned with NWRO and cooperated with it in a number of direct actions against the political establishment. Others, such as PUSH and NTO, became visibly linked with NWRO in the early 1970s for a short period of time. At the local level, the Black Panthers were probably the WRO's most visible political ally among the black organizations.

This lack of racial solidarity in the social movement sector may thus have lessened the political impact of the National Welfare Rights movement, both by withholding resources for the organization and by weakening the political base required to bring about NWRO's goal of an adequate guaranteed income system in the United States. Although specific support for NWRO and welfare rights never gained many adherents among black organizations, the challenge of welfare reform remained on many of their agendas long after NWRO's demise.

Just as class and gender antagonisms among black groups surfaced to exacerbate cleavages among potential racial allies, so did class and race contradictions heighten the tensions and weaken the bonding between NWRO and women's organizations, both black and white. These potential peer alliances of women in a male-dominated society were undermined by historical social conflicts stemming from race and class differences. These long-standing cleavages and lack of cooperation also helped to undermine the power and resources of the welfare rights movement. Only in the late 1970s, after the demise of NWRO, did some signs of increased bonding between the poor and nonpoor women begin to emerge.

NWRO AND WOMEN'S ORGANIZATIONS

Given the fact that NWRO's consituency was overwhelmingly black and female, gender solidarity was a potential basis for gaining additional outside support from black and white women's organizations. Black women's involvement in the racial struggle in the United States had occurred historically across class lines, suggesting the possibility of ties between the poor women's NWRO and the established and more middle-class black women's organizations. One might predict bonding to a lesser extent between WRO women and predominantly white women's groups, given the deep-seated class and racial schisms. Historical antagonisms between black and white women had been reinforced and aggravated by the dominant/subordinate structures in their relationships as mistress and servant in U.S. society. On the other hand, there was some evidence of periodic cooperation between black and white women in such struggles as the abolition movement, the antilynching campaigns, and the civil rights movement. Even these limited alliances, however, had been fraught with conflicts. Historically, class and racial differences had undermined the common bonds of gender in the struggles for black and women's liberation in a white, male-dominated society.

In the early years of the National Welfare Rights movement, consciousness of women's economic oppression was just beginning to emerge. [94] Poverty was not highlighted as a women's issue, and welfare was not considered as a women's problem. Alliances of poor and nonpoor women, and, more specifically, those between NWRO and women's organizations (both black or white) were rare. Relatively few ties were established and few resources transferred to the WROs either at the national or local levels. Some service-oriented women's church groups contributed some monies to the movement of poor women. Political allies among women's groups, with a few notable exceptions, were not to be found. Only by the middle and latter parts of the 1970s did some evidence of bonding in the political struggle for women's rights begin to emerge. As women's consciousness across racial and class lines began to be raised as a result of economic and political forces, the issues of poverty and welfare became defined increasingly as women's issues and were included in the National Women's Agenda. Tillmon had tried as early as 1968 to single out and gain political support for "welfare as a women's issue," but her appeal had gone largely unheeded by other women leaders at that time. In time her insights and slogan would become integrated into the feminist goals and agendas.

Black women's groups appear to have abstained from participation in the welfare rights movement for two major reasons. First, they apparently did not identify NWRO as a "black women's organization" until the mid-1970s. Most existing groups were oriented toward service and social work, rather than political action. They tended to use social and educational strategies, along with traditional lobbying tactics. Few, it seems, were willing to take the risks of involvement with the stigmatized issue of welfare and with a movement of militant poor women. Clearly, in the early years, differences in constituencies, goals, and strategies played an important part in keeping these two groups of women separated. Second, black women's primary loyalty had always been to the black struggle for freedom. Only by the 1970s was the demand for liberation from gender oppression surfacing and gaining momentum among black women. As black feminists emerged, they took deliberate action to blur class lines and to identify visibly with the plight and struggle of poor women on welfare. Ironically, by then it was too late to save the National Welfare Rights movement. The poor women as challengers of the welfare system were now fragmented and without national leadership. The challenge to reform the welfare system remained.

Predominantly white women's groups, both the traditionalists and the new feminists,* in general had a similar pattern of limited interaction with NWRO. They, too, displayed the dominant attitude to blacks and those on welfare. While some white groups participated in the welfare reform struggle and provided some resources for the movement organization, on the whole their involvement was negligible and had little impact on NWRO's rise and fall. Only when women's consciousness of economic oppression across class lines gained momentum in the mid- and late 1970s did "welfare as a women's issue" become incorporated in the U.S. National Women's Agenda.† As more women's groups—both black and white—identified the common sources of economic oppression in the plight of the underpaid working women, unemployed women, displaced homemakers, separated or divorced women, single mothers, the elderly, and retired women of all races did welfare and poverty gain legitimacy as political agenda items for all women's groups. Ironically, as rising recognition of common grievance emerged among various groups of women, the social protest of poor women was rapidly dissipating. By 1980 the welfare rights movement lay scattered and becalmed.

Over the years, various social forces helped to diminish the schisms among women and increase their political solidarity. In the

---

*Traditionalists are defined here as women's groups whose mission is directed primarily to providing services and education (including political education, such as is the case with the League of Women Voters) and who are long-established organizations. Feminists are defined here as those groups whose major goals are directed to social change and social action to bring about greater economic, political, and social equality for women in a male-dominated society. Clearly, there is overlapping in some cases.

†See p. 265 on the U.S. National Women's Agenda.

process, growing numbers of women's groups united around the welfare reform issue, if not the welfare rights movement. Out of the civil rights movement came the rising consciousness of the pervasive inequality between black females and males in all sectors and the emergence of the black feminist movement in the mid-1970s. Out of the welfare rights and the white, middle-class feminist movements came the poor white women, who earlier had abstained from involvement in either protest. Working women, also affected by these social currents, were beginning to mobilize within and outside the labor movement to fight for their economic rights. Thus, the agendas of black and white women, poor and nonpoor women, and working and unemployed women began to converge around their common but different economic needs in the 1970s. Work and welfare emerged by 1980 as two sides of the same coin, namely, economic oppression of women in the United States.

Social controls within the dominant society, which obscured the gender roots of poverty and welfare in the nation and stigmatized dependency on the state, had functioned effectively for many years to inhibit solidarity among women. Once the myths of welfare and work began to be unmasked by the NWRO protest, the expanding feminist movement, and the unprecedented rise of women in the labor force, women's organizations seemed to be more willing to endorse poverty, if not welfare, as part of the women's political agenda. Some, who at first had supported NWRO out of altruistic concern for others, now joined in the struggle out of enlightened self-interest. The growing realization was that as Tillmon had pointed out much earlier, "every woman is one man away from welfare." Others who had stayed out of the struggle now rejected old labels and stereotypes about welfare women and joined to fight for their own economic rights. The common cause of economic justice for all women was expanding. It had come too late to provide support for NWRO, but in the continuing rounds of welfare reform in the 1980s, women's groups appeared to be emerging as a potential new force within the political arena.

This section begins by identifying the ties that emerged between NWRO and black women's organizations and then analyzes the relationship of welfare rights groups with predominantly white women's organizations, focusing on the common grounds for such alliances and the consequences of these alliances or nonalliances for NWRO's mobilized resources. The final section briefly traces the gradual institutionalization of welfare as a women's issue within the women's liberation movement and the implications for the continuing struggle for welfare reform.

NWRO and Black Women's Organizations

Although similar in terms of its elected leadership and membership along gender and racial lines, WROs and black women's organizations established few ties at either the national or local levels. Class
and status differences, as we have noted, inhibited cooperation with
NWRO. However, class divisions had not always separated poor and
nonpoor black women. Black women, according to various writers,
had an extensive background of commitment to helping their less fortunate "sisters." Gerda Lerner, for example, documents how since
the days of slavery, black women in the United States had organized
to fight for many causes including poor relief. [95] She emphasizes
that, in fact, the rise of "the national black women's club movement"
was in part spurred by "the urgent needs of the poor who depended
on private relief" as well as "the presence of several generations of
educated women with some leisure." [96] The infamous period of lynch-
ings in the United States, extending from Reconstruction into the
1950s, had also given rise to black women's organizations in support
of the black struggle against the white system. One such group that
emerged at this time was the National Association of Colored Women,
whose membership included "working women, tenant farmwives and
poor women." [97] Most groups were integrated across class lines in
the black struggles throughout the years. Another reason for the
growth of black women's organizations and their concern about the
needs of the poor stemmed from their exclusion as "fully participating
members of American society." Cynthia Neverdon-Morton adds that,
as a consequence, they established "social service programs for poor
and uneducated blacks." [98] In these organizations, they were expected
"to perform services which were considered 'women's work.'" Thus,
most of the black women's organizations adapted within the white,
male-dominated society and worked to integrate and aid the poor
within their movements.

Despite the handicaps imposed by the dominant groups, black
women joined black men and white women, playing important roles
in the movements for abolition of slavery and the promotion of wom-
en's suffrage in the nineteenth and twentieth centuries. Sexism on
the part of black men and racism on the part of white women, however, resulted in separation and the formation of an independent black
women's club movement. [99] In the civil rights movement in the 1960s,
Diane Lewis observes that black women "played a critical role" in a
movement that was "male inspired and male led." [100] At that time,
there was "very little public discussion of the problems, objectives
and concerns of black women." [101] Black women were "counseled
patience and conciliation at what they perceived as deliberate divisive
tactics by the dominant society." [102] Eleanor Norton Holmes points

out also that black women were accused of "selling out if they were interested in women's liberation."[103] Lewis adds that "historically, their interests as blacks have taken precedence over their interests as women. A shift in power relations between the races had to come before changes in the structural relationship between the sexes."[104]

Women's issues remained largely outside the political arena, and women's actions were limited to service roles, as Neverdon-Morton has pointed out. Some, however, refused the constraints of service and developed political strategies to address their social concerns. Mary Church Terrell, president of the National Organization of Colored Women, for example, observed that the political role "was the most difficult one for the black woman to fill on a national level."[105] Political involvement, however, raised the risks for all black women's organizations. Thus, black women's groups were generally identified, not as political, but as social or service organizations.* These constraints also inhibited the participation of these groups in the politically oriented movement for welfare rights.

While there was historical precedence for cooperation between poor and nonpoor black women, various factors functioned to weaken the ties between these two groups. Primary loyalty to the civil rights movement, rather than to the welfare rights movement, was one factor. Another involved the political constraints on black women that relegated most of their efforts to social services rather than to political action. Another factor was the reluctance of black women to identify NWRO as a women's movement or a black movement. Finally, some have suggested that the lack of participation stemmed, in part, from the antiwelfare ethic that pervaded middle-class black organizations.[106] For these reasons, black women and their organizations played a very limited role in NWRO. By the late 1970s, however, there were signs that this trend had begun to shift, as black feminists incorporated the issue of welfare into their agendas and poor women into their groups and linked up with the broader women's movement.

The only data available on cooperation between WRO groups and black women's organizations were the brief and limited interactions

---

*The Directory of National Black Organizations (New York: AFRAM, 1972), compiled with the help of a Black Women's Community Development Foundation grant in 1972, lists about 225 black organizations. They are classified under the categories of business/economics, civic, education, foundations, fraternal, political, professional/occupational, and religious. Of the 28 black women's organizations listed, all fell within the fraternal or professional classifications. NWRO was listed as the only political organization. By 1978 there were numerous black feminist groups.

of the welfare rights women with the National Council of Negro Women, the Household Technicians of America, and two black feminist groups. In all these cases, the ties emerged only in the final years of the movement, mostly at the national level. The alliances were short-lived and had little or no impact on NWRO's resources. In all cases, while there were common bonds of race and gender, class and occupational status created schisms among these groups of women, as goals and strategies diverged.

NWRO/National Council of Negro Women

The National Council of Negro Women, unlike NWRO, was an established and respected organization, ranking as one of the largest and oldest groups of black women in the United States. Founded in 1935 by Mary McCleod, by the end of the 1970s it was the only black women's group to be included among the 15 most prestigious and politically influential black organizations in the United States.[107] As an "umbrella group of 17 national organizations," in 1979 it claimed over 4 million black women as members in 200 local chapters around the country.[108] At the close of this decade, its stated purpose was "to harness woman power to fight oppressive and demoralizing poverty, unemployment and racism, hunger and malnutrition, unfair housing and unresponsive social services" and to "drive . . . toward self-reliance."[109] Its major thrust was fighting racism, although there appeared to be rising awareness that black women faced the "double jeopardy of racism and sexism." Dorothy Height, its president, insisted, however, that she could not support any struggle that pitted the black woman against the black man. For her, the key to survival and liberation of blacks in the United States was "unity."[110] Her struggle was for "human revolution significant enough to eliminate racism as well as sexism," since she felt that "nothing less can mean true liberation in the daily lives of all Black people."[111] The solution was "to work for the liberation of the whole black family."

Structurally, the National Council of Negro Women's membership meshed closely with that of NWRO, although the latter was limited to the poor. However, NWRO was a single-issue movement, focusing on welfare. The National Council addressed itself to such issues as poverty, hunger, and racism, which were more congruent with the espoused values of U.S. society. The National Council also emphasized self-reliance and independence, while NWRO focused on welfare rights, which implied dependency on the state rather than self-sufficiency. The National Council differed from NWRO in numerous other ways. Relatively speaking, it had many more resources than NWRO in terms of members, money, networks, and social prestige and recognition within the political arena. Its strategies for reform emphasized educational and service programs and lobbying in

Washington. NWRO, at least in its earlier years, chose less traditional political strategies and tactics that involved militant actions
against the established authorities. Only later did the welfare rights
movement shift to lobbying in Washington and in the state capitols.
Its public image was one of militant protest. All these differences
exacerbated schisms between these racial and gender peers and inhibited coalition formation across class lines.

Thus, linkages between NWRO and the National Council of Negro
Women at the national level were very limited. Only two events indicate any kind of interaction between these two groups. In 1973 at its
annual convention, in an effort to mobilize more support among wom-
en, NWRO singled out eight women and their organizations to receive
awards. Height and the National Council of Negro Women was one of
them. Coming shortly after Wiley's resignation and the "takeover"
by the women at the national level, this appears to have been a symbolic gesture of "sisterhood," as well as an effort to create stronger
ties with the established organizations of black women. In the final
months, as NWRO women struggled to find new sources of support,
the National Council of Negro Women responded with a $500 donation
to the Tillmon "Half-a-Chance Campaign."

At the local level in New Jersey, there was no evidence of cooperation between WROs and local chapters of the National Council of
Negro Women or any other group in the black women's club movement.
Although it is difficult, and perhaps hazardous, to generalize from
these limited data, conversations with participants in NWRO from
various parts of the country seem to confirm that abstention from the
welfare rights movement was probably the general pattern.

NWRO/Household Technicians of America

One group of predominantly black poor women that did align itself with NWRO, through the National Committee on Household Employment (NCHE), was the Household Technicians of America. The
ties, however, were more symbolic than substantive. Led by Edith
Sloan, the director of the National Committee, this organization had
been established in 1965, originally to increase the national supply of
household workers for middle-class, suburban homemakers. Structurally, its constituency closely meshed with that of NWRO. Its
members were overwhelmingly poor black women. Most were without husbands. Since the majority possessed few skills, they were
relegated to the lowest-paying jobs and wages.[112]

The goals of the Household Technicians were to promote the
welfare of household workers by lobbying "in Congress and in the
streets." Like NWRO, this organization did not reject militant tactics but at the same time endorsed the more traditional political pressures. Its thrust, unlike that of NWRO, was on jobs for women as a

means to become economically independent. More specifically, it called for "respectable wages, fringe benefits, and good working conditions."[113]

Given its common structure and similar goals and strategies, it is not surprising that this group of predominantly black poor women identified with and joined NWRO women in their fight for an adequate income. Politically, the Household Technicians constituted the most visible and continuous alliance between NWRO and a black women's organization.[114] Given its limited economic and political resources, its ties with NWRO were confined to participation in conferences and conventions from 1972 to 1974. By 1980, the movement of Household Technicians was alive and growing, while the movement of poor women on welfare lay splintered and becalmed. Greater support for workers than for recipients accounted in part for this differential in outcomes of the two groups. By 1979, NCHE had become an integral component of the National Urban League and had "forty-one affiliates in twenty-five states."[115] For a short period, however, NCHE was a symbolic partner of NWRO.

NWRO/Black Feminists

Black feminists and their support of poor women in their struggle for welfare rights arrived too late in the mid-1970s to help save NWRO. They did, however, provide new impetus and legitimacy to the cause of welfare as a women's issue by incorporating this problem into their agendas and some NWRO leaders and poor women into their organizations.

As the polls have shown, black women have "been stronger supporters of the idea of women's liberation than white women." In 1972, 62 percent of black women, compared to 45 percent of white women, supported the "strengthen[ing] or chang[ing of] women's status in society." By 1974 that gap had narrowed (67 percent black and 55 percent white), widening slightly again in 1980 (77 percent black and 62 percent white). This continuing rise in support of efforts to strengthen women's status in society was evident among both black and white women, with many of those previously listed as "not sure" having shifted to being in "favor of it." (See Table 5.1.) While black women ranked higher than white women in their support of women's liberation, their political mobilization as women was inhibited by their primary loyalty to the black struggle and the human rights struggle. This began to show some signs of changing in the 1970s.[116] As Celestine Ware had predicted ten years earlier, as more and more black women became "disillusioned by their oppression in the Black militant movement," both the "lower-class and college-educated black women" linked up with the feminist movement.[117]

TABLE 5.1

Public Opinion of Efforts to Strengthen or Change Women's Status in Society
(in percent)

	1970			1972			1974			1980*		
	White	Black	Difference	White	Black	Difference	White	Black	Difference	White	Black	Difference
Men												
Favor	41	52	-11	50	47	+3	62	67	-5	—	—	—
Oppose	40	27	+13	37	27	+10	20	13	+7	—	—	—
Not sure	19	21	-2	26	13	+13	18	21	-3	—	—	—
Women												
Favor	37	60	-23	45	62	-17	55	67	-12	62	77	-15
Oppose	46	20	+26	39	22	+17	27	14	+13	26	14	+12
Not sure	17	20	-3	16	16	0	18	19	-1	12	9	+3

*1980 data on males not available by race. Of all men, 64 percent favor, 23 percent oppose, and 13 percent are not sure.

Sources: 1970, 1972, 1974—Roper Organization, 1974, 3:3; 1980—The 1980 Virginia Slims American Women's Poll (Roper Organization, 1980).

The growing consensus among many black feminists by the end of the 1970s was that racism and sexism had to be attacked concurrently, not consecutively. Florence Kennedy, a black feminist leader and lawyer, urged black men to "hurry along and join" the black feminist movement instead of trying to inhibit it and/or criticize it. She did not agree with those who stated that "we have first to get rid of racism." For her, the two issues of discrimination and oppression had to be fought simultaneously. [118] Several others, including Shirley Chisholm and Maya Angelou, supported the view of fighting for black women's rights at all levels and in all sectors. [119] Margaret Sloan, a cofounder of the National Black Feminist Organization, asserted that "there can't be liberation for half a race," emphasizing that "Black women have suffered cruelly in this society from living the phenomenon of being black and female in a country that is both racist and sexist." [120] By 1975, at the International Women's Year celebration in Mexico City, the consensus was that "elimination of racism is just as important as elimination of sexism." This trend was further observed and documented by the black sociologist, Diane Lewis, who stated in 1977 that "there are recent indications that a growing number of black women have become more responsive to the issue of women's rights. During the past few years black women's organizations have emerged whose specific aim is to combat sexism and racism." [121] She concluded that black women were beginning "to perceive the way both sex inequality and race inequality affect their lives." Continuing inequalities between black men and women in U.S. society had made the latter "sensitive to the obstacle of sexism." [122] Consequently, there was "growing responsiveness to feminism" by black women and an accelerating pace in the organization of black feminist groups. [123]

In terms of structure, Lewis noted that, while black feminist groups tended to be led by middle-class women, their memberships "cross cut class lines," and "include welfare recipients, maids, and the unemployed, as well as high income earners." This integration in terms of class, Lewis pointed out, was achieved by black feminists but not by white feminists, who failed to "transcend class lines and eradicate labels." [124] Rising solidarity among poor and middle-class black women stemmed from common economic experiences. Increasing awareness, she added, had come in part from the efforts of NWRO. "For poor women, as a black welfare mother knows," she emphasized, "women's liberation is 'a matter of survival,' a perception increasingly held by such groups devoted to removing obstacles to the legitimate interests of poor black women as the National Welfare Rights Organization." As a result of the "successes of the black liberation movement" and the "shared experience of racism, a sense of common interest is beginning to emerge which may increasingly include all classes of black women." [125]

Thus, with the rise of black feminists in the mid-1970s, NWRO had potential political allies with common structures (based on race and gender) and similar goals. Ironically, however, although NWRO's women leaders welcomed this support in 1974, what they needed desperately at this period of financial crisis was money and organizational resources to keep the national movement alive. Since black feminist groups were just beginning to emerge, they had little to share with NWRO. Consequently, they remained only symbolic political allies in the final years of the movement.

For example, the National Black Feminist Organization, which emerged in 1973, wanted, among other things, "to demolish myths about the black woman's relation to her family, to black men and to racism."[126] Its constituency included women from all classes and many different occupations. Within one year, it mobilized 2,000 members in ten chapters around the country.[127] While the organization had few resources to place at the disposal of the financially troubled NWRO, it did provide political and moral support to the movement by sending one of its representatives, Margaret Sloan, to speak on feminist politics at the 1974 NWRO conference, its final meeting as a national movement.[128]

Another black feminist group that established ties with NWRO was the Coalition of 100 Black Women. This group, organized in the spring of 1974, also united poor and nonpoor black women "to deal with social issues" and "to lend credibility to the women's movement which . . . was not being taken seriously . . . as a political and revolutionary force." At the outset, the black feminists invited Sanders, the current chair of NWRO at the time, to join "as one of the 100 Black Women."[129] As with the National Black Feminist Organization, however, the linkages were symbolic, rather than substantive, in terms of resources provided to NWRO. Like other organizations, the coalition incorporated the issue of welfare into its broad agenda, defining it as a survival problem for many black women in poverty. Support of welfare rights as a separate movement of poor women, however, was not forthcoming, principally, it is suggested, because by then NWRO as a national movement was weakened and beset by internal problems. Support from this group had emerged too late to undergird the declining movement.

NWRO and White Women's Organizations

Solidarity between poor black women and middle-class white women in the welfare rights movement was also minimal. While a "pattern of cooperation between white and black women . . . on issues of human rights" had existed historically in the United States, as recorded by several writers, specific support for WROs and NWRO by white, middle-class women's groups* was relatively limited. Historically, alliances between white and black women were undermined by racial and class antagonisms. Catherine Stimpson notes that the history of racism among white feminists in the long struggle for suffrage was not easily forgotten. [130] In addition, when black men got the vote and women did not, racial tensions increased and gender solidarity diminished. Stimpson adds that for a short while "most feminists preserved a vague ideal of sisterhood." Eventually, this "sisterhood proved fragile," as the "solidarity between feminists and blacks gave way to a sexual solidarity, which, in turn, gave way to a primitive racial and class solidarity." As she points out, "a thoroughly ugly white supremacy infested the [feminist] movement" in those early years. As self-interests collided and the issue of power within the movement arose, "morality and compassion went underground."

Another writer who describes the historical conflicts between black and white women in reform movements in the United States is Rosalyn Terborg-Penn. She writes that discrimination existed against "Afro-American women reformers" within the woman's rights movement in the nineteenth and early twentieth centuries, despite the "rhetoric of female solidarity." Terborg-Penn emphasizes that black women were not disinterested, as their low participation might suggest. Rather, examination of "the actual experiences of black women who attempted to join the organizations of white feminists" indicates clearly that woman's rights organizations "actively discriminated against blacks."[131]

Lewis suggests that the source of such conflicts was rooted in the contrasting "deference and power and authority between black and white women," which created among black women a "distrust of white women."[132] The common mistress/servant roles, highlighting the dominant/subordinate power relationships in the daily lives of many women, reinforced differences in power and prestige, rather than the common bonds as women. These deep-seated and historical racial and class antagonisms among women continued into the late twentieth century, inhibiting the development of a well-integrated feminist movement, as well as support for NWRO by middle-class, white women.

Differences in structure and ideology between NWRO and middle-class women's organizations exacerbated the schisms. Structurally,

---

*In this discussion of NWRO and white women's organizations, the assumption is made that the latter were predominantly white in their membership and leadership, even though it is clear that most were racially integrated and had some black and Hispanic participants.

NWRO was made up of poor women who were mostly black. Unlike other women's groups, it was led and organized by men who seemed to support women's traditional roles in the family rather than their employment in the labor force. NWRO emphasized the right to welfare and the right to a guaranteed annual income from the state for women with dependent children. Privileged white women, on the other hand, reflecting the dominant values and norms, tended to reject this right and collaborated with dominant males in the stigmatization of those dependent on public assistance.

In general, most women, poor and nonpoor alike, defined the problems of poverty and dependency as being rooted in personal deficiencies in and failures of the poor women themselves, rather than in the systemic and rampant racism and sexism in U.S. society. Consequently, white, middle-class women, reflecting dominant male values, emphasized work and/or husbands as the best alternatives to public welfare for poor women. In their analyses, they tended to neglect the effects of racial and sex discrimination in education and employment within U.S. society. Expanding the right to work outside the home, rather than the right to welfare, was one of the major goals of the middle-class women's movement in the 1960s and 1970s. For growing numbers of educated and privileged white women in the labor force, a guaranteed income seemed to contradict their thrust for economic independence and perpetuate women's dependency on governmental largess, which was largely controlled by men. Welfare and welfare rights appeared to many women as the opposite of what they were interested in supporting in the mid-1960s and early 1970s.

Another point of contention between these two groups was the issue of women staying home to raise children. NWRO women called for the right to choose to remain at home as child rearers, given their limited job opportunities in the labor market. For many poor women, as William Chafe points out, "a world in which men were able to provide for the family and women had the option of tending the home represented a goal to be sought rather than a fate to be avoided."[133] For NWRO women, the burden of raising children and being breadwinners fell on them as single parents. For many welfare rights women, staying home to raise their own children with income from public assistance was a rational alternative, given dead-end jobs, low wages, and lack of child care. In addition, many repeatedly called for expanded opportunities for education, training, and better jobs to ensure economic independence. Yet, for large numbers of middle-class women, NWRO's demand for welfare as a right remained an anathema. They did not understand the reality of lives of poor women, so vividly described by Tillmon.

> We've been raised to expect to work, all our lives, for
> nothing. We're the worst educated, the least skilled and
> the lowest paid people there are. We're the most liable
> to disease, disability, early death, and unemployment.
> And we've got to carry alone the whole responsibility for
> our children. Bit by bit, society has pecked away at our
> independence and pride, and then, when we're picked nearly
> clean, it blames us for being "dependent."[134]

Only as more women from all walks of life began to experience, or
fear the possibility of, falling into poverty as a result of divorce,
separation, or aging did solidarity begin to emerge between poor
women on welfare and the more privileged women. Economic needs,
as the institutions of work and marriage changed, became a common
basis for concern and action.

Bonds between predominantly white women's groups and NWRO
also remained tenuous because the welfare rights movement, as we
have seen, was identified largely as a "black" movement. Racial discrimination in U.S. society thus helped to aggravate the differences
and obscure the commonality of women's economic problems.

Differences in goals also exacerbated the cleavages between
the welfare rights movement and other women's organizations. In
the 1970s, most of the major, middle-class women's organizations
were focusing their time, energy, and resources on the fight for the
passage of the Equal Rights Amendment (ERA). NWRO, on the other
hand, was fighting for "basic needs," and was only peripherally involved in the ERA issue. Furthermore, as the ERA struggle was
gaining momentum and adherents in the 1970s, NWRO was beginning
to decline. While NWRO leaders endorsed the ERA, their remaining
energies were directed to fighting for the survival of their organization and for their families. Only when the question of basic economic
needs became an issue for a broader spectrum of women (displaced
homemakers; battered women; teenage mothers; unemployed women;
divorced, separated, and widowed women; and the elderly and retired
women) did welfare begin to gain legitimacy within the women's organizations as an issue of vital concern to growing numbers within their
ranks.

Differences in strategies and tactics also created tensions and
lessened the likelihood of alliances between the organized poor women
and their potential female allies in the middle class. NWRO's early
militant tactics and agitation in the "streets" collided with the more
traditional strategies of education and lobbying for social change by
the privileged women's organizations. By the late 1970s, however,
demonstrations within the feminist movement were signs that middle-
class women might be shifting to a strategy of protest. For example,

the march in Washington, D. C. , in support of the extension of the voting period on the ERA brought 100,000 women to Washington in the summer of 1978. In Illinois similar demonstrations for the passage of the ERA attracted from 50,000 to 100,000 women and their supporters in May 1980.[135]

Perhaps most significantly, little cooperation emerged between NWRO and white women's organizations because no one at first defined welfare as a women's issue. Within NWRO it was called a "poor people's" problem. As Glassman notes:

> It does not see itself as a women's movement; rather it is a movement that happens to have as its constituency mostly women. Because of this view welfare rights movements rarely describe or analyze the welfare problem as a woman's problem but rather as part of the national problems of poverty and racial oppression. While pushing naturally for a guaranteed income and an end to repressive controls . . . , they do not concern themselves with the role of women in the economy, or the status of the family.[136]

Few white, middle-class women's groups saw any connection between welfare and their agendas. For many whites, including women, welfare was a "black" issue. For many blacks, including women, it was a "class" issue. Only when the myths of welfare began to be unmasked and the reality of the structure of poverty revealed did women's economic vulnerability gain visibility and attract greater concern. By 1980 "the economy [had become] a women's issue."[137]

Thus, structural differences resulted in divergent goals, strategies, and tactics for NWRO and other women's organizations. Differences, rather than commonalities, were emphasized in the early years. The lack of consciousness of women's common problems as a "minority group"[138] within a male-dominated society inhibited cooperation between NWRO and its white "sister" organizations. Historically grounded racial and class cleavages underscored differences and kept the women separated. Only in the later years—too late to affect NWRO—was there recognition of welfare as one of the major economic problems faced by growing numbers of women.

However, some ties, although minimal, did emerge between NWRO and a few women's groups. We begin by examining the relationship of NWRO with "service-oriented," church-related women's agencies. We then analyze its alliances with the "politically oriented" organizations, such as the League of Women Voters, the women's peace organizations, and the white feminist organizations. The focus is not only on the ties and exchanges that may have emerged in the alliances between welfare rights and women's organizations but also the extent to which different groups incorporated the issue of welfare and the principle of welfare as a women's issue into their agendas. Some organizations within the feminist movement that had no ties with NWRO but that did adopt welfare and/or poverty as a major concern are also examined in order to document the broadening concern by women's groups about this issue. While the interaction between NWRO and white women's organizations was very limited, by the close of the 1970s welfare had been officially adopted as part of the National Women's Agenda,* endorsed by over 100 organizations in the United States. Therefore, NWRO had an indirect impact on the women's movement. Welfare was adopted as a political issue as a result of both growing understanding of welfare in terms of self-interest for all women and the demands of the representatives of poor women from various groups, including WROs, for inclusion and specification of their needs.[139]

NWRO/Church-Related Organizations

At the national and local levels, organized church women in the white Protestant denominations were among the first to respond to the welfare rights appeal for economic and political support. The United Methodist Women, according to several sources, was one of the organizations that quickly mobilized some of its resources for welfare rights groups, especially for those in New York City.[140] National staff members of the United Methodist Women announced in 1971 that "as women we recognized similarities with NWRO who had similar needs and problems."[141]

These church women provided "financial help and field support" in the early years amounting to about $30,000.[142] Thereafter, contributions declined. In terms of NWRO budgetary needs, and the contributions of the white liberal churches as a whole, the amount was relatively small. Yet, it was symbolic and timely for the poor women. Political support for NWRO was mobilized among its church members through educational strategies, such as meetings, conferences, and use of denominational publications and media. Through their networks, they distributed NWRO materials and newsletters, as well as their own analysis of the welfare issue. Members were encouraged to join the movement as Friends of WRO and to help defeat the Nixon FAP. The United Methodist Women also supported NWRO by sending representatives to its conferences and undertaking the responsibility for trying to mobilize other women's divisions within the main-line denominations.[143] Few responded to this call.[144]

---

*See p. 265 on the National Women's Agenda.

The United Methodist Women were by far the most visibly involved of the church-related women's groups, but relatively speaking, their contributions were more symbolic than substantive. However, individual church women, both at the national and local levels, appear to have played significant roles in helping to organize and support WRO groups throughout the country. [145]

The Young Women's Christian Association (YWCA), a quasi-religious, middle-class, service agency, was also peripherally involved in the movement of welfare rights. In 1971 it had shifted from focusing emphasis on changing interpersonal relationships to organizing to bring about "basic change in power relations." As a result, this new emphasis on "equity and empowerment" coincided with that of NWRO. [146] Furthermore, as a racially integrated organization dedicated to the elimination of racism through educational and service programs, its structure, goals, and strategies meshed quite closely with those of NWRO. Its concerns for the economic needs of women also enhanced the bonds between these two groups.

In the late 1960s, it donated some monies to NWRO to help its leaders attend conferences and sent its own representatives to NWRO's meetings. [147] It also joined NWRO in lobbying against FAP, calling it "humiliating, demeaning and [having] racist bias directed at women and children, especially poor black women and those of other minorities." [148] As was the case with women's church groups, its support of NWRO was relatively limited, although indications are that there was greater interaction and cooperation between WROs and YWCAs at the local level. [149] Thus, as both these service-oriented, church-related groups moved toward more endorsement of social action in the 1960s, they established some ties with NWRO. Relatively speaking, however, their support was minimal.

NWRO/League of Women Voters

Among the more politically oriented groups, the League of Women Voters became deeply involved in the welfare reform struggle—but not with the welfare rights movement. It functioned independently of NWRO and used its resources to educate its predominantly white, middle-class constituency about the welfare issue by publishing fact sheets and holding workshops and forums. As individuals, several of its leaders at the local, state, and national levels actively supported NWRO, many as Friends of Welfare Rights. [150] Organizationally, however, because of tax constraints by the federal government, formal ties with NWRO were precluded. In its lobbying for reform, the League of Women Voters first endorsed NWRO's plan for a guaranteed income of $5,500 for a family of four but later switched to the Ribicoff plan for $3,000, which it argued was more politically feasible and at least "a-foot-in-the-door." This stance infuriated NWRO leaders. [151] In the final days of the FAP struggle, the league rejoined NWRO and others to help defeat the Nixon plan, which by then it felt had become "too restrictive." [152] As a respected, middle-class organization, it provided legitimation for the welfare rights goals and indirectly helped to mobilize some needed resources for WRO groups. The league's involvement in the welfare issue led it back into the women's movement, when, in its "work for minorities," it "discovered that women had the most minority problems of all." [153]

Thus, as interest in welfare reform subsided after the defeat of FAP in October 1972, and new political issues began to surface (such as the ratification of ERA), the League of Women Voters shifted its attention and resources from the needs of poor women on welfare to greater concentration on women's issues in general. [154] By 1977, when welfare reform was reintroduced by the Carter administration, the League of Women Voters identified welfare as a women's problem. They reentered the struggle, noting that "poverty is the overriding fact of life for an increasing number of women and their children . . . and as the number of families headed by women grows, poverty will become increasingly a women's problem." [155] The League of Women Voters thus provided some episodic political support for NWRO's goals but not for its national movement organization.

NWRO/Women's Peace Movement

Women's groups in the "peace" movement constituted another political ally of NWRO. Peace and the redirecting of priorities from "warfare to welfare" were the themes that bridged the ideological gap between these two women's groups. Women in the peace movement, mostly white and middle class, were active and continuous political supporters of the welfare rights movement after 1968. While NWRO rarely publicized in its communications and newsletter any of its outside support, it did highlight its cooperation with peace groups. [156] The common cause that united these two partners was the goal to redirect military expenditures to social welfare programs.

Ties between the two groups developed both at the national and local levels. At the national level, Wiley was invited to play a prominent role in the peace coalitions, and NWRO women leaders were paid guests at international peace conferences in different parts of the world. At the local level, WROs benefited from the contributions of the Women's International League for Peace and Freedom and SANE. [157] Roxanne Jones, a WRO chair in Philadelphia, for example, reported that the women in the peace movement had joined the welfare rights mothers in joint protests against the welfare policy makers in the state. As a result, there was a "great feeling of common cause" between the two groups in 1971. Although the ties were tenuous and scattered, the women in the peace movement and in WRO seem to have established some bonds for political support of each other's causes.

NWRO/White Feminists

NWRO's relationship with white feminist organizations at both the national and local levels was at best limited. Structurally and ideologically, the gaps were wide. Structurally, their memberships differed in terms of class and race. NWRO was, as we have seen, overwhelmingly poor and black; feminist organizations were predominantly middle class and white. Organizationally, NWRO was a movement of poor women developed and organized primarily by men. Feminist groups were created and led by women in their struggle for equality between the sexes. NWRO's goal of welfare rights was at first highly criticized by feminists for emphasizing an institution that perpetuated economic dependence, rather than economic independence, of women.[158] These divergent structures and political perspectives limited cooperation between the poor and nonpoor women in the feminist movement.

Other areas of conflict over women's needs also weakened the potential alliances between welfare rights women and the feminists. For example, in the area of protective laws for women, NWRO organizers in general believed that poor women, relegated to low-paying, menial occupations, were more vulnerable to exploitation in the labor force and therefore needed "protection." Feminists, on the other hand, identified protective laws as another institutionalized barrier to occupational equality. They were "the most ardent and well-known advocates of the antiprotective law position."[159] Critics of this position stated that middle-class women "largely ignore many of [poor women's] more critical problems." More specifically, NWRO considered "the abolition of the protective laws a potential catastrophe for welfare women," since it was apprehensive about "potential exploitation that could result if all worker protection is removed and mandatory work requirements were enforced."[160] The WIN legislation in 1967 and the Talmadge amendments in 1971 and 1973 (which forced AFDC mothers to register for work) underlined the reality of such fears within NWRO. Without unionization, it was felt that the loss of protective laws could prove to be disastrous for women. Feminists, on the other hand, argued that elimination of protection would benefit all women, since these laws "seriously interfere with their right to economic independence especially when many Black and white women in the lower classes are family heads and must support their families."[161] Thus, unequal competition for scarce jobs in the labor market and the debate over work or welfare for women at first heightened the tensions between poor women and middle-class feminists.

With more and more women entering the labor force in the 1970s, some suggested that increased competition for jobs would divide white women and black women, rather than unite them.[162] Economist Heather Ross predicted "a growing rift between the poor and the non-poor [women]," especially "as the latter increase their labor force participation, [and] the former go on welfare and reduce theirs."[163] For welfare rights women, the issue of domestic work in the homes of middle- and upper-class women was an issue that underscored the cleavage between the poor and nonpoor women. Sanders explained that "nobody wants to do domestic work" for other people. She stated that for years she had cleaned other people's houses. "Now," she said, "I don't clean anybody's house but my own. And I don't want to force any other woman to do it either."[164] Yet, policy makers had strengthened this potential rift between the poor women and the more affluent ones by creating a "tax incentive" for household employers who hired welfare recipients as domestic workers in an effort to reduce the public assistance rolls.[165]

In terms of priority of goals, there were also differences between the movements of poor women and the feminists. For NWRO the major issues were greater welfare benefits for female-headed families and, ultimately, a guaranteed income for the poor. For the feminists, it was the ERA. Tillmon called on the feminists to support NWRO's "Guaranteed Adequate Income Plan" to help "eliminate sexism from welfare."[166] Feminists, on the other hand, appealed for unity around the ERA to eliminate the oppression of women, arguing that "the ERA would provide the sorely needed constitutional mandate for challenging the sexism that puts women in poverty, keeps them there, and creates a welfare system that barely allows them to survive, while subjecting them to abuse and degradation."[167] While NWRO leaders openly supported the ERA, it ranked low in their list of priorities for the poor women's movement. Their major objectives, as we have seen, were to meet the basic needs of their families, such as adequate income, food, clothing, and shelter. Another major objective was to minimize and neutralize as much as possible the repressive tactics of the welfare authorities that governed their daily lives and those of their children. Tillmon pointed out that while "Women's Liberation is a matter of concern" for many "middle-class women in the country, for women on welfare it is a matter of survival."[168]

Another source of tension that inhibited ties between the poor and nonpoor women was the model of alliances within the welfare rights movement developed by its organizers. The role of outsiders was limited and circumscribed. Friends of Welfare Rights were asked to assume a supportive role in the cause in which only the poor were deemed to be functioning out of self-interest. While some of the more traditional women's organizations were willing to accept this service role in the struggle for poor women's rights, the feminists, fighting for their own rights in a male-dominated society, demanded an equal partnership, not a dominant/subordinate relationship with another group in the political arena. Feminists spoke out against the "compassion trap" in patriarchal systems in which women were socialized to derive rewards vicariously and inconspicuously in the "service" of other people's causes. The fight for equal rights was one based on enlightened self-interest and not on altruism, as so often had been the case in the women's participation in the civil rights struggle. The feminists wanted egalitarian alliances. At first this kind of relationship was unacceptable to NWRO. [169] Some of NWRO's women leaders distrusted the feminist movement, asserting that they saw in it "little concern for poor women." [170] Black welfare women also feared dominance in a coalition with an elite feminist group at a time when NWRO was struggling to build its own identity and organization within the political arena.

Despite these many sources of real and potential conflict and disagreement, there were some underlying bases for cooperation. Tillmon, as head of NWRO, had always supported women's economic independence through paid work as one solution to poor women's continued dependence on welfare. She suggested that welfare be replaced by "paying women a living wage for doing the work they were already doing—childrearing and housekeeping." [171] Child care was another area in which the needs of NWRO women and middle-class feminists overlapped. Tillmon pointed out that "one of the first priorities" of her welfare rights group in California had been a child-care center. [172] Sanders and several other WRO leaders also supported child care as a top priority for NWRO, because of their concern for adequate care for their children. [173] The common goals of adequate jobs and child care thus provided a potential common ground for cooperation. However, NWRO's male organizers emphasized "jobs for men" and "welfare for women." [174] This initial thrust by NWRO collided sharply with the feminist objectives and thus, in the early years, inhibited the formation of any alliances between the two movements of women.

By the early 1970s, economic conditions and the demography of the labor force were changing rapidly. As divorce rates soared, unprecedented numbers of white women were joining the ranks of single-headed families with dependent children. As single parents, the specter of economic dependence on welfare began to loom as a possible reality for increasing numbers. Poor women and more affluent women, left without spouses to support them, were finding that they shared a common destiny as "displaced homemakers" at some point in their lives. A high unemployment rate, restricted job opportunities, accelerating divorce rates, and pervasive sex and race discrimination in the labor market that contributed to women's low wages were converging to strengthen the bonds among women from all walks of life.

Although there were common issues and increasing solidarity among women around economic issues in the 1970s, in the early years both NWRO and the feminist organizations were fledgling movements struggling to mobilize as political challengers of the system. While more independent financially because of its middle-class constituency, the feminist movement still had little to offer NWRO other than symbolic, political support. By middecade, not only national but worldwide forces were emerging to unify women across class and racial lines. The year 1975 was designated and celebrated as the International Women's Year and the 1975-85 decade, as the Women's Decade. Thus, women's economic and social problems, rather than their racial and class differences that historically had kept them apart, were becoming the sources of common cause and protest by the 1980s. As Glassman predicted in 1970, "As the movement for women's liberation spreads out from the middle-class and into other sectors of the society, the welfare rights women are its potential base among the female poor."[175] In the early 1970s, Tillmon appealed to feminists to help NWRO in its political struggle. Some listened and responded. Others listened but did not yet hear a common drummer. Among the former were the National Women's Political Caucus and, to a lesser degree, the National Organization of Women.

NWRO/NWPC. The National Women's Political Caucus (NWPC) emerged in 1970 with NWRO as one of its charter members, "dedicated to increasing the political power of women."[176] Sanders, representing NWRO, appealed in this coalition of feminists "for women to come together as one unit," noting that various economic issues affected all women.[177] From the outset, the NWPC integrated its policy council with poor and nonpoor women and with representatives from various racial and ethnic groups. It was still, however, dominated by white women. It chose as its first goal the passage of the ERA, and Sanders of NWRO "wholeheartedly agreed with the formation of the political caucus" and its goals.[178] It had on its agenda, as did NWRO, the passage of a guaranteed income plan and the defeat of forced work for poor women.[179]

Interaction between NWRO and the NWPC, however, remained more symbolic than substantive. Linkages were mainly between individual leaders of both movements at the national level. Gloria Steinem, Bella Abzug, Florence Kennedy, and others participated as speakers in NWRO conventions and workshops in 1971-73, promoting cooperation between all women "to combat mutual problems."[180] At the local level, ties were also very limited and episodic. Poor women's groups sought support from the middle-class feminists in terms

of funds and other organizational resources, not just symbolic political support. Little assistance was forthcoming. For example, in
1974, when the news of the slaying of Alberta Williams King, the wife
of Martin Luther King, Sr., was announced at a meeting of the Wom-
en's Political Caucus in Kansas, the WRO leader of Wichita appealed
for funds on the basis of their espoused solidarity as women. "Show
me," she said, "that you are my sisters by helping send me to St.
Louis."[181] The result was the passage of a resolution of sympathy
and a collection of "$255 in her memory" to be "given to members of
the Wichita Welfare Rights Organization to help pay their expenses to
the National Welfare Rights Organization meeting in St. Louis."[182]
In Minnesota there were some reports of joint actions but not of specific support of the WROs.

By 1973, two years after the formation of NWPC, Sanders com-
plained that this feminist organization was "ignoring NWRO and the
needs of poor women."[183] It is clear that white, middle-class members of NWPC did not see their role as economic supporters of NWRO.
At best they considered themselves to be equal partners in the political struggle for equal rights for women in U.S. society. Financial
contributions to WROs, when they occurred, appear to have been
based not on local or state NWPC policy but, rather, on individuals'
reactions to the appeals of poor black women.

Another indirect link with NWRO was established when Audrey
Colom, a former member of NWRO's staff, was elected the first black
president of the National Women's Political Caucus in 1975.[184] By
1980 she had become a recognized leader within the national feminist
movement. NWRO leaders counted this as a loss, rather than a gain,
for they felt that she had been "co-opted" and had failed to use her
influence and prestige in support of the welfare rights movement across the country.[185]

NWPC eventually established a Welfare Reform Task Force in
the mid-1970s and fought alongside NWRO against Nixon's FAP.[186]
It also endorsed employment as the solution to "costly welfare programs" and argued that the AFDC program "should concentrate on
helping women become self-supporting rather than provide meager assistance to children."[187] The middle-class feminist's bias in favor
of work, rather than of welfare, was once again highlighted within
this movement organization.

As NWPC grew and expanded its membership base and budget,
NWRO declined.[188] For NWRO the alliance with the feminists in
NWPC resulted in few economic or political resources for the organization or its goals for a guaranteed income system and adequate
child care for poor women. At best the short-lived partnership between poor and nonpoor women may have increased NWRO's legitimacy
and that of the welfare rights cause among some middle-class, women

leaders. It may also have helped to redefine "welfare as a women's issue," for which Tillmon had long argued. For individual leaders in NWRO, participation in NWPC appears to have shifted the poor women's strategy to electoral politics and "working through the system" to achieve their goals. While NWPC may have helped to make welfare reform part of the women's agenda, it may also have detracted from NWRO's specific goal for a guaranteed income for poor people by calling for jobs and training for poor women rather than income re- distribution through a new transfer system. Most significant, per- haps, in this alliance was the inclusion of poor women in the coalition for women's political rights and the adoption of welfare as a concern for women. By the late 1970s, NWPC members had "reasserted [their] support of welfare reform, even though their major thrust as a movement organization was to see that more women got elected to office."[189] In 1980 welfare reform continued to be monitored as a women's issue.

NWRO/NOW. The relationship between NWRO and NOW was even more tenuous than that between NWRO and NWPC. Unlike NWPC, which included the welfare rights organization as a coalition partner, NOW had no formal ties and few informal contacts with NWRO at the national and local levels. Jo Freeman reports that the two movements of women emerged coincidentally on the same day, June 30, 1966.[190] While NOW, like NWRO, had adopted an "inclusive" principle in terms of racial and class participation in the movement, the two member- ships were in sharp contrast. NOW was made up of predominantly white, middle-class women, while NWRO consisted mostly of black, poor women. Structurally, NOW was a group of women organized and led by women, while NWRO was created and controlled largely by men. NOW focused specifically on the grievances of women in U.S. society. NWRO focused on those of poor people in general and AFDC women in particular.

In its agenda, however, NOW included the struggle against the oppression of black women in the United States, declaring that black women were "the victims of the double discrimination of race and sex," which relegated them to the "lowest paid service occupations." NOW's Statement of Purpose also acknowledged that women's prob- lems were tied to the "broader questions of social justice" and that their solution "requires concerted action by many groups." It called upon "other organizations committed to such goals to support [the] effort toward equality of women." Among the original six task forces set up to carry out these objectives were "Equal Opportunity for Em- ployment" and the "War for Women in Poverty."[191] Theoretically, therefore, NOW from its birth was committed to helping resolve the problems of poor, minority women as well as those of middle-class, white women. In reality, it failed to attract many poor or black women.

Over the years, attempts were made by NOW leaders to close this gap and to integrate the movement and its concerns across racial and class lines. In New Jersey, for example, some efforts were made to organize in the urban areas. [192] The Newark NOW, established in May 1975, reported that its membership included "Blacks, whites and Hispanics." It also noted that there were "professional workers, unemployed, clerical workers, welfare recipients, etc., in the organization, which means that we represent a cross-section of the population in the area."[193] Despite this commitment to inclusiveness, in practice NOW's structures and programs reflected middle-class perspectives that inhibited the development of coalitions between poor and nonpoor women. Few blacks, much less poor black women, sought to join local NOW chapters. Although at least one attempt was made by national leaders to establish ties between NWRO and NOW, it did not succeed.

According to one report, the president of NOW in 1970, Karen DeCrow, invited Wiley to speak at the NOW's national board meeting to explore ways in which the two movements might cooperate. This attempt backfired when it became clear to the feminist leaders that the two movements were poles apart in terms of their goals for women in U. S. society. Wiley is reported to have "started out by saying that NWRO's primary goal was to place the black male back where he belonged—at the head of the family, not economic independence for women." According to this NOW board member, the feminists' reaction was that "he blew it!" They realized that "he just didn't have his consciousness raised at that time." Later, many felt that because "he was a sensitive, intelligent person," he would "have moved in his way of feeling, had he lived."[194]

This incident underscores the wide gap between the two movements' goals. NWRO emphasized women's traditional role and dependence on men and thus clashed sharply with NOW's thrust for women's economic independence through paid work in the labor market. NWRO's organizers and planners at that time apparently supported the traditional male and female stereotypes, while the feminists were organized to change them. NWRO's justification for its stand was that black poor women's choices were extremely restricted within the economy. Relegated to the lowest-paying and menial jobs, poor black women saw child rearing and a guaranteed income as more attractive and rational alternatives. Some feminists attacked this reasoning. Judith Levin and Patricia Vergatta, for example, argued that NWRO and the welfare system perpetuated the present social role of women that made them economically and socially dependent on men. [195] They added that "the real tragedy of welfare is not that a

woman is 'forced to work'" but rather "the coercion of <u>neglect.</u>"
From their point of view, "Welfare women should have the same
choices as the rest of society . . . the right to earn and achieve."
They felt that the "right to stay home" was a "hollow choice" and
ultimately denied the poor woman "the necessary resources she needs
to develop her children."

Although NWRO and NOW never established any formal ties or
alliances, the rising concerns of some of the poor women leaders for
employment opportunities, rather than welfare, brought the two movements closer together. Tillmon had long endorsed economic independence for women and the right of women to choose when to have children and whether to pursue employment outside the home along with
child-rearing responsibilities.[196] Tillmon emphasized that work was
not the issue. It was the choice of where and when to work, which,
she pointed out, was unequally distributed among women in U.S.
society. Poor women (and men), she said, had always had to work
in order to survive. A rich woman, such as the "society lady from
Scarsdale," could stay home, if she were married and supported by
a man. She added that the dominant society punished those who
"failed" to attract and keep a man. Tillmon challenged middle-class
women not to "put down other women for being on welfare" and called
for greater empathy and understanding among poor and nonpoor wom-
en. She urged feminists to "stop for a minute and think what would
happen to you and your kids if you suddenly had no husband and no
savings." Where would their monies and support come from? She
appealed to them to get the facts on welfare and learn how poor women
were "suffering from sexism." She warned middle-class women that,
if they did not learn from the struggle of women on welfare, sooner
or later they might have to suffer a similar fate: to live on welfare
"because you are a woman."[197]

Over the years, as political and economic conditions changed,
pushing more women into poverty, NOW began to focus more on welfare and the concerns of poor women.[198] In 1973, having been criticized for its middle-class bias, NOW adopted a resolution on poverty
as a women's issue and called for a standard minimum wage, child
development programs, and the overhaul of welfare programs.[199]
NOW also joined NWRO in lobbying against FAP, opposing the requirement that women accept jobs at 75 percent of the minimum wage.
NOW argued that "one of the reasons that many of these women are on
welfare in the first place is that the wage structure for women is too
low." NOW's proposed solution was to change the economic status of
women by enabling them to get decent jobs at adequate wages. Along
with NWRO, NOW also testified against the "forced work" requirements in the WIN/Talmadge legislation and against the proposed food-
stamp cuts as well as in support of abortion for all women and day-
care.[200]

Although there were several issues that united the poor and non-poor women in the two movements, WRO women leaders were generally critical of NOW's lack of specific support for their organizations and actions.[201] Only in a few states were there reports of some ties between NOW and WROs.[202] In general, the report from WRO leaders around the country was that local NOW groups had not been receptive to cooperating with WROs. In New Jersey, for example, little contact was established with NOW. Kidd, the chair of NJWRO, criticized the women in FWROs who deserted the welfare rights movement to work for their own liberation in the women's movement and then failed to get support for the poor women.[203] One problem was the different expectations. At best, NOW groups might have accepted the WRO women as political allies in joint actions on issues of mutual interest. WROs, however, tended to expect that the organized, middle-class women should be able and willing to provide financial support and "services," a role which most middle-class women rejected. The "auxiliary" role was not acceptable to NOW leaders.*

Toward the end of the 1970s, NOW began to take some action around poor women's needs, seeking to make the feminist organization more inclusive, in accordance with its stated principles. DeCrow, in her address to the annual convention in 1977, highlighted "poverty as a women's issue," pointing out the "outrageous discriminations against women in income, employment, taxation, and welfare programs." She emphasized that "most women are poor and most of the poor are women."[204] In the "second round" of welfare reform in 1977, NOW once again fought for legislation that reflected the basic needs of poor women and their children. NOW leaders criticized legislators for ignoring the fact that "the problem of poverty in the United States is primarily an issue of women and their dependent children" and for seeking solutions to poverty "by employing men."[205] Eleanor Smeal, the president of NOW (who succeeded DeCrow), rejected the arbitrary classification of women with small children as "unemployables" in the proposed Carter "welfare reform,"[206] which would deny them "access to ancillary unemployment benefits" (available to the "employables"), including "training and retraining for other careers."[207]

Although the NOW Task Force on Poverty continued to call for more recognition by feminists that poverty "oppresses ALL WOMEN," the issue of welfare remained "unpopular" within NOW.[208] However,

---

*By 1979, however, after having been criticized by a New York City Welfare Rights group, NOW-NY voted to "commit more of its time and resources to aiding these women" ("NOW-NY Holds Conference on Urban Women," Women's Agenda, December 1978, p. 5).

its leaders at the national level continued to lobby against the inadequacies of the Carter administration's proposals, contending that they

> perpetuated the outrageously sexist treatment of poor women
> by stripping them of control over their lives and their children's lives, by denying them equal access to training and
> jobs, by failing to eliminate gender stereotyping and use of
> sexist language, by completely ignoring the economic value
> of work done in the home, and by condemning mothers with
> young children to subsisting on a below poverty level income.[209]

NOW underscored the fact that there was "an indisputable relationship between being female and being poor" and that this was especially "devastating" for black, Hispanic, and aged women.[210]

Given NOW's top priority for the passage of ERA, its leaders highlighted the fact that the passage of ERA was also closely related to their fight for welfare reform. They called on NOW members to continue the struggle "for the rights and wellbeing of millions of women," suggesting that NOW groups "contact welfare rights groups, [and] poverty law centers" around the issue of welfare reform. At the local level, there appears to have been little response.[211]

By 1980 the movement of welfare rights remained atomized, but NOW continued to expand. From 55,000 paid-up members in 1976, NOW had surpassed 100,000 by 1980. Its annual budget was close to $2.5 million and rising.[212] While its membership included some poor and minority women, it was "still white and middle-class."[213]

While NWRO was active as a national movement organization of poor women, interactions with NOW were rare. Yet it is clear that these two, contrasting women's movements had an impact on each other. NWRO left its imprint on NOW and the feminist movement in at least three ways. First, as Freeman suggested, NWRO educated NOW and raised its consciousness about "welfare as a women's issue."[214] While some leaders in NOW had identified the gender roots of poverty as early as 1966, it was only the prodding of WRO women leaders, such as Tillmon, Sanders, and others, that helped to make this a visible issue within the feminist movement. It never, however, became a popular issue in the middle-class women's movement, although from 1973 on the data indicate that the major feminist groups in the country (at least at the national level) were increasingly incorporating welfare and poverty in their political agendas. Second, NWRO, through Tillmon, contributed what was to become a major slogan of the women's liberation movement, namely, "Every woman is one man away from welfare." This, according to Freeman, symbolized the epitome of woman's dependence on man.[215] Third, after the demise of NWRO in 1975, a few of NWRO's women leaders joined feminist organizations, potentially strengthening the ties between poor and nonpoor women.

NOW, on the other hand, seems to have raised the consciousness of poor women to sexism in society. Welfare at first had rarely been defined by welfare rights members, organizers, and supporters as a women's issue. Symbolically, some changes by the NWRO women seem to reflect this shift in perspective. For example, the language in their letters and publications changed over time. The word chairman, used during the first five years of the movement when NWRO was run by Wiley and his predominantly male staff, was replaced with chairlady in 1972 and later with chairwoman.[216] After Wiley's resignation in 1973, the term the ladies was changed to the women, womanpower replaced mother power, and Mrs. was replaced by Ms.[217]

Other evidence of rising consciousness of sexism within the movement was reflected in the power shifts within the top leadership within NWRO, as described in Chapter 2. From 1966 to the end of 1972, when Wiley resigned from NWRO, there was growing support by the women leaders for liberation from male and middle-class dominance, both at the national and local levels. NWRO's women leaders gradually began to change their definition of the movement from one of "poor people" to one of "poor women," identifying their struggle by 1973 as "Women Waging War for Survival." When Wiley resigned, one woman on the Executive Committee stated, "This is a woman's movement and we make the decisions."[218]

Thus, while the link with the feminists in NWPC and NOW were tenuous at best, and the limited interactions added little to NWRO's resources over the years, it is clear that the feminists were actively involved in the political struggle for welfare reform, aligning themselves many times in support of NWRO's position. The feminists, however, failed to attract poor women to their movement organization. They also refused to accept the role of servicing and supporting the WROs of poor women. Nevertheless, the two women's movements had reciprocal impact on each other. The feminists seem to have become more conscious of welfare as a women's issue, and NWRO women seem to have become more conscious of their oppression as women within the movement and within the larger society. Both these currents had implications for NWRO and the continuing struggle for welfare reform, as we shall discuss in the final chapter.

Welfare as a Women's Issue

The issues of welfare and poverty continued to gain ground within the women's movement even after the demise of NWRO in 1975.

Paradoxically, while the fragmented movement of welfare rights was no longer able to mobilize support to make a political impact on the welfare system, numerous other women's groups and coalitions were addressing themselves to these issues and identifying them as women's concerns.

The sources of this expanding interest in welfare and poverty were varied, but the principal one seemed to be changing economic conditions. By the end of the 1970s, the economic gap between minority and white women was closing. Fully employed women continued to earn less than fully employed men of either white or minority races.[219] In 1966 the difference in median annual income between minority and white women was $1,203. In 1976 the difference had dropped to $460. Over this ten-year period, 60 percent of the gap had been closed. In 1976 minority women had a median income of $7,825; white women, $8,285. Within the minority group, poverty for black women was critical. Alexis Herman, a black feminist and director of the Women's Bureau of the U.S. Department of Labor, notes that, while the gap between the earnings of black women and white women was smaller in 1978, "the most underreported economic fact is the increasing number of black women who live in poverty."[220] She attributed this to both race and sex discrimination.

While the burden of poverty continued to fall disproportionately on black women, statistics also indicated that increasing numbers of white women were slipping into the lowest income category. With the rise of divorce and separation rates, more white women were moving onto the AFDC rolls.[221] Data from HEW showed that whites on AFDC had climbed from 46.9 percent in 1973 to 50.2 percent in 1977, while blacks had dropped slightly from 45.8 to 44.3 percent.[222]

Another economic factor that was changing rapidly in the 1960s and 1970s and that affected the possible bonding of poor and nonpoor women was the unprecedented influx of white women into the labor force. In 1970 the differential between black and white women's participation rate in the civilian labor force was over 7 percent (49.1 percent for blacks, 41.9 percent for whites). Eight years later, this gap had narrowed to about 4 percent (52.7 percent and 48.6 percent, respectively), as the numbers of white women seeking employment soared. The sharing of common experiences in the labor force, such as concentration in clerical and service jobs (52.8 percent of black and 52.6 percent of white women workers), high unemployment rates in relation to men, rising consciousness of sex discrimination and sexual harassment on the job, and the discrepancy in wages and salaries between women and men, were beginning to strengthen the ties between growing numbers of women by the end of the decade.[223]

Louise Lamphere suggested that this "new convergence" of women's economic needs stemmed in part from the fact that divorce

FIGURE 5.1

Poor Families with a Female Householder, No Husband Present, as a Percent of All Poor Families, 1969 and 1977

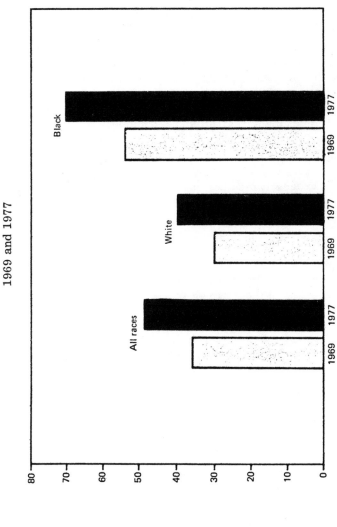

Source: U.S., Bureau of the Census, Population Profile of the U.S., 1978, Current Population Reports Series P-20, no. 336, p. 49.

was no longer a middle-class phenomenon and that both black and white women were becoming female heads of their families, with devastating economic consequences for many.[224] (See Figure 5.1.) In addition, she pointed out, not only middle-class, college-educated women but also "wives of blue collar workers" were "spending an increasing number of years in the workforce." Finally, "working class and black women are increasingly finding themselves isolated in nuclear families, away from networks of kin and neighbors."

Given the convergence of women's economic and social needs, feminist leaders, both white and black, were calling for unity of women across racial and class lines. At the First National Women's Agenda Conference in 1976, Holmes, a black feminist, emphasized that the growing unity among various groups of women "repudiates the myth that such diversity cannot produce a common cause." She felt that despite differences in race, religion, social background, and economic circumstances, alliances could and should evolve around common grievances as women.[225]

By the mid-1970s, new coalitions and organizations of women were emerging and addressing themselves to the plight of poor women. Feminist groups, which had earlier remained uninvolved, were now beginning to join the ranks of those defining welfare as a women's issue. In May 1977 a new coalition of poor and nonpoor women emerged around the combined issues of "women, work, and welfare." The National Council of Women, Work, and Welfare, a spin-off from the welfare rights movement, defined itself as "a non-profit, research and rallying group [that] has been formed to fill [the] void" created by "the disbanding of the National Welfare Rights Organization."[226] It included feminist, church, and welfare rights groups and was established "to focus on the problems, needs, and concerns of poor and working women, setting up a national resource center to inform and educate policymakers and the public in this area." The National Council of Women, Work, and Welfare "pledged to work with Congress to establish a federal floor and standardized payments for AFDC recipients." One of its major goals was "to have children brought out of poverty." Despite its efforts, in 1980 its leaders reported that public concern for welfare as a women's issue was still very limited, even though the statistics available presented uncontestable data that women, especially those in female-headed households, were the most likely to live in poverty. The statement that "poverty is a women's issue" was "well founded in reality and easily documented," but mobilization in support of this cause was not easy, even among women.[227]

By 1977 other feminist groups that had abstained from the welfare reform struggle were taking up this issue as part of their agenda. Women's Equity Action League (WEAL) and the Women's Lobby, for example, spoke out in favor of an adequate guaranteed income and stated that "welfare is a prime women's issue," since almost all of the recipients were women and their dependent children.[228] They also joined with other women's groups to oppose the Carter Better Jobs and Income Plan (BJIP) for welfare reform, stating that any proposal had to incorporate certain principles, namely, that women perform valuable work when they are raising their children and taking care of their homes, that women who head families need and want to work for money while their children are growing up, and that childcare facilities and part-time work are needed for these women.[229]

Another group that emerged and called for support of poor women was the Coalition of Labor Union Women (CLUW). Organized in 1973 to deal with economic issues affecting working women (as a direct result of the women's liberation movement), it linked up with other women's organizations for action to help "the many women who have income below the poverty level, for passage of the Equal Rights Amendment, and for childcare legislation."[230]

Another group joining the women's movement and supporting the rights of poor women was the National Congress of Neighborhood Women.[231] Partly funded by the Comprehensive Employment and Training Act (CETA), it was organized "to help working women in poor neighborhoods." While it considered itself part of the women's movement, many in the organization "did not think of themselves as feminists" and were critical of the women's movement for being an "amorphous middle-class group." They urged NOW and others to help poor women organize within their communities and "to listen to what the needs are . . . and accept that those needs are valid."

Finally, another group of women that emerged in 1973 and supported the right of women to choose to work in their homes raising children was the Housewives for ERA. It endorsed the passage of ERA and asserted that the amendment would enhance the value of "homemaking and the rearing of children." Its members urged legislators and political leaders "to make it [homemaking] an economically secure and dignified role" and to "give legal recognition to the value of the homemakers contribution." Referring specifically to the plight of "women as heads of families," they called for special legislation to ease their economic burdens. They, like Tillmon of NWRO, appealed for the right of women to choose to work in the home or in the labor force without being penalized by society for their particular choices.[232]

The National Women's Agenda, published in 1975 after the celebration of the International Women's Year in Mexico City, also called for the recognition of poverty as a women's issue.[233] It emphasized the "common experience of womenhood," and its publication symbolized, perhaps more than any other event, the institutionalization of poverty as a women's issue by over 100 women's organizations around the country. It called for, among other things, "the establishment of a minimum standard of income and other social benefits for low income and disadvantaged persons, which protect their equity and respect the individual rights and dignity of all women."[234]

One year later, representatives of poor women attending the National Women's Conference rejected the proposed resolution and drafted one of their own entitled "Women, Welfare, and Poverty." It stated:

> The Federal and State governments should assume a role in focusing on welfare and poverty as major women's issues. All welfare reform proposals should be examined specifically for their impact on women. Inequality of opportunity for women must be recognized as a primary factor contributing to the growth of the welfare rolls.

Noting further that "poverty is a major barrier to equality for women" and that "millions of women who depend on income transfer programs or low-paying jobs for their basic life support may be subject to the multiple oppression of sexism, racism . . . poverty," and ageism, it called for the "elimination of poverty" as "a priority of all those working for equal rights for women." It stressed that "just as with other workers, homemakers receiving payments should be afforded the dignity of having that payment called a wage not welfare" (emphasis in original).[235] Welfare was not to be classified as charity but rather as payment for services rendered by homemakers and child rearers in society. This draft resolution was adopted unanimously by 20,000 women present. The final 26-point National Plan of Action, which included this statement by poor women, was "submitted to the President" for action.

Four months later, in April 1978, President Carter established a 40-member National Advisory Committee on Women "to advise him on initiatives needed to promote equality for women."[236] The original committee, headed by Bella Abzug, was short-lived. When the committee criticized Carter's budget priorities and the cutbacks on social-welfare payments that would have a drastic impact on many women, the president dismissed Abzug on January 12, 1979. Reportedly, he was angered by the criticism of his economic policies. A press release prepared by the committee had "warned that the Administration's anti-inflation program will impose additional burdens upon women in increased unemployment, cutbacks in social programs . . . and deferred action on programs addressing poverty and assistance to cities where the majority of women live."[237] Abzug, along with several others who resigned, formed "Women USA" to encourage women to be more deeply developed as a political force and to establish "a nation-wide network of women to lobby on economic, social, and political issues."[238] The president of NWPC, commenting on the new coalition of women, noted that by the end of the decade, "women—old, young, Black, white, and Chicano—who had been on the sidelines are now asking what they can do to help."[239]

While ERA still held center stage for most women's organizations at the start of the 1980s, welfare and poverty as women's issues had been incorporated into the national women's agendas and legitimated as specific concerns for women. There were signs of expanding support among diverse groups of women for ERA based on the belief that it was directly related to women's economic rights. The emphasis of the feminist movement in the mid-1960s on employment rights and NWRO's single focus on welfare seemed to be converging within the women's movement under the broader rubric of economic rights for women. Poverty was being redefined by many women's groups as being rooted in racism, sexism, and ageism in U.S. society. All these actions pointed to a rise in the political solidarity among women at the beginning of the 1980s.[240]

The issues of welfare and poverty appeared to be firmly embedded in the National Women's Agenda for the 1980s. The historical contradications of work versus welfare, which had separated women for generations and inhibited solidarity within the women's movement in the 1960s, by 1980 seemed to be moving toward resolutions. Redefining "mothers as workers" and "welfare as wages" for homemakers seemed to be one possible solution. Greater flexibility in the labor force and elimination of sexism and racism seemed to be another, though distant, solution. Whether sufficient political power could be mobilized by women—poor and nonpoor, black and white alike—to bring about desired changes in the system remained to be seen. The basic question was, as Lamphere pointed out, "whether the converging trends [will] become strong enough to override the differences" among women.[241]

In summary, we have seen that NWRO, although an active, national protest of poor women, did not succeed in mobilizing economic or political resources from black and women's organizations, in comparison to the support gained from the white Protestant churches. Coalitions with black organizations appear to have been inhibited by class and gender cleavages. Alliances with black and white women's organizations were faced with barriers of classism and racism, as well as the lack of consciousness among NWRO organizers, members and leaders of welfare as a women's issue. As feminism gained momentum in U.S. society in the 1970s and NWRO women began to demand more control and jobs within their own movement organization, the common plight of women within the economy and polity became increasingly visible and began to be accepted as an issue by women's organizations. Although NWRO did not last long enough to reap the benefits of this rising tide of support, the problems of welfare and poverty became integrated in the national women's agenda for the 1980s.[242] Black feminists appeared to be emerging in the public and private sectors as important "linking pins" between women and black organizations, as they assumed a vanguard role in highlighting the special needs of poor women, as Tillmon had done in the late 1960s.

Finally, by the 1980s the rising concern in the United States over the state of the family in general, and the single-parent family in particular, seemed to be an area of common cause that might lead to political alliances between blacks and feminists in the future. Both appeared to be committed to strengthening the economic status of female-headed households.[243] Both seemed to identify this as one of the major issues requiring concerted political action to gain governmental support for adequate income, jobs, training, child care and paid abortions for poor women. While there were differences in emphasis, both blacks and feminists agreed that the economic plight of poor women with dependent children had hit crisis proportions.[244] Both called for federal intervention to help solve these problems. For blacks another major strategy was to mobilize support among their organizations for strengthening the "extended family.[245] For feminists the underlying thrust was the elimination of the patriarchal family that they felt reinforced women's subordinate status in society.[246] Despite some deep-seated opposing views on the family issue, their common concern for the plight of poor women with dependent children seemed to indicate a potential base for new alliances in the coming years.

The rising tide of conservatism in the 1980s in U.S. society appeared to be another factor that might well lead to greater political bonding between blacks and feminists in the next decade.[247] Both viewed with alarm the rise of the "new right" with their attack on several issues of great importance to these two groups. Black leaders viewed the growth of the new right and especially the conservative religious organizations as "representing part of a 'frightening' political movement that intended to reduce drastically those social and economic programs of particular benefit to minorities and the poor.[248] Feminists decried "the growth and increasing power of a neofascist right whose chief rallying points are opposition to feminism and sexual freedom, glorification of the traditional patriarchal family, and advocacy of authoritarian and religious values."[249] For conservatives in the new right the soaring rolls of female-headed families, along with other changes in social behavior, signified the collapse of sacred American values and the downfall of the traditional family. From their perspective the federal government was to blame for having undermined patriarchal authority in every sphere of life, and most particularly in the family. The solution, as they saw it, was to reduce government intervention in all areas, restore the authority of the male within the family, eliminate abortion, stop the ERA, bring back prayer in the schools, capital punishment, a balanced budget, and military superiority over the Soviet Union.[250] Clearly, at the beginning of the 1980s decade the nation was becoming increasingly polarized between liberals and conservatives. This social trend suggested that, given common fears and concerns, blacks and feminists, along with others, might well join to oppose the new right and its goals. This revived coalition might have an impact on the continuing struggle for welfare reform and a guaranteed income in the coming decades.

Having analyzed the mobilization of NWRO and its supporters, we now turn to examine the external political struggle that the organized poor women and their allies waged against the welfare authorities, and its consequences for NWRO and the welfare reform debate.

NOTES

1. Anthony Oberschall, Social Conflict and Social Movements (Englewood Cliffs, N.J.: Prentice-Hall, 1973), p. 233. Oberschall notes that "in the North, the class cleavage between the middle and lower-class Blacks was far greater than in the South, the preexisting network of black churches and communal organizations that might have been used to flesh out protest organizations was not present to anything like the degree in the South." See also William Julius Wilson, The Declining Significance of Race: Blacks and Changing American Institutions (Chicago: University of Chicago Press, 1978). Wilson indicates that the gap between blacks on the basis of class has been widening. Also, William Brashler, "The Black Middle Class: Making It," New York Times Magazine, December 3, 1978, pp. 34-36, 138-40, 144-57. Brashler also sees this "[class] division widening into a gulf, something the experts, specifically the Kerner Report in 1968, never anticipated." Also, Dorothy K. Newman et al., Protest, Politics, and Prosperity: Black Americans and White Institutions (New York: Pantheon, 1978).

2. Joseph D. McCarthy and Mayer N. Zald, "Resource Mobilization and Social Movements: A Partial Theory," American Journal of Sociology 82 (May 1977): 1234. These authors suggest that "as the competition within any SMI [social movement industry] increases, the pressure to specialize intensifies. The decision of George Wiley . . . to present the National Welfare Rights Organization aimed at winning rights for black welfare recipients was apparently made partially as a result of the preexisting turf understandings of other civil rights organizations."

3. Ibid. Also see discussion of sources of support for civil rights organizations in Oberschall, Social Conflict, pp. 217-18.

4. Nicholas Kotz and Mary Lynn Kotz, A Passion for Equality: George Wiley and the Movement (New York: W. W. Norton, 1977), p. 253.

5. Ibid.

6. Oberschall, Social Conflict, pp. 217-18.

7. Taped interview with Frances Fox Piven, September 13, 1974, and Bert DeLeeuw, July 1974.

8. Taped interview with Frances Fox Piven, September 13, 1974.

9. Field notes, Ralph Abernathy's speech, July 12, 1974, before the 1974 NWRO Convention in St. Louis, Mo.

10. William Howard Whitaker, "The Determinants of Social Movement Success: A Study of the National Welfare Rights Organization" (Ph.D. diss., Brandeis University, 1970), pp. 170-74.

11. Whitaker, "Social Movement Success," p. 170.

12. Taped interview no. 205.

13. Ibid.

14. Conversation with Johnnie Tillmon, Washington, D.C., May 15, 1973.

15. Taped interview with Johnnie Tillmon, July 30, 1974.

16. Whitaker, "Social Movement Success," p. 171; and taped interview with Johnnie Tillmon, 1974.

17. Whitaker, "Social Movement Success," p. 172.

18. Ibid.

19. Taped interview no. 205.

20. As a matter of fact, various groups of "poor people" competed for the support of the white and black, middle-class, liberal sector. For example, the United Church Board for Homeland Ministries supported several different groups, including Cesar Chavez's United Farmworkers, the SCLC, the American Indians, as well as NWRO, among others. For the organizations of the poor, there were limited liberal sources of financial and political support.

21. Hobart A. Burch, "Conversations with George Wiley," Journal of Social Issues, November-December, 1970, reprint.

22. Ibid., p. 28.

23. Field notes, September 29, 1972.

24. Field notes, December 14, 1973.

25. Field notes, July 1972.

26. Field notes, NWRO Conference, St. Louis, Mo., July 1974.

27. Ibid.

28. Taped interview no. 205.

29. Whitaker, "Social Movement Success," p. 211.

30. Taped interview no. 203.

31. Your Welfare Rights, Rhode Island Manual, June 1966; and Your Welfare Rights, SEDFRE, New Jersey. See also Guida West, "The Welfare Rights Movement in Newark" (Paper, Rutgers University).

32. Interview with Shirley Lacy, December 28, 1971.

33. SEDFRE Proposal, 1966.

34. See August Meier and Elliott Rudwick, CORE: A Study in the Civil Rights Movement, 1942-1968 (New York: Oxford University Press, 1973), pp. 197-98, 335, 411. There was a rupture between CORE and SEDFRE over ideological divergences. "CORE was moving in a more nationalist direction, while SEDF, though sponsoring community organization work, remained committed to interracialism." The split came in February 1966 over an incident between blacks and Jewish supporters. A short time later CORE-SEDF dropped CORE from its name and henceforth was known as the Scholarship, Educational, and Defense Fund for Racial Equality.

35. Guida West, "Twin-Track Coalitions in the Black Power Movement," in Interracial Bonds, ed. Rhoda Goldstein Blumberg and Wendell James Roye (New York: General Hall Press, 1979); and Les Ledbetter, "Panthers Working within System in Oakland," New York Times, July 18, 1977. The Black Panthers membership estimates ranged from a low of 2,000 by the political authorities to a high of 100,000 by its leader, Huey Newton.

36. Field notes, August 15, 1975.

37. Larry R. Jackson and William A. Johnson, Protest by the Poor: The Welfare Rights Movement in New York City (New York: Rand Corporation, 1973), p. 206. See also interview no. 269, 1971.

38. "Iowa Welfare Mothers Maced," Welfare Fighter, December 1969.

39. Whitaker, "Social Movement Success," p. 212.

40. Ibid.

41. Ledbetter, "Panthers Working within System."

42. Letter from Johnnie Tillmon to Friends, March 22, 1973.

43. Field notes, New York, March 1975.

44. Field notes, Montclair, N.J., April 1975.

45. J. Gregory Clemons, "Rutgers Conference Extols Project Excel," Star Ledger (Newark, N.J.), October 15, 1978; Edward B. Fiske, "Jesse Jackson Builds Up Support in a Drive for Student Discipline," New York Times, March 4, 1979; and promotional materials on "PUSH for Excellence," n.d., received March 1979.

46. Directory of National Black Organizations (New York: AFRAM, 1972). Rose Wiley, NTO's associate director, was not related to George Wiley.

47. "Tenants Prepare a National Drive," New York Times, November 7, 1971.

48. "The Poor People's Platform," NWRO, NTO, and SCLC, n.d., distributed July 1972.

49. Taped interview with Hulbert James, 1974.

50. Ernest Hosendolph, "Housing Activists Relatively Quiet," New York Times, March 6, 1976.

51. Kotz and Kotz, Passion for Equality, p. 253.

52. Nathaniel Sheppard, Jr., "Rights Groups Find Growing Racial Gap," New York Times, August 9, 1978; and "Jobs and City Life Are Urban League's Themes," New York Times, July 22, 1973.

53. Sheppard, "Growing Racial Gap."

54. Ibid. See also Oberschall, Social Conflict, pp. 217-18.

55. Taped interview no. 205.

56. Ibid.

57. "Jobs and City Life."

58. Ibid.

59. Taped interview no. 203.

60. Press release, National Urban League, Newark, N.J., July 1969.

61. Interview with James Pawley, chair of the Essex County Urban League, September 22, 1972.

62. Press release, National Urban League, Newark, N.J., July 1969.

63. Interview with James Pawley, September 22, 1972.

64. Ibid.

65. Ibid.

66. Interview with Robert Curvin, Newark, N.J., September 21, 1972.

67. Ibid.

68. Interview with Glenn Hatfield, December 20, 1971.

69. Phillip Nyden, "Welfare and Welfare Rights: An Analysis of Organizations in the Newark Metropolitan Area" (Paper, Drew University, 1972); and field notes, conversation with Montclair WRO leaders, 1972.

70. Field notes, November 9, 1970. See also the "Testimony of Robert B. Hill before the Subcommittee on Public Assistance, U.S. Senate Finance Committee on Perspectives on Welfare Reform," February 7, 1980, in which the National Urban League proposed "a preliminary outline of model welfare legislation that attempts to build on and reinforce the strengths and self-help efforts of low-income families." The proposal was called "The Self-Help Services Act of 1980." U.S., Congress, Senate, Subcommittee on Public Assistance of the Committee on Finance, How to Think about Welfare Reform for the 1980's, 96th Cong., 2d sess., February 6, 7, 1980, pp. 384-90.

71. Guide to Welfare Reform (Washington, D.C.: Food Research and Action Center, 1979), p. 53.

72. Paul Delaney, "Jobs for Minorities Called a Top Issue," New York Times, July 28, 1975.

73. Robert Reinhold, "Civil Rights Has Become More Complicated," New York Times, February 5, 1978.

74. Ibid. See also "The NAACP: How Goes It with America's Oldest Civil Rights Defenders?" RF Illustrated 4 (September 1978): 13-15; Steven V. Roberts, "Financial Crisis Perils Activities of N. A. A. C. P.," New York Times, October 21, 1978; and Thomas A. Johnson, "A. T. & T. Official to Head N. A. A. C. P.'s Fund Drive," New York Times, January 7, 1979.

75. Taped interview no. 151.

76. Taped interview no. 205. These differences in strategy became a continuous source of disagreement between Clarence Mitchell, a nationally recognized lobbyist for NAACP in Washington, D. C., and George Wiley of NWRO. See also Rennie Davis, "The War on Poverty: Notes on Insurgent Response," in The New Student Left, ed. Mitchell Cohen and Dennis Hale (Boston: Beacon Press, 1966), p. 154.

77. See, for example, "South Carolina," Welfare Fighter, November 1971, p. 12. In South Carolina, an alliance was formed between a local chapter of NAACP and a WRO on the issue of "forced work" for mothers with dependent children. All issues of the Welfare Fighter were analyzed to identify reports of cooperation between NWRO and NAACP in various parts of the country.

78. "Bayonets against Mothers in Madison," Welfare Fighter, October 1969.

79. Field notes, September 29, 1972.

80. Taped interview no. 151; and report by George Wiley, New York, September 1972.

81. Taped interview no. 151.

82. Data collected in New Jersey from WRO leaders, 1967-71.

83. Field notes, September 29, 1972.

84. Ibid.

85. Taped interview no. 203.

86. Field notes, New York, May 24, 1972.

87. Ibid.

88. Field notes, NWRO Eastern Regional Meeting, Waterbury, Conn., November 28, 1970.

89. Taped interview no. 203.

90. Ibid.; and taped interview no. 151.

91. Ibid.

92. Taped interview with Frances Fox Piven, September 13, 1974.

93. Letter from Frankie Jeter in Pittsburgh to Friends, July 15, 1975.

94. Judy Klemesrud, "Survey Finds Major Shifts in Attitudes of Women," New York Times, March 13, 1980. The 1980 Virginia Slims Poll included the finding that "a majority of women today [64 percent] approved of most of the efforts to strengthen and change the status of women in society, compared to a minority of women [40 percent] in 1970."

95. Gerda Lerner, Black Women in White America: A Documentary History (New York: Vintage Books, 1973), pp. xviii, 435.

96. Ibid., p. 436.

97. Ibid., p. 437.

98. Cynthia Neverdon-Morton, "The Black Woman's Struggle for Equality in the South, 1895-1925," in The Afro-American Woman: Struggles and Images, ed. Sharon Harley and Rosalyn Terborg-Penn (Port Washington, N.Y.: Kennikat Press, 1978), p. 43.

99. Diane K. Lewis, "A Response to Inequality: Black Women, Racism, and Sexism," Signs 3 (Winter 1977): 348; Lerner, Black Women; Rosalyn Terborg-Penn, "Discrimination against Afro-American Women in the Woman's Movement, 1830-1920," in The Afro-American Woman: Struggles and Images, ed. Sharon Harley and Rosalyn Terborg-Penn (Port Washington, N.Y.: Kennikat Press, 1978), pp. 17-27; and Catherine Stimpson, " 'Thy Neighbor's Wife, Thy Neighbor's Servants': Women's Liberation and Black Civil Rights," in Women in a Sexist Society, ed. Vivian Gornick and Barbara K. Moran (New York: Mentor, 1971), pp. 622-57.

100. Lewis, "Response to Inequality," p. 348.

101. Ibid.

102. Ibid.

103. "Black Feminists Form Group Here," New York Times, August 16, 1973.

104. Lewis, "Response to Inequality," p. 345.

105. Neverdon-Morton, "Black Woman's Struggle," p. 44.

106. Report by George Wiley, September 29, 1972, on "antiwelfare" attitudes of middle-class blacks. See also Brashler, "The Black Middle Class," p. 155; and Wilson, Declining Significance of Race, on the middle-class black "backlash against the 'black underclass.' "

107. Charles Hamilton, "Blacks and Electoral Politics," Social Policy, May-June 1978, pp. 21-27.

108. "An Interview with Dorothy I. Height," Social Policy, September-October 1973, p. 35. See also "Black Women United: Sororities, Alliances, and Pressure Groups," Ms., January 1979, p. 90.

109. "Dorothy I. Height," p. 35.

110. Ibid.

111. Ibid.

112. This entire section is based primarily on Rudolph Wilson, "Aunt Jemima Ain't What She Used to Be," Welfare Fighter, December 1971.

113. Ibid.

114. Field notes, July 1972 and 1973, July 13, 1974, at NWRO's conferences and conventions.

115. "Household Workers," flyer on Ford Foundation film about alternatives, Are You Listening Household Technicians? (New York: Ford Foundation, 1977).

116. See Lewis, "Response to Inequality." Also, John R. Howard, The Cutting Edge: Social Movement and Social Change in America (Philadelphia: J. B. Lippincott, 1974), p. 265; and Toni Morrison, "What the Black Woman Thinks about Women's Lib," New York Times Magazine, August 22, 1971, pp. 14-15, 63-66. At the birth of NWRO on June 30, 1966, Dick Gregory, one of the speakers, emphasized that NWRO was a "human rights" movement not a "civil rights" movement. Race, class, and gender were obscured to minimize divisions and emphasize the common cause of all "humans."

117. Cellestine Ware, Woman Power: The Movement for Women's Liberation (New York: Tower, 1970), p. 95.

118. Field notes, Douglass College, New Brunswick, N. J., September, 23, 1976, Notes on speech given by Flo Kennedy at Voorhees Chapel.

119. Thomas A. Jefferson, "Yale Conference Studies Role of Black Women," New York Times, December 14, 1970; and Shirley Chisholm, "Race, Revolution, and Women," Black Scholar, December 14, 1971, p. 21, reprint.

120. "Black Feminists Form Group Here."

121. Lewis, "Response to Inequality," pp. 339-40, 347.

122. Ibid., p. 358.

123. Ibid., p. 347; and "Black Women United," p. 90. In the Ms. article, out of the 14 black women's organizations listed, there are five described as "political" in purpose: Black Women Organized for Action (1973), National Alliance of Black Feminists (1976), National Black Feminist Organization (1973), National Hookup of Black Women, Inc. (1975), and North Carolina Black Women's Political Caucus (1977). Three are professional organizations: National Association of Black Women Attorneys (1972), National Black Nurses Association, Inc. (1970), and National Association of Negro Business and Professional Women's Clubs (1935). The other six, based on their descriptions, emphasize "service" though it is clear that some of them combine it with political action and others do not. They are Alpha Kappa Alpha (1908), Black Women's Community Development Foundation, Inc. (1967), Delta Sigma Theta Sorority (1913), Links, Inc. (1948), National Council of Negro Women (1935), and National Organization

on Concerns of Black Women (1975). The data base is scant. But analysis and other recent reports by Diane Lewis and Michelle Wallace indicate a proliferation of politically oriented black women's organizations since 1970. This has a potential for impact on the political "welfare" debate, as well as on coalition formation with white feminists. Lewis and Morrison mention NWRO as a black women's movement organization.

124. Lewis, "Response to Inequality," p. 358.

125. Ibid. , pp. 359-60.

126. "Black Feminists Form Group Here."

127. William H. Chafe, Women and Equality: Changing Patterns in American Culture (New York: Oxford University Press, 1977), p. 125.

128. Program Book, 1974 NWRO conference, St. Louis, Mo.

129. Nadine Brozan, "Determined to Foster Change—'As Women and as Blacks,'" New York Times, March 11, 1974.

130. Stimpson, "'Thy Neighbor's Wife,'" pp. 641, 645.

131. Terborg-Penn, "Discrimination against Afro-American Women," p. 17.

132. Lewis, "Response to Inequality," p. 346.

133. Chafe, Women and Equality, p. 200.

134. Johnnie Tillmon, "Welfare Is a Women's Issue," in The First Ms. Reader, ed. Francine Klagsburn (New York: Warner Books, 1973), p. 52.

135. Sandy Roth, "Over 90,000 March in Chicago," National NOW Times, June 1980, p. 13(b).

136. Carol Glassman, "Women in the Welfare System," in Sisterhood Is Powerful, ed. Robin Morgan (New York: Vintage, 1970), p. 114.

137. Susan Podbielski, "Social Action Report: W.O.M.A.N. vs. the Carter Budget," Social Policy, March-April 1979, p. 45.

138. See Helen Mayer Hacker, "Women as a Minority Group," Social Forces, October 1951, pp. 60-69.

139. "National Plan of Action" and "National Women's Agenda," Women's Action Almanac, ed. Jane Williamson, Diane Winston, and Wanda Wooten (New York: William Morrow, 1979), pp. 127-44.

140. Taped interviews nos. 151 and 217; field notes, June 8, 1973; and WPT minutes, October 8, 1970.

141. Field notes, 1971 NWRO Convention, Rhode Island, July 1971.

142. Taped interview no. 151.

143. Field notes, 1971 NWRO Convention, Rhode Island, July 1971.

144. Field notes, 1972 NWRO Conference, Miami Beach, Fla., July 6, 1972.

145. Taped interviews nos. 151 and 153.

146. YWCA ad in the "Banquet Program" book of the 1971 NWRO Convention in Rhode Island.

147. Ibid.

148. Mimeographed statement of the national board of YWCA, February 15, 1972.

149. Field notes, 1968, 1969, and 1970 on YWCA participation in New Jersey; and field notes, WRISC meetings, September 1974.

150. Joan Crowley, chair of the Montclair Friends of Welfare Rights, became the state president of the League of Women Voters in New Jersey in 1979. As vice-president of the league, she held for a number of years the state LWV "portfolio" on welfare. Ann Klein, a supporter of welfare rights, was the state president of the League of Women Voters in New Jersey at the height of the movement. She became the New Jersey commissioner of human resources, in charge of the public assistance programs in the state. Maya Miller, a National League of Women Voters Board member, was a personal friend of George Wiley's and one of the strongest political and financial supporters of NWRO. She was instrumental in organizing the National Council on Women, Work, and Welfare in 1977.

151. "Ribicoff Attempts to Patch Up H. R. 1," Welfare Fighter, November 1971.

152. "Congress Kills FAP," Welfare Fighter, October 1972.

153. "Women's Organizations: It's a Whole New Scene," Family Circle, April 1976, pp. 19-20.

154. Ibid.

155. "To Promote the General Welfare" . . . Unfinished Agenda (Washington, D. C.: League of Women Voters, 1977), pp. 1-8.

156. Analysis of the Welfare Fighter, 1970-74.

157. Flier, "Defend Young America Brunch," December 13, 1970. WRO, SANE, and Friends of WRO united in a educational-political strategy aimed at expanding the middle-class support against the increasingly "repressive" measures taken by New Jersey against welfare recipients. The effort also functioned as a fund-raising vehicle for NWRO. See also "Philadelphia," Welfare Fighter, April-May 1971; and "Women's Organizations," pp. 19-20.

158. Whitaker, "Social Movement Success," p. 202; and Judith Levin and Patricia Vergata, "Welfare Laws and Women: An Analysis of Federal Sexism" (Paper, Rutgers Law School, 1971), pp. 1-54. This solution of jobs for men recalls the much-debated Moynihan report on the Negro family, which attributed the problems of black ghetto families to the absence of the male figure as breadwinner. Ross, criticizing Moynihan's viewpoint, argues that

> it is not the lack of male influence or the limitation of having one versus two parents which is the problem, but the lack of economic resources of female-headed families with children. Moving to help women acquire these resources

for themselves is the most direct solution to the problems they face and which society faces with them.

Heather L. Ross, Poverty: Women and Children Last (Washington, D. C.: Urban Institute, 1975).

159. William Goldstein, Work and Welfare: A Legal Perspective on the Rights of Women on Welfare, Social Welfare Regional Research Institute Publication no. 3 (Boston, 1971), pp. 29-30.

160. Ibid.

161. Constantina Safilios-Rothschild, Women and Social Policy (Englewood Cliffs, N.J.: Prentice-Hall, 1974), p. 67.

162. Goldstein, Work and Welfare.

163. Ross, Poverty, pp. 1-16. Also see Heather Ross and Isabel Sawhill, Time of Transition: The Growth of Families Headed by Women (Washington, D. C.: Urban Institute, 1975).

164. Women's Role in Contemporary Society: The Report of the New York City Commission on Human Rights (New York: Avon, 1972), p. 48.

165. U.S., Department of Labor, Manpower Administration, Tax Credit for Hiring People under WIN (Washington, D.C.: Government Printing Office, 1972).

166. Tillmon, "Welfare Is a Women's Issue," p. 57.

167. Margaret Mason, "Welfare Reform in the 95th Congress," National NOW Times, July 1978, p. 10.

168. Tillmon, "Welfare Is a Women's Issue," p. 52.

169. Conversation with Jo Freeman, New Brunswick, N.J., June 12, 1975.

170. Conversation with Marion Kidd (NJWRO), November 9, 1971.

171. Tillmon, "Welfare Is a Women's Issue," p. 52.

172. Taped interview with Johnnie Tillmon, July 1974; and field notes, report by a white female NWRO organizer, May 15, 1974. Levin and Vergatta, as well as Whitaker, also reported that from the very beginning of the movement, the male organizers focused on the theme of guaranteed income, rather than jobs, for women. These writers note that during the Poor People's Campaign in the spring of 1968, the organizers drew up the demands of NWRO calling for "the repeal of the repressive portions of the 1967 Social Security legislation," "a guaranteed income of $4000 for a family of four," and for "federal funds to create immediately at least three million jobs for men." See Whitaker, "Social Movement Success," p. 197, n. 2; Levin and Vergatta, "Welfare Laws and Women," p. 52; and Lynne B. Iglitzin, "A Study in Patriarchal Politics," American Behavioral Scientist 17 (March–April 1974): 487-505.

173. Women's Role in Contemporary Society, pp. 22-23.

174. See Jo Freeman, The Politics of Women's Liberation (New York: David McKay, 1975).

175. Glassman, "Women in the Welfare System," p. 115.

176. "Goal Set by Women's Political Caucus," New York Times, July 13, 1971.

177. Women's Role in Contemporary Society, pp. 475-83.

178. Ibid., pp. 22-23; and "Beulah—from the Chair," Welfare Fighter, November 1971.

179. Women's Role in Contemporary Society, p. 38.

180. Field notes, "Welfare as a Women's Issue," Workshop led by Gloria Steinem, 1971 NWRO Convention, Rhode Island; and "Convention '71," Welfare Fighter, October 1971.

181. Field notes, personal conversation with WRO leader, July 11, 1974.

182. Eileen Shanahan, "Women's Political Caucus Votes to Alter Membership Structure and Increase Dues Tenfold," New York Times, July 1, 1974.

183. Field notes, meeting in Washington, D.C., January 30, 1973.

184. Field notes, April 17, 1973; "Women's Caucus Leader: Audrey Rowe Colom," New York Times, June 30, 1974; and Mary Breasted, "Women's Caucus Ends on a Cheering Note," New York Times, March 17, 1975. The latter is a report on the New York State Women's Caucus, in which a racial crisis led the Women's Political Caucus to debate and try to ensure greater racial representation of minorities.

185. Field notes, August 15-16, 1975.

186. "A New Chance for Welfare Mothers," Women's Agenda, December 1978.

187. Ibid.

188. "Women's Political Caucus Votes to Alter Membership Structure," New York Times, July 1, 1974; and undated letter from NWPC received August 15, 1978, with latest statistics on national organizations.

189. Robert Lindsey, "Political Gains Cited at Opening of Women's Caucus," New York Times, September 10, 1977.

190. For the birth of NOW, see Freeman, Politics of Women's Liberation, p. 54; and Toni Carabillo, "A Passion for the Possible: An Account of NOW's Founding to Mark Our 10th Anniversary," Do It Now 9 (October 1976): 5-8.

191. Ibid.

192. "NOW Meeting," Star Ledger (Newark, N.J.), May 20, 1975.

193. "Notes from Newman," Newark NOW News, October 1975, p. 4.

194. Conversation with Wilma Scott Heide, first president of NOW, Rutgers University, April 8, 1978; conversation with Jo Freeman, June 11, 1975; and conversation with Karen DeCrow, March 31, 1976.

195. Levin and Vergatta, "Welfare Laws and Women," pp. 1-54.

196. Tillmon, "Welfare Is a Women's Issue," p. 58.

197. Ibid., pp. 54-55, 59.

198. Ross and Sawhill, Time of Transition. See also U. S., Commission on Civil Rights, Social Indicators of Equality for Minorities and Women (Washington, D. C.: Government Printing Office, 1978).

199. Jessie Bernard, Women, Wives, and Mothers: Values and Options (Chicago: Aldine, 1975), p. 184.

200. Conversation with Karen DeCrow, president of NOW, March 31, 1976.

201. "NOW-NY Holds Conference on Urban Women," Women's Agenda, December 1978, p. 5.

202. Susan Hertz, "The Politics of Welfare Mothers Movement: A Case Study," Signs, vol. 2 (Spring 1977).

203. Interview with Marian Kidd, NJWRO, Newark, N. J., November 9, 1971.

204. Karen DeCrow, "From the President," Do It Now 10 (February 1977): 2. See also "Women in the Economy," Jersey Wealer, Women's Equity Action League, New Jersey, April 1975.

205. "Opinion," Do It Now 10 (September-October 1977): 13.

206. Ibid.

207. "Poverty Task Force Prepares for 2nd Decade," Do It Now 10 (January 1977): 6.

208. "Does Welfare Work?" Do It Now 10 (January 1977): 6.

209. Margaret Mason, "Welfare Reform," p. 10.

210. Ibid.

211. Conversation with New Jersey NOW members, April 26, 1979; and Linda Lamendola, "NOW Denies Feminist Movement Undercuts Family Life," Star Ledger (Newark, N. J.), January 4, 1979.

212. "Budgetary Summary," National NOW Times, December 1978-January 1979, p. 18.

213. Lisa Hamel, "NOW Still Growing—But It's Still White and Middle-Class," New York Times, January 24, 1976.

214. Conversation with Jo Freeman, New Brunswick, N. J., June 12, 1975.

215. Ibid.

216. There was, however, periodic differentiation in labels according to the race of the women being described. For example, in a communication on March 18, 1972, the listing has "Mrs." before Coretta King's and Beulah Sanders's names (both black) and "Ms." before Gloria Steinem's and Shirley MacLaine's names (both white).

217. Males within the movement had always addressed the welfare women as "ladies" or "mothers," rarely as "women"—the idiom of the feminists. Tillmon reported that Sampson was the originator of this addressing of welfare women as "ladies." She and other wel-

fare women leaders also used this term to refer to the members of
the movement. For recipients seeking greater respect and dignity
within a society that placed little value on female heads of homes,
this form provided, it might be argued, some measure of respect and
was valued by welfare women. This terminology was rejected, however, by most feminists, as reinforcing the stereotype of women as
fragile and dependent on men.

218. Field notes, August 16, 1975.

219. "Fully Employed Women Continue to Earn Less than Fully
Employed Men of Either White or Minority Races" (Bar graph prepared by the Women's Bureau, Office of the Secretary, U.S. Department of Labor, from data published by the Bureau of the Census,
U.S. Department of Commerce, August 1978).

220. Alexis M. Herman, "Still . . . Small Change for Black
Women," Ms., February 1979, pp. 96-98. Herman points out that

the officially defined poverty level for non-farm families in
1977 was about $6200 and $7300 for families of four or five
persons, respectively. Of the 57.2 million families living
in poverty in March 1978, 10 percent were black. Black
families were four times as likely as white families to be
living in poverty and three and one-half times as likely to
be headed by a woman. Approximately 40% of all Black
families were headed by women in 1978, slightly more than
half of these female-headed families being in poverty.
About 11 percent of white families were headed by women
and about one fourth of these were poor. . . . Of more than
9 million children in black families, 40 percent were in
families living in poverty. The fact remains that [black
women] and their children bear an increasing burden of
poverty.

Based on Bureau of Labor Statistics figures, Herman provides the
following median weekly earnings of workers 16 years and over:

	May 1970 (dollars)		May 1978 (dollars)	
White men	157		279	
Black men	113		218	
White women	95 }	14 dif-	167 }	9 dif-
Black women	81 }	ference	158 }	ference

221. Ross and Sawhill, Time of Transition.

222. Welfare Righter 10 (June 1977): 1.

223. Herman, "Small Change for Black Women," p. 96; and Steven V. Roberts, "Blacks and Women Clash on Access to Jobs and Aid," New York Times, February 20, 1979.

224. Louise Lamphere, "Brief Glimpses of Herstory," in Dialogue on Diversity: A New Agenda for American Women, ed. Barbara Peters and Victoria Samuels (New York: Institute on Pluralism and Group Identity, 1976), p. 19.

225. "The First National Women's Agenda Conference," Women's Agenda, November-December 1976, p. 5.

226. Women's Washington Representative 2 (May 12, 1977): 2.

227. Maureen Whalen, Women, the Poorer Sex (Washington, D.C.: National Council on Women, Work, and Welfare, May 1978), p. 1.

228. "WEAL's Legislative Program," WEAL, Washington, D.C., Spring 1977. Other issues in its 1977 legislative program included, in the order listed, ERA, employment, economic equity, education, health, welfare, and taxes.

229. Nancy Cornblath-Moshe and Carol Burris, "Tip Sheet on Carter's Welfare Plan," Ms., January 1978, pp. 55-56, 81.

230. Jersey Wealer, vol. 4, Special Edition, 1975; and speech by Gloria Johnson, executive officer of CLUW, speaking at a WEAL conference in January 1976.

231. Lisa Hamel, "NOW Still Growing."

232. "Head of Housewives for E.R.A. Says Measure Would Aid Family," New York Times, January 7, 1979; Housewives for ERA (Urbana, Ill.: Housewives for ERA, n.d.); and JoAnn Budde and Joan Krauskopf, Homemakers Need the Equal Rights Amendment (Urbana, Ill.: Housewives for ERA, n.d.).

233. "Summary of Drafts" (Prepared for the National Women's Agenda Conference, Washington, D.C., October 1-2, 1976); and "U.S. Women's Agenda," poster.

234. Ibid.

235. "Women, Welfare, and Poverty" (Paper presented at the National Women's Conference, Houston, Tex., November 1977), pp. 1-2.

236. Judy Klemesrud, "'Houston Plus One': Some Progress, More Work Ahead," New York Times, November 18, 1978.

237. "Excerpts from Panel Statement," New York Times, January 17, 1979.

238. Leslie Bennetts, "Bella Abzug Taking Women's Message to the Nation in a Whirlwind Tour," New York Times, April 7, 1979.

239. Susan Podbielski, "W.O.M.A.N. vs. the Carter Budget: Social Action Report," Social Policy, March-April 1979, p. 44.

240. Roberts, "Blacks and Women Clash."

241. Lamphere, "Brief Glimpses," p. 19.

242. "Women, Welfare, and Poverty," pp. 1-2. Also Jane Williamson, Diane Winston, and Wanda Wooten, eds., Women's Action Almanac: A Complete Resource Guide (New York: William Morrow, 1979), pp. 143-44.

243. James D. Williams, ed., The State of Black America 1979 (New York: National Urban League, 1979), pp. 25-40. Also Williamson, Winston, and Wooten, Women's Action Almanac, pp. 302-3.

244. U.S., Department of Labor, Women Who Head Families: A Socioeconomic Analysis, Special Labor Force Report 213 (Washington, D.C.: Government Printing Office, 1978).

245. Sheila Rule, "Blacks Told to Oppose Evangelicals," New York Times, September 29, 1980. Also Williams, The State of Black America 1979, pp. 187-207. Rule points out that the Congressional Black Caucus conference in 1980 had as its theme "A Salute to the Black Family" and participants were "told of the need for the 'extended family' of all black Americans to pull together and work for national and local policies that would have a positive influence on their stability and growth." Representative Cardiss Collins, Democrat of Illinois, is the chair of the Congressional Black Caucus.

246. Bernard, Women, Wives, and Mothers. See also Betty Friedan, "Feminism Takes a New Turn," New York Times Magazine, November 18, 1979, pp. 40, 92-106. Friedan argues that "feminists at the end of the 1970's are moving to a new frontier: the family." She states that "the women's movement has come just about as far as we can in terms of women alone." She concludes that "the second feminist agenda, the agenda for the 80's, must call for the restructuring of the institutions of home and work." She and other feminists contend that "the future of the family is an overriding feminist issue" (pp. 40, 92). See also Enid Nemy, "Women's Groups: A Forecast for the 80's," New York Times, January 18, 1980, in which Eleanor Smeal, president of NOW, asserts that concern for the needs of homemakers is high on the organization's agenda.

247. Dennis Farney, "'New Right' Is Gaining as Political Movement, Stressing Single Issues," Wall Street Journal, September 11, 1980; and William J. Bennett and Terry Eastland, "The 'New Right' Christians," Wall Street Journal, September 17, 1980. Bennett and Eastland state that "the Christian activists are against abortion, against the ERA, for school prayers, for the traditional family, for capital punishment, for a balanced budget, for military superiority over the Soviet Union." See also Larry Green, "Censorship Grows as Conservatives Take Power," Star Ledger (Newark, N.J.), November 12, 1980; and Philip W. Smith, "Conservatives Eager to Ease Reins on CIA," Star Ledger (Newark, N.J.), November 16, 1980.

248. Rule, "Blacks Told to Oppose Evangelicals."

249. Ellen Willis, "The Rise of the Cultural Right," Social Policy 10 (September-October 1980): 19-20.

250. Bennett and Eastland, "The 'New Right' Christians."

PART III
CONFLICT AND COOPERATION WITH THE WELFARE AUTHORITIES

6

NWRO AND ITS SUPPORTERS VERSUS THE WELFARE AUTHORITIES

To achieve its goal of a guaranteed adequate income for poor people, NWRO and its supporters engaged in protest against the welfare power structures, namely the welfare administrators, legislators, and adjudicators. Three major strategies emerged in this conflict over the years. In the early days, the NWRO organizers devised the "street strategy," or confrontations by the AFDC women with local and state authorities to get more benefits available under the law. As the political climate changed, and legislators and administrators mobilized to change the rules and regulations, NWRO shifted its resources to the "political strategy" of lobbying in Washington against the Family Assistance Plan (FAP). Finally, throughout its history, NWRO utilized the "legal strategy" to expand the rights of welfare recipients by test cases in the courts, with the Legal Services lawyers and "backup centers" as their principal allies. These external conflicts, together with the rising internal struggles within the movement organization, gradually exhausted NWRO's mobilized resources, as the political establishment developed various counteroffensives to try to halt the soaring AFDC rolls and to quell the welfare rights protest.

NWRO, like other protest movements, was confronted with two simultaneous problems: building and maintaining its national organization and planning and carrying out the protest against the welfare authorities. Organizational maintenance competed with goal attainment for its scarce resources. In the process of trying to meet these two needs, tensions increased, resulting in the loss of members, organizers, supporters, and their monies, as we have discussed in previous chapters. As the political authorities at the state and national levels increased the social controls against the poor in general and NWRO in particular, participants in the movement sought alternative partnerships for achieving their goals. In the process, NWRO linked up with the federal government to increase its funds, and organizers and supporters left the movement to form new grass-roots organizations and coalitions with working people and the middle class, resulting in the decline of protest by the welfare rights women.

Over the years, the costs of cooperation with NWRO for its allies rose, as political, economic, and social conditions changed. The actions and rhetoric of the national and state political leaders exacerbated the general hostility felt toward dependent women on welfare. The deepening economic recession in 1974/75 created a climate in which there was rising concern about the "right to work" rather than the "right to welfare." Finally, the social drift toward individualistic, rather than collectivist, solutions to social problems in the 1970s within the public and private sectors also undermined support for NWRO that had been more accessible during the socially oriented 1960s.

We begin with an overview of the origins of the welfare system in the United States, focusing on the AFDC program and the changing principles with respect to women's role in society. We then examine the different strategies of NWRO and its allies against the welfare administrators, legislators, and the courts to determine how they changed over time in reaction to the counteroffensives of the political elites and how this affected NWRO's base of support.

AN OVERVIEW OF THE WELFARE SYSTEM

Poverty in general and welfare in particular have periodically surfaced as political issues, as the socioeconomic conditions in the United States have changed and agitation by the poor has increased. Piven and Cloward assert that "relief-giving" has functioned to regulate "the political and economic behavior of the poor," being "expanded during occasional outbreaks of civil disorder produced by mass unemployment, and then abolished or contracted when political stability is restored."[1] They describe relief policies in the United States as being cyclical—liberal or restrictive—"depending on the problems of regulation in the larger society with which government must contend." Joe Feagin also sees welfare policy as being a "roller coaster phenomenon" in terms of the political attention devoted to it.[2] Few topics, he notes, "have generated more mixed feelings or even hostility." In the 1930s, the Great Depression thrust the problem of poverty into the political arena. Despite opposition, this eventually led to the adoption of a federal/state welfare system to provide public assistance to people in need as a result of the drastic economic dislocations. With the passage of the Social Security Act of 1935, the political leaders instituted a federal/state partnership through various income-transfer programs for the poor.[3] Under this act, the states would be provided with federal revenues in exchange for developing and administering welfare programs for different groups in need that adhered to established federal guidelines. States that failed to comply with the guidelines could theoretically be penalized by withdrawal of the federal grants. It was a cooperative effort between the federal and state governments to find a solution to the economic and political problems brought about by the Great Depression.

The original federal grants-in-aid to the states were not universal but categorical. Public assistance was limited to certain groups: the blind, the aged, and children. These were classified as "unemployable" and dependent and therefore labeled the "deserving poor." Aid was to be provided selectively, given "the assumption that relief had to be restricted and that the major reasons for poverty that should concern government were blindness, old age, and dependent motherhood."[4] Over the years, the public assistance programs were expanded to include the "permanently and totally disabled," adults caring for dependent children, and families with unemployed fathers (the "intact," as opposed to single-parent, families).[5]

Opposition to federal government intervention into the economy and to the institutionalization of a federal welfare system was strong. Many felt that President Franklin Roosevelt and the Congress, in passing the Social Security Act in 1935, had gone too far and that it was "too radical—a violation of the traditional American concepts of self-help and individual responsibility, and therefore a threat to individual liberty and the American way of life."[6] Centralized social solutions, rather than the local and individualistic approaches that had been used traditionally to solve the problems of the poor, were resisted. Only the growing economic plight of millions in the 1930s and the threat of social disorder forced governmental action. As Irving Louis Horowitz points out, "The role of government began to change dramatically" as it "sought to improve not only business conditions but the condition of the population as a whole, even if this meant a curb on profits."[7] This was to set the stage for "the growth of social welfare programs" during the next three decades "under the Fair Deal, the New Frontier, and the Great Society" of the Truman, Kennedy, and Johnson Democratic administrations, respectively.

Advocates of federal support argued that the Social Security Act of 1935 was "a conservative measure that fell short of its title."[8] The measure, this group felt, "did nothing about fundamental social and economic problems, including the question of income redistribution." Millions of people still remained unprotected, and there were no revenues allotted for health insurance. Criticism by the right-wing opponents of governmental intervention and collectivist solutions was dampened by defining the social policy as a temporary measure to alleviate the poverty caused by the depression. As soon as the economy was back in full swing, these federal measures could be abolished. Critics on the left were assuaged by explanations that the public assistance programs were a beginning, a foot in the door, which could be amended in time to better meet the needs of the poor and unemployed.

Despite these criticisms from both ends of the political continuum, the law was held to be constitutional by the U.S. Supreme Court in 1937 in two separate decisions.[9] The intent of the statute was not only to "prevent destitution and dependency" but also to preserve "individual freedom and human dignity."[10] Federal intervention was to provide the monies and set standardized guidelines. The states were to be given extensive administrative discretion and power.

This "welfare" law symbolized the apparent political shift of the dominant leaders from defining poverty as a "question of individual weakness" to having it "recognized as a fundamental social and economic problem."[11] Theoretically, at least, "For the first time in the modern period, the American people as a whole accepted the assumption that a large number of people had a right (which could be legally enforced) to public benefits, or at least that failure to provide such benefits was socially and economically short-sighted."[12] As Walter Traetner notes, "In either case, the charitable and the temporary gave way to the just and the permanent, and the dominance of private charity over public welfare came to an end."[13] "For the first time in American history," he adds, "relief became a major permanent item in the federal budget, one that continued to grow each year."

AFDC, the program under Title IV of the act, became and remained the largest welfare program, providing benefits to needy dependent children who had only one parent present. The overwhelming majority of the AFDC families were headed by poor women. For almost 30 years, welfare in general and the program of AFDC in particular received relatively little political attention as the rolls remained fairly stable. In the 1960s, this began to change. Concern about the breakup of the families resulted in the 1961 amendments to the Social Security Act, which allowed families with unemployed fathers (AFDC-UP) to become eligible for welfare.[14] The following year, with no signs that the "welfare problem" would disappear, legislators enacted other amendments providing unlimited "social services" to multiproblem families to eliminate the continuing public dependency. Kahn notes that these were "the most extensive amendments since the enactment of the system in 1935."[15]

By the 1960s the civil rights protests and the rising turmoil in the cities thrust poverty and welfare back into the political arena during the Kennedy and Johnson administrations.[16] Unlike the 1930s, however, the 1960s was a period of relative affluence, and political leaders were rediscovering poverty as a political issue. Traetner states that "President Johnson's verbal declaration of war on poverty in 1964 only put the highest official sanction on what had already become a vogue."[17] Earlier, President Kennedy had set the tone in his inaugural address of 1961 when he asked the country to "bear the burden of a long twilight struggle against the common enemies of man: tyranny, poverty, disease, and war" and to extend the "hand of hope" to the "poor and depressed." According to Traetner, "Such statements aroused many citizens, especially the nation's young people" and gave impetus to their social involvement in the 1960s.[18] Horowitz points out that not only was there a change in attitude and policy toward equity since the 1930s, as reflected in "the growth of welfare programs," but the thrust for "economic parity" also spilled over into government involvement in "racial, ethnic, and sexual parity."[19]

By 1967, however, legislators, angered by the rising protests of the blacks in the urban areas and the turmoil in the streets caused by the welfare poor, began to take action to revise their strategies toward poverty and welfare. The previous amendments that had provided open-ended services to families of the poor had failed to reverse the rise of the AFDC rolls. Consequently, new programs had to be found. From "social services," the tide shifted to "employment" for the poor in order to make them economically independent. For the AFDC program, this meant, in fact, a new emphasis on employment of mothers with dependent children. The 1967 amendments, as Horowitz points out, "carried a clear signal that Congress was changing its expectations about work by women who head families."[20]

In 1935, as Schorr notes, women on AFDC originally had been given the choice of "staying at home to care for [their] children and taking a job away from home."[21] There were incentives "to attract women out of the labor market, leaving more jobs for men." Theoretically, at least, the women had a right to choose.[22] By 1967 this began to change. The Work Incentive Program (labeled WIN by the legislators and WIP by NWRO) required all individuals (primarily women) receiving AFDC to register for work and training as a condition for receiving public assistance. The assumptions were that child rearing was not productive or full-time work and that women, as able-bodied workers, had to be motivated to move out of the home and into the labor market. While women with children under six years of age were exempted, the public policy redefined AFDC women as "employable" but, paradoxically, gave first priority to men in the WIN training and jobs. Putting AFDC mothers to work in the labor force was now defined by legislators as the solution to the welfare problem. Various incentives to "push" poor women into the labor force were built into the new amendments.[23]

Thus, over a 30-year period, the emphasis by legislators and other political leaders shifted from the "maternal ethnic" and women's role in the home (as spelled out in the original legislation) to the "work ethic" and women's role in the labor force. The legitimacy of "dependency" on the state by poor mothers with dependent children gradually eroded, as the political, economic, and social conditions changed. Given these shifts and the inherent contradictions in the AFDC program, the time was ripe for protest.

NWRO AND ITS SUPPORTERS
VERSUS THE ADMINISTRATORS

NWRO and its supporters, responding to grievances of the poor and the contradictions in the legislation and administration of the AFDC program, developed strategies of confrontation and cooperation with welfare administrators at the local, state, and national levels in order to reform the existing system. Direct actions against the welfare departments came to be known as the "street strategy," while those involving negotiation with the opponents were labeled strategies of "cooperation" or "accommodation" by their advocates and "cooptation" by their critics. The consequences of these different models of interaction varied over the years and had differing impacts on NWRO's resources.

The Street Strategy

NWRO's direct actions against welfare administrators were designed not only to maximize the benefits of those already enrolled in the program but also to attract members to the movement organization and add more poor people to the rolls. For the first three years (1966-69), protests and sit-ins at local welfare departments, planned and implemented by NWRO's organizers, were the principal strategies used against the welfare authorities.[24] This choice was based on the assumption that, in order for the poor to create power, defiance and protest were necessary. Given the fact that the poor were a numerical minority "for the first time in history," political and electoral strategies to bring about change were viewed at best as ineffective and at worst as a waste of time and resources.

Cloward and Piven asserted that the welfare system had only functioned because in practice it was not implemented in accordance to the law in the books.[25] Legislators and administrators had created welfare laws and regulations on the premise that charity by taxpayers to the poor had to be tightly regulated to prevent abuse and erosion of the work ethic. Various social controls were instituted to keep the rolls down. Information on eligibility and application processes was highly guarded. Rules and regulations were changed so rapidly that few had any way of determining their rights under the law. Finally, by intimidating and stigmatizing those who did apply with threats of denial or termination of benefits, welfare administrators and caseworkers within the system wielded tremendous power over the poor and helped to limit the dispensation of welfare monies.

As a result, by the mid-1960s, less than half of the eligible were enrolled. A system theoretically created to improve the wellbeing of the destitute, in fact penalized the most disadvantaged and turned many of its administrators and workers into "overseers" rather than advocates of the rights of the poor. Steiner, in a brilliant analysis and comparison of income-transfer systems, shows how the welfare system, unlike other programs (such as veterans benefits), minimizes the distribution of information on rights and benefits to its clients.[26] Unlike the veterans pension system, which defines its benefits as an "earned right" and searches out those who are eligible, the AFDC program does not take any steps to inform the poor of their eligibility.

The Cloward and Piven strategy, which led to the birth of the National Welfare Rights movement, was thus designed to create a political crisis by massive recruitment of the eligible poor to demand their rights under the law. The expectation was that, as the welfare rolls soared, the taxpayers would revolt at the increased cost and the federal government would intervene and implement a guaranteed adequate income in place of the present system. In the process, the welfare poor would gain through the redistribution of income and would also become less stigmatized, as welfare became defined as a right in fact as well as in theory. Jackson and Johnson point out that "the long-term result of this strategy, it was hoped, would be the replacement by the federal government of existing state and local welfare administrations and institution of some form of guaranteed income maintenance system."[27] With large numbers of recipients demanding legal benefits and protesting in the welfare departments, Cloward and Piven suggested that changes could be brought about that would be beneficial to the poor. Wiley, while accepting their basic theory, modified some of their strategies. He used the welfare system's resources to attract members and build a national movement organization.

There were other basic differences between the Cloward and Piven strategy and the one selected by Wiley. Cloward and Piven did not believe that success of their strategy depended on building a bureaucratic movement organization, underscoring the inherent difficulty in maintaining incentives for poor people to continue their participation after they had joined.[28] They also felt that the emphasis should be not only on expanding the benefits to those already enrolled but, more important, on helping the eligible nonrecipients to join the program. Wiley, on the other hand, believed that it was necessary to create a movement organization and to use the welfare system's resources to build its membership. Unlike Cloward and Piven, his thrust and that of NWRO was to help those already in the AFDC program to demand and gain more benefits. In general, there was little information available on what rights the poor women had to "special benefits" from the welfare departments. NWRO gathered this information and disseminated it only to those who would first join the movement and pay their dues. With this "private benefit" or "selective incentive" for members only, NWRO's numbers at first expanded rapidly.[29] As this information on special benefits became public knowledge and the welfare rolls soared, the legislators changed the laws, in many cases eliminating or restricting these monies, thus eradicating the major organizing "handle" for NWRO.

Despite these basic differences between Wiley and Cloward and Piven, the planners and organizers of NWRO set about mobilizing the AFDC women around the country to confront their local welfare departments. Using Alinsky's strategy, NWRO began to try to force the welfare system "to live by its own rules," as the poor organized "to act in their own self-interest."[30]

One of the first welfare rights strategies in New York City was to organize a massive campaign for winter clothing in the fall of 1966. The objective was "to force the machinery to a halt [and] to force the [welfare] centers to negotiate" with the organized WRO women.[31] It was to be "very militant and very political, aimed toward the welfare department, and toward a deliberate use of tactics that would disrupt the centers." This effort in 1966 "disrupted normal operations" in four centers in New York City.[32] It was a well-organized effort with hundreds of clients bused in daily. There were provisions of coffee and sandwiches, a specially installed telephone system, and a public relations spokesperson to meet the needs of the protestors and the surprised public and media. This operation consumed "several thousand dollars" contributed by the middle-class supporters and the time and energy of Mobilization for Youth (MFY) organizers working along with the poor. The public reaction and strong attacks on MFY's organization of social protests among welfare clients led to MFY's withdrawal. The public was indignant that an agency receiving federal funds should turn around and attack the federal welfare system.

Although in New York City the welfare rights activity was based on the Cloward and Piven model that "emphasized the general fiscal crisis with scant regard for the simultaneous development of organization," elsewhere NWRO organizers were trained to ask how the strategy would help to build NWRO and its membership base.[33] In most parts of the country, as discussed in Chapter 3, the Boston model of organizing recipients constituted "the basic organizing tech-

niques employed by NWRO across the nation."[34] This model emphasized the strengthening of the movement by adding members to its
grass-roots base.

As organizers provided information on special benefits to clients,
confrontations at local welfare centers proliferated. In New Jersey,
as in various parts of the country, there were sit-ins and sleep-ins
by the WRO women at the welfare departments, as well as marches,
rallies, and demonstrations. In New York City, the greatest number
of protests occurred during 1967/68 and then declined. Additional
strategies and tactics were developed to attract members and prepare
them for the protests. Special training sessions were set up in some
areas in which the poor women and their supporters rewrote the public
assistance manuals in lay language and then used these booklets (entitled Your Welfare Rights) to bring more members into their organizations and recruit them for protests.[35]

The turmoil in the streets at first attracted the media, and the
reports in the daily press brought greater visibility to NWRO's cause
and rising recognition of its growing power among the poor. This
publicity also seems temporarily to have aided NWRO in expanding
its membership among the poor. By 1969 it reported a paid-up membership of 25,000 or about 1 percent of the total AFDC adult population. It was, if not the largest, "the most vocal and most publicized
nationwide organization of the poor" by 1970.[36] Mobilization of poor
women on AFDC seemed to be eroding the hegemony of the welfare
administrators. Armed with information and support from organizers
and other outsiders, the AFDC women legally "raided" the welfare
coffers for benefits available to them under the law. Thus, this
street strategy added to NWRO's members, supporters, and recognition, even as it stimulated public hostility and provided the impetus
for counteroffensives by the welfare authorities.

The street strategy of NWRO and its allies also had consequences
for the poor in general, in contrast to those who chose to join NWRO.
Millions of dollars were paid out during the months of turmoil to increasing numbers of poor people. Steiner reports that in April 1967,
a year before the drive began in New York City, "$3.08 million in
grants had been made."[37] One year later, when the drive began, the
outlays by the welfare department had reached $8.07 million. Two
months later in June 1968, "more than $13 million was paid out in
special grants." Sar Levitan and Robert Taggart note that "the percentage change in real expenditures for public assistance was 69 percent from 1965 to 1970."[38] Whitaker also finds that this turmoil by
the poor increased the cost to the welfare department by "$20 million
per year in 1969 to an estimated $90 million in fiscal 1968 under pres-
sure of welfare rights campaigning."[39] The consequences of this
street strategy were, as Jackson and Johnson point out, "private bene-

fits to the membership and public benefits to the poverty population as a whole. "[40]

Although some assessed the resulting "public benefits" to the poverty population in general as an "unfortunate fact" for NWRO, since they decreased the incentives for membership in the movement, Wiley felt there had been several gains.[41] Even "where there had been no law or policy change, the impact [had] been considerable," in his view.[42] Not only had the welfare mothers benefited substantively through the added monies but they also had gained better treatment as a result of organization and protest in the streets. Wiley noted that welfare officials were "a little more cautious" and gave "a little fairer treatment" to those seeking assistance.[43] The protest also "created a cadre of politicized and battle-tested women," increasing the participation of a generally excluded group in the political arena.[44] Politization of the women also lessened, if not eliminated, the stigma of public assistance by redefining it as a "right" rather than a "handout."

Political agitation in the streets had also added to NWRO's resources by increasing its membership, allies, monies, visibility, and ligitimation within the political arena. Protest also helped NWRO gain recognition and legitimation among its peer groups: the Southern Christian Leadership Conference (SCLC), the Black Panthers, the United Farmworkers, and some women's organizations. It was also recognized as a bargaining agent for the welfare poor by its opponents, namely, the welfare administrations at the local and national levels. HEW routinized negotiation sessions with NWRO, and some local welfare departments accepted WROs as legitimate advocates for clients. Politically and socially, therefore, there were both individual and organizational gains from the street strategy during the early years of the movement.

From the standpoint of the welfare authorities and the general public, this redistribution of income to the welfare women and their dependent children was costly. The financial burden on the tax revenues of the government rose as the number of welfare applications and acceptances grew.[45] (See Tables 6.1 and 6.2.) Welfare rights activities in 1967/68 had a major impact on the level of application, both direct and indirect, since increased numbers of eligible families applied as a result of more information, wider publicity in the media, the apparent lessening of the stigma of public dependency.[46] Welfare administrators bemoaned the rising rolls and costs. They kept saying, "It can't go on, it can't go on, but it does."[47] These words were "echoed across the country," as public welfare rolls reached "levels that would have been unimaginable two or three years ago." By 1970 the rate of increase in the rolls had doubled and the welfare costs for the Nixon administration were expected to "exceed the budgeted amount

TABLE 6.1

Public Aid Payments, 1960 to 1978
(in millions of dollars)

	1960	1965	1970	1972	1973	1974[a]	1975	1976	1977	1978
Payments for year[b]	3,282	4,611	14,365	19,775	21,205	25,536	30,490	33,044	35,360	n.a.
Public assistance	3,282	4,611	14,365	19,775	21,205	20,290	24,612	26,976	29,056	n.a.
Families with dependent children	1,001	1,660	4,853	6,909	7,212	7,917	9,211	10,140	10,603	10,729
Old age	1,630	1,601	1,862	1,877	1,743	—	—	—	—	—
Blind	86	85	98	106	104	—	—	—	—	—
Disabled	237	418	1,000	1,391	1,610	—	—	—	—	—
Supplemental Security income										
Aged	x	x	x	x	x	5,246	5,878	6,068	6,304	6,552
Blind	x	x	x	x	x	2,503	2,605	2,508	2,448	2,433
Disabled	x	x	x	x	x	130	131	138	146	152
Medical assistance[c]	6	588	5,923	8,708	9,807	11,476	14,177	15,544	17,140	n.a.
Emergency assistance[d]	x	x	11	44	39	64	78	56	66	81
General assistance	322	259	618	740	689	825	1,138	1,228	1,238	1,205

n.a. = not available
x = not applicable

[a] Beginning 1974, program for old age, blind, and disabled replaced by Supplemental Security income program in 50 states and the District of Columbia.
[b] Includes vendor payments for medical care, that is, payments made directly to suppliers of medical care.
[c] Medical assistance for the aged program initiated in November 1960; terminated in 1969. Medical assistance program initiated in January 1966. Intermediate care facilities program initiated in 1968; transferred to medical assistance program in 1972.
[d] Emergency assistance initiated in 1968.

Source: U.S., Bureau of the Census, Statistical Abstract of the United States: 1979, 100th ed. (Washington, D.C.: Government Printing Office, 1979), p. 352.

TABLE 6.2

Recipients of and Average Monthly Cash Payments under Public Assistance and Supplemental Security Income, 1950 to 1978

	1950	1955	1960	1965	1970	1974[a]	1975	1976	1977	1978
Recipients of payments										
Aid to dependent children										
Families	651	602	803	1,054	2,552	3,323	3,566	3,585	3,547	3,481
Recipients[b]	2,233	2,192	3,073	4,396	9,659	11,022	11,401	11,203	10,780	10,325
Children	1,661	1,661	2,370	3,316	7,033	7,901	8,105	7,903	7,572	7,211
Old Age assistance	2,786	2,538	2,305	2,087	2,082	—	—	—	—	—
SSI for the aged	x	x	x	x	x	2,286	2,307	2,148	2,051	1,968
Aid for the blind	97	104	107	85	81	—	—	—	—	—
SSI for the blind	x	x	x	x	x	75	75	76	77	77
Aid to permanently, totally disabled	69	41	369	557	935	—	—	—	—	—
SSI for the disabled	x	x	x	x	x	1,636	1,933	2,012	2,109	2,172
General assistance cases	431	314	431	310	547	585	692	685	654	621
Per 1,000 children under 18: AFDC[c] (number)	34	30	35	45	87	113	119	120	118	114
Average monthly payment (dollars)										
Aid to dependent children										
Families	71	85	108	137	190	216	229	242	250	256
Recipients[b]	21	23	28	33	50	65	72	77	82	86
Old age assistance	43	50	59	63	78	—	—	—	—	—
SSI for the aged	x	x	x	x	x	91	91	94	97	100
Aid to the blind	46	56	67	81	104	—	—	—	—	—
SSI for the blind	x	x	x	x	x	141	147	153	159	164
Aid to permanently, totally disabled	44	49	56	67	98	—	—	—	—	—
SSI for the disabled	x	x	x	x	x	142	141	146	150	155
General assistance cases	47	55	72	69	112	140	144	154	156	157

x = not applicable

[a] Supplemental Security income (SSI) was instituted in 1974. The program integrated into one the programs for old age, blind, and disabled. SSI data are for federally administered payments only; excludes vendor payments for medical care, that is, payments made directly to suppliers of medical care.

[b] Includes the children and one or both parents or one caretaker other than a parent in families where the needs of such adults were considered in determining the amount of assistance.

[c] Aid to families with dependent children program.

Notes: Number of recipients are given in thousands, except as indicated. Number of recipients are given as of December, rates as of June.

Source: U.S., Bureau of the Census, Statistical Abstract of the United States: 1979, 100th ed. (Washington, D.C.: Government Printing Office, 1979), p. 352.

298

by $1 billion. "[48] While some administrators ascribed the welfare explosion to the rise in unemployment, they acknowledged that a prime factor for this phenomenon appeared to be "a changing outlook among many poor and the near poor," who were being told by organizers that "it's nothing to be ashamed of. "[49]

Given the asymmetry of power between the challengers and the welfare authorities, the fiscal crises soon gave rise to counteroffensives. The agitation brought on increased social controls at all levels, beginning in 1968 "with the forced replacement of 'special benefits' with 'flat grants'* in several states. "[50] Political leaders rationalized this shift in strategy as being beneficial not only to the taxpayers (who would save with reduced welfare costs) but also to the clients, since the "simplified" system would theoretically make it less demeaning. This, they argued, would eliminate some of the discretionary and arbitrary power of caseworkers and supervisors. Concern for the client's well-being, however, had rarely surfaced before the welfare rights agitation.

State legislatures not only instituted cutbacks on benefits but also revised eligibility criteria. In 1969 NWRO attacked these actions as being "some of the most punitive regressive and shortsighted legislation in history." It asserted that the flat grants† led to "vicious cutbacks which hurt the poor in order to benefit the affluent. "[51] The mounting public concern over soaring welfare costs, however, contributed to the necessary political conditions for the tightening of social controls. One NWRO official noted that "as soon as there was a reversal of attitudes and public opinion, we got the flat grants, the work programs, and the whole repressive bag of tricks. "[52] State politicians, echoing the rhetoric of the president and other national leaders, called for the elimination of ineligibles from the welfare rolls, cutbacks of benefits, increased forced work, and the use of fraud squads. Richard Rogin, writing in the New York Times Magazine in November 1970, reported that "a welfare backlash was alive in the land. "[53] He added that "legislators have been voting for budget cuts and Congress is after stringent work requirements in any reform measure." The adoption of flat grants proliferated across the coun-

---

*Special benefits were an open-ended allotment. Flat grants constituted a single lump sum to meet standardized family requirements of those on AFDC. There was no room for bargaining.

†Under the new plan, a family of four previously receiving $222 a month would now receive $208. Before, a family of six received about $6 a day for food. Now, it would get only $4 per day, or about $0.66 for each member of the family per day. Families would no longer receive $100 per person for an annual clothing allowance. Medical benefits were also reduced (NOW!, May 2, 1969).

try. Proposed and/or real cuts were reported in Illinois, New Jersey, West Virginia, California, Connecticut, Delaware, Rhode Island, New York, and South Carolina. [54] Wiley, writing in the <u>Welfare Fighter</u> at the end of 1970, forecast even more serious slashes in 1971. [55]

At the urging of NWRO and its organizers, welfare rights women did not remain passive. Organizers hurried to mobilize the poor women to fight back against the repressive measures of the government. [56] In New York City, for example, this counteroffensive by the welfare administrators and legislators resulted in added protest. There were "demonstrations and rushes against the police barricades, sit-ins, and acts of vandalism," which led to arrests of many. Welfare mothers in Wisconsin "seized the State Legislature protesting welfare appropriation cuts." [57] According to one report, "about two thousand people stormed through the front door and forcibly entered the empty chambers of the state assembly" in September 1969, after "a week-long ninety-mile march from Milwaukee to Madison by welfare mothers and supporters." The reaction of the political establishment was to call in the national guardsmen. "Armed with fixed bayonets and riot guns," they ended the sit-in, giving the incident nationwide visibility in the media. [58] In California, agitation in the streets and protests for additional benefits for AFDC women and their families also resulted in increased social controls by the state and the continuation of cutbacks on entitlements. [59] In Minnesota, sit-ins in the welfare department in 1969 by the state WRO and its supporters also "culminated in the arrest of several leaders for disorderly conduct, and in the rejection of the group's demands for winter clothing." In New Jersey, similar turmoil in 1969 failed to stop the flat grants or stem the cutbacks by the welfare authorities. Although the counteroffensive of flat grants by the welfare authorities had led to a rise in protests in 1969, these failed to stem the tide of increased controls by the government.

With the elimination of the special grants and the rise in other repressive measures and arrests, the costs to NWRO members escalated, and many poor women began to drop out of the movement. One NWRO official noted that these actions by the political establishment had a significant impact on the movement organization's membership and grass-roots base. He stated: "When there was no real 'payoff' anymore—no more money—members left. We were left only with the leaders." [60] Organizers in NWRO tried to stem this withdrawal by developing new targets and new strategies and tactics that might create new incentives for participation in the movement. For example, James, one of the leading organizers in New York City, changed the protest from attack on the welfare departments to attacks on the major department stores during the Christmas season in which the welfare rights women would demand to be given credit. The purpose of this new strategy was to find a substitute for the special grants for members and to attract publicity in the media. It was hoped that this added visibility would mobilize more members and allies. The welfare mothers were encouraged to purchase clothing in the stores for their children and demand credit. The strategy, with one or two exceptions, did not succeed. Most stores refused to cooperate with NWRO.[61]

Protests in the next two years decreased, as NWRO began to shift its resources and energies to lobbying in Washington. One final effort to counter the repressive actions of the welfare authorities by NWRO took place in Nevada in 1971. In response to state action to restrict eligibility and reduce the rolls, Wiley, in answering the Nevada WRO's appeal for help, decided to stage a major counteroffensive to set an example for the rest of the country. NWRO's decision to allocate a substantial amount of its limited resources to this fight in Nevada was based on the assumption that "a successful challenge there might deter other states from following the same course. And, if other states could not be deterred, the Nevada experience would at least produce a cadre of organizers, recipients and lawyers who could move to assist beleaguered recipients in other states."[62] Rather than relying only on the strategy of "turmoil," NWRO combined street demonstrations, lobbying, and court actions to win its case. NWRO joined the state WRO; appealed for support from middle-class allies; and mobilized political, financial, and legal resources to reverse the actions of the state against the poor women on welfare. Demonstrations and court battles followed.

Operation Nevada, as it was called, began in December 1970, when "George Miller, Director of the Nevada Department of Welfare, thought he had found an answer to the [welfare] crisis." According to Sylvia Law and NWRO reports, the Nevada welfare administrator "turned the theory of Ronald Reagan" (the governor of California who had been repeatedly attacking the welfare recipients) into concrete action when he launched a major campaign against welfare "cheaters."[63] The crisis began on January 1, 1971, when 3,000 "Nevada mothers and children failed to receive their monthly checks." Miller claimed that after an audit, "21 percent of the people receiving aid had been terminated for cheating." Miller's audit and cuts in the rolls were clearly in violation of the law, in terms of investigative and termination procedures. Satisfied with the "success" of his plan, Miller promptly notified other state welfare commissioners of his strategy, urging them to take similar action and implement "their own investigations." The assumption was that large sums could be saved by eliminating "the welfare cheaters."

At the request of the small local WRO group and the Legal Services in the area, NWRO urged Edward Sparer, a long-time Friend of NWRO and its general counsel, to mobilize "Operation Nevada." Almost immediately, WRO leaders, organizers, lawyers, law students, and other supporters (including such prominent figures as Sammy Davis, Jr., Ralph Abernathy, Gloria Steinem, Jane Fonda, and David Dellinger) went to Nevada in support of the welfare rights cause. The activities proceeded on several fronts. Poor women were called on to tell their stories in public forums. Training sessions were set up to inform them of their rights. Demonstrations and rallies were staged at welfare centers and on "the strip." Hearings and lawsuits were filed in the federal courts. Despite attempts by the police to inhibit the mobilization of welfare women and their supporters, the political and legal strategies finally brought about a successful outcome for NWRO.

Victory came through the courts. "On March 20, [1971] the Federal District Court issued an order reinstating everyone who had been terminated or reduced in the 'audit.'" The court ruled that "as a result of the precipitous action . . . the Administrator and his staff ran roughshod over the constitutional rights of eligible and ineligible recipients alike." NWRO members, leaders, and supporters were jubilant and celebrated this as a "total victory," even though the media had failed to cover this contest between the poor and welfare authorities, thus lessening the effectiveness of this political action. One of Operation Nevada's aims had been to make the Nevada case of "repression" a national example, and NWRO had counted heavily on large-scale media coverage. According to NWRO officials, the eastern liberal press remained silent during the protest, failing to document this conflict between the poor and nonpoor. As a "silent witness," it in fact sided with NWRO's opponents.

The nationwide tide of more social controls for those on welfare continued unabated. Similar audits of welfare mothers followed in Nebraska, New Mexico, Rhode Island, and elsewhere. National coverage was "practically non-existent." In Nevada, NWRO leaders pointed out that the media was only interested in the "stars" who appeared on "the strip" as supporters of NWRO. Sylvia Law suggests that "perhaps the most effective deterrent to the other States was the cost to Nevada of defending their action." Operation Nevada highlighted NWRO's ability to fight back and involve the state in a lengthy, expensive federal suit and endless, expensive fair hearings as mandated by the Constitution.

Despite its visible rewards, Operation Nevada was not without its costs for NWRO.[64] While the crisis had mobilized some supporters, the expenditures of this campaign further depleted the limited resources of the movement. The tremendous effort to stop and reverse the actions of the welfare authorities in Nevada exhausted NWRO's dwindling budget. Operation Nevada was NWRO's last major

protest against a state welfare administration's counteroffensive.
The actions against the welfare mothers continued, for in 1971 the
national and state public officials were well aware "in which direction
the wind blows. "[65] There was little sympathy in the political arena
for NWRO's demands or for the tactics of turmoil of the women on
welfare. States were caught between rising welfare costs and "inadequate state resources," and, therefore, it was "not surprising that
they should move against the vulnerable poor. "[66]

For a few years, then, the street strategy added to NWRO's resources by providing instant benefits for individual members and
(later) nonmembers alike. Temporarily, it strengthened the welfare
rights movement politically by increasing its grass-roots base, expanding the number of supporters in the liberal sector, and gaining
visibility and recognition within the political arena. For a short period of time, NWRO became a challenger of the welfare system, but
counteroffensives by the welfare power structures soon halted its protests. As the special grants were eliminated, few chose to join NWRO.
As protests led to arrests and other counteroffensives by the state,
the risks of participating in the street turmoil became too high in relation to the rewards. As the grass-roots base of NWRO withered,
its middle-class allies also began to withdraw their support. Thus,
the dialectics of the welfare conflict led to temporary "victories" for
NWRO at the local level followed by counterattacks initiated by the
welfare authorities that gradually eroded NWRO's membership,
allies, and funds.

At the national level, some confrontations against HEW by NWRO
leaders also occurred in the early years. In 1967 they took over the
office of the secretary of HEW, Robert Finch, and gained press coverage for their actions. Later, however, NWRO's strategy shifted to
negotiation with the national welfare administrators.

Cooperation and Negotiation

While NWRO's protest against welfare administrators was one
way of mobilizing members and bringing about changes in the system,
another strategy involved bargaining for increased benefits, more
favorable regulations, and the expansion of in-kind resources for the
poor. Some advocates of this strategy, such as Wiley and others on
his staff, contended that these negotiations with the welfare authorities
reduced restrictive regulations and in many ways maximized the benefits for the poor. Critics of this strategy, such as Cloward and Piven,
opposed these ties with the authorities, warning that it was "cooptation," the tested means used by the governing elites to diffuse protest. [67] Piven pointed out that whenever "the American political sys-

tem deals with the movements of the poor, if it deals with them at all, it is not by giving mass benefits to the poor, but by making a little place in the upper echelons for the leaders of the poor."[68] They then become "deceived into thinking they have power—that their 'conversational' roles lead to power change." Piven concluded that "when WRO leaders are willing to wander into these higher realms and sit down and negotiate with the Secretary of HEW, with members of liberals in Congress, and don't stay with the grassroots, time and money are wasted. Nothing changes."[69] As protest diminished, negotiations increased, and internal conflict within NWRO led to some loss of resources.

This strategy of accommodation to the political establishment had both costs and benefits for NWRO. As an organization, NWRO gained some monies, information, and recognition by the political leaders in Washington. Its negotiating team of women also gained temporary status and social mobility within the movement organization. On the other hand, NWRO lost some of its leaders and organizers, who disagreed with this strategy. Cooperation with the governmental agencies appears also to have attenuated the strategy of protest, as opponents became bargainers on "the other side of the table."

One of NWRO's objectives was to gain political recognition and legitimacy as the representative of the organized poor.[70] As a result, its organizers and women leaders attempted to bargain with administrators at the national and local levels for monies and more decision-making power on the welfare rules and regulations. Another objective was to try to get federal funds to help run the national programs. In 1968 NWRO signed a contract with the Department of Labor during the final weeks of the Johnson administration. NWRO was to monitor and train women in the WIN program, which was designed to get poor women off welfare and into the work force. Wiley and James saw this cooperative effort as a means of gaining recognition and, at the same time, filling NWRO's coffers. Government officials, on the other hand, saw potential rewards in having NWRO provide an inexpensive self-policing of the WIN program.[71] The monetary costs were small. The greater risk was in bestowing legitimacy on NWRO and its goals.[72] It was clear that, in practice, the two parties in the contract perceived their respective rewards quite differently. The government expected greater cooperation among the women on welfare with the WIN program. NWRO expected to use the monies to teach the women their rights and to strengthen its own national organization.

Internal conflict erupted over this decision to cooperate with "the enemy," as the critics labeled HEW. NWRO was accused of hypocrisy for reversing its previous stand on WIN. Earlier, NWRO had been adamantly opposed to it, labeling it "WIP" to highlight the "slave labor" aspects of the policy. Wiley himself had once called it a "horror show."[73] In 1967 NWRO members and leaders, encouraged by the middle-class organizers and staff, had staged sit-ins at the hearings of the Senate Finance Committee in order to protest WIN. Wiley had also demonstrated with the WRO women leaders in front of Congressman Wilbur Mills's home in May 1968 in order to protest the "forced work" amendments of the proposed legislation. Consequently, this turnabout by NWRO did not sit well with some members and groups within the movement organization.

The Philadelphia WRO, one of the largest welfare rights groups at that time, attacked Wiley and the national leaders for signing the contract, contending that one cannot "take government money and stay free." Others, who had "a different political philosophy than Wiley and the national leaders," also rejected it.[74] Wiley, however, stood firm, stating that NWRO needed the monies to build its national organization. NWRO envisioned opening more field offices, subsidizing staff and salaries, and paying for telephone communications across the nation. Relatively speaking, the contract would bring in a substantial amount of money with very few strings attached.[75] The only requirement was that they mention WIN. According to Jackson and Johnson, "The federal government was certainly aware that a substantial portion of the contract funds would be used to strengthen the organization of NWRO."[76] The grant was accepted and lasted for about six months, through the fiscal year ending in June 1969. Thus, the strategy of "cooperation" with the authorities added to the internal tensions within the movement, resulting in the loss of some members and supporters. On the other hand, however, it also added temporarily to NWRO's financial resources.

Cooperation and negotiations between NWRO and government officials in Washington continued for several years. John Twiname, the HEW official responsible for public assistance, and his staff met regularly with NWRO leaders, recognizing it as "the principal group representing the poor."[77] In February 1969 NWRO's Executive Committee also met with the HEW Secretary Finch "to discuss matters of mutual concern."[78] This was a far cry from the sit-ins and takeover of these offices in the summer of 1967. Meetings took place not only with HEW secretaries and their staff but also at least once with Moynihan.[79] Five months before President Nixon officially introduced the Moynihan-conceived $1,600 FAP, NWRO leaders urged his administration at a February 1969 meeting "to guarantee an income of $6-7000 a year for a family of four." Paradoxically, the access to and interaction with the political leaders in Washington was greater during the Nixon administration than during the Johnson administration, which had initiated the War on Poverty. Whitaker suggests that "this probably reflected increased concern over NWRO growth."[80]

In the process of ongoing negotiations with HEW, the NWRO Executive Committee attempted unsuccessfully to win additional monies from the federal government. A request for funds in 1969 "to train NWRO leaders in health issues" was lost when Secretary Finch at the last minute vetoed the $100,000 contract.[81] Some middle-class organizers in NWRO supported this development of the art of "grantsmanship." The argument was that the government during the civil rights years had been a source of monies to many black protest groups. Wiley openly discussed the NWRO approach of negotiation with the government and defended it as beneficial to the poor. He emphasized that the thrust was always to increase benefits by monitoring the regulations and bringing "specific complaints of illegal practices and regulations counter to Federal law to Secretary Finch's attention."[82]

As the HEW leadership changed over the years, so did its interaction with NWRO. The Nixon landslide victory in November 1972 gave the administration a "mandate" to pursue its policies without bargaining with the organized poor. By then, NWRO was no longer seen as a threat to the social order and was labeled by many as a becalmed movement. Agitation in the streets had decreased, and Wiley had resigned. Consequently, the ties between HEW and NWRO began to deteriorate, since there was "particular difficulty in resolving differences."[83] By 1973 the new secretary of HEW in the Nixon administration, Casper Weinberger, made it plain that these meetings with NWRO were no longer of interest to his department. He refused to listen to NWRO's arguments that state welfare administrators had privileged access to the secretary, whereas the representatives of the poor were totally excluded. Said one NWRO negotiator, "Before we could call up 'our lackeys' in HEW, but now nobody there will talk to me." He added that the regulations coming out of the department were "all designed to attack primarily the AFDC caseload and to threaten the organizable recipients. . . [and] to break up Welfare Rights and NWRO." He also commented on how much HEW had changed since the advent of the new secretary.[84] Whereas Robert Finch and his successor, Elliott Richardson, had been labeled good administrators, Weinberger had quickly been nicknamed "CAP the Knife" and "The Tomb" by NWRO members and leaders for his actions in slashing the welfare budgets.[85] Some felt that the new policy was a "cynical gesture by Nixon" and was designed to "mutilate" HEW and "to cut expenses of social programs to the bone."[86] Regardless of intent, these actions by the political leaders in the government clearly reflected the powerlessness of NWRO in the negotiation process.

Cooperation with the welfare administrators occurred not only at the national level but also at the local level. Lacking resources, WRO leaders, sometimes aided by their middle-class Friends, sought

to cooperate with the public welfare authorities to obtain more benefits and to increase the WROs political power on welfare boards. In
New Jersey, for example, WROs and FWROs waged an intensive
campaign in early 1969 to gain a seat on the county welfare board for
a black welfare mother from Newark. Although they succeeded,
breaking precedent for the first time in the 35-year-old history of the
welfare system in the state, it quickly became clear to the advocates
of this strategy that one black welfare mother on a county welfare
board would not alter the pattern of decision making and the decisions
governing the lives of the poor. Tokenism reflected and reinforced
the powerlessness of the welfare rights women and their supporters
in their efforts to change the structure of the system.

Other WRO groups throughout the country also combined the
strategies of conflict and cooperation with the welfare authorities as
a means of mobilizing monies for organizational survival. Wiley reported in 1972 that several WROs had become involved in the game of
"grantsmanship." The Baltimore and Philadelphia WROs had contracts for day care and job training from the federal government, the
Pittsburgh WRO had received "training monies" for its "Project
HOPE," and the Newark WROs were competing against each other
for "Model Cities" monies. [87] Thus, at times, funds from outside
sources, especially the federal government, appear to have exacerbated power struggles within the movement and weakened solidarity
among the organized poor women. In some ways, this resembled the
classic strategy of "divide and conquer," which continued to be an effective means of social control.

Some WROs, however, appear to have survived as a result of
cooperation with federal agencies and the receipt of grants. Without
support from NWRO or the liberal Friends, many local WROs ac-
commodated the political realities and sought monies where they were
available. With these federal grants, however small, some were able
to provide incentives for membership and strengthen, at least temporarily, their local organizations. WROs, as Wiley had ultimately
concluded, were more concerned with local problems and solutions
than with lobbying for long-range changes in national legislation. [88]

It was clear, however, that by 1973 some NWRO leaders, who
had previously supported this strategy of accommodation, were becoming critical of such alliances. The debate was raised repeatedly as
to whether they were "being bought by the establishment." One Executive Committee member reluctantly admitted that NWRO "has lost
many good people this way."[89] Some questioned the impact of federally subsidized WRO groups by asking, "How do you hang onto their
loyalty once they're inside the system and being paid by the system?"[90]
These critics of ties with the government stated that WROs had "to
remain free to tell what is really happening. That's the only way we
can change things."[91]

One indirect consequence of NWRO's cooperation with the federal government was the attack by white radicals, who made attempts to take over NWRO from 1971 to 1973. This internal conflict split the leadership, fragmented the movement, increased the tensions between the local and national offices, created enormous confusion among welfare rights members and their supporters, and (because of the radicals' violent tactics in some parts of the country) frightened many into withdrawing from the movement. While white radicals had been involved in welfare rights since its early days, their participation had ended after a few months. In Newark, for example, Tom Hayden of the Students for a Democratic Society (SDS) and his colleagues had organized the Newark Community Action Plan (NCAP) in 1966. The thrust of SDS was to organize and empower the black and poor in this city. After the riots in 1967, most had moved away. In late 1971 a group of white radical organizers infiltrated the movement and attempted to "divide, destroy and take over NWRO." Called NU-WRO, they reportedly belonged to the National Caucus of Labor Committees (NCLC), which planned to "rebuild" NWRO so that it would represent the interests of "all unemployed workers, veterans, prisoners, et al."[92]

Their strategy was to create dissension within the ranks of the WROs, attack the national headquarters and its leaders, and appeal to current supporters of NWRO to switch their allegiance. They disrupted meetings and printed and distributed materials that contradicted statements and news sent out by NWRO. They secured mailing lists of members and supporters and carried out an intensive mail, phone, and personal contact campaign to undermine the welfare rights movement. The Labor Caucus charged NWRO leaders with joining in a conspiracy with the Nixon administration to destroy the movement.[93] It accused NWRO officers of being paid agents of the government who were working to wipe out the movement of poor people. From NWRO's perspective, NU-WRO was seen as a timely strategy by its enemies to wipe out their weakened and fragile movement in the final years.

The consequences of this attack from the left were very damaging for NWRO. Several state WRO leaders were won over by the Labor Caucus, reportedly with ample monetary incentives, travel opportunities, recognition, and arguments that the national NWRO leaders had never really cared about local needs or the need for grassroots organizing. Middle-class supporters around the country, frightened and totally confused by the violent incidents staged by the NU-WRO and by its radical rhetoric, found additional reasons for withdrawing from NWRO. One white church official stated that some began to feel that it "would be dangerous for the churches to be affiliated with NWRO." Others noted that "this was the goal that the Labor Caucus wanted to achieve—to break up, split up and create lack of confidence among the aupport groups for NWRO." The result was that in a number of instances "they did succeed . . . in helping discredit an organization that was already having all kinds of difficulties."[94]

These white radicals thus successfully used the argument that NWRO was tied to the government to drive a wedge within the movement in 1971-73, when it was at its most vulnerable point. As a result, NWRO lost most of its few remaining mobilized resources: members, leaders, supporters, and legitimacy among its allies.[95]

By the early 1970s the street agitation and sit-ins had, in part, given way to more traditional strategies of negotiating with and accommodating the welfare administrators, lobbying with legislators, and fighting for change through class-action suits in the courts. Some of the negotiations had the payoffs of federal grants for special training and day-care projects for WRO groups. These gained in importance as middle-class sources of support withered away. Bargaining for monies, space in the welfare departments for advocacy, and seats on the welfare boards apparently were some of the strategies used by local WROs. These strategies continued even after the demise of the national movement organization in March 1975. While some WROs rejected this strategy of cooperation with the welfare authorities, others felt that there was enough leeway to maneuver within the federal contracts that enabled them to "do the job" and still get enough resources to stay alive. "Grantsmanship"—and accommodation—thus became means of organizational survival.

Over the years, protest at the local level almost totally disappeared. In a few places, episodic confrontations against the state were reported in Pennsylvania, Texas, and New York even as late as 1980.[96] One NWRO organizer "disagreed with people who think that NWRO was coopted from time to time by different groups." He felt that "in many ways NWRO got as much mileage out of the use of those groups as the groups got out of NWRO."[97] Others warned of the "need . . . to beware of the seductive climate of Washington."[98] NWRO leaders were well aware that political authorities had many resources with which to defuse protest. The dominant ideology that condemned and stigmatized welfarism, the economic resources and the recognition accorded to those working within the establishment, the tax-exempt bonuses for middle-class supporters, the monies for poor people's survival, all could be manipulated by the government to inhibit or promote attachment to the movement by members and supporters. As the political conditions became increasingly hostile, as reflected in the rhetoric and actions of the Nixon administration, many withdrew.[99] As a consequence, NWRO's resources declined.

Both protest and negotiations were part of the strategies employed by NWRO and its affiliates to increase its resources and bring about needed reforms in the system, given the unequal power relations

in the conflict. Both strategies in some ways added temporarily to
NWRO's resources, but neither succeeded in bringing about permanent change in the welfare system. At best, they helped increase the
monies distributed to the AFDC mothers in some parts of the country
for a short period of time, raise the visibility of their grievances,
and place the welfare issue in the political arena. In some instances,
these strategies helped some WROs to survive as local organizations
representing the needs of the welfare poor, even as the national mobilization of poor women declined.

NWRO AND ITS SUPPORTERS
VERSUS THE LEGISLATORS

With the introduction of FAP by the Nixon administration in
1969, the welfare rights conflict moved from the streets into the
suites in Washington, D.C. In the next three years, NWRO shifted
its resources from local agitation and grass-roots organizing to national lobbying and negotiating, which resulted in the final defeat of
FAP as well as the decline of its own base constituency. As such,
this external conflict with the welfare authorities was costly to the
movement organization and had an impact on its demise. Both internal neglect by NWRO leaders and counteroffensives by the political
authorities interacted to weaken NWRO's power, by eroding the numbers of members and supporters. Not only did its base constituency
decline but organizers and leaders such as Cloward, Piven, and Wiley,
finally withdrew their support. Given this turn of events by the end of
1972, NWRO's mobilized resources had practically vanished. It continued to struggle to revitalize its base for the next two years but ultimately was forced to close down its national headquarters in 1975.
Nevertheless, for three years (1969-72), NWRO entered the political
arena to fight a "welfare reform" proposed by the political establishment that it deemed totally inadequate.

FAP was the national counteroffensive of the Nixon administration to the welfare rights protest. It was an effort by governing political authorities to resolve the welfare crisis that was being attacked
by all sectors in U.S. society, from liberals to conservatives, from
administrators to recipients, from the nonpoor to the poor. NWRO
claimed that FAP was a direct reaction to its agitation in the streets
in the mid- and late 1960s. It contended that the threat of social disorder and the political and economic costs of welfare had finally led
political leaders to come forth with an alternative plan to the current
welfare system.[100] FAP was introduced to the public by Nixon on
August 8, 1969, in a national television address. He proposed that the
existing welfare system, which he described as a "colossal failure,"

be abolished and that FAP be adopted in its place.[101] Moynihan, the
architect of the plan and a presidential assistant, called it a solution
to the problem of "dependency," which was reflected in the soaring
numbers of AFDC families.[102] It was, in fact, a form of guaranteed
income, although for political reasons the president made it very
clear that it "was not a 'guaranteed income.'"[103]

FAP was carefully designed to appeal to the sacred U.S. value
of the family and to obscure its effects on income redistribution.
Moynihan emphasizes that "what was at issue . . . [was] not welfare
reform but income redistribution." Income redistribution, as he
points out, "goes to the heart of politics: who gets what and how."[104]
According to Moynihan, the FAP "provided for the redistribution of
income toward Blacks, Mexicans, Indians, toward Southern whites,
toward families with children" (emphasis in the original). In many
ways, it was a revolutionary concept. Introduced by a Republican
president, it was the first major welfare reform proposed in 35
years. President Nixon was well aware of this paradox but noted that
"Tory men and liberal policies are what have changed the world."[105]
Nixon seemed to enjoy such contradictions. As one observer noted,
here was a Republican president proposing a guaranteed income for
the poor, when he had been "elected in significant measure out of dis-
taste for the dependent poor."[106] From NWRO's perspective, although it subscribed to the principle of a guaranteed income, FAP
was totally inadequate. As a result, NWRO set about to mobilize
members and supporters to develop a political strategy to defeat it
by lobbying in Washington.

Specifically, FAP called for a cash benefit of $1,600 per year
for a family of four, plus $800 in food stamps. It required partici-
pants to register for and accept work, excluding only mothers with
small children under the age of six. Provisions for child care were
limited. As soon as it was introduced in August 1969, its supporters
and opponents began to surface for what was to turn out to be a long,
drawn-out political battle.

Some praised FAP as being "surprisingly revolutionary," especially for a Republican president.[107] Others termed it "the most
important change in our times in the American Poor Law and the first
step toward a radical goal of a guaranteed income for all."[108] Mitchell Ginsberg, New York City's human resources administrator, stated
that "despite major limitations," it might in fact "represent the beginning of a turnabout in national policy."[109] He criticized the benefit amount as being "woefully inadequate" but praised the coverage of
the "working poor." He also argued against forcing "welfare mothers
to accept employment," which in his opinion was "unfortunate, un-
necessary and unenforceable." One "average taxpayer" on the street
reacted positively to the proposal, stating that he liked "the idea of a

work program." In his opinion, "every able-bodied man and woman should work for whatever relief is given." "In other words," he added, "no work, no money, except for the sick and disabled." He approved of the "job training idea" but could not accept "Mr. Nixon's income supplementation." His views were reflected in the general public opinion polls that year, which found that "80% of Americans favor legislation requiring employable recipients, including mothers with school-age children, to work."[110]

NWRO's reaction, and that of many of its strongest supporters, was entirely negative. Wiley emphasized the "inadequacy of the bill," underscoring that what was needed was a bill that was "universal in scope" and that would provide adequate income for all in need. Yet, at the same time, he went on to "give credit to the President for having initiated the bill."[111] Cloward not only criticized the legislation's low payments but also decried "the President's talk about work, work, work [which] reinforces all the erroneous impressions about welfare." Cloward added that "most people who go on and off the welfare rolls are already working." In the long run, he felt "it could lead to enormous amounts of coercion to force people into marginal jobs."[112] To Sparer, the founder of the Columbia Center for Social Welfare Policy and Law and a strong supporter of NWRO, the proposal was "a step backwards." He felt that "the Nixon plan, under the guise of work incentive notions, re-establishes an old poor law principle—that of 'less eligibility'—under which the needy unemployable must always get less than the needy employables." He added that only "when we provide enough good jobs and a decent grant to the needy . . . will [we] be over the hill in welfare." Carl Rachlin, the general counsel of NWRO, asserted that "the Nixon proposal clearly calls into question the Administration's credibility in the eyes of poor people." He underscored that its "income maintenance standard" was one "no one can survive on" and that, while the present system was "an atrocity," the "new one would only seem to give the states greater freedom to act oppressively with job mandates and so forth."

Tillmon called FAP simply "disguised repression."[113] She listed several basic flaws in the proposed legislation. She pointed out that 45 states plus the District of Columbia were paying AFDC families more than that proposed by President Nixon. She also criticized FAP for discriminating against the AFDC women and children in favor of the aged, blind, and disabled. For example, "an aged couple"—just two people—would receive almost exactly the same amount as an AFDC family of four. Finally, she added, poor mothers would not be given the choice of staying home with their children (unless the children were under six years of age) or going to work. FAP would require them to register for work, regardless of availability of adequate child care and without any designated labor standards for wages and working conditions. Consequently, NWRO and its allies developed several concurrent strategies in order to "Zap Fap."

In Congress, NWRO testified, unsuccessfully, in the House and Senate for an increase in the "money allotment of the Nixon Welfare Bill."[114] It introduced its own legislation for a guaranteed income in April 1970, which according to Wiley, was "drastically different from Nixon's Plan."[115] Unlike the Nixon administration, which sought to minimize the "guaranteed income" aspect of FAP, NWRO used no euphemisms. Its bill was called the "Guaranteed Adequate Income Bill," and it had no "categories" for eligibility except need. Benefit levels, unlike those in FAP, were based on the Bureau of Labor Statistics (BLS) estimates of what is "adequate" income and were adjusted "as the cost of living goes up."[116] In 1970, for example, NWRO called for $5,500 for a family of four per year. In 1971 the amount was increased to $6,500 and two years later to $7,500, reflecting the changing BLS figures and the rising cost of living.

For three years NWRO struggled to defeat the Nixon proposal. Part of its political strategy was to mobilize liberals in support of its position. Wiley noted that one of the biggest problems was trying to "convince liberals that the Administration bill is not a major reform of the welfare system."[117] Middle-class supporters were urged to join NWRO to "Zap Fap" by contributing resources, both financial and political. Friends of WRO throughout the country were alerted and urged to live on a welfare budget, or, as its promotional poster stated, to "Live Like a Dog" ($0.19 a meal per person) on the Nixon plan. This campaign was directed at attracting media visibility as an inexpensive and effective way of mobilizing more supporters. It was also designed to raise monies for NWRO, since the money saved by eating "on welfare budgets" would allow middle-class Friends to contribute their food savings to NWRO. NWRO gained some publicity but little monies from these efforts. A number of senators and representatives in Washington, D.C., and their spouses held a press conference after having tried to live on a welfare food budget for a week. Similar local efforts in New Jersey and New York were not as successful in attracting "stars" in the political arena and therefore did not receive much publicity. In New Jersey, the monies collected were only about $1,000.

Another part of NWRO's political strategy to defeat FAP was to move toward coalition building. NWRO, as discussed in Chapter 4, formed a coalition with UCC in the spring of 1970. UCC was asked to enlist the support of additional allies among middle-class church constituencies, social agencies, and other potential liberal groups. As the result of this activation of its networks, UCC was successful, to a large extent, in mobilizing liberals to exert their political pressures in Congress to defeat FAP.

A continuous campaign, coordinated by the WPT of the UCC and the National Council of Churches, was waged from 1970 through 1972. In close cooperation with NWRO, political strategy sessions were set up for the liberal activists; training sessions were held for new lobbyists; and social-policy analyses, contrasting the various welfare reform bills in Congress with NWRO's and FAP, were distributed to potential allies. [118] Through the networks of the Protestant denominations, continuous alerts on the latest FAP legislative developments were sent to Friends throughout the country. Appeals were made for individuals and organizations to write to Congress or to visit their representatives to express their opposition to FAP. The white church media, publications, periodicals, and radio shows were utilized to enlist middle-class support in this political fight.

At the same time, using their power and access to congressional representatives, liberal church coalitions sent their analyses and comparisons of the various welfare reform bills to all the political leaders in Congress. White church executives and heads of social-welfare agencies also testified in Washington and personally contacted the key movers in Congress and HEW in an effort to stop FAP from becoming law. NWRO, through Wiley and its Executive Committee members, was also continuously working in this same direction "on the Hill."[119] It was a massive campaign on the part of NWRO and some of its major allies.

Liberal support was, however, not solidly behind NWRO's position. In many ways, the lack of political solidarity in the liberal sector weakened the extensive mobilization efforts of NWRO and some of its supporters. At the outset, several liberal groups chose to defect from the original coalition organized by NWRO and the National Council of Churches. They joined others in the Nixon camp in support of FAP. The rationalization of some of the defectors was that FAP represented at least "a foot in the door" in terms of welfare reform. The principle, they insisted, was correct. The major flaw was the low level of benefits, but this, they felt, would be easily readjusted upward, once the bill had been enacted and the regulations implemented.

The costs of such a national income-transfer program also divided the supporters in the liberal camp who favored some kind of a guaranteed income system. Liberals split into various welfare reform factions, as additional and more acceptable plans were introduced into Congress. [120] Senator Abraham Ribicoff's amendments in 1971 called for $3,000 (per family of four per year) to be gradually increased to $4,000 by 1974. Congressman Donald Fraser's plan, a "middle-of-the-road" proposal, adopted $3,600 as its level. Senator Fred Harris's bill suggested an initial income level of $2,520, to be raised over three years to the poverty level. All these fell between Nixon's low of $2,400* and NWRO's high of $6,500.[121]

The alternative welfare bills had greater appeal than NWRO's "Guaranteed Adequate Income Bill," not only because of their projected lower costs but because of their labels and basic assumptions. FAP and others emphasized the family needs and obscured the idea of a guaranteed income. The Harris bill, for example, was called the "Family Income and Work Incentive Act of 1972," and Fraser's bill was named the "Family Stability Act." All addressed the issue of "family and/or work" and reflected in their titles that all able-bodied adults would be expected to work. If they refused, the implication was that they could be denied benefits.

NWRO's bill adopted a different philosophy. It assumed that people in general want to work and, therefore, incorporated "no work requirement" but rather a "positive work incentive." The strategy was to use "a carrot" rather than "a stick," unlike FAP.

While the goals of the bills were similar, the specific details and strategies differed. On a continuum of overall economic and political benefits for recipients, NWRO's bill fell at one extreme and FAP, at the other, with the liberal proposals (by Ribicoff, Fraser, and Harris), ranging from $3,000 to $4,000, somewhere in between. Despite this pluralism, the final political contest centered around those who favored Nixon's plan, or the amended FAP plan (known as the Ribicoff amendments), and those who opposed it.

While UCC, through its WPT, took a public stand in support of NWRO's guaranteed income plan, voting for a policy statement endorsing $5,500 (later revised to $6,500 in 1971), some white Protestant groups and the Catholics either remained outside the debate or joined the Nixon camp in support of the "modified" FAP.[122] UCC stated that, in its opinion, FAP was "worse than the present system."[123] The Presbyterians, Methodists, and the National Council of Churches also endorsed this stand. Most others favored some modified version and leaned toward or actually joined the Nixon advocates. Church groups supporting the Harris or Fraser plans or NWRO's plan justified their stand on moral grounds, stating that they could not support the "inadequate benefits" of Nixon's FAP.[124]

Debate over support or nonsupport of FAP or NWRO's "$5,500 plan" continued unabated for months within the white denominational

---

*Originally, the Nixon plan called for $1,600, plus $800 in food stamps. When it was reintroduced as H.R. 1, the level was increased to $2,400, and the food stamps were "cashed in," or included, in the total benefit.

sector. UCC reaffirmed its adopted policy in support of NWRO throughout the three-year fight. Cognizant, however, of the realities of politics, NWRO agreed that it would not condemn those who lined up with the Harris or Fraser plans (which called for slightly lower benefits than NWRO's plan) but could not condone those who supported the Ribicoff amendments, which it felt simply constituted a watered-down version of the Nixon plan. NWRO condemned the Catholic and Lutheran churches, the American Jewish Committee, and the League of Women Voters for deserting its cause and siding with the Ribicoff camp. [125] It described "the Ribicoff coalition [as] an elite coalition," pointing out that "what they call welfare reform is totally unaccept-able to poor folk."[126]

The political strategy also entailed mobilizing peer allies. Dur-ing this period, NWRO sought to build coalitions with the United Farm-workers, the American Indians, black organizations, and women's organizations. In 1972, in an attempt to mobilize support for its Guaranteed Income Plan, NWRO formed a coalition with SCLC and the National Tenants Organization (NTO) and presented a Poor People's Platform to the Democratic National Convention. All items on the Poor People's Platform were endorsed by the convention, except NWRO's call for $5,500 for a family of four. Various black groups, including the National Urban League, and women's organizations, especially the organized feminists, testified independently on FAP, highlighting many of the same inadequacies that made it unacceptable to NWRO. Blacks called attention to its negative impact on the large black and poor population. Women's groups underscored the detri-mental effects of FAP on poor women with dependent children, citing as especially harmful the low benefits, lack of child-care provisions, and "forced work" requirements.

In the final months of the struggle, NWRO tried to mobilize public support to defeat FAP by "media staging" and demonstrations. This, too, was part of its political strategy but deviated from the more traditional approaches of lobbying the coalition building. NWRO mobilized its supporters to demonstrate in Washington with the "Chil-dren's March for Survival" in March 1972, using as its theme the negative impact of the Nixon FAP on children. Its slogan was "Nixon doesn't care," which was suggested by a child and adopted by NWRO leaders. The hope was that this theme of "children" would win more supporters, as the media helped to disseminate the inadequacy of Nixon's bill and its effects on millions of children on AFDC. The strategy failed. The eastern liberal press, perhaps sensing the public's lessened interest in the "wornout topic of welfare," "blacked out" both the demonstration and the press conference for testimony by WRO children. [127]

Despite the use of the multifaceted political strategy by NWRO and its allies to defeat FAP, an amended bill was eventually passed

by the House and Senate in October 1972, more than three years after President Nixon had first introduced his plan for replacing the
welfare system. Discouragement and disappointment swept through
the movement. Many felt that there was no stopping the bill. NWRO
leaders, however, would not give up. Wiley recalls that "after having
suffered a crushing defeat at the hands of Russel Long [head of the
Senate Finance Committee] Welfare Rights lobbyists were discour-
aged." That Columbus Day weekend in 1972, "the outlook was gloomy
indeed" for the poor women and their allies. Wiley pointed out that
"there were many who thought [NWRO] should give up the fight at this
point and turn our energies to develop grassroots resistance." However, he added, "We had invested three years of hard effort in trying to defeat FAP," and so the decision was made "to put a last ditch
effort towards defeating Titles IV and V" of the Social Security amendments. These sections included FAP and other test plans, "the Byrd-
Roth tests and drastic restrictions on rights."[128]

A last minute effort was made to mobilize the support of congressional allies to strike out Titles IV and V. Over the Columbus
Day weekend, telegrams were sent to Senator George McGovern "ur-
gently requesting that he and [Sargent] Shriver intervene on behalf of
poor people." According to Wiley, the McGovern aides "brushed the
telegram aside."[129] This was a reversal of McGovern's previous
public support of NWRO. NWRO retaliated by threatening to stage a
sit-in at the McGovern Presidential Headquarters if a positive response was not forthcoming. This threat to the Democratic presidential candidate, according to Wiley, brought the desired results.
NWRO succeeded in contacting McGovern and Senator Edward Kennedy,
who were asked to persuade Congressman Mills (head of the powerful
House Ways and Means Committee) and other top congressional representatives not to accept Titles IV and V of the Social Security
amendments of 1972.

At the same time, the press—the New York Times, Boston
Globe, and Washington Post—were thoroughly briefed on the repressive
contents of the Senate bill by Wiley. This resulted in wide news coverage "on aspects of the legislation crucial to poor people which at
that time had been hidden from public view." The middle-class political networks were reactivated. Friends of WRO all over the country telephoned or sent telegrams to the House Conference Committee
members.[130] According to Wiley, Senators McGovern and Kennedy
spoke to Mills in person, urging him to strike out Title IV (FAP) and
Title V (the "restrictive" measures, as assessed by NWRO and its
allies).

As the fight entered its final phase, allies from the Nixon camp
and some of those supporting the Ribicoff amendments rejoined NWRO
and its Friends to defeat FAP. FAP, now in the House/Senate Con-

ference Committee, was in the last stage of the political debate. For
the first time in this public policy deliberation, the congressional
Black Caucus "voted unanimously to wage a fight on behalf of welfare
recipients" to defeat the portion of the legislation that was objected
to by NWRO. Aligning itself with NWRO for the first time, the Black
Caucus promised that they "would use every means at their command
to jam up the procedures of the House of Representatives" to block
passage of the bill until Congress adjourned. Not only racial solidarity emerged in the terminal period of this conflict but also some
signs of increasing support from women's organizations. Some wom-
en's groups rallied against FAP and moved back into the NWRO/liberal
camp. The League of Women Voters, for example, redefined the final
bill as being "too repressive" and voted to throw its political weight
along with NWRO to defeat it in conference. Earlier, the league had
left the NWRO coalition and joined the supporters of the Ribicoff plan.
Labor, through the United Auto Workers, the AFL-CIO, the Leadership Conference on Civil Rights, and "a host of other organizations"
that also had remained largely outside the struggle, rallied around
NWRO to lobby against "the repressive sections of the bill."[131]

At the last minute, therefore, NWRO succeeded in building a
liberal coalition sufficiently strong to help kill FAP. The increasingly repressive actions by some congressional leaders tipped the
political scales and brought back into NWRO's camp previous supporters, as well as some new ones. This new configuration of power
within the liberal sector in support of NWRO seemed to have emerged
as a result of these restrictive acts by its opponents in Congress.
Wiley noted that "Senator Long had succeeded in making the bill so
repressive that he united all the liberal forces for the first time to
back the Welfare Rights position."[132] While the liberals claimed that
FAP was too meager and repressive, the conservatives asserted that
it was overly generous and permissive. Given this wide spectrum of
political feeling against FAP, it collapsed. The combination of liberal
pressures from various groups "caused the House conferees to reject
the Senate version of Title IV and V, and, since [Senator Russell]
Long was opposed to the House version, because he regarded it as
too liberal, Titles IV and V were struck from the bill."

NWRO claimed this as a "Welfare Rights victory" and explained
it in terms of "good organization and strategy." It praised the cooperation of its middle-class supporters as well as the efforts of its
members throughout the country. Wiley stated that "it could not have
been done without grassroots Welfare Rights Organizations all over
the country prepared to work in this lobby. It could not have been
done without Friends and supporters working in concern" with NWRO.
He underscored, however, the grim reality of the future. If Richard
Nixon were reelected in November 1972 (a few weeks hence), the

struggle would have to continue. NWRO "would have it to do over again the next four years." Two weeks later, as NWRO predicted, Nixon was reelected in a landslide victory. He promised to revive the welfare legislation, but this never materialized, since, in the following months, his administration was immersed in the Watergate scandal that eventually led to his resignation. Welfare, once his top domestic priority, was placed on a back burner.

By then, the national movement for welfare rights no longer had the resources to remain in the political arena to keep the issue of a guaranteed income alive. Its coffers were empty, it was deeply in debt, and its supporters were gone. Despite its rhetoric about grass-roots support during the final phase of the FAP struggle, its constituency base was seriously weakened.[133] The few WRO groups that remained were isolated and scattered, lacking in resources and neglected by the national offices. Liberal supporters, confronted with Nixon's presidential victory and the prospect of fighting the issue of income redistribution again, were shifting partners and issues. They were "tired of welfare," according to one observer.[134] Ginsberg noted that "the nation seems bored with the subject of poverty."[135] In 1973/74 the issue for liberals was no longer welfare rights, but rather "full employment rights." Horowitz and Katz suggest that "it may have been the displacement of the Johnson-Democratic era with the Nixon-Republican era that brought to an abrupt halt the war on poverty," which they note "was wound down almost as rapidly as it had been initially mounted."[136] Just as the lack of concern for poverty increased, so did interest in welfare reform go by the wayside by the mid-1970s.

At the federal level, welfare thus remained "simmering . . . during a long period of inattention" from 1975 through 1976.[137] With the victory of Jimmy Carter in the 1976 presidential election, the Democrats gained control of the White House and the Congress, and the issue of welfare reform resurfaced. On August 6, 1977, President Carter sent his message on welfare reform to Congress, beginning what appeared to be the "second round" of the debate, almost eight years to the date after Nixon had submitted his FAP.[138] It was introduced into Congress one month later as the "Better Jobs and Income Program." The emphasis of the Carter proposal, like that of the Nixon proposal, was on employment as a solution to poverty. The term welfare was deliberately excluded from its title to minimize political opposition.[139] The substance of the Carter plan was "a consolidated cash assistance program" combined with "uniform national rules and a work opportunity program to assure a job or training slot for every primary earner in a welfare family."[140] It called for a grant level of $4,200 for a family of four for those "not expected to work [NEWs] and $2,300 for those "expected to work [EWs]."

Reactions were varied. The liberal press called it a "bold, intelligent and humane plan."[141] Legislators and other political leaders responded generally in favorable terms. Moynihan, the architect of the original FAP, at first called the plan "superbly crafted" and then two months later labeled it "grievously disappointing."[142] He "expressed doubt that it could attract the necessary Congressional support." He criticized the benefit level as being too low and the fiscal relief to the cities, including New York City, as being much less than had been projected. He concluded by stating that, given "the current 'climate' on welfare revision," he did not expect support to be forthcoming.[143] Black leaders assessed it cautiously as "encouraging" and "praiseworthy," adding that it did not go far enough.[144]

While welfare rights women and their supporters had strong views about this new proposal, few were asked to express their opinions in the liberal press. Cloward, in an article written by Roger Wilkins in the New York Times, stated that he did not see the Carter plan or any of the other parallel proposals as "welfare reform." He pointed out that in the mid-1970s, "the people who talk about reform are either governors who want fiscal relief, or a lot of other people who really want to reduce the welfare rolls." In his opinion, that was not reform.[145] Various others, including members of labor unions, social workers, public welfare administrators, and blacks,* claimed to be unhappy with the Carter plan.[146] Welfare rights women organized their own public forum to criticize Carter's plan, since few, if any, had been asked for their opinions. At the WRO convention in Little Rock in 1976, they delineated its various flaws: the benefits were too low, day-care provisions were totally inadequate, and jobs and training were too vague and dead-ended.[147] Evans, now working with the Commission for Racial Justice of UCC, spoke out against the plan, stating that JIP, as he called it (instead of BJIP), "represents outright fraud on the people of this nation who have cried out for true welfare reform." He explained that he had labeled the proposal JIP because in actuality it "gyps those of us who have fought and struggled over the years for an adequate income program and finally convinced ourselves that Jimmy Carter would provide the poor of this nation with a way out of the poverty and degradation that the present welfare system has forced them into, for the last forty-two years." He listed all the weaknesses of the bill, highlighting its inadequate

---

*More specifically, these groups included the executive council of the AFL-CIO, the National Association of Social Workers, the National Council of State Public Welfare Administrators, the Congressional Black Caucus, the National Association of Counties, and the executive director of the National Urban League.

benefits, the social devaluation of child rearing, and the lack of any guarantee for "recipient's rights."[148]

The Center for Social Welfare Policy and Law, reflecting the views of welfare recipients and their advocates, stated that Carter's proposal fell short of "the five basic principles for true welfare reform," namely, "decent jobs for all who can work; adequate income for all; universal coverage; a simplified, fair and responsive administration; and fair and realistic funding." Their assessment of BJIP was that "it did not guarantee an adequate income for all, it did not guarantee a decent job for all who wish to work," and it was "nonresponsive to current needs." Another major criticism was that it did not "treat those with equal needs equally."[149]

Middle-class feminists also spoke out against the Carter BJIP. NOW and WEAL criticized the lack of attention to women's needs, and the assumption that males, rather than females, should be given the first opportunity to obtain jobs. NOW pointed out that Carter was trying "to solve the problems of women in poverty by providing men with jobs." The "traditional American family" had been described by one spokesperson and advocate of the plan, as "two parents and children in which the family head goes out to work and makes enough of a living to keep the family together." He added that "the major thrust of any program ought to be to support this as the predominant situation for Americans." In reality, as feminists pointed out, "fewer than a third of American families" fit this stereotype. Smeal, president of NOW, suggested that the Carter administration was now "going to try to promote among the poor a family model the middle-class cannot afford and the higher classes have rejected."[150]

Since NWRO had not been in operation as a national movement after 1975, MEJ took the initiative in mobilizing support in the fall of 1977 to fight against the inadequacies of the Carter plan and other welfare reform proposals that were being introduced into Congress.[151] While there was general consensus that the BJIP had to be strengthened, there were debates over which strategy and tactics to develop for this second round of welfare reform. MEJ urged poor people's groups to "stay out of the Congressional area." They cautioned grass-roots groups against engaging in the political process "in which they have little, if any, power." They underscored that welfare had reemerged as a political issue in 1977/78, not because of the legislators' "concern about maldistribution of income" or interest in the fact that the "poor are getting poorer," but because of pressure "from states for fiscal relief" and from the public for elimination of "welfare fraud" and the desire to "force recipients to work."[152]

MEJ's proposed strategy was to organize everyone possible at the grass-roots level to "demand real jobs that will pay a decent income, accomplish a meaningful purpose and protect workers' rights."

MEJ leaders argued that traditional lobbying, as had been attempted in the original FAP struggle, would be a waste of time, energy, and resources. They did not preclude, however, "the possibility of mobilizing to defeat the Carter proposals later on." They concluded that, as old-time organizers of NWRO, it was clear that "the handles around which [they had] organized in the 1960's" were no longer available. The Carter plan, however, "because of its complexity and its promise of jobs," opened up "a new range of organizing possibilities." MEJ called on poor people to spend their time and efforts in organizing "the millions of poor who share an uncertain future." Having learned from its experience with FAP, MEJ felt that the strengthening of a mass base constituency of poor people offered a much better chance for mobilizing effective political power than lobbying in the halls of Congress to influence political leaders.

Church supporters rallied quickly to join the renewed struggle for welfare reform. Early in 1978, a coalition of religious groups and welfare rights representatives met in Washington to develop plans for mobilizing middle-class people across the country. Spearheaded by the National Council of Churches (Division of Church and Society), it sought "to pursue welfare reform within the context of social welfare policy, including the need for full employment and health care as a national policy."[153] Welfare, employment, and health care were its principal concerns. Plans were tabled a few months later, however, when it became evident that welfare reform was not moving at the national level and that church constituencies were reluctant to provide any support for "welfare reform."[154]

During the final years of the 1970s, welfare once again remained "simmering" in Congress. With the 1980 presidential elections on the horizon, welfare reform was not a popular subject. Among political leaders, enthusiasm for any comprehensive and expensive national welfare legislation was waning, given the Carter administration's increasing emphasis on a "balanced budget." Yet, at the same time, cities and states were crying for fiscal relief from the rising welfare costs as the inflation rate hit double digits.

By the end of 1979, there was growing consensus that any welfare reform legislation had to incorporate certain components. First, a national minimum benefit level in AFDC had to be established (at about 65 percent of the poverty level).* Second, the AFDC-UP program for two-parent families had to be mandated (rather than volun-

---

*These components were incorporated in the welfare reform bill (H.R. 4904) passed by the House in November 1979. The poverty level in 1979 was about $7,330 in annual income for a family of four. Thus, 65 percent would be about $4,764.

tary). Third, tax credits for the working poor (the Earned Income Tax Credit) had to be expanded. Finally, the emphasis had to be on work, rather than welfare, as a solution for AFDC women with dependent children. A government report in 1978 emphasized that, while in the past efforts had been directed at "the extension of cash welfare benefits as a primary method of assistance," the new thrust was now "on training, employment, and employment-related benefits" for the "principal earner" in families with inadequate income. In the long run, this strategy, it was felt, would be less costly, since "job and training opportunities" would provide income to the poor and at the same time "buil[d] human capital and provid[e] useful goods and services to society as well."[155]

Conflict between congressional leaders and the Carter administration over welfare reform increased in the spring of 1979, reinforcing the general views of various groups and observers that welfare reform was stalemated.[156] Moynihan's position on the subject of welfare had "changed fundamentally" since 1969. Moynihan "freely acknowledge[d]" that his position in 1979 "contradicts the position he had 10 years ago." Now, as the senator from New York, he explained that his concerns were for "the more urgent plight of the Northeast," rather than for the low-benefit states in the South, which had been his primary focus in FAP. He stated that he was "tired" of "trying to force on the South a system that its politicians do not want." He added also that food stamps now had "gone far to ease the plight of the poor" and that the assumption that a guaranteed income system "would prevent breakup of families or provide work incentives" was being questioned in light of recent findings by social scientists. Finally, there was little incentive for "Northern liberals . . . to raise benefit levels in the South, because it is no longer felt that poor people come north to get on welfare." Since Moynihan was a crucial ally for getting welfare reform through Congress, the Carter administration was "dismayed, disheartened, and even angered" by Moynihan's statements. Most observers of the political scene doubted there would be any more action in the next two years. * Tinkering with the

---

*In August 1979 Congress was "considering two radically different approaches to changes in the program of Aid to Families with Dependent Children." One was a Carter proposal similar to his original BJIP. The other was a "block grant" approach, which was also opposed by the poor and their supporters. In November 1979 the major welfare bill passed by the House was H.R. 4904, but it was not considered in the Senate before adjournment. President Carter recommended "a one-year deferral." He also recommended specific changes in AFDC to reduce expenditures for 1981 and thereafter, as

original legislation continued, but the question of basic reform remained unresolved as the Reagan administration took power in January 1981.

In sum, the political strategy of NWRO and its allies against the welfare authorities lasted from 1969 through 1972, the years during which FAP was being debated. After FAP was defeated, as a result of concentrated efforts by NWRO and its Friends as well as resistance to the proposal by conservatives, there was a lull between 1973 and 1976, when there was little or no action on welfare reform. From 1976 through 1978 there was some mobilization for political action by some former supporters of NWRO and scattered leaders of WROs, as a result of the efforts of MEJ and the National Council of Churches. With the waning of interest in Washington, D.C., for welfare reform, and greater concern for a balanced budget in 1981/82, there was little activity at the national level by challengers and their allies or the political leaders in Congress. In general, then, the political strategy against the welfare authorities waged by the poor and nonpoor allies had succeeded in temporarily halting the implementation of what was defined as an "inadequate plan." A continuing network of concerned liberals appeared to be monitoring future actions, ready to remobilize to counter new offensives by the political establishment.

In the meantime, for poor women on welfare and their children, the prospect of adequate income or jobs from the federal government in 1980 remained bleak. Political leaders, reflecting the general climate in the country, saw little need to allocate the government's scarce resources to this powerless group in society. Few voices were being raised to dispute them. The tide of conservatism was rising. There were only scattered reports of protest among AFDC mothers for jobs and income. [157] At the beginning of the new decade, poor women were once again dispersed and the movement becalmed. The political strategy of NWRO had functioned to stem the tide of repression for a few years, but, by 1980 the political climate had greatly

---

well as "reduction in the funding levels for food stamps and child nutrition, low-income energy assistance and unemployment compensation." Congress, according to one report, in its budget recommendations for 1981, is likely to propose "even bigger cuts than the President proposes in the budget authorization for needs-based programs, such as AFDC." These potential actions by Congress in 1980 could "cause major losses in poor peoples programs" (memorandums to Welfare Specialists [August 1979 and April 1980] by the Center on Social Welfare Policy and Law, New York and Washington, D.C.).

changed since the turbulent 1960s. Turmoil had subsided. However, the issue of welfare reform, while muted and barely alive in the legislative branch, continued to be fought in the lower courts, unlike the early years, when the action centered in the highest court of the land.

NWRO AND ITS SUPPORTERS
VERSUS THE COURTS

Another concurrent strategy initiated in the 1960s to bring about welfare reform was the legal strategy, or intervention through the courts. NWRO in coalition with Legal Services lawyers and backup centers funded by the Office of Economic Opportunity (OEO) challenged the welfare system and brought about major changes in a few years. As NWRO's successes mounted, opposition within Congress, which had established and funded the Legal Services programs, emerged. As the structure and orientation of the Supreme Court moved to the right, NWRO's victories declined. Their efforts then shifted to the state courts and legislative and administrative branches. By the early 1970s, the political climate was becoming less tolerant of the demands of the black and poor—and especially of those of poor women on welfare. From their inception, Legal Services groups and their lawyers remained NWRO's, as well as local WRO's, most continuous ally, contributing to the resources of the national movement both directly and indirectly and also working independently for the rights of poor people.

Legal Services was established in 1964 as part of the federally funded OEO program, a part of the Johnson administration's War on Poverty. Levitan called "the OEO legal services program one of the most significant, and certainly the most controversial programs funded initially as part of CAP."[158] Historically, as J. Skelly Wright pointed out in 1969, "the courts had failed the poor." In U.S. society, Wright contended, the law had always "worked a hardship on those least able to withstand it." He added that "rather than helping the poor surmount their poverty, the law has all too frequently served to perpetuate and even exacerbate their despair and helplessness." Quoting the late Senator Robert Kennedy, he described the poor person's view of the law as follows: "The poor man looks upon the lawyer as an enemy. . . . For him the law is always taking something away."[159] In the mid-1960s, the War on Poverty established Legal Services to help solve some of these problems.

Legal Services was designed to include lawyers as well as poor people in its structure. There were advisory boards at the local level with at least one-third of the seats reserved for the poor or their representatives. There were also national advisory councils, whose structure and orientation changed and gradually became more inclusive of the poor. The first, the National Advisory Board, comprised of American Bar Association members, was established in 1965. The second such board, the Project Advisory Board, established in 1967, included lawyers from various Legal Services groups around the country. The third, in 1971, was the National Clients Council, whose members, individuals eligible for Legal Services, were charged to act as liaisons between the poverty community and lawyers working to provide legal assistance to its citizens. The National Clients Council was an "innovative attempt" supported by federal funds. It was rapidly becoming an "ombudsman" on behalf of the poor by the beginning of the 1980s. [160]

Over the years, the Legal Services program was funded at increasingly higher levels, giving impetus to its rapid expansion. Its budget rose from $24.8 million in 1964 to $71.5 million in 1974. [161] In 1975, after restructured into the Legal Services Corporation during the Nixon and Ford administrations, its budget continued to grow. [162] By 1979 it had reached $270 million. [163] Its paid lawyers working on poverty issues numbered over 2,000 at its height, and its offices rose to 800 throughout the country, later declining to about 300 by 1979. [164]

With the advent of the Nixon administration in 1969, the OEO programs came under increasing attack by the president and his allies in Congress and in his administration. The strategy of the Nixon administration, unlike that of its predecessor, was to dismantle OEO programs, especially Legal Services, which had been so successful in many parts of the country in its challenges of welfare laws and regulations in the courts. [165] Legislative and administrative court suits, however, delayed the final restructuring of Legal Services until after Nixon's reelection in 1972.

From 1966 through the beginning of the 1970s, NWRO and Legal Services lawyers in local offices and national backup centers cooperated in class-action suits to bring about welfare reform through the courts. There were mutual benefits for both partners in this coalition. Legal Services had the legal expertise. WROs had the clients and the issues. [166] Legal Services in many areas also provided WROs with the use of its office space, telephones, and other supplies. In some places, it helped WROs print lay welfare manuals used for organizing the welfare poor. The ties also included participation by Legal Services lawyers in NWRO conventions, in which they ran workshops for poverty lawyers, WRO members, and Friends of WROs. The alliance of NWRO with Legal Services enhanced NWRO's power and prestige and yet made few demands on its mobilized resources. The legal expenses were borne by Legal Services, with NWRO's contribution being cases and clients. Cooperation provided

NWRO with judicial "victories" that were added to its list of street
and political successes. Legal Services, thus, in many ways increased NWRO's mobilized resources through its prestige, visibility,
and recognition within the political arena and, indirectly, through the
monies and material needs provided to local WROs where such alliances evolved. These cooperative efforts, as we shall discuss below, resulted in landmark decisions in the U.S. Supreme Court,
which helped to reform the welfare system. It was a continuous alliance, which endured at the local level long after the demise of the
national movement.

NWRO leaders, however, had mixed feelings about this partnership. The immediate payoffs were often offset by underlying conflicts, generally stemming from class, race, and gender contradictions. Most poverty lawyers were middle-class, white, and male,
in contrast to the predominantly poor, black, and female constituency
of NWRO. Tillmon, while endorsing the alliance with Legal Services,
at the same time was wary of the role of outsiders in the movement
of poor women.[167] Jeter, another national female leader in NWRO,
asserted that many WROs throughout the country had had problems
with Legal Services.[168] There were, she stated, tensions between
the black women on welfare and the white, middle-class lawyers,
just as there had been between WROs and white organizers. Although
rarely conflict-free, these alliances, nevertheless, seem to have
flourished, and legal support appears to have been welcomed once
the rules of cooperation had been established.[169]

The coalition between NWRO and Legal Services survived even
as NWRO's resources declined and continued even after NWRO had to
close down its national headquarters. This may partly be explained
by the fact that Legal Services was a federally funded program, which,
despite attacks, continued to be renewed from year to year. The
basis for the partnership was not economic, but political. Another
possible reason for the stability of this alliance between the poor and
nonpoor was that each partner had its own independent agenda and interaction between the two groups was limited, thus lessening the potential conflicts.

While many of the welfare rights leaders were critical at times
of this support by the poverty lawyers, asserting that they tended to
dominate too much, middle-class participants and observers were
almost unanimous in their praise of Legal Services. Cloward and
Piven called the poverty lawyers the "lead actors in bringing about a
new welfare era . . . and creating a new 'poor' law."[170] Robert
Lekachman, the nationally known economist and supporter of the
cause of the poor, noted that "if we could choose to preserve one
strategy, that has succeeded, I would pick up one program—Legal
Services—which was capable of increasing justice wholesale." He

added in 1973 that "that is precisely why it was [being] eliminated.
. . . Legal Services never cost much money but caused a lot of trouble, especially the backup centers."[171] Elizabeth Wickenden, a noted
analyst of social-welfare policy and an advocate of welfare reform,
called Legal Services "the most successful instrument of social
change."[172] Others also suggested that the legal strategy ultimately
had greater impact for WROs and their members than any other strategy. Naomi Streshinsky stated that "close collaboration with Legal
Services has given welfare rights groups both a sense of power and
also an actual part in altering policies and procedures."[173] She
added that "in fact, many informants said that it would be difficult to
separate the effects of welfare rights pressure from those brought in
concert with poverty lawyers." Despite tensions, NWRO cooperated
with Legal Services lawyers at the local and national levels in challenging welfare laws and regulations and trying to use the courts to
bring about social change.

Historically, Wickenden noted that "welfare policies have rarely
been challenged in the courts by individuals or groups who feel their
rights had been abridged."[174] Generally, she added, groups had exerted "their influence at the point of legislative or administrative decision rather than seeking court review of such policy." In 1965
Wickenden encouraged lawyers to consider a "legal strategy" to bring
about change. At the same time, Charles Reich at Yale University
had just published a seminal essay on welfare law, highlighting the
violation of the rights of poor people who were dependent on welfare.[175]

The idea of free legal services for the poor had evolved in 1963
when the Vera Foundation was asked to devise a community legal-aid
service for MFY in Harlem.[176] Sparer, perhaps the foremost welfare rights lawyer in the country, the counsel for NWRO, and the
founder and first director of the Center on Social Welfare Policy and
Law at Columbia University, became the major strategist in developing class-action suits to reform the welfare system. The legal strategy against the welfare authorities complemented NWRO's street and
political strategies and lasted long after the first two had ended.
Through class-action suits against the government, several important
legal victories were won by NWRO and the poverty lawyers.

In 1965 Wright pointed out that "a new philosophy of social welfare" seemed to be emerging, which defined "dependency a condition
ordinarily beyond the control of the individual and seeks to establish
the status of welfare benefits as rights, based on the notion that
everyone is entitled to a share of the common wealth." Wright, endorsing this new orientation, said that it seemed justified since others
received "government subsidies and largess, not as a matter of privilege or charity but as a matter of entitlement."[177] Yet the poor per-

son, unlike other citizens, was "singled out for special, degrading supervision and control."[178] He felt that it was "absolutely essential" that political leaders and the public "cease to treat the welfare recipient as society's child and instead bring him back into the mainstream so that he and society can be relieved of the burdens of welfare." He placed part of the burden and the blame on the courts, accusing them of having a double standard—"one for aid to business and the farmer, and a very different one for welfare." Quoting Reich, he added: "There is a law for the poor and a law for the rest of us. Receipt of government aid by the poor carries a stigma, whereas receipt of government aid by the rest of the economy has been made into a virtue." He criticized the courts for "continu[ing] to apply ancient legal doctrines which merely compound the plight of the poverty-stricken" and urged his colleagues to "modif[y] or abando[n]" them.[179]

Copying the "sequential test case" strategy used by the NAACP Legal Defense Fund in the civil rights movement, Sparer and his colleagues set out to attempt to change the welfare system through constitutional tests of welfare laws and regulations.[180] In 1969, in Shapiro v. Thompson, the Supreme Court struck down the AFDC residency requirement.[181] As Sampson observed, "This case was remarkable because it represented the first time in more than thirty years of history of the AFDC program that a welfare recipient had been able to get a lawyer and get into a federal court on a constitutional issue!"[182] Residency requirements allowed the welfare authorities to deny benefits to poor people who had migrated recently from another state. The rationale for such laws was that it prevented states with high benefits from attracting large numbers of welfare recipients from states with much lower benefits. In the decision of Shapiro v. Thompson, states were no longer allowed, under the Constitution's guarantee of "equal protection of the laws," to distinguish between old and new residents.[183] One poverty lawyer suggested that this "decision . . . did more to alleviate poverty than anything else we had done."[184]

Other class-action suits and victories followed. By the summer of 1970, however, the tide began to turn. Sparer's strategy of sequential test cases had had as its principal objective getting the Supreme Court to "recogniz[e] the inadequacy of the welfare grant." The final step would be for the Supreme Court to read a "right to life" into the equal protection clause of the Fourteenth Amendment of the Constitution. This would then guarantee an adequate minimum payment for every needy individual in society.[185]

In less than three years, welfare rights and Legal Services had won major victories in the "man-in-the-house" decision (King v. Smith, 1968), the invalidation of residency requirements (Shapiro v. Thompson, 1969), and the right to a fair hearing before termination of benefits (Goldberg v. Kelly, 1970).[186] These decisions, with the Supreme Court siding with NWRO and its lawyers, "eliminated harsh substitute-parent rules, which denied welfare to a mother who . . . was caught with a man in her home after being abandoned by her husband" and also "ended the so-called 'midnight-raids' in which welfare investigators hunted after-hours for a man-in-the-house."[187]

In April 1970 the winning streak ended. The suit selected to establish a "bridge to a constitutional right to welfare" finally reached the Supreme Court, and the Legal Services lawyers lost. The Supreme Court ruled five to three that "it is not unconstitutional for states to set limits on the amount of welfare benefits that any family may collect."[188] The Dandridge v. Williams decision in 1970 was a grave setback for Legal Services lawyers and NWRO. The Court stated that "the Constitution does not empower this Court to second guess state officials charged with the difficult responsibility of allocating limited public welfare funds among the myriad of potential recipients."[189] Justices William O. Douglas, William J. Brennan, and Thurgood Marshall dissented, declaring that the benefit limit was unlawful under the Social Security statutes.

For Sparer and his colleagues and allies in NWRO, this was an unexpected blow, for the "right to life" concept was considered by the poverty lawyers as "the single most dramatic change in American society since the abolition of slavery." This concept, if accepted by the Court, would have "affected the lives of as many Americans" as did those of collective bargaining and desegregation upheld in earlier decades.[190] NWRO's reaction was a bitter one. Its leaders stated that the "Court had begun to turn its back on us." They explained to their constituency that the adoption of an "absolute maximum" on grants for poor women and their families meant that "new children would get no money at all."[191]

Samuel Krislov, in analyzing this decision, noted that it came "at a time when popular political support for welfare was manifestly on the wane." He added that "judicial action is not . . . effectively invoked to shore up an ebbing social tide."[192] What the OEO lawyers attempted to do was "to gain judicial acceptance of a doctrine for which popular support was fading," and this turned out to be "just another abortive attempt to retire 'into the judiciary as a stronghold.'" He conceded that the "doctrine of 'the right to life' was not suited to rapid judicial acceptance." He suggested that "major social change which is for temporary or permanent reasons unobtainable from the 'popular' branches of government may be endowed with greater legitimacy when made by the courts if the shift from majoritarian to normative judgment is spread out over time."[193] NWRO and OEO lawyers, he felt, had moved too fast. After 1970 the legal victories for NWRO and the movement of poor women declined.

In 1971 NWRO and Legal Services lawyers had another legal setback. The Wyman v. James decision, a six to three ruling, stated that "welfare officials could insist on the right to inspect recipients' homes and cut off aid to those who refused."[194] The Court recommended that the caseworker be seen not as a sleuth but as a friend. More significantly, it reestablished and reaffirmed the concept of welfare as public charity and not as a right. The public, said Justice Harry Blackmun, as a provider to the poor, "rightly expects" to know how "charitable funds are utilized, and put to work." Again, in this decision, Justices Douglas, Marshall, and Brennan dissented, with Douglas stating that this resulted in the use of government largess to "buy up constitutional rights from poor people."

NWRO once again decried this as a violation of the privacy of poor people—and especially that of women and children—calling the decision "patronizing and insulting to welfare recipients."[195] Bitterly, NWRO leaders suggested that this decision would be "hailed as a victory for anti-welfare forces." Justice Douglas, criticizing the decision, stated that "it is a strange law indeed which safeguards the businessman [who receives government subsidies] at his place of work from warrantless searches, but will not do the same thing for a mother in her home."[196] Underlying his opinion was the unequal treatment of poor women based on their class and gender within the welfare system. For this group, dependency meant forfeiting privacy in their lives.

Others publicized their objections to this ruling. Attorneys on the case stated in a letter to the New York Times that "no other group of citizens is asked to sacrifice privacy," but that now the Supreme Court was ruling "that welfare recipients [and, more specifically, AFDC women] are to be treated differently." They concluded that "the opinion marks the beginning of a frightening era in the Court and in the country."[197]

Over the years, the structure of the Court changed. The Warren Court, in operation from 1953 to 1969, was perceived by NWRO and advocates of the poor as "the ultimate recourse of the disadvantaged and of minorities treated by narrow-minded and legalistic lower court judges."[198] The Burger Court, which succeeded the Warren Court, changed structurally and ideologically, as five seats were filled by Republican presidents. President Nixon appointed those of Chief Justice Warren E. Burger (1969), Justice Blackmun (1970), Justice Lewis F. Powell, Jr., (1971), and Justice William Rehnquist (1971). President Ford appointed Justice John Paul Stevens (1975). Critics of the Burger Court in the 1970s argued that it was "far removed from the egalitarian and activist Warren Court . . . in the 1960's."[199]

For poor women and their allies, the Legal Services lawyers, this apparent shift to the right by the welfare adjudicators after 1970

was "bad news."[200] With the loss of the appeal on the constitution-
ality of the "right to welfare," followed by the reversal on the "rights
to privacy" for recipients, the trend appeared to be increasingly less
favorable toward poor women. Setbacks for welfare reform in the
high Court in the United States tightened the social controls and raised
the risks of protest, thus dampening the mobilization of poor women.

As Legal Services' victories proliferated in the late 1960s,
pressures began to mount within the Nixon administration to disband
the program. Congresswoman Edith Green pointed out in 1973 that
"the [Legal Services] 'backup centers' were the cutting edge of social
change in the country."[201] This had not been the intent of the original
legislation, according to her. In a lengthy congressional session, the
legislators in Washington voted to "limi[t] the scope of the program
and the activities of its lawyers." They also restricted its political
activities and barred Legal Services from lobbying before legislative
bodies.[202] The most drastic attempt was a move to eliminate the research "backup centers" that specialized in poverty law and disseminated information to NWRO and its FWRO network. The Center for
Social Welfare Policy and Law in New York was a central source for
policy analysis used by middle-class activists and supporters as well
as NWRO leaders. While it was not closed down, its activities were
curtailed.

The entire program of Legal Services, in fact, was restructured
and its "activism" restricted in the 1970s. Levitan points out that
"in its brief, but stormy, history, the legal services program made
friends among the poor and disenfranchised, but made many enemies
in the established power bases."[203] In place of Legal Services in
OEO, the quasi-public and independent Legal Services Corporation
was established. This new structure "provided more direction from
the state and national levels." Restraints were placed on the actions
of the Legal Services Corporation and its field offices and their personnel throughout the country. Legal Services could no longer sue
on behalf of its clients in class-action suits, and political activism
by Legal Services lawyers was banned. Representation of the poor
on the Legal Services Board was excluded. The resulting outcry by
many of WRO's liberal supporters, and poor women's organizations,
resulted in the revitalization of the National Clients Council in 1976
as an advisory arm of the Legal Services Corporation.

Conflicts, inherent in any coalition (especially in the alliances
of unlike partners), were, as we have discussed, a source of tension
in the partnerships between poor women and Legal Services lawyers.
The representatives of the law, historically viewed as "the enemy"
by the poor, were not readily accepted with trust and open arms.
While Legal Services accomplished much in a short period to change
some of these negative feelings, tensions between the welfare rights

women and the middle-class lawyers did not fully disappear. This was reflected, for instance, in 1977, as the National Clients Council gained momentum, while the National Welfare Rights movement remained splintered and becalmed. Some WRO leaders felt that these close ties with the federal government tended to inhibit, rather than facilitate, the chances of reviving their national movement. Others, however, felt that participation in the National Clients Council presented an opportunity to establish a direct link with the "power people in Washington."[204] One WRO member suggested that it was important for "WRO leaders to be in the forefront of what's going on at the national level through their close ties with the Legal Services Corporation."[205] She did not see the National Clients Council as a threat to the remobilization of NWRO. In fact, she added, the council might facilitate the reorganization of poor women and provide the basis for renewed action on all fronts.

In some parts of the country, there were signs by 1977 of competition between the rising National Clients Council and the becalmed welfare rights movement. At a WRO convention in Little Rock that year, participants criticized the council for running a conference concurrently with the meeting organized by the welfare rights women. Some felt that the council undermined the renewed effort of WRO women to revitalize their national movement. They said that Legal Services was absorbing members and leaders into a new structure that had many more resources available to offer as incentives than did the remaining, uncoordinated WRO groups in the country. Consequently, the council was viewed by some as a competing group that had emerged out of the Legal Services program. While this may, in fact, have been the case, the reality was that, by the end of the 1970s, there did not seem to be the necessary support among the poor women and their nonpoor allies for rebirth of the movement.

Over the many years of the welfare reform struggle, NWRO's alliance with Legal Services contributed to the liberalization of the welfare laws and regulations, especially with the momentous series of class-action suits and favorable decisions in the Supreme Court.[206] After 1970 the victories in the Court and in the legislative arena had declined and seriously dampened this strategy for welfare reform. Many poverty lawyers, because of the changed nature and actions of the Supreme Court, had begun to avoid it and to move to state courts and legislatures to advance the cause of their clients.[207] The legal strategy within the Supreme Court had, for a short period, achieved remarkable benefits for the poverty population as a whole, and the Legal Services program had undergirded the welfare rights movement throughout the country.

While it is true that none of the strategies adopted by NWRO (the street, political, and legal strategies) had succeeded in bringing about NWRO's goal of a guaranteed income for poor people, the welfare rights movement had, in less than ten years, brought about the transfer of millions of dollars of public monies to the poor. These monies might never have reached them without a combination of all of these actions. Martin and Rein point out that "participation, litigation, political protest are each weak in isolation, but together can provide a framework of arguments and pressures sympathetic to reform."[208]

In sum, the external conflict of NWRO and its allies with the welfare administrators, legislators, and adjudicators in the mid-1960s and 1970s mobilized and transferred resources not only to the movement organization of poor women but also to the poor in general. Through protest in the streets and in the welfare offices, and through "media-staging" for the press and increased political visibility, the movement expanded its membership base, enlisted supporters, and for a few years became recognized as the legitimate representative of poor people and, more specifically, of women on AFDC.

By 1972 the political conditions had changed dramatically. The mood and policies of the welfare authorities and political leaders in the federal and state governments gradually became more restrictive in terms of the demands of the black and poor. Numerous social controls were instituted. Flat grants replaced the more flexible special benefits allotments. States instituted cutbacks. "Workfare," not "welfare," became the catchword of the dominant leaders and the public in general. Fraud squads proliferated. In the process of waging the struggle against FAP, NWRO exhausted all its resources. Its grass-roots base withered, partially out of neglect. Wiley, in disagreement with the women leaders, resigned and created a competing movement organization, MEJ. Most liberal allies vanished, looking for new partners to support their redefined goals for economic justice.

Under the Republican administrations in the first half of the 1970s, the War on Poverty, which had provided numerous resources for NWRO, was dismantled and replaced with revenue-sharing block grants to the states. By the early 1970s, the antiwelfare rhetoric of political leaders dominated the domestic political scene and helped to turn the tide against NWRO. For a short period, the hopes of welfare rights activists were raised with the victory at the polls of the Carter administration, which promised welfare reform.* After a

---

*In 1979 President Carter appointed a new secretary of HEW, Patricia Harris, the first woman and first black to serve in this post. In many ways, her initial statements about the thrust of her department seemed to mesh with the long-espoused goals of the welfare

flurry of renewed interest by the new president and Congress in the late 1970s, the political issue of welfare reform had once again receded to the background by 1980. During the 1980 presidential elections, the welfare issue remained muted. Inflation and the foreign crises in Iran and Afghanistan dominated the headlines and the concerns of the public. Whereas the 1960s had been a time of affluence in terms of low unemployment and inflation rates, the 1970s had been hit by the worst recession since the Great Depression of the 1930s. Deteriorating economic conditions, including rising inflation and unemployment, and a general pessimism about the future outlook of the country marked the beginning of the 1980s. The emerging themes seemed to emphasize scarcity, conservation, and a balanced budget within the governing sector. Economic and political crises had thus cast a shadow over the possibility of any significant income redistribution and assistance for the poor in the coming decade, especially with the landslide victory of Ronald Reagan and other conservatives in the 1980 elections.

By then little remained of the National Welfare Rights movement. A few scattered groups continued in some parts of the country, with most of the activity at the local level. Law suits were still being filed on the behalf of poor people and WROs by the Legal Services lawyers, mainly with the support of the Center for Social Welfare Policy and Law. The three branches of government, with some exceptions, seemed at best frustrated and at worst openly hostile toward welfare reform and the burden of its escalating costs. Aside from sporadic racial flareups, the cities remained mostly quiet.[209] Liberals in the white churches were silent, while conservatives were gaining new power and visibility through mobilization and political action. Civil rights groups were mobilizing for more jobs and organizational survival in an increasingly conservative climate. Feminists, struggling against a backlash, were concentrating most of their resources on a final attempt to gain passage of the ERA. Black feminists were only in the initial stages of becoming a national movement. Welfare rights, as a protest of poor women, lay fragmented, but still alive, although with little support from any sector.

---

rights women. She stated that she hoped "that the American people will learn to think of welfare, not in patronizing terms of charity and dependence, but in terms of essential income security available to all of us who may be unlucky at some time in our lives." Her aim was "to move this country from the soul-destroying concept of welfare . . . toward a concept of common well-being for all in need" (Martin Tolchin, "Mrs. Harris to Seek Reconciliation of Blacks and Jews," New York Times, August 30, 1979). Her term was brief because Carter was defeated by Ronald Reagan in the November 1980 presidential election.

The 1970s, unlike the turbulent 1960s, had come to be defined as the "Me" decade. Some were predicting a new direction for the 1980s, a shift from the polarization of the 1960s and the narcissism of the 1970s to increased social consciousness and action based on enlightened self-interest in the 1980s.[210] Others were not so optomistic, given the political and economic conditions.[211] Thus, changes in the political environment had contributed to NWRO's rise and fall and, more specifically, its mobilization and subsequent loss of needed resources.

NOTES

1. Frances Fox Piven and Richard A. Cloward, Regulating the Poor: The Functions of Public Welfare (New York: Pantheon Books, 1971), p. xiii.

2. Joe R. Feagin, Subordinating the Poor: Welfare and American Beliefs (Englewood Cliffs, N.J.: Prentice-Hall, 1975), p. 1. For an excellent history of social welfare, see also Walter I. Traetner, From Poor Law to Welfare State (New York: Free Press, 1974).

3. Social Security Act of 1935, 42 U.S.C., Section 301 et seq. (1970).

4. Feagin, Subordinating the Poor, p. 60.

5. AFDC-UP stands for Aid to Families with Dependent Children with Unemployed Parent, but only fathers are included in the unemployed category. The public assistance laws were changed in 1961 to include financial support for intact families in which the male was present but unemployed—AFDC-UP—but it never gained wide acceptance either by the states or by men. Only 25 of the states had adopted this voluntary program by 1969. Of the 1 million families expected to apply for help, there were never any more than 80,000 in this program. See Mildred Rein, Conflicting Aims in AFDC-UP (Boston: Social Welfare Regional Research Institute, 1972). There were objections from various sectors to placing males into dependency statuses. Men were socialized to be independent and the breadwinners within the family structure. The National Conference of Catholic Charities, for example, criticized the idea of placing men in "the much maligned category of relief recipient." The stigma of dependency for men, however, was one of the factors that inhibited the enrollment and undermined the "success" of this social policy. Mildred Rein adds:

> Aside from times of very high unemployment [when they
> applied in huge numbers] . . . factors such as the stigma
> of public assistance and the need to sacrifice almost all

their resources prevented many from use of UP to any significant extent. Those who took advantage of UP were only
a very small proportion of the unemployed men in the population who were fathers of families.

6. Traetner, Welfare State, p. 240.

7. Irving Louis Horowitz, ed., Equity, Income, and Policy:
Comparative Studies in Three Worlds of Development (New York:
Praeger, 1977), p. 23.

8. Traetner, Welfare State, p. 240.

9. Ibid., p. 241.

10. Ibid., p. 242.

11. Ibid.

12. Ibid.

13. Ibid.

14. Rein, Conflicting Aims in AFDC-UP, p. 1.

15. Alfred J. Kahn, Studies in Social Policy and Planning (New
York: Russell Sage Foundation, 1969), p. 114.

16. In the introduction to Susan Sheehan's The Welfare Mother
(Boston: Houghton Mifflin, 1976), Michael Harrington writes, "And,
as far as I can figure out, it was in response to the renewed interest
generated by the [Dwight] MacDonald review [in the New Yorker] that
John F. Kennedy borrowed a copy of The Other America from Walter
Heller, read some other analyses, and decided to launch his attack
on poverty." See also, Peter Marris and Martin Rein, Dilemmas of
Social Reform: Poverty and Community Action in the United States,
2d ed. (Chicago: Aldine, 1973), p. 245.

17. Traetner, Welfare State, p. 253.

18. Ibid., pp. 253-54.

19. Horowitz, Equity, Income, and Policy, pp. 2-3.

20. Ibid., p. 23.

21. Alvin L. Schorr, Explorations in Social Policy (New York:
Basic Books, 1968), p. 27.

22. Goals of the National Welfare Rights Organization, NOW!,
August 21, 1968.

23. Horowitz, Equity, Income, and Policy, p. 23; Michael
Useem, Protest Movements in America (Indianapolis: Bobbs-Merrill,
1975), p. 48.

24. Larry A. Jackson and William A. Johnson, Protest by the
Poor: The Welfare Rights Movement in New York City (New York:
Rand Corporation, 1973), p. 150. These authors report that "from
the beginning, there was disagreement within the MFY over the appropriate tactics to be used in forcing the welfare department to implement
desired reforms as quickly as possible." They add that there were
two approaches, namely, the "traditional professional social-work
approach and a more militant disruptive style of protest." The former

emphasized orderly requests and "negotiations between client leaders MFY staff, and the Department of Social Services." (Note the "two against one" advocacy model.) It rejected "disruption of the local welfare centers." The other approach was to "flood" one welfare center with requests for winter clothing and "generate administrative chaos." In this way, a "crisis situation would be created." The basic principle was that of a "strike." A strike withholds "production, services, labor." Welfare clients "could curtail welfare services by legitimately using services." The hoped-for result was a contract between a "welfare union" of clients and the welfare department, which would recognize this "union" as the "sole bargaining agent" for these city clients. Eventually, they envisioned that this movement would expand and that a "national welfare clients union" would emerge.

25. Richard A. Cloward and Frances Fox Piven, "The Weight of the Poor: A Strategy to End Poverty," The Nation, May 2, 1966, reprint.

26. Gilbert Y. Steiner, The State of Welfare (Washington, D.C.: Brookings Institution, 1971), pp. 239-40.

27. Jackson and Johnson, Protest by the Poor, p. 152; Useem, Protest Movements in America, p. 48.

28. "Strategy of Crisis: A Dialogue," American Child 48 (Summer 1966): 26-27.

29. Mancur Olson, Jr., The Logic of Collective Action: Public Goods and the Theory of Groups (Cambridge, Mass.: Harvard University Press, 1965), p. 51.

30. Steiner, State of Welfare, p. 313.

31. Jackson and Johnson, Protest by the Poor, p. 154.

32. Ibid., p. 156.

33. William Howard Whitaker, "The Determinants of Social Movement Success: A Study of the National Welfare Rights Organization" (Ph.D. diss., Brandeis University, 1970), p. 234.

34. Ibid. See also Lawrence Neil Bailis, Bread or Justice: Grassroots Organizing in the Welfare Rights Movement (Lexington, Mass.: D. C. Heath, 1974), chap. 3.

35. Personal interview no. 269 at the Essex County Welfare Department, N.J., December 9, 1971; Jackson and Johnson, Protest by the Poor, p. 62.

36. Whitaker, "Social Movement Success," p. 238.

37. Steiner, State of Welfare, pp. 297-98.

38. Sar A. Levitan and Robert Taggart, The Promise of Greatness (Cambridge, Mass.: Harvard University Press, 1976), p. 35.

39. Whitaker, "Social Movement Success," pp. 242-43.

40. Jackson and Johnson, Protest by the Poor, pp. 238, 283.

41. Ibid., p. 208.

42. Hobart A. Burch, "Conversations with George Wiley," Journal of Social Issues, November/December 1970, p. 8.

43. Ibid.

44. Susan Hertz, "The Politics of the Welfare Mothers Movement: A Case Study," Signs 2 (Spring 1977): 600-1.

45. Whitaker, "Social Movement Success," pp. 242-43.

46. Jackson and Johnson, Protest by the Poor, p. 72.

47. James Welsh, "Poor Have New Outlook," Star Ledger (Newark, N.J.), November 3, 1970.

48. Ibid.

49. Ibid.

50. Steiner, State of Welfare, p. 298.

51. "State Legislatures Cut Welfare Budgets," NOW! 2 (May 1969).

52. Field notes, April 17, 1973.

53. Richard Rogin, "Now It's Welfare Lib," New York Times Magazine, September 27, 1970, p. 73.

54. Welfare Fighter, March 1970 and November 1971.

55. George Wiley, "Director's Corner," Welfare Fighter, December/January 1971, p. 10.

56. See Whitaker, "Social Movement Success," p. 175, who states that the "flat grant organizing document was prepared by Hulbert James, then of New York, and openly called for closing down welfare offices, disruption, harassment and increased militancy. It was widely quoted in newspaper attacks around the country.

57. "Bayonets Against Mothers in Madison," Welfare Fighter 1 (October 1969). See also Jackson and Johnson, Protest by the Poor, p. 66.

58. Jackson and Johnson, Protest by the Poor, p. 66.

59. Naomi Streshinsky, "Welfare Rights Organizations and Public Welfare Systems: An Interaction Study" (D.S.W. diss., University of California at Berkeley, 1970). Streshinsky describes the activity of the WROs in California against the welfare department and the reactions of the welfare department to this outside agitation in the late 1960s.

60. Field notes, April 17, 1973.

61. Steiner, State of Welfare, p. 300.

62. Sylvia Law, "Operation Nevada: Crisis in Welfare," Welfare Law News, Center for Social Welfare Policy and Law, New York, November 1972, pp. 3-5. This section is based on this article and on the "Operation Nevada" report of NWRO, dated February 7, 1971.

63. Ibid.

64. Field notes, September 29, 1972.

65. Law, "Operation Nevada."

66. Frances Fox Piven and Richard A. Cloward, "A Movement on Welfare," New York Times, August 31, 1973.

67. Field notes, workshop at the 1971 NWRO Convention, Providence, R.I., July 1971.

68. Ibid.

69. Ibid.

70. Jackson and Johnson, Protest by the Poor, pp. 70-71.

71. Rogin, "Now It's Welfare Lib," p. 76.

72. Streshinsky, "Welfare Rights Organizations."

73. Field notes, April 17, 1973.

74. Jackson and Johnson, Protest by the Poor, pp. 70-71.

75. Whitaker, "Social Movement Success," p. 177. See also Streshinsky, "Welfare Rights Organizations," p. 99; "Insights of a Welfare Mother," Journal of Social Issues, January/February 1971, p. 23, reprint.

76. Jackson and Johnson, Protest by the Poor, pp. 70-71.

77. Rogin, "Now It's Welfare Lib," p. 75; Jackson and Johnson, Protest by the Poor, p. 72.

78. Rogin, "Now It's Welfare Lib," p. 76.

79. Whitaker, "Social Movement Success," pp. 163, 177.

80. Ibid.

81. "Client Health Committee Meets," Welfare Fighter, November 1969; Rogin, "Now It's Welfare Lib," p. 76.

82. Statement by George Wiley, prepared for delivery at the Institute for Black Elected Officials, Washington, D.C., September 13, 1969; "NCC's Meet in Atlanta," Welfare Fighter, November 1970; speech by Beulah Sanders before the National Council of Churches, Houston, Tex., December 1972, pp. 1-7.

83. Memorandum from D. . . . L. . . . to "All Center Staff," NWRO Legal Committee, re the NWRO committee meeting with HEW Secretary Weinberger, n.d. (postmarked envelope, April 23, 1973).

84. Field notes, May 1, 1973.

85. Field notes, April 17, 1973.

86. Ibid.

87. Field notes, Spetember 29, 1972; "They Said It Couldn't Be Done," Welfare Reporter, WROAC, Pittsburgh, Pa., April 1977.

88. Burch, "Conversations with George Wiley."

89. Field notes, November 19, 1973.

90. Field notes, August 15, 1975.

91. Field notes, 1974 NWRO Convention, St. Louis, Mo., July 12, 1974.

92. "Estimated Budget 1973," memorandum from Don Snider of Labor Caucus, February/March 1973.

93. The Organizer, the National Caucus of Labor Committees, February 1973.

94. Taped interview no. 214, New York, 1974.

95. There were some accounts in the press about this. See "Welfare Rights Dissidents F[or]m Separate Committee," New York

Times, March 13, 1973; "Welfare Group Seeks Unity for Fight Ahead," Star Ledger (Newark, N.J.), March 15, 1973; Joey Johnson, "Labor Committee Conference Blasted as 'Fraud' by WRO," Philadelphia Tribune, April 7, 1973; Pamela Haynes, "Right On," Philadelphia Tribune, April 3, 1973. Data were collected from fieldwork, interviews, as well as material in the Labor Caucus memorandums and newsletters received in 1971, 1972, 1973. Some Friends of WRO and leaders of NWRO "believed that this attack by the Labor Caucus [was] really an infiltration by the CIA or FBI. . . . They [were] very seriously out to undermine NWRO" (Field notes, Buffalo, N.Y., May 1, 1973.)

96. Sheila Rule, "Relief Recipients Rally in Albany for Aid Increase," New York Times, March 15, 1979. See also Welfare Righter, March 1980, which states that Frankie Jeter, WROAC chair, and the last woman to head NWRO, was arrested in demonstrations against the welfare authorities.

97. Taped interview no. 205, New York City, 1974.

98. Memorandum from Interfaith Strategy Consultation for Welfare Reform, Washington, D.C., February 23, 1973.

99. Letter from Frankie Jeter, chair of WROAC and chair of NWRO, n.d. (received middle of July 1975).

100. Welfare Fighter, December 1969, pp. 4-5.

101. James Welsh, "Welfare Reform: Born, August 8, 1969; Died, October 4, 1972," New York Times Magazine, January 7, 1973, p. 4.

102. Daniel Patrick Moynihan, The Politics of a Guaranteed Income: The Nixon Administration and the Family Assistance Plan (New York: Random House, 1973), p. 17.

103. Ibid., pp. 10-11.

104. Ibid., p. 355.

105. Peter Russell and Leonard Ross, "The Politics of the Guaranteed Income," the New York Times Book Review, January 14, 1973, p. 1.

106. Ibid.

107. Rogin, "Now It's Welfare Lib."

108. David Hapgood, "Beyond Welfare," Washington Monthly, May 1970, reprint.

109. "Experts and the Average Citizen View Welfare Plans," New York Times, August 16, 1969. See also the remarks of Michael Harrington, Wilbur Cohen, Richard Cloward, Edward Sparer, Carl Rachlin, and "an average taxpayer."

110. New York Times, October 13, 1969.

111. William May, "Group Urges Change in Nixon Welfare Plan," Evening Star (Newark, N.J.), March 18, 1970.

112. New York Times, August 16, 1969. Remarks by Richard Cloward, Edward Sparer, and Carl Rachlin in this paragraph.

113. Johnnie Tillmon, "Welfare Is a Women's Issue," The First Ms. Reader, ed. Francine Klageburn (New York: Warner Books, 1973), pp. 57, 114. This entire section on Johnnie Tillmon's opinions is based on this article.

114. "Sanders Testifies Before the House," Welfare Fighter, November 1969. The article states that George Wiley, Beulah Sanders, and Carl Rachlin, NWRO's general counsel, testified against the bill before the House Ways and Means Committee on October 27, 1969. See the NWRO report, "Support and Political Activity," submitted without date in June 1970 to the WPT, p. 5.

115. Burch, "Conversations with George Wiley," pp. 9-10.

116. Tillmon, "Welfare Is a Woman's Issue."

117. William May, "Group Urges Change in the Nixon Welfare Plan," Evening Star (Newark, N.J.), March 18, 1970.

118. The principal guaranteed income plans were introduced by Nixon, Ribicoff, Fraser, Harris, and NWRO.

119. Taped interview no. 214, 1974.

120. Jodie T. Allen, Perspectives on Income Maintenance: Where Do We Go From Here and How Far? (Washington, D.C.: Urban Institute, 1972), pp. 3-4. She states that NWRO's $5,500 plan would have cost $71 billion and would have included 37 million families and 132 million people in 1972.

121. Moynihan, Guaranteed Income, p. 453.

122. Ibid., pp. 296-302, argues that "the major religious organizations . . . welcomed the FAP proposal." He adds further, "as time passed, this unity fractured as Protestant support began to give way to doubts." On Spetember 12, 1969, the National Council of Churches General Board "adopted a resolution welcoming the [FAP] proposal." The Catholic response was "warmer." Moynihan says the National Conference of Catholic Charities "hailed the event and called on Catholics to work hard for enactment of the legislation." The U.S. Catholic Conference in April 1970 "urged the passage of the bill" asking, nonetheless, that the $1,600 "be increased." Later, however, "Protestant support steadily eroded until it was understood in Washington that the National Council did not favor FAP."

123. Paul Sherry, Hobart Burch, and Mel Turner, "UCC/NWRO," in Voluntarism in America's Future (Washington, D.C.: Center for Voluntary Society, 1972), p. 42.

124. Ibid.

125. Welfare Fighter, November 1971.

126. Ibid.

127. "Congress Kills FAP," Welfare Fighter, October 1972.

128. Ibid.

129. McGovern had been politically hurt in the 1972 presidential campaign when he had openly come out for a guaranteed income of

$1,000 per person, or $4,000 for a family of four in the McGovern/ Humphrey debates. Senator McGovern had, however, supported NWRO visibly at NWRO's 1971 and 1972 conventions and had introduced NWRO's guaranteed income bill in 1971.

130. Welfare Fighter, November 1972.

131. Memorandum from Audrey Colom and John Kinney, "FAP Is Not Dead: What Can We Do?" October 12, 1972.

132. Ibid.

133. Field notes, March 8, 1973.

134. William F. Farrell, "Welfare Reforms Near a Standstill," New York Times, January 18, 1976. Mitchell Ginsberg, speaking about the welfare rights movement, said, "We're kind of sick and tired of the problem."

135. Mitchell I. Ginsberg and Norman V. Lourie, "The Current Status of the Human Services," Public Welfare, Summer 1974, p. 28, reprint.

136. Irving Louis Horowitz and James Everett Katz, Social Science and Public Policy in the United States (New York: Praeger, 1975), p. 138.

137. Ernest Holsendolph, "Welfare Rolls Stable but Bill Soars," New York Times, January 4, 1976; "Issues: '76 Welfare," New York Times, April 2, 1976; Farrell, "Welfare Reform Near a Standstill"; Elizabeth Wickenden, Washington Notes #22 (National Voluntary Health and Social Welfare Organization), 1976.

138. David E. Rosenbaum, "Carter Asks New Welfare System with Emphasis on Required Work, New York Could Save $527 Million," New York Times, August 7, 1977; "Text of White House Message to Congress on Proposal to Overhaul Welfare System," New York Times, August 7, 1977; Robert Reinhold, "Criticism Deflected by White House Plan," New York Times, August 7, 1977; Elizabeth Wickenden, Washington Notes #23, March 31, 1977, mimeographed report.

139. Rosenbaum, "Carter Asks New Welfare System."

140. Welfare Reform and the 95th Congress (Washington, D.C.: American Public Welfare Association, 1978), p. 3.

141. "The Good, the Best, and Welfare Reform," New York Times, August 9, 1977.

142. Edward C. Burks, "Moynihan Terms President's Plan on Relief System 'Disappointing,'" New York Times, October 1, 1977.

143. Ibid.

144. Reinhold, "White House Plan."

145. Roger Wilkins, "Welfare Reform: So Much Talk, So Little Action," New York Times, December 12, 1977.

146. Reinhold, "White House Plan."

147. Field notes, Little Rock, Ark., August 6, 1977.

148. Faith Evans, "The Carter JIP Proposals: A Step Back-wards," in Better Jobs and Income? (New York: United Church of Christ Commission for Racial Justice, 1977).

149. "Administration's Welfare Reform Plan," memorandum to Welfare Specialists #77/48, Center on Social Welfare Policy and Law, August 23, 1977, pp. 2, 5, and 25.

150. Toni Carabillo, "'Promises, Promises': A NOW Observer Assesses the Carter Presidency," Do It NOW 10 (September/October 1977): 13.

151. "Better Jobs & Income: A Series of Grassroots Conferences to Explore the Impact of the Carter Welfare Reform Proposals—And Develop a Response." MEJ, Washington, D.C., n.d. (received October 11, 1977), mimeographed.

152. Bert DeLeeuw and Madeline Adamson, "What to Do about Welfare Reform," Just Economics 5 (October 1977): 7.

153. "Program on Welfare Rights—1978-80," Health and Welfare Working Group, National Council of Churches, Division of Church and Society, n.d., pp. 1-4.

154. Field notes, March–September 1978.

155. "Planning Information for Employment Opportunities Pilot Program: Welfare Reform Demonstrations," U.S., Department of Labor, August 1, 1978, pp. 1, 11. The "principal earner" was de-fined as the "adult in the household who had the largest earned income during the 6-month period preceding application."

156. Steven R. Weisman, "Clash Between Carter and Moynihan Slows Welfare Reform Plan," New York Times, April 1, 1979. This entire discussion is based on this article. See also "Current Devel-opments in Federal Welfare Legislation," in Memorandum to Welfare Specialists (Washington, D.C.: Center on Social Welfare Policy and Law, 1979).

157. "Picketers Hit Hiring by Eastern Airlines," Boston Globe, November 28, 1978; "20 Cities Protest Eastern Job Shutout," Eastern Boston Community News, December 5, 1978; attachments to letter from Fair Welfare, Boston, Mass., January 12, 1979; "Jobs and Jus-tice," Social Policy, November/December 1978, p. 58; "Suit by a Welfare Group Charges New York Grants are Inadequate," New York Times, March 27, 1979; Welfare Righter, March 1980.

158. Sar A. Levitan, Programs in Aid of the Poor, 3d ed. (Bal-timore: Johns Hopkins University Press, 1976), pp. 81-82.

159. J. Skelly Wright, "The Courts Have Failed the Poor," New York Times Magazine, March 9, 1969, p. 26.

160. Carl Patrick McCarthy, "The Consequences of Legal Advo-cacy: OEO's Lawyers and the Poor" (Ph.D. diss., University of California at Berkeley, 1974), quoting from Richard Blumenthal and Mark Soler, "Legal Services Corporation: Curtailing Political Inter-vention," Yale Law Journal 81 (December 1971): 231-86.

161. Robert Plotnick and Felicity Skidmore, Progress Against Poverty (New York: Academic Press, 1975), p. 8.

162. Memorandum from Center on Social Welfare Policy and Law, January 13, 1976.

163. "Position Announcement," memorandum from the Legal Service Corporation announcing job vacancy for LSC president, Washington, D.C., February 29, 1979.

164. Rogin, "Now It's Welfare Lib," p. 31; Jackson and Johnson, Protest by the Poor, p. 39; Legal Services Corporation memorandum, February 27, 1979.

165. Field notes on the speech given by Robert Lekachman at the "Convocation of Conscience," Washington, D.C., May 9, 1973.

166. Streshinsky, "Welfare Rights Organizations," p. 102.

167. Taped interview with Johnnie Tillmon, July 1974.

168. Field notes, August 15, 1975.

169. Participant observation in New Jersey and conversations with WRO members at NWRO meetings.

170. Rogin, "Now It's Welfare Lib," p. 31.

171. Field notes, Washington, D.C., May 9, 1973.

172. Field notes, February 22, 1973.

173. Streshinsky, "Welfare Rights Organizations," pp. 102, 184.

174. Elizabeth Wickenden, Poverty and Law: The Constitutional Rights of Assistance Recipients (New York: National Assembly for Social Welfare and Development, 1965), p. 6 (mimeographed).

175. Charles A. Reich, "Individual Rights and Social Welfare: The Emerging Legal Issues," Yale Law Journal 74 (June 1965): 1245-57.

176. Samuel Krislov, "The OEO Lawyers Fail to Constitutional-ize a Right to Welfare: A Study in the Uses and Limits of the Judicial Process," Minnesota Law Review 58 (1973): 215-16.

177. Wright, "Courts Have Failed the Poor," p. 110.

178. Ibid., p. 112.

179. Ibid., p. 250.

180. Krislov, "OEO Lawyers Fail," pp. 222-23.

181. U.S., Commission on Civil Rights, Women and Poverty (Chicago: Allied Printing, 1974), p. 61.

182. Timothy Sampson, Welfare: A Handbook for Friend and Foe (Philadelphia: Pilgrim Press, 1972), p. 126.

183. "Justices to Weigh Curb on Welfare," New York Times, January 16, 1968.

184. "State Residency Regulations Face Test in Supreme Court," Newark Evening News, February 21, 1971. See also Krislov, "OEO Lawyers Fail," p. 222; "Welfare Residency Rule Voided," Newark Evening News, April 12, 1969; "Welfare and the Law," NOW! (May 1969).

185. Mark R. Arnold, "The Good War That Might Have Been," New York Times Magazine, September 29, 1974; Krislov, "OEO Lawyers Fail," pp. 223-25. Also see Israel Shenker, "Guarantee of 'Right to Live' is Urged," New York Times.

186. U.S., Commission on Civil Rights, Women and Poverty. See also idem, Women Still in Poverty; U.S., Joint Economic Committee, Subcommittee on Economic Growth and Stabilization, American Women Workers in a Full Employment Economy, 95th Cong., 1st sess., September 15, 1977.

187. Rogin, "Now It's Welfare Lib," pp. 31, 73.

188. Krislov, "OEO Lawyers Fail," p. 228. Also see "Welfare Recipients Set Back by Court," Newark Evening News, April 7, 1970.

189. "High Court Backs a Family Ceiling for Welfare Aid," New York Times, April 7, 1970.

190. Krislov, "OEO Lawyers Fail," p. 228.

191. "Know Your Welfare Rights," Welfare Fighter, April 1970.

192. Krislov, "OEO Lawyers Fail," pp. 236-37.

193. Ibid.

194. Francis X. Cline, "Welfare Official Rules Out 'Raids,'" New York Times, January 14, 1971.

195. "Supreme Court Decision," Welfare Righter, January 1971.

196. "High Court Rules Welfare Homes May be Inspected," New York Times, January 13, 1971.

197. "Welfare vs. Human Dignity," New York Times, February 5, 1971, (letter to the editor by Jonathan Weiss, David Gilman, Christopher Clancy). See also Charles A. Reich, "Midnight Welfare Searches and the Social Security Act," Yale Law Review 72 (June 1963): reprint.

198. Nathan Lewin, "Avoiding the Supreme Court," New York Times Magazine, October 17, 1976, p. 31.

199. Lesley Oelsner, "Carter Will Be Able to Influence High Court Despite Nixon Legacy," New York Times, November 30, 1976. For various articles on opinions about changes in attitudes and actions of the Burger Court, see Aryeh Neier, "Liberties Diminished during 1976," Civil Liberties, January 1977, special issues; Lewin, "Avoiding the Supreme Court"; Warren Weaver, Jr., "4 Nixon Justices Dominate Decisions," New York Times, July 3, 1975; William K. Stevens, "The Professor's Computer Foretells Court's Dealings," New York Times, July 26, 1974 (This is a study by a professor of Michigan State University evaluating the Supreme Court justices' decisions based on three criteria: freedom, equality, and New Deal Economics. On his scale, Justices Douglas, Brennan, and Marshall [in that order] received the highest ratings in the Supreme Court decisions.); Lesley Oelsner, "Justices Back Tomorrow to Face Abortion and Death Penalty

Issues," New York Times, October 3, 1976; Warren Weaver, Jr.,
"Nixon's Appointees to High Court Voting Less as a Bloc with Burger," New York Times, July 5, 1978; "Suit by a Welfare Group
Charges New York Grants are Inadequate," New York Times, March
27, 1979; Lesley Oelsner, "Recent Supreme Court Rulings Have Set
Back Women's Rights," New York Times, July 18, 1977; Mary Ellen
Gale, "Supreme Court: Six Blind Men," Village Voice, July 11,
1977; "Excerpts from Justice Marshall's Arguments," ACLU reprint,
1977; Roger Wilkins, "End to Medicaid Abortion Funds: A Change in
the Social Landscape," New York Times, October 11, 1977; Phyllis
N. Segal, "A Feminist Perspective," Civil Rights Digest, Summer
1978; "Current Supreme Court Cases Relating to Welfare," Center
for Social Welfare Policy and Law, Washington, D.C., March 21,
1979; Linda Greenhouse, "High Court Voids Alimony Laws Requiring
Only Husbands to Pay," New York Times, March 6, 1979; "Toward
Equal Rights," New York Times, March 13, 1975 (editorial).

200. Warren Weaver, Jr., "The 'Burger Court' Is Still a Court
in Transition," New York Times, May 18, 1975. See also Fred
Graham, "Supreme Court in Recent Term Began Swing to the Right
Sought by Nixon," New York Times, July 2, 1972.

201. "House Takes Knife to Legal Services for Poor," Star
Ledger (Newark, N.J.), June 23, 1973.

202. Ibid.

203. Levitan, Programs in Aid of the Poor, p. 82.

204. Field notes, Little Rock, Ark., August 6, 1977.

205. Ibid.

206. Marris and Rein, Dilemmas of Social Reform, pp. 267-68,
289.

207. Weaver, "Nixon's Appointees."

208. Marris and Rein, Dilemmas of Social Reform, p. 295.

209. "Fire and Fury in Miami," Time, June 2, 1980, pp. 10-20;
John M. Crewdson, "Guard Reinforced to Curb Miami Riot; 15 Dead
over 3 Days," New York Times, May 20, 1980; Susan Harrigan and
Charles W. Stevens, "Miami Blacks, in a City of Little Industry,
Feel Particularly Powerless," Wall Street Journal, May 22, 1980;
Jonathan Kaufman, "In Big-City Ghettos, Life Is Often Worse than
in the '60s Tumult," Wall Street Journal, May 23, 1980.

210. Andrew Cherlin, "The 'Me' Movement," New York Times,
June 22, 1978; Tim O'Brien, "Bradley Promises Cheering Backers
to 'Restore Trust in Government,'" Star Ledger (Newark, N.J.),
November 8, 1978 (this article attributed the "we" decade to Bill Bradley, after his successful election as New Jersey's senator in November 1978); "Proposition 13, Bakke, and the Selfish Spirit," Ad-
herent 5 (August 1978): 105, editorial comment; "New Times Magazine Ending Publication; 'Me' Decade Blamed," New York Times,

November 16, 1978; John Herbers, "Radicals of the '60s, Now 'Progressive,' Recall Past and Plan for Future," New York Times, July 17, 1978; Adam Clymer, "More Conservatives Share 'Liberal' View," New York Times, January 22, 1978; Arthur Schlesinger, Jr., "Is Liberalism Dead?" New York Times Magazine, March 30, 1980.

211. Steven V. Roberts, "A Congressional Generation Gap Emerges on Role of Government," New York Times, April 1, 1979.

PART IV
THE CHANGING SOCIOPOLITICAL CLIMATE

7

THE CHANGING SOCIOPOLITICAL CLIMATE:
FROM COLLECTIVISM TO INDIVIDUALISM

During the decade of 1966-76, the changing sociopolitical climate in the United States also had an impact on NWRO's mobilized resources. More specifically, changes in social attitudes and behavior of the welfare authorities involved in determining and carrying out public policy, of NWRO's own supporters and of the public in general, mirrored and modeled a cultural drift toward greater emphasis on individualistic strategies for dealing with social problems and a political trend to localism and decentralization in contrast to the collectivism and centralization of social policy in the 1960s. Since continued support for NWRO's goals and strategies for welfare reform depended largely on a social milieu receptive to collectivism, as well as on centralized policies by the federal government favoring expansion of social-welfare programs, the shift to individualism and the decline of liberalism emerged as social currents that also helped to erode NWRO's resources and the protest of poor women. This chapter reviews some of the major policy shifts within the political establishment, the Protestant denominations, and black and women's groups, as well as public opinion polls on poverty and welfare during this period.

THE POLITICAL ESTABLISHMENT

In his inaugural address in January 1961, President Kennedy set the tone for his administration and demonstrated his personal support for collectivism by appealing to citizens to work together to help solve the nation's problems. He appealed to citizens by saying, "Ask not what your country can do for you, but what you can do for your country." The underlying focus was on the country and its people and the need for cooperation in finding social solutions. Eight years later, in January 1969, President Nixon in his inaugural address used similar words but reversed the emphasis. He said, "Let us measure what we do for others, by what we do for ourselves." The call in 1969 was now for individuals to care for themselves and learn to solve their own problems. The implication was that government intervention should be minimized and that social ills would be more easily and efficiently resolved if individuals assumed responsibility for many of their problems and lessened their dependency on the public ruling bodies. The assumption was that the sum of such individual "self-help" actions might ultimately result in the collective good for all. Another assumption underlining this laissez-faire perspective was that equal opportunities existed for all. Thus, the orientations of these two consecutive administrations from their earliest days were in sharp contrast to each other.

This shift was apparent in the difference between the social policies adopted by the Kennedy and Johnson administrations in the mid- and late 1960s and those of the Nixon administration in the early part of the 1970s. This period in the political history of the United States coincides with the major years of protest by the National Welfare Rights movement, which was active, as we have seen, from 1966 through 1975. After President Kennedy's assassination in 1963, President Johnson assumed the leadership of the country and announced that he would continue to support the same political philosophy as that of his predecessor and would propose policies to help the poor and needy. He tried to put into effect his beliefs by fashioning and implementing the Great Society programs, which turned out to be the source of support for the mobilization of NWRO.

During the Johnson administration, social policies, such as the War on Poverty, directed the nation's attention to the legitimate needs of blacks and the poor, as several writers have documented.[1] Levitan and Taggart, for instance, pointed out that critics of the Great Society programs felt that individuals should assume more responsibility for meeting their needs and that "those in need somehow deserve their fate."[2] These critics, they added, also felt that "there are natural processes at work which cannot be altered . . . [and] they must always continue." On the other hand, "The fundamental hypothesis of the Great Society is that such conditions are not foreordained but are rather supported by public policies and private actions which can and should be changed."[3] Noting that "two of the major aims of the Great Society were to alleviate poverty and to improve the lot of the nation's Blacks,"[4] they added that Johnson's program was "based on the belief that the future is not predetermined but can be molded by our energies and resources, and that our nation is not condemned to passive acceptance of inequality of opportunity, poverty, hunger, urban blight, high unemployment and other ills."[5] Thus, the Great Society, under the Johnson administration, clearly reflected a belief and a commitment to federal intervention to solve major social problems in U.S. society, especially poverty and racism.

In contrast, when President Nixon and his Republican administration assumed power in 1969, the political orientation reflected in
most of its rhetoric and actions (with some notable exceptions) shifted
from emphasis on collectivism and centralization to individualism and
decentralization for domestic policy. Three terms reflected these
new directions in federal social policies during this period: decentralization, workfare, and individualism.

Decentralization of social programs emerged in the Nixon and
Ford Republican administrations from 1969 through 1976, as these
two presidents sought to replace the Great Society programs of the
preceding administrations with "revenue sharing" for the cities and
states. Levitan and Taggart pointed out that both "challenged the
categorical programs as duplicative, wasteful, and ill-considered,
preferring revenue-sharing as an alternative, 'comprehensive' solution. Implicit was a decentralization of authority to the state and
local level under the auspices of elected officials."[6] Moreover, Nixon
and Ford believed that greater well-being for the nation's citizens
depended on reliance "on the market processes," given their assumption that "tampering with the engines of economic betterment would be
self-defeating." They wanted "to 'leave well enough alone' or to try
to reverse the momentum of governmental growth." Control over national programs was to be returned to the state and local governments.
It was hoped that this would lead to a reduction of the federal bureaucracy and the redistribution of power to the lower levels. Fear of big
government and its consequences was reflected in this political philosophy and the subsequent policy actions. Revenue sharing, unlike the
Great Society programs, rested on the principle that government
would turn over monies "to be spent at the discretion of the states
and localities (general revenue sharing) and for "specific and broad
program areas" (special revenue sharing).[7]

Revenue-sharing programs were generally very popular with
the state and local officials but were attacked by NWRO members and
supporters.[8] Governors and mayors expected to receive millions of
additional dollars from the federal treasury, most of it to be used at
their own discretion within some broad contextual guidelines. For
the welfare rights members and their supporters, it meant the dismantling of programs that had, despite numerous criticisms, added
to the resources of the poor.

The shift from the Great Society to Nixon's New Federalism,
in which revenue sharing was the "chief instrument," began slowly
at first and was signaled primarily with statements and pronouncements
about proposed changes. President Nixon made his intentions clear as
soon as he took office. The Great Society programs were to be phased
out and replaced by revenue sharing. Many of the Great Society goals
were renounced, and the welfare system was singled out as a "colossal

failure." A few months later, Nixon introduced the Family Assistance Plan (FAP). He also announced that the antipoverty agency would be dismantled and dispersed.[9] Although many feared "that the protective Johnsonian bear hug would soon become the Nixon stranglehold," Nixon did not "move to kill OEO for four years," during which time he was "heavily influenced by the theories of Daniel Patrick Moynihan —his house Democrat."[10]

Nixon's landslide reelection in 1972, however, changed his actions dramatically. This event "affected OEO like no event since the escalation of the War in Vietnam."[11] This is vividly reflected in the monies spent on poverty programs during the Johnson and the Nixon administrations. Expenditures by the federal government on programs benefiting the poor almost doubled from 1964 to 1969 (from almost $8 billion to almost $16 billion) and then doubled again in the next five years.[12] Levitan and Taggart point out, however, that "the real rate of growth . . . declined from 77 percent during the Great Society years to 45 percent during the Nixon years."[13] The continuation of the poverty programs during the Nixon years was not, according to these social-policy analysts, "a reflection of deep commitment to the antipoverty effort," but rather the consequences of the deteriorating economic conditions. The onset of a recession in 1969 resulted in many more being eligible for welfare, food stamps, and unemployment.[14] Levitan and Taggart conclude that, "while it may be difficult to clearly categorize the antipoverty efforts of the Great Society and the Nixon years, there was a difference in emphasis."[15]

NWRO and its supporters were vocal in their opinions about the Nixon administration's actions. Wiley attacked Nixon's budget priorities, asserting that he was trying to publicly redefine "all poor people as the enemy." He decried the "tremendous retreat on the part of the Federal Government from subsidizing programs that help the majority of the people in the country."[16] Cloward and Piven asserted that Nixon's rhetoric and policies had exacerbated the plight of the poor and that as a political move to win the presidential election, he "overtook popular sentiment," which had shifted with the turmoil of the 1960s, and "led the attack on the Black and poor."[17] Another NWRO ally, the economist Lekachman, asserted that President Nixon had "offered the country the most coherent conservative program in the whole history of the nation since McKinley and Howard Taft." According to Lekachman, Nixon ultimately terminated 115 programs using "three principal justifications: (1) the program had accomplished its purpose; (2) the program had failed to accomplish its purpose; and (3) the program, although worthy, was best carried on at the local level through revenue sharing." He also observed that "FAP, once hailed as the centerpiece of an American revolution, disappeared and there are no more recommendations for welfare reform."[18]

The shift from centralization to decentralization by the Nixon administration—from the Great Society programs to the New Federalism's revenue sharing—had an impact on the National Welfare Rights movement. As we noted previously, the OEO programs, which had contributed various needed resources for NWRO, were dismantled. As a result, the movement lost organizers, monies, and other supports provided by the CAP and VISTA programs.

A second theme in the Nixon administration that indicated a shift away from collectivism and toward individualism was the emphasis on "workfare," rather than "welfare," as a solution to poor people's problems. Paradoxically, President Nixon, a Republican who supported limited government intervention in the economy, was the first president in 35 years to introduce radical proposals for reform of the welfare system. While his FAP was in fact a guaranteed income proposal (albeit inadequate, according to NWRO), Nixon throughout the political debate deemphasized this aspect of the legislation and underscored the bill's principle of workfare as an answer to the problem of rising welfare rolls and public costs. Even his "radical," centralized solution of FAP "was . . . pervaded by the ideology of individualism," as Feagin points out.[19]

The reality that most individuals on welfare were poor women with dependent children failed to deter the administration from attempting to resolve their problems through workfare. Abundant data on the lack of jobs for women (especially those with limited skills and education), the lack of child-care facilities, and the failure of the WIN training programs did not inhibit the policy makers' decision to highlight workfare as the ultimate solution for welfare dependency. The consequences of this rhetoric and these actions was, as Piven and Cloward suggest, an increase in public antagonism toward the poor and the blacks, especially poor women on welfare.[20] Levitan and Taggart also underscore the consequences of the workfare rhetoric and policy.[21] They note that "[as] 'workfare' was increasingly emphasized, the mean real cash income of four-person AFDC families with employed adults rose 8 percent between 1969 and 1973; but for those without a worker it fell 6 percent." They add that "it is important to remember that one in eight AFDC mothers was employed in 1973. They gained while the other seven-eighths who could not find jobs suffered."

Workfare, however, was not a new concept created by the Nixon administration. It had been formally integrated into the welfare amendments to the Social Security Act of 1967 in the Work Incentive Program (WIN). Originally, WIN had been passed to provide "placement services to employable AFDC recipients [and] training for those with handicaps."[22] At first the emphasis during the Johnson years was on training. During the Nixon administration, WIN II (also called the

Talmadge amendments) in 1971 reinforced the provisions of workfare and increasingly deemphasized training in favor of rapid placement in low paying jobs with no future."[23] According to the U.S. Commission on Civil Rights, the emphasis was now "on reducing welfare costs rather than increasing recipients' potential for self-support."[24] Many states and welfare administrations, sensing the hostile mood of the country and its political leaders toward women on welfare, followed suit and tightened their social controls. Levitan and Taggart note that "some states reduced their benefit levels," and "more restrictive application procedures" resulted in the "doubling [of] the rejection rate between 1970 and 1973."[25] Cloward called it a period of repression, with HEW "promulgat[ing] regulations that are a throwback to the period before Welfare Rights came alive."[26] Over the years, the concept of workfare had gained increasingly coercive overtones, as the emphasis shifted from social support to social control. As Levitan and Taggart point out, "workfare versus welfare" became "one of the major national issues of the late 1960s and early 1970's."[27]

One prime example of this change in attitude and behavior by the political leaders was the implementation of the "work experiment" called Incentives for Independence. In this pilot program, the secretary of HEW, Weinberger, allowed the governors of New York, California, and Illinois to test a means of motivating poor people on relief to learn new ways of living. Individuals on welfare were to be given daily opportunities to earn monies and add to their monthly grants (though never to exceed the maximum benefit level) by accumulating points for good behavior, as defined by the state and federal agents. According to this plan, the more the poor conformed to the dominant codes, the more their benefits would be increased. On the other hand, those who chose to reject these "rules of the game" would be penalized by having to survive on severely reduced grants.

NWRO and its supporters lashed out against this social experiment on poor people, labeling it the Brownie Points Plan and claiming that it dehumanized families in poverty and further violated their rights as citizens.[28] This experiment once again emphasized the workfare policy of getting individuals to change their behaviors and attitudes, rather than dealing with the basic problems in the economy that failed to provide sufficient training, jobs, or adequate wages for millions of people in the country. Workfare, then, was a social policy reflecting an individualistic perspective rather than a collectivist approach to solutions of the welfare problem. Its implementation by the political authorities during the 1970s heightened the public antagonisms toward the individuals dependent on public relief and undergirded the dominant stereotypes of "welfare loafers and chiselers" living high off taxpayers' monies. This public hostility, mirroring the rhetoric and actions of the nation's leaders, further contributed to the erosion of support for NWRO. Since 1969 <u>workfare</u> has become the password in all succeeding administrations in the continuing debate on welfare reform.

The third theme that marked the shift away from collectivism in the 1970s was the emphasis on the rhetoric of individualism by the Ford administration. Upon assuming the presidency, following the Watergate scandal and Nixon's resignation in August 1974, Ford described his vision of "a third American century in which the individual, not the Government, makes personal decisions." He added that he "was proud of a free economic system, which corrects its own errors, controlled by the marketplace of free and enlightened consumerism."[29] He repeatedly emphasized individualism and individual freedoms in his speeches, insisting that government bureaucracies could "stifle individual initiative." He concluded that in the United States "our sovereign is the citizen."[30]

Another political leader in the Ford administration who oversaw the welfare programs was Weinberger, secretary of HEW under Presidents Nixon and Ford. He also supported the ideology of individualism and opposed the welfare state. In his opinion, the solutions to the problems that beset the nation could be found, not in "more social programs" by the federal government, but in "more economic growth." He warned of "egalitarian tyranny" in the search for "equal opportunity." In his definition, "Equal opportunity means the right to compete equally for the rewards of excellence, not share in its fruits regardless of efforts."[31] He, like the president, reflected the direction and consistency of his predecessor in believing that "almost anything can be better handled by private enterprise than by government, but, if government intervention is unavoidable, local or state is preferable to federal."[32] The underlying theme was rugged individualism and reliance on the market economy.

Thus, as Levitan and Taggart suggest, there was during the Nixon-Ford years a "dialectical swing away from the 1960s social thinking."[33] The trends were toward decentralization of authority, workfare instead of welfare, and reliance on individualism and the self-directing market economy. This contrasted sharply with the preceding Democratic administrations, whose thrust had been to expand and centralize the social-welfare programs and to nourish social responsibility for those in need. Given this swing of the political pendulum, support for NWRO's goals and constituency suffered losses, as federally funded poverty programs were slashed and the rhetoric of individualism and workfare increased.

THE SUPPORTERS

Similar social currents were also observed among NWRO's liberal supporters. During this period, Protestant denominations began to shift power and authority from their national bureaucracies to the local and state judicatories. Some suggested that this decentralization was the result of the growing economic crisis within the churches as memberships and monies declined. A few contended that this reflected a backlash by the local constituencies against the social activism of church leaders in the 1960s. Others disputed this explanation.

Regardless of the sources of this policy shift, by the early 1970s, it was clear that many Protestant denominational leaders were devising new strategies to minimize membership attrition. Increasing attention was being given to the promotion of "evangelism" and the reduction of the visibility of social action. The latter emphasized social concerns and collectivist actions, while the former focused on individual needs and organizational maintenance. One church executive called this the "pietistic trend in the country" in 1973.[34] Another critic of this shift in emphasis and resources by many of the Protestant churches stressed the difficulty in 1975 of trying to promote social justice in a climate "dominated by piety and charity."[35] Churches, which had been among NWRO's principal supporters, by the mid-1970s were moving away from welfare rights and toward the broader and more abstract goal of economic justice. Where social-action monies still existed, they appeared to be used to help organize poor workers in the South. The emphasis in the religious sector, as in the political establishment, was on work and workers, not on AFDC women and welfare.

Organized black and women's groups, some of which had supported NWRO or the welfare reform goal, were also showing signs of moving with the currents of the day. Most were emphasizing the rights of individuals to jobs and full employment, rather than to welfare. Unlike the political establishment, however, these groups also urged that the solutions to some major social problems could best be achieved through collective efforts to break down the racial and sex barriers, using the power of centralized government to bring this about. While feminists were focusing on the needs of the individual woman, by the 1980s they were also emphasizing that all political issues were the concern of women. Black feminist groups were also emerging to call attention to the triple jeopardy of being black, poor, and female and to the plight of many women as single heads of households. This growing pool of potential supporters for the welfare rights cause as a women's issue, however, had come too late to provide any substantial support for NWRO. Their peripheral involvement in the movement had thus also indirectly served to lessen NWRO's mobilized power.

THE PUBLIC

The move away from collectivism within U.S. society in the 1970s was also reflected in the rise of self-help and self-awareness movements and in the public attitudes and priorities for social programs. Edwin Schur observed a significant shift from social action to self-awareness during the decade of 1965-75.[36] In his book, The Awareness Trap, Schur described how, by the mid-1970s, self-help strategies to solve problems through individual self-awareness techniques began to proliferate. Self-awareness, he noted, became the "new panacea." This rising movement of self-awareness, he suggested, had "struck the more basic notes in the American character," partially because of the strong "themes of individualism and personal responsibility" found in U.S. society.[37] As an individualistic strategy, it appealed to many, especially after the widespread and exhausting collective agitation in the 1960s. Within these new social currents, Schur noted that self-awareness emphasized the improvement of the individual rather than the conditions of society.[38] He regretfully concluded that this reflected less dedication to social ideals and that self-help as a way to bring about social change was an illusion. Only collective action, he felt, would produce changed conditions.[39]

Public opinion polls during this same period also confirmed to a degree the trend against welfarism and centralization. The public, however, seemed somewhat ambivalent about the needs of the poor, in general supporting some assistance to the producers and contributors in society and, at the same time, the maintenance of social controls on the undeserving categories of the poor. In part, this stemmed from the competing U.S. values of social responsibility for the deserving poor and rugged individualism and responsibility for oneself. These attitudes also seemed to be rooted in the deteriorating economic conditions in the country. People were concerned about rising taxes and costs of big government.

William Watts and Lloyd Free, in their surveys of public opinion on domestic matters from 1964 to 1974, found that U.S. residents support governmental intervention and solutions on matters that relate to their self-interest and on issues and policies that had been in operation for a long time.[40] In general the public seemed to be placing more reliance on the state and local levels of government than on the federal government. These public polls also revealed that citizens thought that the government was chiefly to blame for the recession and double-digit inflation and that people were cautious about increasing the use of public funds to alleviate the problem of unemployment.[41]

With respect to the welfare issue, the U.S. public stated in 1974 that "helping low-income families through welfare programs" should be maintained at the current level, despite rising inflation. In fact,

Watts and Free pointed out that welfare for the poor received "the lowest score on any question about spending to alleviate domestic problems"[42] (emphasis in the original). Republicans, in general, favored reductions in expenditures for welfare programs, while Democrats, "in sharp contrast," favored increased spending. Blacks registered the highest support for these programs.[43] When respondents were asked whether individuals should be blamed for being poor because of lack of effort on their part or not criticized for their poverty because of social conditions beyond their control, "a large majority thought that lack of effort, either by itself or combined with circumstances, was at the root of poverty, and not circumstances alone." This finding seemed to reinforce the prevalence of "the Puritan belief that virtue brings material rewards, while poverty is evidence of sin." Watts and Free concluded that "the ideological vestiges of this outlook probably continue to the present day to influence the social judgments of many Americans."[44]

Paradoxically, however, these polls also indicated that, while people in the United States wanted the "welfare load held down," they did not favor ending their obligation to the needy. In fact, Watts and Free suggested that perhaps the public is now "receptive to a new attack on this problem—the concept of a minimum family income."[45] Nearly one-half of the respondents (47 percent) supported a federal guaranteed income for families with workers earning very low wages.[46] Most of the supporters of this new concept were to be found in the large eastern cities among Democrats, liberals, those under 30, blacks, and women (especially those with jobs).[47]

These social analysts, however, pointed to a disquieting self-centered and individualistic trend in terms of the ordering of priorities in domestic issues. Concern for the unemployed "rated below the establishing of more parks and recreation areas." Aiding "low-income families and Black Americans was given lower priority than building better highways." Finally, "With the sole exception of the elderly, the degree of compassion Americans as a whole feel toward the more disadvantaged groups of our society—the trouble-beset residents of our central cities, the unemployed, and particularly the poor and Blacks—is marked by relative restraint."[48] In fact, Watts and Free emphasized that "the problem of Black Americans was at the very bottom of the list of American concerns and the need to improve the situation of Black Americans received the next to lowest rating on government spending for domestic purposes."[49]

The public, according to these polls, was also critical of the efficacy of the spending by big government and were not ready for an all-out attack on domestic issues that would require great economizing and sacrifices by family and individuals.[50] It did, however, seem to take for granted the major social programs started through the New

Deal, the Fair Deal, the New Frontier, and the Great Society programs of the Roosevelt, Truman, Kennedy, and Johnson administrations, respectively. The respondents were willing to spend their tax
dollars for programs that were "compatible with the traditional American commitment to equality of opportunity" but not for programs that
go "beyond equality of opportunity, in the direction of an egalitarian
society."[51] In 1979 Daniel Yankelovich and Larry Kagan also reported
finding that there was support for policies and programs by government based on merit but not on need. [52]

Another study of public opinion polls also supports the thesis
that an emphasis on individualism during the decade of the NWRO's
rise and fall was not diminishing, but increasing. Feagin, in his
study of the "work-oriented ideology of individualism" in the United
States from 1969 to 1972 (the years of the great debate over FAP),
found that "individualism persists in the United States and has had a
shaping effect, direct and indirect, on private and public approaches
to dealing with poor persons."[53] He also documented that, although
present-day U.S. residents may be more willing than those in years
past to accept some governmental action on behalf of the poor, there
are definite limits. Feagin also pointed out that individualism, as
measured in both surveys (1969 and 1972), "was found to relate
strongly to negativism toward traditional welfare programs and alternative poor relief approaches."[54] Most respondents tended to "indi-
vidualize or personalize social problems to a substantial degree,
viewing problems in terms of immoral or character-defective individuals." He added that of these attitudes individualism seemed to be
"a persisting constraint on the development and implementation of
new public policies for aiding the poor" and that their origins dated
back several centuries. Referring specifically to the struggle for
welfare reform in the late 1960s and the early 1970s, Feagin noted
that FAP, as well as the programs of the War on Poverty, were "pervaded by concerns for the work ethic and the maintenance of the institutions of capitalism."[55] In such a climate, he concluded, it has been
very difficult to mobilize support for any new innovations in social
policy to aid the poor.

During the NWRO years (1966-75), therefore, the political climate, as reflected in the actions and rhetoric of the welfare authorities and NWRO supporters (principally, the white Protestant churches)
as well as in public opinion polls, seems to have shifted from supportive policies and attitudes toward the poor in the early years to greater
emphasis on the need for individuals to be responsible for their own
economic well-being. Social policies of the Nixon administration,
emphasizing localism, revenue sharing, workfare, and individuals'
responsibility in relief programs, contrasted sharply with the earlier
policies of the Johnson administration in the 1960s. This change in

the general climate of opinion, especially at the federal level but also within the general public as well, seems to have added to NWRO's obstacles in mobilizing and maintaining its needed resources for protest in the latter years. Unlike the 1960s, the 1970s—the "me" decade—seems to have been characterized by a political tide that brought decreasing support for programs for the poor and black, and especially for poor women on welfare.

Among NWRO's supporters, this shift in emphasis was also apparent. White Protestant churches, NWRO's major middle-class allies, adopted policies emphasizing evangelism, rather than social-action programs dealing with welfare. This gradually eroded the base of support for the protest of poor women. The spin-off organizations from the welfare rights movement, such as the Movement for Economic Justice at the national level and the Arkansas Community Organizations for Reform Now at the local level, also siphoned off organizers, members, leaders, and monies.[56] (See Chapter 3.) These "competing" movement organizations subscribed to goals and strategies of mobilization that were more in line with the accepted U.S. value system, emphasizing the needs of low- and middle-income groups and attracting them around self-interest economic issues, not welfare. Similarly, during this period, blacks and women (with some exceptions) also gave top priority to the issues of "jobs and employment" and avoided to a great extent the welfare issue. These attitudes and actions of limited or nonparticipation in the protest also diminished the potential resources of NWRO, as existing coalitions floundered and others failed to materialize within NWRO's social-movement sector.

Finally, the public in general, as can be seen from several polls and analyses, tended to accept social-welfare policies by the federal government only when there were clear elements of self-interest included in them. Attitudes toward the welfare poor, and women with dependent children in particular, remained unchanged. Public hostility—especially to the "undeserving" poor—did not abate. Both Feagin, in his study of welfare and individualism,[57] and Watts and Free, in their surveys of public opinion on domestic issues,[58] found individualistic explanations for poverty still deeply embedded in U.S. society. Consequently, collective solutions to redistribute income and change economic structures would be very difficult to achieve at this time. Feagin noted that "individualistic interpretations mesh well with attempts to maintain the existing status quo." "Structural interpretations," on the other hand, "lend themselves to major attempts at substantial reforms of society."[59]

The 1970s, which began with a vital protest movement of poor women on welfare, closed with few signs of continuing support for collectivist actions in this area. Since the turmoil of the 1960s, collectivism had declined and individualism had resurfaced, as reflected in the rise of new self-awareness movements and the narcissism of the "me" decade of the 1970s. This shift in the sociopolitical climate thus appears to have also contributed to the loss of resources by NWRO.

NOTES

1. Irving Louis Horowitz, "Social Welfare, State Power, and the Limits to Equity," in Equity, Income, and Policy: Comparative Studies in Three Worlds of Development, ed. Irving Louis Horowitz (New York: Praeger, 1977); Irving Louis Horowitz and James Everett Katz, Social Science and Public Policy in the United States (New York: Praeger, 1975); Sar A. Levitan and Robert Taggart, The Promise of Greatness: The Social Programs of the Last Decade and Their Major Achievements (Cambridge, Mass.: Harvard University Press, 1976); Peter Marris and Martin Rein, Dilemmas of Social Reform: Poverty and Community Action in the United States, 2d ed. (Chicago: Aldine, 1973); and Robert D. Plotnick and Felicity Skidmore, Progress against Poverty: A Review of the 1964-1974 Decade (New York: Academic Press, 1975).

2. Levitan and Taggart, Promise of Greatness, p. 7.

3. Ibid., p. 8.

4. Ibid., p. 11.

5. Ibid., p. 12.

6. Ibid., p. 30.

7. William Watts and Lloyd A. Free, State of the Nation, 1974 (Washington, D.C.: Potomac, 1974), p. 55.

8. Taped radio interview between Paul Sherry (United Church of Christ) and George Wiley (NWRO), "Always on Sunday," New York, April 15, 1973.

9. Levitan and Taggart, Promise of Greatness, pp. 192-93.

10. Mark R. Arnold, "The Good War That Might Have Been," New York Times Magazine, September 29, 1974, p. 64.

11. Ibid., p. 66.

12. Ibid.

13. Levitan and Taggart, Promise of Greatness, p. 193.

14. Ibid., pp. 195-96.

15. Ibid.

16. Taped radio interview between Sherry and Wiley, April 15, 1973.

17. Frances Fox Piven and Richard A. Cloward, "A Movement on Welfare," New York Times, August 31, 1973.

18. Field notes on the speech given by Robert Lekachman at the Convocation of Conscience, Washington, D.C., May 9, 1973.

19. Joe R. Feagin, Subordinating the Poor: Welfare and American Beliefs (Englewood Cliffs, N.J.: Prentice-Hall, 1975), p. 166.

20. Piven and Cloward, "Movement on Welfare,"

21. Levitan and Taggart, Promise of Greatness, p. 78.

22. U.S., Commission on Civil Rights, Women and Poverty (Chicago: Allied Printing, 1974), p. 20.

23. Ibid., p. 33.

24. U.S., Commission on Civil Rights, Women and Poverty, p. 32.

25. Levitan and Taggart, Promise of Greatness, pp. 52-53.

26. Taped radio interview by Paul Sherry with guests Helen Webber of United Church of Christ-Welfare Priority Team and Richard Cloward on August 11, 1973 (three days after the death of George Wiley in a boating accident).

27. Levitan and Taggart, Promise of Greatness, p. 53.

28. "New York Operation Starts Moving," Welfare Fighter, December 1971, pp. 1, 5; and John Darton, "State Confirms It Has Dropped 'Brownie Points' Welfare Plan," New York Times, November 5, 1971.

29. James M. Naughton, "Ford Vows Curb on Social Outlays," New York Times, September 14, 1975.

30. "Ford Dedicates Third Century to the Individual," Star Ledger (Newark, N.J.), July 5, 1975.

31. Casper Weinberger, "Do More Public Programs Equal Freedom?" Chronicle of Higher Education, August 1975.

32. Elizabeth Wickenden, Washington Notes #17, mimeographed (National Voluntary Health and Social Welfare Organization, July 23, 1975).

33. Levitan and Taggart, Promise of Greatness, p. 275.

34. Jovelino Ramos, "What Happened to Justice?" NCC Chronicles 1 (Fall 1975): 5.

35. Field notes, Washington, D.C., January 31, 1973.

36. Edwin Schur, The Awareness Trap: Self Absorption instead of Social Change (New York: Quadrangle, 1976), p. 1.

37. Ibid., p. 5.

38. Ibid., p. 99.

39. Ibid., pp. 192-93.

40. Watts and Free, State of the Nation, p. 76.

41. Ibid., p. 132.

42. Ibid., p. 283.

43. Ibid., p. 284.

44. Ibid., p. 285.

45. Ibid.

46. Ibid.

47. Ibid., p. 286.

48. Ibid., p. 278.

49. Ibid.

50. Ibid., pp. 1, 298. This poll was conducted "prior to the trauma of the Watergate affair in 1974."

51. Ibid., p. 311.

52. Daniel Yankelovich and Larry Kagan, "One Year Later: What It Is and What It Isn't—Two Views on Proposition 13," Social Policy, May–June 1979, pp. 19–23. Another study by the Rand Corporation (sponsored by the Ford Foundation) in December 1979 reported that public opinion polls over the past several years "showed support for cutbacks that affected groups with little political power, such as welfare recipients and the aged." See "Study Finds Relative Drop in Government Spending," New York Times, December 2, 1979.

53. Feagin, Subordinating the Poor, pp. 163–65.

54. Ibid.

55. Ibid.

56. John Herbers, "Activist Groups Intensify Role in Presidential Race," New York Times, April 27, 1980. The Association of Community Organizations for Reform Now, an organization founded by Wade Rathke, an exorganizer of NWRO, has since its founding in the early 1970s "spread to 20 states, opened an office in Washington and become active in a number of large cities, including Philadelphia, Pittsburgh and Detroit." It is a "racially mixed organization of low-income and moderate income people," and, as "a grass-roots political movement," it is known in Arkansas for "its ability to inflict pain on public officials, utilities, banks and landlords in its efforts to help the poor."

57. Feagin, Subordinating the Poor, pp. 163–65.

58. Watts and Free, State of the Nation.

59. Feagin, Subordinating the Poor, p. 163.

8

SUMMARY AND CONCLUSIONS

SUMMARY

The central thesis explored in this book was that the National Welfare Rights movement's mobilized resources declined as a result of internal and external conflicts and a shift in the political climate. It was argued that internal structural contradictions based on class, race, and gender increased the costs for participants in this political conflict that eventually led to the loss of organizers, leaders, members, and supporters and their monies. The external struggle with the welfare authorities within the local, state, and federal governments further eroded NWRO's limited resources, as political lobbying diverted efforts from local organizing, resulting in the attrition of its base constituency. During the period of the welfare rights protest, the sociopolitical forces, as reflected in the actions and attitudes of political leaders, NWRO supporters, and the public in general, increasingly shifted to more individualistic means for solving the welfare problem. Collectivism in the 1960s gave way to greater emphasis on individualism in the 1970s. The interaction of these internal and external conditions thus gradually eroded NWRO's mobilized resources after almost eight years of organized protest to reform the welfare system.

Parts I and II covered the mobilization strategies of poor women and their supporters. Part I began by tracing the rise and decline of NWRO's resources and the internal conflicts involved in these processes. Emerging in June 1966 with its roots in the civil rights and poverty rights movements, NWRO was able to attract and mobilize AFDC women as members as well as middle-class organizers, social scientists and other intellectuals, lawyers, and church supporters with a wide spectrum of economic and political resources. Led by Wiley, a charismatic black leader and a former professor of chemistry at Syracuse University, the national protest expanded with the support of other intellectuals and activists, such as Cloward and Piven

366

of Columbia University and many others. White Protestant churches, foundations, and the federal government (through the OEO programs) provided monies, lawyers, organizers, and networks to NWRO.

The civil rights movement at the beginning of the 1960s also provided some of the needed political conditions for the rise of the welfare rights protest. From CORE came NWRO's national leader, Wiley. In addition, black and white organizers, previously involved in the black struggle but now in limbo as the racial protest subsided, became another available resource to NWRO. An extensive network of liberal, middle-class supporters committed to racial justice emerged as another resource to enhance NWRO's organization in the mid-1960s. Finally, the resulting politization of blacks in the civil rights struggle facilitated the mobilization of black women in the inner cities, who formed the core membership of the welfare rights movement.

In addition to these propitious conditions within the social-movement sector, the federal government, under the Johnson administration, created a supportive political climate within the nation as it attempted to address the needs of the blacks and the poor. The Economic Opportunity Act of 1964, which institutionalized the War on Poverty, not only channeled funds, organizers, and poverty lawyers into the inner cities but also legitimated the goals of the welfare poor in the mid-1960s. The conditions in both the private and public sectors thus were conducive to the rise of the National Welfare Rights movement, given the deep-seated grievances of the poor in the United States.

The contradictions within the national movement organization, reflecting those within the larger society, however, contributed to internal tensions and widened cleavages between blacks and whites, poor and nonpoor, and women and men working together within the movement. The national protest designed to be run by the poor and for the poor in reality became dominated by the nonpoor, or the outsiders. While endorsing racial inclusiveness, NWRO turned out to be almost exclusively a black organization. Planned as a movement for all the poor, in practice its membership was made up overwhelmingly of poor women on welfare. Organized and led by men, conflicts over male dominance in a women's movement gradually surfaced and led to fragmentation. Racial, class, and gender contradictions thus eroded cooperation, exacerbating internal tensions that initially had been present but muted.

For the first few years, NWRO's resources expanded. Its membership and staff grew. Middle-class supporters joined the movement, contributing millions of dollars to the cause, as well as time and various kinds of expertise. Turmoil and agitation in the streets brought NWRO visibility in the media and recognition as a bargaining agent for the organized poor in the political arena. By the late 1960s, it was recognized by both opponents and supporters as a bona fide challenger of the welfare system in the United States.

With the advent of the Nixon administration in 1969, the political climate in Washington began to change. Rather than continuing the War on Poverty and the expansion of social programs benefiting the poor and black, the new administration began to dismantle them. Welfare rights protest at the grass-roots level, resulting in soaring numbers of the welfare rolls and skyrocketing costs, triggered counteroffensives by welfare administrators, legislators, and adjudicators. As political leaders were beginning to tighten social controls on the welfare poor and their supporters, internal conflicts also began to surface. These internal and external pressures together weakened the solidarity and cooperation within the movement.

Racial, class, and gender contradictions gradually contributed to the decline of NWRO's mobilized resources. Racial and class conflicts led to the loss of white advisers, staff, and organizers, heightening NWRO's image as a black movement. Organizers left, and some started spin-off organizations that indirectly competed with NWRO. Without field organizers and with only limited attention paid to grass-roots expansion, NWRO's base constituency suffered attrition. When NWRO devoted its resources to lobbying against FAP, it antagonized some supporters and organizers. One consequence was the final severance of ties by Cloward and Piven with the welfare rights cause.

Finally, Wiley also resigned, as strategic conflicts with the women leaders, who were supported by Evans, came to a crisis. Not only did this result in the immediate loss of NWRO's charismatic leader and the financial support he had been able to mobilize among white liberals but it also gave rise to another new movement of poor people—MEJ—which in many ways became a competitor of NWRO for scarce resources. By March 1975 NWRO, with its funds and support gone, was forced to close its national headquarters in Washington, D.C. Only a few local WROs continued to function. However, these were scattered throughout the country, and, without national visibility or recognition, the power of the welfare rights movement declined.

Part II examined the sources and consequences of the cooperation and conflicts between NWRO and its middle-class supporters in the struggle for welfare reform. Chapter 4 focused on the mobilization of the Friends of Welfare Rights mostly rooted in church-related efforts, at the national and local levels. The rise and fall of these coalitions between the poor and nonpoor were traced, and their consequences for the WROs and the national movement in general, examined. First, the national alliances between NWRO and white Protestant church agencies were analyzed to determine the exchange that developed and the resources provided by the religious sector to NWRO. Support, it was found, came primarily from IFCO, an arm of the National Council of Churches, and from UCC.

The alliance between NWRO and IFCO emerged partly as a result of existing ties between its black leaders, Walker of IFCO and Wiley of NWRO. IFCO, established by white church leaders as a means of supporting black community organizations in the turbulent 1960s, needed entree into the inner city, as well as black organizers, both of which NWRO could provide. Wiley, in turn, needed funds for NWRO and entree into white denominations in order to mobilize additional monies and political support for the movement. With the common goal of empowering grass-roots organizations, especially of the black and poor, this coalition added over $500,000 to NWRO's coffers in three years and opened the doors for Wiley to some of the Protestant agencies.

Internal conflicts and external forces, however, finally led to the rupture of the ties between these two partners. Tensions over NWRO's loose administrative practices, declining church support for IFCO, and harassment of the church foundation by the Internal Revenue Service led to the withdrawal of IFCO's monetary support for NWRO. This loss of resources, a mainstay for NWRO during the early years, was a major setback for the movement organization.

UCC, another major supporter, established a formal alliance with NWRO in the welfare rights struggle in 1970 through its newly created WPT. This partnership between the poor and nonpoor, lasting over three years, had explicit benefits for both partners: economic and political support for NWRO and political and ideological rewards for the white church activists in a period when social action was still a viable strategy within the Protestant denominations. Acceptance as an equal, but separate, partner in the protest movement of the poor and black, when whites were being excluded, became another incentive for white church liberals. The economic thrust of NWRO's goals also provided an added attraction for middle-class church activists, who saw the need to shift the political struggle from civil rights to economic rights of the poor in the late 1960s.

While it lasted, this coalition between NWRO and UCC mobilized substantial economic and political resources for the welfare rights movement. Over $500,000 was transferred to NWRO in three years. Access to foundation and other denominational monies significantly added to NWRO's resources. The alliance also succeeded in mobilizing other middle-class constituencies to help NWRO lobby to defeat FAP. The coalition failed, however, in its efforts to achieve its major goal of an adequate guaranteed income for the poor.

Over the years, political and economic changes within NWRO, within the main-line denominations, and within society as a whole

raised the costs of participation for the church activists. By the end
of 1972, the church liberals saw welfare rights as a losing strategy.
In their view, NWRO no longer represented an inclusive movement of
poor people. Its base constituency continued to be primarily black
and had been eroding continuously rather than expanding. With the
loss of Wiley, another incentive vanished. As a movement of poor
women on welfare, with an entrenched leadership seemingly resis-
tant to changes that threatened its power, NWRO lost its attractiveness as a political ally. Furthermore, white churches, suffering
from declining memberships, were being pressured internally to decrease the visibility of their social activism and to increase resources
for the development of "evangelism" in their own constituencies. The
risks of overidentification with welfare rights had risen over the years
and had created internal conflicts within the UCC. Attacks on NWRO
by the radical Labor Caucus Committee had exacerbated the fears of
the church leaders about their association with the protest of poor
women. Alliance with NWRO by 1972/73 had thus become a liability,
when once, during the heyday of social action in the 1960s by the
churches, it had been considered an asset.

The twin-track coalition model, with its highly visible and regu-
larized interaction between two unlike, but equal partners, by 1972
had become too costly for the middle-class supporters. With Wiley's
resignation from NWRO and Nixon's landslide victory in November
1972, UCC leaders came to the conclusion that it was necessary to
shift strategies to accommodate the new political realities within their
denominations and within the broader political arena. To achieve the
desired economic goals for poor people in the country, they felt that
a different means had to be found. New partners were needed in the
ongoing political struggle, since church leaders foresaw at least four
more years under a conservative administration with little hope of
expanded social-welfare expenditures. In their view, new alliances
and broader coalitions were essential to hold the line on existing income-transfer programs for the poor and mobilize for the "second
round" of welfare reform in 1976, the next presidential election year.
Therefore, the goal in 1973 was changed from welfare rights to economic justice and full employment to attract more allies to a majoritarian coalition for economic change.

While a guaranteed adequate income still remained top priority
for the main-line Protestant churches, the strategy to achieve this
national goal was redesigned. First, the relationship with NWRO
was terminated. Second, the issues of welfare and welfare rights
were made less visible and were subsumed under the broader and
less controversial issue of economic justice. Third, new political
partners were sought among the working poor, low-income groups,
labor organizations, black civil rights groups, and feminist orga-

nizations. At the national level, the thrust was now for a majoritarian coalition around the "right to work," rather than the "right to welfare." Both the issue of welfare rights, never a popular cause, and the movement organization of poor women were reassessed as liabilities in the 1970s.

At the local and state levels, the coalitions between groups of WROs and FWROs also emerged for short periods of time to counter the actions of the welfare authorities. The primary function of the middle-class Friends, as designed by NWRO's organizers, was not political, but financial. They were expected to contribute monies and services in exchange for participation in the movement of poor women. At first, their political role was deliberately restricted to maximize control by the poor within their own movement. While Friends of WRO were sought as supporters, they were also perceived as a potential threat to recipient hegemony. There was always the risk, it was felt, that middle-class Friends might end up dominating the movement of the poor.

Despite NWRO's stated guidelines for parallel alliances between the organized welfare rights groups and their Friends (the outsiders), different models of cooperation emerged within the movement, with varying political and economic consequences for the organized poor women. Twin-track coalitions, as envisaged by NWRO, were designed to be egalitarian alliances between unequals, with specific roles assigned to each: a leadership role for the poor and a supportive one for the nonpoor. In practice, these coalitions were tenuous and beset by internal tensions. Monies and other support rarely met the rising expectations of the local WROs and NWRO headquarters. Criticisms of Friends' attempts to dominate and control were widespread. Alliances observed were generally short-lived. At best, they served to legitimate the cause of welfare rights at the local level and to mobilize middle-class support for welfare reform. Separation usually resulted in spin-off, middle-class coalitions in which the welfare rights women were relegated to a much lesser role in the decision-making process. Generally, the new umbrella coalitions subsumed the issue of welfare under less controversial agendas, enhanced the power of the middle-class supporters, and decreased the control of poor women within the struggle for welfare rights. The challenge continued, but the structure of the challengers changed.

Integrated alliances, in contrast to the parallel coalitions of WRO and the Friends of WRO, incorporated from the start both the poor and nonpoor into one organization and theoretically shared the decision-making power. The limited data available indicate, however, that they, like the twin-track coalitions, tended to be dominated by the middle-class Friends and provided few resources to the WROs, except perhaps middle-class legitimation of the cause and some organizational support.

At the other extreme of the continuum of cooperation between the poor and nonpoor were the independent, middle-class coalitions for welfare reform that excluded the poor and rejected welfare women as allies. In such cases, local WROs gained nothing from these participants in the welfare reform movement. In fact, they detracted from the WROs' efforts to mobilize outside support. In Missouri, the independent, middle-class coalition for welfare reform achieved an increase in the benefit level for the poor ($20 additional per recipient per month) through lobbying and negotiations with political leaders. Critics called it a paternalistic model that undermined the protest of poor women. Middle-class participation in the welfare rights struggle at the local and state levels thus appears to have failed to add to the resources of the movement organization. At best, it mobilized some middle-class support for welfare reform and at times temporarily stalled restrictive laws and regulations.

In Chapter 5 other sources of support for NWRO were examined. The ties that emerged, or failed to emerge, between welfare rights and black and women's organizations were explored. Given NWRO's predominantly black and female structure, these groups were seen as representing potential peer allies, as other minority-power groups within a white, male-dominated society. Class, race, and gender cleavages, however, it was found, inhibited the formation of many such alliances between NWRO and black and feminist organizations, despite some common grounds for grievances.

At best, black organizations provided some political support to NWRO in the struggle for welfare reform. The black groups with poor constituencies were more noticeably involved than those with more middle-class orientations and memberships. SCLC, PUSH, NTO, and the Black Panthers were more visible in the struggle than the more traditional civil rights groups. SCLC, PUSH, and NTO cooperated with NWRO at the national level, while the Black Panthers were more active at the local level. The middle-class black groups were more peripheral as supporters of welfare rights. The National Urban League was active in Newark for one year after the 1967 riots. The NAACP and the black churches remained, for the most part, totally disengaged from the welfare rights protest. Competition for scarce resources and class and gender antagonisms appear to have eroded political solidarity among blacks. With limited organizational resources and largely dependent on white liberal support, most black groups were unable, if not unwilling, to provide NWRO with financial support or to become visibly identified with it as a political ally. The antiwelfare ethic that permeates this society, along with other factors, effectively inhibited racial solidarity across class lines. Moreover, the tradition of male dominance and leadership precluded ties with a movement led by poor women.

Women's organizations were also another potential source of economic and political support for NWRO, given its predominantly female constituency. However, ties with women's organizations— both black and white—were also tenuous and rare. Black, middle-class women's organizations were largely uninvolved in the welfare rights movement until its final years, although some joined independently in the welfare reform debate. The National Council of Negro Women, for example, testified in behalf of NWRO's position on FAP and provided $500 to NWRO in 1974. The most politically visible and supportive black women's group was NCHE, whose membership, consisting of poor, mostly black, working women, was much like NWRO's own base constituency.

With the emergence of black feminists in 1973, new signs of solidarity between the poor and nonpoor black women began to surface. By the mid- and late 1970s, poor women, as members, and welfare, as a priority agenda item, were being incorporated as integral parts of the new, black, feminist organizations. Class barriers, which previously had undermined the bonding between black females, seemed to be breaking down. Paradoxically, just as this concern by black feminists with the welfare issue was on the rise, NWRO and its national movement were declining. As a result, black feminists' participation in the welfare rights struggle during 1966-75 was very limited and had little, if any, impact on NWRO's resources.

Predominantly white women's organizations also played a peripheral role in NWRO's rise and fall, and a somewhat more active role in the welfare reform debate. The most involved in contributing resources directly to NWRO were women's church groups within the predominantly white denominations. The United Methodist Women, through their national staff, and the United Presbyterian Women appear to have been the largest contributors of monies and the most salient of these supporters in the national political debate in Washington. The YWCA, a quasi-religious organization, was also a small contributor of monies and political support. Together, their gifts to the welfare rights struggle never amounted to more than a few thousand dollars, a relatively small amount in contrast to the donations from other denominational agencies, which controlled greater assets within the churches.

Solidarity between the black, welfare rights women and the white, middle-class feminists was almost nonexistent, especially in the earlier years of the movement. Both movements had emerged at the same time in the mid-1960s but had adopted different goals, strategies, and constituencies. However, after 1971, NWRO became increasingly involved with some of the national feminist organizations through the efforts of Wiley, who was pursuing a strategy of coalition politics to defeat Nixon's FAP. In time, some interlocking of the two movements emerged, as some of the NWRO leaders became active participants in the feminist organizations, especially after the NWRO offices in Washington closed. Organizationally, however, there were never any formal ties established. As with that of the black feminists, the white women's liberation movement, while adopting poverty as an agenda item for women, did not accept welfare as a women's issue until after the mid-1970s, despite Tillmon's appeal for support and bonding as women. Consequently, the impact of white women's organizations on NWRO was negligible. At best, some became "carriers" and later advocates of NWRO's concerns after the demise of the national movement of poor women.

In general, then, both black and white women's cooperation with NWRO was very limited and peripheral. Female bonding appears to have been relatively weak in comparison to the support provided by the white, male-dominated, main-line denominations and foundations that were long established. Gender solidarity appears to have been inhibited primarily by race and class antagonisms but also because both NWRO and feminist movements were fledgling organizations at the same period of time. Both were struggling to mobilize a constituency base and to attack the inequities they saw in the system.

By the end of the decade, however, this trend seemed to be reversing. Female bonding seemed to be on the rise among the poor and nonpoor women, both black and white. The demands of poor women and the proliferation of "common grievances," as feminism expanded, seemed to be creating a climate in which enhanced political cooperation among women, transcending major differences across socioeconomic lines, was possible. While deep-seated racial and class antagonisms among these different groups remained sources of conflict between women, by the end of the 1970s, the issues of poverty and welfare had become integrated into the national black and white feminist agendas. Given a common cause based on similar economic and social grievances and a seemingly increased cohesiveness as women, a new base of political support appeared to be emerging for the upcoming rounds of welfare reform under the succeeding administrations. There were, however, few signs that these resources would bring about the revitalization of the poor women's movement. At best, their cause, redefined as a common concern for women and their families, might emerge more prominently in the feminist and black agendas in the coming years.

The external conflict and the changing political conditions affecting NWRO's mobilized resources were examined in Part III. In Chapter 6, the political struggle of NWRO and its allies against the welfare policy makers was analyzed within three different contexts: NWRO's confrontations with welfare administrators, with welfare legislators, and with welfare adjudicators.

Political interaction with welfare administrators resulted in both conflict and cooperation, which had varying results for NWRO's members and organizations. At the local level, direct actions (the street strategy) against the welfare departments for special benefits temporarily increased the resources of individual poor women and their families around the country. During 1966-69, millions of dollars flowed from the welfare departments to the poor. For a short while, these economic benefits, used by NWRO as private incentives for expanding its movement base, brought about the growth of its membership, which peaked during this period. Protest by welfare mothers also added to its members, since this raised NWRO's visibility in the media.

On the other hand, this agitation also antagonized legislators, administrators, and the public. Counteroffensives by the welfare authorities quickly emerged to thwart the "raid" on its treasuries. Laws and regulations were changed to cut the costs of expanding welfare rolls. Special benefits were replaced with inflexible flat grants, and eligibility rules were tightened. At the same time, local and state welfare administrators, mirroring the behavior of national political leaders in Congress and in the Nixon administration, began escalating their antiwelfare rhetoric and instituting additional social controls. This was epitomized in the actions taken by the welfare authorities in Nevada in 1971, which resulted in the final offensive by NWRO to counteract and halt this rising repression of the poor. Welfare administrators also initiated demonstration projects called "Incentives for Independence" in some parts of the country to motivate (or, from NWRO's perspective, to control) the poor by awarding "brownie points" and added monetary benefits for certain approved social behaviors as defined by the dominant leaders. These increased social controls by the welfare authorities led to attrition in NWRO's membership, since, without immediate economic payoffs and with rising penalties, few chose to remain involved.

At the national level, interaction between NWRO and HEW administrators also resulted in some confrontations as well as negotiations. Cooperation with the Department of Labor added some monies to the movement as well as recognition of NWRO as a bona fide bargaining agent for poor people. However, at the same time, it led to the defection of some WRO groups and individuals from the movement. It also provided the rationale for attacks by the white radical Labor Caucus Committee, which criticized NWRO for having been co-opted by the political establishment. This further weakened the movement organization as new cleavages emerged.

The political confrontation of NWRO and its allies with the legislators at the national level, consisting primarily of lobbying efforts to defeat the administration's FAP, lasted for over three years (1969-72) and also consumed NWRO's limited resources. This struggle reduced ties with its local grass-roots base, exhausted its monies, antagonized some of its supporters, and created internal friction between the national and local leadership. At the same time, however, the external FAP conflict mobilized some liberal, middle-class support for NWRO's lobbying efforts that contributed (along with the conservative opposition) to the defeat of the Nixon proposal. While the political strategy to defeat FAP succeeded in attracting some supporters among the poor and nonpoor to NWRO's camp, others were lost as differences over tactics emerged. Liberals split on which bill to support. Some liberals chose to support NWRO's position, but others selected the more moderate plans, which were less generous than NWRO's but also less restrictive than the FAP proposal. Consequently, given all the alternatives, the potential political allies divided among various camps, thus undermining NWRO's concerted efforts to "zap FAP." As a result, FAP almost became law in October 1972. The Social Security amendments (which included FAP under Title IV) were approved by both houses. Only the united and last-minute actions of NWRO and several of its allies within and outside the government succeeded in mobilizing sufficient support to have FAP withdrawn from the 1972 Social Security amendments at the final joint conference meeting.

By the end of this three-year struggle to defeat FAP, NWRO's mobilized resources were exhausted. Its membership had declined, the movement was suffering from internal conflicts, and solidarity among the welfare rights women, staff, and organizers was on the wane both at the local and national levels. Friction among NWRO leaders finally led to Wiley's resignation in December 1972 and the rise of MEJ, another competitor within the social-movement sector. Supporters also withdrew, many expressing their weariness with the welfare issue and their criticisms of NWRO's narrowed base and focus in the economic rights struggle. Church allies switched to mobilizing the working poor and middle-class constituencies around "full employment" and "jobs" rather than "welfare reform." NWRO, its resources decimated, was no longer perceived as a viable political ally in the redefined movement for economic justice, which had been organized primarily by its former middle-class organizers and supporters.

In another arena, NWRO and Légal Services lawyers engaged in court battles to modify the welfare system by changing its laws and regulations. While the legal strategy was employed both at the state and national levels, in the early years, the major victories were won in the U.S. Supreme Court. From 1966 through 1969, several major decisions by the Warren Court expanded the rights of welfare recipients. By 1970, however, even in this arena the tide had begun to turn against NWRO and the welfare poor. Unlike the Warren Court in the 1960s, the new Burger Court decided against the welfare recipients. Nevertheless, cooperation between NWRO and poverty lawyers had resulted in some major decisions altering the welfare system and adding to the rights of the poor. Challenges of existing administrative regulations also contributed to some modifications in the system that may have tempered, at least temporarily, some of the more restrictive actions by the welfare authorities.

The alliance of NWRO and Legal Services had a limited impact on the movement organization's resources, since the partnership was not based on a financial or material exchange. In the long run, however, this relationship between the poor and nonpoor turned out to be the most continuous one within the movement, lasting long after all other alliances had dissolved. It was a clearly delineated exchange in which poverty lawyers gained access to welfare cases and plaintiffs, while AFDC mothers and other poor people received not only personal legal advice but also support in mobilizing class-action suits to reform the welfare laws. At the local level, this coalition, although not devoid of conflicts, had payoffs for both sides. While its stated goal was to aid all the poor in legal matters, the informal political coalition of NWRO and Legal Services enhanced the movement's resources in many inconspicuous and indirect ways. At the same time, the two forces joined together and won many victories that, to some extent, reformed the welfare system.

The successes of NWRO and Legal Services antagonized policy makers, who felt that the federal government should not be subsidizing its own legal adversaries. Outraged congressional leaders demanded that the power of the poverty rights lawyers be curtailed. As a result, with the Nixon landslide reelection in 1972, measures were initiated to restructure Legal Services. This counteroffensive by the political elites affected the amount of support Legal Services was able to provide directly or indirectly to WROs and its continuing use of class-action suits in the courts. Restrictions were imposed on the legal and political activities of the federally funded poverty lawyers and their backup centers. Dependent on the federal government for survival, these legal OEO programs were vulnerable to attacks by political leaders at all levels. In 1975 the Legal Services Corporation was established, replacing the previous programs and adding several constraints to the poverty lawyers' social actions. The new thrust was for service to individual clients rather than law reform and political action. These legislative outcomes in the 1970s affecting NWRO's legal allies, combined with changes in the later welfare rulings by the U.S. Supreme Court, also helped to reduce NWRO's mobilized resources over the years.

Chapter 7, in Part IV, examined the changing sociopolitical climate from 1966 through 1980 and the drift from collectivism and centralization in the 1960s to individualism and localism in the 1970s. These conditions were also found to have eroded NWRO's base of support, enhanced counteroffensives by its foes, and hastened its decline. The actions and rhetoric of welfare authorities and liberal supporters (including the white churches, social scientists, and others) and the general public's opinion of poverty and welfare indicated a shift, if not a reversal, in the political momentum for aid to the poor. Dismantling of the poverty programs and restrictions on Legal Services by the Nixon administration affected NWRO's resources. Shifts in policy from social action to evangelism among liberal Protestant denominations also reflected this general political-cultural shift from collectivism to individualism.

In the 1970s, which came to be known as the "me decade," the direction was inward (individualistic) instead of outward (social/collectivistic), as it had been in the 1960s. Such sociopolitical changes had a direct impact on NWRO's resources since many previous allies chose to withdraw support from the movement. Black and women's organizations, most of which had remained on the periphery of the conflict over welfare rights, while showing signs of increased concern over welfare and poverty, still seemed reluctant to single out these issues as major priorities in their fight for economic rights for their constituencies. Public opinion polls also confirmed the strong prevailing feelings against "welfarism" and in favor of "individualism." Feagin found a negative correlation between the two, reporting that individualism remained firmly entrenched in the United States in the 1970s.[1] Watts and Free, in the State of the Union surveys in 1972 and 1974, also supported this thesis but revealed some rising public support in 1974 for a guaranteed jobs system.[2] By the end of the 1970s, another survey of public opinion reported in the New York Times showed that the U.S. public remained deeply "antagonistic to the concept of public welfare" but "displayed deep compassion for those who are destitute and helpless."[3] Thus, the U.S. paradox of caring for the needy but penalizing them for economic dependence on the state remained.

Within society at large, the cultural trend toward self-help and self-awareness also reflected the public's rising emphasis on individualistic solutions and the definition of problems in personal, rather than social and systemic, terms. Whereas in the 1960s, the personal was political, in the 1970s, the personal had become the individual's problem. Schur, among others, documented the proliferation of self-awareness and self-help movements and its negative implications for collectivist solutions for achieving social change.[4]

NWRO's foes within the political establishment, as well as the general public, seemed increasingly concerned about the rights of individuals. There was a general distrust of big government and centralized solutions, especially after the Watergate scandal in 1974. NWRO's supporters, and potential allies, while mobilizing against the cutbacks on social-welfare programs, were also retrenching their resources and focusing primarily on their organizational needs for survival. Foundations, which had been in the vanguard of support for the poor in the inner cities in the late 1950s and 1960s, had begun to restrict their contributions and involvement in these areas in the deteriorating economic climate and more conservative political era of the 1970s.[5] In such a climate, support for welfare rights and a guaranteed income system for the poor vanished. At best, there was some backing for federal subsidies and policies that emphasized the work ethic rather than the welfare ethic. Public service jobs and training for the economically disadvantaged (such as WIN and CETA), which were designed to reduce dependency on the government and promote economic self-sufficiency, gained wide political support from various sectors, while expansion of benefit levels for AFDC mothers and other social-welfare expenditures for public assistance generally did not. Welfare, still defined by the dominant sector as a "handout," continued to be rejected by the public as the solution to poverty, except for the limited categories of the "deserving" and unemployable poor (the aged, the disabled, and young children). Heightened anti-welfarism, exacerbated by the deteriorating economic conditions in the mid-1970s, thus further eroded the support for NWRO and its final years.

As the 1970s came to a close, the welfare rights movement lay dormant. Fragmented and transformed, only a few scattered groups continued to function independently at the local level. Supporters and political leaders had moved on to other issues. The issue of welfare had receded from the foreground of the political arena, despite some early attempts by the Carter administration to introduce its own welfare reform proposals. In the presidential elections in 1980, the issue of welfare was rarely mentioned. Inflation, unemployment, and foreign policy were top priorities. For the Carter administration, the thrust was for a balanced budget and curtailment of social-welfare programs, which suggested to some critics that the Democratic party had "reverted to the economic policies of Herbert Hoover."[6] At best, the problems of poor women and their dependent children now attracted the interest of only a few. At worst, actions by administrators, legislators, and the U.S. Supreme Court (in its decision against the use of Medicaid funds for abortions) reinforced the fears of many that social controls over the poor were being tightened by political leaders within a rising tide of conservatism.

Under these changed conditions, most friends and foes of NWRO had shifted their attention and resources elsewhere. Moynihan suggested that, in the 1980s, U.S. society might have to face up to the end of "middle-class altruism." Arthur Schlesinger, Jr., underscored, on the other hand, "the inherent cyclical rhythm in our public affairs, the continuing alternation between conservatism and innovations."[7] He noted that, in the 1970s, the country had been "in the depressive phase of the cycle" but that this phase would not continue forever. The coming decades might well bring, once again, the rise of liberalism.

CONCLUSIONS

The analysis of the data on the National Welfare Rights movement from 1966 to 1980 supports the central thesis that both internal and external conflicts interacted to bring about the decline of this social protest of poor women. Similar assessments by the major actors in the movement reinforce this conclusion. The analysis also sheds new light on the sources of the conflicts and how these affected NWRO's successes and failures, revealing the impact of outsiders on the protest of the poor. In concluding, we seek to summarize briefly some of the major causes of NWRO's decline. NWRO's impact on the political establishment and its policies for the poor as well as on its own members, supporters, and the poor in general, will also be examined. Finally, we will list some social trends that may have a bearing on the future of the welfare rights protest in the coming decades.

In general, members and supporters of NWRO tended to identify similar causes leading to the decline of the protest movement. At the same time, however, their emphasis varied, with some stressing the internal factors; others, the external conditions; and still others, a combination of the two. Within the core group, NWRO women leaders generally attributed the movement's downfall at the national level to the internal financial problems and the loss of Wiley's leadership, which contributed to the withdrawal of liberal support.[8] NWRO's organizers for the most part suggest that loss of resources occurred because the movement was "programmatically strung out around the country" and because the organization had begun to "serve itself" rather than maintaining and using its limited resources to achieve its long-range goals.[9]

Wiley, as NWRO's foremost organizer and coordinator, "attributed the decline to the repressive nature of the welfare system and its discouraging effect among welfare rights organizations and leaders."[10] At the same time, he acknowledged that internal conflicts had also weakened NWRO. He pointed out "three things that went wrong": the counteroffensives of welfare authorities that made organizing much more difficult; the entrenchment of the women leaders and their resistance to cooperating with other groups, which, in his opinion, "obstructed people's affiliation with NWRO"; and, finally, the difficulty of recruiting and keeping "good organizers" as involvement in "welfare rights became less voguish." Wiley concluded that the organization "was not able to respond to these changes" and, as a result, collapsed.[11]

Bert DeLeeuw, another national staff member and Wiley's successor as head of the new MEJ, suggested that NWRO's refusal to cooperate with other protest organizations had decreased its power and effectiveness in attracting wider support for its cause. He felt, however, that the biggest handicaps for the movement organization had been its "welfare" label and the loss of Wiley's leadership. Along with others, he noted that, with Wiley's resignation, NWRO's allies and monies disappeared. [12]

Middle-class supporters and intellectuals offered other explanations for NWRO's demise. Cloward and Piven, the social scientists who were the major architects of this protest, concluded that NWRO's shift from mass protest and civil disobedience to an electoral and lobbying strategy had adverse effects on the movement and its power to bring about change. They argued further that NWRO's national organization became a "superstructure" that, as they had originally feared, inhibited, rather than enhanced, its ability to remain a viable challenger within the political arena. The development of a national bureaucracy within NWRO, they suggested, rapidly consumed its meager resources and exacerbated conflict. They emphasized, however, that exogenous, rather than endogenous, factors were responsible for NWRO's downfall. According to Cloward and Piven, the adverse political conditions, as reflected in the actions of the national leaders in Washington during the 1970s were the critical forces that undermined the protest of the poor on welfare. [13] Kotz and Kotz, journalists and observers of NWRO, also attributed NWRO's decline to the "public hostility" within the society, which "once directed towards the civil rights movement and anti-poverty programs was by 1970 clearly focused on welfare." [14] "The question," they contended, "became one of how long could NWRO sustain growth and vitality against this kind of opposition."

White church leaders who were active supporters of the movement suggested that lack of leadership development and Wiley's resignation were probably the principal factors contributing to NWRO's decline. One church official explained that NWRO had never planned ahead, and, as existing national leadership became entrenched, no means was available for the rise of new leaders. Supporting this view was another observer in the religious sector, who suggested that, as NWRO matured, "it lost its vitality, became rigidified, with an entrenched power structure." This, in his opinion, eroded its middle-class support. The increasingly exclusive, rather than inclusive, strategies of leaders and members had, he explained, detrimental effects on the mobilization of liberal support for the welfare rights cause. Others felt, however, that Wiley's resignation provided the fatal blow to NWRO. In sum, the factors singled out by the NWRO women leaders, their organizers and staff, and their allies strongly support the thesis that NWRO's demise was rooted in both external and internal conflicts within the movement that interacted over time to dissipate the movement's mobilized resources.

These general observations by a few of the participants in this protest do not, however, explain the sources of conflicts within the movement and within the larger society that resulted in these changes and undermined NWRO's power. Analysis of the data strongly suggests that structural contradictions, reflecting those in the broader society, were the major underlying cause of the internal tensions and clashes. Racial, class, and gender conflicts within the national core group, as well as at the local level, resulted in the loss of organizers, leaders, and monies.

After the racial clashes in 1969 within NWRO, most of the white staff and organizers withdrew from the movement. Some went on to organize new movements of the working poor (such as ACORN and other grass-roots organizations), which indirectly, if not directly, siphoned off support for NWRO. These conflicts were also rooted in class differences and surfaced repeatedly around the issue of who was to rule within the movement of poor women: blacks or whites, the poor or the middle-class supporters, the women or the men. Gender and class conflicts, in combination with the changing external political conditions, also led to the resignation of Wiley and the takeover of the national movement leadership by WRO women. In every instance, the underlying struggle seemed to have been for the decision-making power within these "equal" partnerships of nonpeers. The resolution of such internal contradictions resulted in the loss of needed resources for the movement organization but enhanced the political power of the poor women.

Similarly, intragroup conflicts between NWRO and its coalition partners also inhibited cooperation and dissipated the mobilization of the political and economic resources of the movement. Coalitions with white church liberals turned out to be tenuous and fraught with increasing tensions as the poor women and their nonpoor allies struggled to define and apply new "rules" for working together as equal partners. In addition, as political conditions within the society changed, conflicts arose within the ranks of the white Protestant denominations, which led to curtailment of social action in general and welfare rights in particular. Although many church leaders had been in the forefront of the black struggle in the 1960s, by the beginning of the 1970s declining membership and increasing tensions within their own ranks, as well as changed conditions within NWRO and Washington, led them to reassess their role in the welfare rights movement. As a result, the close ties with NWRO, symbolized by the FWROs at the national and local levels, came to an end. Alternative partners were sought to achieve desired economic goals. From support for welfare rights, white liberal churches shifted their resources to the fight for economic justice for the working poor, blacks, women, and other minorities. The churches also increased allocations for the development of "evangelism" in their own, middle-class constituency. Although there were some efforts to mesh these two thrusts and legitimate continued support of welfare rights, this failed to materialize. The consequence for NWRO was the loss of major, middle-class allies and their resources.

For the most part, coalitions with black and women's groups, NWRO's potential peer allies, also failed to materialize, given the historical antagonisms of race, gender, and class. When they did emerge, their contributions were relatively insignificant in contrast to the white churches' involvement. This lack of solidarity was partly rooted in the fact that these movement organizations were, like NWRO, on the periphery of political and economic power, having few, if any, resources to share with others. At best, if they chose, they could provide some visible political unity with welfare rights, which some did. When alliances did emerge, they tended to be episodic and unstable. The demands of their own constituencies conflicted at times with the goals and strategies of NWRO. Thus, structural and ideological differences overrode their common economic and social grievances as minority-power groups in U.S. society. Competition among these various groups undermined the potential resources and cohesiveness of the movement.

While participation by supporters expanded NWRO's resources as well as its conflicts, abstention by potential allies also had an impact on the movement's political and economic power. Those who chose to remain on the periphery of the struggle as "witnesses" contributed little or nothing to strengthening NWRO as an organized protest of the poor. Some worked independently to achieve NWRO's goals but failed to link up with the movement. The absence of, or limited involvement by, some black, women's, labor, and religious organizations weakened the protest. Lack of cooperation within the political movement reduced NWRO's legitimacy as a national representative of poor people. Few, in fact, defined it as such. Blacks perceived NWRO as a white, middle-class protest; feminists defined it as a paternalistic, male-dominated movement; and the working poor in labor unions saw the welfare poor as a potential threat to their jobs and wages. However, by the end of the 1970s, some new trends were emerging. Blacks, feminists, and some women in the labor movements were beginning to give more prominence to the welfare issue in view of its impact on their own constituencies.

The external conflict of NWRO and its allies with the welfare authorities also reduced its resources, even though confrontations and turmoil in the early years helped to mobilize members and supporters. Counteroffensives by the political establishment soon raised the costs of participation. As a result, many of the poor women dropped out. The strategy of lobbying and negotiating in Washington reduced attention to NWRO's grass-roots base, even while it increased the monies and recognition for the movement organization and limited the restrictive actions by the political leaders. The legal strategy, made possible by the support of Legal Services, appears to be the only one that did not create too much internal conflict and led to victories, in terms of Supreme Court and many lower court decisions that expanded the rights of the poor.

Finally, the sociopolitical climate and conflicts with the dominant values and goals, as reflected in public opinion polls, also helped to dissipate NWRO's resources. Political conservatism, expressed in the dismantling of poverty programs and in calls for decentralization and individualism, also had a negative impact on the welfare rights protest.

The analysis of these data, however, does not indicate that the movement was a failure, despite its many setbacks. Clearly, if one evaluates NWRO's success or failure merely in terms of achievement or nonachievement of its long-range goals, it did not succeed. A national guaranteed income system for poor people by 1980 had not yet replaced the existing piecemeal welfare system. Yet, if one examines NWRO's impact on its opponents, allies, members, and the poor in general, the data reveal that, as Wilkins points out, it left "indelible marks on America's political system."[15]

Politically, NWRO successfully forced leaders to reopen the debate and reestablish the principles of the "right to welfare" and the "right to work" for poor people. NWRO's actions also reinforced the principle of the right of poor people to participate in the political policy decisions that affect their lives and those of their families. More concretely, the welfare rights protest made policy makers reconsider and reevaluate several public policy programs that have an impact on poor people. As such, NWRO helped to shape and broaden a number of in-kind and income-transfer programs that benefited millions of the poor (see Tables 6.1 and 6.2).

For example, in the food stamp program, NWRO fought successfully to raise the proposed benefit level and to incorporate a cost-of-living clause. By the end of the 1970s, this was recognized as probably the largest guaranteed income program in the country. By 1980 this in-kind transfer program had been modified to provide cash instead of stamps for the poor earning more than the poverty level used for welfare recipients.

NWRO and its allies also succeeded in having nutrition and health regulations implemented by HEW that expanded programs for mothers with infants and all poor children (the Women, Infants, and Children Nutrition program [WIC] and Early Periodic Screening,

Diagnosis and Treatment [EPSDT] program). The Earned Income Tax Credit (EITC) for the working poor, which was adopted in the mid-1970s, was also an indirect effect of NWRO's protests for more assistance for the working poor. The EITC, in fact, institutionalized a small negative income tax for low-wage earners, which was a form of a guaranteed income regardless of its limited level.

Another income-transfer program that was modified and destigmatized, at least partly as a result of the welfare rights movement, was the public assistance component for the aged, blind, and disabled. In 1974 these "adult categories" were transferred from the welfare departments and placed under Social Security, decreasing their visibility and stigma as part of the welfare program. The new SSI program was, in fact, a guaranteed supplemental security income for the "deserving" poor. (See Table 6.1.)

NWRO also appears to have had an indirect impact on the adoption of revenue-sharing programs that addressed the need for guaranteed jobs for poor people. The introduction of the CETA in the mid-1970s created public service jobs for thousands. While millions remained out of work, given the limited scope of this public program, it nonetheless institutionalized the right to work and the responsibility of the federal government to intervene in the economy to attenuate the effects of cyclical and long-term unemployment in a free enterprise system.

Thus, while welfare reform and guaranteed income and jobs for the residual category of women with dependent children—the AFDC component—remained stalled in the halls of Congress in 1980, public policies providing some guaranteed income, jobs, and other in-kind benefits for the working poor, the unemployed, the aged and disabled, and children seemed to be expanding, albeit slowly and at very low benefit levels. Mothers with dependent children, categorized now as "able-bodied" nonproducers, despite their contributions in the home, continued to be penalized with an inadequate and stigmatized public subsidy. Yet, there were signs that a few political leaders were moving to reduce some of these penalties, if not substantively, at least symbolically. Administrative actions at the national and local levels eliminated the word welfare from the titles of government departments and replaced it with the new term human services.* Thus,

---

*The 27-year-old Department of Health, Education and Welfare was transformed on May 4, 1980, into two parts—the Department of Health and Human Services (HHS) and the new Department of Education. Similarly, a few years earlier, the New Jersey agency handling welfare became the Department of Human Services. In some local welfare departments, the word welfare was also being eliminated.

both real and symbolic actions by political leaders seemed to indicate a trend toward the federalizing of income and jobs for the "deserving" poor and the continuing acceptance of limited tinkering with the AFDC and WIN workfare programs, which primarily affect poor women and their dependent children. Ironically, demographic data revealed the "feminization of poverty" by 1980.[16]

The National Welfare Rights movement had an impact not only on various public policies that increased the benefits for poor people but also on its participants. It raised awareness among black and white churches and civil rights and feminist groups that welfare was not only a poor people's issue, not only a black problem, but more specifically a "women's" issue. It also brought to the surface the recognition of the impact of welfare programs on growing numbers of families. By the 1980s, at least in some sectors, the right to income, through jobs or government subsidies, was gaining adherents, especially as deteriorating economic conditions dissipated the resources of the family.

Participation in the welfare rights protest appears also to have politicized a large number of poor black women and, to a lesser extent, some poor white women. Involvement in NWRO helped many to redefine their economic condition as rooted in systemic rather than individual pathologies. Some NWRO leaders gained career opportunities and, through the art of grantsmanship, mobilized small federal grants to sustain and expand their activities at the local level. Many others, however, were not as fortunate and remain trapped in economic dependency on the state.

Finally, NWRO had an impact on the lives of the poor in general and AFDC women (and some men) and their children in particular, most of whom probably had never heard of or participated in the welfare rights struggle. In economic terms, NWRO's protest succeeded in these few years in transferring millions of dollars and in-kind benefits to poor female-headed families and others. By reopening the debate on the right to welfare and income and the right to work, public subsidies to the poor lost some of their stigma, thus helping to expand applications for assistance. Similarly, the continuing efforts of the Legal Services lawyers, and especially the Center for Social Welfare Policy and Law, helped to expand eligibility rights and to curtail

---

("Education Dept. Begins as H.E.W. Splits Today," New York Times, May 4, 1980). It is interesting to note that these changes occurred after women assumed the leadership positions in these departments (Patricia Harris in HHS and Ann Klein in New Jersey). This does not imply, however, that they personally were the cause of such changes.

arbitrary terminations of support. Whereas only about one-third of the eligible poor were on the welfare rolls at the start of the movement in 1966, nearly 90 percent were receiving some assistance by the end of the 1970s.[17] Thus, NWRO was in the vanguard of expanding the economic rights of the poor during this era.

In conclusion, the analysis of these data raises some questions and points to some trends about possible future coalitions within the becalmed, but still unresolved, welfare rights struggle. Questions arise as to who will participate, what alliances are likely to emerge and around what issues, and how future movements will address goals similar to those of NWRO. Current indications are that welfare rights will not be revitalized as a separate movement of poor women. Rather, it appears that poor women and their concerns will more likely become incorporated into existing protest movements that are, or seem to be, moving in the direction of integrating the issues of poverty and welfare.

One alternative, it seems, would be for poor women to become part of the feminist movement, especially as attention to economic issues rises within this protest group. Given the fact that welfare is being incorporated as a women's issue in growing numbers of women's coalitions, it would seem probable that, despite racial and class tensions, poor women may gradually become integrated in various sectors of the expanding feminist movement. Demographic projections suggest increases in the number of single parents, widows, and displaced homemakers—the groups most vulnerable to poverty. This trend would enhance the likelihood that welfare and other guaranteed government supports would gain legitimacy and prominence within the context of the feminists' goal of economic equality. In the growing black feminist movement, which incorporated from the outset the issue of poverty as a central concern and poor women as an integral part of its constituency, the chances seem high that welfare, and other NWRO issues, will continue to be addressed. As part of the broader feminist movement, black feminists may become the "linking pin" between the white, middle-class and the poor, black women's protests. Similarly, feminist/socialists, primarily white women, have also adopted the issue of women's poverty into their agendas, and this group may become a bridge that will unite poor white women with the broader movement.

Poor black women, however, may choose to join and use the black civil rights movement as a forum for their concerns. If the current, internal class debate within the black movement leads to greater unity and solidarity, it may be very likely that poverty and welfare rights, along with job rights, will be clearly advocated by this protest group.[18] The rise of women into leadership positions within the black movement will also give greater impetus to the support for welfare issues. Although only a small sector of the black protest movement was actively involved in the welfare rights struggle, the demands of poor blacks, if economic conditions continue to deteriorate, may also bring welfare concerns to the fore.

A less likely, but still possible, alternative for poor women as challengers of the system would be for them to become part of the local grass-roots movements, especially the spin-offs from NWRO, such as ACORN and MEJ. In the past, these movements have tended to avoid the welfare issue and have focused on low-income and working-class groups. Some WRO groups have joined this movement, but the dominance of whites and middle-class organizers and members seems to have inhibited, and may continue to inhibit, participation by poor black women. However, as AFDC women in WIN and CETA work programs join the fight for jobs and adequate income, they may, as some already apparently have, become participants in the rising movement for "Jobs and Justice." For this to come about, concerted efforts will have to be made to attract this group into this protest.

The National Clients Council, an arm of the federally funded Legal Services Corporation, provides another alternative for political activism by poor women and for promotion of their personal and family needs. Given its dependency on government support, its chances of achieving comprehensive changes in the economic rights of poor people seem to be slim. At best, it would appear that this movement organization of poor people institutionalized by the political establishment may establish another forum for poor people in general and poor women in particular to voice their grievances, as it continues the historical ties between the disadvantaged and the poverty lawyers.

In light of these various alternatives, the question arises as to the possibility of a broadly based coalition as a carrier of the goals initiated by NWRO, in order to maximize political power. Feminists and blacks, who played only a peripheral role in the welfare rights protest, seem clearly to be in the vanguard of this continuing struggle, as we suggested above. Other groups, such as the local grass-roots coalitions in the "Jobs and Justice" movement, seem to be other likely candidates for a broad-based coalition. Labor unions, who also abstained from the protest of poor women, may in the future become an active ally, especially if the unprecedented influx of women into the labor force continues. Many of the issues raised by NWRO concern not only the poor, "unemployed" women but also working women, given their economic vulnerability in U.S. society. As women at home become redefined as unemployed or as employed homemakers—rather than displaced homemakers—they may gain the support of labor unions, since they would represent a potential pool of future workers and labor union members.

Similarly, liberal white churches may be expected to join, and perhaps emerge as one of the catalysts, in a renewed protest for economic rights. Rising conservatism within religious institutions may temporarily restrict social activism and limit the numbers of churches and denominations involved. However, given their historical participation in progressive social struggles, one would expect the churches to assume a visible role in any future protest by the poor and the disadvantaged.

The emergence of a broad-based, majoritarian coalition for economic rights that might be the future carrier of the welfare rights concerns is dependent on the availability of resources from protest movement organizations and their supporters, which hinges in turn on favorable political and economic conditions within society. Ideally, as has been learned from NWRO's history, a liberal political climate and an economy of affluence would provide the necessary social context within which protest for income redistribution might emerge. Given the current projections of scarcity in the coming decade and the conservative political scene at the beginning of the 1980s, it seems unlikely that widespread mobilization will occur in the near future, since resources of outsiders, both within the public and private sectors, will be at a premium. Under such conditions one would expect to find increased competition among potential allies. On the other hand, the rising conservative tide may also result in stronger bonds and coalitions among liberals.

One issue that is gaining visibility within the political arena, and that may catalyze protest by both liberals and conservatives, is the question of the family's economic and social rights.[19] Such an issue appears to be gathering momentum among black and white feminists, among blacks and other minorities, and among church and labor groups. Social scientists and political leaders also have been actively promoting this issue as a social problem. Liberals and conservatives, with almost polar views on the definition of and solutions to the "family problem," are also providing impetus for this emerging conflict. The debate centers around the changing nature of the structure of the family and its social, economic, and political consequences. In general, the liberals' major concerns are with the deteriorating economic condition of the family, the need for social supports for single and two-parent families, such as child care, flexible working hours, and greater job and training opportunities given the large influx of women into the labor market.[20] Liberals argue in favor of government intervention to guarantee and expand such social policies as well as the right of poor and nonpoor women to control reproduction to promote the well-being of their families. While adolescent pregnancy is of concern to a broad spectrum of groups within society, in general the liberal perspective underscores the need for expanded sex education in the schools and home to stem the rise of births among very young girls. Consequently, under the rubric of the "family crisis" various welfare rights concerns are subsumed, including the right to adequate income and social supports for traditional and nontraditional families.

Conservatives, on the other hand, tend to view the rise of divorce, separation, and adolescent pregnancy, resulting in the proliferation of female-headed households, as a clear indication that the traditional values and authority within the family are being eroded. The primary culprit from the conservative point of view is the government, which through its social policies on welfare, abortion, sex education, school prayer, and affirmative action, has invaded the rights of the family and destroyed the traditional patriarchal structure of authority. The conservative perspective sees the need to halt such government intervention, to eliminate abortion rights, and to restore the traditional nuclear family, the male as head of the family, and religion in the schools. Clearly, these two political groups are polarized in the way they define and seek solutions to strengthen the family in society.

In the past politicians and social scientists in government have sought to use the family crisis as a means for mobilizing support for welfare reform among both liberals and conservatives. While this tactic failed in the 1970s in the FAP debate, in the next decade it seems likely that it will be used once again in the continuing struggle for welfare reform. Given the worsening polarization within the political arena, it may be that in the coming years the emphasis of welfare rights will shift to family rights and the role of government and its social policy impact on the family. The outcome of this conflict will depend once again, as it did in the NWRO struggle, on the resources mobilized by its challengers and opponents.

What then is the outlook in the 1980s for the continuation of the welfare rights protest? Based on the analysis of NWRO's protest and the current social, economic, and political conditions, it seems unlikely that political leaders will consider any comprehensive restructuring of the welfare system in the near future. Welfare reform will probably remain simmering on a back burner within the political arena until social turmoil by the poor and their supporters once again threatens the fabric of U.S. society. Limited tinkering will continue, but no major guaranteed income program is likely to occur in the next few years. Political authorities will continue to define the welfare problem and its solution in terms of "relief for the cities" and "workfare" for the poor. Conservatives will fight for social policies that reinforce the traditional patriarchal family structure and reduce governmental intervention. Liberals, as supporters of the poor, such as the social activists in the main-line denominations, foundations, and academia, will most likely continue to mobilize around economic justice in general, and family rights in particular, because of the hostile climate toward welfare and other social programs for the poor. Black and women's groups, and possibly labor (given the rising number of working women), will play increasingly important roles in the continuing contest for welfare reform, given the "feminization of poverty" in the United States.

Poor women will also continue to be involved in the ongoing struggle for welfare reform. While scattered groups of welfare rights women remain active in some parts of the country, there are few signs that they will be able to mobilize the necessary resources to reemerge as a national movement. Indications are that poor women and their special issues will become absorbed into the movements of feminists, blacks, and the working poor (especially organized labor women). In none of these, however, does it appear that welfare alone will be used as a central mobilizing "handle."

Feminists, despite repeated efforts to integrate welfare and poverty into their agendas, have not succeeded in the past in concentrating their scarce resources on the economic needs of poor women. The condition of unemployed and underemployed women in the home and in the labor force, while gaining visibility and recognition within the movement, has received relatively little attention compared with other priorities, such as the ERA. As black feminists join in this struggle, this is likely to change.

It is clear that, given the social reality of welfare as a women's issue, at least for some years to come, women will have to remain the the challengers in this struggle. They will have to continue to lead the fight for their own welfare and economic rights. Others may choose to join and support this struggle. Ultimately, however, feminists from all walks of life, both black and white, young and old, in the home or in the labor market, will have to unite to continue and complete the struggle for welfare rights begun by the NWRO women in the 1960s.

NOTES

1. Joe R. Feagin, Subordinating the Poor: Welfare and American Beliefs (Englewood Cliffs, N.J.: Prentice-Hall, 1975).
2. William Watts and Lloyd A. Free, State of the Nation, 1974 (Washington, D.C.: Potomac, 1974).
3. Robert Reinhold, "Public Found against Welfare Idea but in Favor of What Programs Do," New York Times, August 3, 1977.
4. Edwin Schur, The Awareness Trap: Self Absorption instead of Social Change (New York: Quadrangle, 1976); Christopher Lasch, The Culture of Narcissism: American Life in an Age of Diminishing Expectations (New York: W. W. Norton, 1978).

5. Kathleen Teltsch, "For Ford Foundation Head, Grappling Is Worth Effort," New York Times, May 20, 1980; Kathleen Teltsch, "Foundation and Businesses Start Self-Help Corporation," New York Times, May 23, 1980; Kathleen Teltsch, "Foundation Urges More Philanthropy by Business," New York Times, May 25, 1980; Kathleen Teltsch, "A Believer in Self-Help for City Ills," New York Times, May 26, 1980. In all of these articles, the thrust of the coalition of businesses with the Ford Foundation (and possibly others)—a nonprofit corporation called the Local Initiatives Support Corporation—is "to assist promising self-help neighborhood groups in revitalizing blighted areas in cities across the country." The emphasis at the beginning of the 1980s is on localism and self-help, with some support from outsiders. The Ford Foundation is the country's "wealthiest private philanthropy," and "it has often been the pacesetter for a number of the country's 22,500 foundations." Franklin Thomas, the first black president of the Ford Foundation, stated that among the "major future concerns" for foundations in the 1980s would be "women's rights and the struggle of black and Hispanic Americans as linked issues that should be addressed simultaneously through a concerted effort to help 'those who are discriminated against, whether based on race, sex or whatever.'" See also "Local Initiatives," Ford Foundation Letter 2 (June 1, 1980).

6. Adam Clymer, "Jackson, Attacking Carter, Says Reagan May Win," New York Times, May 23, 1980. Senator Jackson warned that Ronald Reagan might win the November elections because working people believe the Democratic party "is no longer the Party of Roosevelt and Truman" and that it "no longer offers a coherent and comprehensive program for social progress at home."

7. Arthur Schlesinger, Jr., "Is Liberalism Dead?," New York Times Magazine, March 30, 1980. The subtitle states, "No, says the author, a well-known liberal himself. Conservatism may appear to be sweeping the land, but liberalism has been essential to American democracy, and it is going to surface again."

8. Field notes, November 11, 1972; July 30, 1974; September 11, 1974; and August 15, 1975.

9. Paul Sherry, Hobart Burch, and Mel Turner, "UCC/NWRO," in Voluntarism in America's Future (Washington, D.C.: Center for a Voluntary Society, 1972), p. 39; Richard Rogin, "Now It's Welfare Lib," New York Times Magazine, September 27, 1970, p. 85.

10. Lucy Komisar, Down and Out in the U.S.A.: A History of Social Welfare (New York: New Viewpoints, 1974), p. 182.

11. Nicholas Kotz and Mary Lynn Kotz, A Passion for Equality: George Wiley and the Movement (New York: W. W. Norton, 1977), p. 291.

12. Taped interview with Bert DeLeeuw, July 1974.

13. Personal interview with Frances Fox Piven, New York City, September 1974. See also Frances Fox Piven and Richard A. Cloward, Poor People's Movements: Why They Succeed, How They Fail (New York: Pantheon Books, 1977).

14. Kotz and Kotz, Passion for Equality, pp. 285-86.

15. Roger Wilkins, "Books of the Times," New York Times, September 14, 1977 (book review of Kotz and Kotz, Passion for Equality).

16. A 1980 report states that

> To the extent that there have been "winners" in the War on Poverty during the 1970s, they have been male—mainly white. What one writer has called the "feminization of poverty" has become one of the most compelling social facts of the decade. And at the same time, relatedly, the chances of poverty have also increased for blacks, relative to whites."

The writer and the study referred to in this quotation is Doiana Pearce, "The Feminization of Poverty—Women, Work, and Welfare," (unpublished manuscript, Department of Sociology, University of Illinois, Chicago Circle), 1978. (National Advisory Council on Economic Opportunity, Twelfth Report, Critical Choices for the 80's [Washington, D.C.: U.S. Government Printing Office, 1980], p. 17.)

17. Spencer Rich, "Figures Show End of Era in Social Program Growth," Washington Post, February 13, 1979.

18. For arguments showing that gaps between the black middle-class and the black poor are widening, see William Julius Wilson, The Declining Significance of Race: Blacks and Changing American Institutions (Chicago: University of Chicago Press, 1978). Also William Brasher, "The Black Middle Class: Making It," New York Times Magazine, December 3, 1978. For newspaper articles on intraracial conflicts between the black middle class and the black poor, see Thomas A. Johnson, "Leaders Fear Blacks Will Shun Election and Lose Political Impact," New York Times, May 23, 1980, where William A. Jones, head of the National Black Pastor's Conference, asserts that "certain black organizations" have not stood on the side of the poor "in the face of opposition from segments of the white community, both Christian and non-Christian." Another black minister, Herbert Daughtry in Brooklyn, argues that the "crucial black issues of the 1980's" will be the struggle for leadership "between the grassroots leaders or the people propped up in positions of power by whites." Another article, Kent D. Smith, "Lawyer Shocks NAACP," Montclair Times (Montclair, N.J.), May 22, 1980, quotes Raymond A. Brown, noted black trial lawyer, as making a "searing attack" on

middle-class blacks in NAACP who he contends are "more concerned with assimilating into white society than dealing with the plight of the larger and less fortunate black community." Finally, Vernon Jordan in his "Introduction" to The State of Black America, 1979 decries the assertion that those blacks who have "made it" are neglecting the ones who have not and argues that, in a 1978 survey of "2,000 highly successful blacks," 75 percent had supported the civil rights movement and 67 percent made a "concerted effort to support black business." He contends that, "far from being isolated from the mass of Black America, the black middle class is an integral part of it." See The State of Black America, 1979, ed. James D. Williams (National Urban League, 1979), pp. iv-v.

19. "Poll Finds People Feel Family Life on Decline," New York Times, June 3, 1980; "Poll Shows Faith in Strong Family Is Threatened," Star Ledger (Newark, N.J.), June 3, 1980. Both of these articles report on a Gallup poll commissioned by the White House Conference on Families that states that "the majority of Americans favored changes in tax, health, welfare, and housing laws to give more consideration to families" (emphasis added). Using a "representative sample of 1592 adults—married, single and divorced—[the poll] uncovered a 'mandate for change'" in four areas, namely, tax, welfare, health, and child-care policies. In terms of policies affecting both the family and employment, U.S. residents were found to want "more flexible working hours, a four-day work week, more sick leave, employer-provided child care, tax credits for working mothers."

20. Suzanne Schiffman, "Making It Easier To Be a Working Parent," New York Times, November 24, 1980.

APPENDIX I

In social-movement theories, few social scientists have explicitly noted the triadic nature of social protest, the power distribution within the triad, and the consequences for its outcome. Some have indirectly alluded to this characteristic of conflict. Heberle suggests, for instance, that "informal unofficial subgroupings within a larger social movement may be of as great importance for an understanding of its functioning as the official or formal organization."[1] Gamson calls attention to the principal actors in social protest as the "partisan groups" versus the "authorities" and the uncommitted or committed public.[2] More recently, he refers to the triadic nature of social protest by identifying the actors as the "challengers" and their "allies" joined against the "authorities."[3] Lipsky suggests that one of the major problems of the powerless is "to activate third parties" in order to "create bargaining resources."[4] Oberschall, in his study of social conflict, also emphasizes that "the mobilizing effects of intermediate groups are not adequately recognized in mass society theory."[5] Noting that "outside support for initiating and sustaining mobilization for attaining the collective good" is not uncommon (for instance, "Marx's theory of bourgeois ideologists and intellectuals who join the anticapitalist movement of the working class"),[6] he suggests that

> all groups engage in conflict, whether they are threatened
> and therefore have to organize defensively or whether they
> initiate a process of confrontation, are faced with the twin
> problem of mobilizing their members' commitments and
> resources for the achievement of collective goals against
> outside resistance and/or recruiting new members or other-
> wise gaining sympathy, support, and outside help from
> third parties, the uncommitted, and the frequently apathetic
> public.[7] [Emphasis added]

Zald and Ash, in their analysis of social-movement organizations (MOs), also refer indirectly to the triadic structure of conflict, and more specifically social protest, by noting that the "environment of MOs consists of two major segments . . . one broader segment . . . members and backers . . . and the target structures . . . which the movement organization wishes to change"[8] (emphasis added).

More recently, McCarthy and Zald focus attention on the role of outsiders and supporters and their consequences for social movements. The traditional view has been that social movements are dependent on their participating members for their resources and survival. They find, however, that the trend nowadays is for resources to be provided by supporters in churches, foundations, and government itself. Independence from a mass support base implies dependence on other sources. The consequences for social protest are critical, as they point out.

> If it is displeased, a source controlling major amounts of organizational funds can destroy a social movement organization overnight. . . . Foundations, churches, and government agencies are involved in a web of institutional controls that prohibit them from getting too far out of line. Consequently, though it may appear obvious, we believe that the bulk of the institution-backed participatory revolution is meliorative rather than radical in intent. [9]

They suggest that such financial dependence on outside supporters directs "dissent into legitimate channels." Regardless of the motives, the consequences of such support end up as social control of the protesters, both by their friends and allies and by the authorities that dominate the system. At times, however, radical groups may benefit indirectly from such support as resources are diverted from ameliorative programs resources to other more militant groups.

Both the protesters and their allies are linked to the state authorities through existing laws and regulations that exert social control and help keep them in line. Rules that govern the funding by churches and foundations to different groups, and the political elite's ability to change those rules, have a profound effect on the resources available to protesters, whether channeled directly or indirectly through their allies in the struggle. [10] McCarthy and Zald suggest that such "professional social movement activity" by churches, foundations, and other friendly groups "could quite rapidly be reversed if the political elite were determined to bring about such a change." [11] They add that "whereas classical analysis predicts more activity in less prosperous times, [their] analysis predicts just the reverse." The reciprocal lines of interaction between the protesters, their supporters, and the target structures in the federal government thus underscore the triadic nature of social protest in general and NWRO's struggle in particular.

In developing the resource mobilization theory, McCarthy and Zald emphasize the need to examine the role of outsiders in the analysis of social movements. [12] They differentiate participants who are in a position to benefit directly from the social movement organization (SMO) goals (potential beneficiaries) from those who are not. Conscience adherents and conscience constituents are those who do not stand to gain directly from the SMO. The latter are directly involved as supporters; the former are favorable to the movement but

as yet uninvolved.[13] McCarthy and Zald suggest that the "partition-
ing of groups into mass or elite and conscience or beneficiary by-
stander publics, adherents, constituents, and opponents allows us to
describe more systematically the resource mobilization styles and
dilemmas of specific SMOs."[14] They propose a number of hypotheses
linking the interaction among these various groups with the SMO's
gain or loss of resources.[15]

Similarly, Useem in his work on social protest in the United
States describes the principal actors as the "base constituency" of the
protest organization (or what I call the core group), the "secondary
constituencies," and the "targets" within the dominant system.[16]
The base constituency consists of all those "sharing the same subordinate class position," and the secondary constituencies are

> groups whose interests are identified with neither the
> status quo nor social change within an institution. . . .
> Their marginal or mixed interests allow them to play roles
> ranging from that of a neutral third party to one of open sup-
> porter, and both the protest organization and its opposition
> tend to view these intermediate groups as potentially impor-
> tant allies—or enemies. . . . However, latent interests fre-
> quently link secondary constituencies to one side or the
> other, and intense class conflict can force them to act on
> these interests, whatever the pleadings of the protest orga-
> nization and its opposition.[17]

The measure of a protest movement's potential strength depends in
part, then, on "whether secondary constituencies are likely to lend
support during periods of intense conflict."[18] Useem, describing
the asymmetry of power in protest movements between the base constituency's resources and that of the dominant regime, adds that mobilization barriers are critical factors in the collapse of a protest
movement. Without effective mobilization of members and supporters,
the demise of the protest organization generally is inevitable. Along
similar lines, Horowitz has noted that much social protest and social-
movement literature is written quite apart from considerations of
political power.[19] It is this dampening of political variables that
leads to an underestimation of organizational asymmetry in social protest movements.

The conceptualization of conflict as triadic, rather than linear,
was first suggested by Simmel and later expanded by Caplow. Both,
to some extent, examined the triads within political struggles, not
only the visible external triad of the protesters and their allies against
the target structures but also the less noticeable triadic conflicts that
emerged within organizations.

Discussing Simmel's pioneering work in conflict and cooperation, Caplow noted that Simmel viewed social interaction as triangular rather than linear.[20] His was a "geometrical model of interaction." While Simmel never used the terms dyad or triad, he expressed concern over "patterns of social relationships involving three elements." Nor did he ever discuss coalitions directly. He was, however, very interested in "the role of the third party added to a dyad" and the ensuing cooperation and conflict that resulted in this triadic interaction.

In triads Simmel emphasized that "differences in power [were] both causes and consequences of the catalytic influence of a third party on the relationship between unequals."[21] Simmel also suggested that there were three possible roles for the "third members": as mediators, as tertius gaudens, and as oppressors. The mediators intervened to stop conflict. The tertius gaudens (whose support is sought by both sides) entered the conflict or political arena to further their own interest and would "sacrifice the interests of the group to . . . [their] private program." The oppressors intervened to divide the other two for their own purposes and to achieve their goals.[22]

Another property of the triad noted by Simmel was that the triad was not rigid or static but, rather, fluid and dynamic. Not only was the "triad in a continuous situation," almost as "in a game of musical chairs," but the audience also played an important part, as participants moved in and out of the triad, or remained as observers.[23] Some eventually might choose to join one of the sides to strengthen its power with additional resources. When this happened, the power distribution within the triad could potentially be altered, at times enough to change the outcome in the triadic struggle.

Expanding on Simmel's ideas about triads and conflict, Caplow posited that

> at some stage most conflicts can be diagrammed as a triad composed of a pair of combatants and an uncommitted witness to whom each of the combatants appeal for support. The outcome of the conflict is often decided by the formation of a coalition between one of the combatants and the witness.[24]

Caplow emphasized the dynamic nature of the process of interaction within the triad. Conflict and cooperation were both present. "The geometry of triads," he stated, "is full of surprises, for in most triadic situations a coalition of two against one can convert strength into weakness and weakness into strength." The outcome of the conflict is often decided by the formation of coalitions of two against one. He adds that "the whole point of triad theory" is that "different configurations of power lead to different outcomes."

Another aspect of triads underscored by Caplow was that such coalitions always fell into two categories: those between like partners and an unlike opponent; and those between unlike partners against an opponent who is like one of the partners.[25] The coalitions of unlike partners, while generally a "winning coalition," paradoxically were also generally unstable alliances because there was "always . . . some flavor of betrayal, however slight." The "fundamental dilemma of coalition formation" in a triadic setting was the choice of partners: the choice of forming a winning coalition with unlike partners and "the desire for a like partner and unlike opponent." Like partners provided immediate, built-in incentives for participation, given peer solidarity and the lessened risks of domination by a stronger ally. Coalitions with unlike partners, however, held out the long-range reward of greater probability of goal achievement (given access to more resources) but also heightened the dangers of control by the stronger partner. Observations within triads in a family led Caplow to conclude that winning coalitions were generally those between unlike partners, based on different status determinants of generation and gender.* Coalitions between like partners, he found, were "seldom profitable."

Similar dilemmas were identified in organizational triads. Choices of partners within the organization, as well as of the organization within the larger environment, resulted in different risks and rewards. There were immediate and long-range payoffs as well as costs in different alliances. Tensions between personal and group needs affected such choices as organizations emerged. Caplow also noted that the structural basis on which alliances are formed might alternate. For instance,

> Although a given coalition may predominate on the basis
> of some balance of power and likeness, other coalitions
> will appear in the same primary triad in response to oc-
> casions that emphasize other kinds of likeness and unlike-
> ness.[26]

The basis might be generation, gender, occupation, or any other determinant of status and power. "This alternation of coalitions," he added, accounted for much of the vitality in the triad and may in fact add to its cohesiveness. On the other hand, he cautioned, it may become the source of "perennial instability and tension" within the triadic system. Coalitions in triads are, thus, tenuous and unstable,

---

*I suggest this also applies to differentiation on the basis of race and class.

reflecting a continuous process of fusion and fission of different allies and varying combinations of "two against one." Hence, as the power of distribution shifts, the outcomes in different episodes vary.

Moving from the level of the family and organizations to the global level of conflict and cooperation, Caplow noted that when the struggle erupts, some immediately choose sides, while others remain as witnesses.

> There may also be multiple witnesses of a conflict, each witness forming a distinct triad with the two antagonists and thus there may be a considerable number of these triads at the scene of a particular conflict. The witness to an organized conflict is both an observer and a potential intervener. We would not classify as witnesses those observers who are so detached from the situation or so weak in relation to the antagonists that they cannot influence the outcome. The witness may intervene by interrupting the conflict or by forming a coalition with one of the antagonists. If he puts a stop to the conflict, he may have protected the probable loser. If he forms a coalition, his intention is to decide the conflict in favor of his partner. Even if he decides to abstain the witness may determine the outcome of the conflict either because he allows the stronger contestant to proceed to victory without interference, or because his abstention causes a sudden loss of strength for the side on whose behalf he was expected to intervene. [27]

As the struggle continues, "more and more of them will be drawn in until most members of the system are involved." Caplow continued,

> The witness who joins a conflict by forming a coalition with one of the antagonists almost always hopes and expects that the new coalition will dominate the triad, but the outcome of any conflict is inherently uncertain and there is always a possibility that the intervention will fail, either because the strength of the parties has been miscalculated or because a new witness, attracted by the conflict in its modified form, intervenes in turn. [28]

Combining the concepts of triadic conflicts and resource mobilization with protest movement theories, the National Welfare Rights movement is analyzed in the preceding chapters by defining the three major actors in the triad as A (NWRO's opponents or the welfare authorities within the dominant system); B (NWRO's elite supporters, such as the middle-class churches and foundations); and C (the core group of protesters, NWRO's base constituency of poor women, or the challengers belonging to the same subordinate class with the social system).* (Local and state, as well as national protests, form similar triadic conflicts.) According to Caplow, in such a conflict the power distribution within the triad would be described as $A > B > C$.

Peer allies (as measured in terms of comparable power and status within the dominant system) would be symbolized as follows: peer allies of the base constituency or core group (C) would be identified as C' (C-prime). In this study, for example, potential and actual peer allies of the organized poor women are assumed to be organized groups of blacks, women, the working poor, and other minority-power organizations. The peer groups of the middle-class Friends of Welfare Rights (B) would be symbolized by B' (B-prime) and would include various liberal, middle-class organizations and agencies that joined the Friends in support of NWRO. A-primes (A') would thus be the peer allies of the target structures, including those that sided with the welfare authorities and political leaders, opposing the actions and goals of NWRO. While theoretically this portrays a rigid categorization of groups, in practice it is acknowledged that individuals may well fit into two or more categories, which may weaken the analytical power of the model by introducing an element of arbitrary choice in the classification of the members of the triad. For example, a middle-class Friends group, with a large constituency of feminists might well be defined as a nonpeer supporter (B) or as a peer ally, a feminist organization (C'). To minimize this overlap, we focus on groups rather than individuals in trying to classify on the basis of status and power.

Within such a theoretical framework, a social protest movement is thus conceptualized as a dynamic and changing configuration of movement organizations, some closely resembling the core group in terms of power and status, others differing from it. At different times, some become active participants, others remain witness, and still others join and later withdraw, depending on the particular episode under investigation. Such choices affect the power distribution and outcomes within the triadic conflict.

Power within this framework is defined as mobilized resources, both material and nonmaterial, needed to achieve the stated goals. Mobilized resources are in this analysis members, leaders, organizers, supporters, monies, and other needed organizational facilities.[29]

In a social protest movement, it is posited that coalitions between like and unlike status groups emerge in an effort to mobilize and maximize scarce resources to achieve a mutually desired goal or

---

*The symbols A, B, and C are taken from Caplow's work.

goals. In order for these coalitions to arise, however, the assumption is that there are immediate, as well as long-range, incentives to attract participants. Rewards are needed to create solidarity to build and sustain organized protest for any limited period of time. It is also assumed that there are risks, which, like the rewards, fluctuate over time and in different episodes, as conditions within the movement and within the broader society change. As internal and external tensions ebb and flow, the risks and rewards also rise and fall, affecting the formation and dissolution of coalitions within the social protest movement. As alternatives emerge, these tensions also alter the number and nature of alliances within the movement and the larger society and, consequently, the power distribution within the triad. Therefore, it is expected that, as coalitions emerge or dissolve, the mobilized resources of the protest will increase or decrease, depending to a large extent on the intensity of both internal and external conflicts.

Within social protest movements, internal conflicts arise <u>within</u> the core group, <u>between</u> the core-group leadership and its rank-and-file member organizations, and <u>between</u> the core protest organization and its peer and nonpeer allies as a result of structural and ideological contradictions. Within NWRO, for example, the anomalies in terms of race, class, and gender within the movement at various levels and between different groups (blacks and whites, the poor and nonpoor, and females and males) eventually led to conflicts that increased the costs for participation and eroded the movement's mobilized resources. Cooperation was inhibited as allies competed for scarce resources and control. Similarly, conflicts between NWRO and its nonpoor allies over strategies and tactics also resulted in further splintering within the movement and a loss of power for the organized women on welfare within the political arena. Peer bonding among blacks, women, and the working poor, which might have been predicted to emerge (given NWRO's predominant membership of poor black women), in fact was practically nonexistent, as conflicts and competition for scarce resources between "like" partners erupted across racial, class, and gender lines. Thus, cooperation led to internal conflict between potential allies within the movement and contributed to the erosion of NWRO's mobilized resources.

While conflict among "like" partners tends to weaken solidarity and contribute to the loss of power for the protesters, cooperation with allies and opponents in the dominant sector may also lead to conflict and ultimately to accommodation. While the movement may temporarily gain added resources through negotiations with its opponents and coalitions with its Friends, such strategies at the same time may create internal conflicts and fragmentation, with a consequent loss of members and supporters who oppose such tactics. As allies come and go, the structure and the resources of the protest movement, and thus its power within the arena, fluctuate. The outcomes of different episodes in the struggle will thus vary, according to the power distribution within the triad. Caplow suggested that in organizational triads "the man in the middle" is a critical actor in the final outcome.[30]

In applying this framework of two against one to social protest, the major thrust of this analysis of the National Welfare Rights movement is, first, to identify the major actors in the triadic conflict. Then, the relative positions of each in terms of power and status within the society are specified. Finally, we identify and trace the changing interaction and configurations of power that emerged, as allies joined, abstained, or withdrew from NWRO's protest against the welfare authorities. By analyzing these processes of mobilization and demobilization within this triadic conflict of the poor and their allies against the ruling power structure, we are better able to explain the rise and fall of NWRO.

NOTES

1. Rudolf Heberle, Social Movements: An Introduction to Political Sociology (New York: Appleton-Century-Crofts, 1951), pp. 272, 279.

2. William A. Gamson, Power and Discontent (Homewood, Ill.: Dorsey Press, 1968), pp. 191-94.

3. William A. Gamson, The Strategy of Social Protest (Homewood, Ill.: Dorsey Press, 1975), p. 140.

4. Michael Lipsky, "Protest as a Political Resource," American Political Science Review 62 (1968): 1144.

5. Anthony Oberschall, Social Conflict and Social Movements (Englewood Cliffs, N.J.: Prentice-Hall, 1973), p. 106.

6. Ibid., p. 115.

7. Ibid., p. 290.

8. Mayer N. Zald and Roberta Ash, "Social Movement Organizations: Growth, Decay and Change," Social Forces 44 (March 1966): 329-30.

9. John D. McCarthy and Mayer N. Zald, The Trend of Social Movements in America: Professionalization and Resource Mobilization (Morristown, N.J.: General Learning Press, 1973), p. 26.

10. Ibid., p. 27.

11. Ibid.

12. John D. McCarthy and Mayer N. Zald, "Resource Mobilization and Social Movements: A Partial Theory," American Journal of Sociology 82 (May 1977): 1215-16.

13. Ibid., pp. 1221-22.

14. Ibid., p. 1223.

15. Ibid., pp. 1225-31.

16. Michal Useem, Protest Movements in America (Indianapolis: Bobbs-Merrill, 1975), pp. 33-34.

17. Ibid., pp. 34-35.

18. Ibid., p. 46.

19. Irving Louis Horowitz, Foundations of Political Sociology (New York: Harper & Row, 1972), pp. 11-18.

20. Theodore Caplow, Two against One: Coalitions in Triad (Englewood Cliffs, N.J.: Prentice-Hall, 1968), pp. 12-20. This discussion of Georg Simmel's theory is based on Caplow's chapter entitled "In Praise of Georg Simmel."

21. Ibid., p. 19.

22. Ibid., p. 20.

23. Ibid., p. 19.

24. Ibid., pp. 9-10.

25. Ibid., p. 67.

26. Ibid.

27. Ibid., pp. 149-50.

28. Ibid.

29. Hubert A. Blalock, Jr., Toward a Theory of Minority-Group Relations (New York: Capricorn Books, 1967), pp. 110-13. See also Gamson, Power and Discontent, p. 73; McCarthy and Zald, "Resource Mobilization," p. 1216; and Oberschall, Social Conflict, pp. 113-18.

30. Caplow, Two against One, p. 57.

APPENDIX II

Harry C. Bredemeier and Judy Getis,[1] in explaining the prisoner's dilemma, compare it to "the fundamental human dilemma" of interdependence and autonomy. They highlight that "human beings are on the one hand inescapably interdependent, and on the other hand autonomous. Everyone's success in achieving his own goals, whatever they might be, is dependent on what other people do, and no one has certain control over what those others will do. 'The others' are in the same position vis-à-vis 'everyone'" (emphasis in the original). This, they add, is basically the prisoner's dilemma in game theory.

More specifically, the prisoner's dilemma is described as a case in which two suspects are apprehended for a crime and immediately separated from each other. Without enough evidence to convict them at a trial, the attorney general attempts to get each to confess. Negotiating with each alone, he offers them the choices of confessing or not confessing. Either choice will result in different rewards and costs for the individual and the couple (the social unit). If both refuse to confess, the attorney general will book them on a minor charge and both will receive one year each in jail (Box I). "If they both confess, they will be prosecuted, but he will recommend less than the most severe [eight years] sentence" (Box IV). However, if one confesses and the other does not, the confessor will receive a lenient (three months) sentence and the other will get ten years (Box II or III). The cost/reward matrix would be as follows:

Prisoner 1   Prisoner 2

	Not Confess	Confess
Not Confess	1 year each I	10 years for 1 3 months for 2 II
Confess	III 3 months for 1 10 years for 2	IV 8 years each

The problem for each prisoner is whether to confess or not to confess. There is no way to know what the other will do. If the prisoners choose to maximize their collective, rather than individual, inter-

405

ests by cooperating and not confessing, each will come out with a one-year sentence. This is the best collective outcome. But lacking information on what the other will do, there is always the risk that one will confess and get off with only a three-month sentence, while the other is penalized with ten years in jail for acting for the collective good. It is a difficult, but real, choice.

Bredemeier and Getis point out that "nearly all of the social problems with which [human beings] are confronted stem either from the failure to find a solution to this basic problem of interdependence-cum-autonomy or from dissatisfaction with the solution." They suggest "that there must be social arrangements that will induce people to give up short run individual benefits for the sake of longer run collective ones (from which, of course, the individuals benefit individually, also, as the game illustrates)."

A similar dilemma exists in coalition building in social movements: how to become socially organized to achieve one's collective goals and at the same time maintain one's autonomy. Coalitional efforts within the welfare rights movement clearly illustrate this dilemma.

NOTE

1. The following discussion is based on Harry C. Bredemeier and Judith Getis, eds., Environments, People and Inequalities: Some Current Problems (New York: John Wiley & Sons, 1973), pp. 4-6.

SELECTED BIBLIOGRAPHY

Aaron, Henry J. Why Is Welfare So Hard to Reform? Washington, D.C.: Brookings Institution, 1973.

Alinsky, Saul D. Reveille for Radicals. New York: Vintage Books, 1969.

_____. Rules for Radicals: A Pragmatic Primer for Realistic Radicals. New York: Vintage Books, 1971.

All about NWRO. Washington, D.C.: National Welfare Rights Organization, 1969.

Allen, Jodie T. Perspectives on Income Maintenance: Where Do We Go from Here and How Far? Washington, D.C.: Urban Institute, 1972.

Ash, Roberta. Social Movements in America. Chicago: Markham, 1972.

Austin, David, Barry Bluestone, Martin Lowenthal, and Martin Rein. The Dilemmas of Welfare Reform. Boston: Social Welfare Regional Research Institute, Institute of Human Sciences, 1972.

Bailis, Lawrence Neil. Bread or Justice: Grassroots Organizing in the Welfare Rights Movement. Lexington, Mass.: D. C. Heath, 1974.

Barth, Michael C., George J. Carcagno, and John L. Palmer. Toward an Effective Income Support System: Problems, Prospects, and Choices. Madison, Wis.: Institute of Research on Poverty, University of Wisconsin, 1974.

Baxandall, Rosalyn, Linda Gordon, and Susan Reverby, eds. America's Working Women: A Documentary History—1600 to the Present. New York: Vintage Books, 1976.

Bell, Inge Powell. CORE and the Strategy of Non-Violence. New York: Random House, 1968.

Bennett, Lerone, Jr. Confrontation: Black and White. Baltimore: Penguin Books, 1968.

"The Black Sexism Debate." Black Scholar, May–June 1979.

Blalock, Hubert M., Jr. Toward a Theory of Minority Group Relations. New York: Capricorn Books, 1967.

Blau, Peter M. Exchange and Power in Social Life. New York: John
   Wiley & Sons, 1967.

_____. "Orientation toward Clients in a Public Welfare Agency." In
   Social Welfare Institutions, edited by Mayer N. Zald, pp. 654–
   70. New York: John Wiley & Sons, 1965.

Bernard, Jessie. Women, Wives, and Mothers: Values and Options.
   Chicago: Aldine, 1975.

Bluestone, Barry, William M. Murphy, and Mary Stevenson. Low
   Wages and the Working Poor. Ann Arbor: Institute of Labor
   and Industrial Relations, University of Michigan, 1973.

Blumer, Herbert. "Social Movements." In Principles of Sociology,
   edited by Alfred M. Lee, 2d ed., pp. 199–220. New York:
   Barnes & Noble, 1962.

_____. "Social Problems as Collective Behavior." Social Problems
   8 (1971): 298–305.

Brager, George. "Organizing the Unaffiliated in a Low-Income Area."
   In Social Welfare Institutions, edited by Mayer N. Zald, pp.
   644–53. New York: John Wiley & Sons, 1965.

Bremer, Robert. "Shifting Attitudes." In Social Welfare Institutions,
   edited by Mayer N. Zald, pp. 23–37. New York: John Wiley &
   Sons, 1965.

Brinton, Crane. The Anatomy of Revolution. New York: Vintage
   Books, 1952.

Burch, Hobart A. "Conversations with George Wiley." Journal of
   Social Issues, November–December 1970, pp. 10–20.

Burkey, Richard M. Racial Discrimination and the Public Policy in
   the United States. Lexington, Mass.: D. C. Heath, 1971.

Cade, Toni, ed. The Black Woman: An Anthology. New York: New
   American Library, 1970.

Cameron, Colin. Attitudes of the Poor and Attitudes towards the Poor: Annotated Bibliography. Madison: Institute for Research on Poverty, University of Wisconsin, 1975.

Cameron, William. Modern Social Movements: A Sociological Outline. New York: Random House, 1966.

Caplow, Theodore. "Further Developments of a Theory of Coalitions in Triad." American Journal of Sociology 64 (March 1969): 488-93.

_____. The Sociology of Work. New York: McGraw-Hill, 1954.

_____. "A Theory of Coalitions in Triad." American Sociological Review 21 (August 1956): 489-93.

_____. Two against One: Coalitions in Triad. Englewood Cliffs, N.J.: Prentice-Hall, 1968.

Carmichael, Stokely, and Charles V. Hamilton. Black Power: The Politics of Liberation. New York: Vintage Books, 1967.

Carroll, Jackson W., Douglas W. Johnson, and Martin E. Marty. Religion in America: 1950 to the Present. New York: Harper & Row, 1979.

Chafe, William H. The American Woman: Her Changing Social, Economic, and Political Roles, 1920-1970. New York: Oxford University Press, 1975.

_____. Women and Equality: Changing Patterns in American Culture. New York: Oxford University Press, 1977.

Clark, Kenneth B. Dark Ghetto: Dilemmas of Social Power. New York: Harper & Row, 1967.

Clark, Kenneth B., and Carl Gershman. "The Black Plight: Race or Class? A Debate between Kenneth B. Clark and Carl Gershman." New York Times Magazine, October 5, 1980, pp. 22-26, 28, 30, 33, 90-96, 98-99, 102, 104, 105, 109.

Cloward, Richard A., and Frances Fox Piven. "Dissensus Politics: A Strategy for Winning Economic Rights." New Republic, April 20, 1968, reprint, pp. 2-6.

_____. "Hidden Protest: The Channeling of Female Innovation and Resistance." Signs 4 (Summer 1979): 651-69.

_____. "Migraticn, Politics, and Welfare." Saturday Review, November 16, 1968, pp. 31-35, reprint.

_____. The Politics of Turmoil: Poverty, Race, and the Urban Crisis. New York: Pantheon Books, 1974.

_____. "Rent Strike: Disrupting the Slum System." New Republic, December 2, 1967, reprint.

_____. "The Weapon of Poverty: Birth of a Movement." Nation, May 8, 1967, reprint.

_____. "The Weight of the Poor: A Strategy to End Poverty." Nation, May 2, 1966, pp. 510-17, reprint.

_____. "Welfare Reform Again." New York Times, April 11, 1977.

_____. "Who Should Be Organized? 'Citizen Action' vs 'Jobs and Justice.'" Working Papers, May-June 1979, pp. 35-40, reprint.

_____. "Workers and Welfare: The Poor against Themselves." Nation, November 25, 1968, reprint.

Coleman, James S. Community Conflict. New York: Free Press, 1957.

Cox, Harvey. "The 'New Breed' in American Churches: Sources of Social Activism in American Religion." In Religion in America, edited by William McLoughlin and R. N. Bellah, pp. 368-82. Boston: Houghton Mifflin, 1968.

Directory of National Black Organizations. New York: AFRAM, 1972.

Dixon, Vernon J., and Badi Foster. Beyond Black and White: An Alternate America. Boston: Little, Brown, 1971.

Elman, Richard M. The Poorhouse State. New York: Dell, 1968.

Epstein, Cynthia Fuchs. Woman's Place. Berkeley: University of California Press, 1971.

Etizioni, Amitai. The Active Society. New York: Free Press, 1968.

Fager, Charles. White Reflections on Black Power. Grand Rapids, Mich.: William B. Erdmanns, 1967.

Feagin, Joe R. Subordinating the Poor: Welfare and American Beliefs. Englewood Cliffs, N.J.: Prentice-Hall, 1975.

Fernandez, John. "Black Unity: An Analysis of Black-White Cooperation." Honors thesis, Harvard University, 1969.

Freeman, Jo. The Politics of Women's Liberation. New York: David McKay, 1975.

Friends of Welfare Rights. Correspondence with chair of Friends of Welfare Rights in Chicago, 1970.

_____. Correspondence with chair of Friends of Welfare Rights in Pittsburgh, 1970.

_____. Field notes in New Jersey, 1968-72.

Gamson, William A. "An Experimental Test of a Theory of Coalition Formation." American Sociological Review 26 (1961): 565-73.

_____. Power and Discontent. Homewood, Ill.: Dorsey Press, 1968.

_____. The Strategy of Social Protest. Homewood, Ill.: Dorsey Press, 1975.

_____. "A Theory of Coalition Formation." American Sociological Review 26 (1961): 373-82.

Gans, Herbert J. More Equality. New York: Vintage Books, 1973.

_____. "The Positive Functions of Poverty." American Journal of Sociology 78 (September 1972): 275-89.

_____. "Three Ways to Solve the Welfare Problem." New York Times Magazine, March 7, 1971, pp. 26-27, 94-97, 100.

_____. "Toward the Equality Revolution." Current Magazine, December 1968, pp. 6-14.

Gelb, Joyce and Alice Sardell. "Organizing the Poor: A Brief Analysis of the Politics of the Welfare Rights Movement." Policy Studies Journal 3 (Summer 1975): 346-54.

_____. "Strategies for the Powerless: The Welfare Rights Movement in New York City." Speech delivered at the 1973 Annual Meeting of the American Political Science Association, New Orleans, La., September 4-8. Mimeographed.

Gerlach, Luther P., and Virginia H. Hine. People, Power, Change: Movements of Social Transformation. Indianapolis: Bobbs-Merrill, 1970.

Ginsberg, Mitchell I., and Norman V. Lourie. "The Current Status of Human Services." Public Welfare, Summer 1974, pp. 27-32, 76, reprint.

Glassman, Carol. "Women in the Welfare System." In Sisterhood Is Powerful, edited by Robin Morgan, pp. 102-14. New York: Vintage Books, 1970.

Glazer, Nathan. " 'Regulating' the Poor—Or Ruining Them." New York Magazine, November 8, 1971, pp. 55-58.

"Goals and Structure." Mimeographed. Newark, N.J.: New Jersey Ad Hoc Coalition for Welfare Reform, 1970.

"Goals of NWRO." Washington, D.C.: National Welfare Rights Organization, 1968.

Goldstein, William. Work and Welfare: A Legal Perspective on the Rights of Women on Welfare. Social Welfare Regional Research Institute Publication no. 3. Boston, 1971.

Goodwin, Leonard. Can Social Science Help Resolve National Problems? Welfare, a Case in Point. New York: Free Press, 1975.

_____. Do the Poor Want to Work? Washington, D.C.: Brookings Institution, 1972.

Gornick, Vivian, and Barbara K. Moran, eds. Woman in Sexist Society. New York: Basic Books, 1972.

Gottlieb, Naomi. The Welfare Bind. New York: Columbia University Press, 1974.

Gouldner, Alvin W. "The Norm of Reciprocity." American Sociological Review 25 (1960): 161-78.

Governor's Select Commission on Civil Disorder. Report for Action. New Jersey, 1968.

Gray Paper No. 5, Issues for Action. "Welfare: End of the Line for Women." Mimeographed. Oakland, Calif.: Older Women's League Educational Fund, May 1980.

Greenwood, Elma. How Churches Fight Poverty. New York: Friendship Press, 1967.

Gurr, T. D. Why Men Rebel. Princeton, N.J.: Princeton University Press, 1970.

Gusfield, Joseph. Protest, Reform, and Revolt: A Reader in Social Movements. New York: John Wiley & Sons, 1970.

_____. Symbolic Crusade: Status Politics and the American Temperance Movement. Urbana: University of Illinois Press, 1963.

Hacker, Helen Mayer. "Women as a Minority Group." Social Forces, October 1951, pp. 60-69.

Hamilton, Laurie S., and John E. Muthard. Reducing Economic Dependency among Welfare Recipients: A Review of Vocational Rehabilitation and Manpower Training Research. Gainesville: Regional Rehabilitation Research Institute, University of Florida, 1973.

Harrington, Michael. The Other America: Poverty in the United States. Baltimore: Penguin Books, 1963.

_____. Socialism. New York: Bantam Books, 1972.

Harris, Robert. Welfare Reform and Social Insurance: Program Issues and Budget Impacts. Washington, D.C.: Urban Institute, 1977. Reprint.

Hayden, Thomas. Rebellion in Newark. New York: Vintage Books, 1967.

Heberle, Rudolf. "Observations on the Sociology of Social Movements." In Readings in Sociology, edited by Alfred M. Lee. New York: Barnes and Noble, 1951.

_____. Social Movements: An Introduction to Political Sociology. New York: Appleton-Century-Crofts, 1951.

Hertz, Susan. "The Politics of the Welfare Mothers Movement: A Case Study." Signs 2 (Spring 1977): 600–11.

Holtzman, Abraham. The Townsend Movement: A Political Study. New York: Bookman, 1963.

Horowitz, Irving Louis. Foundations of Political Sociology. New York: Harper & Row, 1972.

Horowitz, Irving Louis, ed. Equity, Income, and Policy: Comparative Studies in Three Worlds of Development. New York: Praeger, 1977.

Horowitz, Irving Louis, and James Everett Katz. Social Science and Public Policy in the United States. New York: Praeger, 1975.

Howard, John R. The Cutting Edge: Social Movement and Social Change in America. Philadelphia: J. B. Lippincott, 1974.

Howe, Florence, ed. Women and the Power to Change. New York: McGraw-Hill, 1975.

Isaac, Larry, and William R. Kelly. "Racial Insurgency, the State and Welfare Expansion: Local and National Level Evidence from the Postwar United States." Paper presented at the Society for the Study of Social Problems Convention, New York, August 1980.

Jackson, Larry R., and William A. Johnson. Protest by the Poor: The Welfare Rights Movement in New York City. New York: Rand Corporation, 1973.

Jenness, Linda, ed. Feminism and Socialism. New York: Pathfinder Press, 1973.

Just Economics. Issues published 1973 through 1977 by the Movement of Economic Justice, Washington, D.C.

Kahn, Alfred J. Studies in Social Policy and Planning. New York: Russell Sage Foundation, 1969.

Kahn, S. How People Get Power: Organizing Oppressed Communities for Action. New York: McGraw-Hill, 1970.

Kain, John F., ed. Race and Poverty: The Economics of Discrimination. Englewood Cliffs, N.J.: Prentice-Hall, 1969.

Killian, Lewis M. The Impossible Revolution?: Black Power and the American Dream. New York: Random House, 1968.

King, C. Wendell. Social Movements in the United States. New York: Random House, 1952.

Knowles, Louis L., and Kenneth Prewitt, eds. Institutional Racism in America. Englewood Cliffs, N.J.: Prentice-Hall, 1969.

Komisar, Lucy. Down and Under in the U.S.A.: A History of Social Welfare. New York: New Viewpoints, 1974.

_____. "Where Feminism Will Lead." Civil Rights Digest 6 (Spring 1974): 2-11.

Kornhauser, William. The Politics of Mass Society. Glencoe, Ill.: Free Press, 1959.

Kotz, Nicholas, and Mary Lynn Kotz. A Passion for Equality: George Wiley and the Movement. New York: W. W. Norton, 1977.

Kreps, Juanita M. Women and the American Economy. Englewood Cliffs, N.J.: Prentice-Hall, 1976.

Krislov, Samuel. "The OEO Lawyers Fail to Constitutionalize a Right to Welfare: A Study in the Uses and Limits of the Judicial Process." Minnesota Law Review 58 (1973): 211-45.

Kurzman, Paul A. The Mississippi Experience: Strategies for Welfare Rights Action. New York: Association Press, 1971.

LaRue, Linda J. M. "Black Liberation and Women's Lib." Trans-Action 8 (November-December 1970): 59-64.

Lasch, Christopher. The Culture of Narcissism: American Life in an Age of Diminishing Expectations. New York: Warner Books, 1979.

Lasswell, Harold D. Politics: Who Gets What, When, How. New York: Meridian Books, 1971.

Lekachman, Robert. "Acquiescence for Now." Social Policy 10 (May-June 1980): 35.

Lenin, V. I. What Is to Be Done? New York: International, 1969.

Lenski, Gerhard. The Religious Factor. Rev. ed. Garden City, N.Y.: Doubleday, 1963.

Lerner, Gerda. Black Women in White America: A Documentary History. New York: Vintage Books, 1973.

Levens, Helene. "Bread and Justice: A Participant Observer Study of a Welfare Rights Organization." Ph.D. dissertation, University of Wisconsin, 1971.

Levin, Judith, and Patricia Vergatta. "Welfare Laws and Women: An Analysis of Federal Sexism." Paper, Rutgers Law School, 1971.

Levitan, Sar A. Design of Federal Antipoverty Strategy. Ann Arbor: Institute of Labor and Industrial Relations, University of Michigan, 1967.

_____. Programs in Aid of the Poor. 3d ed. Baltimore: Johns Hopkins University Press, 1976.

Levitan, Sar A., and Robert Taggart. "The Great Society Fallout." Society 13 (September-October 1976): 66-72.

_____. The Promise of Greatness: The Social Programs of the Last Decade and Their Major Achievements. Cambridge, Mass.: Harvard University Press, 1976.

Levy, Charles. Voluntary Servitude: Whites in the Negro Movement. New York: Appleton-Century-Crofts, 1968.

Lewis, Diane K. "A Response to Inequality: Black Women, Racism, and Sexism." Signs 3 (Winter 1977): 339-61.

Lipman-Blumen, Jean, and Jessie Bernard. Sex Roles and Social Policy: A Complex Social Science Equation. Beverly Hills, Calif.: Sage, 1979.

Lipset, Seymour Martin. Agrarian Socialism: The Cooperative Commonwealth Federation in Saskatchewan: A Study in Political Sociology. Rev. ed. Berkeley: University of California Press, 1971.

Lipsky, Michael. "Protest as a Political Resource." American Political Science Review 62 (1968): 1144-58.

Lofland, John. Doomsday Cult: A Study of Conversion, Proselytization, and Maintenance of Faith. Englewood Cliffs, N.J.: Prentice-Hall, 1966.

Lowenthal, Martin. Work and Welfare: An Overview. Boston: Social Welfare Regional Research Institute, Institute of Human Sciences, 1971.

McCarthy, John D., and Mayer N. Zald. "Resource Mobilization and Social Movements: A Partial Theory." American Journal of Sociology 82 (May 1977): 1212-41.

_____. The Trend of Social Movements in America: Professionalization and Resource Mobilization. Morristown, N.J.: General Learning Press, 1973.

Marris, Peter, and Martin Rein. Dilemmas of Social Reform: Poverty and Community Action in the United States. 2d ed. Chicago: Aldine, 1973.

Martin, George. "The Emergence and Development of a Social Movement Organization among the Underclass: A Case Study of the National Welfare Rights Organization." Ph.D. dissertation, University of Chicago, 1972.

Marx, Gary, and Michael Useem. "Majority Involvement in Minority Movements: Civil Rights, Abolition, and Untouchability." Journal of Social Issues 27 (1971): 81-104.

Meier, August, and Francis L. Broderick, eds. Black Protest in the Twentieth Century. 2d ed. Indianapolis: Bobbs-Merrill, 1971.

Meier, August, and Elliott Rudwick, eds. Black Protest in the Sixties. Chicago: Quadrangle Books, 1970.

_____. CORE: A Study in the Civil Rights Movement, 1942-1968. New York: Oxford University Press, 1973.

Merton, Robert K. Social Theory and Social Structure. New York: Free Press, 1968.

Michels, Robert. Political Parties: A Sociological Study of the Oligarchical Tendencies of Modern Democracy. New York: Dover, 1959.

Miller, S. M. "Turmoil and/or Acquiescence for the 1980's." Social Policy 10 (May–June 1980): 22–25.

Miller, S. M., and Pamela Roby. The Future of Inequality. New York: Basic Books, 1970.

Mills, C. Wright. The Power Elite. New York: Oxford University Press, 1959.

Morgan, Robin, ed. Sisterhood Is Powerful. New York: Random House, 1970.

Morrison, Toni. "What the Black Woman Thinks about Women's Lib." New York Times Magazine, August 22, 1971, pp. 14–15, 63–64, 66.

Moynihan, Daniel Patrick. Maximum Feasible Misunderstanding. New York: Free Press, 1970.

_____. The Politics of a Guaranteed Income: The Nixon Administration and the Family Assistance Plan. New York: Random House, 1973.

Murphy, Irene. Public Policy and the Status of Women. Lexington, Mass.: Lexington Books, 1974.

National Advisory Council on Economic Opportunity. Critical Choices for the 80's. 12th Report. Washington, D.C.: U.S. Government Printing Office, 1980.

National Welfare Rights Organization. Conferences and conventions, program books, packets, taped workshops. Eastern Regional Conferences: 1970 (Connecticut), 1971 (New York, N.Y.), 1972 (Baltimore, Md.), 1975 (Pittsburgh). National Conventions and Conferences: 1971 (Rhode Island), 1972 (Miami Beach, Fla.), 1973 (Washington, D.C.), 1974 (St. Louis, Mo.), 1977 (Little Rock, Ark.).

Neverdon-Morton, Cynthia. "The Black Women's Struggle for Equality in the South, 1895–1925." In The Afro-American Woman: Struggles and Images, edited by Sharon Harley and Rosalyn Terborg-Penn, pp. 43–57. Port Washington, N.Y.: Kennikat Press, 1978.

New York City Commission on Human Rights. Women's Role in Contemporary Society. New York: Hearst Corporation, 1972.

The 1980 Virginia Slims American Women's Opinion Poll: A Survey of Contemporary Attitudes. Roper Organization, 1980.

The 1972 Virginia Slims American Women's Opinion Poll. Louis Harris and Associates, 1972.

Nyden, Philip. "Welfare and Welfare Rights: An Analysis of Organizations in the Newark Metropolitan Area." Paper, Drew University, 1972.

Oberschall, Anthony. Social Conflict and Social Movements. Englewood Cliffs, N.J.: Prentice-Hall, 1973.

Ohlin, Lloyd E. "Indigenous Social Movements." In Social Welfare Institutions, edited by Mayer N. Zald, pp. 180-85. New York: John Wiley & Sons, 1965.

Olson, Mancur, Jr. The Logic of Collective Action: Public Goods and the Theory of Groups. Cambridge, Mass.: Harvard University Press, 1965.

Pinckney, Alphonso. The Committed: White Activists in the Civil Rights Movement. New Haven, Conn.: College and University Press, 1968.

Piven, Frances Fox. "Who Does the Advocate Planner Serve?" Social Policy, May-June 1970, pp. 32-37.

Piven, Frances Fox, and Richard A. Cloward. "A Movement on Welfare." New York Times, August 31, 1973.

_____. Poor People's Movements: Why They Succeed, How They Fail. New York: Pantheon Books, 1977.

_____. Regulating the Poor: The Functions of Public Welfare. New York: Pantheon Books, 1971.

Plotnick, Robert D., and Felicity Skidmore. Progress against Poverty: A Review of the 1964-1974 Decade. New York: Academic Press, 1975.

President's Commission on Income Maintenance Programs. Poverty Amid Plenty: The American Paradox. Washington, D.C.: U.S. Government Printing Office, 1969.

President's Commission on National Goals. Goals for Americans. Englewood Cliffs, N.J.: Prentice-Hall, 1964.

Presser, Harriet B., and Wendy Baldwin. "Child Care as a Constraint on Employment: Prevalence, Correlates, and Bearing on the Work and Fertility Nexus." American Journal of Sociology 85 (March 1980): 1202-13.

Prestage, Jewel L. "Political Behavior of American Black Women: An Overview." In The Black Woman, edited by La Frances Rogers-Rose. Beverly Hills, Calif.: Sage, 1980, pp. 233-45.

Rainwater, Lee, and William L. Yancey. The Moynihan Report and the Politics of Controversy. Cambridge, Mass.: MIT Press, 1969.

Rapoport, Anatol. "Game Theory and Human Conflict." In The Nature of Human Conflict, edited by Elton McNeil, pp. 195-226. Englewood Cliffs, N.J.: Prentice-Hall, 1965.

Reich, Charles A. "Individual Rights and Social Welfare: The Emerging Legal Issues." Yale Law Journal 74 (June 1965): 1245-57.

Rein, Mildred. Conflicting Aims in AFDC-UP. Boston: Social Welfare Regional Research Institute, Institute of Human Sciences, 1972.

Rein, Mildred, and Barbara Wishnov. Patterns of Work and Welfare in AFDC. Boston: Social Welfare Regional Research Institute, Institute of Human Sciences, 1971.

Report from the Steering Committee of the Arden House Conference on Public Welfare. 1967.

Report of the National Advisory Commission on Civil Disorders. New York: Bantam Books, 1968.

Research and Policy Committee of the Committee for Economic Development. Improving the Public Welfare System. New York: Committee for Economic Development, 1970.

_____. Reshaping Government in Metropolitan Areas. New York: Committee for Economic Development, 1960.

_____. Training and Jobs for the Urban Poor. New York: Committee for Economic Development, 1970.

Rights Writer. Issues published March 1970 through June 1972 by the New Jersey Friends of Welfare Rights. Mimeographed.

Robinson, Pat, et al. "On the Position of Poor Black Women in This Country." In The Black Woman, edited by Toni Cade, pp. 194-97. New York: New American Library, 1970.

Rodgers-Rose, La Frances, ed. The Black Woman. Beverly Hills, Calif.: Sage, 1980.

Rogin, Richard. "Now It's Welfare Lib." New York Times Magazine, September 27, 1970, pp. 73, 75-76, 80-83, 85, 87.

Ross, Heather L. Poverty: Women and Children Last. Washington, D.C.: Urban Institute, 1973.

Ross, Heather, and Isabel Sawhill. Time of Transition: The Growth of Families Headed by Women. Washington, D.C.: Urban Institute, 1975.

Rudolph, Robert. "Foes of New Welfare Laws Claim Bias against Blacks." Star Ledger (Newark, N.J.), January 18, 1972.

Ryan, William. Blaming the Victim. New York: Random House, 1971.

Safilios-Rothschild, Constantina. Women and Social Policy. Englewood Cliffs, N.J.: Prentice-Hall, 1974.

Sampson, Timothy J. Welfare: A Handbook for Friend and Foe. Philadelphia: Pilgrim Press, 1972.

Sanders, Marion K., ed. The Professional Radical: Conversations with Saul Alinsky. New York: Harper & Row, 1970.

Schlesinger, Arthur, Jr. "Is Liberalism Dead?" New York Times Magazine, March 30, 1980, pp. 42-43 ff.

Scholen, Ken. "Making a Difference: A Model." Colloquy, October 1973, pp. 32-33.

Schorr, Alvin L. Explorations in Social Policy. New York: Basic Books, 1968.

Schur, Edwin. The Awareness Trap: Self Absorption instead of Social Change. New York: Quadrangle Books, 1976.

Seligman, Ben B. Permanent Poverty. Chicago: Quadrangle Books, 1970.

Selznick, Philip. TVA and the Grass Roots. New York: Harper & Row, 1966.

"Separate but Equal Groups Seen Remedy for Social Ills." Newark Evening News, May 6, 1969.

Sexton, Patricia Cayo. "Workers (Female) Arise!" Dissent, Summer 1974, pp. 380-95.

Shenker, Israel. "For Alinsky, Organizers Clutch Key to the Future." New York Times, January 6, 1971.

_____. "Guarantee of 'Right to Live' Is Urged." New York Times, September 29, 1969.

Sherry, Paul. "A Strategy for Social Change." Crisis, November 1972, pp. 299-303.

Sherry, Paul, Hobart A. Burch, and Mel Turner. "UCC/NWRO." In Voluntarism in America's Future, pp. 36-44. Washington, D. C.: Center for a Voluntary Society, 1972.

Simmel, Georg. Conflict and the Web of Group Affiliations, translated by Kurt H. Wolff and Reinhard Bendix. New York: Free Press, 1955.

_____. On Individuality and Social Forms, edited by Donald N. Levine. Chicago: University of Chicago Press, 1971.

_____. The Sociology of Georg Simmel, edited and translated by Kurt Wolff. New York: Free Press, 1950.

Smelser, Neil J. The Sociology of Economic Life. Englewood Cliffs, N. J.: Prentice-Hall, 1963.

_____. Theory of Collective Behavior. New York: Free Press, 1971.

Smith, Georgina M. On Welfare. Plainfield, N. J.: Interstate Printing, 1967.

Smith, Ralph E. Women in the Labor Force in 1990. Washington, D. C.: Urban Institute, 1979.

Sobel, Lester A., ed. Welfare and the Poor. New York: Facts on File, 1977.

Solomon, Barbara Bryant. Black Empowerment: Social Work in Oppressed Communities. New York: Columbia University Press, 1976.

Sparer, Edward V. "The Illegality of Poverty." Social Policy, March-April 1971, pp. 49-53.

_____. "The Right to Welfare." In The Rights of Americans, edited by N. Dorsen, pp. 65-93.

Spencer, Anne Carol. "A History of the National Welfare Rights Organization." Paper, University of Pennsylvania, 1976.

Staples, Robert. The Black Woman in America. Chicago: Nelson-Hall, 1973.

Staples, Robert, ed. The Black Family: Essays and Studies. 2d ed. Belmont, Calif.: Wadsworth, 1978.

Stein, Bruno. On Relief. New York: Basic Books, 1971.

Steiner, Gilbert Y. The State of Welfare. Washington, D.C.: Brookings Institution, 1971.

Stimpson, Catherine. "'Thy Neighbor's Wife, Thy Neighbor's Servants': Women's Liberation and Black Civil Rights." In Women in a Sexist Society, edited by Vivian Gornick and Barbara K. Moran, pp. 622-57. New York: Mentor Books, 1971.

Stone, Chuck. Black Political Power in America. New York: Dell, 1970.

Storey, James R. The Need for Welfare Reform. Washington, D.C.: Urban Institute, 1978. Reprint.

"Strategy of Crisis: A Dialogue." American Child 48 (Summer 1966): 20-32.

Street, David, George T. Martin, Jr., and Laura Kramer Gordon. The Welfare Industry: Functionaries and Recipients of Public Aid. Beverly Hills, Calif.: Sage, 1979.

Streshinsky, Naomi Gottlieb. "Welfare Rights Organizations and the Public Welfare System: An Interaction Study." Ph.D. dissertation, University of California, 1970.

Sullivan, Ronald. "U.S. Court Backs Cutbacks in Aid to the Working Poor." New York Times, October 5, 1972.

Taylor, William L. Hanging Together: Equality in an Urban Nation. New York: Simon and Schuster, 1971.

Theobald, Robert, ed. The Guaranteed Income: Next Step in Socioeconomic Evolution? New York: Doubleday, 1967.

"There Must Be a Better Way." Newsweek, February 8, 1971, pp. 22-30.

Therkildsen, Paul T. Public Assistance and American Values. Albuquerque: University of New Mexico Press, 1964.

Tillmon, Johnnie. "Insights of a Welfare Mother." Journal of Social Issues, January-February 1971, pp. 13-23, reprint.

_____. "Welfare Is a Women's Issue." In The First Ms. Reader, edited by Francine Klagsburn, pp. 51-59. New York: Warner Books, 1975.

Titmuss, Richard M. Social Policy. New York: Pantheon Books, 1974.

Tocqueville, Alexis de, and Gustave de Beaumont. Tocqueville and Beaumont on Social Reform, edited and translated by Seymour Drescher. New York: Harper, 1968.

Traetner, Walter I. From Poor Law to Welfare State. New York: Free Press, 1974.

Tumin, Melvin M. Social Stratification. Englewood Cliffs, N.J.: Prentice-Hall, 1967.

Turner, Jonathan H., and Charles E. Starnes. Inequality: Privilege and Poverty in America. Pacific Palisades, Calif.: Goodyear, 1976.

Turner, Ralph H., and Lewis M. Killian. Collective Behavior. Englewood Cliffs, N.J.: Prentice-Hall, 1957.

U.S., Commission on Civil Rights. Social Indicators of Equality for Minorities and Women. Washington, D.C.: Government Printing Office, 1978.

_____. Women and Poverty. Chicago: Allied Printing, 1974.

_____. Women Still in Poverty. Washington, D.C.: Government Printing Office, 1979.

U.S., Congress, Joint Economic Committee. The Economics of Federal Subsidy Programs, 92nd Cong., 1st sess., January 11, 1972.

U.S., Congress, Joint Economic Committee, Subcommittee on Economic Growth and Stabilization. American Women Workers in a Full Employment Economy, 95th Cong., 1st sess., September 15, 1977.

U.S., Congress, Senate, Subcommittee on Public Assistance of the Committee on Finance. How to Think about Welfare Reform for the 1980's, 96th Cong., 2d sess., February 6 and 7, 1980.

U.S., Department of Health, Education and Welfare. Having the Power, We Have the Duty. Washington, D.C.: Government Printing Office, 1966.

U.S., Department of Labor. Employment and Economic Issues of Low Income Women: Report of a Project. Washington, D.C.: Government Printing Office, 1978.

_____. 1975 Handbook on Women Workers. Washington, D.C.: Government Printing Office, 1975.

Urban America, Inc., and the Urban Coalition. One Year Later. New York: Frederick Praeger, 1969.

Useem, Michael. Protest Movements in America. Indianapolis: Bobbs-Merrill, 1975.

The Virginia Slims American Women's Opinion Poll. Louis Harris and Associates, 1970.

The Virginia Slims American Women's Opinion Poll: A Survey of the Attitudes of Women on Marriage, Divorce, the Family and America's Changing Sexual Morality. Vol. 3. Roper Organization, 1974.

Wallace, Michelle. Black Macho and the Myth of the Super Woman. New York: Dial Press, 1979.

Ware, Celestine. Woman Power: The Movement for Women's Liberation. New York: Tower, 1970.

Watts, William, and Lloyd A. Free. State of the Nation, 1974. Washington, D. C.: Potomac, 1974.

Waxman, Chaim, ed. Poverty: Power and Politics. New York:
Universal Library, 1968.

Weber, Max. The Theory of Social and Economic Organization,
translated by A. M. Henderson and edited by Talcott Parsons.
Glencoe, Ill.: Free Press, 1969.

Weisman, Steven R. "What Is a Conservative?" New York Times
Magazine, August 31, 1980, pp. 12-15, 34.

Welfare Fighter. Issues published 1969 through 1974 by the National
Welfare Rights Organization, Washington, D. C.

Welfare Priority Team. Reports, minutes, and other research papers
and analyses. New York: United Church Board of Homeland
Ministries, 1970-73.

Welfare Righter. Issues published 1974 through 1980 by the Welfare
Rights Organization of Allegheny County, Pa.

"Welfare Rights." In Grapevine. New York: Joint Strategy Action
Committee, 1972, pp. 1-4.

"Welfare: Trying to End the Nightmare." Time, February 8, 1971,
pp. 14-23.

West, Guida. "Twin-Track Coalitions in the Black Power Movement."
In Interracial Bonds, edited by Rhoda Goldstein Blumberg and
Wendell James Roye, pp. 71-87. Bayside, N.Y.: General Hall
Press, 1979.

Whitaker, William Howard. "The Determinants of Social Movement
Success: A Study of the National Welfare Rights Organization."
Ph.D. dissertation, Brandeis University, 1970.

White House Conference on Families. Listening to America's Families: Action for the 80's. Washington, D. C.: U. S. Government
Printing Office, 1980.

Wickenden, Elizabeth. "Poverty and Law: The Constitutional Rights of Assistance Recipients." Mimeographed. New York: National Assembly for Social Welfare and Development, 1965.

Wilensky, Harold L., and Charles N. Lebeaux. Industrial Society and Social Welfare. New York: Free Press, 1965.

Williams, James D., ed. The State of Black America 1979. New York: National Urban League, 1979.

Williamson, Jane, Diane Winston, and Wanda Wooten, eds. Women's Action Almanac: A Complete Resource Guide. New York: William Morrow, 1979.

Wilson, John. Introduction to Social Movements. New York: Basic Books, 1973.

Wilson, William Julius. The Declining Significance of Race: Blacks and Changing American Institutions. Chicago: University of Chicago Press, 1978.

Women's Role in Contemporary Society: The Report of the New York City Commission on Human Rights. New York: Avon, 1972.

Wright, J. Skelly. "The Courts Have Failed the Poor." New York Times Magazine, March 9, 1969, pp. 26–27 ff.

Wright, Nathan, Jr. Black Power and Urban Unrest. New York: Hawthorn Books, 1968.

_____. Let's Work Together. New York: Hawthorn Books, 1968.

Zakuta, Leo. A Protest Movement Becalmed: A Study of Change in the CCF. Toronto: University of Toronto Press, 1964.

Zald, M. N., and J. D. McCarthy. "Notes on Cooperation and Competition amongst Social Movement Organizations." Paper, Vanderbilt University, 1974.

Zald, Mayer, and Roberta Ash. "Social Movement Organizations: Growth, Decay, and Change." Social Forces 44 (March 1966): 327–41.

Zinn, Howard. SNCC: The New Abolitionists. Boston: Beacon Press, 1964.

INDEX

428

black dominance, 151
Black Economic Development Council
  (BEDC), 151
black families (see families, black)
black feminist movement, 210, 235,
  238, 373, 387
black feminists, 234, 238-39, 240-43,
  268, 335, 358, 373, 387, 391
black leaders (see leaders, black)
black liberation, 233
Black Manifesto, 153
black middle class, 228, 238
black nationalism, 20, 44, 60, 78, 106
black organizations, 4, 10, 15, 153,
  210-32, 358, 372, 378, 383, 391 (see
  also black churches; Black Panthers,
  Congress for Racial Equality; Interreligious Foundation for Community
  Organization; National Association
  for the Advancement of Colored People; National Tenants' Organization;
  People United to Save Humanity;
  Southern Christian Leadership Conference; Urban League)
Black Panthers, 109, 219, 232, 296,
  372
black population, 6
black poverty, 22, 42
black power, 20, 44, 105, 149, 155,
  211-12
black revolution, 108
black separatism, 105, 179
black staff (see NWRO, informal leaders of; NWRO, staff of)
black women, 44, 47-48, 233-43, 373,
  381 (see also women)
black women's club movement, 236-37,
  239
black women's organizations, 232-33,
  236-43, 267
black workers, 222
black working class, 24
Blackmun, Harry A. (Justice), 331
blacks, urban, 19, 22
blind, 16, 289 (see also aged, blind,
  and disabled)
black grant approach, 334

bonding (see class, solidarity; gen-
  der solidarity; racial solidarity;
  solidarity)
Boston Globe, 317
Boston model, 59, 96-97, 101,
  294-95
Brennan, William J., Jr. (Justice),
  330, 331
Brookins, Louise, 93
Brooklyn Welfare Rights Organiza-
  tion (BWRO), 103-4
Brown Berets, 228
Brownie Points Plan, 357, 375
Burch, Hobart, 170, 181
Bureau of Labor Statistics (BLS)
  Lower Standard Budget, 41, 42
Burger Court, 331, 376
Burson, Joyce, 103, 108
Byrd-Roth tests, 317

cadre organizations, 36-37, 41
Cahill, William (Governor), 192
California, 19, 22, 49, 60, 83, 84,
  300, 301
California Welfare Rights Organi-
  zation (WRO), 83-84
Camden, New Jersey, 32
Campaign for Human Development,
  31, 126
campaign for winter clothing, 294,
  300
capitalism, 361
Carmichael, Stokely, 105
"CAP the Knife," 306
Caplow, Theodore, 8, 9
Carter, Jimmy (President), 266,
  319, 320
Carter Democratic administration,
  129, 177, 250, 260, 321, 322,
  323, 334, 379
Carter welfare reform, 259-60,
  319-21, 322, 323, 334-35 (see
  also Better Jobs and Income
  Plan)
Catholic church, 31, 126; and contributions to IFCO, 152; and FAP,
  315-16; as Friends of WRO, 146;

and Rhode Island WRO, 196; and
ROWEL, 198; and SCAN, 192 (see
also Campaign for Human Development; National Catholic Conference
on Interracial Justice; U.S. Catholic
Conference)
Cavanaugh, Bertha, 45
Center for Social Welfare Policy and
Law, 321, 328, 332, 335, 386
centralization, 176, 351-63
Chafe, William, 245
challengers, 6, 7, 15, 64, 299, 303,
324, 368, 381, 391
Chambers, Ed, 193
charity, 16, 90, 98, 225, 290, 292,
329, 331, 358
Chavez, Cesar, 223
Chicago, 39, 47, 111, 214
Chicanos, 42, 157, 267
child care, 5, 18, 19, 48, 49, 83, 86,
88-89, 91-94, 96, 102, 245, 253,
255, 265, 268, 311, 312, 316, 355,
389 (see also day care)
child rearing as work, 89-91, 265
children: and FAP, 312, 316; assistance to, 255; care for, 253; choice
to have, 258; dependent, 17, 290; dependent and crippled, 16; elimination
of poverty among, 264; helpless, 18;
illegitimate, 18; needs of, 88, 94; on
AFDC, 38, 290; rearing of, 265; resources for, 258; rights of, 168;
special programs for, 222; staying
home to raise, 245
Children's March for Survival, 31, 119,
316
Chisholm, Shirley (Congresswoman),
111, 242
church agencies, 22, 23
church constituency (see constituency
development)
churches, 1, 8, 28, 34, 52, 63, 123,
126, 127, 145-78, 191, 192, 196,
248, 370, 377, 389 (see also Catholic
church; Jewish support; Protestant
churches)
Churchman's Seminar on the Public
Welfare Crisis, 187

citizen action organizing, 128 (see
also Arkansas Community Organizations for Reform Now; Jobs
and Justice; Movement for Economic Justice)
Citizens' Crusade against Poverty,
26
Citizen's Lobby for Economic Justice, 124-25
"Citywide," 107
civil disorder, 17, 288
civil rights activists, 37
civil rights movement, 1, 4, 20,
24-25, 41, 44, 83, 145-46, 149,
150, 155, 162, 176, 179, 180,
211-12, 213-14, 216, 221, 228,
230-31, 233, 235, 238, 253, 335,
367, 370, 381, 387
class, 3, 57, 58, 62, 63, 77, 78-
79, 81-83, 113, 130, 236, 239,
242, 331, 366; -action suits, 102,
328, 329, 333; antagonisms, 228,
232, 233, 244, 383; cleavages,
211, 247, 367; conflicts, 382;
differences, 254; divisions, 236;
schisms, 233; solidarity, 211,
244, 246
classism, 25, 48
Cloward, Richard A., 4, 16, 17,
19, 20, 24, 25-28, 37-38, 40, 45,
51, 63, 80, 89, 95, 99, 100, 117,
129, 288, 292-94, 303, 310, 312,
320, 327, 354, 355, 366, 368, 381
Coalition of Labor Union Women
(CLUW), 265
Coalition of 100 Black Women, 243
coalition politics, 184
coalitions: configuration of, 7, 9;
equal partnership, 148, 156, 177;
of ethnic groups, 150; in FAP
campaign, 314, 316, 322; independent, 178-86, 197-202, 372;
integrated, 116, 178-86, 195-97,
371; legal services, 325-36; majoritarian, 116, 389; of middle-
class church groups, 198; minority-power groups and, 111;
NWRO and [black and women's

430

303, 310, 368, 375, 377, 380, 383
(see also strategy, of social control)
courts, 6, 96, 102, 197, 302, 325-36
Cox, Harvey, 148-49
Curvin, Robert, 58, 218, 226

Dandridge v. Williams, 330
Davis, Sammy, Jr., 302
Day, Edwin, 41, 60, 231
day care, 48, 93, 168, 258, 307, 309,
  320 (see also child care)
decade of affluence, 1
decentralization, 176, 351-63, 384
DeCrow, Karen, 257, 259
Delaware, 300
DeLeeuw, Bert, 107, 112, 126, 127-
  30, 181, 183, 381
Dellinger, David, 302
Dellums, Ronald (Congressman), 110,
  111
demobilization, process of, 9
democracy, 81
Democratic National Convention, 111,
  120, 222, 316
dependency, problem of, 18, 88, 92,
  114, 235, 245, 251, 253, 257, 261,
  292, 311, 328, 352
dependent children (see families, female-headed)
depression (see Great Depression)
Des Moines Black Panther Party, 219
desegregation, 330
deserted mothers, 18
deserving poor, 3, 16, 289, 359, 379,
  385, 386
deviants, 98, 99, 112, 212
direct action, 292 (see also strategy,
  "street")
Directory of National Black Organizations, 151
disabled, 3, 289 (see also aged, blind,
  and disabled; Supplemental Security
  Income)
displaced homemakers, 234, 246, 253,
  387, 388
divorce, 48, 246, 253, 262
divorced women (see women, divorced)

dominance, by white activists,
  178, 192
domination by nonpoor, 162 (see also
  also middle-class dominance;
  white dominance)
Douglas, William O. (Justice),
  330, 331
Downtown Welfare Advocate Center
  (DWAC), 48
Duncan, Ruby, 93
dyad, 9

Early Periodic Screening, Diagnosis, and Treatment (EPSDT),
  384-85
Earned Income Tax Credit (EITC),
  384
earned right, 293
eastern liberal press, 302, 316,
  320 (see media)
economic: conditions, 1, 4, 19,
  20, 22-23, 24, 34, 78, 127, 175,
  184, 354, 379, 386; dependence,
  34, 161, 179, 193, 331, 378, 386;
  development, 150, 167; independence, 5, 18, 226; justice, 3, 5,
  7, 25, 48, 119, 124, 127, 155,
  167, 169, 210, 220, 235, 334,
  358, 370, 376, 383, 390; needs of
  black poor, 24; parity, 291; security, 222; security programs,
  16, 167
Economic and Racial Justice Priority
  Team (ERJPT), 167, 168, 169,
  171, 177
Economic Opportunity Act of 1964,
  21, 367
economically immobile, 89, 93
economy: of affluence, 3; of
  scarcity, 4
ecumenical support, 174, 176
education, 48-49, 83, 221, 245
egalitarian tyranny, 357
elderly, 116, 184, 246, 360
elected officers (see leaders,
  elected; leaders, formal)
electoral strategy (see strategy,
  electoral)

432

eligibility for welfare, 292-93, 299
employable, 291, 312
employment as solution to poverty, 89, 291, 311-12, 355
employment for poor, 291 (see also jobs; Work Incentive Program; workfare)
employment of mothers with dependent children, 291-92, 311
entrenched female leadership (see leaders, entrenched female)
Episcopalians, 31, 150
Equal Rights Amendment (ERA), 246-47, 250, 252, 254, 260, 265, 267, 335, 391
equality of women, 256
Essex County Welfare Board, 189
ethnic parity, 291
evangelism (see strategy, of evangelism)
Evans, Faith: as associate director of NWRO, 63, 123; and Better Jobs and Income Plan, 320; and cleavages among blacks, 231; in conflict with Wiley, 118-23, 368; as executive director of NWRO, 62; as fund raiser for NWRO, 36, 55, 122-23; as organizer of NWRO, 118; poverty background of, 118-19; as representative on NCC, 118; and resignation from Executive Committee, 121-22; as supporter of elected leaders, 118; and WPT, 167; and WRISC, 175
"Every woman is one man away from welfare," 47, 260
exclusive movement, 3
Executive Committee, 39, 45, 49-50, 53, 55-59, 307, 314
external conflicts (see Family Assistance Plan; strategy, of confrontation; strategy, legal; strategy, of lobbying; strategy, street)

factionalism, 226
Fair Deal, 289, 361
fair hearings, 302, 329
families: AFDC, 96, 98, 290, 312; black, 47, 229, 238, 257; extended, 268; and FAP, 314-15; female-headed, 23, 33, 38, 40, 47, 48, 86-89, 93, 116, 250, 264, 265, 268, 386, 390; guaranteed income for, 160, 224; intact, 86, 289; nontraditional, 390; poor, 83, 86; single-parent, 86, 253, 268, 289, 358, 387, 389; traditional, 86, 93, 321, 390; two-parent, 86, 289, 389; with unemployed father, 289
family, 5, 6, 17, 40, 214, 229, 243, 246; crisis in, 390; economic and social rights of, 389; impact on, 386; limits on welfare for, 330; patriarchal, 268-69; rights, of, 390; of welfare, 319
Family Assistance Plan (FAP), 115, 119, 120, 155, 162, 183, 184, 185, 189, 217, 222, 224, 248, 249, 250, 255, 258, 287, 305, 310-11, 312-20, 322, 323, 324, 334, 354, 355, 361, 368, 369, 373, 375, 376, 390
Family Income and Work Incentive Act of 1972, 315
Family Stability Act, 315
Farmer, James, 24, 25
farmworkers movement, 83, 107, 159, 176, 178, 184, 296, 316
fathers, unemployed, 17, 86, 93, 290
Feagin, Joe R., 288, 355, 361, 362, 378
Federal Bureau of Investigation (FBI), 219
female-headed families (see families, female-headed)
female solidarity (see gender, solidarity)
feminism, 115, 374
feminist: consciousness, 115; movement, 48-49, 210, 235, 240, 244, 246, 374, 387; organization, 192, 370-71
feminist/socialists, 48, 387
feminists, 48, 115, 184, 234, 240-44, 251-69, 335, 358, 370, 383, 386, 388, 389, 391

Wiley, 28, 30, 34, 35, 118, 122–23; by women, 123 (see also Half-a-Chance campaign; Welfare Rights Information and Support Community)

fusion and fission, 9, 202

gender, 3, 58, 62–79, 82, 113, 130, 213, 260, 331, 366; neutral language and, 46–47, 260–61

gender: cleavages, 232, 367, 372–73, 382–83; discrimination, 18, 253, 256, 262, 264; oppression, 242; solidarity, 232–35, 239, 244, 250–51, 253–54, 262, 264, 373–74

Ginsberg, Mitchell, 311–12, 319

Glassman, Carol, 47, 247, 254

Glynn, Tom, 103, 107

goal: attainment, 287; displacement, 160

Goldberg v. Kelly, 329–30

government: expenditures on programs for poor, 354–55, 360–61, 375; intervention, 16, 22, 269, 289, 290, 352, 357, 359, 389–90; largess, 328, 331

Grace, Ruby, 48

grants-in-aid, 289

grantsmanship, 52, 306, 309, 386

grass-roots: grievances, 22; organizing, 27, 318

Gray, Jesse, 221

Gray Panthers, 112

Great Depression, 16, 21, 125, 288–89, 335

Great Society programs, 1, 21, 33, 180, 231, 289, 352–55, 361

Greater Newark Council of Churches, 187

Green, Edith (Congresswoman), 332

Gregory, Dick, 44, 111

grievances, 1, 6, 7, 22, 40, 97–100, 367

guaranteed: income, 6, 7, 10, 15, 17, 20, 26, 27, 38, 39, 42, 86–89, 95–96, 116, 147, 154, 159–61, 168–70, 177, 214, 215, 221–24, 245, 252, 254, 256, 257, 269, 293, 311–13, 319, 323, 334, 355, 370, 379, 384–85, 390; jobs, 378, 385

Half-a-Chance Campaign, 35–36, 112, 176

Handbook of Public Assistance, The, 88

Harlem, 23, 24, 328

Harrington, Michael, 21

Harris, Fred (Senator), 314–16

Hatfield, Glenn, 188, 192–93

"Having the power, we have the duty," 21

Hayden, Tom, 308

health, 6, 168–69, 289, 322, 384

Health and Welfare Division of United Church Board for Homeland Ministries, 159, 163, 166, 171

Health and Welfare Working Group, 177

Height, Dorothy, 238, 239

Herman, Alexis, 262

Hispanics, 45, 55, 57, 111, 125, 257, 260 (see also Chicanos; Mexicans)

historical ties between church and poor, 147–50

Holmes, Eleanor Norton, 237–38, 264

homemakers, 266, 267

Hoover, Herbert, 379

Horowitz, Irving Louis, 289, 291, 319

House Ways and Means Committee, 317

Household Technicians of America, 238, 239–40

Household Workers, 110

households headed by women (see families, female-headed)

housewives: for ERA, 265; suburban, 239; wages of, 91

housing, 124, 238

H.R. 1, 189

human rights, 243; movement, 22; struggle, 240

hunger, 6, 238, 352

ideology, 76, 80–81, 147–50, 160, 186, 212, 361

Illinois, 58, 300, 356

Incentives for Independence, 356, 375

incentives for participation, 37, 40–41, 49, 51, 78, 100, 175, 180, 184, 185, 293, 300

income redistribution, 5, 24, 95, 121, 124, 156, 256, 289, 293, 296, 311, 319, 335, 389

income transfer programs, 288, 293, 314

indirect contributions to NWRO, 164

individual donations, 30, 63

individualism, 10, 116, 176, 351–63, 366, 378–80, 384

Industrial Areas Foundation, 153, 193

ineligibles, 299

inequality of opportunity, 352

inflation, 1, 7, 20, 335, 359, 379

injustice, 192 (see also social, justice)

insiders, 20, 57–58, 85

integration (see racial, integration)

integrationists, 247 (see racial, integration)

intellectuals, 25, 366, 381

internal conflicts: between black and white women, 232–33; in Boston model, 100–1; class and gender as basis for, 113–23, 130; in CORE, 25; and interracial structure, 105–6; within NWRO, 36, 40, 49, 57, 64, 76–123, 124–31, 168, 304, 307, 366; between NWRO and [black churches, 228–31; black organizations, 211–32; black women's organizations, 232–43; CORE, 217–19; IFCO, 153–54, 369; Legal Services, 325–36; NAACP, 227–28; NTO, 221–23; SCLC, 213–17; Urban League, 225–27; white women's organizations, 243–62]; race and class as basis for, 105–13; race, class, and gender as basis for, 82–105; between Tillmon and Sampson, 83–84; between Wiley and black leaders, 25; between Wiley and Faith Evans, 119–23; between WRO and Friends of WRO, 178–202

Internal Revenue Service, 153–54, 183, 369

International Women's Decade, 254

International Women's Year, 48, 242, 254, 265

interracial cooperation, 109

interracialism, 20, 25, 44, 105, 213

Interreligious Foundation for Community Organization (IFCO), 31, 111, 118, 150–54, 183, 201, 229, 369; Good Housekeeping seal of approval, 153

Iowa, 219

Iran, 335

Jackson, Jesse, 110, 112, 220–21

Jackson, Larry, 23, 293, 295, 305

James, Hulbert, 32, 36, 62, 107, 108, 112, 173–74, 180, 185, 219, 300, 304

Jefferson, Kim, 187

Jeter, Frankie, 55, 231, 327

Jewish support, 32, 152, 192, 198

JIP, 320 (see also Better Jobs and Income Plan)

jobs, 27, 48, 83, 87–92, 116, 130, 168, 212, 215, 220, 223, 227, 229, 239, 245, 251–52, 258, 291, 307, 320, 321, 355–56, 376, 387, 389

Jobs and Justice, 129–30, 388

Johnnie Tillmon model, 96–97, 101–5

Johnson, Lyndon (President): administration of, 1, 19–20, 21, 33, 149, 183, 289, 290, 304, 305, 319, 325, 352, 354, 357, 361, 367; and poverty, 1, 82, 149, 290, 305, 319, 325, 352, 354, 357, 361, 367

Johnson, William, 23, 293, 295–96, 305

Jones, Roxanne, 251

Jordan, Vernon, 223, 224, 227

Just Economics, 128

Kagan, Larry, 361

Kahn, Alfred, 21, 290

Katz, James Everett, 319

Ministry of Welfare Rights, 173 (see also Welfare Rights Information and Support Community)
Minnesota, 300
minority-power groups, 210, 383
Misseduc Foundation, 126, 151
Mississippi, 19
Missouri, 197-200, 372
Mobilization against Hunger, 189-91
Mobilization for Youth (MFY), 23, 294, 328
Model Cities program, 226, 307
monies, 1, 10, 20, 28-36, 40-41, 63, 114, 117, 118, 147, 155, 156, 162, 171-72, 181, 188, 192, 193, 225-26, 304-5, 334, 369, 375
Montclair, New Jersey, 193 n
Morristown, New Jersey, 193 n
motherpower, 46
mothers as workers, 267
mothers with dependent children (see families, female-headed)
Movement for Economic Justice (MEJ), 35, 62, 112, 124-31, 168, 334, 362, 368, 376, 381, 388
Moynihan, Daniel Patrick, 20, 22, 88, 90, 184, 189, 305, 311, 320, 323, 354, 379

NAACP Legal Defense Fund, 329
narcissism, 60, 336, 363
National Advisory Committee on Women, 266
National Association for the Advancement of Colored People (NAACP), 110, 227-28, 372
National Association of Colored Women, 236
National Association of Social Workers, 111, 224
National Black Coalition, 151
National Black Feminist Organization, 242, 243
national black women's club movement, 236
National Catholic Conference for Interracial Justice, 31

National Caucus of Labor Committees (NCLC), 308
National Clients Council, 326, 332, 333, 388
National Committee for Household Employees, 112
National Committee of Black Churchmen, 151, 229
National Committee on Household Employment (NCHE), 239, 240, 373
National Congress of Neighborhood Women, 265
national convention, 53, 55
National Coordinating Committee of Welfare Rights Groups (NCC), 38, 53, 55, 86, 109, 113, 119
National Council of Churches, 31, 111, 112, 118, 126, 146, 151-52, 175-77, 229, 314-15, 322, 369
National Council of Negro Women, 238-39, 373
National Council of Women, Work, and Welfare, 264
national federation of welfare recipient groups, 37
national Friends network, 154, 172-76, 185-86 (see also Welfare Rights Information and Support Community)
National Friends of WRO, 154, 172-73 (see also Welfare Rights Information and Support Community)
national guardsmen, use of, 300
national health insurance, 124, 289
National Organization of Women (NOW), 254, 256-61, 321; Task Force on Poverty, 259
National Organizers' Conference, 108
National Plan of Action, 266
National Tenants' Organization (NTO), 110, 221-23, 232, 316, 372
National Urban League, 110, 218, 223-27, 240, 316, 372
National Welfare Rights Organization (NWRO): and AFDC, 38, 50;

440

44, 77, 80-82, 105; and PUSH, 220-21; racial conflict in, 105-9; racial integration in, 15, 105; racial separation in, 105; resources of, 20-21; and SCLC, 213-17, 220, 221-22; shadow staff of, 108-9; and Spring Offensive, 110; staff of, 39-40, 57-64, 120-21 (see also leaders, informal); structural contradictions in, 4, 15, 77; as superstructure, 38, 381; supporters of (see supporters); targets, 58 (see adjudicators; administrators; legislators); and UCC, 154-202; and United Methodist Women, 248-49; and unpaid staff, 94; and Urban League, 223-27; and U.S. Supreme Court (see U.S. Supreme Court); and VISTA, 58, 94; Welfare Bill of Rights of, 39, 70-71n; and welfare reform (see welfare reform); and white feminists, 251-61; women leaders in, 47, 49, 89; as a women's movement, 47, 122; and women's organizations (black and white), 232-61; and women's peace movement, 250-51; and YWCA, 249

National Women's Agenda, 26, 233, 234, 248, 264, 265-66, 267

National Women's Conference, 266

National Women's Political Caucus, 254-56, 267

National Women's Rights Organization, 49

Native Americans, 111

Nebraska, 302

negotiation (see strategy, of negotiation)

networks, 1, 20-21, 27, 28, 37, 145, 147, 154, 159n, 162, 171, 172-74, 185, 188, 238, 248, 313-14, 317, 324, 367

Nevada, 93, 301-3, 375 (see also Operation Nevada)

Neverdon-Morton, Cynthia, 237, 238

New Deal, 360-61

New Federalism, 353, 355

New Frontier, 289, 361

New Jersey, 19, 48, 50n, 52, 58, 177, 187-94, 220, 257, 259, 295, 300, 307, 313

New Jersey Department of Human Services, 189, 385n

New Jersey Friends of Welfare Rights (NJFWRO), 188, 190, 192-93, 194

New Jersey State Welfare Rights Organization, 48, 187-88, 191-92, 194

New Mexico, 302

new right, 268-69

New World Foundation, 126

New York City, 23, 28, 31, 48, 50n, 51, 107, 109, 219, 248, 259n, 294, 295, 300, 311

New York State, 24, 45, 50n, 58, 59, 300, 309

New York Times, 299, 317, 320, 331, 378

Newark, 47, 58, 187-88, 189, 193, 218, 219, 226, 307, 308

Newark Community Action Plan (NCAP), 308

Newark National Organization for Women, 257

Newark Welfare Rights Organization, 225-27

Nixon, Richard (President), 16, 111-12, 115-16, 119, 120, 124, 127, 183, 221, 222, 311-12, 317, 318-19, 332, 351, 353-55, 357

Nixon Republican administration, 33, 154, 175, 184, 189, 191, 214-15, 296-99, 305, 308, 309, 310-11, 319, 326, 334, 353-56, 361, 368, 370, 375-76, 377, 378

nonconformists, 99, 180, 191

nonpaternalistic model, 161 (see also paternalism)

NOW!, 109

NOW Task Force on Poverty, 259-60

NU-WRO, 168, 308

Nyden, Philip, 193

Office of Economic Opportunity (OEO), 21-22, 325, 326, 332, 354, 367, 377

Ohio, 23, 26, 50n, 58

Ohio Steering Committee for Adequate Welfare, 23, 26
OIC, 229
Operation Breadbasket, 110
Operation Life, 93
Operation Nevada, 301-3
"organization of organizers," 37
"organization of taxpayers," 124
"organization of women run by women," 103-4
organizational maintenance, 101, 287, 358
organizers: black, 1, 58, 59, 60-61, 106, 153, 218, 367, 369; black women, 59, 77, 103; and Boston model, 97-101; burned out, 60, 100; from civil rights movement, 20, 26, 41, 59, 78; dominance of, 85-86, 95, 99, 106; Faith Evans as one of the, 118; focus on urban areas of, 44-45; former NWRO, 129-30; and Friends of Welfare Rights, 178, 180; indigenous, 22; as informal leaders, 57-63; loss of, 105, 355, 366, 380-81, 382; in MFY, 23-24; mobilization by, 36; model of the 102-3; nonrecipient, 123; in Operation Nevada, 301; as outsiders, 22, 58; pool of, 179; from poverty movement, 20; from social welfare and church agencies, 22, 94; and street strategy, 292-303; and traditional family roles, 93; and twin-track coalitions, 179; on unemployment, 60; VISTA, 94, 355; as volunteers, 60; white, 22, 78, 85, 86, 106; white men, 60-62, 103-4; white, middle-class, 15, 78, 79, 82, 95, 100, 109-10, 367; white, middle-class church, 150; white women, 59, 103; withering away of, 38; and WRO women, 226
Other America, The, 21
outsiders, 5-6, 20, 34, 41, 57-58, 77, 80, 82, 83, 85, 97, 98, 101, 102-3, 104, 105, 107, 117, 124-25, 147, 151, 173, 179, 252, 295, 327, 367, 371, 380, 389
overidentification, 160, 162, 168, 169, 190, 191, 225, 370

parallel coalition (see coalitions, parallel; coalitions, twin-track)
parallel movement organization, 173, 181, 371 (see Welfare Rights Information and Support Community)
participatory democracy, 81, 82
partnerships (see coalitions)
part-time work, 265
Pastreich, Bill, 59, 97, 103
paternalism, 148, 156, 166, 186, 199, 372, 383
patriarchal systems, 253, 390
Patterson, New Jersey, 32, 193n
Pawley, James, 225
peace, 169
peace allies, 49, 192
peace movement, 250-51
peer alliance, 217, 232
peer allies, 10
peer constituencies, 162
peer solidarity (see class, solidarity; gender, solidarity; racial, solidarity; solidarity)
People United to Save Humanity (PUSH), 110, 112, 220-21, 230, 232, 372
Pennsylvania, 50n, 93, 309
Philadelphia, 229
Philadelphia Welfare Rights Organization (WRO), 251, 305, 307
pietistic trend, 358
Pittsburgh Welfare Rights Organization (WRO), 55, 111, 307
Piven, Frances Fox, 4, 16, 17, 19, 20, 24-28, 37-38, 40, 45, 51, 63, 80, 89, 95, 99, 100, 117, 129, 213, 231, 288, 292-94, 303-4, 310, 327, 354, 355, 368, 381
polarization, 106, 108
policy analysis, 163, 332
political: climate, 3-4, 21, 24, 39, 40, 51, 64, 77, 112, 113, 116, 127, 131, 180, 184, 191, 200, 210, 325 (see also sociopolitical climate); crisis, 24, 38; independence, 179; involvement of Friends of WRO, 181, 184-85, 188-89; op-

pression, 148; pragmatism, 186; strategy, 189 (see also Family Assistance Plan; strategy, of lobbying)

politization, 6, 22, 48, 79-80, 94, 105, 115, 296, 367

poor law, 17, 311, 312

Poor People's Campaign, 86, 214, 215

Poor People's Platform, 111, 120, 222, 316

Poor People's War Council on Poverty, 25

Pope, Jackie, 62 n, 108

poverty, 6, 17-18, 19-22, 42, 82-83, 118-19, 125, 192, 213, 233-35, 238, 245-46, 247-48, 250, 260-62, 264-68, 288-91, 319, 320-21, 325, 351, 352, 377-78; law, 332; level, 19, 41-42, 260; programs, 28, 34, 354

Poverty amid Plenty, 19, 21

poverty as a women's issue, 47, 48, 49, 82, 233, 248, 250, 258, 259-60, 265-66 (see also feminization of poverty)

Poverty Rights Action Center (P/RAC), 26-28, 38-39, 53, 60, 86, 126

Powell, Lewis F., Jr. (Justice), 348

power: Alinsky's views on, 80-81; arbitrary, of caseworkers, 299; balance of, 129; between black and white women, 244; of blacks, 24, building, 83, 292; Chambers' views on, 193; of churches, 196, 314; configurations of, 7, 9, 171, 210; contrast between, of NWRO and white liberal churches, 147, 156, 161-62; decline in, 194; differential in, 5; distribution in ROWEL, 199; distribution of, in society, 79; economic, 77, 383; formal, 82, 84; in government, 24; illusion of, 122, 304; of individual women leaders, 116; and internal conflicts, 76; and Johnson administration, 21; within liberal sector, 318; loss of, 116, 118; and majoritarian coalition, 116; mother, 116, 261; of NWRO and Legal Services, 326, 328; of NWRO women, 94; NWRO's declining, 63, 368; in parallel versus integrated coalitions, 191-92; political, 77,

176, 177, 295, 383; political, for welfare recipients, 25; political, of women, 254; for poor people, 36-37, 80, 96; positions of, 80; powerless take, 84; organizers' views on, 80-81; and recognition, 231; redistribution of, within NWRO, 108; reversal of, 38; of Sampson in NWRO, 84; shift of, to middle-class supporters, 187; shifts in, 62, 77, 187, 238, 261; of staff, 85; struggle for, 83; sufficient, to create a crisis, 24; in suffrage movement, 244; symbolic, 113, 115, 123; traditional relations of, in NWRO, 115; unequal partners of, 76; of Wiley, 113-23

power base, 95

Presbyterians, 31, 149, 315

prestige, 3, 84, 116

principal earner, 323

prisoner's dilemma, 194

privacy, 331

private enterprise, 357

private good, 40-41

Project HOPE, 307

protective laws, 251

Protestant churches: in Camden, New Jersey, 32, 126; and contributions to IFCO, 152; and evangelism, 148; and FAP, 314, 315; as financial contributors to NWRO, 30-31, 36, 155, 180, 367, 368-69; and Friends of WRO, 186; as Friends of WRO, 146-47; and liberation of the oppressed, 148; and liberation theology, 148; and political climate, 361; and ROWEL, 198; and SCAN, 192; and service versus social action, 148; shift from social action to evangelism of, 358, 382; shifting policies of, 358; and social gospel movement, 148-49; and support of NWRO, 201-2; and theology about poor, 147-49; and UCC, 158, 174; and WRISC, 174-77

174; for NWRO, 161, 162, 173, 178, 180, 186-94, 303; for organizers, 79-80, 100, 105, 108-9, 113; for SCLC, 217; for UCC, 161-62, 169; for Urban League, 225

Rockefeller, Nelson (Governor of New York), 356

Rogin, Richard, 299

roller coaster phenomenon, 288

Roosevelt, Franklin Delano (President), 16, 289, 361

Ross, Heather, 252

Roundtree, Richard, 110

Rudwick, Elliott, 25

rugged individualism, 4, 357, 359

rules of the game, 152, 157, 159, 181, 186, 201, 214, 215, 225, 327

sacred values, 4, 116, 145, 191

Saduski, Brother Owusu, 112

Sampson, Timothy, 22, 60, 62, 80, 83, 84, 102, 107, 108, 111, 155, 156, 163, 166, 167, 173-74, 175, 178, 179, 181, 329

Sanders, Beulah, 55, 63, 89, 127, 167, 186, 220, 252, 253, 254, 255, 260

SANE, 189, 251

satellites of PUSH, 220

Schlesinger, Arthur, Jr., 379

Scholarship, Educational, and Defense Fund for Racial Equality (SEDFRE), 217-18 (see also Congress for Racial Equality)

Scholen, Ken, 195

Schorr, Alvin, 88, 291

Schur, Edwin, 359, 378

second round of welfare reform, 129, 259, 319, 370

secondary labor market, 129

self-awareness movement, 359, 363, 378

self-development, 151

self-help, 359, 378

self-interest, 152, 154, 160, 174-75, 196-97, 235, 252-53, 294, 336, 359, 362

Senate Finance Committee, 305, 317

separation of poor from nonpoor (see coalitions, twin-track)

separatists (see racial, exclusiveness; racial, separation)

sequential test case, 329-30

service role, 181, 200, 233, 247, 253

sex discrimination (see gender, discrimination; sexism)

sex education, 389-90

sexism, 3, 18, 48, 87, 89-90, 237, 238, 242, 245, 252, 254, 258, 260, 261, 266

sexual parity, 291

shadow staff, 108-9, 119-20

Shapiro v. Thompson, 329

Shriver, Sargent, 317

silent revolution, 88

Simmel, Georg, 8, 147

single-parent families (see families)

single parents, 245

sisterhood, 239, 244

Sixth General Synod of United Church of Christ, 155

slave labor, 5, 305

Sloan, Edith, 112, 239

Sloan, Margaret, 242, 243

Smeal, Eleanor, 284, 321

social: agencies, 192, 196; controls, 7, 17, 235, 332, 334, 356, 359, 368 (see also strategy, of social control); gospel movement, 148, 149; justice, 150, 184, 256, 358; movements, 4, 7-8; policy, 6, 93, 162, 352, 356-57; scientists, 23-24, 38, 46, 87, 323, 366, 377-78, 381; services, 21, 22, 236, 238, 290, 291; welfare agencies, 22, 23, 198

Social Concerns Action Network (SCAN), 191-92, 194

Social Security Act of 1935, 17, 88, 288-90; amendments to [1961, 290; 1962, 21; 1967, 291, 355-56; 1971, 314-15, 317, 356; 1972, 317, 376 (see also Talmadge and Ribicoff amendments)]

social security recipients, 41
social welfare programs, growth of, 289, 291
sociopolitical climate, 1, 9, 10, 16, 19-20, 22, 33, 34, 36, 268, 324-25, 351, 366, 367, 377-80, 384
solidarity, 3, 44, 99, 117, 210, 211, 219, 220, 223, 233, 234-35, 242, 246, 267, 307, 314, 368, 372, 373, 376, 383, 387-88
Somerville, New Jersey, 193 n
Sorren, Jack, 118 n
South Carolina, 93, 300
Southern Christian Leadership Conference (SCLC), 32, 110, 111, 112, 151, 213-17, 220, 221-22, 230, 232, 296, 316, 372
southern whites, 311
Sparer, Edward, 301-2, 312, 328-30
special benefits, 39, 183, 294, 295, 299, 334, 375 (see also special grants)
special grants, 5, 23, 40-41, 49, 95, 99, 196, 300-1, 303 (see also special benefits)
spin-off organizations, 4, 130, 131, 192, 221, 264, 362, 368, 371, 382, 388
Spock, Benjamin, 111
spontaneous support, 180-81
Splain, Mark, 129-30
Spragg, Howard, 111
staff, NWRO (see leaders, informal; National Welfare Rights Organization; organizers)
state courts, 325
State of the Union surveys, 378
statewide network of the Friends of Welfare Rights, 190
status hierarchy, 116
Steinem, Gloria, 254, 301
Steiner, Gilbert, 18 n, 20, 293, 295
stereotypes, 5, 79, 115, 156, 257, 260, 321, 356, 357
Stevens, John (Justice), 331
stigma, 6, 19, 23, 98, 116, 224, 296, 329, 385, 386
stigmatization, 3, 47, 98, 117, 190, 212, 245, 293

Stimpson, Catherine, 244
strategy: of accommodation, 7, 292, 303-10; of agitation, 20, 22, 23, 34, 38; of antipoverty (see War on Poverty); of bargaining, 23, 114, 303-10, 114; of cadre organizations, 36, 301; collaborative, 198; of collective grievances, 40, 99; of confrontation, 10, 23, 27, 99, 102, 198, 215, 219, 225, 287, 292; consumer rights, 95; of cooperation, 292, 303-10, 333 (see cooperation; strategy, of accommodation; strategy, of bargaining; strategy, of co-optation; strategy, of negotiation); of co-optation, 179, 255, 292, 303-10, 375; of credit rights, 95, 301; of crises, 24; of demonstrations, 26-27, 162, 188, 198-99, 225, 227, 295, 300, 301 (see also strategy, street); of divide and conquer, 307; educational, 158, 163, 187, 189, 190, 195, 197, 226, 238-39, 246; electoral, 37, 223, 256, 292, 381; of evangelism, 147, 148, 169, 176, 177, 358, 362, 370, 378, 383; of FAP, 310-25; of formal organization, 36, 37, 39; of grantsmanship, 52, 306, 307, 309; grass-roots organizing, 117 (see also Boston model; Johnnie Tillmon model); of individual grievances, 40, 99; legal, 6, 20, 102, 197, 287, 301, 325-36, 376-78, 384; of legislative cuts, 26-27, 187-202, 266, 299-300, 323-24 n, 334, 355-56; of lobbying, 20, 95, 117, 162, 163, 183, 187, 195, 233, 238-39, 246, 249-50, 267, 287, 301, 307, 309, 310-25, 366, 368, 372, 375, 376, 381, 384 (see also Family Assistance Plan); of local organizing, 51; of mobilizing around economic justice, 124-31, 176, 177; of mobilizing middle-class constituency, 157, 197-202, 369 (see also constituency devel-

opment); of mobilizing middle-class supporters, 180, 185, 189, 370 (see also Friends of Welfare Rights); of mobilizing the welfare poor, 24, 26, 27-28, 37-38, 96-105, 295, 310, 366; of mobilizing the working poor, 125, 128 (see also Movement for Economic Justice; ACORN); of negotiation, 3-4, 7, 114, 162, 292, 303-10, 372, 375, 384; of organizing poor people across racial lines, 26; of political action, 233, 237, 247-48, 249; of political agitation (see strategy, of protest); of protest, 7, 22, 37, 40, 189, 287, 304, 334; of reconciliation, 149-50; of rehabilitation, 21; of rent strikes, 95; of social action, 147, 148, 149, 155-56, 160, 164, 176, 177, 182, 216, 249, 358, 362, 369, 370, 378, 382, 389; of social control, 219, 287, 292-93, 299, 300, 302, 307, 332, 334, 356, 375 (see also strategy, of bargaining; strategy, of co-optation, strategy, of fraud squads; strategy, of legislative cuts; strategy, of negotiation); of social service, 21, 101, 102, 147, 148, 149, 175, 181, 224, 233, 236, 237, 238-39, 247, 249; street, 6, 7, 95, 96, 102, 180, 223, 239, 292, 303, 375; twofold, 157, 165, 166, 187, 194; of utility rights, 95; of welfare rights, 26, 28-29, 116, 152, 157, 160, 162, 163-64, 165, 167, 169-70, 176
"Strategy to End Poverty, A," 20, 24, 25, 63, 80
Streshinsky, Naomi, 328
student movement, 78
Student National Coordinating Council (SNCC), 60, 107
students, 37, 158, 184, 191
Students for a Democratic Society (SDS), 22, 308
subordinate role, 179, 184
substitute-parent rules, 330
suburban support, 187

success, 6, 24, 40, 81, 97, 100, 189, 192, 195, 197, 199, 201, 232, 242, 301, 302, 325, 377, 380
Sullivan, Leon, 229
superstructure, 38, 381
Supplemental Security Income (SSI), 17, 385
supporters, 4, 5, 7, 8, 15, 20, 46, 88, 112, 123, 130, 174, 175, 176, 178-202, 228-31, 236-61, 287, 300, 303, 308-9, 332, 351, 358

tactics: direct action, 20; sit-ins, 20 (see also strategy)
Taggart, Robert, 295, 352, 353, 354, 355, 356, 357
Talmadge amendments, 251, 258, 356
targets, 5, 9, 58, 198-99
tax: credits for working poor, 323; incentive for household employers, 252; reform, 124
tax-exempt status, 154
teenage mothers, 246
Terborg-Penn, Rosalyn, 244
Terrell, Mary Church, 237
Texas, 104, 309
Theobald, Robert, 111
theoreticians, 20 (see also social, scientists)
third parties, 8
Thomas, Bruce, 60
Tillmon, Johnnie: and ANC mothers in California, 83-84; and appeal to feminists, 254, 258, 260, 374; and apprenticeship programs, in Watts, 92; as associate director, 62, 94, 118n; as chair of NWRO, 39, 55; and children, 92, 253; and Child Care Development Center, 92; and child rearing as work, 89, 265; and conflict with Timothy Sampson, 83-84, 102; and description of lives of poor women, 246; as executive director, 62, 121,

122; and fund raising, 40; and Half-a-
Chance campaign, 35-36, 239; and
jobs for poor women, 91-92, 253; and
Johnnie Tillmon model for organizing
poor women, 96-97, 101-5; and Legal
Services Support, 327; at Little Rock
Convention (1977), 53; and MEJ, 127;
and National Council of Negro Women,
239; and need for choices for poor
women, 89-90, 258, 265; and needs of
poor women, 268; and NOW, 47; and
NWRO conference (1976),   and
partnership with Wiley, 115; and role
of middle-class supporters, 180, 186;
and San Francisco Convention (1975),
53; and SCLC, 214-15; and support of
interracialism, 44, 55; and views on
FAP, 312; and views on solution to
welfare problem, 90-92; and views on
women's liberation, 252-53; and welfare as a woman's issue, 233; and
work background, 89-90; and WRISC,
175
tinkering with the welfare system, 7,
21, 323-24, 386, 390
tokenism, 189, 193, 307
Tory men and liberal policies, 311
traditionalists, 234
Traetner, Walter, 290, 291
triadic conflict, 8, 9, 10
triads, 8, 9
triage, 170
trickle-down strategy, 161, 165-66, 176
triple jeopardy, 358
troika, 150
Truman, Harry (President), 289, 361
Turner, Mel, 63
Twiname, John, 305
twin-track coalitions (see coalitions,
twin-track)
two-against-one strategy, 9, 102

underemployed: organizing the, 95,
129; women, 391
undeserving poor, 359, 362
unemployable, 289, 312
unemployed: black women who are, 4,
15, 242; Johnnie Tillmon and the, 22;

in MEJ, 129-30; in NOW, 257;
organizing the, 95, 116; parent
(see AFDC-UP); public assistance
programs for, 290, 385; public
opinion polls, 360; women who are,
234, 246, 391
unemployed parent (see AFDC-UP)
unemployment, 1, 7, 17, 18, 19,
20, 38, 125, 238, 246, 253, 259,
262, 266, 288, 299, 324 n, 335,
352, 354, 359, 379
unionization, 251
unions (see labor unions)
United Auto Workers, 195, 318
United Church (see United Church
of Christ)
United Church Board of Homeland
Ministries, 111, 154 n, 155, 164,
167
United Church of Christ (UCC):
and Better Jobs and Income Plan,
320; and FAP, 315; as financial
contributor to NWRO, 31; and
IFCO, 150; and mobilization of
middle class, 313; NWRO staff
liaison to, 62-63; and SCLC, 215-
16; Welfare Priority Team, 146,
154-71, 369
United Farmworkers movement,
32, 83, 107
United Methodist Church (see
Methodists)
United Methodist Women, 248
United Presbyterians (see Presbyterians)
United Presbyterian Women, 373
United Welfare Groups of Essex
County, 218
universalistic strategy, 149-50
urban crisis, 188
urban Democratic coalition, 24
Urban League (see National Urban
League)
Urban League in Essex County,
225, 226-27
urban riots, 92, 184, 187, 188,
194, 224, 335
Urban Training Institute, 188, 190

U.S. Bureau of Labor Statistics (BLS), 41-42, 313
U.S. Catholic Conference, 31-32
U.S. Commission on Civil Rights, 356
U.S. Department of Agriculture, poverty level, 41-42
U.S. Department of Education, 385 n
U.S. Department of Health and Human Services, 385 n
U.S. Department of Health, Education, and Welfare (HEW), 114, 117, 262, 296, 303, 305, 306, 334 n, 356, 375, 384, 385 n
U.S. Department of Labor, 33, 118, 183, 304, 375; Women's Bureau, 262
U.S. Supreme Court, 20, 290, 325-36, 376, 377, 379, 384
utility rights (see strategy, of utility rights)

Vera Foundation, 328
Vergata, Patricia, 257
veterans' benefits, 293
Vietnam War, 222, 354
Virginia, 50, 95
visibility, 48, 51, 99, 114, 116, 125, 153, 157, 162, 174, 180, 190, 191, 200, 201, 221, 223, 225, 232, 295, 296, 300, 301, 303, 310, 313, 334, 367, 368, 370, 375, 385, 389, 391
VISTA, 58, 94, 97, 355
Volunteer Service Program, 157
volunteers, 22, 58, 158
voter registration, 102

wage supplements, 93
wages for women, 258, 262, 266, 267
Walk for Decent Welfare, 26
Walker, Lucius, 151, 152-53
War for Women in Poverty, 256
War on Poverty, 1, 20-21, 23, 26, 82, 149, 179, 180, 290-91, 305, 325, 334, 352, 361, 367, 368
Ware, Celestine, 240
Warren Court, 331, 376
Washington Post, The, 317
Watergate, 175, 319, 357, 378

Watts, 22, 83, 91-92, 102
Watts, William, 359-60, 362, 378
Weinberger, Caspar, 306, 356, 357
welfare and political authorities, 5, 6, 10, 19, 23, 27, 40, 46, 63, 92, 99, 156, 159, 162, 183, 186, 223, 351
Welfare Bill of Rights, 39, 82 n
welfare: as a black issue, 18, 247; definition of, 15-16, 91 n; eligibles, 23, 24, 38, 296; as a women's issue, 3, 78, 90, 122, 233, 234, 235, 240, 247, 249, 256, 258, 260, 261-69, 373, 387, 391
welfare bureaucracy, 23
welfare costs, 295, 296, 299
welfare crisis, 23, 24
welfare explosion, 299
Welfare Fighter, The, 109, 118 n, 123, 128, 185, 300
welfare law, 290
Welfare Priority Team, 62, 63, 146, 154-71, 198, 201, 314, 315, 369
welfare reform, 6, 7, 111, 115, 147, 154, 155, 156, 157, 159, 160-63, 165, 167, 169, 171, 176-77, 183, 184, 187, 191, 192, 194, 210, 224, 227, 234, 235, 249, 250, 256, 259, 260, 261, 269, 314, 320, 322, 323, 324, 325, 334, 335, 351, 354, 357, 390, 391
welfare rights (welfare as a right), 4, 7, 15, 19, 21, 23, 24, 39
Welfare Rights Information and Support Community (WRISC), 35, 171-78
welfare rights, lay manuals, 23, 195, 217-18, 295
Welfare Rights Organizations groups (WRO), 40, 41, 45, 49, 51-52, 57, 58, 63, 82
welfare separatism, 41
welfare state, 357
welfare system, 288-92
West Virginia, 300

Westfield, New Jersey, 193 n
Whitaker, William H. , 41, 59, 95, 106, 179, 184, 214, 295, 305
white: dominance, 106-7; feminist movement, 235, 251-61; feminists, 244, 251-61; liberals (see liberals); main-line churches (see Protestant churches); poverty, 42; racism, 106; radicals, 308, 309; supremacy, 244; women, 44, 47-49 (see also women's organizations)
women's organizations, 233-34, 243-67
Wichita Welfare Rights Organization (WRO), 255
Wickenden, Elizabeth, 328
widows, 18, 246, 387
Wiley, George: and adequate income, 89; and Alinsky-strategy of organizing, 80-81; attacks on Nicon's budget priorities of, 354; belief in racial inclusiveness and interracialism of, 25-26, 42, 44, 60, 81; and Black Caucus in NWRO, 107-8; and black churhces, 31, 228-32; and black image, 109-10, 112; and black leaders, 114, as black male organizer, 59, 77; and Boston model of organizing, 104-5; and burnout of organizers, 60, 100; as "captain of the ship," 113; and Cesar Chavez, 223; and changed political climate, 116; charismatic leadership of, 71, 123, 130-31, 368; and Chicago Conference on Guaranteed Income, 26; and Children's March for Survival, 110; and Citizens' Crusade against Poverty, 26; and Citizens' Lobby for Economic Justice, 125, 126; and Cloward and Piven's strategy, 27, 28; and collapse of NWRO, 380-81; and commitment to Welfare Rights, 114; and conflict with Executive Committee, 113-23; and conflict with Faith Evans, 118-23; and conflict with women leaders, 80; and CORE, 24-25, 106, 217, 367; as criticized by NWRO leaders, 169; death of, 126, 128; as decision maker, 85; and de-

pendency on liberal funds, 34, 179, 180; and editors of major newspapers, 317; and employment of poor women, 88-89, 93; and estimate of poverty population, 42, 44; and Executive Committee, 108; as executive director, 28-30, 59, 62, 107, 366; and FAP, 312, 314, 317, 318, 373-74; in favor of formal organization, 36, 37, 39; and freeze on hiring, 118; and Friends of Welfare Rights, 145, 180, 183, 185; as fund raiser, 32, 34-35, 51, 63, 114, 118; and impact of street strategy, 295-96; as informal leader, 63; as integrationist, 25; and Johnnie Tillmon model of organizing, 104-5; and MEJ, 35, 112, 124-31; middle-class background of, 62, 118; and mobilization of liberal resources, 28, 30, 380; and NAACP, 228; and need to include working poor, 116, 124, 155; and NOW's National Board meeting, 257; and NTO, 221-23; and NWRO's debt, 28; and Operation Nevada, 301-3; and organization of grass roots, 38-39; and outside organizers, 37-38, 104; and participatory democracy in movement, 37; and peace coalition, 251; and pluralists movement, 44; and Poor People's Platform, 222; and Poverty Rights Action Center, 26-27; and power within NWRO, 114-15, 120; and racial tensions within NWRO, 106-9; and Rathke (ACORN), 100; resignation from NWRO of, 32, 35, 36, 51, 63, 95, 111, 121, 125, 165, 168, 169, 186, 220, 222, 376; and role of outsiders, 38, 104, 117, 180; and SCLC, 213-14; and search for new allies, 124; and shadow staff, 108-9;

ABOUT THE AUTHOR

GUIDA (MARGARIDA) WEST is Assistant Professor of Sociology at Rutgers University, New Brunswick, New Jersey. Until 1980 she was Coordinator of Continuing Education for Women at the Division of Continuing Education, Rutgers University.

Dr. West has published in the area of sociology of race relations, welfare, and women's rights. Most recently her article "Twin-Track Coalitions in the Black Power Movement" appeared in the book Interracial Bonds, edited by Rhoda Goldstein Blumberg and Wendell James Roye (1979).

Dr. West holds a B.A. from Barnard College, an M.A. from Columbia University, and a Ph.D. from Rutgers University.